THE ECONOMICS OF EUROPEAN INTEGRATION

THE ECONOMICS OF EUROPEAN INTEGRATION

(THEORY, PRACTICE, POLICY)

WILLEM MOLLE

Dartmouth

Aldershot • Brookfield USA • Hong Kong • Singapore • Sydney

HC
241.2
M63
1990b

© W. Molle 1990

All rights reserved. No part of this publication may be reproduced, stored in a retrieval system, or transmitted in any form or by any means, electronic, mechanical, photocopying, recording, or otherwise without the prior permission of Dartmouth Publishing Company Limited.

Published by
Dartmouth Publishing Company Limited
Gower House
Croft Road
Aldershot
Hants GU11 3HR
England

Dartmouth Publishing Company
Old Post Road
Brookfield
Vermont 05036
USA

ROBERT MANNING
STROZIER LIBRARY

MAR 6 1991

Tallahassee, Florida

British Library Cataloguing in Publication Data

Molle, W. T. M. (Willem T M), 1942-
    The economics of European integration : (theory, practice, policy).
    1.   European Community countries. Economic integration
    I.   Title
    337.142

    ISBN 1-85521-149-1
    ISBN 1-85521-153-X pbk

Library of Congress Cataloging-in-Publication Data

Molle, Willem.
   The economics of European integration : theory, practice, policy / Willem Molle.
      p. cm.
   Includes bibliographical references and indexes.
   ISBN 1-85521-149-1. – – ISBN 1-85521-153-X (pbk.)
    1. European Economic Community. 2. Europe– –Economic integration– –History.   3. Monetary policy– –European Economic Community countries.   I. Title.
   HC241.2.M58   1990
   337.1' 42– –dc20

Printed in Great Britain by
Billing & Sons Ltd, Worcester

CONTENTS

v

List of Tables

List of Figures

Foreword

Integration is among the most pervasive tendencies in the economic development of Europe. Hence more and more people are confronted with the bewildering complexity of the functioning of the EC. I have tried in this book to offer a systematic and thorough, yet readable treatment of the aspects of European Economic Integration. My first aim was to explain the logic of the dynamic processes, place the wide variety of issues in a robust conceptual structure, and lay the theoretical foundations for analysis. The next was to present key data and case studies to illustrate how the segments of the economy have evolved under conditions of integration. My final objective was to show how the EC and national governments influence the process by policy measures.

In writing this book I have been supported by many. Its present form owes much to my European and American *students* at the Centre of European Studies of The University of Limburg in Maastrict and at the other Universities in various European countries where I have lectured. Many of their critical comments on earlier versions of this text have resulted in this adapted version which is better suited to students' needs.

Colleagues have helped me by suggestions to include new material or to present the existing material in a different way. Foremost among them was Aad van Mourik, who, using earlier versions for his lecturing courses, had reason to scrutinise all the parts thoroughly. He made valuable suggestions and discovered some errors that had slunk into the text. Other useful comments on the complete text came from Michael Emerson and an anonymous reviewer. Among the many others kind enough to give their comments on individual parts of the book, I will mention here Dirk Strijker for agriculture, Henk de Jong for manufacturing, Peter Odell for energy, Bo Herman for services, Peter Blok for transport, Jacques Pelkmans for the internal market, Peter Coffey for monetary matters, Bernard Seidel for social policy, Leo Klaassen for regional policy, and Jacob Kol for external policy. Their expertise in their own fields has made it possible for me to cover areas far beyond the territory I could possibly have hoped to become an expert in myself. I thank them all for their help and encouragement. Needless to say that all remaining errors and shortcomings are my responsibility alone.

A difficulty encountered in writing about the EC is that the text in preparation needs continuous adjustment. The burden this puts on the author is shouldered off onto those who come later in the production line. A particular word of thanks goes to Attie Elderson, who, during the genesis of this work, has put the continuously changing text into correct English, signalling weak spots and suggesting improvements in passing.

The EC policy environment and the response of firms and individuals have recently changed so drastically owing to the rapid pace of the integration process that all books on the subject need to be updated at the very moment of publication. I have tried to attenuate the difficulty for readers in two ways. First by highlighting the long trends and the structural factors not susceptible to much change, next by giving references that may be the starting point for readers who want to update the parts they are particularly interested in.

WILLEM MOLLE

PART I
GENERAL ISSUES

1 Introduction

Opening remarks

Progressive integration has been one of the most characteristic aspects of economic development in the last few decades, worldwide and in Europe, where it has found expression notably in the European Communities (EC). The EC has had a direct and profound influence on the economy of member states and third countries.

European unity is widely approved of in European business circles and by the European population. For thirty years, opinion polls have steadily shown that the great majority of Europeans consider European integration, on the whole, a good thing to strive for. The ideal of unity, sprung from political motives, has been kept alive by the general feeling that economic solidarity is a must.

Much has been written about integration, of which the importance is generally recognised, in particular about its political, legal and economic aspects. In the last few decades, economic integration has been a pet subject in the theory of international economic relations, as witnessed by the number of specialised books on the subject.

Recently, the idea of economic integration has quickly spread to several sectors of the economy (agriculture, energy, manufacturing industry, transportation) and to such aspects as market regulation, monetary control, or even regional equilibrium. In all those fields, the body of specialised literature is rapidly growing. However, this literature is inconvenient to *students of the integration process per se* because it is addressed to sector specialists rather than integration 'specialists'. And because sub-disciplines seem slow to share their experiences and results with others (what little exchange there is, is mostly concerned with policy aspects), the actual significance of European economic integration is difficult to get hold of.

The present volume sets out to accomplish a *systematic analysis of economic integration in Europe,* extending it beyond the traditional area of international economic relations, to economic sectors, regions, etc. It is based mostly on the results of theoretical and empirical studies of a large number of colleagues, and to some extent also on original research by the author. The book addresses primarily two groups of readers:

- students of economics, principally the increasing numbers who are following courses on European integration. To facilitate its use as a text for such courses, the book has been organised to serve as a general introduction into the dynamics of integration, covering in a systematic and coherent way a variety of discrete areas such as agriculture, trade, or monetary matters. Additionally, it addresses students of economics specialising in industrial economics, international economic relations, monetary and financial economics, and other specific fields, who find themselves increasingly confronted with the European dimension of their specialty; in this book they will find a general framework for the study of their own specialism.[1] To facilitate deeper and more complete treatment starting from this text, references to more specific literature are added. Whilst not claiming complete coverage we have tried to include at least the most relevant 'classical' and recent literature.
- all those interested in the economic aspects of European integration in the widest sense, including the increasing number of persons who in their professional activities are faced with questions as to the organisation and functioning of the EC economy (researchers, consultants, journalists). To facilitate their access to the material, the book has been written in such a way that only a basic knowledge of economics is needed; the use of mathematics has been reduced to a minimum.[2]

Definition of the subject

As the title suggests, three words are central to this book: Economics, European, and Integration. All three call for some clarification.
    As to *economics*, we will

- go into the theoretical principles of economic phenomena associated with integration processes;
- describe the development of the various parts of the European economy, under conditions of integration;
- analyse public intervention in the economic process, that is to say, discuss policy aspects.

These three elements will recur in all parts of the book. In each chapter, we shall present, with respect to the aspect of the economy under discussion, both the actual state of integration and some important descriptive figures, weaving in theoretical elements as we go. The institutional framework and the intervention of the national and European layers of government will also be recorded. Attempts will be made to evaluate the processes described in economic terms.

The word *European* will in principle refer to the whole geographical entity of Europe, but in practice Western Europe will be the focus. Indeed, the dynamism of the integration processes in the west was much larger than in the 'centrally planned' economic systems of Eastern Europe. The European Community, extended since its foundation from six to nine, then to ten, and finally to 12 states, constitutes the core of Western Europe.

Integration, is taken here to indicate the gradual elimination of economic frontiers between countries. The usual stages are distinguished. At the first stage, goods traffic among partners is liberalised. This stage is followed by the liberalisation of movement of production factors. Co-ordination of the national policies, with regard to economic sectors but also to such aspects as exchange rates, is the objective at the third stage. The various integration stages will be a recurrent theme of the book. Taking a dynamic view of integration, we shall describe not only the present state of the European economy but also its development through time, using selected statistical series on the one hand, and drawing lessons from case studies of earlier developments on the other.

European integration is not an isolated process; it takes place in a world in which international relations are more and more interwoven. Therefore, we must keep an eye open to *external aspects*. Speaking of labour migration, for instance, we will discuss not only internal migration within the EC, but also migration from and to third countries. The same goes for goods and capital markets. The natural consequence is that we will include in the analysis not only the policy pursued with respect to the internal market but also, for instance, external trade policy.

Organisation of the volume

The book is divided into six parts.

Part I contains a *general introduction* into the problems. Chapter 2 introduces the essential concepts related to economic integration. The present manifestations of economic integration have a long history. Because historical developments can help us better to understand present processes, Chapter 3 sketches the history of European economic integration, pointing out that for some time integration has mainly proceeded within the institutional framework of the European Community. The situation in the EC being frequently our point of reference, the objectives and the organisation, functioning, and legal and administrative competencies of the various institutions of the EC are given full treatment in Chapter 4, which completes the first part of the book.

Part II is devoted entirely to the *theoretical treatment of integration phenomena*. We will follow the framework of Balassa (1961), progressing from goods-market through factor-market integration to policy integration. First of all, Chapter 5 discusses the theory of the customs union based on the theory of international goods trade. The movements of production factors form the second major component of theory, which we will develop in particular for capital-market integration (Chapter 6). The third component is the integration of national policy. The theoretical elaboration of that subject has so far been largely done in international (monetary) economics. However, other elements are also needed, elements to be borrowed from the theory of market regulation, public-sector economics, and other disciplines. Chapter 7 undertakes an attempt to unite the dispersed elements of theory in one integrative framework of theoretical concepts for the higher stages of integration. While Part II discusses the general theory of integration, the other relevant theoretical aspects of each specific subject will be given a brief treatment in the chapters of subsequent parts, often woven into the presentation of empirical results. These parts are set up in such a way that they can be read without previous study of Part II.

Part III is concerned with the *three freedoms* (goods and services, labour, capital) on which the Common Market is based, an entire chapter being devoted to each. Chapter 8 deals with free movement of goods; Chapter 9 with free movement of the production factor: labour; Chapter 10 with free capital movement. The freedom to provide services has not been given a special chapter in this part, although many arguments plead for it, for example the growing importance of services in the economy. The lack of relevant data and operational concepts preclude for the moment an analysis on a footing with goods. This shortcoming may be compensated in part by the elements we have introduced in the chapter on services in the next part. The discussion of the three freedoms reveals that for the Common Market to function properly, economic integration has to extend to other areas. It seems useful to keep two things apart: on the one hand the regulation of markets – measures rather directly concerned with the functioning of enterprise – and, on the other, the more general matters of socio-economic environment.

In **Part IV** the regulation of markets will be extensively dealt with. Each chapter will discuss one of the broad *sectors of economic activity* (agriculture, manufacturing industry, energy, services, transport). This breakdown follows the famous Clark (1957)/Chenery (1960)/Kuznets (1966) approach, which describes the change of the sectoral composition of an economy with increasing per-capita income levels. Countries with low incomes will spend much on food, hence the agricultural sector will be dominant. Next, the share of manufacturing will expand; finally, at high income levels, the demand for leisure will rise and the share of services increase. We have further detailed the breakdown for two sectors, namely energy and transport, in view of the special position these sectors hold in the integration process. Indeed, inspired by the idea that socio-economic conditions call for a specific organisation of markets and specific policies, the European treaties give different rules for these two sectors. We will describe the EC policies together with the sectors' development under conditions of integration, referring, wherever useful, to theoretical notions specific to the sector concerned.

Part V discusses the *conditions that must be fulfilled for a balanced growth of the integrated economy.* We will distinguish several policy fields along the lines of the well-known Musgravian (Musgrave and Musgrave, 1985) triad: allocation, stabilisation and redistribution. Under the heading of allocation we shall discuss the general aspects of the policies aiming at a well-functioning internal market (such as competition, tax, and market-intervention policies). Under the heading of stabilisation will be treated the co-ordination of macro-economic and monetary policy. The redistribution function as such is also too general a notion; we will break it down into regional and social policies.

All three policy fields have important internal and external aspects (for monetary stabilisation policy, for example, the internal aspect applies to the exchange rates of currencies of member countries, the external aspect to the exchange rate of all member countries towards a third currency). The external relations of nations are a well-established field of economic thought and analysis.[3] In line with this we have opted for the separate treatment of the external aspects of both allocation, stabilisation and redistribution policies. This choice is reinforced by the need to define the emerging identity of an integration area on the international scene. Under the heading of external relations, the whole array of policies, from trade to defence, will be reviewed. Here, too, theoretical and policy elements will be mixed with the results of empirical research.

Part VI finally contains an *evaluation* or appraisal of the results presented in Parts III to V in the light of the conceptual and theoretical notions of Parts I and II. Here, as in the earlier chapters of the book discussing the advantages of integration, use will be made of well known concepts of welfare economics (see among others, Mishan, 1982). A short presentation of the prospects for the future development of the European integration process completes the book.

Notes

1   To that end, the material of the book has been organised and presented to allow fruitful study of individual subjects without having to go through the complete text.
2   Only basic knowledge of linear equations and their graphical representation and the essentials of regression analysis is required to understand the complete text.
3   See in this respect the huge volume of literature on international trade relations.

2 Fundamental Concepts

General

Purpose and progress of economic integration

The expression 'economic integration' covers a variety of notions. It may refer to the absorption of a company in a larger concern. It may have a spatial aspect, for instance if it refers to the integration of regional economies in a national one. In this book, economic integration is always used with respect to international economic relations, to indicate the combination of the economies of several sovereign states in one entity.

Economic integration is not an *objective* in itself, but serves higher objectives. The immediate, economic, objective is to raise the prosperity of all co-operating units. In the rest of this book we will go into the details of the theoretical foundations of, and the empirical evidence for, the relative increase of welfare through integration. The farther-reaching objective is one of peace policy; namely, to lessen the chance of armed conflicts among partners. We mention in passing that substantial empirical support exists for the statement that economic integration reduces conflicts between nations. Polacheck (1980), using data for 30 countries in the 1958–1967 period, showed that doubling the trade between two countries leads to a 20 per cent decline in the frequency of hostilities.[1]

Used in a *static* sense, 'economic integration' represents a situation in which the national components of a larger economy are no longer separated by economic frontiers but function together as an entity. Used in a *dynamic* sense it indicates the gradual elimination of economic frontiers among member states (that is to say, the abolition of national discrimination), with the formerly separate national economic entities gradually merging into a larger whole. The dynamic interpretation is the more usual, and the one to be used in this book. Of course, the static meaning of the expression will apply in full once the integration process has passed through its stages and reached its object.

9

Objects of integration

Economic integration is basically the integration of markets. Economists make a distinction between markets of goods and services on the
one hand, and markets of production factors (labour, capital, entrepre-
neurship) on the other.

Free movement of goods and services is the basic principle of economic
integration. As is well known from classical international trade theory,[2] the free exchange of goods promises a positive effect on the
prosperity of all concerned. It permits consumers to choose the cheapest good, generally widens the choice, and creates the conditions for
further gain through economies of scale, etc.

The obvious welfare gains from the liberalisation of product markets are a good economic reason to start integration with that object.
However, integration schemes tend to follow a political logic rather
than an economic one. The political reasons to begin integration at the
goods market are:

- a lasting coalition between sectors demanding protection and
  sectors and consumers demanding cheap imports is hard to accomplish;
- substitute instruments (such as industrial policy, non-tariff barriers, and administrative procedures) can be used to intervene in
  the economic process;
- vital political issues like growth policy and income redistribution are guaranteed to remain within national jurisdiction.

Free movement of production factors can be seen as another basic
element of economic integration. One argument for it is that it permits
optimum allocation of labour and capital. Sometimes, certain production factors are missing from the spot where otherwise production
would be most economical. To overcome that problem, entrepreneurs
are apt to shift their capital from places of low return to more promising
places. The same is true of labour: employees will migrate to regions
where their labour is more needed and therefore better rewarded. A
second argument is that an enlarged market of production factors
favours new production possibilities which in turn permit new, more
modern or more efficient uses of production factors (new forms of
credit, new occupations, etc.).

The choice of production factors as the object of the second stage in
the integration process is partly based on the economic advantages that
spring from such integration. But here, too, we have to consider the
political logic. The integration of labour markets seems to be the
obvious choice in periods of a general shortage of labour (for instance
the EC in the 1960s, see Chapter 9). A tangle of national regulations for

wages, social security, etc. seems to leave politicians sufficient opportunities for practical intervention on the national level for them to accept general principles on the European level. With capital-market integration the issue of direct investments seems straightforward; many politicians may hope to attract new foreign investment in that way. For other capital movements the willingness to integrate is less obvious because integration would imply giving up the control of sensitive macro-economic instruments.

Policy approximation is the next stage of economic integration. In an economy which leaves production and distribution entirely to the market, the elimination of obstacles to the movement of goods and production factors among countries would suffice to achieve full economic integration. Not so in modern economies, which are almost invariably of the mixed type, the government frequently intervening in the economy. In economies of the mixed type, integration cannot be achieved without harmonising the policies pursued by the governments of the individual states. Policy making is on the whole more difficult to integrate than markets for goods, services and production factors. Politicians are likely to be the more unwilling to give up their intervention power, the more such elements are involved as employment policy or budgetary policies (referring to expenditure on schools, subsidies, as well as revenues from taxes). Moreover, national civil servants tend to uphold their way of operating interventional schemes as the most efficient, and since their very existence depends on complicated sets of rules, they are hardly inclined, in general, to co-operate towards harmonised policy. Thus, the conditions for a common currency or monetary integration will not readily be met. That is one reason why currency integration is mostly introduced at a late stage of integration. Even later comes the integration of points that touch the very heart of a nation's sovereignty, in particular the acceptance of a common defence policy.

Positive and negative integration

With respect to modern mixed economies, Tinbergen (1954) distinguished negative integration (that is, the elimination of obstacles), and positive integration (that is, the creation of equal conditions for the functioning of the integrated parts of the economy). The former's demand on policy will be relatively simple (deregulation, liberalisation), but the latter will always involve more complex forms of government policy (harmonisation, co-ordination). Let us look somewhat closer at the differences.

Negative-integration measures are often of the simple 'Thou shalt not' type. They can be clearly defined, and once negotiated and laid down in treaties, they are henceforth binding on governments, companies and private persons. There is no need for permanent decision-making machinery. Whether these measures are respected is for the courts to check, to which individuals may appeal if infringements damage their interests.

Positive integration is more involved. It often takes the form of vaguely defined obligations requiring public institutions to take action. Such obligations leave ample room for interpretation as to scope and timing. They may, moreover, be reversed if the policy environment changes. As a consequence, they hold much uncertainty for private economic agents, who cannot derive any legal rights from them. Positive integration is the domain of politics and bureaucracy rather than law. No wonder then that positive integration does not present a built-in stimulus for progress. Because politicians are more likely to opt for positive rather than negative integration, progress is likely to be slower, the higher the stage of integration, that is the farther integration proceeds on the path towards a Full Economic Union.

Stages of economic integration

Integration can apply merely to product markets, to markets of production factors as well, and finally to different areas of economic policy. The higher the form of integration chosen, the higher the institutional demands to be fulfilled. Largely following the sequence of Balassa's (1961) classical work, we can describe the most important stages, by increasing degree of integration, as follows:

- In the *free-trade area* (FTA), all such trade impediments as import duties and quantitative restrictions are abolished among partners. Internal goods traffic is then free, but each country can apply its own customs tariff with respect to third countries. To avoid trade deflection (goods entering the FTA through the country with the lowest external tariff) internationally traded goods must be accompanied by so-called 'certificates of origin' indicating in which country the good has been manufactured. That enables customs officers at frontiers between member countries with different outer tariffs, to determine whether duties or levies are still due (on goods originating from a third country), or whether the merchandise originates from another member state and can therefore be imported duty-free.
- In the *customs union* (CU), as in the free-trade area, all obstacles to the free traffic of goods among partner countries are removed. Moreover, one common external tariff is agreed upon, which does away with the certificates of origin at internal borders. Once a good has been admitted anywhere to the customs union, it may circulate freely.

- The *common market* (CM) is first of all a customs union. Moreover, production factors, that is, labour and capital, may move freely within the CM. That definition leaves various options as to the relation with third countries; different national regulations (comparable to the FTA), or a common regulation (comparable to the CU). Combinations of common policies (for instance for labour) and national policies (for example for capital) *vis-à-vis* third countries are possible.
- The *economic union* (EU) implies not only a common market but also a high degree of co-ordination or even unification of the most important areas of economic policy, market regulation as well as macro-economic and monetary policies and income redistribution policies. Not only is a common trade policy pursued towards third countries, but external policies concerning production factors and economic sectors are also developed.
- The *monetary union* (MU) is a form of co-operation which on top of a common market (notably free movement of capital) creates either irrevocably fixed exchange rates and full convertibility of the currencies of the member states, or one common currency circulating in all member states. Such a union implies quite a high degree of integration of macro-economic and budget policies.
- The *economic and monetary union* (EMU) combines the characteristics of the monetary union and the economic union. In view of the close interweaving of monetary and macro policies, integration evolves mostly simultaneously for both policy fields.
- *Full economic union* (FEU) implies the complete unification of the economies involved, and a common policy for many important matters. The situation is then virtually the same as that within one country. Given the many areas integrated, political integration (for example, in the form of a confederacy) is often implied.

The transitions between the various stages of integration are fluent and cannot always be clearly defined.[3] The first stages, FTA, CU and CM, seem to refer to market integration in a classical laisser-faire setting, the higher stages (EU, MU, FEU) to policy integration. In practice, however, the former three stages are unlikely to stabilise without some form of policy integration as well (for instance, safety regulations for a FTA, commercial policy for a CU, or social and monetary policies for a CM (Pelkmans, 1980). So, between a customs union and full integration, a variety of practical solutions for concrete integration problems are likely to occur.

The seven stages of integration just sketched have two characteristics in common. They abolish discrimination among actors from partner economies (internal goal). They may thereby maintain or introduce some form of discrimination with respect to actors from economies of third countries (external goal).

Degrees of policy integration

All forms of integration described above require permanent agreements among participating states with respect to procedures to arrive at resolutions and to the implementation of rules. In other words, they call for partners to agree on the rules of the game. For an efficient policy integration, common institutions (international organisations) are created. However, for the higher forms of integration, such as a common market, the mere creation of an institution is not sufficient: they require transfer of power from national to union institutions.

All forms of integration diminish the freedom of action of the member states' policy–makers. The higher the form of integration, the greater the restrictions and loss of national competences. The following hierarchy of policy co-operation is usually adopted:

- *Information*: partners agree to inform one another about the aims and instruments of the policies they (intend to) pursue. This information may be used by partners to change their policy to achieve a more coherent set of policies. However, partners reserve full freedom to act as they think fit, and the national competence is virtually unaltered.
- *Consultation*: partners agree that they are obliged not only to inform but also to seek the opinion and advice of others about the policies they intend to execute. In mutual analysis and discussion of proposals the coherence is actively promoted. Although formally the sovereignty of national governments remains intact, in practice their competences are affected.
- *Co-ordination* goes beyond this, because it commits partners to agreement on the (sets of) actions needed to accomplish a coherent policy for the group. If common goals are fixed some authors prefer the term *co-operation*. Co-ordination often means the adaptation of regulation to make sure that they are consistent internationally (for example, the social security rights of migrant labour). It may involve the *harmonisation* (that is, the limitation of the diversity) of national laws and administrative rules. It may lead to *convergence* of the target variables of policy (for example, the reduction of the differences of national inflation rates). Although agreements reached by co-ordination may not always be enforceable (no sanctions), they nevertheless limit the scope and type of policy actions nations may undertake, and hence imply limitation of national competences.
- *Unification*: either the abolition of national instruments (and

their replacement with union instruments for the whole area) or the adoption of identical instruments for all partners. Here the national competence to choose instruments is abolished.

Goods markets

Advantages

Fully integrated goods markets imply a situation of free trade among member states. People aim for free trade because they expect economic advantages from it, namely:[4]

- more production and more prosperity through better allocation of production factors, each country specialising in the products for which they have a comparative advantage;
- more efficient production thanks to scale economies and keener competition;
- improved 'terms of trade' (price level of imported goods with respect to exported goods) for the whole group in respect of the rest of the world.

Integration of goods markets implies first of all the removal of (all) impediments to free internal goods trade. In modern mixed economies such negative integration is not sufficient, however. For the market to function adequately, there must be common rules for competition on the internal market and for trade with third countries.

Obstacles to free trade

The free-trade area has been defined before as a situation where there are neither customs duties or levies with similar effect, nor quantitative restrictions or indeed any factor impeding the free internal movement of goods[5] (the latter are often taken together under the heading of non-tariff barriers, or NTB).[6] They can be described as follows:

- Customs duties or import duties are sums levied on imports of goods, making the goods more expensive on the internal market. Such levies may be based on value or quantity. They may be indicated in percentages or vary according to the price level aspired to domestically;
- Levies of similar effect are import levies disguised as administrative costs, storage costs or test costs imposed by the customs;
- Quantitative restrictions (QR) are ceilings put on the volume of imports of a certain good allowed into a country in a certain

period (quota), sometimes expressed in money values. A special type is the so-called 'tariff quota', which is the maximum quantity which may be imported at a certain tariff, all quantities beyond that coming under a higher tariff;

- Currency restrictions mean that no foreign currency is made available to enable importers to pay for goods bought abroad;
- Other non-tariff impediments are all those measures or situations (such as fiscal treatment, legal regulations, safety norms, state monopolies, public tenders, etc.) which ensure a country's own products' preferential treatment over foreign products on the domestic market.

Motives for obstacles

Obstacles to free trade are mostly meant to protect a country's own trade and industry against competition from abroad, and therefore come under the heading of *protection*. Protection can be combined with free trade. A customs union, for instance, prevents free trade with outside countries by a common external tariff and/or other protectionist measures, while leaving internal trade free.

Like individual countries, a customs union may hope to benefit from protection against third countries, that is, from *import restrictions*. From the extensive literature we have distilled the following arguments in favour of such measures:

- Independence from other countries as far as strategic goods are concerned, a point much stressed in the past and especially in times of war;
- The possibility of nurturing so-called 'infant industries'. The idea is that young companies and sectors which are not yet competitive should be sheltered in infancy in order to develop into adult companies holding their own in international competition;
- Defence against dumping. The healthy industrial structure of an economy may be spoiled when foreign goods are dumped on the market at prices below the cost in the country of origin. Even if the action is temporary, the economy may be weakened beyond resilience;
- Defence against social dumping. If wages in the exporting country remain below productivity, the labour factor is said to be exploited; importation from such a country is held by some to uphold such practices and is therefore not permissible;
- Employment boosting. If the production factors in the union are not fully occupied, protection can turn the demand towards do-

mestic goods, so that more labour is put to work and social costs are avoided;
- Diversification of the economic structure. Countries specialised in one or a few products tend to be very vulnerable; marketing problems of such products lead to instant loss of virtually all income from abroad. That argument applies to small developing countries rather than to large industrialised states;
- Shouldering-off balance-of-payment problems. Import restrictions reduce the amount to be paid abroad, which helps to avoid adjustments of the industrial structure and accompanying social costs and societal friction (caused by wage reduction and a restrictive policy, etc.).

Pleas for *export restriction* have also been heard. The underlying ideas vary considerably. The arguments most frequently heard are the following:

- Some goods are strategically important and must not fall into the hands of other nations; that is true not only of military goods (weapons) but also of incorporated knowledge (computers) or systems;
- Exportation of raw materials means the consolidation of a colonial situation; a levy on exports will hopefully increase the people's inclination to process the materials themselves. If not, then at any rate the revenues can be used to start other productions;
- If too much of a product is exported, the importing country may be induced to take protective measures against a series of other products; rather than that, a nation may accept a 'voluntary' restriction of the exports of that one product.

In anticipation of further discussion, let it be pointed out that most arguments for protection[7] do not hold water: protection in general has a negative effect on prosperity.

Service markets

Forms of integration

The integration of service markets proceeds in ways that are in agreement with the characteristics of this sector. Following Bhagwati (1987a) and others, we have distinguished three types of international transaction. We will consider service markets to be integrated if:

- consumers of one country can move freely to producers in another country to receive the service offered; personal services (such as staying at a seaside resort) and retail services (such as Dutch people shopping in Paris) are cases in point;
- producers of one country can move freely to a foreign country to provide their services there; managing a construction site, but also a plumber fixing a problem in a house across the border, are cases in point;
- in cases where no spatial move of either producer or consumer is needed because the service is rendered through transborder flows of information, integration is considered to exist if a consumer in country A is free to contract a service (for instance an insurance policy) with a company in country B.

The transaction costs involved in international service trade are often considerable, and not all services are susceptible to economies of scale. Hence, even without restrictions, services tend to be traded less than goods. However, as technological progress in telecommunication lowers the transaction costs, integration may be expected to intensify, particularly for the third category of transactions.

Advantages

The standard arguments for the integration of service markets are similar to the ones used for goods:

- Comparative advantages of countries determine international specialisation patterns, and higher international specialisation raises the efficiency of resource allocation and hence income. In other words, consumers will have more choice and the products produced and consumed will be better matched (Shelp 1981).
- Economies of scale and scope will be better exploited (for instance in banking through spreading risks).

As with goods, the liberalisation of international trade in services alone does not suffice to integrate markets. Most of these markets have been regulated for several reasons (to protect consumers, for example), and a certain degree of harmonisation of the rules is necessary to avoid distortions. In much the same way, competition rules must be enforced and the relations to third countries defined.

Obstacles

The obstacles to free trade in services are mostly comparable to those in goods trade. However, as the value of a border-crossing service is harder to control than that of a good, tariffs are seldom practised, and restrictions on the trade in services are mostly of the non-tariff type. Moreover, because the provision of some types of service across the border involves direct investments, a set of restrictions to entry of markets is relevant too.[8]

Trade in services can be hampered by the following instruments:

- quantitative restriction (for instance, in advertising, air transport);
- subsidies (for instance in construction);
- government procurement (for instance, construction, data processing);
- currency controls on transfers to foreign countries for services provided;
- restrictions on the qualification of manpower required to perform certain services (legal, medical);
- technical requirements for capital goods (transport, for example);
- customs valuation problems for goods required to perform services (for instance, plumbers' tools).

Entry restrictions on the professions or restrictions on setting up in business are the second category of barriers. These can take the following forms:

- restrictions on the right of foreign firms to set up or take over subsidiary companies;
- exclusion of foreign firms from certain types of activity;
- discriminatory performance requirements;
- selective taxation;
- restrictions on the transfer of profits.

Motives for obstacles

Most of the obstacles are allegedly drawn up to *protect consumers*. A few examples from different sectors may illustrate this:

- In banking and insurance, regulation serves to limit the risk of insolvency through surveillance of private operators by (semi) public organisations (Central Banks, among others). Since foreign suppliers are hard to control, access to the national market is barred to them;
- In air transport, the safety of the passenger is the main concern. Standards are accompanied by mutual import controls in the form of landing rights;
- In communication and energy (electricity), services are regu-

lated to protect consumers from unfair pricing by a 'natural' monopolist;
- In medical services, the interests of the patient are protected by the enforcement of standards for the qualifications of personnel (medical doctors, etc.).

Although the arguments are valid, they are not convincing, and other policy measures can be devised with the same effect for the safety and health of consumers while leaving international competition free. Many other obstacles, however, overtly aim at *protecting national companies*. There are several reasons to do so:

- Strategic importance. An example is maritime transport, where international trade is restricted by a complex system of cargo reservation; a national merchant navy is thought to be necessary in times of war to provide the country with essential goods;
- Economic policy: the control of macro-economic policy (through the banking system);
- Enhancing the national prestige (civil aviation);
- Control of key technologies (telecommunication), and safeguarding cultural values (movies, television).

However, even if consumer protection is the official reason, one is inclined to believe that the real motive is to protect domestic producers (for instance, construction, software, electricity generation, etc.).

Production factors: labour markets

Forms of integration

There is free international movement of employed persons if:

- nationals of one member state may unrestrictedly look for and accept a job in another;
- self-employed people from one member state are free to settle in another member state, there to exert their profession or activity.

There are as yet no generally accepted notions to capture the various *forms* in which the labour market may be integrated, but here, too, a distinction can be made along the lines of free-trade area and customs union. While in a Free Labour Movement Zone(FLMZ) as well as in a Labour Market Union (LMU), employed persons would be free to accept a job in any of the partner countries, in the former, participant countries would be free to establish their own conditions with respect to third countries, while in the latter that competency would have been transferred to the union. In the former case, therefore, employed persons from third countries admitted to one member state would not automatically have the right to move freely into other member states. With the fully integrated labour markets in a union, that last limitation does not exist. Full labour-market integration means, indeed, that among partner countries (all) restrictions are abolished. But to achieve real integration, measures of positive integration are needed as well. Such positive integration will mostly be realised by co-ordinating labour-market and employment policies as well as social policies and taxes.

Advantages of integration

The advantages hoped for from the free movements of labour (that is to say, the integration of labour markets), depend on the type of exchange chosen. In general terms, the following advantages are expected from *permanent migration*:

- for employed persons, a better chance to capitalise on their specific qualities, and in consequence, an increase of the potential supply of qualified labour;
- for those demanding labour, better possibilities of choosing a technology with an optimum capital/labour ratio from the management point of view;
- levelling of differences in production costs as far as they were due to the compartmentation of the labour market.

In the case of *temporary migration* a distinction must be made between advantages to the emigration country and to the immigration country (Scott, 1967; Kindleberger *et al.* 1979; Macmillan, 1982).

Emigration countries expect three major advantages: (1) to ease their unemployment situation (and lower the budgetary cost of unemployment benefits), (2) to ease their budget and balance-of-payments problems through remittances, and (3) to improve the quality of the labour force. The employment effect has often been only temporary. The regular income transfers have indeed permitted the purchase of more goods. The transfer of savings, which also seemed promising, has proved rather disappointing in terms of investments in the emigration country, for too much money has been invested for purposes that are not directly productive. Emigration countries had also hoped for advantages in the form of professional training. Again, reality often does not come up to expectation: the training obtained tends to be less than hoped for, and returning migrants frequently fail to find a suitable job.

Immigration countries hope to gain a direct production effect: by adding foreign workers with skills that are scarce to their own manpower in places where investments require it, they are able to make the most of their own manpower. Sometimes the advantages are manifest only in times of cyclical heights, but they may also be of a more structural nature. Immigration may also have a redistributive welfare effect: the larger labour supply lowers the wage rate of the indigenous labour force; the additional income is shared by capital and foreign labour. Moreover, the pressure on inflation is diminished due to relaxation of labour scarcity.

The profitable effects of international migration may well be distributed unevenly, and therefore the voices pleading restriction may be louder than those pleading full freedom. *The outcome is often free movement of labour within a common market, but a policy of restriction towards third countries.* This is the more likely as the common market is supplemented with some form of redistribution mechanism which could offset the potential negative effects of emigration for the less developed member countries.

Restrictions

To control the international exchange of labour, most governments use permits as a tool (comparable to quantitative restrictions in the exchange of goods), forbidding all immigration without a permit. The permit may be accompanied by all kinds of restriction, sometimes defined so sharply that in practice no immigration is feasible. The mere abolition of such permits does not mean that factor markets are integrated. There are, indeed, several methods to impede migration of workers; they can be divided into the following categories:

- Limiting the access to functions and professions, achieved by direct conditions (stipulating, for instance, that foreign nationals cannot be lawyers), but also in a subtler way. One way is to set professional demands which foreigners cannot satisfy (for instance because foreign certificates are not recognised); another, to make public labour-exchange services accessible to a country's own nationals only.
- Accommodation conditions. To accept a job, a person must have accommodation. To foreigners a residence permit can be refused or made hard to get. Restrictions can also be imposed on obtaining residential accommodation or schooling for children, etc.
- Creating financial disadvantages, for instance by imposing higher taxes, or charging premiums for social security without granting

rights to benefits. Finally, the transfer of earnings can be restricted (foreign currency).

Motives for impediments

Opponents to the free movement of the production factor 'labour' raise certain arguments, which are mostly directed against *immigration*. The following arguments are frequently heard:

- immigration puts pressure on wages: at equal demand, additional supply leads to lower prices;
- it increases unemployment: demand remaining the same, additional supply expels existing supply;
- it raises government expenditure, because foreigners often need costlier social equipment (education, housing, for instance) and make more demands on social security than nationals;
- it causes societal disruption: cultural differences tend to disturb the social equilibrium;
- it causes regional disparities: labour tends to move to concentrations of economic activities;
- it has an adverse effect on the balance of payments via increased invisible imports (remittances);
- the cost of recruitment and travel is high.

On the other hand, arguments are also raised against *emigration*, such as:

- loss of human capital essential to the development of the economy;
- depopulation of certain regions, causing waste of societal capital;
- opportunity cost of foregone output.

Developed countries rarely inhibit emigration, but to developing countries there may be valid arguments to do so. To circumvent direct controls, Bhagwati (1987b) proposed an emigration tax.

Production factors: capital markets

Forms of integration

The movement of the production factor 'capital' can be considered free if entrepreneurs can satisfy their need for capital, and investors can offer their disposable capital, in the country where conditions are most favourable.

Once more a parallel can be drawn with free-trade areas and customs unions. A free-capital movement area (FCMA) would then be a zone within which capital can move freely, each state making its own rules with respect to third countries. In a 'capital market union' (CMU), on the contrary, there would be a common policy concerning the union's financial relations with third countries. Given the inter-wovenness of the capital market with monetary policy, a certain integration of mutual monetary relations, and co-ordination of the monetary relations with third countries, would be implied.

The integration of capital markets can be defined first of all as removing constraints on foreign exchange, discriminatory tax measures, and other obstacles. This is the so-called negative integration. Since capital is highly mobile and apt to go where the returns are highest, positive integration will also be needed, that is, the integration of capital markets by co-ordinating or harmonising the rules which govern their organisation and functioning, such as prudential regulations for bank credit, payments, etc.

Advantages of integration

Integration of capital markets is aspired to because:

- it diminishes the risk of disturbances such as tend to occur in small markets;
- it increases the supply of capital, because better investing prospects mobilise additional savings, the investor being free to choose the combination most favourable for him in terms of return, solidity and liquidity;
- it enables those who are in need of capital to raise larger amounts in forms better tailored to their specific needs;
- it makes for equal production conditions and thus fewer disturbances of competition in the common market.

Impediments

We can distinguish three groups of instruments to restrict the importation and exportation of capital, whether or not speculative (compare Woolly, 1974):

- *Market-oriented instruments* (resembling tariffs in goods trade, as they influence the price of capital):
  split-currency markets, with a more (or less) favourable rate of exchange for current payments than for capital transactions;

lower (even negative) interests on foreign deposits, caused
by taxes on interest or deposits, or otherwise.
- *Administrative and legal instruments* (comparable to quantitative
restrictions and non-tariff barriers):

  securities: trade may be impeded through reserving the
  right to hold stocks and bonds to persons or institutions of
  a given nationality and restricting non-residents' purchases
  of domestic securities; moreover, restrictions may be put on
  domestic investment and pension fund investments in foreign securities;

  bank deposits may be hindered by a ceiling on deposits kept
  by foreigners, or, alternatively, by restrictions on residents'
  deposits in foreign countries.
- *Other instruments:*

  currency restrictions on certain transactions, the authorities
  allotting only limited amounts of foreign currency for given
  capital transactions;

  taxes or levies on the acquirement of foreign currency, tax
  withheld on foreign investment, or heavier taxes on foreign
  profits than on domestic ones;

  profits and interests transfers may be hindered by an obligation to reinvest in the host country all profits made with
  foreign capital, and by committing exporters to return as
  soon as possible (for instance, within five years) any capital
  drained off abroad.

Motives for impediments

Arguments to restrict capital movements are based mostly on the
disadvantages associated with long-term capital drain-offs (Cairncross, 1973; Swoboda, 1976). The most frequently heard reasons for
governments to feel they should impede the *outflow* of capital are the
following:

- The capital flow is the bloodstream of the national economy.
Capital drain-offs will reinforce the economies of other countries
to the detriment of the country's own economy (for instance,
with domestic investment the government is able to tax the
ensuing revenue). Moreover, the government often wishes to
reserve to itself the national capital market.
- The loss of currency reserves jeopardises the ability to meet other
international obligations; this is particularly relevant when the
balance of payment is in disequilibrium, and authorities are
trying to prevent changes in the exchange rate.
- The outflow of capital has repercussions on the internal equilib-

rium, for instance the interest rate, an argument mainly associated with the price of capital. A large outflow of capital may compel a high rate of interest when a low rate would be recommendable for the internal economy.
- The outflow of capital disturbs the external equilibrium and frustrates monetary policy: it may lead to currency devaluation even though the rate of exchange as such is not unbalanced. In that way, the nation might be compelled to more expensive imports and imported inflation.

Rather paradoxically, arguments are also raised against the *importation of capital*, such as:

- Capital is power; therefore, capital in foreign hands means loss of authority over one's own economy.
- Disturbance of the internal and external equilibrium: a large inflow of capital may entail a lower rate of interest than the monetary authorities think adequate for internal equilibrium, in the sense of prohibiting a scarce-money policy with reasonable interest rates. To avoid such an inflow, the authorities may consider upward adaptation of the rate of exchange; however, that weakens the export position.

Finally, there are arguments pleading against both the *importation and the exportation* of capital:

- The possible disturbance of equilibrium by short-term capital transactions. We have already pointed out the disturbances that may be the result of exportation of capital. Capital imports can be disturbing because they are often of a speculative nature, that is anticipating changes in the rates of interest and/or the exchange rates of currency;
- Perversity: free movement of capital does not lead to optimum allocation, but to concentration in countries with a large market where capital is already in abundant supply, while states with smaller markets are deprived of capital.[9]

The *welfare effects* of capital restrictions are rather complicated; we will come back to them later (see, among others, Phylaktis and Wood, 1984). To speak a simple 'yes or no', on economic considerations, to the restriction of international capital flows is not possible from an economics point of view. Anyway, the experience with controls has shown them in the long run to be ineffective instruments to prevent structural adjustments to the balance of payments. The arguments for fighting speculative capital movements, on the contrary, are on the whole economically sound, but for that purpose other instruments may be more effective (see chapter 17 on monetary policy).

Policy; positive integration

Economic reasons for positive integration

In the previous sections we have seen that the creation of a customs union of nations which used to have closed internal markets, generally leads to higher production and lower costs within the union, and thus to more prosperity, mainly because economic resources are used more efficiently. We have also seen that the elimination of impediments to labour and capital flows can be advantageous.

Such measures of negative integration must be completed by positive integration, that is to say that public authorities must lay down rules lest third countries, companies and persons by their actions prevent the advantages from being fully realised. In all European countries, there has been progressive government control of economic life. The regulations diverge widely among countries, which is a great nuisance to companies that operate internationally. Therefore, as the economic integration progresses, the national regulating systems must be integrated to form a policy framework which can give the greatest support to integrated economic activities.

The first question is then at what stage such policy areas should be integrated. An answer to that question may be obtained by applying the general *principle of subsidiarity*, which stipulates that a policy should be executed at the lowest level of government. If that is inefficient and compensation mechanisms fail, it should be handed over to the next higher level, for instance from a regional to the central government (see, among others, Oates, 1972). That happens when the spill-over of important cost or benefit elements to other areas leads, respectively, to the over- or under-supply of public goods. As integration advances, spill-over effects are likely to increase in importance and hence more competences need to be transferred to the community level.

A second question concerns the type of policy that may be affected. To answer that question we will follow Buchanan (1968) and Musgrave and Musgrave (1985) in *breaking down public policy into three functions*, namely:

- allocation of resources, requiring mainly micro-economic policy instruments aiming at the efficient use of resources. This function comprises all policies aiming at the proper functioning of the internal market;
- stabilisation, requiring mainly macro-economic and monetary

policy instruments to attain such objectives as high growth rates, price stability, and full employment;
- redistribution of income, requiring policies that aim to ensure to different social groups (social policy) and regional groups a fair share in the benefits of integration should the market mechanisms fail to achieve an equitable outcome;
- external relations should be added, as at each stage of integration the union defines itself *vis-à-vis* the Third World through commercial policies in a customs union up to defence in a full political union.

If the first two policies are essential to gather the full benefit of integration, the third is indispensable to gain the necessary political support from all participants in an integration scheme[10] and the fourth to establish an international identity.

Most people agree that for a balanced integration process, the transfer of the four functions to higher layers of government should run more or less in parallel; however, allocation and external policies may be somewhat ahead of stabilisation and redistribution because their relation to the earlier stages of integration is more straightforward.

Dynamics of further integration

By their very dynamics, the lower forms of integration tend to bring forth more advanced forms. A few examples may be illuminating.

The wish to make the *customs union* work is an obvious impulse to policy integration. Externally, the setting of a common external tariff and its regular adjustment to changed circumstances call for a common trade policy. Moreover, negotiations with third countries can be conducted to more advantage by the customs union acting as an entity than by each member state on its own. Internally, tariffs and quotas appear to be easier to abolish than non-tariff obstacles, such as higher taxes on foreign goods than on domestic ones (wine against beer), technical norms (allegedly meant to safeguard workers and consumers, but actually supporting the country's own production), priority to national companies for (government) orders, etc. To remove such obstacles, regulations must be harmonised in such widely divergent fields as taxation and safety, regulations which are often deeply rooted in countries' legal, institutional and social structure. For the internal market to function properly, measures are also needed to prevent competition distortion. Competition can be limited by companies (agreements) as well as governments (state support, export subsidies, etc.). Hence the need for a common competition policy, with rules for private and public sectors. Such a policy affects other areas as well:

equal competitive conditions for companies require a degree of harmonisation of consumer policy (concerning responsibility, for instance) but also of environmental policy (avoiding unnecessary costs; pollution abatement).

The establishment and functioning of a *common market* also give strong impulses towards the co-ordination of policy. Free movement of workers requires in practice the mutual recognition of diplomas or certificates of professional proficiency, for free professions as well as employed persons. Measures of social security must be harmonised lest different claims for sickness, accident, old-age and other benefits should in practice make a mockery of the free movement. Free movement of capital necessitates the elimination of some administrative obstacles, such as exchange control, and legal ones, such as company laws. In the fiscal sphere, too, some adjustment will be necessary to prevent capital from flowing to states with a favourable tax regime. Finally, the mobility of capital demands the adjustment of monetary policies (rates of exchange, interest, etc.) to diminish economic disturbances caused by speculation. In principle, capital is more mobile than labour. The creation of a common market may lead to concentrated investments in certain regions, and growing unemployment in others. Such situations call for measures of social and regional policy, co-ordinated on the level of the common market.

In working towards an *economic and monetary union*, integration extends into different policy areas. The most important is the wish to stimulate economic growth. One way to do so is to lower transaction costs for firms by introducing a single currency. Another way is to conduct a research and technology policy which encourages innovation and thus the creation of new sales prospects. Any national measures to that effect must be co-ordinated to avoid similar, or even conflicting, developments at different places. Another way is to foster favourable and stable conditions. As the free movement of goods and factors renders the economies of member states more mutually dependent, economic or fiscal measures taken by one member state become more likely to affect all others, perhaps conflicting with their policy. Because member states no longer have authority to counteract such disturbances by measures of trade policy, they may resort to budgetary and monetary instruments. To prevent an escalation of such measures in all countries, which again would make for disturbances, co-ordination of the macro-economic and monetary policies of member states becomes imperative.

Finally, economic integration favours integration in other areas from *political motives*. Economics and politics being in many ways interwoven, the common trade policy could induce member states to co-ordinate their foreign policy and their defence policy as well. Thus, economic integration may pave the way to political integration.

Welfare effects of advanced integration

Several times we have pointed out the advantages of the primary forms of integration, namely, of the goods markets and the markets of production factors. Anticipating the more theoretical discussion in Chapters 5 to 7, we have pointed out that all partners may profit from the establishment of a customs union. The theory also admits that the profit of integrated product markets is enhanced if the internal movement of the production factors 'capital and labour' is liberalised. The fact is well established that to let markets function properly, a certain level of positive integration is needed. It means that such policies as competition policy and trade policy have to be integrated to some extent.

However, *progressive integration is not always favourable to national prosperity*. Advantages in some respects may indeed be offset by great disadvantages in others, for instance the jeopardy to certain social objectives. Thus, the harmonisation of taxes (considered necessary to the undisturbed movement of capital) may bring about a shift from direct to indirect taxes in some countries, so that the tax system can no longer be used to lessen income inequality. Whether the positive effects of an abundant goods supply outweigh the drawbacks of, for example, regionally concentrated unemployment, depends entirely on how much store is set on the realisation of certain social objectives.

One argument for progressive integration, however, springs from political rather than economic theory (Pryce, 1973; Jansen and De Vree, 1985). It is based principally on an analysis of the factors underlying the political dynamics of integration, the outcome of which is that under the conditions prevailing in Western Europe, a free-trade area and a customs union are unstable forms of co-operation, which can function only if progressing continuously towards further integration. When the progress stagnates, forces opposed to the union's 'rules of the game' may gain weight and combine with others to become a serious threat to the freedoms achieved.[11] Disintegration could then be prevented only by further integration.

Summary and conclusions

- Economic integration is a dynamic process in which the economies of partner states become more and more interwoven.
- Economic integration is aspired to because it yields economic advantages: higher growth, hence more prosperity, and because it reduces considerably the chance of armed conflicts among partners.
- In the process of economic integration can be distinguished the

main stages: the customs union, the common market, and the economic and monetary union, representing the integration of, progressively, the markets of goods and services; of production factors; and finally of commercial policy, sectoral policy, macro-economic policy, and monetary policy.

- The removal of the numerous measures which impede the free movement of goods and production factors among member states is called negative integration.
- In modern mixed economies, the government intervenes in many ways in the economy. The co-ordination (harmonisation) or unification of government regulations, which the higher forms of integration especially require, is called positive integration.

Notes

1 Hirsch (1981) suggests that countries feel obliged to adopt a peaceful attitude when a 'balance of prosperity' is created instead of a 'balance of deterrence'.
2 For a description, see, for instance, Södersten (1980), chapters 1, 5, 8 and 12.
3 That the distinction made is not always found back in practice has already been recognised by Balassa (1976). Others have remarked that the various stages distinguished here can be split up further: see for example, Pelkmans (1986) for the CM and Gros (1989) for the MU.
4 The theoretical implications of these points will be taken up in Chapter 5, the practical aspects in Chapter 8.
5 Absence of tariffs and QR is generally sufficient to speak of a free-trade area; the complete liberalisation of goods trade involves supplementary measures, which we will discuss in Chapter 16.
6 Non-tariff barriers are very common, because international agreements forbid countries to have recourse to tariffs. The negative effects are similar to those of tariffs; see, for instance, Krauss (1979); Greenaway (1983). For a more thorough treatment of voluntary export restraints (VERs), see Jones (1984).
7 The arguments for protection and the (lack of) economic base for them have been extensively studied in the literature. We refer here only to the authoritative work of Corden (1971, 1974), the handbook by Caves and Jones (1984), the case studies by Meyer (1973), the political economy approach of Frey (1985), the inventory of the OECD (1985) and the European study of new protectionism by Page (1981).
8 A detailed description of these types of trade barrier for different sectors can be found in OECD 1981b, 1983a, 1984a, 1985b and 1986a.
9 See in that respect, among others, the study by Meyer (1967) of the difference in efficiency of financial agents in large and small markets.
10 We will take up this breakdown into functions in Part V of the book dealing with each function in a separate chapter.
11 Compare also Lindberg and Scheingold (1970).

3 Short History

Introduction

Economic integration was defined in the previous chapter as a process of economic unification of national economies. The expression has become so current, especially with respect to Europe, that it gives the impression of a fundamental notion with a long historical background. Actually, the term was used for the first time in 1930, or rather, its negative counterpart, 'economic disintegration'. In a positive sense the term does not occur until after the Second World War.[1] That the term is new does not mean that the process of economic integration and disintegration is also new. On the contrary, it has been going on all through modern European history, as will become clear from the brief sketch in this chapter.[2] Two stimulating factors can be observed (Pollard, 1981a) to have always been present, namely:

- *Technological progress.* Long-term economic development is determined by some autonomous factors, of which technology is the most important. Mechanisation and automation of the production process have completely changed production methods. Advances in energy technology, for instance, led to the replacement of human and animal power with steam and later with electricity. With respect to transport, horse-drawn vehicles gave way to railways and lorries. As a result, goods can now be produced and distributed cheaply in large numbers. But production in large series makes first exportation, and next integration, imperative. The exchange of technical knowledge and capital also press towards more economic integration;
- *Political idealism.* The conception of Europe as a separate entity, separate in particular from Asia, is very old (Chabod, 1961; Duroselle, 1965), and has been developed and deepened through the ages. Especially since the Middle Ages there has been virtually no period in which statesmen or philosophers did not point to the common European heritage and the necessity of more 'political' unity in Europe. The arguments have become louder as the national states became stronger. Notably since the Second

World War, economic integration has been appreciably accelerated by political pressure.

In the course of history, the weight of these two main elements of the dynamics of European economic integration has constantly shifted. Consequently, there have been periods in which developments favoured integration, and others in which integration seemed to stagnate or even to be reversed. A separate section will be devoted to each. The chapter will be concluded with a brief summary.

Until 1815, a traditional world with little integration

From the Middle Ages to the French Revolution

In the early Middle Ages, the European economy was marked by a great fragmentation of markets. The feudal system had made all regions almost perfectly self-supporting. Under the influence of urban development in the twelfth century, the system was gradually adapted.

First the *movement of goods*, that is, trade among regions and countries was slowly resumed (Pirenne, 1927). In the following centuries trade expanded steadily but remained of limited scope, being mostly concerned with luxury goods. There were three reasons for this:

- Countless obstacles like tolls, different weights and measures and coins, staple rights and the privileges of merchant groups obtained within countries. These were comparable to those now prevailing among states, for national frontiers did not yet have the economic function they have now. Tolls were levied at bridges, town gates, locks, etc. rather than at the national frontier. In the late Middle Ages, the citizens of all towns tried to obtain privileges so as to evade tolls and other trade obstacles. The resulting patchwork of privileges for various groups heralded in a way the complex systems of trade discrimination by country groups that we know today.
- Primitive transportation means. On land, everything had to be hauled by waggon and pack animal. Most tradesmen preferred the cheaper waterway: across the sea or along the river. The fleets of river barges and seagoing vessels were already quite large, but the tonnages of the vessels remained small.
- Economic policy was a movement opposing international integration. The aim of mercantilist policy was primarily to be as much as possible self-sufficient, and next, to achieve the highest possible export surplus. To that end, goods trade among countries was limited by import levies, export embargos (on strategic

goods), etc. Evidently, the arguments for old mercantilist and modern protectionist policies are much alike. With mercantilism, no greater internal integration was achieved, however, for local tolls continued to be levied for all goods, domestic or foreign.

The *movement of production factors* was also very limited in the early Middle Ages. The movement of labour was hampered because virtually the entire population, with the exception of the nobility and the clergy, was bound by law to a certain place (serfdom). In the course of the Middle Ages, citizens fought for, and gained, the right to move and trade freely everywhere. In principle, the movement of capital was free in this period. In practice, however, the transfer of money was much hindered by the defective monetary system and the limited means to convey money from one place to another. From an early date, money traffic consisted not only of payments for commercial transactions, but also of money loans, mostly loans to princes to cover their military expenditure. Investments in transport infrastructure were mostly made and financed locally.

The innovations of the French Revolution

The French Revolution, a political event, was soon developed by the citizens, who became all-powerful, into an economic revolution, totally upsetting the 'feudal' economy. The following measures show clearly the essence of this revolution: *the integration of the regional and local economies into a national economy:*

- abolition of all rules impeding the free traffic of goods, instantly followed by the abolition of all seigneurial rights and serfdom;
- shift of customs duties to the outer frontiers;
- creation of quota systems and tariffs to protect national production;
- abolition of all privileges of companies and guilds, and of rules about the manner of production;
- introduction of a uniform system of weights and measures;
- introduction of new legal rules for trade;
- construction of new infrastructure.

Owing to the national character of these measures, at first economic integration increased internally but decreased externally. During the Napoleonic regime the above novelties were introduced all over the European sub-continent. Moreover, the so-called 'continental system' was created, intended to make the continent independent of Britain.

The ensuing selective international integration was the fruit of a politico-military concept rather than economic logic.

With the downfall of Napoleon's empire, the continental system broke down as well. Once more, British goods could be sold on the continent, and given Britain's technological leadership, a whole range of new industries on the continent had to be closed down. That put free trade, and international integration, in a bad light. On the other hand, measures like the removal of tolls, which had fostered economic integration on the national level, were found useful and were maintained practically everywhere in Europe.

Fading concept of Europe

The late Middle Ages can be characterised as a period during which the pan-European ideas of Empire and Papacy were more and more fading, giving way to a *growing nationalism*. The idea of a Europe acting as a unity receded to the background, to reappear only when the common heritage was immediately threatened from outside. In concrete terms, the threat came from the Turks, steadily encroaching upon East Europe. To take a European stand against them was pleaded more than once (among others by the diplomat Piccolini from Siena in the 15th century), but only when the Turks threatened Vienna was collective action taken: the Turks were beaten by a European coalition. Internal threats to peace also inspired some advocates of a united Europe. They looked for a way to avoid the internal armed conflicts which constantly ravaged Europe. Out of the long range of illustrous men who devoted themselves to the creation of some type of European Federal State, we will mention only Sully, Leibniz, Penn, Bentham, Kant, von Gentz, and Saint Pierre. However, all their plans came to nothing, and their worthy goals avoiding the constant wars for the hegemony in Europe, frontiers or heritages, or trade privileges failed to come about. The clearest evidence of that failure is found in the Napoleonic wars concluding this period.

1815 – 1870: progressive integration following the Industrial Revolution

Theory and policy

In the period after 1815, the economic policy of many European countries was greatly influenced by the successful model of Great Britain. That country, with an open economy of long standing, was the first to accomplish a drastic industrial revolution. This was the period in which the ideas of *free trade* were given a theoretical foundation and a political shape. Great classical economists such as Smith, Ricardo and Mill emphasised in their work that free national and international trade would lead to the greatest possible prosperity. They paved the way for political aspirations towards free trade (Gomes, 1987). Obstacles to the free movement of goods, persons and capital were increasingly felt as suffocating. That was especially true in areas such as Germany, Austria and Italy, where economic frontiers were dividing a space felt to be culturally united. To such areas, economic integration spelled a way to political unity.

Germany took up the problem of trade obstacles by means of the *Zollverein*. Under Prussian leadership a customs union was created in 1834 and gradually expanded. It implied the abolition of all duties at inner borders, and a duty levied on the outer frontier which was low for 'European' and high for colonial goods. Gradually more and more states in central and south Germany joined this union. The fast industrialisation which commenced in Germany in this period contributed much to the success of this type of integration, and was itself stimulated again by progressive integration.[3]

It is interesting to see how integration was progressing even among countries that were clearly independent from one another. Most European countries adopted more liberal external policies. Britain, as leader in industrial technology, initially prohibited the exportation of machinery and the emigration of skilled workers. Nevertheless, British craftsmen went to work in other countries of Europe, often with the help of smuggled machinery. Because the prohibition could not be enforced, Britain abolished all legal barriers to the emigration of skilled workers in 1825 and of capital goods in 1842. It moved further towards free trade with the abolition of the Navigation Acts and the Corn Laws. 'Protection or free trade' had become the central theme of discussions between politicians and economists in many countries, and until the middle of the century the free-traders were in the ascendency. Pollard (1981b) remarks that the successful coalition of philosophers and politicians heralded a decisive stage in history:

> Unlike some earlier examples of freedom from frontier control it was not based on the technical inability to levy duties or to the insignificant quantity of traffic, but on the conscious decision of modern governments to encourage the closer integration of European economic life by opening out the opportunities to international trade and competition.

Total external trade increased rapidly (see Table 3.1). Intra-European trade in this period relied strongly on sectoral specialisation, itself the result of different technologies practised in different countries. At the end of the period international trade, migration and capital movement were practically free all over Europe.

Technology and diplomacy

While integration was clearly stimulated by *industrialisation*, founded on technological innovation, and by the ensuing rapid economic growth, the rapid industrialisation marking most West European countries in this period (see Figure 3.1) was in turn fostered by the progressive integration. Indeed, the application of modern technology made further specialisation not only possible but also desirable (see Table 3.1).

Table 3.1   Some indicators of European economic development, 1810–1870

Indicator	1810	1830	1850	1870
Gross National Product per head (index 1900=100)	47	53	62	79
Industrial production (index 1900=100)	n.a.	20	33	51
Production of pig iron (MT/y)	1	2	4	10
Production of coal (MT/y)	20	29	67	180
Proportion of urban population (%)	13	25	n.a.	n.a.
Share of exports in GNP (%)	3	4	7	11
Share of foreign investment in GNP (%)	–	1	2	3
Railway track (x 1,000 km)	–	–	24	105

Source: Bairoch (1976)
n.a. = not available

A second important component of the 'natural techno-economic process' is the *means of transportation and communication* and in particular the railways. The tremendous accumulation of capital required for the construction of railways was sometimes warranted only if transport nodes and feeding points were also internationally connected; moreover, to be feasible, railway transport had to be liberalised to a high degree. River transport, too, was liberalised: the new, larger steamships called for flexible exploitation. Successive international agreements ensured free navigation on the Rhine (Central Committee for Rhine Navigation, 1815, and Mannheim Treaty, 1868), the Danube, the Scheldt, etc.

Attempts were also made, in this same period, at *monetary integration* (Bartel, 1974). The large states of Western Europe had often reached a considerable degree of internal monetary integration (as early as the 13th century, Louis the Saint, King of France, introduced one single coin, the Ecu, for his entire kingdom!). After the Napoleonic wars, practically every country had developed its own national currency system. International monetary co-operation was set up by the German (Holtfrerich, 1989) and Italian states (Sannucci, 1989) before unification and by the Latin Monetary Union, which was based on the French Franc and to which the Belgian, Swiss, Italian and later the Greek and Spanish currencies were joined. All these systems suffered from the lack of mechanisms obliging the participants to consultation and co-ordination. These experiences show that a monetary union seems to have to go hand in hand with political union in order to be successful (see also Hamada, 1985).

The *form* in which integration was expressed varied in the course of the years. International integration had always been a more or less

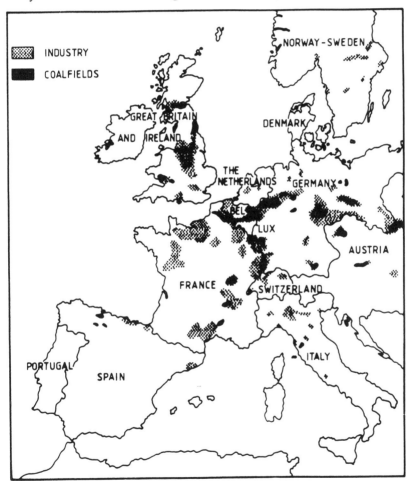

Figure 3.1   European industry around 1870

factual process partly consolidated in bilateral agreements. This continued in the period under discussion, for instance with the famous Cobden–Chevalier free-trade treaty of 1860 which gave French industry access to cheaper and better coal and iron from Britain. It was copied by many other countries for similar matters. Its importance lies in its unconditional most-favoured-nation clause, which had considerable implications for Europe-wide tariff reductions.[4] These treaties were drawn up and implemented through the usual diplomatic channels, no permanent bodies being created for the purpose. Postal services and telecommunications are noteworthy exceptions; only for them was the need for positive integration already so great at the time as to warrant the setting up of an international organisation.

Monarchist ideologies and socialist utopia

In the period after the Napoleonic wars, three widely different initiatives were taken towards lasting peace in Europe.

The first, *monarchist* and anti-revolutionary in nature, was the Holy Alliance. The objective of this bond of heads of state was to prevent revolutionary troubles in, and wars between, European states. To that end, the monarchs consulted regularly with one another, and in some instances decided to act collectively. The Holy Alliance indeed made but little impact — the system fell apart after some time through internal conflicts and lack of a strong institutional organisation.

A second attempt came from the *philosophical* corner. From a visionary utopian analysis of the developing industrial society, Saint Simon concluded that the political organisation should be left to representatives of trade and industry, in particular manufacturing industry and banks. In his view, for a satisfactory development, a peaceful international community in Europe was an absolute condition. Saint Simon's ideas and their elaboration by the Saint Simonists were not translated into action and made little impact at the time.

Nor did a third movement to unite Europe, of a more *democratic and republican* nature, have a successful outcome. Manzini, theorist of Italian unity, was perhaps the most important representative of a movement aiming to accomplish in Europe a fraternal collaboration of free peoples (Giovine Europa).

Other suggestions by intellectuals for some form of political integration (almost invariably involving economic integration) in Europe hardly found any response at the time.

1870 – 1914: stagnating integration

Depression and protectionism

The long period of growth came to a sudden end around 1870, in a depression which has been compared to the Great Depression of 1930.

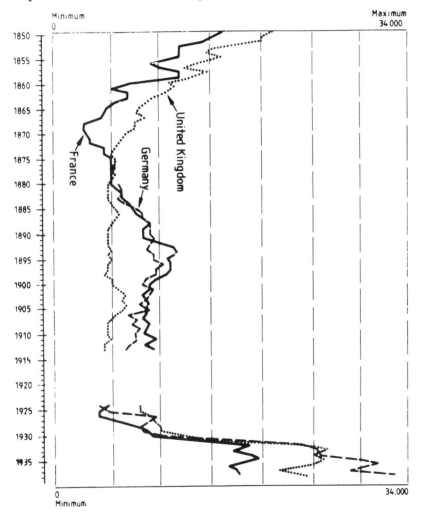

Figure 3.2 Evolution of British, French and German average tariff rates of protection, 1850–1938

Source: Messerlin and Becuwe (1986)

Many governments responded to it in a *protectionist* fashion. The French–German war and the Italian fight for unity had completely upset the situation. The powers demanding more protection for economic reasons were reinforced by a desire for autarky of mostly political and military inspiration. As a result, at many places attempts were made to curtail the existing freedoms of trade and traffic; straight tariff and subsidy wars were fought between some countries (see left-hand side of Figure 3.2). Having become far better organised than before, national states found themselves in a better position to impose taxes and customs duties, regulate their social affairs, and to pursue a protectionist, nationalist policy.

In spite of such protectionist inclinations, *trade* increased at the same rate as production (see row 3 Table 3.2). Some countries soon found out that complete autarky was an illusion, given the international specialisation which had developed. Not different natural endowment, but far-reaching sectoral specialisation had become the main reason for goods trade, a specialisation based on economies of scale and technological leadership. Improved transportation techniques (leading, among other things, to lower freight rates) also made for continued economic integration in Europe; the railway and canal networks proliferated in this period (see Table 3.2). However, in the construction of infrastructure, nationalist tendencies were becoming more and more manifest.

Table 3.2   **Some indicators of European economic development between 1870 and 1910**

Indicator	1870	1880	1890	1900	1910
Gross National Product per head (index)	79	80	85	100	110
Industrial production (index)	51	61	77	100	136
Production of pig iron (MT/y)	10	14	17	25	37
Coal production (MT/y)	180	217	328	438	574
Share of exports in GNP (%)	11	13	13	11	13
Share of total foreign investment in GNP (%)	3	4	4	4	5
Ocean freight rates (index)	212	180	127	100	83
Railway track (x 1000 km)	105	169	225	292	351

Source: Bairoch (1976)

The *free movement of production factors,* that is, of workers and capital, next to goods, was taking shape in this period. International migration referred mainly to seasonal workers. Several thousands of Italians were employed in France, Germany and Austria. Some hundreds of thousands of Poles went to Germany every year, as did quite a number of other East Europeans. Many of them were employed in manufacturing industry, the mining industry or the construction trade, but many also filled the jobs in agriculture left open by the urbanising rural population. Many specialised labourers tended to move from country to country to operate special machines in regions and countries starting up new industrial projects. Capital was moving practically freely. In this period, Europe became the banker of the world. Its total stock of foreign investment rose significantly to arrive in 1913 at a level that exceeded its GDP. Annual flows amounted to more than 5 per cent of GDP in 1913. Outgoing capital was oriented for about a quarter towards other European countries, a quarter to the USA and half to the rest of the world.

In the period under discussion, banking organised itself internationally for the purpose of large investment projects: railways in Russia, textile factories in Silesia, but also government loans. As a consequence, the total foreign investment of European countries increased sharply (Table 3.2). In this period, the automatic rules of the gold standard governed the monetary relations of all major industrialised countries. Free trade, free movement of capital, and fixed exchange rates were achieved by abstaining from an independent monetary policy (Hawtrey, 1947; Bordo and Schwartz, 1984).

The European idea

In the last part of the 19th century, there were hardly any movements to promote the idea of a united Europe. Though not typically European, an important anti-nationalist movement should perhaps be pointed out, namely, the Socialist International. This movement suggested that the popular masses had nothing to gain either from an armed conflict or from economic conflicts among capitalists of various countries. Successive versions of the Socialist International proved unable, however, to translate suggestions into a clear plan of action, let alone make the plan operational. Once more, the self-interest of national 'sections' proved the main obstacle to practical internationalisation.

The almost complete lack of utopias and proposals for concrete actions for the unity of Europe should not make us forget that most Europeans at the time continued to take the cultural unity of their part of the world more or less for granted. In spite of wide differences among nations, neither literary and artistic trends nor great spiritual movements were confined to any one nation; they were part of one common European cultural world (Duroselle, 1987) – a conception which in economics, and especially politics, was still a long way off.

International organisation and co-ordination

At the turn of the century, forms of integrated policy (positive integration) were practised for the first time, international institutions being founded for the purpose. It was the logical outcome of increased government intervention in the economy combined with intensified international exchange. Not surprisingly, this policy integration concerned only areas directly connected with international trade or conditions of international competition.

- *Transportation.* The technical standardisation of railway equipment was mainly due to the British system of measures being adopted by most states. The co-ordination of other elements, such as the exchange of rolling stock, the treatment of goods, time schedules, etc., was accomplished in international committees.
- *Post and telecommunication* were among the first elements for which international organisations were created. The International Telecommunication Union (1865) and the Universal Postal Union (1874) were established to harmonise internationally all national regulations with respect to rates, procedures, infrastructure (cables), etc. The harmonisation has contributed much to the fast growth of PTT traffic.
- *Agriculture and fishery.* Several attempts were made at international co-ordination and regulation; a first limited success was the regulation of trade in sugar (premiums being abolished). An effort was made to achieve one European tariff for foodstuffs, to protect European producers against competition, on the European market, from new producer countries.
- *Social policies.* Efforts towards integration were inspired largely by the fear that the improvement of social services and work conditions in one country would put that country at a competitive disadvantage. Much later, after the First World War, the problem was the subject at various conferences which finally led to the creation of the International Labour Office. The abolition of slavery was among the first steps towards social-policy integration: in 1890, a General Act against Slavery was signed.

Some hesitant steps were taken to bring about some co-ordination in other areas by diplomatic deals, but they were mostly not very successful and will therefore not be elaborated on here.

1914 – 1945: disintegration

The First World War and the peace treaty

With the outbreak of the *First World War*, a process of disintegration was set in motion. During the war, every country emphasised the need for autarky: to depend economically on foreign countries makes a country vulnerable in military terms. The result was a steep drop in international trade. Not only did free trade suffer from the war, the movement of production factors was also more and more curtailed. Under the pressure of conscription, among other things, the free movement of persons collapsed completely. Capital was more and more contained within national borders by a multitude of national rules. The international loans concluded in this period were concerned exclusively with the assistance of one government by another.

The state began to interfere intensively with trade and industry, organising it for purposes of war. Because the control was strictly national, a co-ordinated policy was practically impossible. Even within a bloc, integration was shunned for fear of disloyalty of allied states. Any agreements concluded between the members of each bloc covered only restricted areas. For instance, during the First World War the Allies only co-ordinated the use of shipping tonnage and made some attempt at specialising production (Monnet, 1976).

The *Peace Treaty of Versailles* even consolidated the disintegration. The central theme of this treaty was the nations' right to self-determination. On that basis, many new states were formed in Europe, which instantly began to quarrel about frontiers, debts, minorities, etc. The result was a great length of new frontiers (some 11,000 km) with corresponding customs barriers. To support the autonomy of the national economies, most barriers were drawn up sky-high (see right-hand side of Figure 3.2). Thus, the industrial and transportation structures were forced to adapt themselves to a multitude of small territories. Factories were built at uneconomic locations, railways rerouted, etc.

The period between the two world wars

After the First World War some countries (notably Germany) were left with enormous debts, leading to serious balance-of-payment troubles. These troubles were aggravated by low prices and diminishing sales prospects on export markets. Under such circumstances, non-competitive companies, traditionally in favour of protection, grasped their chance, and the enormous unemployment consolidated the *protectionist tendencies*. This movement spread quickly over Europe and as a consequence, imports were reduced to almost half the pre-war level;

this in turn led to a decrease in exports as well (as illustrated by Table 3.3). An even greater decrease happened to international capital movements, that fell back to about one-fifth of their pre-war level.

Table 3.3   Some indicators of European* economic development 1913–1938

Indicator	1913	1920	1930	1938
Gross National Product per head (index 1938=100)	n.a.	73	89	100
Industrial production (index 1938=100)	n.a.	61	86	100
Production of pig iron (MT/y)	39	21	36	38
Coal production (MT/y)	498	392	480	481
Share of exports in GNP (%)	16	9	9	6
Share of total foreign investment in GNP (%)	5	n.a.	1	1
Railway track (x 1000 km)	193	189	197	199

Source: calculated on the basis of figures given in OECD (1964), Bairoch (1976), Mitchell (1984)
* Only present EC12 countries
n.a. = not available

The disadvantages of the economic disintegration were increasingly recognised and attempts were undertaken to reunite certain groups of states. The plan to unite the old Habsburg states in a customs union failed (Ponteroso Conference), as did a world-wide free-trade scheme in which 29 states agreed to abolish all trade restrictions within six months and never impose them again (Conference of Geneva, 1927). The League of Nations, founded by the Allies, came into operation in 1920; its object was to maintain peace in Europe. The League developed some activity in economic and social affairs (among others it created the ILO, the International Labour Organisation). However, all those initiatives hardly made an impact.

So severe were the obstacles to international trade and payments in this period of general disintegration that we have been able to find only one example of *positive integration*. The Bank for International Payments, a joint venture of the central banks in Europe, was founded in 1930 to facilitate payments, quite a feat in a period of great monetary disorder (inflation, devaluation race, downfall of the gold standard, etc.).

In the 1920s a slight improvement on some points raised hopes for a period of more intensive integration. However, as Table 3.3 indicates, during the 1920s, average dependency on trade remained virtually stable. Even that comparatively modest integration was curtailed by the *Depression of the 1930s.* The USA's introduction of the very high

Smoot–Hawley tariff in 1930 sparked off a further wave of protectionist measures in Europe, leading to tariffs of unprecedented height (see Figure 3.2) and the multiplication of the number of quotas.

The *gold standard*, which had not worked very well in this period, collapsed (Britain left gold in 1931; other countries soon followed). A period of currency competition ensued, one devaluation following upon the other. All attempts to solve the crisis by international agreements failed.

To overcome the Depression, national states began to intervene even more than before in the economy, and Keynes (1936) furnished the theoretical foundation. National solutions (armament, infrastructural works) to the unemployment problem were governed by national circumstances, and once more the economy was often made subservient to military objectives.

The idea of a united Europe

During and between the two world wars, short-term economic thinking (fight against unemployment) and strategic-military thinking (autarky was believed to be safer than integration) were dominant; however, some enlightened spirits began to see that nationalism only breeds economic problems and is a permanent threat to peace. The best known attempt of this period to solve the problem in a European perspective was the *Pan Europe Movement*, led by Coudenhove–Calergi. Although this movement had quite a lot of response, it shared with comparable activities the weakness of keeping rather aloof of the political reality of the time and of being too utopian.

Initiatives towards European unity from leading statesmen seemed more promising, in principle. There was, for instance, the plan for a European federation which Briand, French prime minister in 1930, after consultation with the German Stresemann, submitted to the League of Nations. The scheme was well received, but the support was soon found to be very superficial. It failed to stir the masses in any nation; nationalism had sunk too deeply in the consciousness of the average citizen. Even such weak attempts were heard of less and less in the 1930s, when *fascist movements* were organising themselves along downright nationalist lines, more and more straining international relations to the test, and finally even trying to impose the hegemony of the Axis powers on Europe by military force – hardly a situation to foster a true European vision.

1945 – the present: a new upsurge of integration

Europe and world policy

 The Second World War brought about a measure of integration. On the side of the Axis powers it was achieved by enlisting the economies of territories occupied by Germany in the German war efforts. The integration concerned not only products (agricultural as well as industrial): production factors were forcefully integrated as well (Arbeitseinsatz, war loans). On the side of the Allies some integration could also be perceived: once more, production and means of transportation were to some extent normalised for the sake of the war effort. The integration efforts hardly touched the other sectors of the economy.

The terrors of war inspired attempts to improve the relations among nations by creating a number of *international organisations*. The lesson from the experience with the League of Nations was that all large countries would have to be members of the central organisation, in this case the United Nations. A range of other bodies was founded, some of them associated with the United Nations (UNO). The World Bank (IRBD) and the International Monetary Fund (IMF) deserve to be mentioned in particular. Their combined task was to ensure well regulated international monetary relations (Conference of Bretton Woods). That meant fixed exchange rates between currencies. Countries that through temporary balance-of-payment problems found it hard to maintain these fixed exchange rates could obtain hard-currency loans. Since then, the IMF has expanded its scope and has become the place for co-ordination and consultation in the international monetary sphere.

The GATT, the General Agreement of Tariffs and Trade, was to guard against the provocation of trade wars by high customs barriers. One important instrument operated by the GATT was the so-called most-favoured nation clause, according to which any favourable tariff which two countries accord to each other is essentially valid for all other participants in the General Agreement. The GATT has accomplished a considerable world-wide tariff decrease; many non-tariff impediments have been eliminated as well.

Integration, which had come to a halt during the war, was gradually re-established in this period. First there was a move towards free trade, next towards convertibility of currencies and free capital movements, with exchange rates pegged to the dollar. The monetary and macroeconomic co-ordination schemes of the IMF and OECD (see subsequent section) could not cope with the emerging inconsistencies, and in the 1970s the Bretton Woods system collapsed. The experiences of the period lead to the conclusion (Padoa-Schioppa, 1987) that free movement of goods and capital cannot be combined with pegged exchange rates and independent macro-economic policy making of member countries.

After the Allied victory *Europe was cut in two.* If at first the spheres of influence of the western Allies and the Soviet Union were not precisely delineated, soon afterwards the outbreak of the Cold War, the revolutions in some East European countries and the refusal of Russia and its confederates to accept Marshall Aid, led to the very sharp dividing line which goes by the name of Iron Curtain. Economic integration of European countries from the Western bloc with those from the Eastern bloc was thus excluded for a long time. The only platform where 'integration' of East and West was still a point of discussion, was the Economic Commission for Europe (ECE), a regional organisation of the United Nations. Its role has been very modest, however. Any further integration has proceeded within each separate bloc. Some integration of the economies of Eastern Europe has taken place in the framework of the Council of Mutual Economic Assistance (CMEA or Comecon), a different organisation from that chosen in the West (Kozma, 1982; Pinder, 1986). We will concentrate henceforth on Western Europe.

The pursuit of European unity

Already during the Second World War, the pursuit of intensive *economic integration was put on a political–idealistic footing.*[5] Especially in circles of the Resistance the conviction was growing that nationalism was at the roots of the disaster which fascism had wrought in Europe. Therefore, Europe should be rebuilt in a sphere of increased international integration, especially in economic terms.

The Ventotene Manifest published in 1941 by personalities grouped around Spinelli is perhaps the best known of the ideas fostered by the Resistance. It led more or less directly to the Geneva Declaration of 1944, which confirmed the principles of an Atlantic Charter and proposed a federal solution for the whole of Europe (including Eastern Europe). For the first time the sentiments initially expressed by some members of the Resistance, appeared to be attractive to large groups of people.

A whole series of initiatives for European integration were fostered by these sentiments, many of which found active support from leading politicians in all West European countries. The first result was the creation of the Council of Europe, and the Union Parlementaire Européenne the second. Many groups continued to submit proposals and to campaign for a more far-reaching European unity.

The movements varied widely in objective and organisation. International pacifism, European federalism and economic functionalism were joined, however, into one *European Movement* (Lipgens, 1982). The generally felt need for economic integration soon generated a favourable climate to create, with US support, the OECD. However, after some time the United Kingdom appeared to set greater store by an empire than a European orientation, and the British gradually with-drew from initiatives towards greater European integration.

That continental nations continued to strive for closer co-operation is not surprising. Most initiatives were inspired by the hope to elimi-nate forever the potential war threat of the French–German differ-ences. That political aim was to be achieved, not through unrealistic plans for complete political union, but through a *strategy of gradual economic integration.* That seemed the most practical as very good economic reasons pushed into that direction anyway (Bourrinet, 1981). Such a strategy was the basis of the plan launched on 9 May, 1950, by the French minister Schuman, to join the French and German basic in-dustries together under a High Authority. The road Europe took at that moment towards economic and political integration and has followed since, was indicated by Schuman in his famous declaration and con-sisted in the creation of a factual solidarity based on practical realisa-tions.

During the negotiations about the European Coal and Steel Commu-nity (ECSC), the French initiator of the Plan, Monnet, persuaded the parties to transfer much of their national authority to ECSC bodies. The success was due to the heavy support the plan received from leading politicians (Adenauer, de Gasperi, etc.). After the successful creation of the ECSC, new initiatives were taken to found an European Defence Community (EDC) and a European Political Community (EPC). The ratification of the treaties for these two communities miscarried even-tually in the French parliament. The pressure of the Europeans was then once more brought to bear on the economic sector, leading, after the Spaak report and the Messina Conference, to the establishment, in 1958, of the European Economic Community (Jansen and De Vree, 1985).

In the past, voices pleading integration had hardly found any response. Now that all nations were feeling the chafing war scars, these voices had at last gained sufficient political weight to be heeded. Moreover, the basis for further integration had been enlarged as the social differences among European countries gradually became less outspoken, a development that gained momentum in the post-war decades (Kaelble, 1986).

European organisations

The ravages of war made it clear that Europe's only chance of survival lay in progressive economic integration. To that end some important multinational agreements were concluded and some international bodies, widely different in structure and authority,[6] created (see for instance, Palmer and Lambert 1968). Examples are the Council of Europe, concerned in particular with cultural affairs and human rights, and the West European Union, mainly occupied with defence. Four others deal more specifically with economic integration.

The *Benelux Economic Union (1944)*, which joins together The Netherlands, Belgium and Luxemburg, has a long history. Unsuccessful attempts at creating a Benelux customs union had already been made in 1919 and 1932. The present agreement provides for a customs union as well as an economic union. The customs union took a relatively short time to realise; the economic union is still being worked at. The importance of the Benelux lies in particular in the opportunity it gives to gain experience in certain forms of integration, an experience which has proved useful for the establishment and extension of the European Community.

The *OEEC*, Organisation for European Economic Cooperation (1948), later reorganised to become the *OECD*, was created to administer Marshall Aid. To prevent the tremendous currency deficit of the European nations from disrupting international trade and payments, the European Payment Union was established. It undertook the clearance of bilateral currency surpluses and deficits, and provided credit facilities. The OEEC aimed for trade liberalisation by the elimination of all manner of obstacles. The OEEC further provided for some co-ordination of national policies, for instance on the macro-economic level and with respect to manufacturing industry and energy, constituting a clear, albeit light, form of positive integration. The type of organisation chosen, namely full inter-government collaboration with a modest secretariat, to many European nations seemed too limited and too weak to foster further economic integration. These nations kept looking for other ways to consolidate the integration. To that end, the OEEC was extended and relaunched in 1961 under the new name of Organisation for Economic Co-operation and Development (*OECD*); at present it comprises the entire industrialised Western world (Western Europe, the United States, Canada, Australia, New Zealand and Japan).

The *European Community* was established in 1952 by the Treaty of Paris, which created the European Coal and Steel Community (ECSC). Its objective was to withdraw the French and German basic industries from the national authority and place them under a European High Authority. Besides France and Germany, the Benelux countries and Italy joined the pact. The UK, having serious reservations about its supra-national character, kept aloof. The sectoral limitation of the ECSC was felt to be a serious practical handicap, and a fuller economic integration was aimed at. It was achieved when the European Economic Community (EEC) was created in 1958 by the Treaty of Rome.

The member states were the same six mentioned before, the UK again keeping apart. With the EEC, European integration reached a decisive stage in its development, for the Treaty of Rome provides for drastic forms of integration. First of all, a complete customs union. Next, free movement of persons and capital. Finally, an integrated policy in a number of important areas (agriculture, transportation). In that same year (1958), the same countries also founded the European Atomic Energy Community (EAEC). In the 1960s, the executive bodies of the ECSC, the EEC and the EAEC were combined. In the 1970s, economic integration within the European Community (EC) was extended to encompass monetary co-ordination, regional development, etc.

The *European Free Trade Association* (EFTA) was created in 1959 in Stockholm under the leadership of the UK by the remaining nations of Western Europe. While recognising the advantages of further integration, these countries could not, for different reasons, accept the organisation of the Communities. The objectives of EFTA went far less than those of the EC, only a free-trade zone being established. The institutional organisation of the EFTA was no other than the usual intergovernmental structure of most international organisations. In the course of the 1960s the advantages of such integration as was being realised in the EC became rapidly evident to other European countries as well. So, in 1972, the United Kingdom, Denmark and Ireland left the EFTA to join the EC. In 1981, Greece was admitted, followed on 1st January, 1986, by Spain and Portugal. At present, the EFTA is only a free-trade agreement between the remaining six small West European countries.

Summary and conclusions

- In an historical perspective, the economic integration of Europe has been not so much an objective as a by-product of technological progress on the one hand and aspirations to political unity on the other.
- Technical and economic factors (for instance large-scale production attended by mechanisation and automation, and the development of new means of transportation such as trains and lorries), were the principal stimulus to progressive economic integration in Europe.
- A political and idealistic pursuit of European unity can be observed throughout history; it has been strongly inspired by the need for peace. Its influence on practical economic integration remained slight, however. Indeed, not until after the Second World War did the European idea become really effective.[7]
- History proves that integration cannot only cease to make prog-

ress, it can also, once achieved, be reversed. Especially in times of economic depression and decline, the forces pleading against integration tend to become stronger and harder to resist.

- Welfare gains due to the opening-up of markets appear to be very substantial (resource allocation).
- Integration of goods and factor markets creates a demand for macro-economic and monetary integration (stabilisation). However, integration on those scores has been effective only under strict rules and in a strong institutional setting.
- Integration does not automatically lead to the satisfactory distribution of welfare among the participants. To safeguard cohesion and solidarity to the union, some form of support to the weaker participants has to be given (redistribution).
- Many institutional ways to realise economic integration have been tested. The European Community has emerged as the leading organisation.

Notes

1   For a discussion of the meaning of the term, see Herbst (1986).
2   The organisation of the subject matter of this chapter has been largely borrowed from Pollard (1981a); the passage concerning the 'ideology' of European unification leans in particular on the standard volume by Brugmans (1970).
3   Italy had the same experience after its unification.
4   See Chapter 19 for the present relevance of the clause.
5   See Machlup (1977) for a review of the contributions of historians (Chapter 5), political economists (Chapter 6), statesmen, men of affairs and men of letters (Chapter 7), Committee members and organisation staff (Chapter 8), and economic theorists (Chapter 9).
6   For a more complete review, see van Meerhaeghe (1980), or MacBean and Snowden (1981).
7   For a description of the perceptions of Europe in history, see A. Rijksbaron *et al.* (eds) 1987.

4 Institutional Economics of the European Community

Objectives and means

The treaties

Economic integration in Western Europe is fostered mainly in the legal and institutional framework drawn up by the European Community. Therefore, to understand the nature, depth and rate of the integration, one needs to be familiar with that framework. The *Treaties of Paris* (1951), creating the European Coal and Steel Community (ECSC) and *Rome* (1957), creating the European Economic Community (EEC) and the European Atomic Energy Community (Euratom), provided the three elements from which the European Community was built.

The Community is primarily an association of member states, the participating states having kept their sovereignty and competence in essential areas. The member states are represented in the Council of Ministers, as in all traditional intergovernmental international organisations, the dominant institution where final decisions are made. But the Community has also some clear federal traits: it has developed its *own system of laws* and its institutions exercise a *clearly defined authority* in several areas.[1] European Community law, being instantly and equally applicable in all member states, is neither national nor international; it used at one time to be called supra-national. Similarly, three of the EC institutions – the Commission, the Court of Justice and the Parliament – founded by virtue of the treaties, were said to be supra-national in nature, being endowed with powers between those of an intergovernmental international organisation like the OECD (with only a general secretariat to assist the ministers at their task), and those of a strong federal government (the United States of America, for instance) leaving only limited authority to the member states.

While the ECSC and Euratom treaties were envisaging only a limited form of sectoral integration, the EEC Treaty is concerned essentially with the *entire economy*. It is not surprising, therefore, that of the three, this last treaty has become the most important, in fact the source of most of the Community legislation issued since 1958. Structural economic changes by which coal (energy) and steel (manufacturing industry) lost much of their weight, have reinforced that tendency.

Different means for different objectives

The European Community's tasks (art. 3 EEC) are threefold:

- to establish a *customs union* (CU) by: 'the elimination, as between Member States, of customs duties and of quantitative restrictions on import and export of goods, and of all other measures having equivalent effect and the establishment of a common customs tariff';
- to realise a *common market* (CM) by 'the abolition, as between Member States, of obstacles to freedom of movement for persons, services and capital';
- to create an *economic union* (EU) by gradually unifying (foreign trade, competition, agriculture and transportation) or harmonising (macro-economic policy co-ordination) the economic policies of the member states, and by harmonising national legislations to the extent necessary for the CM to function.

The steps described here are elaborated in further chapters of the EEC Treaty. The Treaty is not exhaustive; indeed, article 235 stipulates that to achieve Community objectives, the Community can, if required, take appropriate measures in areas not envisaged in the Treaty. That has indeed happened – redistribution policies created by the foundation of the Regional Fund (on the initiative of the United Kingdom) and the stabilisation policies reinforced by the creation of the European Monetary System (on the initiative of Germany and France) are cases in point.

Remarkably enough, while explicitly regulating negative integration, the Treaty indicates only the general underlying principles of positive integration. The negative-integration measures, needed to ensure the free movement of goods, services, labour and capital became operational at the time foreseen in the Treaty. The implementation of positive integration (unification, harmonisation and co-ordination of policies), on the contrary, was left to the Community institutions. Indeed, in that respect the EEC Treaty offered no more than a framework; positive integration cannot be attained until further regulations in the sense of the relevant articles in the Treaty have been adopted.

Steady progress towards new objectives

The founders of the European Communities believed that the creation of a Common Market would entail further economic, or policy, integration, which would in the event, more or less compulsively, result in political integration. That expectation has not been entirely fulfilled.[2] True, the achievement of negative integration has given an impetus to positive integration, but the latter has not always come about. There are factors that explain why the *progress of positive or policy integration* is slower than that of negative integration.

For one thing, the *decision-making process* involves (apart from Commission, Parliament and Council) many interest groups. Views of these actors often diverge. This handicap worsened as the differences among states grew wider after the expansion of the EC from six to nine and later to 12 member states.

An even more important factor is the development of the *welfare state*. In a simple economy, where the state confines itself to maintaining law and order and safety, negative integration is often all that is needed. History has known several examples of successful integration of that type. However, the EC was created at a moment in time when the state was becoming more and more active everywhere. Increased government intervention covered not only such 'classical' areas as industry and energy, but also social security, the environment, the consumer, safety, regional equilibrium, income reallocation, etc. An evolution towards more state intervention could be observed, to a greater or lesser extent, in all member states at the same time, whatever their prevailing political conceptions of the role of the state in the economy.[3] Unfortunately, not until negative integration was well under way and positive integration was in order, was the fact realised that the many policy measures which member states had independently taken in the meantime, made positive integration a lot harder.

A third factor is the *procedure* followed to realise the necessary policy integration. In the late seventies and early eighties, state intervention, increasing in variety and intensity, has impeded the integration of goods and production-factor markets, replacing the tariffs and quantitative restriction just abolished with new obstacles. Of the abounding examples, we mention: quality standards imposed on goods by national legislation are an impediment to intra-Community trade; different environmental laws cause different investment costs of fixed production equipment; different labour legislation makes for different production costs. Now to remove such obstacles by progressive harmonisation of a great variety of detailed national regulations is a cumbersome process. Therefore, the accent has recently been put on deregulation and the competition of national rules that are mutually recognised (see Chapter 16) rather than harmonisation.

Finally there is the problem of *national sovereignty*. As policy co-ordination and harmonisation become more urgent as integration is progressing, more and more areas which used to be the exclusive responsibility of member states are coming under common control. At the same time, however, resistance against co-ordination and harmonising measures is gaining strength, the claim being that progressive inroads are being made into vital competences.

Unequal progress for different policy areas

Economic integration is steadily progressing, but at different rates for different sectors of policy. The causes are political and institutional rather than economic.

For one thing, the *treaties* explicitly prescribe common policies for a few policy sectors only, and keep silent about others. In areas where the EC did not get the necessary powers, progress was bound to be slow or non-existent. There are some exceptions. A common policy has been realised for some aspects not mentioned in the treaties (regional development, for example), whereas up to recently little progress had been made for aspects on which the Rome Treaty *is* explicit (transportation, for instance).

Actually, the main cause of sectorally divergent integration is *the sectorial segmentation of the institutional structure of the EC* (Faber and Breyer, 1980). This structure is the subject of the next section, but some characteristics of the workings of Council of Ministers, the Commission, Parliament and the Court of Justice should be mentioned here. Negative integration could be carried through smoothly because every citizen or legal person has recourse to the Court of Justice to enforce respect of the regulations concerned. Positive integration, on the contrary, requires the collaboration of the Commission, the Council and Parliament, and a final decision of the Council of Ministers. These tend to segment policy-making by area: the 'expert' Council (of agriculture, for instance) co-operates with the expert Directorate General of the Commission and the expert committee of Parliament. The same happens with the areas of transport, industry, monetary policy, etc. Conditions for one sector being often very different than those for another sector, different solutions will be the result.

The *priority ministers often give to the consistency of national policy over the consistency on the European level* (WRR, 1986) reinforces this. During negotiations in the Council, every minister tends to use what elbow room he has within the co-ordinated policy of his own country to arrive at an acceptable compromise on the European level. If a compromise is out of the question because the nations are at cross purposes, nothing will be accomplished even if the Treaty requires it; transportation is a case in point. How sometimes a fundamental decision can force a breakthrough is illustrated by the European involvement in regional assistance, which was conditional for a compromise between the EC6 and the new members (notably the United Kingdom). Sometimes, progress can only be made by abandoning the idea of equal forms for all member states in favour of a set-up which permits different roles to individual countries. That is the solution adopted, for instance, for the European Monetary System, in which member states participate in different ways.

The different rates of integration in the sub-areas of the economy is interesting not only from a political but also from an economic point of view, because the gaps and inconsistencies entailed have caused many problems to companies, citizens and authorities. The following parts of the book describe how integration has progressed in the various sectors; the final chapter will survey the whole.

The institutions

Different treaties, common institutions

The four *most important institutions* of the European Communities are the Council of Ministers, the Commission (or, for the ECSC, the High Authority), Parliament (formally called the Assembly) and the Court of Justice. The Treaty of Paris, creating the European Coal and Steel Community, also provided for four institutions: a Council of Ministers, a High Authority, an Assembly (the European Parliament), and a Court of Justice. Later, when the Treaties of Rome had called Euratom and the European Economic Community into being, the European Parliament and the Court of Justice went on to act also for the new Communities, but the Rome Treaties provided for separate executive bodies, namely Commissions (comparable to the ECSC's High Authority) and Councils. That situation – separate Commissions and Councils, common Parliament and Court of Justice – continued until 1967, when a new treaty merged the executive bodies of the three Communities as well. We shall describe the workings of these institutions in some detail hereafter.[4]

Three other institutions exist. The European Court of Auditors (ECA) examines the accounts of all revenue and expenditure of the Community, to determine not only whether all revenue has been received and all expenditure incurred in a lawful manner, but also whether the financial management has been sound. The Economic and Social Committee (ESC), composed of representatives of employees and employers, professionals and consumers, advises the Commission and the Council on their policy plans. The European Investment Bank (EIB) grants credits to business companies and governments. As the functioning of these three is not essential to the understanding of our subject matter, they will just be mentioned in passing.

Although institutions are merged, treaties are not. Indeed, the merged bodies have continued to act by the legal rules and procedures valid for the individual Communities, as the matter in hand requires. That situation has long been considered unsatisfactory,[5] and plans have been made to merge the Treaties into one, with a single set of legal rules. The European Parliament even proposed an entirely new treaty for a European Union, which, as the name indicates, would not only encompass the existing three Communities, but envisage a much intensified integration of Europe. To discuss the proposal, an intergovernmental meeting was convened in 1985. Instead of working out a completely new treaty as Parliament had suggested, this meeting confined itself to drawing up a 'Single European Act' (SEA) (CEC, 1986a). This SEA has been ratified since. It amends the Treaty of Rome by

- codifying the Communities' authority in some areas, such as regional development, monetary union, R&D, environment and foreign policy;
- introducing some measures intended to speed up the institutions' decision making, particularly with respect to the internal market (see Chapter 16);
- reinforcing the democratic procedures of the EC (art. 149, cooperation procedure between EP and CEC), and
- codifying the role of the *European Council*.[6] This institution had developed in the course of the years from the 'European Summits'. It consists of the heads of the governments, and meets at least two times a year, once in the country assuming the presidency, for the purpose of elaborating any important strategic decisions and giving new impulse to the work of the Council.

Although formally there are still three different Communities, for simplicity's sake the term of 'European Community' is used to indicate both the group of 12 member states and the total system drawn up on the basis of the three treaties. We will follow that usage from now on.

Figure 4.1 gives a schematic representation of the institutional system.

The special position of the Commission and the Council

The Commission and the Council occupy a special position in the institutional framework, because they are jointly responsible for the following tasks:

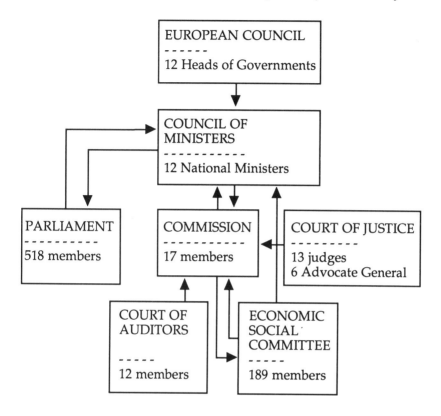

Figure 4.1 The EC Institutional system

- to co-ordinate national policies;
- to issue regulations and directives and take decisions in the policy areas foreseen in the treaties;
- to give form and substance to Community policy wherever the treaties have not done so;
- to supervise the observation of the treaties and the implementation of decisions.

In practice, there is some division of work; the Council co-ordinates and determines the strategy to be adopted, while the Commission takes care of daily operations and controls and supervises the observation of the treaties. The difference is one of accent only, for the Commission helps to prepare Council decisions, and often consults the Council or the representatives of the national governments on the execution of its tasks. Indeed, Council and Commission perform their duties in constant consultation (article 15 of the Merger treaty).

The Commission

Composition and procedure

The Commission consists of 17 members, appointed, after mutual consultation, by the governments of the member states for a four-year period. The largest countries (Germany, France, the United Kingdom, Italy, Spain) appoint two members each; the smaller ones (Belgium, Denmark, The Netherlands, Ireland, Portugal, Greece, Luxemburg) one each. The treaties stipulate that members shall be chosen on the ground of their 'general competence' and that their independence must be beyond doubt. Although one member acts as president and six others are vice-presidents, all members have the same powers, none being subordinate to any of the others. Decisions are made by majority vote.

Once appointed, the *members of the Commission have a Community responsibility*, that is to say, they must not set themselves up as representatives of their own country. For that reason, a member state cannot call 'its' Commissioner to account, or withdraw him. Nor can the Commission as a whole be dismissed by the Council of Ministers. However, the Commission is accountable to the European Parliament, and can be forced to resign as a body only by a motion of censure of the Parliament. In that case, the governments of the member states must appoint a new Commission (this has never happened yet).

The Commission occupies a *special position* in the system of the Community. It cannot be compared to the secretariat of other intergovernmental institutions, which can only prepare decisions and implement them by delegation of authority of the representatives of member states. Nor can the Commission be compared to the government of a sovereign member state, which has full executive power, whereas the Commission shares its powers with the Council of Ministers.

To perform its task, the Commission has at its disposal an international staff (informally called the Eurocracy), for the greater part established in Brussels. Each member of the Commission is responsible for one policy sector, or, in more concrete terms, for the work of one or more Directorates General (comparable to national ministerial departments). At the moment, a total of over 10,000 officials are employed in the Commission's services, many of whom are engaged in translating work.

The Commission serves the Community in a general sense, but two of its functions and competences will now be studied in some detail.

Executive body

Some of the Commission's executive powers have been bestowed on it by the treaties, others by the Council. The *executive tasks conferred upon the Commission by the treaties* are limited; most are concerned with the customs union, others with the co-ordination of investments, the supervision of prices in the coal and steel sector, the fight against monopolies and competition distortion due to government support, the supply of fission material to, and the control of, nuclear installations.

The *powers given or transferred to the Commission by the Council* are more numerous. Nearly all Council decisions contain articles which call for implementation by the Commission. However, the Council tends to take a narrow view of the executive tasks to be entrusted to the Commission, and to reserve to itself all decisions which in some respect might have important consequences. Wherever that is out of the question on efficiency considerations, the Council is apt to tie up the Commission's executive task with some form of consultation, for instance with the so-called 'management committees', composed of national experts (of, for instance, agricultural markets or harmonisation). A proposal of the Commission agreed to by the majority of the management committee need not be submitted to the Council and can be carried out immediately. Commission proposals not accepted by the management committee have to be submitted to the Council, which then decides by qualified majority.

Another important executive task of the Commission is the *implementation of the Community budget*, including that of the so-called 'structural funds' (Agricultural, Regional, Social, and Development Funds). The Commission is also authorised to raise loans to finance investments in energy, industrial and infrastructure projects envisaged to help realise certain policy objectives.

Representing the Community interest

The Commission is sometimes called the *engine of the Community*, because it develops new policies, that is, proposes new regulations, directives and decisions. That is so because the Rome Treaty is a framework treaty: it has outlined the objectives, to be elaborated by the executive bodies. The Commission can exert strong pressure because, in general, the Council can only act on proposals from the Commission. To fulfil its role effectively, the Commission is represented in the meetings of the Council and COREPER (see next section).

The role of initiator is a highly important one, for it is that role which enables the Commission to *safeguard the Community interest against the national interests dominating the Council.* Admittedly, the Commission is not the sole actor here. For one thing, the European Council (of heads of government) has reserved to itself part of the initiating of new developments. For another, the Commission often sounds the Council for agreement before formally submitting its proposals.

The role of guardian of the Community interest is also manifest in the Commission's responsibility for the *enforcement of Community law.* To that end the Commission supervises the correct implementation of treaties and decisions. The authority to gather information was bestowed on it in the Treaty. When the Commission finds, through an inquiry, that a company, individual or member state has violated the EC rules, it invites that company, individual or member state to explain its behaviour. If no satisfactory explanation is given, the member state or individual will be invited to stop the violation. In some cases a fine is imposed. Should that remain without result, then the Commission will institute legal proceedings before the Court.

The Council of Ministers

Composition and procedure

The *Council of Ministers consists of representatives of the governments of member states.* The composition of the Council varies with the matter in hand. In general, the Council consists of the Ministers of Foreign Affairs of the 12 member states, but the 12 Ministers of Agriculture or Transportation or Finance can also *act as the Council* of the European Communities. The Council of Ministers meets as often as it considers necessary – mostly in Brussels, sometimes in Luxemburg. The member states take the presidency in turns, for six months each; a fixed order has been agreed upon.

Every member state has only one representative in the Council, but dependent on the size of the countries, the representatives have different *numbers of votes.* Very important decisions are taken unanimously, others in principle by a qualified majority of votes. The total number of votes is 76; they are distributed as follows:

10: Germany, France, Italy and the United Kingdom
 8: Spain
 5: The Netherlands, Belgium, Greece, Portugal
 3: Denmark, Ireland
 2: Luxemburg

A proposal of the Commission must be supported by at least 54 votes in the Council to be accepted; in some cases these 54 votes must come from at least eight member states. Some questions explicitly foreseen in the Treaty require unanimity. In practice, unanimity is often tried for by persevering with the negotiations for as long as is necessary to find a compromise acceptable to all. Naturally, such a procedure slows down decision making a great deal, and is not conducive to clear and consistent outcomes. To improve the decision making, the 'Single European Act' established that some decisions about the internal market, regional policy, and research and technology will be made by qualified majority.

The ministers on the *Council are accountable to their national parliaments and not to the European Parliament* (EP). There is, however, some dialogue between the two bodies: during each session of the EP one day is reserved for a debate between the EP and the Council on topical subjects.

The Council has a separate staff of European officials who prepare the meetings. It is a small staff compared to that of the Commission. Important to the preparatory work is the *Committee of Permanent Representatives,* often indicated by the French acronym of COREPER. This Committee meets almost every week in task-oriented workgroups, in which civil servants of national departments also take part. COREPER deals with the Commission's proposals. If COREPER is agreeable to the proposal, the Council's final decision is no more than a formality. If not, the proposal is further negotiated in the complete Council of Ministers. That can take a long time, several days – and nights!

Tasks and competences

According to the Treaties, the Council's first concern is to co-ordinate the economic policy of the member states; in practice that implies the co-ordination of many different policy areas. The Council has furthermore been given the *'power to take decisions'*, in other words, the Council has the final say in Community legislation. Finally, the Council is competent to regulate the Community's relations with other countries by treaties. In actual fact, it is mostly the Commission which acts as negotiator for the Community as a whole, by the mandate given to it by the Council; the final decision is the Council's.

The Council of (Foreign) Ministers also acts as a consultative body at the meetings of the European Political Co-operation. The EPC is a framework for dealing with problems of international diplomacy. It has evolved as a loose co-operation, distinct from the EC institutional machinery, but has been integrated in the EC by the Single European Act (art. 30). Both Commission and Parliament are associated with the work of the Council of Ministers with respect to diplomatic matters (see Chapters 19 and 20).

The European Parliament

Composition and procedure

The *members* of the European Parliament (EP) are elected directly, as they have been since 1979, for a term of five years. In most countries the election proceeds by proportional representation. There are 518 members. Large countries, like the United Kingdom, France and Germany, have 81 members each; a medium-size country like The Netherlands has 25 members, and small countries, like Ireland, 15. Each member has one vote. The Parliament elects from its members a president and 14 vice-presidents, who together constitute the 'Bureau', the executive body responsible for the agenda, competence of committees, etc.

From the start, EP members have grouped themselves not by national delegations, but along *party-political lines* (Social Democrats, Christian Democrats, Liberals, etc.). The preliminary work of the Parliament is carried on in the parliamentary committees, which may be standing or temporary, general or special. From their members, the committees choose rapporteurs, who report on subjects to be treated in the full Parliament. Most reports contain a draft resolution, to be voted on by the full EP.

The seat of the Parliament is a bone of contention. The secretariat, the Parliament's own clerical staff, is established in Luxemburg. The Parliament's plenary sessions (during one week of every month) are mostly held in Strasbourg, while the Committees most often meet in Brussels. The situation is very inefficient and expensive. A majority of EP members would prefer to conduct all their activities in Brussels, but there are still legal obstacles to this.

Tasks and competences

The tasks and competences of the EP refer to three areas, namely: (1) decision making (legislation), (2) budget, and (3) control, and vary greatly among the three (see van Schendelen 1984). In practice they remain far below the competence of most national parliaments. Therefore, the EP strives constantly to extend its authority, on the argument that only the European Parliament can make up for the democratic gaps in EC decision making (the Council of Ministers is not accountable to the European Parliament, while each individual Minister tries to circumvent accountability to his national parliament by the argument that the negotiations in the EC obliged him to act as he did).

With respect to *legislation* the EP has only an advisory capacity. The EP discusses the proposals of the Commission and draws up an advisory report, which is submitted to Commission and Council. However, the role of the EP has been strengthened by the Single European Act (SEA), which stipulates that for many subjects the Council can reject amendments of the EP only unanimously. If the Council wants to go against the advice of the EP about Commission proposals with important financial implications, reconciliation of the standpoints is tried for by consultation. Parliamentary approval is required for the conclusion of treaties and for extension of the Community.

With respect to the *budget*, the competence of the EP is more extensive. It can accept the complete budget or reject it. The EP has different powers regarding the various parts of the budget. With regard to expenditure necessarily resulting from the treaty ('obligatory' expenditure) it can only propose modifications. With regard to other expenditure, however, it can amend the draft budget.

The *control* powers of the EP are limited, the major aspect being that the Commission has to account to the EP for its actions. It does so in answer to spoken or written questions, and in the discussion of its Annual General Report. In the extreme, the EP can force the Commission to resign by a motion of censure. The Council is not accountable to the EP, but the two bodies are in continuous dialogue.

Court of Justice

Composition and procedure

The Treaties of Paris and Rome have established an original legal order. Rights can be conferred and obligations imposed directly on citizens and authorities of member states by Community law; member states do not need to intervene for these provisions to take effect. On the other hand, citizens can appeal to Community rules in national courts. The *consistent application of Community law all over the EC evidently called for a supreme body* to settle the conflicts which were sure to arise. To that end, the European Court of Justice was established, the highest authority within the Community. The national judge is subordinated to the European Court of Justice. The Court consists of thirteen Judges, five Advocates General, and a Registrar. Judges and advocates general are appointed by member-state governments, by mutual agreement, for a period of six years. They must satisfy the requirements valid in their own country for the fulfilment of the highest legal functions. They must be entirely independent and cannot be dismissed.[7]

When a question is put before the Court, the *procedure* is as follows. First, an advocate general is appointed to prepare the decision of the Court. He analyses the matter and relates the facts to the relevant legal rules. He then publicly draws his independent and impartial conclusions, which form the basis for the consultations and judgement of the Court. Actually, the Court has no legal and police staff of its own; it relies on the goodwill of all member states involved for the enforcement of its rulings. The judgement of the Court is directly applicable in all member states.

Tasks and competences

The Court's task is to ensure the proper interpretation and application of Community law. It concerns both the treaties and the derived legislation, that is to say, all regulations, directives and decisions (see next section).

Who has access to the European Court? Member states and Community institutions (Council, Commission and Parliament) have unlimited access. Natural and legal persons (companies, for instance) can only initiate proceedings in cases where an act (or the failure to act) of the Commission and/or of the Council affects their interests directly. In a national lawsuit, too, judgement may depend on relevant Community law. Persons can request a national judge who is not sure about the interpretation of Community law, to demand, before pronouncing judgement, a 'preliminary ruling' from the European Court of Justice (art. 177 EEC).

The *subject matters* put before the Court are concentrated in four areas: agriculture, internal market, competition, and social. The agricultural matters mostly concern the application of the very extensive EC regulation in the field. As regards the internal market, the Court has repudiated, in many judgements, any form of protectionism with respect to free movement of goods and services within the Community. With respect to indirect protectionist measures, such as administrative rules, taxes, etc. it has often ruled against member states as well. In that way, the Court has contributed much to the realisation of the Common Market. The Court has been very active in the area of competition. Undistorted competition is one of the most important objects of the Treaties. The Commission can act against violations of fair competition, imposing fines if necessary. Companies who disagree may submit their case to the Court. They have frequently done so, and a very extensive jurisprudence with respect to competition has accumulated. Finally, social matters relating, for instance, to the free movement of employed and self-employed and to equal treatment of men and women have been important areas of Court ruling. In these

four areas, among others, the judgements of the Court have prevented
the erosion of the intentions laid down in the Treaties.[8]

Laws and rules, decision making

Legal instruments

The EC knows Regulations, Directives, Decisions, and Recommendations (art. 189 EEC), always issued by the Council and the Commission.[9]

- A *Regulation* is general in its application; it is binding in its
  entirety and directly applicable in all member states. This means
  that national legislation, if existent, is overruled by EC regulations; indeed, EC law takes precedence over national law. The
  national governments have no right nor need to take action once
  a matter has been settled by an EC regulation, for it is automatically valid in all member states.
- A *Directive* is binding as to the result to be achieved upon each
  member state to which it is addressed, but leaves the national
  authorities the choice of form and methods. So, to implement
  directives, action by member states is needed in the form of national laws and decrees.
- A *Decision* is binding in its entirety upon those to whom it is
  addressed.
- *Recommendations* and opinions have no binding force.

The process of legislation in the EC

Decisions about regulations and directives are made by a procedure
that differs according to the matter in hand. The so-called *traditional
procedure* applies to matters like free movement of persons, fiscal
harmonisation, environmental protection, structural funds, etc. It consists of the following steps (see Figure 4.2):

1. *Preparation*
   - The Commission elaborates a planned proposal with the help of
     its staff; work discussions with national experts are often held
     already at this stage;
   - The Commission presents its opinions and outlines its planned
     strategy in communications to the Council and the Parliament;
   - The Council and the Parliament communicate their reactions to
     the Commission; the Commission revises its plans, establishes

its proposal and submits it to the Council in the shape of draft regulations or directives.

2. *Consultation*
   - The Council sends the proposal to the Economic and Social Committee and to the Parliament;
   - ESC and EP take notice of the opinions of the Commission, decide on their recommendations, and advise the Council.

3. *Negotiation*
   - The Committee of permanent representatives (COREPER) initiates the administrative preliminaries to the Council's decision. Most of the work is done in workgroups composed of national officials, created for the purpose, in which officials of the Commission are always represented. Any amendments proposed will be submitted by the COREPER to the Council, together with the ESC and EP recommendations. In practice, this is the most time-consuming stage of decision making, and also the stage where the matter may come to a standstill;
   - the Council initiates the political preliminaries of decision making, in the presence of members of the Commission. The Ministers continue to negotiate about matters not agreed upon in COREPER. At this stage, the Commission often submits adapted proposals. Sometimes a package deal is the only way to reach an agreement.

4. *Enactment*
   - The Council decides. This must be by qualified majority; to change a proposition of the Commission, unanimity is required;
   - The regulation, directive, etc. is enacted by publication in the *Official Journal* of the European Communities.

A second procedure called *co-operation* (introduced by the Single Act) gives a more important role to the European Parliament and does away with the unanimity rule in the Council. It applies to some well specified fields: internal market, health and safety, protection of workers, and the implementation of certain programmes (such as the Regional Fund, Research and Development, etc.). This procedure is largely the same as the classical one for stages one and two. For stages three and four the following holds.

3a. *Co-operation*
   - the Council then establishes a 'common position' by qualified majority, and communicates this to the EP.
   - The European Parliament may:
     (i) agree to the proposal (simple majority);
     (ii) amend or reject the proposal by absolute majority of votes.
   - The European Commission then decides whether or not to

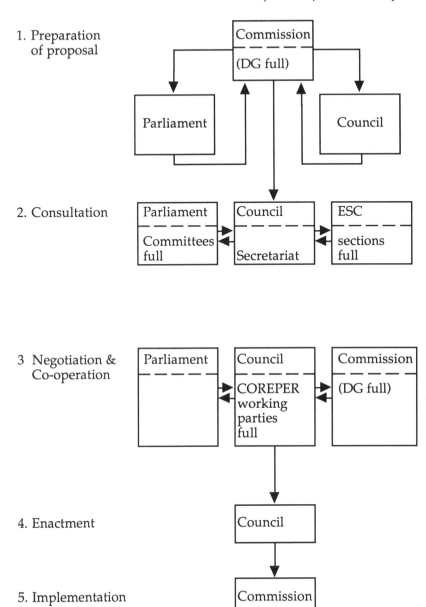

Figure 4.2 The Community's legislation-making process

endorse the amendments of the Parliament, and informs the Council of its decision.

4a. *Enactment*

- The Council decides. Unanimity is required for proposals that have been rejected by the EP, for amendments of the EP that are not endorsed by the Commission and for rejecting amendments of the EP supported by the Commission. A qualified majority is sufficient for a decision on EP amendments which the Commission supports.
- Regulations, directives or decisions adopted are then enacted by publication in the *Official Journal*.

The practice

The processes described above are not the most efficient ways to reach decisions. In the past, quite a few *proposals have been made to speed up the decision-making process of the Council,* for it is there that most stagnations occur. Central to all such proposals is the extension of the majority principle for Council votes. Although the 'Single European Act' has extended the application of that principle, on many important questions unanimity is still required. In the past this requirement of unanimity was often paralysing because there was a tendency not only to lay down the general principles but also to arrange technical details. National officials have been leaning very heavily on that point (hence the delay in COREPER), because their main concern is national acceptance and the consistency of national policy. Recently there is much more attention on the principles (see for example, Chapter 16) than the details and decision making has been quicker.

The process tends to lead to *inconsistent policy making on the European level* (WRR 1986). The Commission, although responsible for the aspect of consistency of Community actions, is not well equipped to fulfil that task because of

- its heterogeneous composition; its members are largely autonomous in their own fields and have not been chosen to execute a certain programme, but appointed by the member states from different political parties.
- its limited power; the Council of Ministers, having assumed a larger part of the task of co-ordinating Community policy, has many difficulties in fulfilling it on account of the 'segmentation' into 'professional' councils of ministers where sectoral interests prevail.[10]

With such a decision-making structure it is hardly surprising that integration has developed by widely divergent models and to varying degrees in different areas, as we shall see in the chapters dealing with the Common Market (Part III), Sectors of Activity (Part IV) and the Economic Union (Part V).

Budget

General

The cost of international institutions is almost invariably paid from member states' contributions, each country paying a fixed percentage of total expenses. Most international organisations only incur staff and household expenses, larger outlays for special programmes being taken care of by those member states wanting to participate. With the European Community, things are different, on two essential counts. For one thing, apart from 'secretarial expenses', the EC has large programmes to execute and finance. For another, since 1979 the EC has had its own resources. These are pre-federal traits of the EC, which we referred to earlier. Nevertheless, the budget of the Community cannot be compared to that of a national state, because:

- it can *hardly serve any specific sectoral purposes*. Indeed, with the small budget divided among a long list of programmes in different fields, no more than a little influence can be exerted on the economy in specific areas, by subsidies to certain branches of industry, infrastructural development, medical care, etc. The only exception is agriculture, which devours huge sums.
- it cannot be used either as an *instrument of macro-economic policy*, for Article 199 of the EEC Treaty reads explicitly: 'The revenues and expenditure shown in the budget shall be in balance'. That means that the EC's macro-economic policy stretches only to the co-ordination of the corresponding policies conducted by the member states. Moreover the total weight of the EC budget (about one per cent of EC Gross Domestic Product against some 40 per cent of GDP in some member states; total EC budget being about 2.6 per cent of national budgets) is too small for an effective macro policy.

We will now go briefly into the means, expenses and procedures of the EC budget.

The means

The EC differs from most other international organisations in that it has its own funds. Unlike most federal and confederal structures, the EC cannot itself levy taxes, having no fiscal sovereignty. Its revenues consist essentially of EC claims on fiscal and para-fiscal levies of the member states.

The Community's own resources, from which it is almost entirely financed, consist of VAT, customs duties, GNP related income, agricultural levies, and some various other components of little quantitative importance (about 3 per cent). The first four merit some detailed attention (the shares mentioned are 1989 budget figures).

- *Customs duties* were the EC's first own income. They are levied from products imported from outside the Community. The member states levying these duties will often be the ones most favourably situated for importation into Europe, not necessarily the ones to which the goods are destined (think, for instance, of German imports through the Dutch port of Rotterdam). In such a case, to allocate the duties to one member state seems unjust; so, from 1971 (the old six) they have flowed into the EC treasury. They account for somewhat over 20 per cent of total EC income. They have decreased through time as external tariffs of the EC have been lowered continuously (Chapter 8).
- *Agricultural levies and contributions.* Special types of import levies are the variable agricultural duties levied at the outer frontiers of the EC to adjust the price level of imported produce to EC prices. Duties and contributions are levied from internal EC produce as well, to control production and thus limit the need for financing from the Agricultural Fund. Once more, logically these levies accumulate to the Community. They contribute a relatively small portion, about 5 per cent, to total income. The levies have also tended to decrease as the EC has become increasingly a net exporter of agricultural produce (see Chapter 11).
- *Value-Added Tax.* A uniform basis has been established for value-added tax in all member states. A fixed percentage (at present 1.4) has to be transferred to the EC. Value-added tax represents the lion's share (some 60 per cent) of EC income. It was introduced in 1960 to replace fixed national contributions.[11] Because the importance of the other two items decreases, the share of VAT perforce increases.
- *GNP related income.* Since 1988 each member state pays a certain percentage of its GDP to the EC budget; this percentage is fixed every year. Through this mechanism the contributions to the EC budget tend to take better relative wealth levels of each member into account, thereby limiting the need for redistributive measures on the expenditure side. This fourth source of income represents some 9 per cent of the total.

Expenditure

Between 1973 and 1983 (the period in which the EC was composed of nine member states), the total budget rose by about 5.5 per cent a year, a substantial real increase, given the fact that prices rose by about 2.7 per cent only. It was needed primarily to cope with the expansion of the existing policy area (agriculture) and the introduction of new ones (regions, for instance). In the 1989 budget, the expenses totalled about 45,000 million Ecu.

- *Agriculture and Fishery* absorb a very large portion (two-thirds) of the total budget, mainly through the European Agricultural Fund's outlays for guaranteed prices. Because of the way decisions are made in the EC, these outlays are very difficult to control effectively. Voices raised against a policy claiming so large a portion of the available means for the financing of surplus productions have not yet become loud enough to bring about a significant change (Chapter 11).
- *Regional policy* now demands about 10 per cent of expenditure. This new policy was drawn up in 1973; the expenses of the European Regional Development Fund (ERDF) have grown rapidly to cope with the need for more cohesion (see Chapter 19).
- *Social policy* accounts for some 7 per cent of expenditure, of which 90 per cent is through the European Social Fund (ESF). In spite of the serious depression, the costs of this policy have risen but slightly in the past 15 years.
- *Energy, manufacturing industry, transportation and research* cover about 3 per cent of the outlay. No large funds have been created; the amounts are spent directly on programmes.
- *Development aid* is another relatively important item accounting for 2 per cent of expenditure. Besides, the European Development Fund (EDF) (not included in the budget) grants credits to developing countries.
- *Running costs*: these come to some 5 per cent of the total budget.

In 1988 the decision was made that by 1993 the structural funds (destined in particular for regional and social policy) will be doubled, while the cost of agriculture will be reduced considerably.

The procedure

The Community's overall budget is established by an involved procedure;[12] the main steps are:

1 *First reading*
- The Commission establishes a preliminary draft budget, taking into account the guidelines of the Council of Ministers and the European Parliament, and submits it to the Council of Ministers.
- The Council goes into consultation about the preliminary draft, amends it if necessary, and turns it into a draft budget (acting by qualified majority). The draft is then sent to the European Parliament.
- The Parliament discusses the draft budget. It can only propose modification to the Council as far as the so-called 'compulsory expenditure' is concerned, that is to say, expenses springing from the legal commitments of the Community towards third parties (farmers enjoying guaranteed prices, developing countries with which co-operation agreements are in force, etc.). The European Parliament can amend the budget as regards so-called 'non-compulsory expenditure', that is to say, outlays associated with, for instance, regional development. (At the onset of the budget procedure, the Commission computes the maximum percentage by which such categories of outlay may increase from one year to another.)

2 *Second reading*
- The Council of Ministers receives the draft budget with proposals and amendments for a second reading. It must reach a qualified majority to adopt or reject the amendments and modifications proposed by the Parliament. The Council is fully competent to reject EP modifications with respect to compulsory outlays. Decisions on that score are final. If it rejects the amendments with respect to non-compulsory expenditure, the draft budget is again forwarded to Parliament together with a report on the deliberations.
- Parliament deals with the second reading of the budget. It may reinstate the amendments rejected by the Council, provided it acts by majority of the members and three-fifths of the votes cast. At the end of the second reading the Parliament may reject the budget, which happened for the first time in the 1980 budget and again in the 1985 budget.
- To avoid such conflicts, smooth the procedures and take the increasing influence of Parliament into consideration, a conciliation procedure between Parliament, Council and Commission has developed.

3 *Adoption*
- After a final round of negotiations between Council and Parliament, in which the Council decides on compulsory and Parliament on non-compulsory expenditure, the president of the

European Parliament signs the budget, thus formalising its adoption.

Evaluation

The European budget has some specific features which distinguish it from national budgets:

- *Important allocation, no stabilisation, and small redistribution and external functions* (see Chapter 2). Contrary to national budgets, the EC budget is not used for macro-economic policy making. Its redistributive function has developed with the increasing expenditure on regional and social policies. (We will look further into the redistributive function in Chapter 18.)
- *Responsible institutions*: the EC has a bicephalous budget authority, vested in the Council of Ministers and in the European Parliament. The Commission is involved only in the proposition of a draft budget.
- *Fragmented decisions with budgetary consequences.* Many decisions bearing on expenses are made, on the basis of the treaties, by specialised Councils of Ministers (for instance, Agriculture). Moreover, some decisions of the Commission entail expenses. Many expense categories (for instance, the Agricultural Guarantee Fund) depend on market and monetary developments. The Council of Ministers for the Budget draws up the framework for the budget but cannot make sure that other decision making is consistent with it.
- *Absence of an integral framework for evaluating alternative policies.* The split-up of expenses between 'compulsory' and 'other' implies that if the budget estimates of the former are exceeded, either the budget of the latter has to be reduced or higher revenues have to be found, for the Treaty obliges the EC to keep the budget in balance. In either case, political decisions to carry out certain programmes are put in jeopardy.
- *Insufficiency of controls.* Many executive functions of the EC involve the participation of member states, which makes the control function of the budget difficult to accomplish. The European Court of Auditors, charged with the control of expenditure and revenues and endowed with powers of investigation with regard to Community institutions as well as national administrative bodies, reports every year on the most important deficiencies, but to remove their causes has proved extremely difficult.

Summary and conclusions

- The objective of the European Community is to create among the member states not only a Customs Union but also a Common Market. Moreover, an Economic and Monetary Union is to be aimed for, and eventually even a European Union.
- The Community has its own institutions as well as its own decision-making mechanism with some pre-federal traits.
- The treaties of Paris and Rome provide for measures of negative integration: the elimination of all obstacles to the internal free movement of goods, services, active persons and, as far as necessary to ensure a good performance of the customs union, also of capital. Such negative integration imposes legal restrictions on the actions of member states, companies and persons.
- Besides, the treaties enjoin upon the Community to pursue a common policy in many areas, that is, they oblige the EC to take the road of 'positive integration', indicating the procedures to be adopted. However, they are vague as to the objectives and timetables, and fail to provide efficient machinery for coherent action.
- Positive integration is confronted with many difficulties of which we mention: (1) the considerable state intervention in the economy, (2) the transfer of weighty competences to the EC, (3) the activity of pressure groups, (4) the priority of internal national political equilibrium over consistency of Community policies.
- Thus, advanced positive integration, while indispensable to safeguard the results of negative integration already achieved, is hard to realise. The original treaties have not provided solutions to problems that are due to sluggishness. The Single European Act has however made an important contribution to more efficient and rapid decision making.

Notes

1 For a short and handy description of the basics of the system, see the publications of the Commission CEC (1984a) and CEC (1986b). For a comparison with other organisations: Van Meerhaeghe (1980).
2 For a public-choice description of the difficulties of international co-operation, see Frey (1984), chapter 7; in chapter 8, he discusses the functioning of international organisations.
3 The societal context of policy making varies much among the countries of the EC; see, for example, the introductory text of Lane and Ersson (1987); Harding and others (1986) is also interesting.
4 See for an insider's view: Noel (1988).
5 For a more elaborate discussion of the political aspects of the division of tasks between Community institutions and national state institutions, see the contribu-

tions by Hoffmann (1982), Wallace (1982), and for an economist's view the contribution by Pelkmans (1982) to the special issue of the *Journal of Common Market Studies*. See also Wallace *et al.* (1983).

6 Since the Single European Act, the European Council has also formally been part of the EC institutional machinery. The role of the European Council has been described in some detail in Bulmer and Wessels (1986).

7 Further details in another European Documentation brochure: CEC (1986c).

8 Another important group of cases concern the coal and steel sector: for further details on the whole 1953–86 period, see the twentieth General Report of the Commission.

9 These are the terms used by the EEC and Euratom; we will disregard the slightly different terms used by the ECSC for practically the same notions.

10 How serious the damage to consistency can be illustrated by the outcomes of past negotiations in matters of agriculture. In the 1970s and early 1980s, decisions went repeatedly against the principles of the EC, violating the unity of the market, exploding the financial frameworks and jeopardising the integration reached in other areas (for example, monetary). Even a kind of legal restraint imposed by the ministers of finance on the agricultural ministers remained without success.

11 The budget has given rise to heated annual debates about net payers and net receivers, particularly in the United Kingdom, which, despite being below the average EC wealth level, is a 'net payer'. Since 1983 the 1.4 per cent of VAT has got a ceiling for countries like Portugal, Greece, Ireland and the UK in the sense that their VAT basis is set at a maximum of 55 per cent of total GDP.

12 For a thorough treatment see Strasser (1982), and for a succinct one CEC (1986d); Isaacs (1986) is also interesting in this respect.

PART II
THEORETICAL
FOUNDATIONS

5 Customs Union

Introduction

The theory of economic integration is relatively recent. It is based on international trade theory. Classical economists occupied themselves quite frequently with the problems of free trade (Ricardo) and also with preferential trade agreements, and the creation of the German Zollverein in the 19th century gave rise to a theoretical debate on the advantages and disadvantages of protection (List, 'infant industries'). Still, the subject of economic integration remained embedded in a more general economic analysis.

International economic integration actually did not become a separate object of economic thinking until after the Second World War.[1] Viner's book *The Customs Union Issue* (1950) pioneered its development into a separate part of economic science. Since then, the literature on the subject has accumulated, not least because the post-war integration processes greatly stimulated profound theoretical studies.

As the customs union (CU) represents a special case of (internal) free trade and (external) protection, this chapter sets out to *place the CU phenomenon in the perspective of international trade theory* (the neo-classical partial and general equilibrium models), explaining some of its major principles.

Next, we will go into the short-term effects that can be expected from the formation of a CU. In spite of the relevance, in terms of economic theory, of the distinction between free-trade area (FTA) and customs union we made earlier,[2] we will focus on the CU, the FTA stage not having, after all, counted for much in Europe. To explain in essence the static customs-union theory and identify some effects of the CU on welfare,[3] we will *compare the CU with a situation of free trade* and *with a situation of protection*. Moreover, we shall consider some refinements which in the abundant literature have been added to the basic theme. Finally, we will deal with the long-term effects of a CU (estimated in Chapter 8 to be much larger than the short-term ones), giving attention to aspects of competition and changed production, organisation, and marketing techniques.

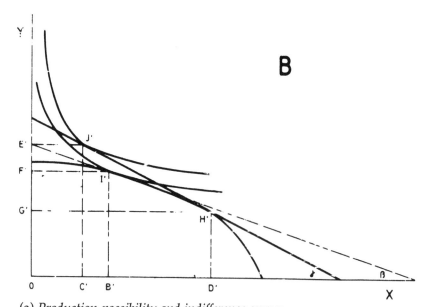

(a) *Production-possibility and indifference curves*
Figure 5.1 Advantages of international trade

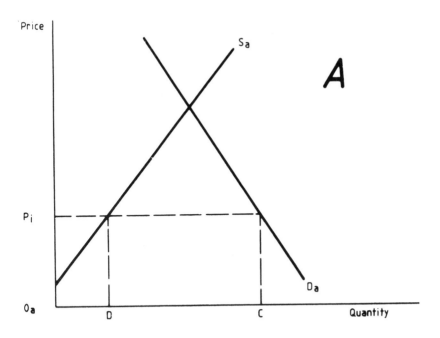

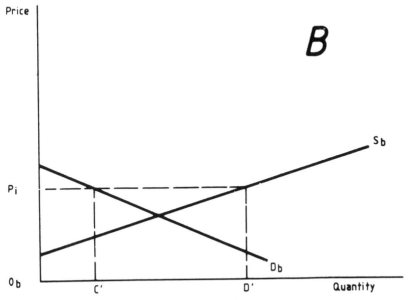

(b) *Supply and demand curves for commodity x*

Free trade versus protection

International trade

The theory of international trade has developed largely from the relatively simple *case of two countries* (A and B) *each producing two products* (*x* and *y*), *with two production factors*, namely labour (*l*) and capital (*c*). Initially, the countries are two *closed economies*. The availability of production factors is different in the two countries, which implies different production costs (comparative cost theory). The upper part of Figure 5.1 represents the situation for both country A (left-hand side) and country B (right-hand side). The concave curves – from the origin's point of view – are the so-called production-possibility or transformation curves, reproducing for either country the combined quantities of goods *x* and *y* that can be produced with the available quantities of production factors. The curves are different for the two countries owing to differences in availability of production factors and technology. The convex curves are the indifference curves of the collective consumers in either country; they represent the combinations of goods *x* and *y* that yield equal utility. We assume that the indifference curves of the two countries are dissimilar (on account of different climates, for instance). In either country, production and consumption will take place where the indifference and transformation curves touch. The price ratios of the goods, given by the tangents α and β, are evidently different for the two countries.

Now suppose the *two countries enter into trade relations*, each country specialising in the production of that commodity for which it needs the smallest relative input of production factors. Specialisation will continue until the price ratios in both countries have become identical (tangent γ). In country A, production will shift from point *I* to point *H* owing to more of *y* and less of *x* being produced, and in country B from *I'* to *H'* because production shifts from *y* to *x*. That such trade increases welfare follows from the indifference curves. Thanks to trade and the changed price ratios, the two curves no longer need to have a point of tangency (touching point) in both countries, and either country can reach a higher indifference curve touching the common price-ratio tangent γ.

We can now indicate *each country's production and trade* as follows. In country A, a quantity equal to O_aD of good *x* will be produced domestically, and a quantity equal to *DC* imported. Of good *y*, however, a quantity O_aG will be produced, of which *OE* will be consumed domestically and *EG* exported. In country B, the situation will be the reverse: once the frontiers have been opened, a quantity equal to O_bD' will be produced and only O_bC' consumed of good x, so that *C'D'* can be exported ($C'D' = CD$), while of good y, OG' is produced and OE' consumed, so that $G'E'$ must be imported ($E'G' = EG$).

The exercise can be done as well with the more familiar *supply and demand curves*. The indifference curves can also be combined with the production-possibility curve to plot demand curves for either product x or y (Lindert 1986). A demand curve for good x shows how the quantity demanded responds to the price of the good (generally downward sloping). In Figure 5.1(b) the demand curves for countries A and B have been drawn (D_a and D_b respectively). The equilibrium situation given in this figure occurs after integration, with a price p_i prevailing for both countries. At that price, demand is O_aC (equal to O_aC in Figure 5.1a) in country A, and O_bC' (equal to O_bC' in Figure 5.1a) in country B. In country A, the supply of good x by home producers is OD, which implies that DC has to be imported (equal to DC in Figure 5.1a). In country B producers are much more efficient (the S_b curve runs below the S_a curve), and at price p_1 they are prepared to supply O_bD' (equals O_bD' of Figure 5.1a). The quantity $C'D'$ (equal to CD) is exported from country B to country A.

The trade effects of a tariff

As briefly indicated above, international trade theory contends (see, among others, Greenaway, 1983; Lindert, 1986) that countries may benefit mutually by specialising in the commodities at which they excel, and also exporting them, while importing those goods which they could produce only at relatively high costs, leaving their production to other nations. That implies that, theoretically, on certain assumptions, prosperity would be greatest if trade were free the world over. In practice, however, world economy is not based on general free trade. On the contrary, most countries have raised barriers in the shape of tariffs, quotas, etc. The *establishment of tariffs affects production patterns and trade flows*; a simple diagram (Figure 5.2), derived from partial-equilibrium analysis, may illustrate them. The diagram contains first of all the traditional supply and demand curves of a given product in country A. The demand curve D_a of the home country (A) is given by the following equation:

$$D_a = -3/2p + 13^1/_2 \qquad (5.1)$$

the home country's supply curve of importables S_a, that is, the supply curve of the domestic producers in country A, is given by:

$$S_a = p - 1^1/_2 \qquad (5.2)$$

We now assume, besides country A, a country W representing the free world market. We further assume a fully elastic supply on the world market, at a price of $p_w = 4$. The assumption of a fully elastic supply implies that this price is unaffected by changes in the supply or demand of country A. In Figure 5.2, S_w is the curve of world supply. For country A, we can envisage a situation of autarky, of free trade, or of protection. Let us consider the effects of each situation on price, demand, production and imports.

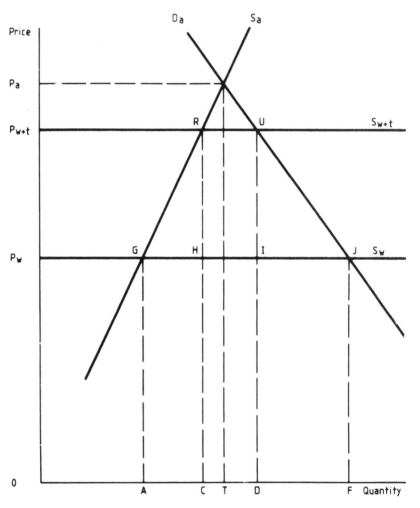

Figure 5.2 Trade effects of a tariff

In the situation of *autarky*, suppliers in A have a 100 per cent market share; they cover total demand in A. In that case, in which country A remains completely closed to the world market, the world-market price p_w is far below the equilibrium price p_a. To achieve isolation, country A needs to operate either a system of import bans or a prohibitive tariff of at least $t = 2.0$. This demonstrates that the country has no comparative advantage for the production of the good in question.

If, on the contrary, country A pursues a policy of *free trade*, the price in A is equal to the low world-market price p_w; the domestic supply is limited, but both demand (*OF*) and imports (*AF* = *GJ*) from the world are considerably higher than in the autarky case. In other words: the market has expanded (to *OF*); the share that A supplies has decreased to *OA* and the market share of imports has increased (from zero to *AF*).

Should country A conduct a *protectionist* policy, establishing a customs tariff t (of, for instance, 1.5 ECU), then national production in A (and hence the market share of A suppliers), national consumption, and imports (and hence the market share of 'world' suppliers) will stabilise somewhere between the two extremes of autarky and free trade. The effects are summarised in the next table.

Table 5.1   Effects of various forms of protection on trade and production of country A

	Autarky	Free trade	Protection
Domestic price (ECU)	$p_a = 6.00$	$p_w = 4.00$	$p_{w+t} = 5.50$
Domestic demand	$OT = 4.50$	$OF = 7.50$	$OD = 5.25$
Domestic production	$OT = 4.50$	$OA = 2.50$	$OC = 4.00$
Imports	$x = 0.00$	$AF = 5.00$	$CD = 1.25$

Welfare effects of the introduction of a tariff

In economic terms, free trade is preferable, the introduction of tariffs having two adverse effects. Figure 5.3 and the numerical examples given in the previous section on free trade and protection illustrate that.

First, the introduction of a tariff by country A, which had practised free trade before, causes a *loss on the producer side*. In the protected economy, goods are produced at a cost ($p_{w+t} = 5.5$ ECU) higher than would have been necessary with free trade ($p_w = 4.0$ ECU). The waste involved in the use of production factors (*GH*) which could be put to

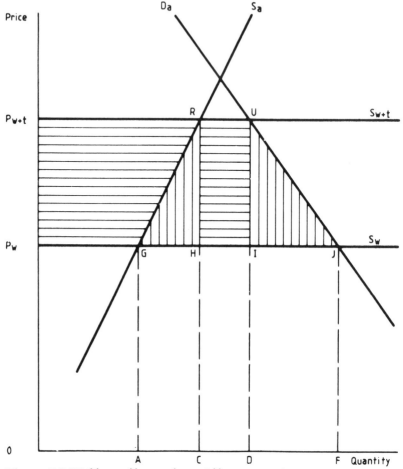

Figure 5.3 Welfare effects of a tariff, country A

better use (cost difference *HR*) elsewhere is represented by the vertically shaded triangle *GHR*. It can be calculated as:

$$1/2(OC - OA)(p_{w+t} - p_w) = (4.00 - 2.50) \times 0.5 \times (5.50 - 4.00) = 1.125 \text{ ECU}$$

Contrary to a widely held belief, an increase in production can thus
entail a loss in efficiency for the economy as a whole.

On the *consumer side,* too, there are additional costs: the consumer pays more (5.5 instead of 4.0 ECU) for the same goods, and the total quantity of goods at his disposal has diminished (OD = 5.25 instead of OF = 7.50). The resulting loss of welfare is measured by the change in consumer surplus, or the area below the demand curve above market prices. (Some consumers would indeed have been willing to pay more for the good.) The net (or deadweight) loss of welfare on the consumer side is calculated as the total effect of a lower quantity (IJ) times a gradually higher price (half of ILJ). This is represented by the vertically shaded triangle UIJ (amounting to 2.25 x 0.5 x 1.5 = 1.688 ECU. There is a redistribution of wealth from consumers to the government, as the latter gets the revenues from customs duties represented by the horizontally shaded square $HIUR$ (amounting to 1.25 x 1.5 = 1.875 ECU), and from consumers to producers: the horizontally shaded area $p_{w+t}RGp_w$ (amounting to 1.5 x 4.00 = 6.00 - 1.125 = 4.875).

Obviously, the above analysis for one commodity and one country can be extended to several goods and several countries. Because the introduction of a tariff by one country is mostly followed by counter-measures of others, the negative welfare effects will be felt in many countries. That the introduction of a tariff works out negatively for overall welfare can also be illustrated with the help of Figure 5.1; indeed, as trade diminishes, countries A and B are forced back to lower indifference curves and thus to lower welfare.

Welfare effects of quantitative restrictions

A quantitative restriction (QR) has in many respects the same welfare effects as a tariff. Under a system of QR, importers are given licences to import a given quantity of goods. On the assumption of full competition, the effects of quantitative restriction can be explained from Figure 5.4.

With free trade, demand would have been OF at a price p_w and an imported quantity of AF. Restriction of the latter to CD = RU will entail a diminished demand, and a market equilibrium in country A at a price of 5.5 ECU and a domestic production of OC. As after the introduction of a tariff, that domestic production increases from OA to OC and consumption drops from OF to OD. From the diagram, this QR is in that respect equivalent to a tariff of t, which is why a QR (CD) is expressed as tariff equivalent (t). There is, however, an important element *which makes a tariff in general preferable to a quota,* if protection is needed at all: in the case of a QR (to, say, RU) the government does not have the benefits which would accrue from a tariff ($HIUR$). At best, the amount involved flows to domestic companies (importers), but it may also accrue as profit to the foreign manufacturers. The only way open to the government to prevent the diversion of welfare from domestic con-

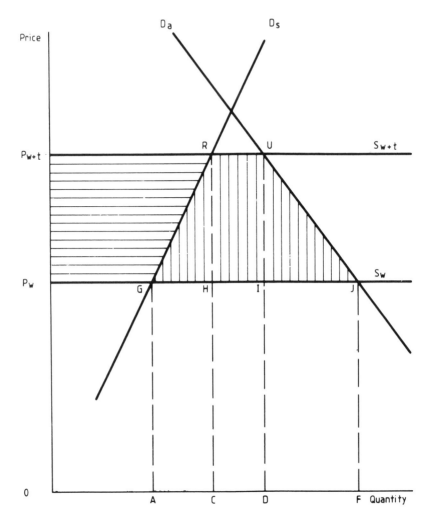

Figure 5.4 Welfare effects of quantitative restrictions, country A

sumers to foreign producers would be to sell the licences by auction. If not, the total welfare loss to country A from the QR are the two triangles *RGH + UIJ* and the square *HIUR*, together vertically shaded. There is again a redistribution effect of $p_{w+t} - p_w RG$ from domestic consumers to domestic producers.

Some exporting countries are now prepared to commit themselves, with respect to importing countries, to so-called VER, *voluntary export*

restraints, because they expect to profit more from small sales at high
unit prices than from large sales at lower unit prices. Again, there is no
government revenue under VER. Why should importing countries
resort to QR or VER rather than to tariffs, which have the advantage of
additional revenue over the two former ? As far as QR is concerned, the
answer is that there is neither perfect competition nor a perfectly elastic
supply. On agricultural markets in particular, the supply is so inelastic
in the short run as to allow a sheer drop in prices; in that case a tariff
would not be effective. The only way to protect the internal market at
given minimum prices may then be to restrict imports to a certain
maximum. The motive for recourse to VER is institutional: the GATT
(see Chapter 19) does not allow the establishment of any new unilateral
trade obstacles in the shape of tariffs; so, if protection is nevertheless
wanted, the relatively costly VER are all that's left. . . .

Short-term static effects

The production and trade effects of altered tariffs after the establishment of a
customs union

Classical international-trade theory teaches us that the best way to
avoid the negative welfare effects of protection is for all countries of the
world to adopt perfect free trade. However, countries, finding progress
on that score too slow, try to adopt as a second-best strategy, a
geographically limited form of free trade as represented by a customs
union.[4] Recall that a customs union implies free trade among partners,
but protection of the entire union against the rest of the world. So we
move from a situation in which country A operates tariffs against all
other countries, to a situation in which it applies tariffs to 'third
countries' only.

The theory of customs unions relates to the gains and losses incurred
by the establishment of such unions. These include first the static short-
term gains from specialisation referred to in the preceding section. The
preceding sections may have given the impression that the introduction of a CU maintaining a tariff wall lower than the average of the ones
existing before, would be unambiguously advantageous to the members and the world as a whole. However, we will demonstrate that this
is too simplistic a view and that both positive and negative effects
occur. In economic terms the creation of the CU is warranted only if the
former outweigh the latter. In political terms it is feasible only if the
advantages and disadvantages are fairly distributed among partners.

Especially Viner's pioneering work (1950) shed light on the effects of
a customs union between countries A and B, by making a distinction
between trade creation and trade diversion. Later, Meade (1955) added

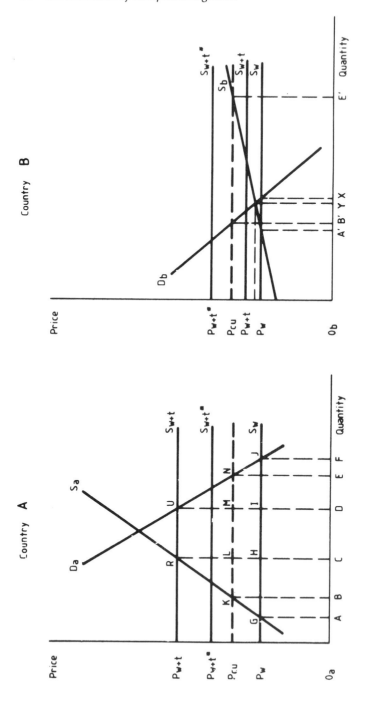

Figure 5.5   Trade and production effects of a customs union, countries A and B

the effect of trade expansion. We can explain these effects as follows.

Trade creation will occur when trade between partners A and B increases. In country A, demand will shift from the expensive protected domestic product to the cheaper product from the partner country, implying a shift from a less efficient to a more efficient producer.

Trade diversion will occur when imports from the efficient or cheap producer 'world market' are replaced with imports from a higher cost (or less efficient) producer, namely, the 'partner country'. That country's products can be sold cheaper in country A than world-market production, because the CU imposes a protective tariff on imports from W, while leaving imports from the partner country free.

Trade expansion will occur because the lower market price in A stimulates total domestic demand, which will be satisfied by foreign trade.

For a better understanding of the nature and volume of these three effects, let us take a close look at Figure 5.5, which gives the situation for country A on the left-hand side and for country B on the right. We assume that the supply from producers in the rest of the world is fully elastic at a price level p_w. The corresponding supply is represented in the diagrams by the horizontal line S_w. As a high-cost producer, country A enables its industry to capture part of the home market by introducing a fairly high tariff. Country B, on the contrary, produces at rather low costs, and needs only a low tariff to permit its producers to cover the entire internal demand. Assume now that countries A and B form a customs union which establishes a common outer tariff t^*, the average of the tariffs of countries A and B. Once the customs union is established, the equilibrium price of total demand and total supply in A+B will be p_{cu}. Country A will buy all its imports (BE) from the partner country, p_{cu} being lower than p_{w+t^*}. Production in country A will be O_aB. Country B, on its side, produces the quantity O_bE', of which $B'E'$ (equal to BE) in excess of its home demand (O_bB'); B can export this quantity to the partner country.

What, then, are the *trade effects of the creation of a customs union* which adopts a common external tariff of t^*? The effects differ according to the initial situation. Let us take the two cases of protection and free trade of the previous section as examples. If protection marks the initial situation of country A, a new trade flow (BE) occurs between partners, of which CD replaces the flow that used to come from other countries in the world. Trade creation is BC and expansion DE. On balance, trade has increased in our example (BC + DE being larger than CD), and international specialisation has intensified accordingly.

Starting from free trade for country A, a negative development occurs. Trade actually diminishes by AB on the producer side, and by EF on the consumer side. Moreover, BE is diverted from the lower-cost world producer to the high-cost partner country. So, for country A this Customs Union has nothing but negative trade effects.

For country B, the situation is somewhat different. The introduction of a common tariff stops the trade that existed between B and W, which implies negative trade creation ($-A'Y$) and expansion ($-YX$) as less efficient home producers take over from more efficient world producers. In terms of production in B there are no trade effects (but for the exports $B'E'$), as there were no imports from the world anyway. The effects of the two cases for the two countries are summarised in the following table.

Table 5.2 Trade effects of a Customs Union, countries A and B

Effect	Starting situation			
	Free trade		Protection	
	A	B	A	B
Creation	-AB	-A'Y	BC	*
Expansion	-EF	-YX	DE	*
Diversion	BE	*	CD	*

* not applicable

Welfare effects of altered tariffs after establishment of a customs union

What are the advantages and disadvantages ensuing from the customs union and the tariff? On the one hand, trade diversion tends to make production less rational, which is a disadvantage. On the other hand, trade creation and trade expansion make production more efficient, which is advantageous. To get an idea of the magnitude of the effects, consider Figure 5.6 and the quantitative examples given earlier, starting from protectionism. We assume that the price for the Customs Union is 4.5 ECU.

For *country A* the advantages on the production side (trade creation *BC*) are represented by the triangle *KLR*. It indicates that the saving on production cost equals, on average, half the difference in costs between home production and that in country B ($p_{w+t} - p_{cu}$), leaving economic resources available for other purposes. In our example, this advantage can be quantified at (5.50 - 4.50) × 1.0 × 0.5 = 0.50 ECU. On the consumption side (trade expansion equal to DE) the advantages are represented by the triangle *MUN*; they amount to (6.75 - 5.25) × 1.0 × 0.5 = 0.75 ECU. Together 1.25 ECU. The disadvantages for country A are represented by the square *HLMI*. For the amount of trade equal to *CD*

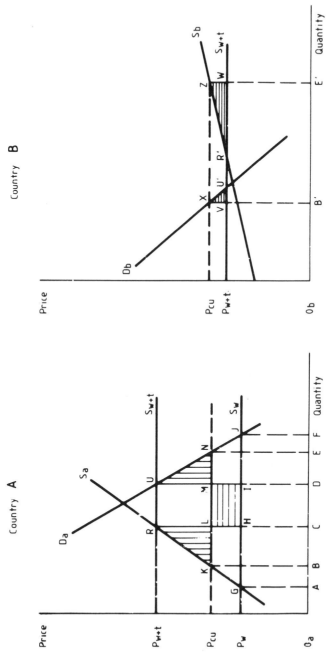

Figure 5.6 Welfare effects of a (trade-diverting) customs union, country A

which has been diverted, production inputs have been higher than necessary. We can compute this disadvantage, in our example, at (5.25 - 4.00) x (4.5 - 4.0) = 0.625 ECU. So, in our example the establishment of a customs union produces a net advantage of 0.625 ECU for country A.

For *country B* the case is quite different. The disadvantages are on the consumer as well as the producer side. The consumer gets less quantity for more money; his loss is indicated by the horizontally shaded little triangle *VXU'* in Figure 5.6. On the producer side, there is a production loss indicated by the horizontally shaded triangle *R'ZW*. The producers in B will of course enjoy a net gain.

Alternative cases can be imagined in which the profits or the losses are heavier. If, for instance, the only effect is trade expansion, there will be larger net advantages, as can be shown by a slight variation of the former example. Assume the supply curve of country B is equal to that of the world. The effects of a customs union between countries A and B will be positive, in fact the reverse of the negative ones found for country A passing from free trade to protectionism (Figure 5.5). By varying the differences between p_{cu} and p_w and the gradient of the supply and demand curves, the reader can work out other examples, to arrive finally at the point where the trade diversion exceeds trade expansion, so that the establishment of a Customs Union produces a net disadvantage to the world as a whole.

The present examples refer to only one product. To judge the economic desirability of a customs union by its static effects, the profits and losses for all products involved need to be calculated, under consideration of the specific circumstances obtaining for each.

Customs union and quantitative restrictions

While a customs union does away with all quantitative restrictions among member states, they can be maintained with respect to third countries. The effects of a customs union with quantitative restrictions are slightly different from those of a customs union with tariffs. Starting from the same example as before we will describe the developments for country A. Suppose in Figure 5.5 there is no question of a tariff equal to $p_{w+t} - p_w$, but of an equivalent quantitative restriction, equal to $CD = RU$. Two cases can be distinguished.

- *All licences had initially been granted for goods from country B*. The effect of a CU between A and B is then that country B crowds out country A, implying a trade creation of *BC* and a trade expansion of *DE*. *CD*, too, continues to be supplied by B (no trade diversion), but at lower prices.
- *All licences had initially been allotted for goods from country W*. Because after the establishment of a customs union there remains

a price difference between country A and the world market, failing further agreements of a common policy of the Customs Union with respect to country W a quantity CD will continue to be imported into country A from the world market. The effect will again be a trade expansion and trade creation equal to *BC* + *DE* (no trade diversion *CD*).

Evidently, the welfare effects of abolishing quantitative restrictions differ from those caused by tariff elimination: the advantages *KLR* and *UMN* obtain in both cases, but the disadvantage *HLMI* does not accrue in the latter case.

The incidence of positive and negative effects

Various factors influence the occurrence of positive and negative effects of a customs union.

- *The production structure*: Two countries can be complementary or competitive. Viner (1950) pointed out already that with complementary production structures, most probably the two countries have already specialised to a high degree in one type of commodity; in that case the advantages of a customs union cannot be very important. If, on the contrary, the production of either country is a potential competitor of the other, specialisation in the products which either country can make best and cheapest is probable, and the advantages are likely to be relatively important.
- *The size of the union*: The more and the larger the countries participating in the CU, that is, the larger its share in total world trade, the better the prospects for division of employment and the smaller the risk of trade diversion (Viner, 1950; Meade, 1955; Tinbergen, 1959).
- *The level of the tariffs*: As the initial tariffs of the trade partners are higher, the attendant inefficiencies will be worse and the welfare effects of the abolition of tariffs greater (Viner, Meade, *op. cit.*). On the other hand, the introduction of high tariffs against third countries will reduce the positive effect.
- *Transportation and transaction costs*: The increased trade has to be realised physically, for which efficient transport is required. Failing that, the transportation costs will replace the tariffs as an obstacle to further specialisation. For that reason, CUs tend to be concluded between contiguous countries (Balassa, 1961). The remark about transportation costs applies to time-consuming clerical procedures at the frontier, and probably as well to the linguistic differences in Europe which tend to make transaction costs between linguistic areas higher than within such areas.

- *Flexibility*: The advantages are greater as both countries can respond more flexibly to new prospects. The reverse also applies: the advantages are smaller if production bottlenecks prevent the full accomplishment of advanced specialisation and the corresponding reallocation of production. We will come back to this point when discussing dynamic effects.

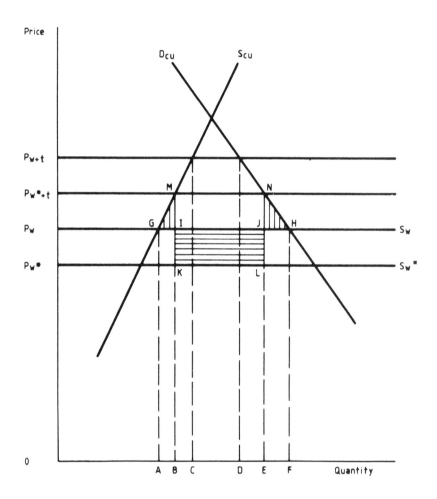

Figure 5.7 Terms-of-trade effect of a tariff for the CU

Terms of trade

So far we have assumed a fully elastic supply function in countries B and W. That may be realistic if a small country A forms a customs union with a large country B, leaving a still larger world market W, but makes no sense for a customs union of several large countries, confronting a small world market.[5]

On the other hand, importing countries united in a customs union can enforce lower supply prices on the world market (for instance by trade restrictions or bargaining power) and thus improve the terms of trade (defined here as export price divided by import price) for the CU. This is illustrated by Figure 5.7, where D_{cu} is the customs union's demand curve and S_{cu} its supply curve. The rest of the world supplies at price p_w any quantity demanded. The CU now introduces a tariff t. That takes the CU price to p_{w+t} and supply in the CU increases from OA to OC. As demand falls from OF to OD, foreign suppliers are confronted with a decrease of their export volume from AF to CD. To prevent such a considerable loss of exports, the third-country producers will cut their prices to $p_w{}^*$, which means they keep an export volume of BE. The customs union can import much cheaper than before; on the assumption of constant prices for CU exports, the CU lands a net gain; its welfare from improved terms of trade is the square $KLJI$; this has to be set against a loss of welfare of the two triangles MGI and JNH.

The example given above is not a realistic one. The supply curve of the world producers, for example, will in practice be upward sloping. For a realistic analysis, the present simple illustration does not suffice, and a wide range of differently shaped supply and demand curves have to be reviewed, which makes the analysis rather complicated. Moreover, substitution effects and income effects due to alterations in the differential prices of imported (tariff-burdened) and exported goods must also be taken into account. We will not go into the literature on the subject, extensive though it is, because the general conclusion must be that no satisfactory method has as yet been developed for a proper analysis of the problem (Wonnacott and Wonnacott, 1981), and that, therefore, *general statements on the effects of the CU on trade and price formation between CU countries and with third countries are out of the question.*

A few rules of thumb can be given, though. A tariff will probably induce producers/importers to lower their prices so as to keep their market share. That means that by introducing a tariff, a country will improve its terms of trade. Now suppose a customs union is concluded between countries A and B and that country B was the cheapest supplier, that is to say, cheaper than either W or A; in that case the customs union may deteriorate A's terms of trade. Finally, on politico-economic grounds a large customs union is arguably in a better position to substantiate its trade policy towards the outer world and to improve its terms of trade than the individual countries. That might produce a net advantage to the entire CU.[6]

Evaluation

In the previous sections, the static effects of a customs union have been considered on the basis of a partial analysis. We found that sometimes the entire world profits from a reduction of tariffs among partners. However, for a number of nations to conclude a CU, a profit must accrue to each of the would-be partners, or, if not, compensation must be given to the country that stands to lose. But even in a country which on balance would benefit, to tip the scales towards a CU those who hope to profit from a CU policy must be politically stronger than those who fear to suffer from it.

We have seen that the static partial equilibrium model enables us in principle to compute some effects of a CU and to prove its partial advantages. However, the static approach has some major drawbacks, from the practical as well as the theoretical point of view, and also regarding its realism. The *practical drawback of the static approach* is that to draw a complete picture of the whole economy of all member states would necessitate the calculation and netting out of the various effects for a virtually infinite number of cases (goods with different elasticities of supply and demand, different tariffs, and hence different *ex-ante* production and imports).

A *more fundamental objection* against partial equilibrium analysis (Corden, 1972a) is that a tariff, and also its abolition, affects the structure of the economy and hence the demand for production factors; this in turn may change the amount producers are prepared to pay for employing them. This argument for a general-equilibrium model of discriminatory trade agreements can be illustrated as follows. Suppose the export sector of country A is labour-intensive and the import sector capital-intensive; the liberalisation of production factors will induce larger imports of capital-intensive goods, so that the scarce capital production factor will be set free in A. The supply of capital remaining equal, this means that capital becomes cheap and labour scarce and thus expensive. In the end, imports may thus cause a reversal of the relative cost of production factors, leading towards a new point of departure for international specialisation (see next chapter.) However, as general-equilibrium models appear to have many shortcomings, we will continue to work with partial-equilibrium analyses.

Finally, we must keep the *lack of realism* in mind: indeed the restrictive assumptions on which the static approach relies seldom hold in practice.[7] On goods markets, perfect competition is disturbed by cartels; adjustment processes are not without cost; factors are to some extent mobile across national frontiers, and not completely mobile within them; unemployment will arise through imperfections, etc. In sum, a better, more dynamic analytic approach has to be looked for.

Long-term restructuring effects

Some distinctions

Besides the factors discussed in the previous section, there are others which are recurrent in the discussion of the advantages and disadvantages of a customs union; Balassa (1961) called them 'dynamic effects'. We prefer the term 'restructuring effects'. They occur because firms, workers and governments do not just sit back but react to the new situation and adapt the structure of production and the economy. On the one hand, firms faced with increased competition will try to lower their costs to stay in the market. On the other, the extended market allows large-scale production at lower average cost. These two effects are considered very important and will be analysed in some detail. Some other effects (internal to the company, such as size, or external to the company such as the industrial environment) are much less developed theoretically and empirically, and will be referred to only in passing. Still others, like the possible negative effects of regional concentration of production, or the (un)employment effects on certain groups of the labour force, will not be discussed here. We should keep in mind, however, that a CU may entail an important restructuring of the economies of the member countries, a process which cannot always be carried through without incurring significant adaptation costs. On the whole, however, the long-term benefits, to be described hereafter, are considered to outweigh by far the short-term costs. For that reason, the groups incurring these costs are given compensation (see Chapter 7, Redistribution) to facilitate the restructuring.

Increased competition and efficiency

In the 1950s, most people in Europe were convinced that the limited competition prevailing in some countries caused production to be less efficiently organised than it could be, or, to put it another way, that the input was higher than would be required for efficient production. The expectation was that the inefficiency would be overcome in a common market. It is the same argument which has lately been used to justify the entry of Spain and Portugal into the EC. Indeed, with the help of Figures 5.8 and 5.9 (suggested by Pelkmans, 1984), we can demonstrate how *improved technical efficiency due to increased competition can have a*

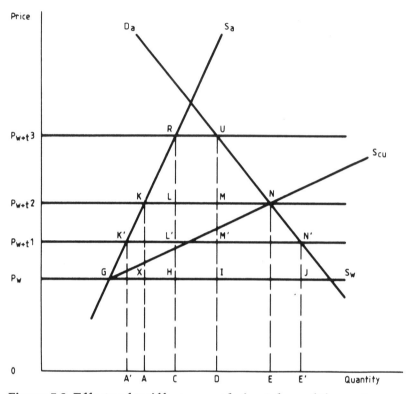

Figure 5.8 Effects of tariffs, account being taken of the customs union supply curve, country A

welfare effect, exceeding many times the limited static effect – two small triangles – we analysed in the previous section.

Figure 5.8 again reproduces the market for good x in country A. Curves S_a and D_a represent, as in Figure 5.5, supply and demand in country A itself. Supply from the world – fully elastic – is once more denoted by S_w. A change has occurred in the supply from country B; it is not indicated by a curve S_b but combined with supply S_a and incorporated in curve S_{cu}, which is valid for the entire customs union. The diagram has been drawn in such a way that the tariff t_2 is just sufficient to avoid any imports from the world market. Now suppose that before the CU was established, country A operated a tariff of t_3. After creation of the CU, the common external tariff will be set at t_2, and further lowering of this common outer tariff to t_1 is envisaged. Let us

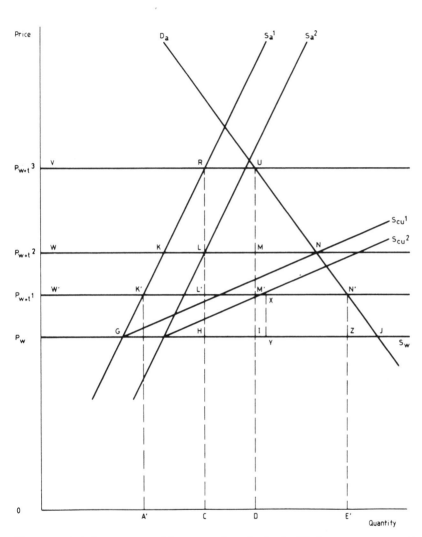

Figure 5.9 Advantages of improved technical efficiency, country A

consider the static welfare effects of this CU; according to the model given in Figure 5.6, the lowering of the initial tariff from t_3 to t_2 would mean a trade-creation effect of *RKL* and a trade-expansion effect of

UMN, against a trade-diversion effect of *HLMI*. As the area of the latter is about equal in size to the combined areas of *RKL* and *UMN*, this CU would be about welfare-neutral. Reducing the tariff further to t_1, triggering off an import quantity *A'C* from the partner country and *CE'* from the world market, would be highly welfare creating, as the combined areas *RK'L'* and *UM'N'* clearly outweigh the area *K'L'HX* (*A'C* being the trade diversion from W to B).

Now this is not the whole story. Manufacturers in A, finding themselves confronted with a great loss of sales markets (from *OC* with tariff t_3 to *OA'* with tariff t_1), rather than accept the loss will accomplish savings on production costs (Figure 5.9). As a result the supply curve of A will move down to S^2_a; the supply curve of the entire CU will drop accordingly (S^2_{cu} in Figure 5.9). The drop has been drawn in such a way that S^2_a cuts through point L.

This effect of a CU on competition and hence on cost levels changes the situation profoundly. The quantity *OC* (the initial production of A) is now produced at a cost of *OW* (= *CL*) instead of *OV* (= *CR*). With tariff t_2, there are no imports from the world. *The cost-reduction*, equal to *VRLW*, is no longer a net welfare effect of *RKL* and a redistribution effect of *VRKW*, but becomes fully a welfare gain, and *renders the net effect of the CU highly positive* (*VRLW* + *UMN* - *HLMI*). With a lower customs tariff, t_1, the effects would be even better. Imports from the world market would then amount to *XN'*, giving a tariff revenue of *XN'ZY*, and more trade creation and expansion: *RL'K'* and *UM'N'* respectively, and far less trade diversion: *HL'M'I*.

Economies of scale

An establishment which can produce larger quantities cheaper than smaller ones, and is constrained in its outlets by a market of limited size, would profit from the extension of the market, for instance by a CU. Figure 5.10 can help us to analyse the effect of 'economies of scale' within one establishment. In this figure, D_a and D_b are the (identical) demand curves for countries A and B, and D_{cu} their common demand curve. S_w is the world supply curve; once more we assume a perfectly elastic supply. Contrary to the demand curves, the supply curves are not the same for countries A and B, country A producing, on average, at higher cost than country B. In both countries the cost decreases as the production increases in volume (definition of 'economy of scale').

We can again analyse *trade effects* for situations of free trade, protection and CU. Free trade appears to be the most advantageous option: at price p_w, countries A (Figure 10a) and B (Figure 10b) both import their total demand (*OQ* for either) from the world market. If, on the contrary, countries A and B both close their markets, in other words, adopt a policy of autarky, country A consumes *OL* at price p_a, country

B consumes OM at price p_b. Evidently, to prevent the national producer from making monopolist profits in this case, the tariffs must not be higher than $(p_a - p_w)$ for country A or higher than $(p_b - p_w)$ for country B (see the discussion of 'made-to-measure tariffs' in Corden, 1972a). The total demand in countries A and B would be $OL + OM$, appreciably less than the $OQ + OQ$ in the case of free trade. Suppose a CU is concluded between countries A and B, and that this CU decides to close its own market to competitors from the rest of the world. Evidently in that case, represented in the left-hand bottom part (Figure 5.10c), demand in the

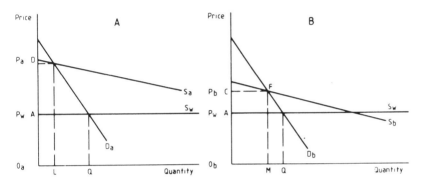

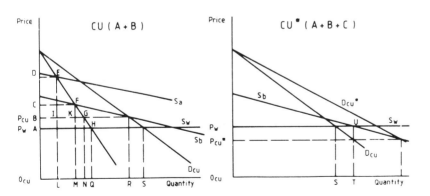

Figure 5.10 Economies of scale in production for individual countries A and B and for customs unions of A and B and of A, B and C

CU could be OR at a price of p_{cu} and a customs tariff of $(p_{cu} - p_w)$. The implication is that country B would take care of the entire production, production in country A being discontinued. The effects of trade creation, diversion and expansion of this CU are in line with the definitions given earlier, albeit that account has to be taken of the slope of the supply curves.

Table 5.3   Trade and production effects of a CU under conditions of economies of scale (countries A and B)

| | Initial situation | | | |
| | Free trade | | Autarky | |
Effect	A	B	A	B
Creation	*	*	$O_{\mathring{a}}L$	*
Expansion	$-NQ$	$-NQ$	LN	MN
Diversion	$O_{cu}N$	$O_{cu}N$	*	*

* not applicable

What are the *welfare effects* of the customs union of A and B in comparison with a state of complete protection and with one of free trade in a situation of economies of scale?

Compared to the case of autarky, consumption in country A becomes ON instead of OL, an advantage equal to $BDEG$. Part of it, namely $BDEI$, is the cost-cutting effect of the 'economies of scale', equalling trade creation; the other part, the triangle EIG, is trade expansion (LN). For country B, consumption becomes ON instead of OM; the advantage is $BCFG$, of which $BCFK$ represents the cost-cutting effect, in this case on domestic production, and FKG the effect of trade expansion (MN).

For the customs union to be an advantageous alternative to overall free trade, the prices of the world producers must be equal to or higher than those of country B. That would be so if a third high-cost country C with a domestic market at least the size of ST joined the CU (the case depicted in Figure 5.10d). The considerable advantage of such a large market achieved by the customs union is that it enhances the international competitiveness of the CU. Indeed this enlarged CU enables the producer in country B to diminish his costs so as to deliver the good to the CU market at $p_{cu}*$. As this price is below p_w, he can start to export his product to the world market. This will permit the CU to abolish the tariff $p_{cu} - p_w$, which leads to a further trade expansion and creation in both countries A and B. (We will come back to these effects in Chapters 12, Manufacturing, and 16, Allocation Policies.)

Do *'economies of scale', as described above, justify the creation of a customs union*? That depends in the end on the net effects for the entire CU, and their division between the partners. In our example, a CU seems favourable on balance, but the losing partner A is likely to demand compensation in terms of money transfers from country B, or to try and achieve a better starting point than country B for other products, so that their manufacture can be concentrated in country A.

Advantages internal to the company

Next to the advantages of the CU discussed up till now, that are internal to the establishment there are three advantages that rather affect the whole company. These apply to the company's size, its growth rate and its learning curve. They are all rather difficult to grasp and quantify in empirical studies. Still, a brief description of them based on many micro-studies may suffice to make the point.

The average *size of companies* may increase after the establishment of a CU because the extension of the market will induce many firms to merge with others for a stronger collective market position. Production may become more efficient because large companies tend to be more efficient than smaller ones, for various reasons. For one thing, large companies are stronger negotiators than smaller ones, and therefore able to make better deals while purchasing their raw materials and intermediary products. They also have easier access to capital and pay relatively less interest. For another thing, they tend to need relatively less manpower because they can, more easily than small companies, shift their staff from one department to another. With respect to their environment and the public authorities (subsidies), large companies have a stronger position than small ones. Large companies are more often in a position to mobilise the resources required for innovation. Finally they are better able than small companies to build up stable market positions, also in export countries. However, these advantages are far from decisive. A small company is often able to respond more flexibly to new market needs, fewer overheads (no bureaucracy), is better equipped to motivate the staff, etc. Moreover, new needs tend to be recognised sooner by small rather than by large companies.

The *growth rate* of companies tends to have a positive effect on efficiency. On the one hand, growing companies tend to have the most up-to-date machinery; moreover, their work force performs better because in growing companies the adaptation of staff is smoother and the atmosphere tends to be more innovative than in companies with a more established pattern. On the other hand, growing companies tend to be unsure about the prospects on entirely new markets, and growth is often paid for dearly. The growth effects of a CU may be enhanced if companies innovate in the manner described here.

Finally, there is the *learning curve*, indicating that companies learn to produce more efficiently by the actual production of greater numbers. Indeed, practice is thought to be the best teacher of how to make things, how to organise production, etc. Learning by doing is different from economies of scale in that the latter give the curve a downward slope, while the former tends to lower the entire curve in the course of time. The first company to produce great quantities will learn so much that it will outrace the others in cutting the costs, and thus gain a profit. To the extent that a CU creates a market in which a company is able to proceed fast along a learning curve, production can be made cheaper in the CU. The welfare implications are illustrated in Figure 5.11.

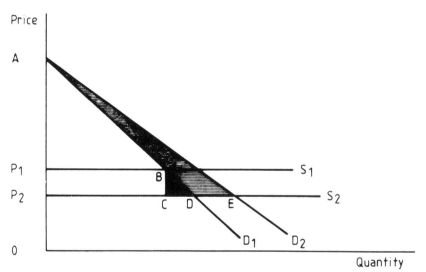

Figure 5.11 Welfare effects of learning

In the first instance, demand is at curve D_1, supply is fully elastic, S_1 (world-wide competition) at price p_1 including a (non-tariff) barrier of $p_1 - p_2$. The abolition of protectionism will bring the prices down to p_2 creating a static welfare gain of the triangle BCD. However, as this expansion permits producers to offer products of higher quality that are better adapted to specific consumer needs, the demand curve will shift to D_2. Evidently, the total welfare gain of removing the protectionist barrier is $ADE + BCD$, which is much greater than the mere static effect.

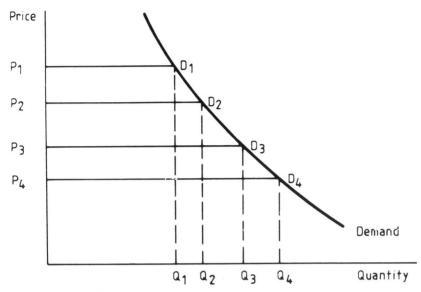

Figure 5.12 Effects of eliminating trade barriers in a customs union

Effects external to the company

It has been argued (among others by Balassa, 1961) that the *industrial interwovenness* of an economy can have a positive effect on total efficiency. When a CU puts a company in a better position, the positive influence is not confined to that company, but extends to all suppliers and buyers. For instance, a successful product innovation may stimulate the suppliers of machines to innovate their production processes, and the suppliers of intermediate products for machines to design better parts. Thus, starting from some key producers, the positive effect of the CU propagates through the whole economy. That effect will, of course, be the greater, the better the various parts of the economy are equipped to respond to the impulse.

Another argument, is that *technical progress* is consolidated by the integration of markets. Stimulated by increased competition, companies will be on the lookout for new producers and new production methods. The enlarged market will also foster the exchange of technical know-how. The ensuing enhanced dynamics will in the end stimulate economic growth.

Effects of the removal of barriers

The effects of the creation of a customs union through the removal of internal barriers to trade may be synoptically represented as in Figure 5.12. As barriers such as tariffs, quotas and other non-tariff barriers are eliminated, domestic producers have to reduce their price to the level of producers in partner countries. The first implication is for them to give up economic rents in the form of excess profits (price moves from p_1 to p_2). If the resulting cost level p_2 is not yet competitive, they will reduce such inefficiencies as overstaffing, excess overheads, etc. As the price goes down to p_3 the demand increases, which may induce new investment. The process of mergers and exit of firms will make room for economies of scale that bring prices down to p_4, permitting demand to increase from Q_1 to Q_4.

Consumers gain from these price reductions (area $p_1D_1p_4D_4$) as they obtain more goods at lower prices. Producers offset the loss by cost reductions. The total welfare gain to the economy is $p_2D_2p_4D_4$ as the excess profits $p_1D_1p_2D_2$ are transferred from producers to consumers. The final gain may be even greater if producers become so efficient (p_4) that they are able to export to third countries. That conclusion rests on the assumption that no country has a comparative advantage over others, and that redundant resources are re-employed.

Summary and conclusions

- The creation of a customs union has some positive and some negative (welfare) *effects*. The creation of a customs union is justified if the former exceed the latter.
- As regards the *short-term effects*, which may concern the consumer as well as the producer and the government, the analysis has shown that (on certain assumptions) the CU is the more positive as the production structures are more competitive, the CU is larger, the initial tariffs were higher, and the transaction costs lower.
- The *long-term restructuring effects* offer better reasons for creating a CU. Competition and economies of scale are the most important effects; among the others are larger companies, growth rates, learning curves, and industrial interwovenness. The latter effects are hard to define and even harder to quantify.

Notes

1   An interesting description of the history of economic thinking on integration is given in Machlup (1977).

2   See for the differences, among others, Robson (1988), Chapters 2 and 3. See this text also for issues of integration of developing countries.

3   Students unfamiliar with the type of analysis cited in these chapters are referred to Part II of Mishan (1982) for a succinct and clear introduction into concepts and methods.

4   World free trade is fostered by GATT; the creation of a customs union is explicitly allowed by the GATT rules (see Chapter 19).

5   EC world trade in agricultural produce (the subject of Chapter 11), for instance, has had an appreciable effect on prices on the world market.

6   For evidence in the EC on this point, see Petith *et al.* (1977).

7   Attempts have also been made to extend the 3 x 2 case (three countries, two commodities) to a 3 x 3 case (three commodities) with a high- and a low-tariff import good (Lloyd, 1982). The results of these exercises are very indeterminate and depend largely on specific sets of assumptions.

6 Common Market

Introduction

In the previous chapter we discussed the integration of goods (commodity) markets. We assumed that production factors are completely mobile within a country, and completely immobile between countries. In Chapter 2 we gave a review of the types of barrier that exist on the international labour and capital markets. If an integration scheme removes the obstacles to free movement among partners not only for goods markets but also for factor markets, the stage of a Common Market (CM) is reached. In this chapter we will discuss the theoretical basis for this stage of integration. We will deal not only with the liberalisation of factor markets, but also with the interrelation of the goods and factor markets that is typical of the Common Market.

The reason to strive for a Common Market is the hope that the freedom of capital and labour to move from activities with a low marginal product to those with a higher one will lead to a more efficient allocation.[1] The next section will discuss to what extent the integration of factor markets helps to equalise factor returns and to create and distribute wealth.

Economic integration does not always proceed by the stages sketched in Chapter 2. In practice this means that trade impediments may persist where international capital and labour markets are already partly integrated. Goods markets and factor markets influence each other in many ways, and consequently the integration of one market affects that of others. How this mutual influencing operates, and how the removal of barriers to either goods or factor movements affects welfare, will be discussed next.

The abstract nature of neo-classical theory is not very well suited to grasping the reality of a world in which entrepreneurial skills and technological innovation vary among nations and the functioning of many markets is far from perfect. So our following step will be to present elements of a theory of international production likely to explain the intricacies of the Common Market better than the loose strands of thought so far developed on the integration of separate markets for goods and production factors.

115

Country A   Country B

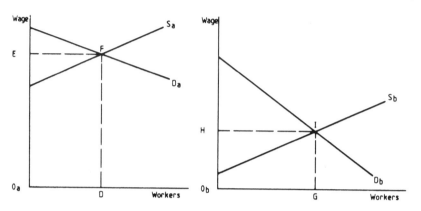

(a) No factor-market integration

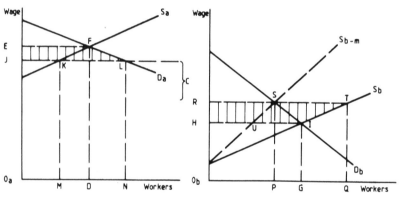

(b) Integration of factor markets, price convergence

Figure 6.1 Effects of movement of production factors

The chapter will be rounded off as usual with a brief summary and some conclusions.

Integration of factor markets; disregard of goods movements

Movement and movement cost; price convergence

The effects of the integration of factor markets can be illustrated by comparing situations with and without movement of factors (Lindert 1986). That is done in Figure 6.1. We have assumed that the world consists of two countries, A and B; the situation for A is depicted on the left-hand side, that for B on the right-hand side. The situation on the factor market is given by the upward sloping curves S_a and S_b representing factor supply, and the downward sloping curves D_a and D_b representing demand for either labour or capital. Together they determine the price of labour (wages) or capital (interest) and the number of workers (amount of capital) employed. We will now work out the effects of integration for the labour market; however, the same reasoning can be applied to capital markets.

- In the non-integrated situation, in which the labour markets of countries A and B are separate, that is, *without migration* (upper part of Figure 6.1), the supply and demand conditions in country A lead to high wages and those in country B to low wages. As was said in Chapter 2, two national labour markets with such different wage levels can be kept separate only by dint of control measures, for instance 'permits' or restricted access to professions.
- In the *integrated situation* (bottom part of Figure 6.1), such barriers are removed. Now workers of country B will move to country A where they earn a higher income. As movement entails costs, both in economic and psychological terms, this will not lead to the complete equalisation of wages. We assume these costs to be equal to C. The inflow of migrant labour into country A pushes the wages down, which leads to a lower domestic supply (O_aM) and a higher domestic demand (O_aN). The difference (MN) indicates the number of migrants from country B in country A. In country B the opposite occurs: the higher wages lead to less demand (O_bP) and increased supply (O_bQ); the difference PQ indicates the number of migrants from country B to country A. The number of out-migrants PQ is of course just equal to the demand for foreign labour created in country A (MN). The new curve of domestic supply of labour S_{b-m} pictures the consequences.

The *welfare effects* of the migration caused by the joining of markets are also illustrated by Figure 6.1. They are fairly intricate and apply to both workers and employers in country A and country B.

Workers from country A lose area *JEKF* because their wages are forced down. (For that reason, many trade unions in developed countries are against immigration.) On the other hand, workers remaining in country B gain from out-migration; there is less competition for jobs, which raises the wage rate from O_bH to O_bR. The gain is the producer surplus above the new supply curve (*HRSU*). The migrants also gain: they earn a higher income in A than they would have in B. However, account should be taken of cost factor C. So, the gain is the area above the old supply curve S_b and below the new one S_{b-m} (*USTI*).

Table 6.1 Welfare effects of integrated production-factor markets

Category	Country	Gains	Losses
Workers	A	*	*JEFK*
Savers	B	*HRSU*	*
	B to A	*USTI*	*
Employers	A	*JEFL*	*
Investors			
	B	*	*HRSI*

*not applicable

Employers in country A gain considerably: the area *JEFK* is redistributed to them from workers, while the area *KFL* is a net gain. In country B, on the contrary, employers are losers: they have to pay higher wages and hence lose profits. Of their consumer surplus (employers are demanders of labour!) they have to hand over area *HRSU* to workers remaining in the country, and area *USI* to migrants.

Countries A and B are clearly in different positions. The receiving country A has a net gain (*KFL*). The sending country B on the contrary has a net loss *USI* (difference between employers' loss and migrant workers' gain). The migrants gain also: *USI* and *STI*. So, the net gain to the world is *KFL* and *STI*; the distribution of welfare among countries depends on the allocation over countries of the gains to migrants.

The reasoning followed here for the movement of labour can also be applied to the movement of capital. It suffices to put savers at the place of workers, investors at the place of employers and to use interest instead of wages etc. The interpretation of the cost difference c for capital movement may be in terms of extra cost of information that will be incurred on investment abroad. The welfare effects of both labour and capital movements are reviewed in Table 6.1.

Movement of factors; full price equalisation

That the integration of factor markets will lead to better allocation of capital and labour can also be illustrated by a somewhat different neo-classical static two-country diagram (again, there is no influence of the rest of the world). In Figure 6.2, the curves of country B mirror those of country A, so that one picture describes the effects of integration on both countries (see Grubel, 1981). The effects of integration of markets for production factors (on the assumption that goods markets are not integrated) can now be illustrated by comparing the situation of Figure 6.2(a), in which there are barriers to movement, with that of Figure 6.2(b), in which these barriers have been removed.

We will first consider the situation of Fig. 6.2(a), in which the capital markets of *countries A and B are completely separated;* in other words, capital is fully immobile between nations.[2] The vertical axis gives the price of capital; with perfect competition on the national markets, this price is equal to the marginal product of capital. The horizontal axis gives the supply of capital (O_aO_b, indicating the total stock of capital at the disposal of the two countries), demand (not indicated in the figure) of capital being given. Country A has a relatively abundant supply, hence a low interest rate; in country B capital is scarcer and hence the interest rate higher. The differential is *ED*. The downward sloping curves for both country A and country B indicate that the marginal product of capital is lower as the capital stock is greater; with a given capital stock (K) in both countries (O_aC for A and O_bC for B) the price of capital R is given for either: R_a for A and R_b for B. We assume there is no unemployment. From this picture the distribution of income can be derived. Total output is $ADCO_a$ for country A and $BECO_b$ for country B (the total production realised at all points on the horizontal axis). It consists of two components – capital income and labour income. Capital income (measured by the quantity of its input times the marginal product of capital at the point where the market is in equilibrium) corresponds to the rectangle O_aCDR_a in country A, and to the rectangle O_bCER_b in country B. The triangles ADR_a and BER_b represent labour income in countries A and B respectively.

What happens when the two countries *integrate their national capital markets?* Figure 6.2(b) illustrates the effects of the removal of obstacles. Owners of capital will now move their capital from the country where it earns a relatively low income (A) to that where interest is higher (B). On the assumption of equal risks and uncertainty for foreign and domestic assets and of no other costs being involved, this will lead to upward pressure on interests in A (smaller supply of capital) and downward pressure in B (greater supply of capital). In the end it will bring about the full equalisation of return on capital in both countries at level R_{cm} (representing the marginal productivity of capital in the Common Market). The capital stock of A declines while that of B increases by the amount CG, equal to A's net foreign asset. So, country A will specialise in savings and country B in investment.

The same approach can be followed for *labour-market integration*. In Figure 6.2(a), R represents wages; they may differ in the two countries because of different endowments with qualified labour and barriers to migration between the two countries. If the latter are taken away, a number GC of workers will move from country A to country B, attracted by the higher wages there. The movement will equalise wages in the two countries.

Even if there were no *differences in factor prices* between the two countries, the removal of controls is likely to favour a better allocation of resources. On capital markets, different liquidity preferences in the two countries will cause the importation of long-term capital and the exportation of short-term capital in A and the reverse in B. On labour markets, the different qualifications may lead to migration of certain categories of active persons from A to B while other professional categories may want to move from B to A.

Welfare effects

The integration of the two markets does not only lead to equal prices, but also has important welfare effects, which are different for different groups and hence lead to distributional disputes.

Total welfare will increase for both countries by the following process. The net domestic product of country A declines by $FDCG$; its net national product, composed of the domestic part AO_aGF and the investment income earned abroad, $GCHF$, increases by FDH. The net domestic product of B increases by $EFGC$. As $CGHF$ must be paid to A, the net gain for B is the triangle EFH. The total net gain from the better allocation of capital through integration corresponds for both countries to the triangle EDF (FDH in A and EFH in B).

The *distribution of income between the main functional categories* (wage income versus capital income) changes when the factor markets are integrated. In country A the part of total income that accrues to labour is reduced in favour of the part that accrues to capital owners (by R_aDFR_{cm}), whereas in B the share of labour increases at the expense of owners of capital (by FER_bR_{cm}). This explains why trade unions tend to welcome incoming investment, but are opposed to domestic investment abroad even if it leads to a higher aggregate income. Of course that effect will come about only if markets function properly, that is if the wages are adjusted downward. If not, the result may be more

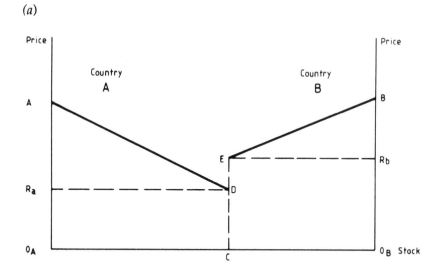

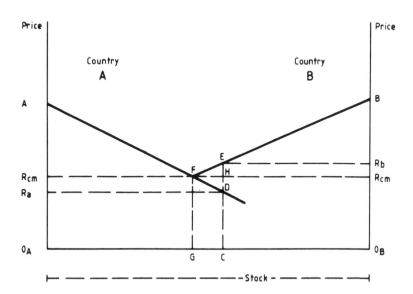

Figures 6.2(a) and 6.2(b). Integration of factor markets; price equalisation

unemployment leading to reduced production, which the growth of capital may fail to compensate in the short run.

Integration is bound to change *government revenue* springing from the taxation of international capital. If country B taxes foreign assets, a proportion of the area *FHCG* remains in B. If it exceeds the net gain of A (the triangle *FDH*), country A will suffer a net loss from opening up its capital market while country B had not done so completely.[3]

The welfare effects of *labour migration* are similar to those of capital movement. On the assumption that the migration is not permanent, the migrants will transfer a labour income *FHCG* to their home country, creating a net gain of *FDH* for country A and *FEH* for country B. Bear in mind, however, that the division of revenues resulting from labour movement may not run fully parallel to that of capital. Since labour will incur subsistence cost while staying abroad, the remittances will be less than *FHCG*, and may even become so small as to offset the gain *FHD* for country A, the emigration country.

Table 6.2 summarises the overall effects.

Table 6.2 Effects of the integration of production-factor markets (letters refer to Figure 6.2)

	Country			
	Segmented Markets		Common Markets	
Indicator	A	B	A	B
Stock (cap. lab.)	O_aC	O_bC	O_aG	O_bG
Price (int. wage)	R_a	R_b	R_{cm}	R_{cm}
Income (first factor)	O_aCDR_a	O_bCER_b	O_aGFR_{cm}	O_bGFR_{cm}
Income (second factor)	ADR_a	BER_b	AFR_{cm}	BFR_{cm}
Net domestic product	$ADCO_a$	$BECO_b$	O_aGFA	O_bGFB
Net national product	$ADCO_a$	$BECO_b$	$AFHC_a$	$BEFHCO_b$
Net gains	–	–	FDH	EFH

The removal of internal constraints and its effects on the balance of payments and welfare

In the previous section we assumed full employment, on the national level, of the two production factors labour and capital. However, that assumption is unlikely to be fulfilled in reality. In small segmented markets specialised labour will be hard put to find sufficient demand for its services, or the necessary capital with which to complement prevailing technological know-how. So in small segmented markets both the supply of and the demand for factors of production may be constrained, with negative effects on production and welfare. By taking away controls on the international movement of labour and capital, both supply and demand can assert themselves, and an efficient allocation of all specialised factors of production will come about.

The 'trade' and welfare effects of removing the constraints on, for example, the capital market, are illustrated by Figure 6.3(a) which gives the supply and demand curves for capital. The supply of capital comes from savers, its demand from investors. Controls on capital imports and exports are making the capital market of country A inefficient. The financial products provided by the banking sector in A being inadequate, potential investors and savers refuse transactions, which implies that some capital remains idle -- indicated in the figure by *AB* (given demand), investment and hence savings being limited to the amount *OA*. The price for the investor, or the borrowing rate, is *OI*, and the lending rate for savers is *OG*. The spread between the two, *GI* or *DF*, is the margin taken by banks for their intermediate role. This margin can be that high because banks are protected from foreign competition. This creates a 'monopoly' permitting banks to earn a monopoly rent of *GIDF* (quantity *OA* times the margin *GI*). Assume now that controls on international capital movements are abolished and thus all inefficiencies in the markets removed. Fear for new entrants from abroad taking away profitable markets will induce banks in the home country to propose new products, better adapted to the wishes of both savers and investors. This will bring additional supply and demand on the market. Let us assume provisionally that the resulting rate of interest (*OH*) is just equal to the interest rate abroad. Both savings and investment will now expand to *OB*. There is an important gain to society as a whole. First investors increase their 'consumer surplus' by the area *HIDC*. Next savers increase their 'producer rent' by the area *GHCF*. Of their monopoly rent *GIDF*, banks lose *HIDE* to investors and *GHEF* to savers. This leaves a net gain to society equal to the triangle *FDC*.

The *effects of partial liberalisation are different.* Under such conditions, the liberalisation of financial markets is unlikely just to balance out home supply and demand at the prevailing world-market price. Figure 6.3(b) represents the situation where the world interest rate *OH* is lower than the domestic-equilibrium rate without international exchange. Now, controls may affect only capital outflows leaving inflows free, or alternatively, affect only capital imports, leaving exports free. Let us analyse the effects of either case on the situation $R_w < R_a$.

In a situation of free outflow and controlled inflow, savers will take the opportunity of getting higher returns on the foreign market (*OH*) than on the domestic market (*OG*), and expand their supply to *OJ*.

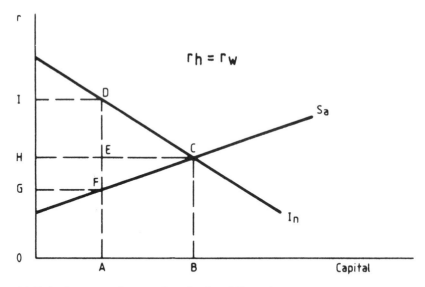

(a) Price home market equals price 'world' market

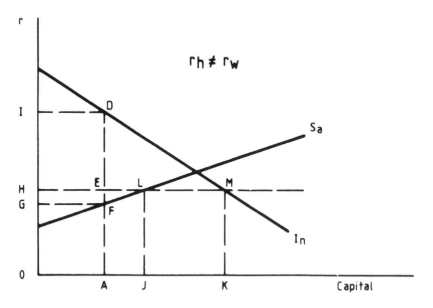

(b) Price home market different from price 'world' market

Figure 6.3 Welfare effects of production factor market integration

Under the pressure, domestic banks will have to diminish their margins from GI ($= FD$) to HI (or DE) to acquire the necessary capital (OA) for making the transaction with the domestic investors. The remaining supply AJ is invested abroad (either directly by savers or indirectly by banks). This will give rise to an inflow of interest payments equal to the area $AELJ$. The 'rent' of savers increases by the area $GHLF$, of which $GHEF$ is gained at the expense (transfer) of the banking sector's monopoly rent, and ELF is the net welfare gain to society.

In the situation of free inflows and controlled outflows, the same reasoning applies. In the closed domestic market, investment was constrained by savings to OA. In the new situation, foreigners will acquire equity (portfolio investment) or companies (direct investment) and get higher returns than on the world market. That inflow will take total investment up to OK instead of OA, the quantity AK being imported, which entails payment of interest on foreign debt corresponding to the area $AKME$. Investors find their 'surplus' increased by the area $HIDM$, of which $HIDE$ is at the expense of monopoly 'rents' of financial intermediaries (that is, a transfer), and the triangle DEM is the net welfare gain.

Evidently, in the situation where both inflows and outflows are liberalised the welfare effects of both can be combined. The net welfare gains (in case the equilibrium interest levels at home are higher than those in the rest of the world as depicted in Figure 6.3 (b)) amount to the area $FDML$.

In Chapter 5 we found that contrary to popular belief, welfare may improve if a good is produced less at home and imported more from abroad, provided that the resources set free are used to produce other goods for which the country has a comparative advantage, thus offsetting the negative balance-of-payment effect. Failing that, total growth will be constrained by the balance of payments. In much the same way we find that a liberalised capital market has positive effects on economic growth (welfare effects) despite an initial deterioration of the balance of payments (from the equilibrium of Figure 6.3(a) to the deficit of $LMKJ$ of Figure 6.3(b). However, if the imported capital is used to create production units, the output of exportables may expand, compensating for the deficit in interest payments.

Other effects

In the foregoing we have shown some welfare effects of liberalising international capital and labour movements. There are other effects, which we will not discuss in detail but which nevertheless call for some attention.

For one thing, factor-market integration may ease the *restructuring* that will follow the liberalisation of trade in a CU. Indeed, new combinations of production factors may often prove impossible with the capital and labour available nationally (by subcategory), and therefore the Common Market may speed up the realisation of the dynamic effects of the CU.

For another, Vinerian effects may occur, this time not in the shape of the creation and diversion of trade, but in the form of the *creation and diversion of labour or capital movements.* Figures 6.3(a) and 6.3(b) could indeed be developed in the same way as Figure 5.2 to demonstrate these effects, an exercise well warranted, as the creation of a Common Market might be bad for world efficiency if a union between countries A and B diverted production factors from third countries. However, for practical reasons we will refrain from going into the matter. As most countries initially restrict labour movements to all third countries alike, the net effect of the liberalisation of labour movement among partner countries is very unlikely to have such an effect. For capital the possibility of diversion seems unlikely as countries with free movement of capital will not easily accept the introduction of a control system discriminating between partners and third countries.

The integration of factor markets will most probably lead to *dynamic effects* (compare goods markets in Chapter 5) by enhancing competition between financial organisations, boosting their economies of scale and raising the quality of their products. Of course, the banking industry in countries with very protected capital markets will suffer from liberalisation, but on the other hand all the activities that use financial products will gain. The gains will be small for multinationals but large for borrowers who until now had no access to foreign markets. The advantages accumulating to governments borrowing in protected markets are likely to diminish as investors find substitutes for domestic government bonds abroad. Finally, the reduced gap between the interest paid by borrowers and the interest received by lenders means that both categories benefit from liberalisation, both investment and savings are stimulated, and better conditions created for future growth. As the dynamic effects of the Common Market are very poorly worked out in theoretical terms, we will not go into the matter further.

Finally there may be an effect of *spatial concentration.* As Kindleberger (1987) shows, at advanced levels of development of financial markets, not only are excess demand and excess supply transferred to the financial centre, but borrowers and lenders move their whole activity there. The effects are shown in Figure 6.4.

The situation before integration is given in Figure 6.4(a). On the left-hand side of the graph, supply (S_l) and demand (D_l) in the small local market mirror the supply (S_c) and demand (D_c) in the large central market indicated on the right-hand side of the graph. Owing to that mirror representation, the supply curve (S_l) goes from bottom centre to upper left, and the demand (D_c) curve from upper centre to bottom left.

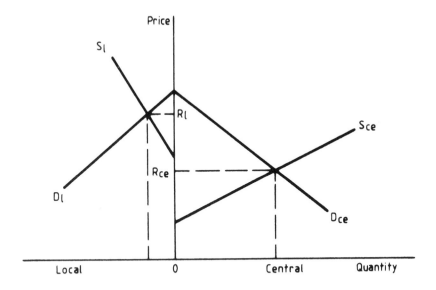

Figure 6.4(a)   Demand and supply of capital in separated small (*l***)
and large (***c***) markets**

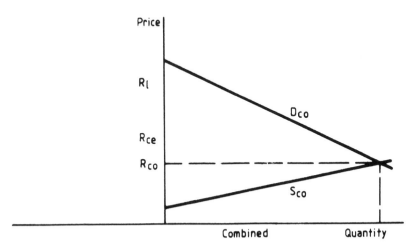

**Figure 6.4(b)   Demand and supply of capital transferred from small
(local) markets to a large (central) one**

After integration of the local and central markets, the central market will take over all activity from the local market (both supply and demand). That situation is given by the 'crossed' lines on the right-hand side of the graph. After integration, savers of both the local and the central areas are prepared to accept a lower rate of return because they will henceforth acquire an asset in a wider, more liquid market (indicated by the downward shift in the combined supply curve of both areas). Integration does not change the curve of borrowers, so the local and central curves of demand have been added up to form the new curve for the common market D_{co}. Borrowers of both areas will thus get a better deal in the central market. The new equilibrium price of capital will lie below the price prevailing on both the local and central capital markets before integration.

Kindleberger observes that this may have considerable influence on the way the integration of capital markets takes shape. Relatively small countries will almost always find it more profitable to integrate with a third large market than with each other, for such a combined market is likely to be less efficient than the external one (see Chapter 10 for the practical relevance of this observation).

Interrelations between goods and factor markets and the effects of barriers to movement

Are goods and factor movements substitutable?

The creation of a Customs Union profoundly affects the labour and capital markets in the two countries concerned, and the integration of production-factor markets affects the production of goods and thus trade. The close relations found to exist between them have induced economists to study the mutual impact of the two forms of integration.

In the 1920s and 1930s, the Swedish economists Heckscher and Ohlin found that on some very strict assumptions, the integration of goods markets will equalise the factor prices. In the 1940s and 1950s, Samuelson[4] developed the theory, which can be summarised as follows. Suppose there are two countries that are differently endowed with the production factors labour and capital. In country A labour is abundant while capital is scarce, which leads to a relatively low price of labour. In country B, on the contrary, capital is abundantly available but labour is scarce; as a result capital is relatively cheap. There is no exchange of goods or of production factors. This situation has an impact on the prices of goods. Suppose there are two products x and y. With the prevailing production technology (identical in both countries) good x is labour-intensive and good y capital-intensive; consequently, product x will be relatively cheap in country A and product y in country B.

Suppose now the two countries start trading with each other while the production factors remain immobile internationally. According to comparative-cost theory, country A will then export good x and country B, good y. The trade relations thus created will affect the production structure of both countries. On the assumption of full internal mobility of production factors, the hope of profit from trade will induce producers in either country to shift resources to the production of the good for which they have a comparative advantage. So, country A will curtail the production of good y and divert the production factors thus set free to sector x, expanding and enabling it to export part of its output. In country B, on the other hand, the production of good y is expanded at the expense of good x.

From the above theoretical exercise, the *movement of goods may be a substitute for the movement of production factors.* This can be elaborated as follows. The change in the production structure entails a change in the demand for production factors, which will in turn lead to a change in relative prices. An amount of capital comes available in country A as the production of good y is reduced; given the technology, relatively small amounts of capital may boost the production of good x considerably. On the assumption of full competition on factor markets (an unlikely assumption especially when wages are at stake), in country A capital will become cheaper and labour more expensive, while in country B the opposite occurs. So in both countries the relatively high factor prices will go down and the relatively low ones up, and in certain conditions complete equalisation of factor prices may even be achieved. In that case, there would be no more incentive for labour and capital to move from one country to another. In other words, the creation of a Customs Union would dispense with the need to create a Common Market; trade is a substitute for factor movement.

On the other hand, *factor movements may also be substitutes for goods trade.* Mundell (1957) has shown that the movement of production factors will alter the relative scarcities of the two production factors in countries A and B, and thus equalise their prices. This will in turn reduce the cost differences between the two countries in the production of goods x and y, thus removing the stimulus to trade in these goods.

However interesting its results, the theory just described is not very helpful for practical purposes (Hufbauer 1968) since its assumptions rarely hold in practice: markets are not characterised by perfect competition; factors are not perfectly mobile; countries are differently endowed with natural resources, etc.

Welfare effects of various types of trade impediments in conditions of capital mobility

If goods and factor movements are substitutes, the question arises whether it is better to integrate goods markets or factor markets, in other words, the question is how to achieve the optimum mix of goods, services, capital and labour movement. Theoretical work on that issue is scarce, and mostly concerned with the relations between Third World and developed countries (Bhagwati 1987b). In Western countries the answers tend to be politically tinged. As migration of labour is considered socially undesirable, most governments would prefer the movement of goods and capital to take care of the equalisation of prices on goods and factor markets. And as the free movement of capital is closely bound up with macro-economic policy making, for which governments are reluctant to give up autonomy, goods trade will in general be preferred to capital movement.

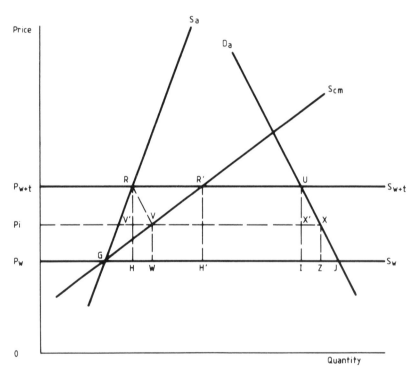

Figure 6.5 Welfare effects of trade impediments with and without capital-market integration

However, some theoretical indications for the optimum choice can be distilled from the effects of trade barriers on welfare, if the analysis described in Chapter 5 is extended to a situation in which capital is free to move from one country to the other. Neary (1987) complemented the well-known partial-equilibrium diagram of Figure 5.2 with a supply curve of goods that comes within reach when industrialists can use foreign capital. In Figure 6.5, the curves D_a, S_w, S_{w+t} and S_a represent, respectively, home demand, world supply without and with a tariff t, and home supply without capital mobility. S_{cm} is the curve representing the supply of country A on the assumption that capital is mobile. This curve passes through point G where free trade obtains, and is more elastic than that of home supply.

Now capital mobility has different welfare effects for tariffs, quantitative restrictions (QR) and voluntary export restraints (VER).

- When a *tariff t* is introduced, consumers suffer a welfare loss of UIJ (compare Figure 5.2), which is equal in both integrated and non-integrated capital markets. However, on the producer side the welfare loss from a tariff increases from the triangle GRH without capital mobility to the much larger triangle $GR'H'$ with capital mobility (see also Neary and Ruane, 1984). In the same operation the government revenue decreases from $HRUI$ to $H'R'UI$.

- Introduction of a *quota RU* raises the price to the level P_{w+t} when the capital markets are segmented, but only to P_i in a situation with capital mobility. That is illustrated by the figure: by drawing a line parallel to D_a through R, intersecting S_{cm} at point V, we apply the same quota (VX equals RU) but arrive at a much lower domestic price P_i. We assume that the quota rights are sold by a system of auctioneering to foreign producers; with capital mobility the government revenue is $WVXZ$, which in the present case is of the same order of magnitude as the revenue the government would get from a tariff under conditions of capital mobility. The welfare cost of a QR under a CM is the total of the areas GVW and XZJ, the loss suffered by consumers being far below the cost of a tariff (the difference being $UIZX$), while to producers the cost (with the present S_{cm} curve) remains about the same (area GRH being approximately equal to area GVW).

- When a *VER* is applied, the assumption regarding government revenue no longer holds. The rent represented by rectangle $HRUI$ in the situation without capital mobility, flows to foreign producers. With capital mobility, the loss to the domestic economy is only $WVXZ$. As $WVXZ$ equals $HV'X'I$, the gain induced by capital mobility is the difference between the two: $V'RUX'$.

Table 6.3   Welfare effects of various trade instruments with (CM) and without (CU) capital mobility (see Figure 6.5)

	Tariff		Policy measures Quota		VER	
Category	CU	CM	CU	CM	CU	CM
Loss to consumers (deadweight)	*UIJ*	*UIJ*	*UIJ*	*XZJ*	*UIJ*	*XZJ*
Loss to producers (deadweight)	*GRH*	*GR'H'*	*GRH*	*GVW*	*GRH*	*GVW*
Government revenue	*HRUI*	*H'R'UI*	*HRUI*	*WVXZ*	–	–

The first *conclusion* from the above analysis is that to introduce capital mobility without abolishing the tariffs spells a loss to the economy, which is one reason why a Customs Union should precede the creation of the Common Capital Market (a view that was also given in Chapter 2). The second is that once tariffs are abolished and capital is made mobile, the costs of applying quotas and VERs are much reduced (which may explain in part why these trade instruments have been so popular under the conditions prevailing in the 1980s).

Production-factor packages; different forms of capital movement with free trade and protection

The theory of international capital movements is not a sufficient base for a study of the dynamics of the Common Market. The reason is that very often capital transactions are not made as portfolio transactions, but in the form of direct investments (DI). Typically, direct investments are internal to the company involved but external to both countries where it operates. DI mostly involve the transfer not only of capital but also of other resources, such as technological know-how, management and marketing skills. It is the expected return on the total of the transferred resources rather than on the capital *per se* that is the rationale for firms to engage in direct foreign investment.

Several approaches have been tried to explain DI, none of which produced satisfactory results.[5] Dunning (1979) forged them together in an eclectic approach. The principal hypothesis of that approach is that *a firm will engage in foreign direct investment if three conditions are satisfied*:

- It possesses net ownership advantage *vis-à-vis* firms of other nationalities in serving particular markets. These ownership advantages largely take the form of the possession of intangible assets – a technological lead, for instance – which are, at least for a period of time, exclusive or specific to the firm possessing them.

- On the assumption that the above condition is satisfied, it must then be more beneficial to the company possessing these advantages to use them itself than to sell or lease them to foreign firms, in other words, it must be more profitable to the firm to internalise its advantages through an extension of its own activities than to externalise them through licensing and similar contracts with foreign firms;
- once these conditions are satisfied, it must be profitable for the firm to utilise these advantages in conjunction with at least some factor inputs (including natural resources) outside its home country; otherwise foreign markets would be served entirely by exports and domestic markets by domestic production.

Assume that *capital movement for direct investment is free between two countries; the type of DI will vary according to whether or not trade in goods is free as well.* Developing the reasoning in Dunning (1980) and using other elements of the theory of Multinational Firms (de Jong 1981, among others) we can distinguish two types of foreign direct investments dependent on the situation with respect to goods trade:

- *Protection.* If country A operates trade impediments, firms from B that want to export to A need a comparative advantage superior to the level of the tariff equivalent of country A's trade barrier. This advantage may be based on superior production technology, on the exclusive right to use a patent for the product, or more generally, on better management or entrepreneurial skills. Exporting firms of country B who judge their advantage real but inferior to the tariff, and firms of B unwilling to have their profit margin taxed away by the tariff, will consider setting up production in country A. This necessitates a direct investment of country B in country A. Many governments are keen to attract such direct investment to further their country's development. Firms in B will invest in A to be able to serve the markets of A. Such investments (often called 'tariff-jumping' investments) are based on product differentiation and tend to be substitutes for trade.
- *Free trade.* Many firms following a strategy of growing through product specialisation opt for operations on several markets, wanting to export to foreign markets from their home base. However this may not always prove the optimum solution, as production in other countries may be less costly. Within the market area, a location will be chosen for each plant that is optimum in view of the prevailing market conditions and other

locational determinants like transport costs, taxes, etc. To cash in on the advantages of international division of labour within the firm (scale economies, use of factors in different countries, etc.), the type of direct investment that could be called 'optimum location seeking' will then be preferred. After production is started, international trade will develop. Some countries will specialise in one good, other countries in others. Often the direction of the investment is contrary to the direction of trade, that is, the exportation of capital goes hand in hand with the importation of goods, and vice versa.

The abolition of tariffs is not a sufficient reason to stop the first type of direct investment. Indeed even in a Customs Union other barriers may persist that are equally important impediments to trade, such as poor access to government contracts, the obligation to comply with national technical norms that oblige firms to keep in close contact with national authorities, etc. (see Chapters 2 and 16). In some cases the type of foreign direct investment that actually occurs is difficult to tell from the observed pattern. On the one hand, firms may have production facilities in a series of countries to jump trade impediments in those countries. On the other hand, they may do the same in a situation of free trade because consumer tastes vary among countries, and technical factors do not push towards production on a very large scale.

Effects on the international distribution of factor returns of removing trade impediments after integration of the capital market

In the previous section we have seen that partial liberalisation of capital markets may precede the liberalisation of goods (commodity) markets. If under these conditions two countries enter into a Customs Union, the welfare effects are more complicated than the ones described in Chapter 5. According to Tironi (1982):

> there are additional gains and losses for the host country which arise from the change in rents earned by foreign companies and that imply a redistribution of income between the latter and the host country. In case of an importable commodity produced by foreign firms where price falls after integration, the host country will gain from the reduction in foreign company rents and vice versa.

Figure 6.6 (which is very similar to Figure 5.2) illustrates the point.
We assume that the whole production in A of good x is realised in the plants created in A by direct investments of foreign firms. Previous to the CU the production is OC, determined by the world market price plus tariff (P_{w+t}). If a CU is formed, with a fully elastic supply from B, the production in A will go down to OB, and quantity BE will be

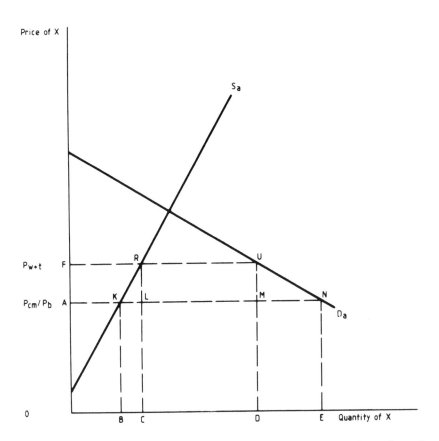

Figure 6.6 Effects on factor earning under partial integration of goods and capital markets

imported from country B. Recall that the creation of a CU produces a net welfare gain of *UMN* on the consumer side and of *RKL* on the producer side. However there is an additional gain for country A of *AFRK*, because this amount (which we assume was previously a remittance of foreign profits of country A to country B, or in welfare economic terms, a rent paid to companies from country B producing in A), is now transformed into an indigenous consumer surplus. This positive effect for country A is termed *foreign-profit diversion effect* (FPDE). Evidently, the effect is the same when more countries are involved and the line *AN* is no longer P_b but becomes P_{cm}.

A similar reasoning can be applied to the case where country A is the most efficient producer. Assume the presence of foreign firms in country A that produce at the price *OA*. Creation of a CU with a country B that up till now has had a very high price level and very high protection implies that a customs tariff for the whole union is set at *AF* and that the new price for the CU as a whole becomes *OF*. The welfare effects will be those of the case analysed in Chapter 5 as one of protectionism. However, with the presence of foreign firms an additional loss is incurred on top of the traditional negative welfare effects of *RKL* and *UMN*. It springs from the part of the consumer surplus *AKRF* that is transformed into additional rents earned by the foreign producer in A and thus transferred abroad. In distinction from the foreign-profit diversion effect, this loss can be called the *foreign-profit creation effect* (FPCE).

The significance of these effects for the advantages of the formation of a Customs Union, depends critically on the origin of the foreign capital. Should the capitalists of the partner country B be the investors in A, then the negative FPCE for country A will be compensated by a net positive effect of the same size for country B; the inverse would apply to the FPDE. In both cases, however, the problem is only one of distribution of wealth, not of net gains for the CU as a whole. The situation is different if the investment in A is owned by capitalists of a third country, when FPCE will become a net loss for the CU as a whole, and FPDE a net welfare gain.

Towards a theory of international production

Interrelations between goods and factor movements

International trade and international movement of production factors, at least of capital, should not be considered in isolation, but tend to be different reflections of the spatial organisation of the production process by private firms. The pattern is shaped by such factors as prevailing technology (which provides the potential for economies of scale), availability and price of factors of production at different locations, the location of demand and the structure of markets, and corporate organisation (see, among others, Helpman and Krugman, 1985; Rugman, 1982).

An interesting model permitting the combination of some of these elements in a simplified view of the international economy is based on the *product life-cycle theory*. This theory distinguishes four stages in the life of each product: (1) introduction, (2) expansion, (3) saturation, and (4) decline. At each stage in this cycle, the companies that produce them show differences in size, profitability, etc.; the markets are differently structured and competition takes on different forms; and the division between capital, labour inputs and returns also displays wide variation. A schematic view constructed from indications in the work of various authors is given in Figure 6.7.

Many elements of this framework are relevant to the process of integration. A CM may speed up innovation and enforce changes in industrial structure (see Chapter 12); it may sharpen competition (for allocation policies see Chapter 16) and thus lead to economies of scale, cost reductions, product improvement and a better export potential (see Chapter 5). New producers are potential competitors on the mass markets, and by innovation and imitation will speed up the passage through the life cycle described above (see Chapter 16).

But it is the bottom part of Figure 6.7 that indicates how the use of differentiated production factors and the location of production and trade take shape internationally. The continuous process is set going by a technical change inspiring the development of a new product. At the first stage of its development this product will need close contact with existing customers, located in developed countries. At the second stage, it will still require special skills to produce and a strong market potential to sell; this means that the production will be located in developed areas where it generates a high value added and sustains high wages. At the maturity stage, margins will fall, and to cut costs, the production will be relocated to areas where wages are lower. The richer countries will change over to new products that are still at an earlier stage of development.

Here again a CM is likely to influence the process. The larger market will offer prospects to specialist producers who would not have been viable in smaller, nationally segmented markets. If the CM presents a sufficient diversity in production environments, it will offer better opportunities for the location of firms in the course of the expansion and saturation stages. Finally, a CM may make it possible to find locations to accommodate within its territory the production of articles at the final stage of their life cycle, and thus postpone the moment of delocation of these activities to third (and Third World) countries.

Divergence or convergence in development?

The neo-classical and Heckscher–Ohlin–Samuelson models lead to the conclusion that factor returns (that is, interests and wages) tend to converge when markets are opened up after the creation of a CU and a CM. However, the outcome of such models depends on many assumptions, the most important probably being that markets function properly and that there are no impediments to movements. The arguments presented in the discussion of labour migration and capital movement (investment behaviour based on technological leads, com-

	Introduction	Expansion
Sales	Small	Fast growth
Products	Very diversified	Few competing concepts
Innovation	Very high product innovation	High product innovation Increasing attention to process innovation
Structure	Few suppliers in separate markets, joint ventures innovation monopolies	New entrants Deconcentration, licencing
Competition	By adapting products to needs to specific clients, pioneering	Imitative improvement Price competition
Profit/Loss	Initial losses; also incidental profits	Considerable profits
Jobs	Little employment, highly qualified	Fast growing number of jobs, decreasing qualifications
Capital/labour ratio	Labour-intensive processes	Intensification of capital input
Location of production	Developed (central) areas	Intermediate areas
Markets	Regional and national markets	Increase of exports; Growing imports from partner countries

Figure 6.7 The product life cycle and international production patterns

Saturation	Fall
Slow growth	Stagnation and decline
Standardised	Only brands different
Low Product innovation accent on process innovation	Absence of innovation
Strong tendencies towards concentration and oligopolies, concerted practices, mergers	Restructuring cartels; diversification through takeovers of young firms in markets with good prospects; splitting-up of firms
Product differentiation High promotion cost	Cut-throat competition, rationalising Collusion
Decreasing profits	Increasing number of companies with loss
Beginning decline in job numbers, simplification of tasks	large-scale reductions in jobs
Large-scale investment in capital-intensive processes	Reduction of labour through closure of the most labour-intensive plants
Low-cost areas	Third world countries
High interpenetration of markets; third-country competition on home markets	High pressure of imports from third world

Figure 6.7 The product life cycle and international production patterns

pany strategies, etc.) have been used by several authors to show that the opposite outcome, that is divergence, is also possible.

The model based on the life cycle of the product may also lead to the conclusion of *convergence* between the levels of development of different areas in the Common Market. It comes about by the gradual absorption of skills and know-how in areas benefiting from direct investment to develop production at the later stages of a product's life cycle. This permits them to develop gradually their own research and innovation, upgrade the quality of the production, at the same time increasing the capacity of their productive system to sustain high wages and high profits.

However, the life-cycle model can also be used to defend the thesis of *divergence* (Myrdal 1956, 1957; Vernon 1966; Hirsch 1974). A simplified description of this model was given by Krugman (1979). He defined two composite commodities: 'new' with a high value added, and 'old' with a low value added. There are two countries: 'North', which is rich, and 'South', which is poor. Capital is mobile and labour is not. Figure 6.8 shows how the capital stock of these two countries is allocated. On the left-hand side of the graph we indicate the situation for North, and on the right-hand side that for South. The curve D_s shows the marginal product of capital in the South, which is also the demand for capital. D_n shows the marginal product of capital in the North, measured in terms of old goods at some given relative price of new goods. At that relative price, the equilibrium return on capital is r_2 with a stock of capital K_s in the South and K_n in the North ($K_n + K_s$ being the total stock of capital).

Now if technical progress leads to the birth of a new good and that new good is much in demand so that the demand for old goods drops, the relative price of new goods rises. The marginal product of capital in the North increases, which can be illustrated by the shift in the curve D_n to $D_{n'}$. As a consequence, the return of capital rises to r_1, and capital moves from South to North ($K_n' > K_n$; $K_s' < K_s$; $K_n' + K_s' = K_n + K_s$). This has consequences for factor prices. The income of northern workers relative to southern workers rises for two reasons. For one thing, the rising relative price of the goods they produce sustains higher wages, and for another, their real wage in terms of output rises because of the reallocation of capital. Southern wages, on the contrary, fall.

The lesson from this is that the technological change in country North triggers off a capital inflow. The rents of the North's monopoly on new goods are collected by the immobile factor of production: labour. So technological change under these conditions equalises the returns on the mobile factor while increasing the inequality of the immobile factors.

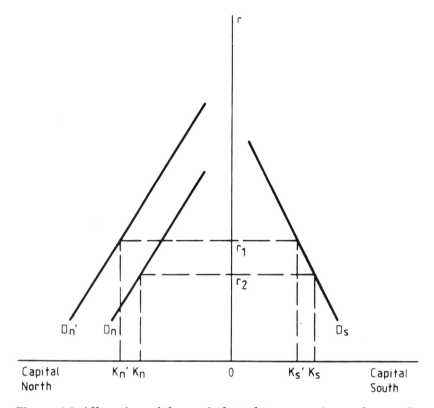

Figure 6.8 Allocation of the capital stock to countries under conditions of technological dominance

Selective labour mobility

In the previous section we have seen the critical importance of the life cycle for a number of phenomena in the international division of production. Presumably, the firms operating in 'Northern' countries in sectors losing their comparative advantage would give up their production and transfer it to lower-wage countries. However, this is not very likely, for parts of the labour force and management will seek to avoid the adaptation cost that is involved, and demand protection against goods imports. If that option is difficult to realise because of international agreements, firms will try to counter lower-price imports in other ways. The most common option is then to cut cost domestically, an option that is feasible only if labour can be imported and effectively paid lower wages than those prevailing in other sections of

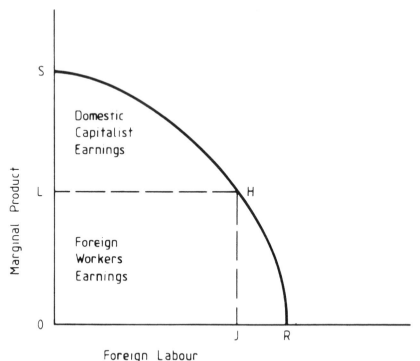

Foreign Labour

Figure 6.9 Labour import in sunset industries

the industry. That can indeed be achieved by allowing the selective in-migration of foreign workers. Bhagwati (1982) used Figure 6.9 to illustrate this option.

In Figure 6.9, *OS* represents the real wages of the domestic labour in country A, which is threatened by low-cost competition from outside. *OZ* represents the lower, fixed real wages at which foreign labour can be imported to execute the parts of the production process that have lost their comparative advantage. *SHR* is the marginal product curve of the labour that is permitted to immigrate (immigration quota *OJ*) given the input of domestic capital and qualified labour. The output in country A is then *SHJO*, of which only *LHJO* accrues to foreign workers, and the rest, *SHL*, to domestic capitalists. The latter effect makes the policy welfare-improving to the labour-importing country.

So, we can conclude that if the internal labour market can be effectively segmented, capitalists and the unions of the remaining domestic labour of the industry in question will bring pressure to bear on the government to import labour and thus postpone the restructur-ing of the sector and its relocation to other countries. In view of the net welfare gain of *SHL*, governments will be inclined to accept such a policy for economic reasons (being pushed in the same direction for electoral reasons as well). However, as the product progresses into later stages of the life cycle, competition of foreign producers is likely to increase, rendering the cost reduction that was made possible by a liberal immigration policy insufficient to keep up the production in country A. Industrialist pressure groups will then cry for protection, supported by both domestic and immigrant labour. After the discussion of the previous sections there is hardly any need to argue that the case for protectionist measures is very weak. Indeed, on top of the well-known welfare losses they would entail (Figure 5.2), a 'foreign-labour income-creation effect' would accrue, similar to the foreign-profit creation effect that occurs when capital is owned by foreigners.

Summary and conclusions

- Integration of national labour and capital markets leads to net welfare gains for the participating countries.
- Under certain conditions the integration of goods markets does away with the need for the integration of factor markets, but these conditions are seldom fulfilled.
- Integration of goods markets should precede the integration of capital markets; indeed the costs of protection of goods markets by tariffs and other instruments are much higher under conditions of free capital flows than under conditions of segmented capital markets.
- The international movement of capital in the form of direct investment is a substitute for goods trade in the case of protection on goods markets, but will create trade in the case of integrated goods markets.
- Trade, direct investment, and migration of labour are all reflections of the decisions of firms as to the international location of their production units. The life-cycle model can give a good succinct description of the spatial patterns that will emerge.
- A Common Market may enhance the development of new sectors and extend the presence of old sectors. Immigration of labour may be resorted to to extend even further the economic life of certain productions in the CM.

Notes

1   Recall that a major argument for controls on capital movements is not the regulation of capital markets, but the stabilisation of exchange rates. However, this motive for capital controls cannot be upheld as the instrument is not efficient for achieving the objectives; in the long run the exchange rate will have to adjust to the

basic economic variables (see Chapter 17). A number of other arguments for capital controls are based on the need to deal with externalities due to market failures and (foreign) government interference (see, among others, Claassen and Wyplosz, 1982). The welfare effects of these controls coupled to goods market controls depend on many factors. However, such complications tend to lose their relevance if all partner countries dismantle their controls, as is the case in a Common Market.

2   A list of instruments that may be used to separate markets is given in Chapter 2; in this case one could think of the use of control or of a foreign capital interest tax in B equal to $ED (= R_b - R_a)$.

3   See for some generalisations of the welfare effects of taxation of foreign-owned firms: Grubel (1974).

4   See for the Heckscher–Ohlin–Samuelson thesis on factor-price equalisation, text-books on international trade such as Södersten (1980, Chapter 4); for a more elaborate treatment Chipman (1966); and for the 'originals': Samuelson (1948, 1949).

5   A more formal mathematical representation of the various theories of FDI is given in Carson (1982).

7 Economic and Monetary Union

Introduction

The development of a Free Trade Area (FTA) into a Full Economic Union (FEU) passes through the stages of the Economic Union (EU) and the Economic and Monetary Union (EMU) (see Chapter 2). In the previous two chapters we have described the gains to be won by the creation of a Customs Union (CU) and a Common Market (CM) through the abolition of impediments to international exchange, a process defined in Chapter 2 as 'negative integration'. We pointed out that such integration cannot be stable without some form of policy or positive integration, which takes us to the higher stages of economic integration.

The most important point to be discussed in this chapter is the *economic rationale for further integration.* Opinions being very divided as to how far further integration is still beneficial to partners in terms of policy, partners in an integration framework tend to apply the principle of subsidiarity, that is, leaving competence as long as possible with the nation states. Transfer of competence will be agreed upon only if it can be proved to make the overall policy process more efficient.

In Chapter 2 we have established that policies aiming at allocational efficiency, macro-economic stability, redistributive equity and external identity are the most important. In the following sections the integration of each of these four policy fields will be conceptually and theoretically underpinned. Under the heading of 'Allocation policies' we will briefly touch upon the why and how of such diverse matters as competition policies, direct intervention in markets, and regulation of access to markets. With respect to stabilisation policies we will go into the advantages of co-operation in monetary and budgetary policies. Finally, we will discuss the rationale and forms of redistribution policies in an international context. For external policies we will indicate what steps have to be taken as the CU moves through the CM towards the stages of EU and EMU.

Allocation policies

Market imperfections and public intervention; the need for a competition policy

In Western industrialised countries, most decisions are left to private economic actors. Market forces (including competition) are allowed to play their role and the price mechanism is largely relied upon to bring about an efficient allocation of resources. However, private actors may collude to put aside competition. Indeed, Adam Smith wrote in his famous book *Wealth of Nations:* 'People of the same trade seldom meet together, even for merriment and diversion, but the conversation ends in a conspiracy against the public or in some contrivance to raise forces'. In these cases, he argues, prosperity is less than with free competition; monopoly spells loss of welfare to consumers.[1] To prevent it, public authorities must take upon themselves to intervene by competition laws and policy (Demsetz, 1982).

The principal *theoretical reason* to pursue competition policies (see, among others, Shepherd, 1985) is indeed the need to avoid the misallocation resulting from:

- *static inefficiency in resource allocation*. A firm charging a price above the real (marginal) cost of production (because of monopolist power) keeps production and consumption below the optimum level (with excess profits to the firm and losses to the consumer);
- *reduced technical efficiency*. Firms producing at lowest cost under conditions of competition will begin to operate inefficiently (through overstaffing, higher wages, lack of response to new opportunities, poor management) in sheltered situations;
- *dynamic inefficiency*. This is an extension of technical inefficiency. To be dynamically efficient requires the constant innovation of production and products.

In this way, the removal of barriers to competition has similar effects as the removal of barriers to trade discussed in Chapter 5. In line with the literature cited there, that on competition indicates that the technical and dynamic efficiency effects are far more important than the static ones (Pelkmans, 1984; Geroski and Jacquemin, 1985).

In a Common Market, national policies are probably insufficient to safeguard competition throughout the union, and hence to maintain the conditions for specialisation, economies of scale, etc. If two firms in different member states agree to refrain from competing on each other's 'home' market, national competition policy probably cannot do anything against it, since firms do not come under the jurisdiction of states where they are not active; yet, such agreements obviously impede the trade between member states. Some form of union competition policy is indeed needed to ensure the fair play of common market forces.

Prices and quantities

In some cases, market forces are not allowed free play, and governments intervene in product markets either by directly prescribing prices and quantities, or by influencing them indirectly.

Direct price and/or quantity controls are practised for several reasons.

- Acute scarcity may drive up the prices of products providing for basic needs, which for social reasons must be kept low. Basic economics teaches that to prevent excess demand in such cases, the quantities need to be controlled as well. Such direct intervention was very common during and just after the Second World War but has now become the exception rather than the rule.
- Natural monopolies (in electricity distribution, for instance) are inclined to charge too high prices and restrict production. Such potential abuse of market power calls for regulation to keep prices at the level that would prevail under competitive conditions.
- Unstable markets (like the one for agricultural products) may call for intervention; to stabilise prices for producers, governments make use of such instruments as guaranteed prices or selling and purchasing from public stocks.
- On social considerations, minimum wage levels, compulsory social security contributions and rules about equal pay for men and women are imposed on labour markets.
- External effects on the consumption of goods (health, environment, for instance) and the existence of public goods lead in some cases to the fixing of prices (for medical and pharmaceutical products, transport, among others).

The intervention in, or regulation of, markets has many negative side effects, and most economists would agree that it should be the exception rather than the rule (see, among others, Breyer, 1984). Moreover, the instruments of regulation should be carefully chosen with a view to the objective one wants to attain.

Nowadays, intervention rather relies on such *indirect instruments* as *taxes and subsidies*. Governments will impose indirect taxes such as excise duties to discourage the consumption of goods with negative external effects (for instance tobacco and liquor on account of their harmful effects on health) while subsidising goods with positive externalities (for instance sports facilities, cultural events, etc.). Taxes and subsidies change the (relative) prices of goods.

Differences in national practices of direct intervention distort trade between partners. If prices and quantities are fixed, evidently governments will want to control imports and exports as well. For such elaborate structural intervention schemes as those in operation for agriculture, organisation on the union level may be inevitable to prevent national compartmentalisation of markets. Indeed, different prices can continue to exist side by side only by dint of compensatory import and export duties equivalent to tariffs, or by such quantitative restrictions as import and export controls, both of which are incompatible with the free internal trade that should characterise the Customs Union.

The same reasoning holds for indirect taxes and subsidies. National systems with different levels and structures of indirect taxation and excise duties will lead to different prices for consumers in different national markets. That situation may encourage sales of goods from low-tax countries to residents of high-tax countries, at the cost of a loss of government revenue in the latter. To prevent this, national indirect taxation systems are usually complemented with trade controls, so that goods leaving the exporting country can be fully 'detaxed' and the duty of the importing country applied to it on access to its market. Evidently, different tax systems lead to controls on international trade; hence the need for harmonisation or even uniformisation.

Quality; regulation of access to markets based on technical specifications etc.

Governments wish to limit market access for several reasons.

- Imperfect information makes it hard for consumers to judge the quality of goods and services, and may also spell material losses and risk to health and safety.
- Production and consumption may have external effects in the shape of costs or benefits to third parties. Environmental damage is a case in point.

To cope with such aspects, governments use various *instruments*.

- For goods, governments mostly rely on the specification of technical standards and norms with which goods must comply (for instance, safety windshields in cars).
- For services, governments tend to set minimum requirements which key persons in a profession must satisfy (for instance pharmacists, lawyers, etc.). Continuous control of a company's finan-

cial soundness is another instrument; such prudential control is applied to financial institutions like banks, pension funds and insurance companies, to whom the public entrusts large sums of money on sometimes long-term contracts.
• Governments may reserve certain activities to themselves or to (state) monopolies, thus blocking the entry of other suppliers. Many social services belong to that category, along with, for instance, defence industries.[2]

That a free market cannot be created by simply removing tariffs and quotas will now be clear. Indeed, states can effectively use national standards (technical specifications) to bar the importation of foreign goods; qualifications, diplomas, etc. to curb the free movement of active persons and services; and prudential control of financial institutions to restrict the movement of capital.

Structural policies

Governments intervene to smooth the continuous restructuring that marks modern economies (Jacquemin and de Jong, 1977), implying the balanced phasing-out of old industries and support to the creation of new activities. There are essentially two strands of *theoretical foundation for the pursuit of an industrial policy* (see for instance; Urban, 1983 and Odagiri, 1986).

The *market-failure theory* states that the perfect-competition model leading to a stable equilibrium does not apply in practice. The reasons are monopolistic behaviour, the existence of public goods, economies of scale, external effects, the cost of gathering information and making adjustments, rigidities, entry barriers, etc. To correct such imperfections and to secure an optimum situation, the government needs to intervene in the market.[3] A classical case in point is the infant-industry argument: a firm should be protected (by subsidies, for instance) from its foreign competitors at the first stage of its development, because only in that way can it grow enough to profit from economies of scale and become competitive. The costs of protection in the first period are compensated by the benefits of production reaped at a later stage (creation of private and tax revenue).

The *growth-cycle theory* (discussed in the previous chapter) takes a more dynamic view of the economy. It finds the reason for government intervention in the incapacity of the economic system to pass smoothly and efficiently through the adaptation stages imposed on it by constant structural changes. At the first stage of new products, public intervention may be beneficial because the market is not well informed, the risks are considered too high for the participants, or the socio-economic cost/benefit ratio is positive while the private one is not, or not sufficiently (externalities). At the second stage of growing products, disturbances may arise from unco-ordinated private decision making (overcapacities); the cost of adjusting capacities to demand levels may be minimised by government intervention. Finally, at the recession stage, the public authorities can steer the sector through the rough waters of capacity reduction.

The quality of the arguments for intervention in the two trains of thought has been severely criticised by several authors in the field. One criticism is that the cost of intervention is often overlooked; another that public authorities are generally no better equipped to evaluate future developments than private decision makers. Many observers, for instance Lindbeck (1981) and Eliasson (1984) consider the economic record of industrial policy so negative as to make it an empty box.

Structural policies can use various *instruments*. Aid (subsidy) to investment and aid to innovation (subsidies to Research and Development; R & D) are the most common; other instruments are the reservation of public procurement to certain firms and restructuring allowances to firms in sectors faced with structural overcapacity. The theory of intervention for structural purposes has been developed in particular for the manufacturing sector, but applies, *mutatis mutandis,* also to other sectors (agriculture, services) and factor markets (think, for instance, of programmes for the (re)training of workers who will be needed in certain new industries, or the retraining of workers made redundant in old industries).

Such measures affect the allocative efficiency of the Union economy. Indeed, structural subsidies to domestic industry can be recalculated in money values per unit of product, with an effect on importers similar to that of tariffs. For that reason, a common stand towards measures of structural policy aid is an obvious necessity in a Customs and in an Economic Union. Common rules for state aids are the obvious first step; at later stages, common programmes for structural change may become a more efficient solution.

Stabilisation; macro and monetary policies

The problem: growing interdependence narrows the scope for independent policies

The creation of the Customs Union and Common Market increases the specialisation of the constituent economies and the exchange of goods, services and production factors. As a result, the economies involved become increasingly interdependent, every country being dependent on its partner-countries and affected by the developments there. Openness has a strong bearing on the degree to which individual governments can influence the economy through budgetary (fiscal) and monetary (exchange-rate) policies. For example, a budgetary policy intended to increase output by increased government spending may be ineffective if the additional purchasing power created is spent on imported rather than domestic goods. A monetary policy that restricts the money supply to keep inflation low may be frustrated by price increases of imported goods as a result of wage inflation in the partner (exporting) country. Interdependence of national economies means that developments on the national scale are apt to have spill-over effects in partner countries, each country giving impulses and feeling the impact of impulses in other countries.

That situation imposes severe constraints on domestic macro-economic and monetary policies, constraints that are reflected in the *reduced ability* to:

- control the instruments of policy (such as the domestic money supply under a regime of fixed exchange rates);
- influence policy targets (such as the level of real output, the level of unemployment and the level of inflation);
- determine the link between targets and instruments.

Now private decision makers in financial markets are very well aware of the reduced effectiveness of policies pursued independently. No longer are they prepared to adapt to policies that are announced but which they do not expect to work. So, public authorities have to put in considerable efforts to remain credible. If they fail, private parties will go on responding to expectations of future exchange rates, irrespective of policy intervention, thus doing away completely with whatever room for manoeuvring there was left to the public authorities. That reinforces the need for partner countries to co-operate to regain collectively the control which they lost individually.

For monetary policy as well, integration will proceed by degrees. Exchange of information on the response of authorities to exchange-rate turbulence is the first degree, the highest being a single currency managed by a Union institution.

The traditional approach

A well known approach to the problems of exchange-rate unification in a situation where national policy-makers envisage different objectives, starts from the Phillips curve, which assumes an inverse relation between wage increases determined by inflation, and employment. This approach, initiated by Fleming (1971) and Corden (1972b), has been developed in geometrical terms by de Grauwe (1975) and is illustrated by Figure 7.1.

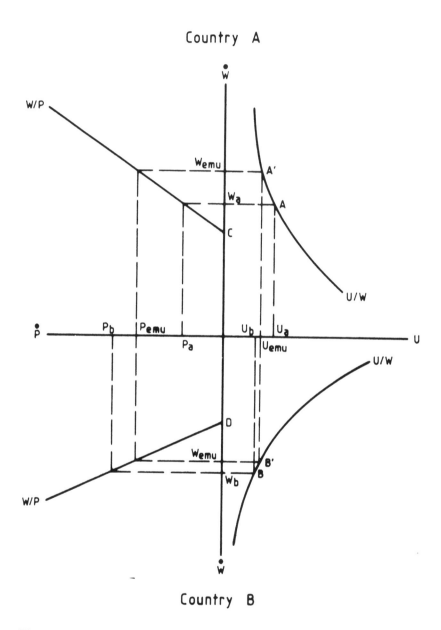

Figure 7.1 Monetary integration in a Phillips world

The *general structure* of Figure 7.1 can be briefly described as follows. The upper half refers to country A, the lower to country B. The w/p curve, which represents the two-way relation between wage increase (w) and price increase (p) is shown in the left-hand part of the figure. Reading from the x- to the y-axis we find that, on the one hand, price increases push up wages; reading from the y- to the x-axis we perceive that, on the other hand, wage increases beyond the rise in productivity push up prices. The intercepts of the w/p curves with the y-axis (sections OC for country A and OD for country B) indicate the increase of productivity. Note that they are assumed to be different for the two countries (higher in country A than in country B). The u/w curve, which gives the two-way relation between wage increase (w) and unemployment (level) (u) is shown in the right-hand part of the figure. The relation from u to w is based on the observation that the higher the unemployment, the lower the pressure on the labour market, and the lower the wage increases. The relation from w to u reflects that the higher the wage growth, the more demand for labour will fall and unemployment increase. Wages have a central role in the set-up given; if we assume that prices (left-hand x-axis) determine wages (y-axis), then these in turn determine unemployment (right-hand x-axis). If we assume wages to be determined by unemployment, then presumably price increases are also governed through the wage variable.

The *situation of independent economies* is characterised by different equilibrium situations in the two countries (no connection between upper and lower halves of the figure). In country A the inflation rate is low (p_a) and the unemployment rate correspondingly high; in country B a much higher inflation rate (p_b) is accepted, with a much lower level of unemployment. Because productivity rises much faster in A than in B, this corresponds to roughly the same nominal wage increases in both countries (w_a and w_b). The equilibrium in the international economic system cannot be sustained at such diverging inflation rates, unless the currency of country B depreciates with respect to that of country A. In the long run, the exchange rates have to be adapted by the difference between the two inflation rates, p_a and p_b (see, among others, Krugman and Obstfeld, 1988, Chapter 14).

The *creation of a Monetary Union* alters the picture (now the upper and lower halves communicate). The irrevocable fixing of exchange rates means that there can no longer be any international difference in inflation rates. So, a Union inflation rate (p_m), presumably lying between p_a and p_b has to be adopted. Through the w/p curve, this determines the wage increases in each country, w_{emu}. These need not be identical for both countries A and B, because of different endowments with factor qualities, technology, etc. Given the position of the u/w curves in A and B, this leads to a Union unemployment rate as well, u_{emu}. Both countries have to move from the points A and B on the u/w curves, which they

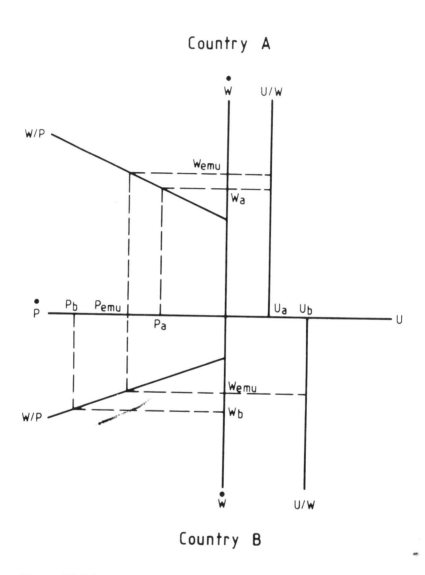

Figure 7.2 Monetary Union in a Friedman/Phelps world

considered optimum, to the sub-optimum points A' and B', and that is felt as a welfare loss.

An alternative view (taken by Friedman and Phelps, among others) is that in the long term there is no such trade-off, and that the relation between prices (through wages) and unemployment is fully inelastic, which means that in the long run unemployment is not influenced by price and wage increases. That situation is illustrated by the vertical u/w curves for countries A and B in Figure 7.2 (adapted from de Grauwe 1975). The position of the u/w curve is assumed different for the two countries, as structural unemployment is higher in country B than in country A. On that assumption, evidently a common inflation rate p_m would affect only the nominal wage changes (w_a increases to w_{emu} in A, and w_b decreases to w_{emu} in B; again, w_{emu} in A need not be equal to w_{emu} in B), but not unemployment. Although the adoption of a lower inflation rate may not cost country B any loss of employment, its acceptance may still be a sub-optimum solution from B's point of view. Indeed, the reduction of nominal wage increases may be very difficult to implement politically, while decreasing inflation may give rise to changes in the behaviour of economic actors. In the same way, to country A the higher inflation rate it has to accept may be sub-optimum (see Chapter 17).

A game-theoretical approach

The traditional approach to monetary integration described in the previous section is not very well suited to the study of macro-economic co-ordination, because it does not account for the *policy reactions of other countries*. Quite a few authors have tried to introduce that element into 'international' macro-models (Cooper, 1983).

However, gradually the fact has become clear that traditional economic modelling is not rich enough to capture the complex interrelationships between private and public economic agents, and in particular the role of expectations and the reactions of other countries. A new approach has therefore been tried, based on game theory (Sachs, 1980; Steinherr, 1984; Buiter and Marston, 1985; Hamada, 1985). Following Sachs (1980) we can illustrate the advantages of co-operation as follows:

Suppose there are only two countries, Germany and France. The growth of GNP (Y) is for either country a simple function of the growth of its own money supply (M) and its partner's (M^*),

Germany: $Y = M + M^*$
France: $Y^* = M^* + M$ (7.1)

the implication being that the external effects are symmetrical and positive. The two countries value the increase of their production (Y) equally positively, and an increase in inflation equally negatively. The utility functions read as follows:

Germany: $U = Y - 2E$
France: $U^* = Y^* + 2E$ (7.2)

where E is the change in the exchange rate (DM per FF) and $E = M - M^*$. Substitution of this and (7.1) into (7.2) gives the following very simple utility functions of the two countries:

$U = -M + 3M^*$
$U^* = M - 3M^*$ (7.3)

Now if we assume increases of money supply from respectively M and M^* to 1 and a decrease to -1, we obtain the following results for different strategies.

Table 7.1 Effects of co-ordinated and non-co-ordinated policies on utility and its distribution among countries

Case	Impulse (M)		Effect (U)	
	Germany (M)	France (M^*)	Germany (U)	France (U^*)
A	+1	+1	2	2
B	+1	-1	-4	4
C	-1	+1	4	-4
D	-1	-1	-2	-2

Clearly, under these very simple conditions, A is the best strategy to follow for both countries, that is to say, for both countries to expand their money supply. This increases total utility by four points, which moreover are divided equally between the two countries. The unco-ordinated strategies B and C are inefficient, as they do not lead to an overall increase in utility, and result in a highly unequal distribution of benefits. Yet, they may be followed in practice because of the dominant views of decision makers. Take for instance Germany: being strongly opposed to inflation this country often refused to embark upon a policy of monetary expansion, whereas France was much less apt to shy away from inflation. Confronted with the danger of imported inflation,

Germany is likely to opt for a strategy to curb M. If France maintains its strategy of expansion, it will lose considerable utility to Germany (case C in Table 7.1). Now to avoid that, France will be forced to adopt similar measures, and the result will be that both countries follow the policies of case D, despite the fact that they are clearly harmful to growth.

Reasons for non-co-ordinated policies

In all types of games in which the policy of one country affects (directly or indirectly) the variables making up the other country's welfare function, better results are possible with a co-operative than with a non-co-operative attitude (Fisher, 1987). That being so, the important question arises why in practice co-operation is the exception rather than the rule. Steinherr (1984) presents the following reasons for *limited progress with policy co-ordination* in an EMU:

- *Uncertain relations between objectives and policy.* Players believe in different models of the real world, for instance monetarists versus Keynesians. Even if they agreed on one basic model, the quantification of the parameters is very difficult, leaving large error margins. Co-ordination can be introduced with success only if conceptual problems can largely be eliminated.
- *Absence of compensation mechanisms.* If under co-ordination country A is not worse off than before while country B stands to reap large benefits, the scheme is unlikely to be considered a good deal by country A. Better deals may be concluded if side payments are made to countries that lose or gain but little from co-operation. If no mechanisms for such payments exist, co-operation may not be realised. If gains and losses from consecutive games tended to compensate each other, such side payments would not be necessary. However, if there is no institutional stability and hence no guarantee that the game be continued, co-operation again is unlikely to come about.
- *Rank and file.* Players (governments) are constrained not only by other players' strategies, but also by their national parliaments and pressure groups. The need to maintain a balance back home may preclude the choice of the optimum solution in the EMU. Therefore, budgetary and income policies may be harder to achieve than monetary policy. The latter is carried out largely by Central Banks, which in some countries are politically fairly independent.
- *High cost of co-ordination.* Negotiations can be long-winded, and conditions may change while they are going on. The adoption of compromise objectives and policies, needed because optimum policies are found not feasible, may incur the highest costs.

Indeed, welfare functions are very hard to define, and the weighing of advantages accruing to one group rather than to another meets with conceptual as well as statistical obstacles.
- *Complexity.* Even in an EMU with a limited number of members and confining its attention to only one or two objectives, the game is already complex. The complexity increases with the number of players (geographical extension of the EMU) and the number of targets (extension of subjects to deal with). The difficulty increases further with the adding of objectives with different time horizons. So, the feasibility of co-ordination depends critically on the limitation of the number of targets.

We can cite one more reason:

- *Lack of awareness of loss of autonomy.* Countries that have traditionally pursued an independent policy tend to be slow to realise that increased international integration has eroded the effectiveness of such policies.

Co-ordination: goals and instruments

What are the principal *goals* that an EMU should strive for ?

The first is the *stability of exchange rates*, needed to create stable conditions for the efficient functioning of markets. The main instrument to arrive at this goal is contained in the very definition of the Monetary Union: the definitive fixing of the exchange rates with the currencies of all partner countries or the adoption of a single common currency.[4] It is understood that there is full and irrevocable convertibility of currencies, which implies that unlimited foreign exchange is available for all international transactions, be they related to trade, services, capital or remittances (essential for CU and CM). The goal of fully fixed exchange rates is not easy to attain, and therefore intermediate solutions have been advocated by which the variability of exchange rates is limited to certain target zones around pivot rates. At a further stage, a so-called 'pseudo union' (Corden, 1972b) may be established, in which exchange rates are fixed but monetary policies not fully integrated; there is no Union monetary authority, and some doubt persists about the durability of the exchange rates.

The *alignment of inflation rates* constitutes the second goal for macroeconomic policy co-ordination. It is derived from the goal of stable exchange rates; indeed in the long run the exchange rate has to be adapted to changes in the inflation rates between two countries thus; to keep the former fixed, the latter have to be aligned. The instruments to be used to arrive at a target rate of inflation for the whole Union are the monetary and budgetary policies. The Union Monetary Authority controls the pool of exchange reserves. Obviously, in a complete EMU with only one currency, there must not be any differences in inflation. That would imply, however, that the money-supply and budgetary policies are agreed upon jointly by partners or decided by Union institutions.[5] In other words, the member states lose all autonomy in that respect. On the way to an EMU, intermediate solutions are likely to be found that gradually reduce the divergence of inflation rates through the co-ordinated use of policy instruments by member states. During the intermediate stage, governments retain some flexibility as to the degree of compliance with the goal, and as to the mix of instruments used.

With respect to the *business cycle*, the question is whether the convergence of the short-run cyclical fluctuations in the economy is a desirable goal. If the cyclical differences come from an exogenous shock, the country affected should not try to realign to its partners. Actually, the effect of the shock will anyway be disseminated to other countries by changes in the imports and exports. If the difference is based on policy measures, whether parallelism is desirable depends on the state of the two economies. If the unemployment figures are high in one country and low in the other, while the opposite is true of inflation, then demand policy should favour opposite directions. In practice, clear-cut rules for co-ordination of objectives and instruments are extremely hard to set. Therefore, the principal mechanism for policy integration at the earlier stages of monetary and macro-economic integration is consultation rather than co-ordination.

The convergence of *growth rates* in the medium or long term is not a desirable goal. For one thing, it cannot mean identical growth rates, as in most integration schemes a major objective is to reduce the difference in wealth levels among partner countries, which requires faster than average growth in low-income countries and slower than average in high-income countries. In the competitive environment that Western economies favour, every country should rather aim at the highest possible long-term growth, irrespective of what partner countries can achieve. Should the equalisation tendencies (that by classical theory would be produced by the integration of markets) fail to establish themselves, then there seems to be a need for the transfer of resources to low-income slow-growth countries by redistribution policies, to create conditions for faster growth. To constrain the growth rates of affluent countries does not seem an advisable policy as it tends to constrain total welfare as well.

Gains and losses

Governments will not give up autonomy in sensitive policy areas to erect an Economic and Monetary Union unless they consider the gains from integration sufficient to make it worth their while. These *gains* can be summarised in three points (Thygesen, 1990):

- *Efficient goods, service, labour and capital markets.* The basic reason for monetary integration is to relieve traders and investors of exchange losses on their international transactions. Stable exchange rates may also lead to greater volumes of trade and investment if the risks of currency fluctuation are taken away, and thus will be a stimulus to growth. Unco-ordinated policies, on the contrary, lead to 'overshooting' in a system of flexible exchange rates, and to largely unnecessary fluctuations in trade, production and investment (Dornbusch, 1976). Morever, the increase in the volume of transactions is likely to improve the financial services needed for payments and hence reduce transaction costs further. The better allocation of available resources will produce welfare gains.
- *An efficient monetary system.* A MU needs far smaller monetary reserves than the group of constituent countries operating individually. For one thing, no stocks need to be kept of currencies of other MU members; for another, peak demands for the currencies of third countries are unlikely to occur in all member countries at the same time. Intervention in foreign-exchange markets by MU authorities is probably more effective than individual actions because of the increased means and the unity of purpose. Finally, the easier management of the system will free part of the resources now tied up in it (both with the monetary authorities and with the banking system).
- *Faster economic growth and curbed inflation* through increased effectiveness of policy instruments. The magnitude of these advantages, which can be won by co-ordinated budgetary and monetary policies, are subject to debate, and some authors consider the dynamic effects to outweigh the static effects discussed earlier (among others, Hughes Hallett,1986).

The *cost* of monetary integration is twofold:

- *Transition from a CM to a MU.* The move towards a common rate of inflation entails adjustment costs. Many countries suppose in their policy the existence of the Phillips curve, which implies that there is in the short run a certain relation between the level of inflation and the level of unemployment. Each country that used to 'choose' independently a combination of these two, now is forced to accept a common inflation rate, and hence accept a different combination of inflation and unemployment. The costs involved depend, of course, on the form of the curve, the discrepancies between independent national targets and the common MU rates, the time period, etc. These costs can be reduced if partners take long enough to realise convergence of national rates for these two variables before passing to the stage of adopting irrevocably fixed exchange rates or a common currency.

* *Continuous reponse to shocks* after the MU has become effective. A MU constrains domestic policy-making; to devalue in response to external shocks (say, a sudden fall in demand for a country's exports or a rise in import prices) is, for instance, no longer feasible. Adjustment in the real sector (actually the lay-off of production factors) is then called for. The cost involved in that adjustment process will depend on the (institutional and social) flexibility of the economy.

Participation

Countries that participate in a Customs Union, and *a fortiori* in a Common Market, will come to realise that the costs of non co-ordinated policies tend to increase. For one thing, the volumes of trade subject to exchange-rate risks have become greater; for another, there are larger flows of capital, which tend to shy away from exchange-rate risks as far as they are of a structural nature, but tend to increase them as far as they are of a speculative nature. That seems to be a good enough reason for CU partners, and even more CM partners, to consider the possibility of eventually progressing to an EMU.

That logic is not found back in the mainstream of literature, however. Rather has the concept of the Optimum Currency Area (OCA), introduced by Mundell (1961), been used to establish *who should take part in a scheme for monetary integration.* Authors have often tried to identify the group of countries likely to form an Optimum Currency Area with the help of one single indicator of the same type as used to determine the stages of integration distinguished earlier (products, production factors, and policy). The most popular indicator is openness of goods markets: pairs of countries with high importation or exportation figures in respect of their domestic consumption are good candidates for an exchange-rate union. Mundell, followed by Ingram (1973), favoured factor mobility as a strategic factor. MacDougall (1977) and Allen (1983), stressing that countries need to develop some form of integrated policy with respect to stabilisation and redistribution before an MU can be sustained, considered the degree of integration on those scores decisive for participation in an OCA. Others, for instance Hamada (1985), even suggest that a full monetary union cannot be sustained without political unification.

The search for optimality on the basis of such criteria as openness to trade, capital, etc. has been severely criticised (by Ishijama, 1975, among others). For one thing, the scores on these criteria are often difficult to measure. For another, which criterion would be best is hard to say; even a combination is of little avail, as we do not know what weights to attach to them. Finally, countries may value their independence so highly that the perceived cost of participation outweighs the advantages of integration. There is also a more institutional reason not to follow up the argument of the Optimum Currency Area. To be viable, an EMU must have a fairly strong institutional structure and real powers. Such a structure is unlikely to be created or sustained among countries that have not acquired some experience with less difficult forms of integration. This implies that countries already forming a CU or a CM will be the best candidates for participation in an EMU.

The question then becomes a much more pragmatic one: *what conditions must be met for CM partners to realise monetary integration?* That depends on the trade-off between the loss of autonomy in certain policy fields and the economic advantages which integration promises, to each member individually and to the union collectively. The loss of political autonomy is not a new phenomenon. We have already seen that countries participating in a Customs Union waive the right to use tariffs, quotas and other trade instruments *vis-à-vis* their partners, and the right to decide on their own to use such instruments towards third countries. In much the same way, partners in a Common Market refrain from using instruments for the control of capital flows to pursue macro-economic objectives. All partners have given up part of their competences because they reckon that the benefits of co-operation would outweigh the loss of manoeuvring room. So, the quantification of gains and losses becomes the essential point of analysis.

Redistribution policies

Economic and social foundations

In a free market economy, distribution of income is determined by the demand for and supply of factor services, and hence depends largely on factor endowments. If we look at persons rather than categories (labour, capital, etc.), we see that endowments or abilities are unequally distributed among the population. Income from labour being largely determined by the ability to perform highly valued tasks, the resulting distribution of income is likely to be highly unequal among persons and households. National governments have tried to bring about a more equal distribution of income by appropriate policies. The idea of distributive justice, initially very popular among representatives of moral and political philosophy, has been increasingly adopted by economists. Chiefly in welfare economics and public finance a theoretical basis for interpersonal redistribution has been developed.

In this book we are concerned not so much with persons as with redistribution among partners in an integration scheme. Recently Findlay (1982) placed the fundamental ideas of different schools of thought on redistribution in a setting of international trade theory. The exercise produces the following three criteria for designing international redistribution schemes:

- *Need* is a moral criterion of distributional justice that has a strong tradition, particularly in Marxist-oriented thinking. In an international context it involves the transfer of resources from rich to poor member states of the union. Many people consider measures of redistribution on the basis of need all the more important as the economic system, left to its own, tends to increase the inequality between the better-off and the poor.[6]
- *Desert* or merit is a more economic criterion often used in a utilitarian view of redistribution. In an international setting its basic idea is that redistribution from richer to poorer states is required up to the point where the gains to union welfare are offset by the losses in economic efficiency incurred by the union as a whole.
- *Belonging* is a legal criterion that restricts the claims for redistribution to participants in schemes of social co-operation for mutual advantage. This has important consequences. Since such schemes coincide traditionally with nation states, claims can be made only by citizens of the specific state involved. Because for participants in economic integration schemes the boundaries of co-operation tend to extend beyond the national framework, to extend distributional justice to citizens of all member states of the Union seems logical.[7]

The foundations for drawing up policies for the redistribution of wealth among partners of an integration scheme have thus been laid. However, the theory to guide the development of specific international redistribution policies on that basis has still to be evolved. So we will limit ourselves in the following sections to some practical set-ups.

Why are redistribution policies necessary?

Countries participate in integration schemes such as a CU or a CM because they expect welfare gains from them. However, there are also costs involved in integration. Resources that are set free need to adapt to other occupations, which often entails the loss of expertise, costs of moving, etc. For some countries the benefits may take long to materialise, whereas the adjustment costs occur immediately. For others,

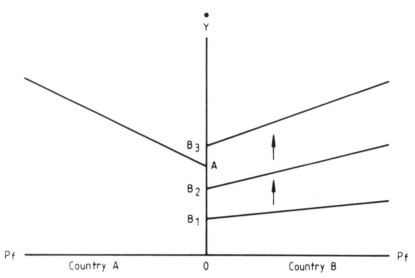

Figure 7.3 Monetary Union and international balanced growth

gains may be quick to come about while the costs are limited. In other words, costs and benefits may be very unequally distributed among countries.

The risks of uneven development across space of the benefits and costs of integration increase with the creation of an EMU. Indeed, in such a union the equilibrium with partner countries can no longer be influenced by exchange-rate and monetary policies, but requires the move of production factors.[8] Now production factors may not always move such as to bring about a better equilibrium. Capital in particular tends to move to those areas that have already secured the best position. Labour may move from low-wage to high-wage countries, but that may entail high social and personal cost. Countries that find incomes sinking below those of others, and understand they are apt to be losers in the integration game, may be inclined to step out. Although solidarity with integration schemes is not determined solely by imme-diate economic gains, for some countries the absence of such gains may become a political factor important enough to inspire compensation schemes. The rationale for such compensation may be indicated by Figure 7.3. Suppose income growth (y) is determined completely by increases in production-factor availability and productivity, together called *pf*. Suppose further that country B is not only a slow-growth (OB_1) but also a low-level-income country, while country A is a not only a fast-growth (OA) but also a high-level-income country. To make income levels in the Union converge, the curve of country B has to move upwards with the intercept moving from point OB_1 through OB_2 to OB_3, which is beyond point OA, this equals structural growth in country A. This can be done only by structural policies raising the level and improving the capacity of production factors in country B.

What form could international redistribution schemes take?

The schemes drawn up in confederations, federations and unitary states for the interregional redistribution of resources differ as to the *combination they use of income instruments* (tax, social security) and *expenditure instruments* (grants, programmes) (MacDougall, 1977). During the pre-federal and small-public-sector-federation steps of institutional integration, redistribution occurs through the expenditure group of instruments rather than through taxes and social-security systems dealing directly with the individual. The reason is that:

- expenditure can be tailored to specific needs (including compensation of negative integration effects);
- governments are generally reluctant to let Unions decide on 'internal' redistribution matters;
- the redistributive power of expenditure is greater than that of income instruments.

There are two main ways to handle the redistribution of funds through the union budget (Musgrave and Musgrave, 1985):

- *General-purpose grants* take the form of block payments from the Union to a member country. The underlying philosophy is one of needs. These have to be evaluated for each individual state against a standard for public-sector programmes and the capacity of the member state to finance them.[9] The Union has no control over the actual use of the funds transferred, which risk being used in a way not expedient to structural improvement.
- *Specific-purpose grants,* not having the same drawback, are the most common. Here the Union decides on the type of programme that should be set up and to which it is prepared to give financial aid. Its inspiration is of the utilitarian type: such grants are considered to lead to optimum welfare in the long run, because they lead to a better allocation of available production factors to whole sections of the economy.

Redistribution schemes should be designed to help along (or alternatively do the least possible harm to) the achievement of the targets of allocation and stabilisation policies. That implies that they must help to create a viable base for future-oriented economic activities. Examples of this type are financial-aid programmes for specific areas, designed to retrain workers who have become redundant because of the structural changes of the economy due to integration. While such schemes are mostly short term, others are of a structural nature. An example of the latter is a programme for the improvement of the infrastructure in regions that are far below the average level of development, aimed at creating the conditions required for self-sustained regional growth.

Transfer payments are very important on the national level. Whether they are so in an international framework naturally depends on the size and composition of the budget of the Union and generally also on the stage of integration.

External policies

The rationale for integration

Integration schemes need to define rules not only for their internal functioning, but also for their external relations. Owing to the high degree of world-wide interdependence, each member country had developed a whole panoply of relations with third countries. Some of these relations, trade for example, will be affected by the creation of a Common Market. All matters that are dealt with internally by the 'union' become at the same time objects of common external policy. The general reason is that common policies tend to be more efficient than individual policies (producing better results with less effort), which justifies giving up a certain degree of individual manoeuvring room. The degree of external policy integration will depend on the advance of internal policy integration. With external policies that are a complement to a clearly defined internal 'union' competence, unification of instruments may be the answer (for instance, a common external customs tariff for a CU). In areas where powers are not yet endowed upon the 'union', for example when countries of a Common Market strive for some stabilisation of the exchange rates of their currencies with those of third countries, consultation or co-ordination is a more likely choice of instrument.

Early stages

By creating a common external tariff, a customs union lays the corner–stone for a common *commercial* policy. Indeed, the common external tariff (CET) needs to be negotiated in the framework of international organisations. Other trade instruments will then be included in the common commercial policy, lest governments unwilling to accept the level of protection provided by the CET impose quotas and other non-tariff barriers. And by raising the level of effective protection for its industry in that way, a country might create a supplementary comparative advantage for its industry on the internal market of the CU, thus disturbing competition.

A Common Market will entail common external policies with respect to the *immigration of labour and movement of capital*. If the CM wants to do away with all internal border controls for workers, it will be forced to adopt as well a common, or at least harmonised, policy for the immigration of workers from third countries. That will lead to a common visa policy for all foreigners, workers or otherwise, for the fully free movement of workers is unlikely to be realised without the introduction of free movement of persons within the Union, which means that, once in the CM, citizens of third countries are also practically free to move within it. The same is true of capital: the abolition of controls at the inner borders means that capital will flow from and to third countries through the member country which gives the easiest access. Until the CM adopts a policy of full openness towards world capital markets, a certain common external capital policy will be needed.

International trade in goods and services and international factor mobility are welfare improving (better static allocation of resources, dynamic effects of competition and innovation. See Figures 5.8 and 5.9 for a graphic illustration of the disciplining effects of import competition on domestic supplies.) Therefore, the external policies of the CU and CM will have to be marked by *openness*. However, as many impediments to trade from the past persist for many countries and competition is distorted on many markets, complete openness may not be the best policy and a more diverse response to the situation on specific segments of goods and factor markets may be best for maximising welfare on the CU and CM level.

Advanced stages

More advanced stages of integration, such as an EMU, are characterised by two features: the fixing of the exchange rates of currencies of partner countries, and the development of a number of common policies.

Allocation policies raise a few problems which call for a common external approach. It has to be made clear, for example, how far firms from outside the CM have to comply to the rules of competition and to technical specifications, how far they may benefit from programmes devised for the structural improvement of the industrial base, etc. In much the same way, the external effects of Union activity need to be co-ordinated; think only of the way world markets may be influenced by schemes to enhance the competitiveness of firms from the CM, or the trade effects of Union market regulation, etc.

Stabilisation policies also have an important external compound. Indeed, the advantages of co-ordination of policies pointed out in a previous section apply not only internally to countries on their way to an EMU, but also to third countries with a high degree of trade interdependence with the EMU. As a common stand carries more weight in international issues, there is a clear need for the CM/EMU to hammer out a common policy of international monetary co-operation (stabilisation of exchange rates).

Redistribution policies are less a matter of external relations; as we have seen, the criterion of belonging tends to reserve univocally the access to such schemes to partners. However, the general ideas of need and desert may be applied internationally as well, leading to a policy of development aid. As aid is often related to trade, common policies may be more efficient than independent ones.

Some common aspects

Mix of goals and improper use of instruments

In the previous sections, we have dealt separately with the aspects of allocational efficiency, macro-economic stability, redistributive equity and external identity. The distinction, so neat in theory, is often blurred in practice in the process of political bargaining.

Indeed, instruments devised to serve policies in one area are often adapted under political pressure to serve other purposes as well. A good example is allocational efficiency. The instrument of guaranteed prices, introduced to make agricultural markets function properly, can easily be used also for redistribution purposes. Whether, and to what extent, redistribution from consumers and taxpayers to producers indeed comes about depends on the relative strength of political pressure groups. Another example is the use of the instruments for the regulation of financial markets to control credit in the framework of stabilisation policies. A final example is state aid for the restructuring of industries that in practice may become an instrument for permanent subsidisation of certain sectors, in order to enhance their 'competitiveness' on external markets. The general rule can be formulated that original objectives are often lost sight of as policies, also common policies, develop.

As combinations of policies, for instance trade and structural policies (Klein, 1985), are often made for specific sectors, for such sectors different sets of combinations of goals and instruments from the four policy areas can be observed. This may lead to the situation that some sectors are exposed to external and internal competition without getting subsidies (allocation) or transfers (redistribution), while other sectors are sheltered from external and internal competition with generous subsidies, with great redistributive effects.

Stages and degrees of integration

In Chapter 2 we made a distinction between several stages and several degrees of integration. There is a certain relation between the two, in the sense that at the early stages, the lower degrees of integration will be applied. On the way to a common allocation policy, member states may begin by consulting one another with respect to certain elements (systems of value-added tax, the structure of tariffs, for example), to end up with the full unification of value added tax rates etc. Between the two stages, harmonisation may be practised. Parallels can be found in external policy, where a Free Trade Area may start with consultations on the external tariff and, passing through the harmonisation of the structure, may end up with the adoption of a Common External Tariff, which makes the Free Trade Area into a Customs Union.

Another option is the distinction within one policy area of cases calling for integration, and others for which partner-state competences are maintained. Examples are the fixing of a Common External Tariff while maintaining partner competence with respect to quotas *vis-à-vis* third countries. So long as the balance between gains and losses of a particular transfer of competence remains doubtful, the lower degrees of integration, like consultation, are likely to be preferred; as soon as that approach shows that the benefits of integration are probably real, the next higher degree of integration will be tried out.

Each successive bit of autonomy lost will make it harder for a member state to achieve the policy mix suited to its specific objectives. Therefore, no progress towards further integration can be hoped for unless clear proof is extended that more stands to be gained from steps towards common allocation, stabilisation and redistribution policies than the direct or indirect costs incurred by loss of autonomy, in terms of taxes, consumer protection, health, and other matters clearly indicated. Therefore, policy integration will vary in extent, nature and combination of elements of allocation, stabilisation, redistribution and external policies according to the prevailing practical political circumstances; there is no theoretical optimum blueprint for the intermediate states between the CM and the FEU.

Summary and conclusions

- The CM cannot function properly without some form of *harmonisation of allocation policies*. Policies concerned with access to markets and the proper functioning of markets will have to be progressively integrated.
- The growing interdependence of the economies of partner countries as a consequence of international trade and factor movements also narrows the scope for independent *stabilisation policies*. The co-ordination of monetary and budget policies that takes account of spill-over effects from one partner to another is then beneficial to all partners as it decreases the fluctuations in the economy (macro-economic stability). The main rationale for such co-operation lies in the removal of exchange-rate uncertainty, which renders the goods and service markets of the Union more efficient. Additional reasons are improved efficiency of capital markets and of the whole system of monetary control. Member countries have some freedom as to the mix of monetary and fiscal instruments they use. Even in a full EMU not all parts of monetary and fiscal policies need to be harmonised. Particularly in the latter area a substantial autonomy may be maintained.
- The proper functioning of a CU or CM requires also some form of co-operation in *redistribution policies* to insure that each member state gets a fair share in the advantages of integration. An EMU puts even higher demands on such distributional policy co-operation, as there the aspects of need and desert will carry more weight; social security may become a Union task.
- The gradual acquisition of more competences in internal matters forces the Union also to define common *external policies* with respect to these matters. Such policies include a common trade policy (CU), common immigration and capital flow policies (CM), a common policy towards key currencies of third countries (EMU), and a common foreign policy (FEU).
- With respect to the *dynamics of integration,* neither the optimum mix of Union and national measures nor the areas where further integration will be more beneficial than sticking to national autonomy, can be determined *a priori* on theoretical grounds.

Notes

1   The same effect can be reached, of course, by potential competition; when existing suppliers fear that potential new suppliers have easy access to the market, they will set their prices with more care. (That contestable market theory is elaborated by Baumol and others, 1982.)

2   Access to markets may also be limited as a consequence of firms' behaviour, for

instance investment and innovation; that will not lead to static inefficient price setting, however (van Wittelloostuyn and Maks, 1988).

3   For a description of the imperfect functioning of markets, see also Wolf (1987).

4   This currency may still take different forms in different countries (Belgian and Luxemburg francs, for instance).

5   Evidently, the exchange rate with all third currencies as well as balance-of-payment questions with the rest of the world will then become matters of common policy, the Union Monetary Authority controlling the pool of exchange reserves.

6   For a short introduction into this school of thought in matters of economic integration, see the second part of the article by Haack (1983).

7   The consequence of such limiting of claims to a well-delimited subset of the world, be it the nation or the Union, is that international transfers to third countries remain acts of charity rather than distributional justice. For that reason, we have included development policies among the external policies (Chapter 19) rather than among redistribution policies (Chapter 18).

8   There are obviously intermediate cases of capital-market and monetary integration where capital is not perfectly mobile nor exchange rates rigidly fixed. These cases make smaller inroads into national competences (Dornbusch, 1980). Some have particular relevance for the EC, as the Community has embarked upon monetary integration schemes before completing the liberalisation of capital markets.

9   In that connection, the need to harmonise social-security schemes (by introducing minimum standards) becomes an issue at advanced stages of economic integration.

PART III
PRODUCTS AND
PRODUCTION FACTORS

8 Goods

Introduction

Since the Second World War, international goods trade has become much freer in Europe thanks, first of all to the activities of the European Community, but also to those of the European Free Trade Association (see Chapter 3).

The most important framework for worldwide liberalisation of trade relations has been GATT, the General Agreement on Tariffs and Trade. Besides, within UNCTAD (United Nations Conference on Trade and Development) there has been some inclination towards free trade, especially with respect to developing countries. How the development of free trade has been accomplished by these international institutions will be sketched in Chapter 19. Here we will explain the EC rules for internal free trade and external trade protection.

The body of the chapter will be devoted to a close analysis of the structure of trade in the EC, the geographical as well as the product structure being commented upon. For the time being, we will confine ourselves to presenting and explaining the changes in the structure of extra- and intra-Community trade under the influence of integration. Trade policy with respect to third countries will be the special subject of chapter 19; policy making with regard to the functioning of the internal EC market is dealt with in Chapter 16.

Having thus covered the quantity aspect of trade under the influence of integration, we will turn to the price aspect, finding out whether or not prices have converged. Finally, we will present a selection from the literature dealing with the question of how liberalised goods movements in Europe affect welfare and commercial as well as economic growth.

Community regime

Treaty

Article 9 of the treaty of the European Economic Community expresses the principles of the free movement of goods in the following words:

> The Community shall be based upon a *customs union*, which shall cover all trade in goods and which shall involve the prohibition between member states of customs duties on imports and exports and of all charges having equivalent effect, and the adoption of a common customs tariff in their relations with third countries.

By that definition, the freedom of movement within the Community extends to goods from third countries for which in the importing member state the administrative conditions have been complied with, and the (common) customs tariffs, or measures of equal effect, settled by the importing member state (article 10). Exceptions to that general rule require extraordinary procedures (article 115), to which no government is entitled by its own discretion.

Article 12-17 EEC stipulates that the abolition of *import duties* and *levies* of equal effect in force between member states was to proceed according to a strict schedule. Thanks to the favourable economic climate that schedule could even be speeded up. A year and a half earlier than foreseen in the treaty, namely, in July 1968, the last internal tariffs among the original six member states were eliminated.

At the same date, the *common external tariff* (CET) came into force. Article 19 EEC had stipulated that for the CET the arithmetical average of the duties applied in the various countries was to be taken as the basis. The national tariffs were gradually adjusted to that CET as the mutual tariffs were broken down. France and Italy in particular had to adjust themselves to freer trade, while the other member states had to introduce more protection against third countries.

Quantitative restrictions and *measures* of equal effect (import, article 30; export, article 34) are forbidden among member states. In accordance with the treaty, they were eliminated before the end of the transition period, that is, before 1969. Quotas for manufactured products had already been completely abolished by the 1st December 1961.

For the three states joining up in 1973 (the United Kingdom, Ireland and Denmark), the transition period terminated in 1977, since when they too have applied the CET, abstaining from quotas and tariffs in intra-Community trade. At the time of writing (1989), Greece, Spain and Portugal were still in a transition period.

The CET system, that is to say the system of tariffs (in value percentages) and quotas, applies in general to all manufactured products. However, the external protection of the agricultural market of the EC is ruled by a separate system of variable levies on imports and subsidies on exports (export restitutions) for variable quantities of produce. Chapter 11 will explain the details of that system.

Level and structure of the CET

Initially, the CET was equal to the weighted average of the tariffs valid in the four customs areas making up the Community of Six (the Benelux counting as one single custom area); it thus reflected the structure and level of all constituent parts.

At the time the Community was founded, its *average common customs tariff* was lower than the tariffs operated by, for example, the United States and Japan. Since then, the CET has been steadily reduced in successive rounds of international (GATT) negotiations on tariffs and quotas (the so-called Dillon round of 1960–1972, the Kennedy round of 1964–1967, and the Tokyo round of 1973–1979). The reduction was entirely in line with the policy laid down in the Treaty (article 110), purporting that the Community wishes '. . . to contribute in the common interest to the harmonious development of world trade, the progressive abolition of restrictions on international trade, and the lowering of customs tariffs'. The average level is now about 3.5 per cent, with far fewer upward deviations than contained in the tariff structure of trade partners.

Apart from the general negotiations mentioned, the EC has negotiated tariff privileges with *certain groups of countries* with which it wants to keep up special relations. The most advanced agreement is the free-trade treaty with EFTA; it was concluded to prevent the creation of the EC, and later the transfer of three EFTA states to the EC in 1973, should entail tremendous diversions of trade in Europe. Furthermore, agreements have been made to allow Mediterranean states free admission of their industrial products to the EC market. The so-called ACP states (African, Caribbean and Pacific states), for which the Community has taken over a special responsibility from the member states concerned (former colonial powers), are permitted free importation into the Community of nearly all their products. Finally, in the framework of UNCTAD an agreement of so-called 'General Preference' has been made with the other developing countries, implying that these countries can freely export their manufactured products to the EC, up to certain quantitative limits. With respect to East-bloc states, the Community unilaterally applies what are called 'most-favoured nation' tariffs. Chapter 19, dealing with the EC's common trade and development policy, will discuss the above agreements in more detail.

Common customs legislation

The elimination of internal obstacles and the introduction of a CET are insufficient to guarantee the efficient working of the customs union. For that purpose, the customs procedures as well as the practices of separate customs administrations have to be harmonised as much as possible. On that score, the treaty is very positive in its commission: article 27 EEC stipulates that before the end of the transition period, the member states shall proceed, as far as necessary, to approximate their legal and administrative customs regulations.

For the *internal market*, it means the elimination, as far as possible, of frontier formalities. They have not been completely abolished because of the different natures and levels of taxation in the member states, the different technical standards imposed on certain goods, and the administrative stipulations based on government measures on a wide spectrum of subjects. We will deal extensively with that problem in Chapter 16.

Externally the introduction of a common customs legislation calls for a uniform way to establish the customs value (on which to apply the tariff), uniform rules to verify the 'origin of goods' (relevant to the tariff, because different agreements have been made with different groups of countries), rules about the collection of money at the frontier or at inland offices, rules with respect to processing trade (relevant to the free importation of goods to be re-exported after processing), and so on, and so forth.

To draw up a common customs legislation is a cumbersome task, in view of the great variety of goods and because customs rules are closely interwoven with other legal and administrative stipulations. A whole series of *EC directives* have been issued for the purpose of further harmonisation, but there are still many differences, especially in practical procedures. An important role is played by the so-called 'Management Committees', on which officials of the Commission sit together with civil servants of member states, and which can give instant answers to questions about the application of rules.

Trade patterns

Relative importance of total foreign trade

International goods trade is essential to the economies of EC member states, as is illustrated by the figures of Table 8.1, representing the relative importance of goods trade in Gross Domestic Product.[1]

First, the table shows that a country's participation in international goods trade depends, in some degree, on the size of its economy. For large countries, the value of goods trade (including intra-Community trade) amounts to about one-fourth of their GDP, while for smaller countries with an open economy (The Netherlands, Belgium, Ireland) it rises to 50 or 60 per cent. The low ratio of Greece is explained by the fact that, historically, Greece has been weak in goods trade, having always applied itself to the exportation of services. To Spain and Portugal, trade in goods is relatively less important than to other comparable EC countries.

Secondly, the figures show very clearly that in 25 years, the international integration of the economies of the EC member states by the exchange of goods has progressed by an average of some 12 percentage points (from about 15 to about 27). This is due not only to the integration between member states; as the bottom line of Table 8.1 indicates, the

Table 8.1 Percentage share of goods imports and exports[a] in total GDP (current prices), 1960–1985

	1960		1970		1980		1985[b]	
	imp.	exp.	imp.	exp.	imp.	exp.	imp.	exp.
Germany	15	16	16	18	21	22	25	29
France	11	11	14	13	19	17	21	19
Italy	13	10	15	13	24	22	25	22
Belgium/Luxemburg	37	34	45	45	50	59	67	64
Netherlands	42	37	43	38	46	43	55	57
United Kingdom	16	14	18	16	25	22	25	22
Denmark	28	23	27	21	28	22	32	30
Ireland	35	23	41	28	66	47	53	55
Greece	17	5	21	7	27	13	31	14
Spain	11	5	13	7	13	9	17	14
Portugal	19	10	24	11	27	15	37	27
EC12 (average)[c]	15	14	18	17	25	23	27	26
Third countries[c]	9	9	10	9	12	11	12	12

Source: Eurostat: *National Accounts* (totals) *1960–1979*, 1983; Basic Statistics; *Trade Statistics*, Luxemburg

[a]   The exports of goods comprise all (national or nationalised) goods carried permanently, free or against payment, from a country's economic territory abroad; for imports, a similar definition applies.

[b]   Estimation.

[c]   On the assumption that the EC consists of 12 member states in all years.

Table 8.2 Percentage shares of EC in total commodity imports and exports of (future) member states

Country	1960[a] imp.	1960[a] exp.	1970[a] imp.	1970[a] exp.	1972[b] imp.	1972[b] exp.	1978/79[b] imp.	1978/79[b] exp.	1981[c] imp.	1981[c] exp.	1985[d] imp.	1985[d] exp.
Germany	31	32	44	41	54	47	50	48	48	47	53	50
France	32	34	49	49	56	56	51	53	48	48	59	54
Italy	29	31	41	43	49	50	45	49	41	43	47	49
The Netherlands	49	48	56	62	62	74	57	73	53	71	56	76
Belgium/Luxemburg	51	53	59	69	71	74	69	73	59	70	69	71
United Kingdom	15	17	20	22	32	30	41	42	39	41	48	49
Ireland	11	8	17	12	69	78	75	78	75	70	72	70
Denmark	39	29	33	23	45	43	50	49	48	47	51	48
Greece	38	31	40	46	55	52	44	49	50	43	49	54
Spain	26	38	33	36	42	46	36	48	29	43	38	54
Portugal	38	22	33	18	46	47	42	57	38	54	47	64
EC[e]	36	38	45	47	54	55	50	54	49	53	54	55

Source: Eurostat, *Basic Statistics of the Community*, various years, Luxemburg

[a] Exports to, and imports from, the six original member states of the EC, also for new member states
[b] Exports to, and imports from, the EC extended to 9 members, also for Greece
[c] Average exports to, and imports from all 10 EC countries
[d] All 12 member states
[e] Average, as if all 12 states had already been members (intra EC trade based on import figures)

integration of the EC as a whole in the world economy has also significantly increased: from 9 to 12 per cent.

Internal trade among member states of the EC

The European Community being a customs union, logically its member states trade more among themselves than with third countries. We know from Chapter 5 that the creation of a customs union may divert, or create, trade flows. Despite measures taken to prevent large-scale shifts (EFTA/EC custom-tariff agreements), trade-creation and trade-diverting effects were experienced at the moments of the formation and enlargement of the EC. Table 8.2 gives an illustration.

For all *six original member states*, the EC share in exports as well as imports rose steeply between 1960 and 1972. From Eurostat figures, trade among the six original EC member states between 1958 and 1972 (the year of the extension with the UK, Ireland and Denmark) can be calculated to have increased ninefold, while goods trade with the rest of the world grew by a factor three. Evidently, in the same period the importance of the EC as a trade partner increased with respect to two of the three new member states (trade with Denmark declined).

After 1972, the year of the *first enlargement*, the picture changes somewhat. The trade of the six original member states with the three new ones increased very fast between 1972 and 1978, but their trade with third countries grew even faster in the same period, as appears from a slight decline in the ratios of the original six between 1972 and 1978 (effect of the first oil crisis). As could be expected, in the period from 1972 to 1979 the EC became more important to the UK, Denmark and Ireland. For the candidate members Greece, Spain and Portugal, however, the relative importance of the European Community to their foreign trade remained fairly constant during the 1960s. The sudden rise of their EC shares observed between 1970 and 1972 is merely a statistical artefact, reflecting the effect of the joining up of the UK, Denmark and Ireland, states with which the three southern countries already had close trade relations. In the 1970s, the degree of integration with the EC varies among the candidates, Portugal in particular having conducted rather a small portion of its total trade with the six original countries (about 25 per cent on average).

The figures for the most recent period, that is, since 1978, show that in practically all member states, old and new, the share of EC imports has declined. This is the effect of the second oil crisis causing a fast rise of the import costs of energy. However, a more structural development *of increased integration of the EC in the world economy* can also be observed, as is evidenced by a more detailed analysis of manufacturing imports by product (Jacquemin and Sapir, 1988). The figures of Greece, how-

Table 8.3 Intra-EC trade (million ECU), by country, 1985

from \ to[1]	BL	DK	D	GR	S	FR	IR	IT	NL	PO	UK	EC12
Belgium/Luxemburg	*	1	14	–	1	14	–	5	11	–	6	52
Denmark	–	*	4	–	–	1	–	1	1	–	3	10
Germany	15	5	*	2	4	25	1	20	19	1	21	113
Greece	–	–	1	*	*	1	–	1	–	–	1	4
Spain	1	–	4	–	*	5	–	2	1	1	3	17
France	11	1	22	1	3	*	1	15	6	1	11	72
Ireland	–	–	1	–	–	1	*	1	1	–	5	9
Italy	3	2	16	1	2	14	–	*	3	1	7	48
Netherlands	15	1	30	1	1	10	1	6	*	–	10	75
Portugal	–	–	1	–	–	1	–	1	1	*	1	5
United Kingdom	5	2	16	1	2	12	6	6	9	1	*	60
EC12	50	11	109	6	13	84	9	58	52	5	68	465

Source: Eurostat, *Monthly Statistics on External Trade,* Series B6, 1 – 1987
[1] Country abbreviation headings follow same order as vertical list

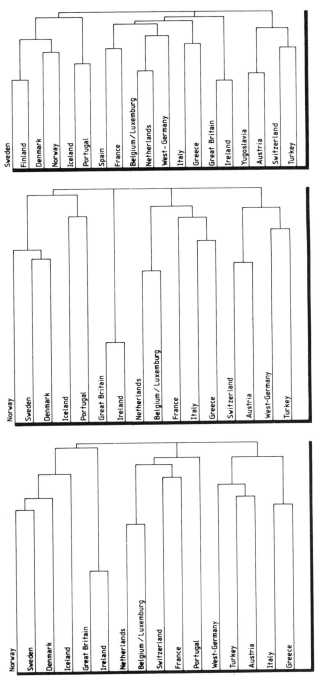

Figure 8.1 Clustering of European countries by trade pattern

ever, suggest an effect in favour of the EC, especially in the import trade, after the country joined the Community.

In the EC12, *intra-community trade* accounts for an average of 55 per cent of the total; the percentage showed a clear rise up to the first oil crisis and has been fairly stable since.

Geographical pattern of internal trade

The geographical structure of internal trade in the present EC of twelve member states is marked by some large flows between some pairs of countries and much smaller flows among others. Table 8.3 records some data of both total exports and total imports of all 12 EC member states.

By far the *largest trade partner* (accounting for one-fourth of the total) on the import as well as the export side is Germany. This country is the largest exporter to the markets of all EC member states, except Ireland. It is, moreover, the largest importer from all countries except Spain and Ireland.

Another striking point is that on the *trade balances* of all member states, the exports to, and imports from, the other members are of the same order of magnitude and fairly equilibrated. We should keep in mind, however, that in particular for small countries, the percentage differences can still be wide. The same (approximate balance of imports and exports) is largely true of the bilateral trade flows, as appears from a pair-wise comparison of columns and rows. Naturally, such a comparison reveals occasional greater discrepancies (for instance The Netherlands versus Germany, The Netherlands versus France, the United Kingdom versus Germany) than are apparent in the totals.

An interesting point to investigate is whether *the integration process has changed the trade orientation of the member states*. Peschel (1985) has analysed this with the help of a linkage procedure clustering the OECD countries. By joining the lines of individual European countries Figure 8.1 shows which countries are integrated the closest (the combinations evolving on the left-hand side), and how these combinations in turn form larger clusters. The further to the right the clustering occurs, the lower the degree of integration. The left-hand picture of 1955 shows that the pre-EC situation predicted neither the formation of the EC6 (Italy, Germany, France and the Benelux belonging to different blocs), nor that of EFTA (whose member countries also belonged to different clusters). Integration did not change that picture very fast: by 1975 the nucleus of the EC (though without Germany) came into being, but EFTA did not emerge. Only in 1981 did trade figures begin to reflect the institutional arrangements: the central cluster of the figure is indeed made up of the member states of EC9, to which Greece and Spain were already associated but from which Denmark was apart.

External trade of the EC, by partner

The European Community (EC12) is the world's largest trade partner.[2] In 1985, exports and imports of the EC (without intra-community trade) amounted to some 18 per cent of total global exports and imports. The figure is slightly lower than that of 1958, when the EC still accounted for 22 per cent of world trade. In the period 1958–1985, when external trade of the EC12 expanded tremendously, both imports and exports rose by a factor 17, which is slightly less than the growth of total world trade.

Of course, the EC's trade relations are much closer with some countries than with others. For example, the Community maintains closer contacts with its Western allies than with the East-bloc countries. Table 8.4 pictures the relative *importance of EC trade with groups of third countries* (without intra-community trade). From the figures given, the first conclusion is that this relative interest has been quite stable through time for each group of countries.

Table 8.4 **Geographical distribution (in percentages) by groups of countries, of the EC12's extra-Community trade in goods, 1958, 1972, 1985**

Country (group)	Imports			Exports		
	1958	1972	1985	1958	1972	1985
EFTA	14	18	20	20	26	22
Other industrial countries	34	34	32	29	34	36
United States	18	19	17	12	19	23
Japan	1	4	7	1	3	3
Rest of OECD	15	11	8	16	12	10
Third World	46	39	38	44	31	34
Mediterranean	7	9	11	12	11	12
ACP	10	8	7	10	7	5
OPEC	17	19	18	12	9	13
Centrally planned economies	6	8	10	7	9	8

Source: Eurostat

Apparently, more than half of EC trade is done with the remaining part of the Western industrialised world. Within that group, the small bloc of countries in the remaining part of Western Europe that adheres to EFTA actually holds a share equal to that of the United States. The significance of Japan as a trade partner is still limited. The other half of EC's external trade is oriented to developing and East-bloc countries. The Third-World countries take pride of place with a share of 40 per cent, while centrally planned economies account for only a small portion (just under 10 per cent). Within the former group, the OPEC holds an important share.

A general question is what *factors determine the relative importance of each group;* A more specific one is why, in the most recent decade, the tendency is no longer for EC member states to get progressively involved with one another, but for their trade with third countries to grow at the same rate. The open character of the EC economy is one cause, the other being the changed international relations expressed, among other things, in the trade policy of the Community. In Chapter 19 we will discuss in detail the policy pursued by the EC with respect to each individual group; some general points may be briefly presented here.

The *developed countries with a market economy* (the Western states) have greatly extended their economic relations with one another, right across the board. The volume of international trade of this group has increased considerably faster than that of production, or did so at any rate up to around 1975 (elasticity lying in the neighbourhood of 1.4). This in consequence of, among other things, the disappearance of many trade barriers. To give an example: since 1983 there have been no barriers (tariffs or quotas) in international trade in industrial goods among the EC and EFTA partners. Trade with other large trade partners, too, has been strongly liberalised (by the reduction of tariffs) in the GATT setting.

The *developing countries* have also profited from a considerable liberalisation of trade. In the dialogue between North and South and by the efforts towards a new international economic order, trade between developed and developing countries is growing. As a matter of fact, the EC has created, through association agreements, very special relations with the group of so-called ACP countries. Trade with OPEC, in particular, has greatly expanded.

The *countries with a centrally planned economy* (like the Soviet Union and the East-European states) for a long time adhered to the principle that trade with 'capitalist' states had to be kept on a low level. They had to confine their imports to products of which they themselves were unable to produce sufficiently (cereals, advanced technology). About ten years ago that strategy was timidly changed. At present the East-bloc countries can be observed to be clearly in favour of openness, a tendency that reflects itself in quite a sizeable trade increase.

External EC trade, by commodity groups

Another point interesting enough for closer inspection is that of the *kinds of commodities* internationally traded by the EC12; Table 8.5 surveys how the patterns developed in a period of more than 20 years.

The structure of EC *import trade* reflects the traditional dependence of Europe on other parts of the world for its raw materials and energy supply. The two oil crises have led to a steep increase in the money value of energy imports and hence of that item's share in total imports (see Chapter 13). The share of the other raw materials has diminished strongly, mostly as a result of reduced prices on the world market and increased efficiency.

Table 8.5 Distribution of EC12's foreign trade by commodity group, 1962 and 1985, in percentages

Commodity group	Imports		Exports	
	1962	1985	1962	1985
Food, drink, tobacco	25	9	9	8
Energy products	16	29	4	5
Raw materials	26	10	4	2
Chemicals	4	5	10	11
Machinery, transport equipment	10	20	37	37
Other manufactured products	17	21	33	31
Miscellaneous	2	6	3	6
Total (million Ecu)	31,500	405,700	26,300	378,500

Source: Eurostat

On the *export side,* manufactured products, with machinery and transport equipment in the lead, are observed to account for about three-quarters of total exports, a share which has been stable throughout.

A major shift in the pattern refers to agricultural produce. Although agricultural imports increased considerably in the period analysed, their relative share dropped steeply, and by 1985 was almost on a level with exports. That development is closely tied up with the common agricultural policy, to be described in Chapter 11.

Shares of the member states

The EC is not homogeneous with respect to foreign trade. The individual member states occupy clearly different positions, which, moreover, are subject to changes in the course of time. Table 8.6 recapitulates these changes.

Table 8.6   Percentage share of member states in EC extra-Community trade

Country	Imports		Exports	
	1958	1985	1958	1985
Germany	19.4	24.1	25.1	31.8
France	16.7	14.2	16.3	15.6
Italy	9.3	15.5	7.8	13.9
The Netherlands	7.4	9.8	6.2	5.9
Belgium/Luxemburg	5.8	5.6	6.3	5.4
United Kingdom	34.0	18.5	33.2	17.8
Ireland	0.7	0.9	0.3	1.1
Denmark	2.2	2.9	2.3	3.3
Greece	1.1	1.7	0.5	0.7
Spain	2.5	5.5	1.2	3.8
Portugal	0.9	1.3	0.8	0.7

Source: Eurostat

The Federal Republic of Germany has become the leader in the EC, not only in total production (GNP) but also in trade. On that score, Germany has indeed outraced the United Kingdom, in 1958 still accounting for one-third of total trade, but reduced, by 1985, through lagging economic growth and structural deficiencies, to a position just ahead of France and Italy. This last country has displayed remarkable growth in foreign trade. The balance of extra-Community trade is positive for Germany and – to a lesser degree – for France, Denmark and Ireland; all other member states show a deficit, as does, for that matter, the EC as a whole (see Table 8.6).

Competitive position of the EC on the international market

Is the pattern of specialisation reproduced in Table 8.5 also indicative of the sectors for which the EC is most competitive on international markets? Indeed, the EC is generally considered strongest in capital-intensive industries (where wage costs are less relevant), and in know-ledge-intensive products (for which other countries do not always have the qualified labour); however, other countries have specialised in those sectors as well. For that reason, the European Community has repeatedly analysed its competitive position, especially in comparison with the United States and Japan (EEC, 1975, 1982, 1985). These studies focus on the sectors of technologically advanced products. The index used is the ratio between two shares, on one hand the share of exports of technologically advanced products in a country's total exports, and on the other hand the share of that country's (or the EC's) total exports in total OECD trade. Table 8.7 surveys the results of that analysis. From the figures, the EC appears to be on a lower level since 1970 than its two competitors, Japan and the USA, and its relative position has weakened further in the course of the years. Japan in particular has consolidated its position very rapidly. That result is confirmed once more by a study by Rollet (1984), who defines a category of products 'mastering tech-nology' – products at the frontier of technology development, with a very high R & D content (computers, telecommunication, robots, etc.), and another category of investment goods which are at the crossroads of different production systems; see also Maillet and Rollet (1986).

Table 8.7 Specialisation index of export trade in high-value tech-nological products, 1963–1983 (OECD = 100)

	1963	1970	1978	1983
EC	1.01	0.94	0.88	0.82
USA	1.27	1.28	1.27	1.26
Japan	0.72	1.07	1.27	1.36

Source CEC, 1982a; *European Economy*, September 1985, page 108.

From a study by the OECD (1987a) the EC is seen to be specialising rather in medium technology products and to hold a neutral position in low technology products. The analysis of Jacquemin and Sapir (1988) shows on the other hand that for the products of the former categories (motor vehicles, wireless and television sets, office machinery, other machinery) the competitive position of the EC on its own market has been gradually eroded. There are many who believe that the deterioration of the EC's position was due to structural weaknesses of its manufacturing industry, which tends to be too small and is confronted with a segmented home market. To remedy that situation, two types of action are taken: an industrial policy specifically aimed at stimulating innovation (see Chapter 12), and a policy focusing on market conditions (see Chapter 16 on the programme on the completing of the internal market by 1992).

Explanation of spatial trade patterns

Some 'traditional' approaches to goods-market integration

Trade theory puts a heavy accent on *comparative advantage*. In practice, the concept is rather difficult to work with, however. Prices and availability of factors are not easy to integrate in our framework with export and import structures. The suggestion has been made first to analyse the so-called 'revealed comparative advantage' (RCA) with the help of an index dividing a country's share in the exports of a given commodity category by its share in the combined exports of a group of countries, and then relate that ratio to relative cost (compare the figures in Tables 8.7 and 8.8). Balassa (1977) is one of those who have followed that approach for the EC, showing the changing trade patterns of the individual member countries. However, as systematically relating these RCA indices to explanatory factors seems difficult, we will not follow his example.

Trade patterns may also be influenced by *trade impediments*. Among these we find structural factors as well as government and private distortions. Tariffs occupy a preponderant place in integration theory (Chapters 2 and 5). Distance has also been cited in that respect (see Chapter 2). An early demonstration of the effects of transport cost in the EC was given, for aggregate trade flows, by Linnemann (1966), who used a gravity-type model, followed by Aitken (1973). On the disaggregate product level, distance has been found by Bröcker (1984) to have a significant effect on trade patterns in the EC in 32 out of 33 manufacturing industries. Bröcker also found significant integration effects (tariff costs) for 14 out of 33 industries. We will come back to the effects of integration through tariff cuts in the last part of this chapter. In recent times the study of goods trade has tended to focus on other aspects, highlighting the role of industrial organisation (see Chapter 12), technology, etc. However, to the author's knowledge, no systematic studies have been made explaining the trade pattern from trade impediments other than tariffs and transport.

Intra-industry specialisation

Contrary to what some had expected, the further opening up of the national markets for manufactured goods by the integration schemes of EC and EFTA and the liberalisation in GATT have not produced specialisation among countries along the lines of traditional trade theory, according to which one country specialised in one good, for instance steel, and the other in other goods, for instance port wines, on the basis of comparative advantages. On the contrary, at the beginning of the 1960s it became clear that the *specialisation occurred within sectors* both countries producing, for example cars, but of a different type. In the early 1960s, Linder (1961) suggested that 'the more similar the demand structures of two countries, the more intensive potentially the trade between these two countries'. Balassa (1966, 1975) showed that trade liberalisation in Europe was in fact accompanied by increases in the extent of intra-industry trade (IIT) among the countries in question. The question how to measure and explain IIT has received much attention in the literature (among others by Grubel and Lloyd, 1975; Tharakan, 1983; Greenaway and Milner, 1986; Kol, 1988).

The *process of IIT* in the course of European integration is illustrated by the results of the studies by Grubel and Lloyd (1975) and Greenaway (1987), summarised in Table 8.8. The development over time of the index figures shows that in all countries and through the 1957–1977 period, IIT has been on the increase. (Similar information for EFTA countries shows the same tendency, but at a lower level; for CMEA the indices are lower, Drabeck and Greenaway, 1984.) The figures reveal a reduction between 1977 and 1980; no satisfactory explanation for it has

Table 8.8 **Average levels[a] of intra-industry trade, in selected EC countries 1959–1980**

	1959	1967	1977	1980
Belgium/Luxemburg	53	63	69	63
France	45	65	76	65
Italy	35	42	58	50
The Netherlands	55	56	67	65
United Kingdom	35	69	72	60
Germany	39	46	64	57

Source: Greenaway (1987)
[a] Grubel and Lloyd indices of IIT at third-digit SITC (Standard International Trade Classification)

yet been found. The results in Table 8.8 are corroborated by Bergstrand (1983), who calculated IIT indexes for the years from 1965 to 1976 for the four large EC countries; he found that on average, in three-quarters of the sectors he analysed IIT had increased, sometimes considerably (30–50 per cent).

Several factors can *explain intra-industry trade.* The first is scale economies; if there is much product differentiation and a wide range of products, each country will produce only a limited subset. Technology is another factor; if R & D produces a rapid turnover of products protected by patents, each country will specialise in different segments of the market. Moreover, the strategies of multinational companies lead to flows of intermediary goods among plants and the delivery of final goods in their distribution systems (Caves, 1982)

Now, *is growth of IIT also due to integration?* A set of studies (see Greenaway,1987) would suggest so, because in the 1959–1980 period intra-EC, intra- industry trade grew more rapidly than total EC intra-industry trade. On the other hand, the comparison of IIT growth in countries participating in integration schemes with that in comparable non-participant countries suggests, but does not prove, an integration effect. Recently Balassa and Bauwens (1988) found however, that economic integration (EC + EFTA) had a clear influence on the level of IIT in Western Europe, together with the factors just cited. Moreover, they found that IIT decreases with increasing distance and differences in culture.

Technology

Modern theory of trade tends to look towards technological and industrial factors for the explanation of trade patterns.

The idea is that the *level of innovation determines the quality of the product, which in turn determines its competitive position on external markets.* This leads to specialisation: some countries specialise in high-tech goods, others in low-tech goods; the latter are generally believed to create less value added.

Within the European Community, countries show a wide variation in innovation efforts, the pattern being that R & D per head is highest in the richer countries and very low in the poorer ones (see Chapter 6). It would be interesting to verify whether that pattern is reflected in the internal trade patterns. An empirical study directly testing that hypothesis has not yet been made, however.

An attempt to explain by technology factors the trade shares held by the wider circle of OECD member states has been undertaken by Soete (1987) for a range of products. His static cross-section model contained such explanatory variables as a country's innovative capacity (country's patents in the USA), factor proportions (gross fixed capital formation divided by employment) and, of course, a distance variable. Although the results clearly indicated a role of the technology variable, such a static analysis cannot give final answers. Better explanations still seem a long way off (Cheng, 1983; Dosi and Soete, 1988).

Price differences

Measuring differences

The degree of integration can be measured not only by the growth of the exchange of goods but also by the degree of convergence reached by their prices in the various countries of the EC.

Under the *law of one price* undistorted markets would result in completely equal prices, and trade would reflect the location of demand and the location of the lowest-cost producers. However, what with transportation cost, collusion practices, tariffs, etc., prices do differ from one (sub) market to another. An interesting study in that respect is the one by Glejser (1972), who compared the prices of a fairly well-defined product set before (1958) and after (1970) the creation of the EC. His results were not very conclusive; out of 36 cases, 15 showed a tendency towards greater disparity and 21 a tendency towards convergence. Work on prices has since been continued by the Commission for reasons of competition policy, and by consumers' organisations who demand that any price cuts be passed to the consumer in all countries of the EC.

To compare price levels in different countries has always been a hazardous undertaking. To be meaningful, such a comparison should be made between products which are not only available in all the countries surveyed, but also representative of all the national (and regional!) consumption patterns. The size of the EC and the historical origins within its borders give rise to a great variety of consumption patterns. In spite of the difficulties, Eurostat has succeeded in putting together a series of comprehensive sets of price data for the Community (EC9). For the present comparison, we have selected from the series those headings of consumer and equipment goods that are broadly representative of final demand in tradeable goods. Part of the price differences among countries spring from the differences in taxes, in particular value-added tax and excises. The comparisons have therefore been made for prices inclusive and exclusive of taxes. For an idea of the magnitude of the price differences among countries and their development through time, coefficients of variation have been calculated; Table 8.9 gives the results.

From the table, price levels evidently differed appreciably from one member state to another. For consumer goods the price dispersion

Table 8.9   Price dispersion (coefficient of variation) in the EC9, by product group, 1975–1985

Category	Without taxes			Taxes included		
	1975	1980	1985	1975	1980	1985
1.1 Food	16.4	15.3	14.4	19.2	18.0	17.3
1.2. Food products subject to excise duty	19.0	21.2	17.0	31.3	38.3	32.7
1.3. Textiles, clothing, footwear	13.7	16.4	12.9	15.8	17.8	13.5
1.4. Durable consumer goods	12.4	13.9	12.3	17.7	17.7	17.4
1.5. Other consumer goods	21.3	21.4	19.3	21.8	20.0	20.1
1 Total consumer goods	16.5	17.1	15.2	20.5	20.9	19.4
2 Equipment goods	13.7	13.8	12.4	13.7	13.8	12.4

Source: Eurostat; Emerson *et al.* (1988), page 120.

came to about one-fifth of the average price in the EC, for investment goods it was less: some 12 per cent. A comparison of the left- and right-hand parts of the table shows that indirect taxes, which vary considerably among countries for the same product, were responsible for about one-quarter of the total price differences. Note that the composite calculation method used reduces the gap considerably; the absolute price differences between maximum and minimum prices are far greater. In 1985 for example, the dispersion of car prices net of tax was 14 per cent, but the absolute difference between countries at either end of the scale (Denmark and the United Kingdom) is 35 per cent; for refrigerators the dispersion is 10 per cent and the highest absolute difference (between Italy and France) 39 per cent.[3]

The trend in the dispersion of prices in the period between 1975 and 1985 is not easy to interpret. The dispersion widened between 1975 and 1980, but narrowed between 1980 and 1985 enough to cancel out the increase previously recorded, with the result that for all products the coefficients were lower in 1985 than in 1975. As the exchange-rate turbulence at the turn of the decade may have distorted the picture for 1980, we will look only at the 1975–1985 indicators. The conclusion is that in that period, prices in the EC tended to converge.

Causes of price differences

Differences in prices among EC countries are due to different factors. One has already been mentioned in the previous section, namely, the differences in indirect *taxes*. However, even net of indirect taxes prices differ considerably; in the case of consumer goods the table shows that for items normally subject to excise duties prices tend to differ more than for other items, which leads to the conclusion that tax structures affect the price structure (net of taxes).

More detailed material, not reproduced in Table 8.9, reveals larger differences for certain goods, like boilers and transport equipment. An interesting observation is that these goods belong to the categories of products that are mainly *purchased by the public sector and which show sizeable differences in technical regulation or standard,* in other words, categories for which trade is subject to non-tariff barriers. Moreover, in those sectors where there are non-tariff barriers, price dispersion has tended to increase in the past 10 years (+5 per cent), while narrowing appreciably in the sectors more open to Community competition (-24 per cent).

These are indications that tax differences and non-tariff barriers need to be removed to achieve further integration.[4] However, even after their removal numerous factors will continue to justify price differences between countries as well as, indeed, within each country. That is the case of, for example, transportation on account of different distribution networks, and of cars on account of regional differences in tastes and competitive pressures. However, these factors do not justify the differences observed in Table 8.9; indeed, an analysis applied to a specific sample of products (Emerson *et al.*, 1988) showed the price dispersion within Germany to be half that in the Community, indicating a large potential for further price convergence in the EC.

Welfare effects

Traditional methods for measuring effects on member countries

One of the most common indicators of integration is the intensity of trade among partners. Growing mutual involvement of that kind is considered a sign of the trade effects of integration schemes. That indicator, which can be applied to member states as well as third countries, has been operated in previous sections of this chapter (see Table 8.3). However, the method being rather crude,[5] more sophisticated ones have been developed to analyse the trade and welfare effects of progressive integration. These methods build on to the theoretical considerations set out in Chapter 5; they are essentially an exercise in completing the accounting frameworks with data about, for instance, cost differences, price elasticities, trade flows, tariffs, and consumption in the countries participating in the CU. At the time of the creation and successive enlargements of the European Community, various attempts were made along those lines.[6]

Two *approaches* can be distinguished. The *ex ante* approach tries to estimate the effects of a planned customs union by forecasting what will happen if the CU is realised and what if it is not realised. Such an approach shares with all prospective studies the drawback that the information from which the effects have to be estimated is incomplete and far from reliable. The *ex post* approach sets out to estimate the effects of a customs union that has already been realised. In that case, historical data can be used, the problem being to establish what would have happened had no CU been formed. To that end, hypothetical situations, known as 'antimonde', have to be created.

To calculate the *trade effects*, the usual procedure of *ex ante* studies is to estimate demand and supply elasticities and compute average tariffs for various sectors, and from the outcomes measure the effects of the transition from different national tariffs to the common CU tariff. Methods varying in sophistication have been applied (Krauss, 1968; Williamson and Bottrill, 1971; Resnick and Truman, 1975; Petith, 1977; Miller and Spencer, 1977, and Viaene, 1982). In the *ex post* approach, the total growth of trade observed in the past is split into normal growth (that is, the growth that would have been achieved without integration), and residual growth, that is, the growth attributed to integration. Again, there are legion methodological problems[7] (Balassa, 1975; Grinols, 1984). Given the sometimes rather crude methods applied, the rather wide variation in the results of these studies is hardly surprising. For the first period of the EC6, from 1955 to 1969, the period of eliminating high tariffs, some estimates assumed a doubling of trade in comparison to a situation without EC. The first enlargement has been estimated to account for a 50 per cent rise in trade between the United Kingdom and the EC. The effect of the recent joining of Spain, which entailed the abolition of low tariffs only, was not more than 5 per cent, perhaps 10 in the somewhat longer run.

A survey of the results of computations of the trade effects allegedly due to the creation of the EC in the 1960s and the 1970s was given by Mayes (1978). Although the quantitative results are hard to compare because of methodological differences, the general impression is that the trade creation has amounted to between 10 and 30 per cent of total EC imports of manufactured goods. Trade diversion is on the whole estimated much lower, at between 2 and 15 per cent. Agriculture is an exception to the general picture; Balassa found considerable trade diversion for this sector. Recent new studies, among which *ex post* studies like the one by Winters (1985), confirm the results of earlier ones and add interesting sophistications with respect to the asymmetrical developments of UK and EC imports and exports.

The next step is the calculation of *income effects*. Only a few authors have actually taken that step. The problem is that the income effects cannot be derived from trade effects without additional information.

From the scarce empirical *ex ante* studies, very low calculated static welfare effects emerge. Verdoorn's (1952) first estimates of the effect of the West European free-trade area on the growth of the collective national incomes of the states involved, amounted to less than 1 per cent. Johnson (1958) also found that the effect of freer trade between the United Kingdom and the other West European countries would probably be around 1 per cent of GNP. Miller and Spencer (1977), studying the UK's entrance into the EC, arrived at an estimate of about 0.15 per cent of GNP of the United Kingdom for the static reallocation effects. Other studies, among which *ex post* studies like Balassa (1975), also found the effects to be slight, in the order of less than 1 per cent.

The studies cited have a number of drawbacks. Many use simplified methods to avoid data problems. Most studies, moreover, confine themselves to manufactured goods, leaving agriculture and services largely out of account. Finally, and that is a major objection, none of these studies has properly come to grips with such dynamic effects of goods-market integration as economies of scale, efficiency, or learning by doing.

Effect of the EC Customs Union on trade with third countries

The formation of a customs union also disturbs the patterns of trade with third countries, as has already been suggested in the previous sections. Only two attempts have been made at tracing the effects of the formation of the initial EC of six; both Sellekaerts (1973) and Balassa (1975) use variants of the *ex post* approach. One study of some importance (Kreinin,1973) has gone into the effects of the first enlargement. Begging the reader to keep the limitations of this approach in mind, we will briefly recapitulate some results.

The *effect of the formation of the EC6* on trade with third countries was studied by Balassa (1975). He found particularly large positive trade-creation effects for machinery, transport equipment, and fuels; negative ones for food (see Chapter 11), chemicals, and other manufactures. The EC formation caused a significant trade gain for associated less developed countries, and somewhat lesser positive trade effects for the United Kingdom and the United States of America. By contrast, net trade-diversion effects occurred for the other developed countries and the centrally planned economies; very small negative effects can be observed for the other EFTA and other LDC groups.

The *effects of the first enlargement* on trade partners have been estimated by Kreinin (1973), on the assumption of a merger of EC6 and EFTA. The analysis was limited to semi-manufactured and manufactured goods. There appeared to be large net trade-diverting effects against third countries; they were heaviest for the group of other developed countries (approximately 20 per cent) and somewhat less heavy for the LDC (approximately 15 per cent). As could be expected, the United Kingdom and the rest of EFTA showed trade-creation effects (some 27 per cent of total 1970 exports).

A macro-model approach

In his two recent publications, Marques-Mendez (1986a, 1986b) presents a model based on the macro-economic effects of changes in trade and in terms of trade. The central variables in the model are the percentage growths of GDP. While circumventing many difficulties besetting previously discussed approaches, the model raises others concerning the correct measurement of the phenomena. Table 8.10 reproduces the results of an estimation of the model for two periods, the first relating to the EC6, the second to the EC9. The first column gives the growth rate actually observed, the second the growth rate that can be attributed to the EC.

Table 8.10 Effects of the integration of manufactured-goods markets on the percentage trend growth rate of EC member states

Period	1961–1972		1974–1981	
	observed	due to EC	observed	due to EC
Germany	4.39	0.80	2.65	−0.78
France	5.40	−4.30	2.66	0.56
Italy	4.97	2.73	2.74	−1.21
Netherlands	5.17	3.40	1.99	−0.69
BLEU*	4.56	2.86	2.03	0.66
UK	–	–	1.24	1.28
Ireland	–	–	3.84	−2.94
Denmark	–	–	1.98	−4.58

* Belgium/Luxemburg Economic Union

From the first and second columns, the *effects of the EC6* appear to be quite substantial, particularly for the smaller countries (which is in line with the suggestions made by Petith, 1977), much larger anyway than the effects calculated by the Vinerian type of study discussed earlier. The result for France is slightly different, probably owing to the large error and residual factor obtaining for that country. Most of the positive effect is due to the growth of the export volume, only partly offset by the change in the propensity to import.

The *effects of the EC9*, represented by the last two columns, present quite a different picture. Of course, the period differs from the preceding one in many respects. At the start of the EC9 most tariffs were lower than at the time of creation of the EC6; besides, a profound need for economic restructuring was recognised, energy prices were on a steep increase, and 'new protectionism' was becoming generally accepted. Although all this warrants the lower growth rates quite naturally, still it seems surprising that the integration of the enlarged EC should have adversely affected growth in most member countries. The explanation is that the propensity to import outweighed in many countries the growth of exports. Moreover, Denmark and the Netherlands, and to a lesser extent Ireland and Italy, were experiencing in this period considerable negative changes in the trade balance. Only the United Kingdom, the largest of the three new member countries, scored differently as to its propensity to import *via-à-vis* its exports. Before concluding that economic integration apparently leads us the wrong way, remember that the results of this model for this period are all susceptible to large error margins of about half the actual growth rates, and that trade effects are not the only effects of economic integration.[8]

Summary and conclusions

- The integration of the economies of EC countries through *the exchange of goods* has greatly increased in the past period, and their mutual involvement has increased more than their involvement with third countries.
- Specialisation took the form not so much of each country concentrating on a specific sector, but of specialisation within sectors *(intra-industry trade)*.
- The *prices* of most goods tended to converge in the 1975–1985 period, in line with theoretical expectations.
- Trade creation has on the whole been considerably greater than trade diversion; on balance, the EC *appears to have contributed clearly to the efficient allocation of production factors in the world*. (That is very evident for manufactured products; for agricultural products certain negative effects are dominant, effects to which we will revert in Chapter 11 on agriculture.)
- Integration as such does not appear to have entailed great static *welfare effects*; the great advantages of the EC have to be found rather in the improvement of the terms of trade, the reduction of costs, and economies of scale.

Notes

1   Naturally one should keep in mind that the goods trade is given at production value and GDP value added. On the other hand, GDP also comprises some activities which do not enter into the international commercial circuit. For lack of basic data, the ratio has not been corrected for these influences, as it should have been.

2   The USA, with an average of 16 per cent of the total, is the second trade power of the world; Japan, with 9 per cent, is much smaller. In relative terms, too, the Community's external trade exceeds that of the USA; for the EC12 external trade amounts to 12 per cent of GNP, for the USA 8 per cent; Japan approaches the EC figure with approximately 11 per cent.

3   These branches will be dealt with in more detail in Chapter 12.

4   The policies pursued to realise the conditions for such a development are discussed in detail in Chapter 16.

5   Compare for instance, Waelbroeck (1976).

6   For a brief review of methods and outcomes, we shall borrow from the surveys made, in particular, by Verdoorn and Schwartz (1972); Balassa (1975); Mayes 1978 and Jones and El Agraa (1981).

7   Note, however, that some of Balassa's methods and definitions (as, for that matter, those of other authors of *ex post* studies) are not directly compatible with the theoretical conception of the CU of Chapter 5. However, a discussion of the details would lead us too far off the main road.

8   In the next chapters we will take up other effects of integration, such as mobile production factors and/or the common policies, particularly agricultural policy. One aspect of integration, namely the effect of stable exchange rates on the volume of trade , will be taken up in Chapter 17, where the effects of policies, particularly monetary policy, will be discussed.

9 Labour

Introduction

In our discussion of the theory of economic integration in Chapter 6 we pointed out that, under certain conditions, the creation of a common market entails movements of labour which in turn have a levelling effect on the price of labour (the wages). In this chapter, we will describe the two phenomena in some detail.[1]

First, however, we will devote a section to *regulation*. Soon after the Second World War, Western Europe fell apart into two groups. The one comprises the countries with many immigrants: France, Germany and Belgium in particular, but also Sweden and Switzerland. The other group contains the emigration countries: Italy, Spain, Portugal, Ireland and Greece. Each country, or group of countries, tried to regulate migration by a complex whole of multinational or bilateral agreements, national legislation and administrative rules and practices. International organisations, such as the International Labour Organisation (ILO), the OECD, the Council of Europe, and the EC each assumed a co-ordinating role. The Council of Europe, taking up the cause of international migrant labourers, tried to safeguard their legal status by drawing up a European Convention to that effect (1977). The European Community went much further, ensuring to EC nationals unrestricted migration for work reasons within the Community. More complicated rules apply to nationals of third countries. The next section will deal at some length with the role of the EC in matters of migration, and the legal points involved, because without that previous knowledge, the working of the European labour market is hard to grasp.

The *exchange of labour among member states through international migration* is the subject of the next section. In Western Europe, labour has always been on the move (see, for instance, Winsemius 1939; Lannes 1956). The movements were often inspired by political motives. The tremendous migration wave just after the Second World War comes immediately to mind; more recent examples of 'political' migration are the repatriation moves of French people from North Africa and of Portuguese citizens from Angola and Mozambique. Migration for economic reasons is distinguished from politically-induced migration in that it is voluntary; mostly, but not always, intended to be temporary; and, finally, concerns mostly workers who leave their families behind. We will briefly indicate the results of studies that have tried to explain labour movements.

With respect to the *price of labour*, we shall devote a separate section to the question of how far wages in the EC have actually been adjusted. We shall see that factor prices have indeed converged but that several factors have been at work to prevent the complete elimination of wage differences among member countries of the EC.

An evaluation of the *welfare effects* and a brief summary of the main findings conclude the chapter.

Community regime

Treaties

Free movement of labour is vested in the Treaty of the European Economic Community, and more particularly in article 7, forbidding in general discrimination because of nationality, and thus stipulating that nationals of other member states shall in principle receive the same treatment on the labour market as a state's own nationals. Numerous regulations and directives contain rules to realise that principle in practice; the Court of Justice's jurisprudence has also contributed a great deal.

With regard to the free migration of labour, a distinction can be made between employed persons and persons practising an activity for their own account and responsibility. The EC Treaty applies the principle of article 7 to both, but works it out differently for either.

With respect to *workers*, articles 48 ff. of the Treaty stipulate that:

> the freedom of movement shall entail the abolition of any discrimination based on nationality between workers of the member states as regards employment, remuneration and other conditions of work and employment. It shall be secured within the EC by the end of the transitional period at the latest (January 1, 1970).

By the definition given in the treaty, a worker is essentially someone who performs work in an employment situation against payment.

To be considered *self-employed*, or *independent*, the person concerned must exercise an economic activity in his own interest and for his own responsibility. Two specific rights are given to the category of self-employed. First, the right of establishment (articles 52 ff.), that is, the right for member-state nationals to set up businesses abroad (agencies, branches or subsidiaries), and the right to take up and pursue activities as self-employed persons and to set up and manage undertakings in a member state, on the same conditions as laid down for its own nationals by the law of the country where the establishment is effected. Second, the right to provide services by nationals of member states who are established in a state of the Community other than that of the person for whom the service is intended. Although the EC Treaty deals with the freedom of establishment and service in separate chapters (2 and 3, Title III), we will combine them here because economically they are not much different. A company can indeed choose either to create an establishment (branch or otherwise), or to exercise the activity from the main establishment.

The rules of the Treaty apply *in principle to all sectors of the economy* unless explicitly excluded. However, the Treaty stipulates (art 55) that:

> this freedom shall not apply to employment in the public sector (art. 48.3) and activities which in that state are connected, even occasionally, with the exercise of official authority .

Given the prominent place which the government now occupies in the economy of many member states, manifest in the large shares of workers with a civil-servant or equivalent status in total employment, large portions of the labour market could thus be excluded from free migration. However, the Court of Justice has pronounced clearly in several verdicts that such an interpretation would be contrary to the intention of the Treaty. The Court has laid down that the notion of 'public sector' must be understood narrowly, as comprising exclusively those positions and tasks which imply direct or indirect involvement in the exercise of public authority, or functions which concern the general interests of the state and in particular its internal and external safety.

By the end of the transition period (1970), a free market for labour and services had indeed been realised as far as the agricultural, manufacturing and craft, and commercial sectors were concerned. The same was not true of banking and insurance, transport, and a large number of professions, sectors for which problems continue to exist. These problems spring, for banks, from the insufficient integration of capital markets; for insurance companies, from the need to protect policy holders; for transport, from the specific rules which the Treaty sets for that sector; and for the professions, from the different qualifications required for access to their practice in different countries (see Chapters 14 and 15). For some years the EC has worked at the abolition of these remaining obstacles (see Chapter 16). The Treaty makes a distinction between the situations during and after the so-called 'transition period', which was to end on January 1, 1970. Some verdicts of the Court have made it clear that at that date, article 7, forbidding discrimination of any kind, will apply in full and can be appealed to directly before the national judge.

Remarkably, the EC Treaty is practically silent about the *price of labour*. Article 48 only indicates that there shall be no discrimination in the remuneration of workers of different nationalities working in the same establishment and country. That does not say anything at all about the differences existing among states.

Regulations, directives and programmes

In the course of the transition period, several regulations (directly applicable in the member states) were issued by the Council to give substance to the general stipulations of article 48 of the Treaty with respect to the free migration of workers. Regulation 1612/68 settles the details of many matters that are essential to the workers' right to freedom of movement. For instance, article 7 of this regulation stipulates that *discrimination is forbidden* not only to the public authorities of member states, but also *to companies, institutions, etc.,* and *to private employers*. That means that all stipulations in collective or individual labour contracts as to conditions, remuneration, dismissal, etc. are null and void by force of law if they contain elements which are discriminating to workers from other member states. That rule has been confirmed several times over by verdicts of the Court.

The same regulation rules the co-operation of the national *Labour Exchange* (article 49a and d of the Treaty), thus substantiating the rule of Community priority, that is to say: member states must pass on to the labour exchanges of other member states any vacancies they cannot themselves fill. During a given period of time, nationals of member states looking for employment will then have priority over workers from third countries.

The Treaty stipulates that the Council shall establish, on the proposal of the Commission, programmes and guidelines to ensure the *right to establishment (art. 54) and the right to render services (art. 63).* Such programmes and guidelines have indeed been drawn up. In the meantime, however, the Court laid down in two verdicts that starting from January 1, 1970, anybody can claim, before the national judge, the direct application of art. 52 with respect to establishment (the Reynders case 2/74), or art. 59 with respect to services (the Van Binsbergen case 33/74), thus confirming that all national stipulations discriminating by nationality are null and void.

The general programmes refer mostly to the elimination of illegal discriminatory regulations subjecting immigrants from other member states to higher taxation, claims of caution money, certificates of solvency, good conduct, criteria for admission to appeal, for the obtaining of licences, etc. Freedom of professional activity thus also comprises the freedom to join professional or sectoral organisations with or without ruling authority. Finally, the programmes concern the elimination of obstacles to good functioning, for instance the recognition of foreign certificates. Much remains to be done on that score; we will take the matter up in the final section.

Like the Treaty, the regulations of the EC contain hardly anything about *remuneration discrepancies* among countries; that remains a matter for national negotiation (CEC 1967).

Third countries

In Chapter 2 we tried to transfer the notions of free-trade area and customs union from goods trade to the movements of production factors, in particular as regards the frontiers between the EC and third countries. While the Treaty clearly lays down a preferential regime for member states as far as goods trade is concerned, it is far less outspoken as to free movement of persons. Neither do the regulations and directives implementing the Treaty give unequivocal rules about the treatment of nationals of third countries (CEC 1979a). Moreover, the situation differs for workers and self-employed persons. From Kapteyn and Verloren van Themaat (1980), the various legal rules can be economically interpreted as follows:

- *Workers*: Regulation 1612/68 seems to imply rather than prescribe the priority of Community workers, so that member states might extend certain EC advantages to workers from third countries. In that case the advantages are restricted to the member state involved; the other member states are not obliged to apply them as well.
- *Establishment*: The right to establish is confined to natural persons who are nationals of a member state. Nationals of third countries are excluded; they are subject to the rules each individual member state cares to issue. The fact that they are established in one member state does not give them the right to establish in other member states. The right to establish in the entire EC does apply to persons who are nationals of a member state but are still residing outside the EC. The right to establish also applies to workers with an EC nationality who want to set up in business in another member state.
- *Services*: The right to free service trade in the entire EC can be claimed only by nationals of member states who are also established in a member state. The right does not apply to nationals of member states established outside the EC. That is logical since neither can they claim, from their foreign location, other free-

doms (goods, capital). Nationals of third countries located in a member state and licensed to render services there, are not entitled to do so in other member states, except if the Council rules to that effect on the proposal of the Commission. This is in line with the regulation for workers, but seems illogical in comparison with the free trade of goods.

Apparently, as far as the movements of persons are concerned, the EC resembles a free-trade area rather than a customs union. Obviously such a situation will be difficult to maintain as physical frontiers are abolished (see Chapter 16); for that reason, an EC admission policy for workers and services from third countries is therefore imperative.

Improving the conditions for the functioning of the European labour market

The rights to freedom of migration for workers, of establishment and service trade, have no meaning unless accompanied by some other rights. The most important are given in arts. 48 and 54 of the EEC Treaty; others have been added later on; they concern the right to continuous social security and pension claims; to admission, sojourn and housing, and to professional education. In view of their economic interest, they will be briefly commented upon here.

One of the most important conditions for the practical achievement of free movement of workers is to prevent the loss of claims to *social security*. To settle the matter, the Council issued in 1971 Regulation 1408/7, dealing with benefit payments to the sick, invalids, old-age pensioners, widows and orphans, in case of work accidents, professional diseases, unemployment, and in view of the family situation. The Regulation lays down principles purporting to prevent negative discrimination of migrating workers in respect of non-migrating colleagues, and the collection of double premiums as well as the payment of double benefits with respect to the same period of insurance. Benefits can be enjoyed in any country, irrespective of where they have been acquired; in other words, a worker who has long been employed in a foreign country, can have his social security benefits transferred to his country of origin when he returns there.

The right to *move to and stay freely in another member state* is defined in directives 68/360 and 73/148; it applies not only to the worker (employed or independent) moving to another country, but also to his or her spouse, children and family relations. The right to stay is not forfeit, in principle, after finishing the professional activity or employment. A closely related right is that to housing, which also exists for workers, self-employed, and their families. It concerns the right to either rent or purchase a dwelling. To independent workers, the right to purchase land and buildings for the purpose of setting up in business is relevant.

The right *to perform payments and capital transactions* is an obvious complement; without the possibility to let one's money pass frontiers for investments and payments and for repatriating profits and transferring wages, the principle of free moves of persons and services would be completely eroded.

For a well-performing labour market, finally, the right to *professional education* or retraining of workers, independents and family members is relevant. The right to *education* (general and professional, and the apprentice system) also applies to the children of foreign workers.

Progressive harmonisation of the criteria for admission to a profession and the related mutual *recognition of diplomas* is a second, equally daunting matter of importance. On the one hand education is generally looked upon as a typical national concern, and the Treaty does not provide for co-operation on that front. On the other hand, with new social claims constantly necessitating changes in educational programmes, harmonisation has to restart again and again.

The fundamental principles of the free movement of workers, laid down in the Treaty and interpreted by the Court, are still encountering *difficulties in actual practice*. Some of these difficulties can be explained from deeply rooted cultural differences, others are of a legal or administrative nature. Moreover, the organisation of the labour market on the level of the Community is still defective. The Commission tries to reduce the remaining obstacles as much as possible by further harmonisation of the rules. Recently this has got a new impetus by the programme for the internal market (1992) that foresees a completely free internal labour market (see Chapter 16).

International exchange of labour (migration)

Migration from and to the six original member states (1958–1973)

Before the creation of the EC, international migration of labour in Western Europe had been on a small scale. In the 1950s, Italy provided about half the supply of migrant labour, while Switzerland and France were the greatest demanders. Moreover, France received some immigrants from North Africa. By the end of the 1950s, the situation was changing. Germany started to recruit foreign labour, at first mainly from Italy.

From 1958 onward, the free movement of labour among the six original member states was gradually introduced. In the period between 1958 and 1973 the labour market was tight in all member states except Italy. That was one reason why the *number of foreign workers staying in the EC* (that is to say, workers originating from one member state of the EC and staying in another) remained, in general, limited. Only Italians migrated north in numbers. However, the recruitment of hundreds of thousands of Italians was not sufficient to provide the economies of the 'northern' member states with enough labour; so, these countries soon extended their recruiting efforts outside the EC. That immigration enabled the EC to keep activities within its borders which otherwise would have had to relocate outside the EC (entailing outward direct investment flows; see Chapter 6). Table 9.1 indicates that the inflow of workers was growing, but that the relative share of the other EC countries, in particular Italy, in the inflow was reduced.

Table 9.1 First work licences[a] granted to foreign workers[b] by the six original EC member states, 1959–1973

Period	Total	of which EC per cent	of which Italy per cent
1958–1961	273 000	60	49
1962-1965	595 000	36	32
1966-1969	565 000	30	26
1970-1973	751 000	26	21

[a] In 1968 abolished for workers from EC countries
[b] Algerians in France not counted
Source: KEG, DGXV Beschäftigung ausländischer Arbeitnehmer, (V264/76-D)

In the peak years 1969–1973, some 570 000 workers from third countries were admitted into the Community every year. The actual figure was considerably higher, because the figures in the table do not include the Algerian immigrants in France. The share of the Italians, who around 1960 still accounted for half the foreign labour in the EC, progressively dropped after that year to about 16 per cent in 1973. The growth of the Italian economy and the reduction of wage differences made that development possible.

Table 9.1, representing stocks, underestimates the *size of the migration flows*. Most work licences were valid for a short period. The holders of such licences, mostly unmarried, unskilled workers, used to arrive at the workplaces of Western Europe, stay for a period of two years, and then return to their home country. Around 1970, nearly one million migrants entered the EC, but about the same number returned home. Taking into account migration to other countries, such as Sweden and Switzerland, and to a lesser extent the United Kingdom, we observe in Western Europe, in that period, a yearly gross migration of between

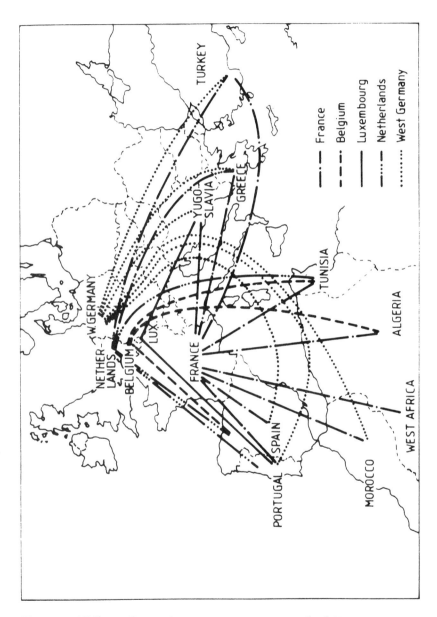

Figure 9.1 Bilateral recruitment agreements; end of 1973

Table 9.2   Estimate of the number of foreign labour in the EC member states, 1960–1980, and their relative importance (%) on the labour market of the host country

	Absolute figures (x 1,000)				Percentage of labour force			
	1960[a]	1970[a]	1973[b]	1980[b]	1960[a]	1970[a]	1973[b]	1980[b]
Germany	461	1727	2519	2072	2	6	11	9
France	1294	1584	1900	1643	6	8	11	9
Netherlands	47	134	121	194	1	3	3	4
Belgium	170	257	211	333	5	7	7	11
Luxemburg	20	27	43	51	16	21	35	37
Italy	20	30	55	57	-	-	-	-
EC6	2012	3759	4849	4350	3	5	7	6
United Kingdom	1233	1815	1751	1606	5	7	7	7
Denmark[c]	15	30	36	48	1	1	2	2
Ireland	1	2	2	2	-	-	-	-
EC9	3261	5606	6638	6006	3	6	8	7
EC12[d]	3300	5600	6600	6000	3	5	6	5

[a]   Labour force
[b]   Dependent workers
[c]   Given the free movement of labour existing between Denmark and Sweden, Norway and Finland, these figures have to be corrected upwards
[d]   Estimate; figures for Spain, Portugal and Greece very low

Sources: 1960 and 1970: *United Nations* (1979, page 324). For Italy, Denmark and Ireland: *national statistics and estimates*. 1973 and 1980: KEG, *Beschäftigung ausländischer Arbeitnehmer*, various years.

two and three million people. In the flows, cyclical patterns can be perceived (Kayser, 1972; Moulaert and Derykere, 1982).

Much of the migration described here was so-called *'organised' migration* through recruitment bureaux of the host countries established in the countries of origin. These bureaux often took upon themselves the organisation of transportation, medical checks and housing. That means that the size and direction of the flows was ultimately determined by policy. Figure 9.1 shows the principal bilateral recruitment agreements existing at the end of 1973, and hence gives an idea of the direction of migrant flows around 1973. It also shows that at the time Western Europe and the southern and eastern flanks of the Mediterranean indeed formed one large market for unskilled labour. In the period 1960–1973, *foreign labour was essential to the economy of European receiving countries*. A first approximation of its importance can be derived from the relative importance of foreign labour on the labour markets of EC member states. In the EC Six, the number of foreigners on the labour market rose between 1960 and 1973 from approximately two million to nearly four million (Table 9.2).[2]

The detailed national data show that between 1960 and 1973 the number of foreign workers rose in particular in Germany (by some two million); therefore that country accounts for most of the rise in the number of foreign workers in the entire EC in that period. If we relate the number of foreign workers to the size of the total labour force, we find that in five of the six member states of the EC (Italy being the exception), in 1970 an average 7 per cent of total labour supply came

Table 9.3 Total number of foreign workers in the 12 member states of the European Community, by country of origin, (millions), and percentage shares in total labour force 1973–1985

	Area	1973[a]	1980[a]	1980[b]	1985[b]
Intra-EC	EC 9	1.8	1.6	1.4	1.2
	EC +3	1.4	1.0	0.9	0.8
	Total EC12	3.2	2.6	2.1	1.9
Extra-EC	Mediterranean	2.0	1.9	1.5	1.4
	Other	1.4	1.5	1.0	0.9
	Total of third countries	3.4	3.4	2.5	2.3
Total		6.6	6.0	4.8	4.3
Per cent share in total labour force	Intra + Extra-EC12	6	5	4	4
	Extra-EC12	3	3	2	2

Sources: [a] KEG, *Beschäftigung ausländischer Arbeitnehmer*, 1975 and 1982
[b] Eurostat (1985); Eurostat (1987)

from third countries, against 3 – 4 per cent in 1960. For certain sectors the dependency was actually much greater; in particular the metal industry, construction and some service sectors (catering) attracted much foreign labour in this period (Bhagwati *et al.*,1984).

The situation at the time of the first enlargement of the EC (1973)

In 1972, the EC was enlarged with the United Kingdom, Ireland and Denmark, and from that year onward, the free mutual exchange of workers could be extended across the nine member states.

Let us see what the situation was at that moment with respect to the *interpenetration of labour markets of the EC member states.* From the few deficient statistics available, Table 9.3 indicates that for 1973 a total of some 1.8 million workers from the then nine EC member states were employed in other EC states. Thus, of a total labour force of about 84 million employed in that year, 2 per cent were working in a member state other than their own. So, the degree of integration of the labour markets in 1973 was still quite modest.

Three types of labour exchange among EC member states can be distinguished. The first refers to a hard core of workers stationed abroad by multinational companies and international organisations, or working as border commuters. A second type refers to emigrated Italians, already discussed in detail in the previous section (about 0.9 million). The third type refers to Irish emigrants (almost half a million of them), traditionally destined to the United Kingdom; that kind of emigration had already been regulated by bilateral agreement before 1973 (see also Böhning, 1972).[3]

The *presence of workers from third countries* in the nine member states of the EC is represented in the bottom part of the first column of Table 9.3. In total there were in 1973 some three million non-EC foreign workers in the EC9, the majority (over two million) originating from Mediterranean countries. Three groups of emigration countries can be identified.

Greece, Spain and Portugal are now members of the EC. A total of 1.4 million nationals of these countries were employed in the nine EC member states in 1973. The destinations of the emigrants show very clear patterns: practically all Portuguese were staying in France, most Spaniards in France but also some in Germany; by far most Greeks were employed in Germany, a very small portion in the United Kingdom. Emigration was highly important to these three countries. In 1973, 19 per cent of the labour force of Portugal, 9 per cent of the Greek and more than 4 per cent of the Spanish workers were employed in the EC9. Salt (1976) mentions that emigrants had transferred from the EC to their home countries sums that equalled 24 per cent of imports for Greece, 9 per cent for Spain, and as much as 37 per cent for Portugal.[4]

The *other Mediterranean countries* constitute the second group of emigration countries. Turkey and Yugoslavia were important emigration countries in 1973 (each accounting for 0.6 million emigrants). Workers from these countries were employed almost exclusively in Germany (Turks to a lesser degree in the Netherlands). Around 1970, between 5 and 8 per cent of the labour force of these countries were staying in the EC. Emigrants from North West Africa (Algeria, Morocco and Tunisia) were rather selective as to their destination, being oriented practically entirely to France and to some extent the Benelux.[5]

Finally, there is a group of immigrants from *other countries*. A small portion of them are citizens of third countries who work for multinational companies or international organisations (Americans, Japanese, and other nationalities). Foreign workers from Central and West African countries also constitute only a limited portion of this group. The main body is formed by the approximately one million foreigners staying in the United Kingdom. Most immigrants into the United Kingdom come from Commonwealth countries. For many of them the status of foreigners, in the legal sense, is far less clear than for other immigrants. For that reason, the figure of about one million Commonwealth immigrants resident in the United Kingdom should be looked upon as merely indicative.

Migration to the enlarged Community

The first enlargement of the Community in 1973 coincided more or less with a changed attitude to migration, and with the end of a long period of stable growth in Western Europe. *The changed economic and socio-cultural situation* in the host countries led to a steep drop in the number of foreign workers (see Table 9.3). The drop was steepest in the 1970s; the figures for the 1980s indicate a continuation of the trend, but at a lesser pace. External economic factors, among others, dictated a drop in GNP; many companies got into difficulties and the tension on the labour market rapidly diminished. These economic factors were reinforced by socio-cultural ones. The concentration of foreign labour in certain areas invoked feelings of *Ueberfremdung*, of being swamped by foreigners; voices were raised to call a halt to further immigration, and the active stimulation of return migration was advocated (Böhning 1979).

Host countries responded in widely different ways. Several member states drew up return-migration schemes, introducing measures of the following four types (Lebon and Falchi, 1980): (1) paying a return premium to the person involved; (2) granting subsidies for professional training in the home country; (3) development aid to projects in countries of origin, and (4) direct personal aid for setting up in business. Moreover, schemes were developed to stimulate the assimilation or improve the integration of workers settled more permanently (that is, whose families were resident in the host country) (Council of Europe, 1980, 1983; Castles and Kosack, 1985; Edye, 1987).

The developments and measures described above have affected migrants differently according to *their country of origin* (compare the second pair of columns of Table 9.3).[7] As regards EC *partners*, the developments seem to indicate an integration effect; that is to say, the phenomenon that migration diminishes as free trade grows.[8] For instance, on balance, 200,000 Italians working in other member states returned home in the 1970s once free trade among the original six had been realised; other countries, too – Belgium, the Netherlands and others – registered a drop in the number of citizens employed in another EC country. Possibly, too, in times of economic depression both workers and employers tend to prefer their own labour market. The increasing number of British employed abroad in the 1970s may be the initial effect of the United Kingdom's progressive integration in the EC, clearly helped along by economic (push-factor) motives; moreover, given the widespread knowledge of the English language, for British people the social distances may well be shorter than for workers from other member states.

Looking at the *three new member states*, we are struck first by the steep drop in the number of workers from Greece, Spain and Portugal employed in the rest of the present EC, totalling almost half a million (about 200 000 Spaniards, 100 000 Portuguese, and 150 000 Greeks).

The number of workers from other *Mediterranean* countries also decreased. In 1980, there were also almost 200,000 fewer Yugoslavians working in the EC than in 1973. On the other hand, the numbers of North Africans and Turks had still risen just a little on balance.

As regards *third countries*, the doubtful measurement of the remaining group (United Kingdom) does not permit a clear-cut conclusion.

The first explanation of these developments is found in the restrictions in the admission policy of the immigration countries (Hammar, 1985). An additional factor may have been the increasing equality of wages (at given productivities) which increased free trade had brought about. Indeed, importation into the EC has been liberalised to a high degree for many products from labour-sending countries.

The determinants of the spatial pattern of migration

Several studies have been undertaken to explain the patterns of international migration described in the previous section. Some are mostly theoretical (see for example, Mueller, 1980); others concentrate on the motives of individual migrants and employers (for instance, OECD 1978), yet others focus on phenomena well known from interregional migration analysis (for instance Klaassen and Drewe, 1973). Molle and

Van Mourik (1988, 1989b) have combined elements from these studies with factors suggested by integration theory, international sociology and modern political economics in a static explanatory model.

The results of the model confirm that international migration to Western Europe is influenced not only by the more traditional factors of wage differences and distance between the sending (LEC) and receiving (LIC) countries (Heijke and Klaassen, 1979), but also by cultural differences between LECs and LICs and immigration restricting measures in receiving countries. Less straightforward is the outcome with respect to the hypotheses concerning degrees of integration. No significant influence emerges of the integration of capital markets, but that may be due to the poor specification of the variable. The relation between trade and migration, on the other hand, was indeed significant and positive. That means that more trade increases the (need for) migration, which is contrary to the generally held view in which the relation is negative (see Chapter 6). The cause for this last partial result may lie in the simplicity of the static model used.

Wage structures, convergence or divergence?

The legal basis: treaties and regulations

Before the Treaty of Rome was drafted, there had been a discussion about the need to harmonise wages and the other elements of manpower costs firms have to pay (such as social-security contributions, holidays, fringe benefits) prior to the liberalisation of labour movements in the EC. Most of those participating in the debate did not recognise such a need, however; consequently the *treaties of the EC are practically silent as to wage formation*. The basic idea of the founding fathers was that wages were to be determined in the process of national bargaining between trade unions and employers, both sides taking account of the international competitive position of the business in question. Nobody thought there was any need for Community bodies to regulate wages on the European level.

There are *a few exceptions* where the EC regulates related matters in order to:

- prevent migrant workers from losing their social security rights (art. 51 EEC);
- enhance the co-operation among member states in such social matters as social security, work conditions, health and safety conditions, etc. (art. 117–118 EEC);
- develop the dialogue between management and labour on the European level which could lead to relations based on agree-

ment (art. 118b EEC). In many European countries the drive of labour unions towards nation-wide bargaining has made regional differences in wages disappear and thus widened the regional differences in unemployment. The same tendency has not manifested itself on the European scale, however. As Seidel (1983) shows, the attitudes of trade unions as well as employers' organisations vary widely among the EC countries, as do the legal frameworks in which they operate and their respective bargaining strengths. Because neither partner has accepted European constraints on their national behaviour, there has been no development of European agreements, despite the trade unions' persistent pleas for them. Evidently, neither have the EC authorities been involved in wage formation;

- make sure that men and women receive equal pay for equal work (art. 119 EEC).

The aspects of social security and work conditions will be left aside for the moment; they will be reviewed in Chapter 18. The remainder of this chapter will deal with the main issue, namely, the way wages in the EC have evolved. The principle of equal pay is important enough to devote a separate section to it.

International differences in wages

Among the countries of the EC there are wide differences in average wages. On the whole they are highly similar to the international differences in Gross Domestic Product (see Table 17.7), with mostly high figures for the countries in Northern Europe, and low ones for the Mediterranean states. Here we are interested not so much in the absolute differences as in their development in the course of the integration process. Economic theory offers elements for theses of decreasing as well as increasing differences in wages among countries.

The *convergence school* is based on the classical, neo-classical and Heckscher–Ohlin–Samuelson models of international trade and factor movements (see Chipman, 1965–1966). The conclusion of that line of thinking is that on severely restricting conditions, the international integration of goods markets, reflected by increasing trade, leads to the equalisation of factor income (see Chapter 6). With respect to labour, that means the equalisation of wages. Some early analyses of the effects of European integration (Meyer and Willgerodt, 1956; Fischer, 1966; Butler, 1967) showed indeed a certain convergence of wage levels.

The *divergence school* maintains that the conditions for equalisation mostly do not obtain. Even in a customs union, trade is impeded by collusive practices, transportation costs, multinational firms monopolising new technology, etc. A system characterised by large initial disparities and rigidities tends towards an increasingly unbalanced situation (Myrdal, 1956, 1957). The technology advance of certain countries implies that they will always select the new products with high value added as soon as they come on the market, pushing away products as soon as their value added drops and no longer sustains high wages. Thus the wage gap that accompanies the technology gap is not only perpetuated but even accentuated. An early representative of these thoughts was Giersch (1949), who was afraid that the liberalisation of goods and factor markets in Europe would have an agglomeration effect. More recently the vision of a Europe falling apart into a rich and dominant core and an impoverished periphery was voiced by Seers and others (1979–1980).

Rigorous testing of the alternative views used to be very difficult because of the deficient data situation. Recently new data have come available, allowing authors to shed some light on the matter. Tovias (1982) showed that wage levels in the founder countries of the EC converged in the period from 1958 to 1971, but failed to prove that this was due to economic integration. To remedy that drawback, Gremmen (1985) related the disparity of wages to the intensity of trade between two EC countries (integration) for the period from 1959 to 1979, finding support for the theorem of factor-price equalisation. Because that type of analysis wanted improvement on several points (van Mourik, 1987), a fresh look at the matter imposed itself. Estimating a more developed model, van Mourik (1989) was able to show that the convergence of the aggregate wage levels in the five largest founder countries of the EC in the 1959–1979 period was primarily due to Italy's catching up with its partners in terms of productivity, but failed to establish a direct link between integration and growth variables.

Industrial and occupational structure

There are *several reasons for the limited convergence of wage levels.* One is the imperfect factor mobility among countries; an idea of the relatively limited migration among the member countries of the EC has indeed been given in the previous section. That lack of mobility is not only an international phenomenon; it does obtain also among sectors of activity and among occupational groups. Impediments to movements are many and manifold; they encompass personal choice, capacities, and discrimination. Personal choice is reflected in the different amenities going with certain jobs, which may offset pay differences, and in the unwillingness of certain persons to pay for the retraining required to move to a better occupation, or to change their place of residence. The capacity factor shows up in the personal qualities (intelligence, skill, etc.) needed for certain jobs and limiting the number of possible entrants. Movements may also be impeded by opaque markets and by the high cost of gathering information. Finally, differences in pay may spring from restrictive practices based for instance on trade-union power or on government regulations issued under pressure of certain groups. Open discrimination is shown by employers refusing to employ, for example, people of a certain race, sex or religion.

The *industrial structure* of wages is very similar in the different countries of the EC, despite large differences among them in trade-union practice, availability of manpower, relative importance of the sector in the total economy, etc. (Butler, 1967; Bouteiller, 1971; Saunders and Marsden, 1981). The causes of that similarity have been analysed by Vassille (1989), who found that branches have the same characteristics as to skill, sex, capital/labour ratio, firm size etc. in different countries. Moreover, the structure is remarkably stable through time (Lebergott, 1947; Reder, 1962; OECD 1965, 1985c). Although the ranking of industries tends to remain the same, there seems to be a slight tendency of convergence towards the mean. The industrial wage structure is indeed stable because the determinant factors are stable through time.

The *occupational structure* of wages shows the same features of similarity and stability as the industrial structure, despite differences in demand for and supply of different grades of labour, different values and cultures, and different intervention by the government (UN/ECE 1967; Phelps-Brown, 1977). The reason is that in all countries occupations requiring more education, experience and skill, or carrying more responsibility, are higher paid than others. The stability is due not only to the persistence of those structural characteristics, but also to the heavy weight of tradition, which determines the notions of the hierarchy of wages and the principles of fair pay, and causes relics from the past to be long preserved.[9]

Equal pay for equal work; sex structure

One of the main *policy objectives*, already expressed in the provisions of the Treaty of Rome (article 119), is that member states shall ensure that men and women shall receive equal pay for equal work, a goal to be achieved by the end of the first stage. However, when the deadline came, almost nothing had been done to end discrimination, and it was again the Court of Justice which in the famous Defrenne case of 1976 declared article 119 directly applicable. That member states had such difficulty reaching a consensus on the specific actions needed suggests that in many member states strong forces were at work to maintain practices far removed from equal pay for equal work. UN/ECE (1980, Chapter 4) gives a good survey of the quantitative differences among European countries, showing a wide variety among countries and industries. In 1972, the differences were markedly higher for non-manual than for manual workers. In the United Kingdom and The Netherlands, the countries with the largest pay differentials, the difference diminished considerably in the 1972–1977 period, probably under the influence of the Equal Pay Acts of 1970 and 1971. In their analysis, Saunders and Marsden (1981) confirm this, as well as the influence of such factors as hours worked, age structure, and sector.

Table 9.4 Female-male earnings differential (ratio) 1972, EC6

Country	Actual ratio	Expected ratio	Unexplained differential
Germany	0.72	0.85	0.13
France	0.75	0.92	0.17
Italy	0.81	0.96	0.15
Netherlands	0.71	0.71	0.00
Belgium	0.74	0.95	0.21
Luxemburg	0.59	0.73	0.14

Source: Kottis (1985)

In an interesting article, Kottis (1985) provides some more detailed information about *wage differences between men and women by industry.* Using figures on average hourly earnings of male and female manual workers in seventy industries in the EC founder countries, she clearly shows how wide the gap was between the principle of equal pay for equal work and the 1972 practice (see Table 9.4). She found that on average, the hourly earnings of women were about one-quarter lower than those of men. Now such differences are not necessarily due to discrimination; they may also spring from men and women doing different work. To identify the influence of work characteristics, Kottis regressed the average earnings of men and women in each industry to a set of characteristics of each group, and found that the differential could largely be explained from factors like less skill, lack of seniority, unfavourable age, and more part-time work. She then used the model to estimate the portion of the pay differential that must be attributed to other factors, including discrimination against women. Column 1 shows the unadjusted earnings ratio between women and men. Column 2 gives the ratio that can be expected from accounting for the factors skill, etc. Column 3 gives the unexplained earnings differential, calculated by subtracting the actual from the expected female–male earnings. From these results, Kottis concludes that the entire differential in The Netherlands, more than half of it in Germany and Luxemburg, about one-third of it in France, and one-fifth in Italy and Belgium, can be attributed to women's unfavourable work characteristics. On the assumption that the unexplained part is largely attributable to discrimination, EC action on the basis of article 119 was needed most urgently in Belgium and somewhat less in Luxemburg, France, Italy and Germany. Moreover, the results show that in all member countries supplementary action was needed to make women overcome the handicaps which affect their work characteristics unfavourably.

There is some partial evidence of the *development of the men-women wage differential through a longer time period.* Schippers and Siegers (1986) found, for example, that the wage rate of women in relation to that of men increased substantially in the 1950–1983 period. Looking for the causes, they estimated a model of macro-economic inspiration. Although they found a limited influence of certain macro-economic variables, their outcomes clearly show that the drop in discrimination was largely due to autonomous factors.[10]

Welfare effects

In Chapters 2 and 6 we have briefly touched upon the cost and benefits of migration, split up for labour-exporting countries (LECs) and labour-importing countries (LICs). In this section we present some results of studies that have tried to come to grips with the net benefit of European integration.

A *labour-importing country* derives benefits from two static effects. The direct production effect relates to the increase in GNP as a result of the employment of immigrant workers. Case studies for France indicate that immigrant workers, forming about 7 per cent of the French wage-earning labour force, contributed about 5 per cent of French GNP in 1971 (Macmillan, 1982). Askari (1974) calculated the contribution of migration to the economic growth of EC countries and came up with figures between 0.02 and 0.08 per cent, or, on average, approximately 1 per cent of total growth. The welfare effects concern mostly the distribution of income between categories. As the more abundant labour supply lowers the wage rate of the indigenous labour force, the extra output is shared by domestic capital and foreign migrants. Returns to capital therefore rise. For France, the magnitude of that effect was calculated between 1.2 and 2.2 per cent of GNP in 1971 (Macmillan, 1982). The dynamic effects of labour migration to LICs are less known (Böhning and Maillat, 1974), but some think that immigration, by taking away certain bottlenecks in the economy, has led to a permanently higher growth rate of GNP (UN/ECE, 1977). Some negative aspects have also been pointed out. One of these is the presumably high cost of social services for immigrants (schools, etc.). However, there is no evidence that immigrants' demands on social (security) services exceed their contributions in times of full employment. On the contrary, both Blitz (1977) and Bourguignon *et al.* (1977) concluded that LICs had saved considerable sums in public services (schools, hospitals, etc.). Negative aspects of migration are that it has prevented the economies of the LICs from adjusting structurally to the new world conditions in comparative advantages. On balance, however, labour-importing countries seem to have benefited from immigration.

For a *labour-exporting country* (LEC), too, the emigration of part of its labour force has significant advantages. First, unemployment decreases. But the loss of manpower it implies has not been as beneficial to LECs as might be expected, as a substantial part of the emigrants have received more education than the average workers in the LECs. Second, emigrants are supposed to have increased skill on return. However, the enhanced quality of human capital has had little positive effects on the economies of LECs. On the one hand, the inability of LECs to offer sufficient employment opportunities to returning skilled workers has led to a net loss of skilled labour. On the other hand, returning migrants are generally disinclined to accept low-status jobs, and frequently set up 'unprofitable' service trades (Papadimetriou, 1978). Migrants' remittances count as a possible third positive effect of labour export. They amount to a considerable proportion of the LECs' GNP and in the short run constitute a very convenient means of financing deficits on the balance of trade. The long-run effects of remittances on the LECs' economies are limited, however, because on the whole they have been used for investment in houses and consumption purposes rather than for productive capital formation. The increased consumption they have made possible has caused substantial price and wage increases and contributed to the misallocation of resources in LECs. And sometimes they have led to an overvalued currency. Interesting in that respect are proposals to introduce an emigration tax (Bhagwati, 1987b), and to transfer financial means to LECs through an 'International Labour Compensatory Facility' (ILO; see also Kennedy Brenner, 1979).

Summary and conclusions

- The interpenetration degree of labour markets (number of foreigners divided by the total number of employed) is less than 2 per cent. If that seems little, we must keep in mind that *the right to free movement has never been intended to create massive migrations of workers.*

- Politically, the EC holds as a *fundamental principle* that nobody must be forced to submit to the socio-cultural and legal adjustments involved in international migration within Europe, and that ideally everyone should find sufficient work in his own country. International capital flows should permit the growth of the national economy needed to that end. Thus, unlike on goods markets, the further integration is not meant to entail large migration flows.
- The fairly wide *wage discrepancies* prevailing among EC member states in 1960 have decreased somewhat in the last decades, which is in line with expectations fostered by the theory of integration.
- *Occupational and industrial wage structures* are very similar in the various countries of the EC, and change only very gradually.

Notes

1   See for the migration of other than active persons the last chapter of this book, which deals, among other things, also with 'Europe of the citizens'. The definition of movement of labour refers to persons residing outside their home country; frontier-zone workers are generally excluded. Although they also reflect the integration of labour markets, their motives are different from those of actual migrants. The co-ordination of policies of national states towards such frontier workers presents particular problems, which for lack of space we cannot discuss here. Those interested in the phenomenon may be referred to the works of Aubrey (1984) and Ricq (1983).

2   In interpreting these data, keep in mind that they should be corrected upwards because of the considerable clandestine migration going on. Some estimate illegal migration at certainly no less than 10 per cent, while others put it nearer to 20 per cent.

3   An interesting aspect of international migration of labour is that it often proceeds stepwise. Many of the present EC12 member states, from which workers migrated in great numbers to prosperous EC countries, themselves know the phenomenon of foreign labour in the form of Pakistanis and North Africans working there in unskilled jobs.

4   These national figures obscure even higher figures for certain regions: in some regions of Portugal, up to half the male labour force appeared to have emigrated to North Europe in 1973. In interpreting these data one should moreover keep in mind that all three countries are traditional emigration countries for destinations other than the EC: Iberians particularly to South America, Greeks to Australia and the United States (UN 1980; Bernard, 1978).

5   The volume of the North African presence in the EC around 1973 is probably incorrectly reproduced in the table, owing to the fact that at one time Algerians were admitted to France without working or residence licence. Some observers estimate the number of employed North Africans resident in France at more than one million.

6   Short descriptions of the situation in the member states as regards immigration and the policy towards aliens are contained in the 'Report on social development' published regularly by the Commission of the European Communities; for a short

summary of the objectives pursued by the Commission with respect to migrants, see CEC (1985a).

7   Despite the efforts of international organisations (for instance OECD, 1986b), the available data do not yet permit a description, in clear series of figures, the development from 1981, when Greece joined the EC, up to 1986, the moment of Spain's and Portugal's joining. Table 9.3 groups the best data available up till now.

8   Very few authors have tried to test these hypotheses quantitatively, although the subject has been debated for a long time (see, for instance, Meyer and Willgerodt, 1956; Mihailovic, 1976).

9   Phelps-Brown (1977) reports the astonishing persistence of the ratio between the pay of a building craftsman and a labourer in the South of England, which remained at about 1.5 throughout the centuries from 1400 to 1900.

10 In view of the persistent male–female discrepancies, some authors, like Warner (1984), have cast doubts on the EC's ability to implement its policies effectively.

10 Capital

Introduction

The attempts made by the Commission of the EC to liberalise capital movement in Europe are in line with more general efforts in the same direction made by other *international* bodies. On the world level, the International Monetary Fund (IMF) is the framework for such efforts; on that of the industrialised world as a whole it is the Organisation for Economic Co-operation and Development (OECD). The IMF's primary aim is the greatest possible freedom to settle all current payments associated with the free movement of goods and services. Indeed, the Bretton-Woods Treaty (by which the IMF was founded) only provides for a very limited liberalisation of capital movement. To the OECD, free capital movement is somewhat more of an objective as such. After a thorough study of the specific aspects of national markets (OECD 1968), the so-called 'Code of Liberalisation of Capital Movements' (OECD, 1982b) was agreed upon. This code divides capital transactions into a number of categories for which different degrees of freedom are envisaged. The European Community also aims at the liberalisation of capital movement, initially only within the limits set by the Treaty of Rome.

The chapter is *set up* as follows. A brief sketch of the situation created by the EC and the general environment in which capital liberalisation in Europe proceeds will be given in the next section. The remainder of this chapter will be on transactions by private enterprise, which are essentially autonomous. Transactions of the public sector are often of a compensating nature; they will be dealt with in Chapter 17, as they come under the heading of monetary policy rather than free movement of capital.

In (long-term) international capital movement, we make a distinction between direct investment and portfolio investment. The main objective of direct investment is to acquire control of, say, a company, which can be done either through equity transactions or through direct capital participation. The objective of portfolio investors (bond and shares), is to make the highest possible profit and spread risk. We will devote separate sections to direct investment and to portfolio investment, the latter with the help of indicators of stock-market integration. Next we shall go into the present patterns of other international capital movements from and to the EC, discussing two important indicators of the degree of integration, namely, the volume of international transactions, and the equalisation of interest, that is, of the price of capital.

A short summary will complete the chapter.

Community regime

Treaty

The liberty of capital movement is laid down in articles 67 to 72 (Chapter IV, Capital) of the Rome Treaty. The most important stipulation is that member states

> shall abolish between themselves all restrictions on the movement of capital belonging to persons resident in Member States and any discrimination based on the nationality or on the place of residence of the parties or of the place where such capital[1] is invested.

However, while the Treaty decrees the most comprehensive freedom of movement for goods and labour, with respect to capital there are restrictions.

Article 67 of the Treaty makes the significant restriction *that discrimination needs to be abolished only 'to the extent necessary to ensure the proper functioning of the Common Market'*. That restriction, consciously introduced by the member states, indicates that member states did not aspire to fully free movement of capital as an object in itself. The reason is that member states dared not give up the right to influence the capital flow,[2] because it is one of the few instruments available to them for the effective control of internal macro-economic and monetary developments. Moreover, full freedom of capital movement is hard to reconcile with the selectivity implicit in the measures of fiscal policy, investment stimulations etc. of many member states. As a consequence, the provisions for freedom of capital are not directly applicable, contrary to those for goods and labour. Indeed, the Treaty does *not* enjoin upon the Community the creation of a veritable European capital market.

The Treaty permits the following *restrictions* of capital movement:

- 'domestic rules governing the capital market and the credit system' (art. 68.2). Entirely in line with the important article 7 we encountered earlier, member states may apply such rules only in a non-discriminating way, in other words, member states must treat residents of other EC nationalities on the same footing as their own residents.

- 'Loans for the direct or indirect financing of a member state or of its regional or local authorities shall not be issued or placed in other member states unless the states concerned have reached agreement thereon' (art. 68.3).
- The safeguard clause permits member states to undo the liberalisation introduced since the creation of the EC 'if movements of capital lead to disturbances in the functioning of the capital market' (art. 73). This has to be authorised by the Commission after consultation of the Monetary Committee.
- Balance of payments problems may justify capital-movement restrictions (art. 108/109).

To the movement of goods applies the basic principle of the greatest possible freedom with respect to traffic with *third countries*. The same principle is not laid down in the Treaty with respect to the external capital policy, it only urges member states to co-ordinate their capital movements with third countries in the framework of the EC. So the integration of the capital market is less far reaching than the goods and labour markets not only internally but also externally (see Chapter 19).

The last point (article 71) to be made is that member states have committed themselves to the

> readiness to *go beyond the degree of liberalisation* of capital movements prescribed by the Treaty, in so far as their economic situation, in particular the situation of their balance of payments, so permits.

Indeed, efforts towards the progressive liberalisation of capital movements have been made ever since the EC was founded, but up to 1987 they had not resulted in agreements reaching beyond the stipulations of the Treaty.

Directives of 1960–1962

With respect to capital movements as well, the Treaty is a framework agreement, setting out some general principles to be complemented later by further rules. Such rules were drawn up at an early date (1960–1962) in the shape of *two directives* by virtue of article 67. They distinguish three groups of transactions by the degree of liberalisation:

- *Fully free.* This category encompasses such transactions as direct investment (making capital available for an establishment abroad), the purchase of real estate, short- and medium-term trade credits, personal transactions like repatriation of earnings and former investments, and the acquisition by non-residents of quoted stocks in another member state. The liberalisation of this group rests on the direct connection with the free movement of goods (short- and medium-term trade credits), of employees and self-employed (personal transactions), and the right to free establishment (direct investments and investments through participation in capital stock).

- *Partly free*. This group comprises the issue and placing of shares listed on the stock market of another member state than the one where the placing body resides; the acquisition of non-quoted shares by those not resident in the same country; shares in investment funds; and finally long-term trade credits. For this group, capital movement is only partly liberalised.
- *No obligation* to liberalise exists with respect to such short-term transactions as the purchase of treasury bonds and other capital stocks and the opening of bank accounts by non-residents. The reason why the principle of free movement is not applied to these transactions is that they may be of a speculative nature and therefore a cause of disturbance. Full and irrevocable liberalisation of these transactions could not be achieved while certain conditions were not fulfilled.

In the mid-1960s, a team of experts reported on the prospects of further liberalisation and integration of markets (Segré *et al.*, 1966). Between 1966 and 1986 many concrete proposals were made, but in practice nothing was achieved. The causes are involved but in the main associated with the possibility provided for in the Treaty of restricting capital movement for reasons of monetary policy.

Progress in deregulation and liberalisation

Although EC regulations on the integration of financial markets ceased to progress in the 1960s (Philip, 1978), actual integration has not stopped since. On the contrary, many member states (Germany, The Netherlands, Belgium, UK) have proceeded with the liberalisation, not only for transactions with partners in the EC, but also for transactions with third countries. Others like France and Italy, went on controlling many capital movements (by virtue of article 73 EEC) in spite of partial liberalisation. The same was true of Ireland, which, however, considers itself in a transition situation (since joining the EC), as are, of course, Greece, Spain and Portugal.

Many and manifold have been the proposals made to improve the European capital market.[3] In the 1980s, the attitude towards international capital transactions has gradually but considerably shifted

(Lamfalussy, 1981) in favour of deregulation and liberalisation. What factors have brought that change about?

First, the *external position* of many European countries has improved, which diminished the *need* for regulation. Indeed, the converging inflation rates and economic policy under the EMS have greatly diminished the risk of balance-of-payment troubles (see Chapter 17). Besides, confidence in the international financial system has been restored.

Next, the *efficiency of the external regulation* turned out to be much poorer than hoped for. Governments had realised that restrictions on capital movement often just delay structural adaptations of the economy that will be necessary anyway in the end and may become more costly if put off. Controls that seem effective in the short run, generally had to be intensified and extended to related fields to counteract the evasive behaviour of economic actors. Moreover, in many countries the costs related to such restrictive regulations had become more manifest. These costs include the salaries not only of those involved in controls, but also of those employed by firms that are working on tasks serving nothing else but those controls (OECD 1980, 1982a).

A third reason for preferring international deregulation was the general tendency to *deregulate national financial markets*. The progressive abolition of restrictions on credit expansion by quotas, or the compulsion for financial institutions to invest in public bonds, was stimulated by the experience in many countries with the negative effects of distortions created by such intervention of the public sector in the market. Many governments have come to rely much more on interest as a mechanism of adaptation. Another important element in that respect is the increased internationalisation of the financial sector and the trade in financial services (see Chapter 14). This has led to the introduction of new financial techniques. Countries aspiring to a role as international financial centres have discovered deregulation as an apt instrument.

A fourth factor is *technological innovation*. The telematics revolution has also greatly affected the financial sector by reducing information and transaction costs. Information on financial markets anywhere in the world is now almost instantly available anywhere else. Standardised electronic transactions are moreover cheaper than those involving lots of paper work.

Last but not least, the development of the largely *unregulated Euromarkets* has had much influence. We make a distinction between the short-term Eurocurrency market and the medium- and long-term Eurobond market. On both markets, a number of very large banks, so-called 'Eurobanks', play a dominant part in new issues. They also handle trade in existing bonds, as the (stock) market for such secondary transactions is rather poorly developed.

Recent EC measures for liberalisation

Inspired by the world-wide trend to liberalise capital markets and by the will to complete the internal market (Chapter 16) and after having discussed the European Commission's new proposals (CEC, 1986c) the EC decided to realise a *free European capital market by 1992* (June 1988 directive). Capital movements in the EC have been fully liberalised by 1990; capital markets of Spain, Ireland, Greece and Portugal have to be opened at the latest by 1992 (if necessary by 1995 for Greece and Portugal). To circumvent new barriers to movement, article 2 obliges member states to notify the Committee of Governors of Central Banks, the Monetary Committee and the Commission of 'measures to regulate bank liquidity which have a specific impact on capital operations carried out by credit institutions with non residents'. These measures 'shall be confined to what is necessary for the purpose of domestic monetary regulation'.

Short-term capital movements may cause *disruptions of the exchange-rate policy* (distinct from the balance-of-payments equilibrium referred to in the safeguard clauses 108 and 109 of the EEC Treaty). If movements of exceptional magnitude occur, Article 3 permits the EC Commission, after consulting the Monetary Committee and the Committee of Governors of Central Banks, to authorise a member state to take protective measures in respect of capital movements. Examples of such movements are operations in securities and other instruments normally dealt with on the monetary market, operations in current and deposit accounts with financial institutions, and short-term financial loans and credits. As monetary co-operation between the EC countries develops further, the escape clauses of article 3 and articles 108–109 EEC may be no longer needed and free capital movement may become unconditional.

To prevent *tax evasion and loss of consumer protection*, member countries may take all requisite measures to prevent infringement of their laws and regulations etc. in the field of taxation and prudential supervision of financial institutions, or to lay down procedures for the declaration of capital movements for purposes of administrative or statistical information.

Improving the conditions for a proper functioning of European financial markets; harmonisation

To be effective, capital-market integration cannot be limited to removing the barriers to investment in foreign stock; it also needs transparent markets and conditions enabling investors and creditors to be informed about the quality of foreign financial products. The 1992 plan

for the completion of the internal capital market contains action programmes to improve these conditions.

The first condition is the harmonisation of *company law*. Indeed,
direct investors (for a take-over), investors in stock (for portfolio
purposes) and subscribers to foreign company loans want to be able to
judge the solvency and profitability of the company in question. In
accordance with article 54 of the EEC Treaty, the Council of Ministers
has adopted a series of directives on company law and are working on
some more. They concern the obligation to publish annual accounts
according to certain specifications, minimum capital requirements, the
qualifications of company auditors, national and international mergers, and the creation of a European company. These directives guarantee that certain minimum rules are respected by all companies. The
EEC rules are stricter for companies listed on the stock exchange than
for others. The directives establishing them concern the minimum requirements for listing, the information to be given with the application
for listing (prospectus) and after admission (half-yearly reports). The
EC is working on directives on the issue of prospectuses, insider
trading, and public take-over bids.

A second important group of rules is concerned with *financial
intermediaries*. A saver who puts his deposit with a foreign bank wants
to be reasonably sure that the bank is trustworthy, and the same is true
of an investor in so-called open-end funds. The most important directive of 1977 ('European Banking Law') lays down uniform criteria for
admission to the banking trade and for the prudential control of banks
in all EC countries. Other directives determine the information banks
have to give in their annual reports, the definition of the term 'own
funds', and the application of common solvency and liquidity ratios,
and even the specification of certain financial products (mortgages, for
instance). Harmonisation has not always been easy owing to differences in the legal status of certain intermediaries, different traditions of
prudential control, and deep-rooted differences in culture (such as the
opposition between the British view of finance as an independent
industry, and that of some continental countries of finance as an
activity that should be put at the service of the real economy).

Direct investments

Position of the EC in the OECD

An international direct investment (DI) is made when a company in
one country transfers capital to another country to create or take over
an establishment there which it wants to control.[4] DIs of some significance are a relatively recent phenomenon: before the war, a 'portfolio

investment' was mostly preferred. Since the Second World War the phenomenon has rapidly gained importance. To give an example: the total stock of foreign investments in OECD countries grew in the 1960s by some 13 per cent a year, a percentage equal to that of the growth of international trade. Between 1967 and 1977 DI grew faster and clearly outpaced trade growth. This section will give attention only to the situation in the industrialised world, although there are also important relations with other groups of countries. Traditionally, industrial countries invest much in Third World countries (especially in primary products and energy). Besides, OPEC countries have recently made sizeable investments abroad (especially in OECD countries).

Table 10.1 Direct foreign investment flows of EC12 by major partner 1969–1986 (billion current Ecu)

	1969/73		1974/78		1979/83		1984/86	
Origin or destination	I	E	I	E	I	E	I	E
EC12	8	8	13	13	20	20	16	16
World	14	13	20	28	29	58	25	66
USA	7	2	9	9	13	31	12	39
Japan	–	–	–	–	1	1	2	1
As a percentage of GFCF*								
EDIE	0.9		0.8		0.8		0.9	
(FDIE+EDIF): 2	1.4		1.5		1.7		2.4	

Source: Eurostat: several issues of *Balance of Payment* (some estimates)
I = inflow into the EC
E = outflow from the EC
* five-year averages.
GFCF = Gross Fixed Capital Formation; EDIE = European Direct Investment in Europe;
FDIE = Foreign Direct Investment in Europe; EDIF = European Direct Investment
    Abroad.

Table 10.1 presents the structure of the development of DI in the EC for the period 1969–1986. Contrary to what one would expect from their relative levels of integration, the DI interactions between the EC and third countries are larger than those among the EC countries themselves. Moreover, that tendency seems to become stronger with time: despite the increased trade and policy integration within the EC (Chapters 8 and 16–19, respectively), DI flows with third countries have grown much faster than those among EC countries. While in 1970 the latter still accounted for around three–fifths of total flows, by 1985 the share had gone down to 35 per cent. A satisfactory explanation of that phenomenon is still wanting.

The relative share of foreign direct investment in total investment (Gross Fixed Capital Formation: GFCF) is very small. DI flows within the EC (EDIE) accounted for no more than 1 per cent in 1969, and that figure remained stable throughout the period of analysis in spite of increased integration. External DI flows (FDIE and EDIF), while not much larger, did show a clear growth, which seemed to accelerate in more recent years.

The role of the EC in international DI has changed with time: a net recipient in the 1950s and 1960s, the EC had proceeded to a balanced situation around 1970, and since then has increasingly accentuated its role as a net direct investor abroad.[5] The main explanation is the increased availability of funds and the growing capacity of EC firms to organise international production. The USA is the main source and destination. EDI in Japan is still very limited. The largest direct investor abroad is the UK, followed by West Germany and The Netherlands, the very countries that relaxed or abolished capital-market controls with respect to third countries at an early date.

Traditionally, the USA is the largest investor in the EC. *Direct investment flows from the USA to the EC* in the 1960s and 1970s have sprung mostly from American companies, who capitalised on their ownership advantage in technology and management, by conquering a portion of the growing European market. Because that market was liberalised internally and protected externally, *in situ* production (that implies direct investment) was preferred to exporting from existing production facilities in the United States. In the terms of Chapter 6 this DI was of the 'tariff jumping' type. The exportation of capital was all the easier because the USA had a strong currency and no balance-of-payments problems. American foreign direct investment was increasingly concentrated on Europe; in 1970, Europe accounted for only about one-third of total American DI abroad; by 1978 its share had expanded to four-fifths. Many authors have tried to assess the effect of the creation of the EC on US direct investment in Europe (USDIE). This effect is visible in the development of US direct investment in the United Kingdom (before it joined the EC) and in the countries on the continent that were EC members. In the 1950–1958 period, the growth rate of US DI was almost equal in both areas. Between 1958 and 1973 the EC growth rate was half as high again as the UK's; after 1973 the two rates became equal again (Whichart, 1981). The first econometric analyses made by Scaperlanda (1967), d'Arge (1969) and Scaperlanda and Mauer (1969) showed considerable scepticism about a possible effect of the CET on the pattern of USDIE; they stressed the importance of access to the EC market. However, later analyses (for instance Schmitz, 1970 and Lunn, 1980), showed that both the external tariff and the size were both important, from which Schmitz and Bieri (1972) concluded that 'the formation of the EC did significantly affect the pattern of US direct investment and product trade in a manner consistent with the tariff discrimination hypothesis' (see Chapter 6). In recent years Japanese DI in Europe seems to be increasingly motivated by fears of a more protectionism stand of the EC.

The recent *DI flow from the EC to the USA* (EDIUS) springs from another cause. Many European companies are now investing directly in the USA to profit from the possibilities offered by the American market for the development of a product at the 'growth stage', the EC market being still too fragmented (see Chapter 16). Moreover, many entrepreneurs believe they need a foothold in the three main centres of the world: EC, USA, Japan (see, for instance, OECD 1987c). The first European companies to follow that strategy were based in countries without balance-of-payments problems: first the United Kingdom, next, especially, Germany and The Netherlands. Now other EC countries have joined in as well.

European direct investments in the EC

Internal direct investment flows have been completely free in the EC since the 1970s. In accordance with the theoretical expectation that *direct investments increase as soon as companies become convinced of the advantages of selecting optimum locations within an enlarged market area* (the 'free-trade' type of Chapter 6), direct investments by companies from the original six in other EC member states increased very fast in the 1966–1970 period (by some 63 per cent in four year; Pelkmans, 1983). That finding, based on rather limited data with respect to capital flows, is corroborated by the observation of Francko (1976) that in the same period the number of subsidiary companies of multinationals in the EC rose from 340 to 774. A comparison of 1970 data with those of 1978 shows that in that period DI grew even faster (multiplying roughly by four). An analysis of the importance of DI in the total economy shows fairly low figures. By our calculation, in 1975 the stock of DI (inward) amounted to some 6 per cent of GDP of the EC, the same figure applying to the EC stock of DI abroad. By 1983 it had increased to an estimated 7 per cent for EC inward and 8.5 per cent for EC-outward DI.

The *flows of DI among EC countries* (EDIE)[6] as given in Table 10.2, show a regular pattern consistent with the theoretical one given in Chapter 6. The poorer member states Greece, Ireland, Italy, Spain and

Portugal are net importers of capital, while the richer countries UK, Germany and The Netherlands, are net exporters of capital. France and Belgium are also net importers of capital. The pattern of intra-EC relations also prevails for EC relations with the rest of the world, with two exceptions: France and Italy move from the camp of net importers to that of net exporters.

Table 10.2 Direct investment flows (in billion Ecu) between the member countries of the European Community, 1975–1983

From\to	FRG	FRA	ITA	NETH	B/L	UK	DEN	IRL	SPA	POR	GRE	EC12
Germany	–	1.8	0.6	0.3	1.8	1.1	0.2	0.1	0.7	0.1	0.1	6.8
France	0.9	–	1.0	0.4	0.9	0.7	0.0	0.0	1.3	0.2	0.0	5.4
Italy	0.1	0.5	–	0.0	0.1	0.0	0.0	0.0	0.1	0.0	0.1	0.9
Netherlands	0.3	1.3	0.2	–	1.1	3.4	0.0	0.5	0.4	0.0	0.0	7.2
Bel/Lux	0.6	1.0	0.5	0.4	–	0.2	0.0	0.0	0.3	0.0	0.0	3.0
Un.Kingdom	1.4	1.4	0.5	1.2	0.6	–	0.2	0.7	0.5	0.1	0.1	6.7
Denmark	0.2	0.0	0.0	0.0	0.0	0.2	–	0.0	0.0	0.0	0.0	0.4
Ireland	0.0	0.0	0.0	0.0	0.0	0.1	0.0	–	0.0	0.0	0.0	0.1
Spain	0.0	0.1	0.0	0.0	0.0	0.0	0.0	0.0	–	0.1	0.0	0.2
Portugal	0.0	0.0	0.0	0.0	0.0	0.0	0.0	0.0	0.0	–	0.0	0.0
Greece	0.0	0.0	0.0	0.0	0.0	0.0	0.0	0.0 ·	0.0	0.0	–	0.0
EC12	3.5	6.1	2.8	2.3	4.5	5.7	0.4	1.3	3.3	0.5	0.3	30.7

Source: Author's own calculations from various statistics

These patterns are highly illustrative of the European integration process. They indicate that there is a net flow of capital towards the less developed EC countries; in other words, they confirm that jobs are indeed going to the people, although formerly people also used to go where the jobs were (see previous chapter). The accession of Spain and Portugal to the EC (CEC, 1988a) has accelerated the present trend for them; both countries have attracted a growing flow of DI, of which most has come from the EC. Apparently the concentration effects which the divergence school had feared (Chapter 6), have not materialised in the recent period.

Molle and Morsink (1990) have estimated a model to test the influence of certain national characteristics on EDIE flows. The *financial strength* of a country proves very important: the largest EDIE flows occur when the origin country shows a net financial resource and the receiving country a high borrowing requirement. Moreover the variable of *ownership advantage* (the R & D expenditure) shows good results (high R & D leads to high outward DI, and vice versa). The hypothesis that integration stimulates DI was validated: for practically all pairs of countries with very little trade, DI was non-existent, which highlights that EDIE is of the optimum-location rather than the tariff-jumping type (Chapter 6). A final important finding is that the downward variability of the exchange rate proved a negative factor and the upward variability a positive factor, which means that monetary integration, creating stable exchange rates, is likely to influence the EDIE flows positively. Finally they found that both geographical and cultural distance were relevant resistance factors.

Direct investment through take-overs

Companies that have decided to expand in other countries than their own have a choice between creating a new subsidiary company or taking over an existing foreign company. The latter strategy has the advantage of immediate access to markets whose specific characteristics are known to the management. Such a take-over often takes the form of a (public) offer to buy all existing shares. This does not make the operation a portfolio investment (see next section) because the essential motive for the transaction is to obtain control of the company.

While by EC regulations this type of DI transaction is completely free in principle, in practice it is not. In many countries (legal) measures or the involvement of banks in their capital protect companies from such take-overs. The fact that some member states have a free market for companies (the UK, for one), while in others (FRG, FR) it is restricted or closed, clearly illustrates that the integration of capital markets in the EC is not complete.

The different regimes have important consequences for the strategy of firms. Table 10.3 shows the performance of the 20 companies of each country that between 1979 and 1988 showed the fastest growth of

Table 10.3 Percentage growth and profitability, 1979–1988

Country	Growth of sales	Tax adjusted profit rate
UK	45	9
France	51	4
The Netherlands	53	5
Germany (FRG)	80	4
USA	48	10
Japan	190	4

Source: De Jong, H.W. (1989).

turnover and profitability. Evidently, companies under a 'liberal' regime (UK, USA) were forced to maximise profits, whereas companies in countries like the FRG could systematically aim at market power through maximising their turnovers. They are free to follow that strategy because their management is not threatened by potential bidders wanting to make a profit by increasing the firm's value through discontinuing its less profitable activities. Of course, in a truly free capital market in Europe, all national differences in legal shelter from take-overs should disappear, and hence the national differences in firms' profit and growth figures flatten out.

Portfolio investment; stock-market integration

Small segmented markets

Investors have wanted to make portfolio investments across the border of their home country for several motives (Ayling, 1986). The first is the wish to diversify (risk pooling), investing in stock with different fluctuations from that on the domestic market. The more segmented national markets are, the greater the advantage of such diversification may be. However, with increasing integration, and hence parallel fluctuations of stock prices, that advantage is bound to disappear. What remains is the possibility to invest in other stock than the ones traded on the home exchange, which comes to no more than product diversification.

The national European stock markets are still fairly segmented (OECD 1987b). Each of them is fairly small, with the exception of that in the UK. The ratio of capitalisation of continental European stock markets to GDP is, on average, only half that of the USA and Japan; the figures do not change if turnover is taken as the indicator instead of capitalisation. The following table gives an idea of the relative sizes of the European stock markets.

Clearly, the United Kingdom dominates the European stock markets, both in terms of capitalisation and in number of companies quoted (half the total). The markets of Germany, The Netherlands and Italy are dominated by large companies. These markets are all heavily regulated on a national basis, which has led to widely different practices, performance and control mechanisms (Stonham, 1982). Moreover, their very smallness often makes them far from efficient.[7]

European governments and the European Commission have given increasing attention to the problem, trying to improve the internal efficiency of stock markets in allocating savings to the borrowing requirements of the corporate sector both on the national and on the European scale. Their efforts have resulted in important changes in the

Table 10.4 Indicators of EC stock markets, 1985

Country	Market capitalisation (1000 m $)	Number of companies quoted	Average size ($)
United Kingdom	331	2460	135
Germany	179	450	397
France	79	582	135
Italy	61	246	248
Netherlands	60	208	288
Belgium	30	214	140
Spain	20	357	56
Denmark	15	217	67
Total for EC12[a]	775	4,734	164

[a] Ireland, Portugal, Greece: very small, omitted here
Source: James Capel & Co. as cited in Corner and Tonks (1987)

organisation of most markets (Stonham, 1987). Markets have been opened to foreign demand for, and supply of, stock; the techniques of trading and dealing, the nature of instruments, and the organisation of participating institutions have been adjusted.

Europe in the world

European integration is part of world integration. The integration of world asset markets is generally measured by correlating of the prices of stock in different countries; the general conclusion of such exercises is that the correlation is low (Adler and Dumas, 1983). In a detailed analysis of an 11 country data set comprising four EC countries, with over 300 individual stock, Cho *et al.*,(1986) again found evidence of limited integration of world markets as well as EC markets. Only for two out of six country pairs (FRG/Netherlands; France/UK) was the integration found to be significant.

An interesting question is whether the *stock markets of Western Europe have become more integrated among themselves than with those of the USA and Japan*. To analyse that, Corner and Tonks (1987) computed the weighted change of the correlation coefficients of European countries among themselves and with the USA and Japan. Table 10.5 gives the results. The table clearly indicates that Germany, The Netherlands and Italy have increased their market integration more on the European than on the world level; the opposite is true of France (only slightly) and the United Kingdom.

Table 10.5 Weighted percentage change in correlation coefficients of five European stock markets with those of the rest of Europe, the United States and Japan

Country	Europe	US + Japan
France	93	105
Germany	37	18
Netherlands	23	15
Italy	121	28
UK	43	78

Source: Corner and Tonks (1987)

The accelerated integration is mainly due to a few major factors. On the European level, the first to be mentioned is the relative stability of exchange rates, which has considerably reduced the risk of international transactions. The second factor, affecting both European and world markets, has been the revolution in information and telecommunications, permitting all relevant information on stock prices to be diffused at high speed. The European Commission is aware of this development and intends to stimulate the integration of the European stock markets by electronic links between the stock exchanges in the EC (Blaise *et al.*, 1981; Duncan and Hall, 1983). The third factor is the

Table 10.6 Correlation coefficients between European stock markets, 1973–1979 and 1980–1986

		France	Germany	Netherlands	Italy	UK
France	1973–9	–	0.49	0.55	0.14	0.73
	1980–6	–	0.94	0.90	0.87	0.87
Germany	1973–9		–	0.95	0.86	0.67
	1980–6		–	0.94	0.88	0.92
Netherlands	1973–9			-	0.73	0.76
	1980–6			-	0.78	0.98
Italy	1973–9				-	0.39
	1980–6				-	0.81
UK	1973–9					-
	1980–6					-

Source: Corner and Tonks (1987)

growing international integration of firms providing financial services, in particular brokers, and the establishment of foreign brokers on national stock exchanges. Notably the United Kingdom has gone very far in that direction, with other countries following slowly.

The integration of the EC stock markets

Arbitrage between markets tends to equalise prices (exchange-rate changes being taken into account). However, several studies have given evidence to the fact that there are nevertheless national factors that cause price differences between two markets. Corner and Tonks (1987) have tested the integration hypothesis by calculating correlation coefficients between the values of the stock-market portfolio (index at the beginning of each month converted into £ sterling) in pairs of EC countries during two time periods: 1973–1979 and 1980–1986. The year 1979 has been chosen because it was the year when EMS came into operation, and also the year in which the United Kingdom relaxed its exchange controls. The results are given in Table 10.6.

The results imply a considerable increase in the integration of European equity markets. Out of the 10 country pairs for which R^2 were calculated in the two periods, seven show a significant increase in R^2 from the first period to the second. The three others concern Italy and Germany; the national factor may have played a role in the behaviour of these countries and further research would be necessary for a satisfactory explanation.

Other capital

Long-term and short-term loans

The integration of long-term and short-term capital markets in the EC had made very little headway till recently owing to the restrictions imposed on capital movements by a number of member countries. Failing the integration by direct dealing between EC countries, a different type of integration has developed in which both countries deal with a third party (see Chapter 6). This has been done through the so-called 'Euromarkets', a misleading term because it actually refers to off-shore capital markets falling outside the control of any monetary authority. These markets, almost non-existent in the early 1960s, have developed very quickly since (Table 10.7).[8]

- The *Eurobond* market concerns long-term bonds that are sold in countries with other denominations than the currency of the country where they are sold. Better efficiency has made the

Table 10.7 Growth of Euromarkets, 1960–1985

Size (10^1 US$)	1960	1965	1970	1975	1980	1985
Eurocurrency (liabilities)	0	17	73	285	851	n.a.
Eurobond	0	1	3	9	23	141

Annual growth (%)	1960–65	1965–70	1970–75	1975–80	1980–85
Eurocurrency	–	34	32	25	n.a.
Eurobond	82	28	24	20	44

n.a. = not available
Source: BIS: Annual reports
       IMF: *International Capital Markets*, various issues

Eurobond markets more competitive for many issues than national capital markets. The success of Eurobonds is based on an inconsistency in regulation: governments tend to limit the access of foreign issuers of bonds to their national markets, but their control of domestic investors purchasing foreign bonds is less stringent or non-effective. So, banking firms active in international investments can bypass national restrictions by issuing bonds and similar debt instruments. Eurobond borrowers range from international institutions and multinational companies to national and municipal governments.

- The *Eurocurrency* market is the short-term equivalent of the Eurobond market. It thrives on the difference in interest levels on deposits: lower than national ones for borrowers and higher than national ones to lenders (Dufey and Giddy, 1981; Clarke and Pulay, 1978; Levi, 1981). Hence their explosive growth: from equalling no more than ten per cent of the domestic US market in 1965, by 1983 the Eurocurrency market had become equal in size (EC figures are not available).

Although little is known about the *origin and destination* of capital on the Euromarkets, the Bank for International Settlement estimates that Western Europe holds a share of some 40 per cent in total demand. Regrettably, there is no way to assess the transactions between European countries, interesting though they are from the integration point of view. Most transactions (some 70 per cent) on the Eurobond and Eurocurrency markets are denominated in US$. The Ecu (see Chapter 17) is the fourth currency after the DM and the Yen.

Interest-rate parity

A number of authors have tried to measure the integration of major financial markets by studying the equalisation of prices. Most of them have extended their investigation not only to the EC but to the whole (developed) world.

The first study we will discuss here deals with the *short-term covered interest parity*, which means equal prices of capital for comparable financial instruments in different markets. Deviations from parity spring from significant barriers to financial transactions, such as controls on capital flows, differences in reserve requirements, and transaction costs. Van den Berghe (1987) has estimated the interdependence between the development of interest on Euromarkets and internal markets. The results for the 1970s show very little integration; Belgium and The Netherlands were in line with international developments, a tendency increasingly applying to Germany and the United Kingdom as well. In the 1980s, on the contrary, the markets of Germany, the United Kingdom, The Netherlands and Belgium have become highly integrated, whereas the integration of the Italian and French markets has remained poor. The results reflect the deregulation of financial markets in the former group of countries. Similar patterns are observed for the American and Japanese markets; for the former, the integration has become almost perfect in the 1980s.

A much stricter test of interest parity refers to the *short-term real interest rates* (RIR). For the real interest rates to be equal among countries there must be no exchange-rate premiums and *ex ante* purchasing-power parity[9] must hold. Some empirical studies have been carried out to find out whether the short-run *ex ante* real interest rates are internationally equal. None of the authors found parity on international markets. Mishkin (1984a, 1984b), who studied seven OECD countries [10] found neither equality at one point in time, nor RIR to move similarly through time. Mark (1985a, 1985b) came to the same conclusion after incorporating taxation effects. These results were confirmed by Gaab *et al.* (1986), Caramazza (1987), and Cumby and Mishkin (1986). The last mentioned authors did, however, find strong evidence of a positive relation between the movements of the real rates in the USA and Europe.

Long-term real interest rates on international markets are less documented than short-term ones. One reason is that comparable financial instruments on Euro and domestic capital markets are hard to find. Following Fukao and Hanazaki (1987), we have estimated the significance of real interest-rate differentials between Germany and five other EC countries. We have made a distinction between the pre-crisis period, with low inflation and fixed exchange rates, the 1973–9 period, when monetary disturbances occurred and capital controls abounded, and 1980–6 when international capital-movement controls were abandoned or relaxed in many countries. The analysis shows that in the second period the differences were fairly large, in particular for the UK and Italy. After the creation of the EMS and the relaxation of the capital-mobility controls, the differences became very small (less than 2 percentage points). The essentials of our findings are given on the bottom row of Table 10.8. So, the conclusion may be that European interest rates have recently shown a clear tendency to converge.

Table 10.8 Convergence of interest rates in the EC 1963–1985

	1963-73	1973-79	1980-86
Short term[a]	0.42	0.61	0.71
Long term[b]	0.94	0.81	0.92

[a] Average correlation coefficient of national rates to Euromarket rates. (*Source*: van den Berghe, 1987; additional estimates)
[b] $100 - x$ (x is the total number of percentage points of absolute differential of interest rates of five EC countries to Germany)

Welfare effects

The empirical evidence on the 'trade' and welfare effects of the integration of European capital markets is very thin. This may be due to the absence of a clear-cut objective; indeed, the markets of EC countries were to be only partly integrated among themselves, and the attitudes of EC member countries towards world integration were very different. Let us briefly review the situation with respect to the three main categories.

The few studies that have analysed the effects of free *direct investment* in the EC, have been limited to the employment effects in both source and destination countries. The latter seem invariably to have benefited from DI. The effect on the former varies from negative when exports from the home bases are replaced, to positive when the penetration into a foreign market actually increases home employment (Buckley and Artisien, 1987). To our knowledge, no studies have been made on the welfare effects of DI.

The potential effects of further integration of the *EC stock market* in the world system were studied by Levy and Sarnet (1970). They observed from experience in the 1950s and 1960s, that the mean return from a portfolio of EC6 country stocks was about 16 per cent at a risk of 25 per cent, while the return on a 'world' portfolio would be 18 per cent at a risk of 8 per cent. A 17 per cent risk was the lowest that could be obtained for a 12 per cent return on EC stocks only. We do not know of any more recent studies of the welfare effects of stock market integration.

Recently an attempt has been made to estimate the welfare effects of the integration of *short-term and long-term capital markets* along the theoretical path indicated by Figure 6.2(b) (Price Waterhouse, 1988). First the Common Market interest rate (R_{cm}) was calculated, and next the size of the triangles *EHF* and *FHD* for each country. For the EC as a whole a beneficial result of 1500 million Ecu was found.

Summary and conclusions

- The *objective* of European capital-market integration was fairly limited and practically restricted to intra-EC direct investment; only lately has the EC tried for complete internal and external freedom of capital movements.
- *Direct investment* in the EC has considerably expanded. The intra-EC pattern of DI shows a net flow from the richer (Northern) states towards the poorer (Southern) states, which should lead to more convergence in the EC.
- *Stock markets* used to be highly segmented; until recently, access to foreign markets was difficult, and the prices on different stock exchanges showed little correlation. With the recent deregulation, integration has progressed considerably.
- *Long-term and short-term loans in the EC* were also segmented. However, an alternative to European integration has developed in that respect with the growth of the practically unregulated off-shore markets. With increasing liberalisation, the national markets in the EC countries tend to align with these 'world' markets.
- The *welfare effects* of the integration of European capital markets are unknown as far as DI and portfolio investment are concerned. A recent estimate of the effects of the integration of short-term and long-term capital markets showed that considerable benefits can be gained.

Notes

1   Capital and *payment* are both financial transactions and are therefore often treated together. Free movement of goods, persons and services presupposes, as we have seen, freedom of payments for such transactions. Indeed, now that the transition period is over, such payments are completely free (article 106 of the Treaty). This freedom cannot be revoked by any Member State. Equally free (article 67, second paragraph) are 'all current payments connected with the movement of capital

between Member States' (that is, payments of interest and dividends), with the proviso, however, that Member States have the right to check whether such bank-note operations are not capital transactions in disguise (Court of Justice).

2   For the way such influencing, mostly through impediments, may be put into practice, see, for instance, OECD (1979) and (1982c).

3   See, among others, Verrijn Stuart (1965), Segré (1966).

4   For the many factors that affect international merger or acquisition decisions (such as taxes, merger regulation, accounting obligations, etc.), see the book by Cooke (1988).

5   This change for the USA is statistically measured by the increase in the Reciprocity indexes of the US/EC direct investments (see Sleuwaegen, 1987).

6   The data have been taken mainly from Dunning and Cantwell (1987), and complemented with balance-of-payment data and data from various other sources, for instance OECD (1987c), Kragenau (1987) and some unpublished sources. Because on the whole, inward investment is documented better than outward investment, the former has been taken as the main basis for our calculations. To arrive at a consistent table, the basic data had to be corrected on several points. Consequently, although the table gives the best possible picture of DI in Europe, the figures in it can be regarded only as indications, or as the likely order of magnitudes.

7   Stonham (1982) reviews some studies undertaken to measure the (in)efficiency of every major stock market in Europe. Although a short conclusion is difficult to draw (what with the variety of hypotheses, data and techniques used), the general impression is clear: European stock markets cannot be called efficient.

8   See: Geist (1979), Johnston (1983), Kane (1982).

9   Several methods have been proposed for measuring real interest rates (nominal rates corrected for inflation) (Atkinson and Chouraqui, 1985). They all suffer from the difficulty of establishing inflation expectations.

10   US, Canada, France, Germany, UK, The Netherlands, and Switzerland.

PART IV
SECTORS OF ACTIVITY

11 Agriculture

Introduction

Those responsible for economic policy always have given special attention to agriculture. Most other sectors of economic activity are the concern of the Ministry of Economic Affairs, but agriculture is honoured by a separate ministry in practically all countries of Europe.

What makes agriculture so special? The answer is threefold: the nature of its products, the structure of its production and the production conditions. Many agricultural *products* are vital necessities, and the wish not to be dependent on others in exceptional circumstances induces many governments to pursue a policy of autarky. Moreover, consumer demand for vital necessities being inelastic (which implies a low price elasticity), markets are easily disturbed and market regulation is resorted to. Among agricultural *production processes*, the technical optimum may not be the feasible one because it is not always compatible with the geological and social conditions, individual farms often being family establishments. Among the extraordinary *production conditions* of agricultural activity, the vagaries of the weather come first: they may cause great fluctuations in production volume, which, demand being inelastic, lead to large price differences. There are, moreover, very many suppliers who, by simultaneously responding to certain signals, may boost market fluctuations.

Given these characteristics, the *agricultural policy* pursued in most countries is for the government to intervene in the market on a large scale, often regulating both prices and quantities. Apart from that, measures to strengthen the structure of agriculture are in most countries elements of agricultural policy. The fact that national agricultural policies tend to be strongly interwoven with social structures and choices (maintaining the viability of small family businesses) or spatial planning (maintaining regional balance), may be responsible for the limited role of agriculture in many integration processes. That does not mean that there is no important world-scale trade in agricultural produce; it only means that until recently, within international organisations there have been hardly any attempts at international harmonising of the organisation of agricultural markets (production and trade). Admittedly, international agreements have been drawn up for certain products, aiming at some control of their world markets, so liable to great fluctuations through speculations and other causes. Such control schemes tend to be specialist in their orientation – to one product – and weak in their institutional structure. The Food and Agriculture Organisation of the UN is concerned in particular with world-wide aspects of food supply. The OECD's concern (for example, OECD 1987d) has been of a co-ordinating nature (exchange of information and cautious adjustment of policy). An organisation like the European Free Trade Association has even excluded agriculture from free traffic. The GATT now tries to formulate world-wide rules for trade in agricultural products.

When the *European Community* was founded, however, agriculture was given a central place, on theoretical as well as political grounds. The theoretical motive was the strong association of the agricultural sector with the rest of the economy; differential prices for agricultural produce, affecting the cost of raw materials as well as labour cost (through food prices), would lead to differential costs in other sectors and could thus disturb competition. The political motive was that as a counterweight to the prospects the Common Market opened to German manufacturing industry, equivalent chances had to be created for French agriculture.

In the next section we will discuss in detail the principles of EC agricultural policy as it has been given substance in the EEC Treaty and in later regulations and directives.[1] However, the system chosen for the EC is neither the only one feasible nor the best one from an economic point of view. To grasp the workings of EC and alternative systems, let us therefore dwell a few moments on some theoretical aspects; the actual structure of the production, trade and consumption of agricultural products in Europe will be dealt with afterwards. The disadvantages of some characteristics of the EC regime will then stand out clearly.

To round off the chapter, some observations will be made about the costs of the present policy and the need for and chances of its improvement.

Community regime

Treaty

The Treaty of Rome states that the Common Market encompasses all agricultural products and that for good performance and development of the Common Market a common agricultural policy must be pursued (art. 3). That policy had to be accomplished in the course of the transition period (that is, between 1958 and 1970) (art. 40). In the articles

38 to 47 the Treaty states the objectives and principles of this common agricultural policy.

The *objectives of the policy are* (art. 39):

- to increase agricultural productivity by promoting technical progress and the optimum use of production factors;
- to ensure a fair standard of living to the agricultural community by increasing their per capita income;
- to stabilise markets;
- to assure the availability of supplies;
- to ensure reasonable consumer prices.

The editors of the Treaties, realising that objectives were to some extent conflicting owing to the conflicting interests of consumers and producers, tried to indicate some priority by the order of the points of article 39. From the position of the first 2 points, to improve the income prospects of the producers is clearly the primary aim.

The Treaty (art. 40) orders Community agencies to elaborate the Common Agricultural Policy (CAP) and gives some instructions how to set about it: a conference of expert representatives of the member states is to be convened to plot the main lines of such a policy. That conference was held in Stresa in 1958; two kinds of policy were found necessary:

- a policy of *market control* (including the following three elements of the treaty);
  - a market regulation, comprising an intervening body, competition rules and rules for foreign trade;
  - a price policy, consisting in the setting of minimum prices by criteria as objective as possible;
  - a fund to pay guaranteed prices (guarantee);
- a *structural policy*;
  - production factors;
  - production conditions;
  - involving a fund for financing this policy at the EC level.

The two kinds of policy were worked out in the 1960s and the early 1970s, and subsequently adopted by the new member states as part of the so-called *acquis communautaire*, that is, the Community attainments.

Policy of market control

The results of the Stresa conference enabled the Commission to submit the first drafts for Green Europe fairly soon, and as early as 1960 the Council could on that basis issue the first regulations. In the course of the years these have been followed by untold regulations, directives and decisions, too detailed to go into here. However, all those implementations of the common policy of market control are based on *three principles*, important enough to be discussed in detail, namely: (1) unity of the European market, (2) priority for the EC's own products on the Common Market, and (3) financial solidarity among member states.

The *unity of the market* means not only the completely free traffic of agricultural products (that is to say, no customs tariffs, quotas, etc.), but also, given the special structure of agriculture, a common organisation setting one price for the whole market and using in all member states the same intervention instruments to regulate the market. One important instrument is the protection of the outer frontiers; another is the guaranteed sale of the domestic production of some major products at a set price. Unity of the market also implies mutual adjustment across the whole Community of instructions with respect to health, control, veterinary care, etc. and supervision to prevent certain, mostly national measures, from distorting competition.

The *priority for EC's own products* implies that the needs of the market are in the first instance provided for by European production; only if that is insufficient will imports be resorted to. Should the world-market price be above the EC price, then the system provides for a subsidy to be paid on imports to avoid upward pressure on the internal price level, and for a levy to be imposed on exports, to prevent their own production from seeping away abroad.

The *financial solidarity* among member states finds expression in the European Agricultural Fund, Guarantee Division. A policy of market control yields (levies) as well as 'costs' money (restitutions, storage costs, etc.). All yields are paid into the European Fund (EAGGF) no matter what member state collects them;all costs are paid from that Fund no matter what member state the amounts flow to. Because in general the returns from levies on agricultural produce are not sufficient to finance all costs, the European Agricultural Fund has to be fed as well from the Community's other own financial means (see Chapter 4).

The issue of a common market regulation does not imply that it is the same for all products. The three most important types of *systems of market control* are:

- *Guarantee schemes and intervention prices* when the world market is screened off. This scheme applies to by far the greater part of production (more than 70 per cent), namely cereals, sugar and dairy products. This type of scheme guarantees a minimum price at which intervention agencies will buy up any domestic supply, the quantities involved being stored and sold when the market situation is favourable. There are broadly similar market schemes for pork, fruit and vegetables, and table wine, but they put the emphasis on storage and processing support rather than on an automatic sales guarantee at fixed prices.

- *Limited free price formation* with the world market screened off. This type of scheme has been introduced for about a quarter of the products, in particular for certain kinds of fruit and vegetables, flowers, eggs and fattened poultry. These products do not count as basic feeds and often have a short production cycle, which is why extraordinary support is not judged necessary and constraining the imports by levies and restrictions thought sufficient.
- *Bonuses* based on the quantity produced. For some other products, for instance those for which international agreements allow no customs levies, a system of subsidies on the value of the produce is sometimes applied. Such a system allows domestic production to be maintained at high producer costs, consumer prices being kept low nevertheless. It is applied, for instance, to oilseeds. Producers of olive oil, too, are given support in proportion to their production volumes. In other cases, subsidies by hectare, number of cattle, etc. are offered. Together these schemes do not account for more than 5 per cent of the total production value of EC agriculture.

From the above, the pivot of most market regulations is the *intervention price*. Since among the objectives of agricultural policy, farmers' incomes have pride of place, it is hardly surprising that intervention prices are mostly set as high as possible. The yearly price settings by the Council, on the proposal of the Commission and after consultation of the European Parliament, have long been the main event of European decision making. The day-to-day implementation of agricultural policy is in the hands of the Commission, but in practice carried on in committees in which representatives of the member states confer. If the Commission decides according to the committee's opinion, the measure becomes valid at once; otherwise it has to be submitted to the Council for consideration.

In the prescribed system, one price prevails throughout the market for a given product in the whole Community. The Community not having a currency of its own, the price must first be expressed in the Ecu, European Currency Unit and next recalculated in the various national currencies. That means that changes in the rate of exchange may cause the price suddenly to rise for farmers in the devaluating country and drop for farmers in the revaluating country. To cushion such changes, the so-called *Monetary Compensatory Amounts* (MCA) have been introduced: a system of levies and restitutions on the interior frontiers, serving to eliminate the effects of sudden price differences on the market, but having the effect of breaking the unity of the common market. This system is to be discontinued however.

Structural policy

If the EC policy of market control was achieved rather rapidly, things were different as far as structural policy was concerned. Given the varied production conditions and national regulations, until the early 1970s the Commission practically confined itself to some co-ordination of the member states' structural policies. Still, a limited number of schemes deemed of common interest by the Council were financed by the Guidance Division of the European Agricultural Fund.

The impulse to a genuine European structural policy for agriculture was given by the so-called '*Mansholt Plan*' (CEC, 1968). Some relevant decisions were made around 1972, and from then on this policy has been gradually extended. At present it concerns three main elements: support to management, improvement of trade channels for agricultural produce, and reduction of regional differences. As is evident from the word structure, the long-term aim of structural policy is to enhance the productivity of agricultural enterprise, an aim that derives directly from the first objective of agricultural policy in article 39 of the Treaty.

Support to good management means first of all support to investments aimed at technical progress, interest subsidies and investment subsidies being the instruments wielded. Improving educational and training possibilities for agriculturalists is another form of support. Rational management is stimulated by support to senior owners of marginal establishments willing to close shop, and infrastructural measures such as improvement of the water economy, reallotment schemes, etc. Finally, quite a network of consulting agencies has been built up, able to give advice on widely diverging matters associated with conducting a business.

Improving the often complicated *structure of sales channels* and processing of agricultural products is indispensable to a well-functioning agricultural sector. In that connection dairy factories, slaughter houses, packing establishments for fruit and vegetables, wine-bottling establishments, auctions, cold-storage warehouses, etc. fulfil important roles besides the trade proper. Therefore, EC structural policy provides for EC subsidies to such establishments for improving their performance. Furthermore, the EC can make funds available for producers to found 'cooperatives' with a view to reinforcing the farmer's position in his negotiations with customers.

The structure of agriculture is much worse in some areas than in others, which is evident from the *large regional discrepancies in productivity*. The agricultural productivity of weak regions cannot be improved by the simple expedient of stimulating the outflow of workers, for these regions mostly have not much to offer in the way of alternative activities. For that reason the EC may sometimes introduce supporting measures, provided they fit in with other regional actions in the framework of an integrated development programme. That point will be taken up in Chapter 18.

The EC measures sketched above are not the only ones to be taken to improve agricultural structure in the Community; indeed the Community's policy is merely complementary, the main responsibility being still with the member states, as is apparent from a comparison of expenditures incurred by the EC and the national budgets.

The costs of the European structural policy are paid from the European Agricultural Fund (EAGGF), Guidance Division. In practice that often means that the EAGGF finances a certain proportion of a programme's total costs. That proportion is on average small in so-called strong areas, but may be as much as 50 or 65 per cent in so-called weak areas. The Guidance Division has for some time been spending considerable sums, especially in comparison to the expenditures of the EC for other sectors.

Sketch of the sector

The sector as a whole

From the fact that agricultural policy is the EC's most elaborate policy area and has always been the focus of interest, one might presume that this sector is the most important in the EC economy. That is no longer true, however. Admittedly, in former days agriculture used to be the most important sector of the economy, but gradually industry and later services have progressively developed, reducing agriculture to a relatively modest position. Table 11.1 shows a steep drop of the relative significance of agriculture in the EC economy in the last 30 years.

Table 11.1 Percentage share of agriculture in total Gross Domestic Product and total employment of the EC12, 1950–1985

Indicator	1950	1960	1970	1980	1985
GDP	n.a.	8	6	4	3
Employment	30	21	13	10	9

Sources: GDP: Eurostat, Review 1970–1975 and 1972–1981; Molle *et al.*, 1980. Employment: 1950–1970 Molle *et al.*, 1980; 1970–1985 OECD Labour Force Statistics
n.a. = not available

At the moment, less than 3 per cent of total Gross Domestic Product is produced by the agricultural sector, with not quite 10 per cent of the total active population of the EC still employed in agriculture, figures which in 1950 were still thrice as high. In the 1950s the shares of agriculture differed widely among the countries of Europe. While in Italy, France and other Mediterranean countries such as Spain, Portugal and Greece the sector was still relatively important, in the United Kingdom it was very modest. The differences, though still there, have shrunk in the course of time.

The main cause of the relative reduction of the agricultural share in the economy is the low *income elasticity* for foodstuffs among the higher income groups. Indeed, as incomes rise, people tend to spend a smaller portion on food. Typical income elasticities of agricultural products in the EC are between 0.1 and 0.3 only, and for some products elasticity is even negative (see for example, Hill and Ingersent, 1982). Because the cost of food is increasingly made up by such industrial activities as processing, packaging and presentation, the share of agricultural products in the economy is even smaller than the elasticities seem to imply (on average: a 1 per cent increase in the price of raw materials leads to a 0.4 per cent increase in consumption price).

Sub-sectors

The broad sector of agriculture hitherto referred to falls into some important branches, namely: (1) agriculture in the narrow sense (that is, cereals); (2) husbandry (meat, milk, dairy products); (3) horticulture (vegetables, fruit, flowers, etc.); (4) viniculture; (5) forestry (wood); and finally (6) fisheries.[2] Each of them can be sub-divided into product

Table 11.2 **Percentage share of some selected product groups in the total production value of agriculture**

Product	EC9 1974	EC10 1985
1 Cereals (mainly wheat)	12	12
2.1 Dairy (mainly milk)	19	19
2.2 Meat (mainly beef and pork)	31	32
3 Vegetables, fruit, olives	13	15
4 Wine	4	5
5 Other	21	17

Source: CEG, *De toestand van de landbouw in de Gemeenschap 1974 and 1986* (The state of agriculture in the Community), Brussels, 1975 and 1987

groups. Table 11.2 indicates their relative importance and the stability of the shares of the four groups through time.

Size of farms

The structure of the agricultural market is characterised by almost perfect competition on the side of supply. Table 11.3 gives an indication of the number of suppliers, in this case the number of farms. The picture is not complete, very small holdings (often run as side activities) not being included.

National and EC measures to improve the structure were among the causes of a rapid decline in the number of establishments in the past 25 years: by nearly 40 per cent. Table 11.3 also shows that small farms in particular have been closed down or taken over, or their land has been put to another use.[3] Agriculture in the countries of the original EC6 was dominated by small farms, while in the United Kingdom and Denmark there were more large establishments. In the EC10 the share of small farms (between 1 and 10 ha) dropped by some 8 percentage points (of a shrinking total!!) in the whole period. In the last few years the decline has been slowing down, owing to, among other things, the worsening prospects of employment outside agriculture. As a result of the developments described, in the EC10 the average establishment size rose by more than half between 1960 and 1985.

Table 11.3 Development of the number and size of agricultural establishments (EC10)

	1960	1970	1980	1985
Number of holdings larger than 1 ha, x 1000	8147	6585	5539	5037
Share of holdings smaller than 10 ha in total area of holdings of over 1 ha (%)	70	66	63	62
Average size of holdings (ha)	11	14	16	17
Area per worker (ha)	6	8	10	13

Source: Eurostat, *Yearbook of Agricultural Statistics 1978–1981; Statistical Yearbook, 1986;* some estimates.

A second indicator of structural change is the *number of persons by hectare of cultivated land.* In the past 25 years the area of land cultivated by farms of more than 1 ha has hardly changed: there has been a slight decline of about 5 per cent. Apart from small differences in definition, the decline in employment discussed in the previous section is therefore an adequate measure of the increase in the number of hectares cultivated by one agricultural worker. By a crude computation (total area of land cultivated in farms of over 1 ha divided by active population in agriculture), each person employed in agriculture in the EC10 corresponded to about 4 ha of cultivated land in 1950, and 13 ha in 1985 – a very large but gradual increase.

Productivity

Another indicator of the changing structure of agriculture is the degree of *mechanisation*. The number of tractors, for instance, has grown rather spectacularly. Account being taken of the contraction of cultivated land, in 1985 there appeared to be three times more tractors for every 1000 ha of cultivated land than 25 years earlier. Total capital use would be the best indicator, but that is difficult to measure, so that we are forced to go by the overall effects.

An idea of *productivity rises* is given by Table 11.4, which shows how the average yields of certain agricultural products increased between 1958 and 1985.

Table 11.4 Average yields of agricultural products, EC10

Product	1958–60	1968–70	1978–80	1984–86
Milk (kg/cow)	2900	3400	4100	4400
Wheat (100 kg/ha)	23	32	48	58
Sugar-beets (100 kg/ha)	400	420	450	510

Sources: LEI, Selected agricultural figures of the EC; Eurostat, *Land Use and Production* 1980; *Yearbook of Agricultural Statistics*, various years

With sugar-beets the rise of productivity is less than 1 per cent a year, with milk and potatoes somewhat less than 2 per cent; the rise of 3.5 per cent achieved with wheat was very high indeed. (For the other cereals the more modest increase of 2 per cent was registered.) All increases are mostly due to better varieties and the use of more fertilizers.

The above picture of the various structural characteristics of agriculture in the whole European Community conceals marked differences among member states. More detailed values of the various indicators by country reveal that the productivity in a country like Greece is poor beside those of northern member states like The Netherlands and Denmark. As far as certain crops are concerned, Italy's productivity still remains below that of the rest of the Community. Corresponding differences are observed in average farm size and number of hectares by person: in 1980, in the EC10, 45 per cent of the farms fell in the category from 1 to 5 ha, in Greece and Italy the corresponding figure was still around 70; against an average 10 ha in the EC10, in Italy no more than 6 ha and in Greece only 3 ha were available per working person.

Market regulation and its effects

Unstable markets

Agricultural markets, as we pointed out earlier, tend to be rather unstable; demand is price inelastic and so is, in the short term, supply. Farmers are small producers compared to the size of the market. They tend to react to price changes without understanding the underlying demand and supply changes. An illustration of the inability of agricultural markets to achieve equilibrium is the so-called *'hog cycle'*, which owes its name to the German economist Hanau who was the first to analyse the phenomenon with respect to the pig market. Figure 11.1 presents the relevant supply and demand curves. Suppose a sudden rise in demand (from D_1 to D_2); supply fails to adjust (it takes some time for pigs to be born and become fit for slaughter). As a consequence, the

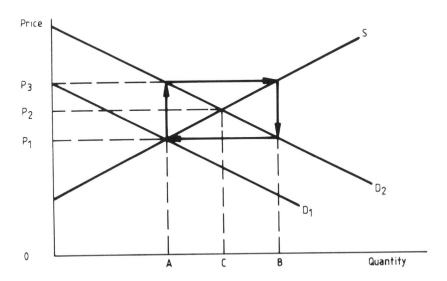

Figure 11.1 Disequilibria on agricultural markets: hog cycle

price rises to P_3 instead of P_2, which would be the new equilibrium price at which the equilibrium quantity OC would be sold. Producers considering the high price P_3 to be the long-term measure, will extend the supply of pigs from OA to OB. However, demanders are not prepared to digest so great a supply at that price, so that the price will drop to the P_1 level. Many producers now decide not to produce at this price; fewer pigs are raised, supply is for some time limited to OA, after which the cycle can start anew. In its pure form the cyclical movement only occurs if the gradient of demand and supply curves are equal. If the gradient of the demand curve is steeper than that of the supply curve, the system is explosive, that is to say, it progressively removes itself from the equilibrium; if the supply curve has a steeper gradient than the demand curve, the system converges (cobweb theorem). The disequilibrium inherent in agricultural markets can give rise to heavy social costs, which is why many countries decided at quite an early date to introduce some kind of control of these markets.

Effects of various systems of market control; production, trade and welfare

There are various systems of market control, most of which influence the price (through guarantees or subsidies, for example), sales (through market organisation), and the access to the market (through import constraints).

In the previous section some features of the *EC system of guaranteed prices* have already been pointed out. How this scheme of market control works at various national (or EC-guaranteed) and world-market prices is shown by Figure 11.2. Here S_{com} is the EC supply curve, which runs a rather level course, implying that a relatively small price increase causes a more than proportional production rise. D_{com} is the demand curve, drawn as rather precipitous, in concordance with the inelasticity of demand for most agricultural products. We can now distinguish four cases corresponding to the four prices in Figures 11.2(a) and 11.2(b).

(1) The price on the world market is P_1, at which price any quantity wanted can be obtained (fully elastic supply). In an entirely open economy, domestic production will now become OA, domestic demand OB, and a quantity AB will be imported, everything at the price P_1. The domestic agricultural production is low in that case, so are consumer prices. Government subsidies do not apply so the taxpayer is not asked for a contribution (Figure 11.2a).

(2) At a guaranteed price P_2, domestic production will rise to OC and demand drop to OD. On the quantity imported, CD, an import levy of $P_2 - P_1$ will be imposed to make prices on the world and EC markets equal. That yields $CD \times (P_2 - P_1)$ in tariff revenue, the

shaded area MNTI of Figure 11.2(a). The consumer is worse off: he consumes less at higher prices (consumer loss ZXNK, deadweight loss NTK). The farmer's gross return, achieved in one transaction, namely through selling to the intervention authority, will amount to XOCM. The area ZXMH represents an extra producer rent transferred to farmers from consumers (HMI deadweight loss).

(3) The price is raised to P_{de}, which indicates the domestic equilibrium between supply and demand. It can be done without creating surpluses and without involving public budget expenses to be borne finally by the taxpayer, albeit at a cost to consumers (Figure 11.2b).

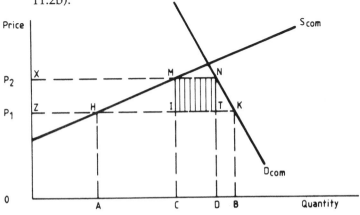

(a) Imports

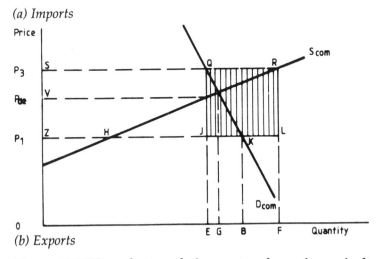

(b) Exports

Figure 11.2 EC market-regulation system for major agricultural products (guarantee prices)

(4)   At a price P_3, the situation changes profoundly, however. Demand will drop to OE entailing an additional loss in consumer surplus as less product becomes available at higher prices. As supply rises to OF, market authorities find themselves compelled to buy up a quantity $OF - OE$ at price P_3. That quantity has to be sold on the world market, which implies an export subsidy (or restitution in the EC jargon) of the difference between the guaranteed price (or intervention price) P_3 and the world-market price P_1. The amount is QJLR, which will be charged to the taxpayer. The gross return to the farmer, achieved in one transaction through selling of production to the intervention authority, will amount to OFRS (Figure 11.2b).

The second type of market regulation to be dealt with is the one that used to be applied among other countries in the United Kingdom, where it was known as the scheme of *deficiency payments*.[4] Slightly altered it is also common within the EC in the form of 'bonus payments'. Figure 11.3 illustrates the working of this scheme, which leaves trade in agricultural produce free.

(1)   At a price P_1 (world-market price) (Figure 11.3a) demand will be OB and domestic production OA. The consumer enjoys high quantities OB at a low price and the government's (taxpayer's) resources are not tapped.

(2)   Now, a country wanting to boost its own production under this scheme, rather than setting high guaranteed prices will grant farmers a kind of subsidy by unit of produce. A subsidy of $P_2 - P_1$ will entail a domestic supply of OC and imports to a quantity of CB. The price remains low for all consumers: P_1. The taxpayer contributes ZXMI. The farmer's gross return consists of two parts: the market part OCIZ and the subsidy part ZXMI. Even less costly is a system that is related not to the production volume but to the difference in cost and revenue. With such a system, based on information on production cost of groups of farms, producers in the OA range would not receive any subsidy, producers at point C the full subsidy $P_2 - P_1$, and producers in the AC range a subsidy that would be just sufficient to cover their cost. Costs to the government (taxpayer): the triangle HIM.

(3)   Because with this system farmers' income-support and price policies remain largely separate, a pressure strong enough to push up the price to P_3 (through subsidies in the order of magnitude of $P_3 - P_1$) is not likely to build up easily; should it happen nevertheless, then the subsidy would work out as a production subsidy for the OB part and as an export subsidy for the BF part (see Figure 11.3b).

From these examples, *different schemes clearly have widely divergent welfare effects*, dependent on the domestic price level and the differences between the domestic guaranteed and the world-market prices.

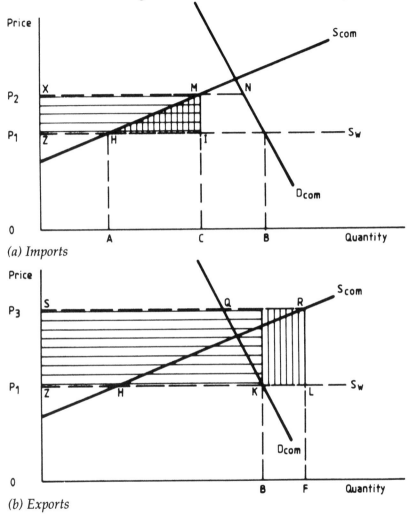

(a) Imports

(b) Exports

Figure 11.3 Alternative market-regulation systems (deficiency payments)

Price policy and the consumer

Before 1964, Common Agricultural Policy made no move towards common prices. In that year the Commission proposed the establishment of common price levels for cereals, pig meat, poultry meat and eggs. The negotiations with the Council were difficult, wheat prices being at the time much higher in Germany than in France and somewhere in between in other countries. Because of the German position, the EC price result was well above the average of all other countries. Later the Council also agreed on prices for fruits and vegetables and for some important other products. The complete price structure, with other cereal prices derived from the high wheat price, became effective in 1968. Because many animals are on a cereal diet, meat prices rose in proportion. Following that trend the EC adopted relatively high prices for other products as well.

EC prices were thus set well above world-market levels, as is illustrated by Table 11.5 for some selected products: on average EC prices appear to be almost double the world-market ones.

Table 11.5 EC agricultural prices as a percentage of world-market prices (five-year averages)

Product	1968[a]–1972	1973–1977	1978–1980[b]
Soft wheat	192	146	167
Hard wheat	222	167	171
Rice	171	117	129
Barley	174	135	173
Maize	159	140	179
Sugar	247	129	165
Beef	140	171	198
Pork	140	123	147
Butter	404	349	367
Olive oil	157	164	200
Oil seeds	153	112	171

Source: Eurostat, *Yearbook of Agricultural Statistics*, various years
[a] 1968: start of the common price system
[b] Later years not published

That does not mean, however, that European consumers pay twice as much for their food than they would without the CAP price system. As a matter of fact, prices on the world market are heavily influenced by the EC system that dumps goods on the world market, bringing down prices there. Should prices in Europe, and hence European production and exports, drop, those on the world market would probably recover to some extent, though not to anywhere near the EC level; even during the commodity-price boom of 1973, many European prices remained well above world level.

Domestic production and world markets

Prices, increased to raise farmers' incomes, do not necessarily entail external problems through subsidised exports; domestic prices can rise to well above world-market levels (P_{de} versus P_1 in Figure 11.2) without giving rise to surplus production (that is, production beyond OG).

The same idea can be expressed in the *self-sufficiency ratio* (SSR). In Figure 11.2, at price P_1 domestic production is below the equilibrium levels of domestic supply and demand, so that the SSR is below 100. On the other hand, at price P_3 domestic production exceeds domestic demand, and hence SSR is above 100. For the period from 1958 to 1984, Table 11.6 indicates the SS ratios for a set of important products. Before the enlargement of 1972, the EC6 increased its self-sufficiency for many products to a considerable degree, in some cases to more than 100 per cent. The first enlargement entailed a drop in self-sufficiency for the EC9, due mostly to Britain's position as a large importer of many agricultural products. Since then, however, the production of practically all commodities has grown considerably. By 1984, the EC had again become a net exporter of many of the products mentioned in the table. Raising the internal prices to P_3 levels had obviously boosted production to levels exceeding demand. A very important line had thus been crossed. Instead of receiving tariff income from levies on imports, the EC increasingly had to pay restitutions to exporters. The appearance of the EC (as well as other countries) as a structural supplier on world markets, where prices tend to fluctuate strongly with changes in demand and supply, has had a downward effect on world market prices.

Apart from internal problems, this causes grave *external conflicts*. Indeed, other exporting countries are increasingly pushed out of existing markets owing to subsidised exports of the EC, or, if they manage to keep their hand in, have to be content with lower prices than they would have had without the EC's 'dumping' activities. The predicament is serious, for the EC gets into conflict not only with developed countries like the United States (about cereals, for example), but also with developing countries which depend very much on the revenues of their exports (of sugar, for example) to pay their imports. Thus, the beneficial effects of EC development policy (see Chapter 19) are partly undone by the detrimental external effects of the CAP. On the other hand, recent analysis, carried out by means of a very large multi-

Table 11.6   Self-sufficiency ratio (SSR, of the European Community for some selected agricultural products, 1958–1985[a] (in.1ex)

Product	EC6		EC9		EC12
	1956-60	1972-73	1973-74	1980-81	1985
Wheat	90	111	103	117	122
Rye	n.a.	105	94	103	112
Barley	84	113	106	114	133
Oats	n.a.	96	95	96	100
Maize	64	67	58	66	84
Cereals, total	85	97	92	103	114
Rice	85	90	98	95	n.a.
Potatoes	101	102	100	101	102
Sugar[ao]	104	116	91	135	125
Vegetables	n.a.	97	93	97	107[b]
Fresh fruit	n.a.	82	80	83	86[b]
Citrus fruit	n.a.	41	42	43	74[b]
Wine	89	101	99	102	107
Cheese	100	102	102	107	108[bc]
Butter	101	118	101	120	129[bc]
Powdered milk					
unskimmed	139	191	208	411	348
skimmed	97	124	137	142	106[bc]
Beef	92	85	92	105	106[c]
Veal	n.a.	104	104	101	112[c]
Pork	100	99	101	101	102[c]
Poultry	93	100	103	109	n.a.
Meat, total	95	92	96	102	101[c]
Eggs	90	100	100	102	102[bc]
Fish	n.a.	74	57	n.a.	n.a.
Oils and fats	n.a.	44	40	43	n.a.

[a]   Bear in mind, in interpreting the SSR, that many of them are much too low, because the EC includes in demand the quantities which it has been forced to sell on the internal market to low-grade users and at special prices. Corrected for this unrealistic demand, the self-sufficiency ratio for powdered milk for example, goes up from 130 to 470

[b]   1984

[c]   EC10.

n.a. = not available

Sources: 1956–1981: Eurostat, *Basic Community Statistics; Yearbook of Agricultural Statistics; Statistical Yearbook Agriculture*; Supply Balances; Animal Production and Crop Production: *Quarterly Statistics*, various issues country multi-product model (Tims, 1987), has shown that the complete abolition of the EC protective system would favour the LDC as a group only slightly. One reason is that as soon as the EC stops dumping its surpluses on the world market, prices there are bound to rise, to the detriment of the many LDCs who are themselves importers of food.

Price policy and the taxpayer

As surpluses accumulate, the government and hence taxpayer are again asked for increasing contributions. With the EC realising net exports of many products during long time spans, import levies do not suffice to compensate for the cost of restitutions. Moreover, as every additional unit of export tends to have a negative effect on world-market prices, the restitution needed per unit increases accordingly. The costs of stockholding are also steadily waxing. Table 11.7 pictures the budgetary cost of the CAP.

Table 11.7 Outlay (in million Ecu) on the European Guidance and Guarantee Fund for Agriculture, 1968–1987

	1968–72	1973–77	1978–82	1983–87
1 Guarantee	10 100	22 800	55 700	99 000
2 Guidance	300	1 000	2 300	3 900
3 EAGGF	10 400	23 800	58 000	102 900
4 Total budget	11 900	30 900	83 500	151 600
1 as a percentage of 3	97	96	96	96
3 as a percentage of 4	88	77	70	68

Source: CEG, *De toestand van de landbouw in de Gemeenschap*, various years.

From the data underlying this table, the EC's total expenditure on agriculture indeed amounts to almost 1 per cent of total GNP in Europe, having risen very sharply between 1972 and 1987 (EC9).

The burden of the budget is shared 'equally' by the member states (see Chapter 4). The benefits of the CAP, however, tend to go to member states with high national self-sufficiency ratios (SSR) (Strijker and de Veer, 1988). In some studies attempts have been made to measure these redistributional effects on the budget (Koester, 1977; Rollo and Warwick, 1979; Buckwell *et al.*, 1982). The group of states with low SSRs being relatively poor, large compensation amounts need to be paid out to them (for instance to the United Kingdom), which upsets the budgetary balance of the EC. If market disequilibria in agriculture could be avoided, the distributional problems would be much easier to handle.

Conflicts and solutions

Problems and conflicts

The European Commission judged (CEC, 1982b) that the common agricultural policy has realised its objectives on many points. Markets have been stabilised (that is to say, supply has been insured, if at rather high prices). Farmers' incomes increased in the period between 1969 and 1979 at about the same rate as the rest of the economy (they would probably also have done so without any policy, at higher social costs for this group but lower cost for consumer and taxpayer). Production has grown rapidly (by about 7 per cent between 1968 and 1973, by about 5 per cent since). On the other hand, there are enormous problems whose solution requires a thorough adjustment of the CAP, for the CAP objectives as laid down in article 39 of the EC treaty contain an inherent conflict. Indeed, the attempt to keep up agricultural incomes by boosting the price levels has led to a large overproduction: surpluses which have to be stocked and for which special campaigns have to be conducted to sell them on EC or world markets.

Contrary to the political evaluation of the CAP just given, its *economic evaluation* shows many negative points. The first group of losers in the EC are the consumers, because they pay more for their products than necessary. A second group incurring welfare losses are the taxpayers. If consumers pay too much for products they need, taxpayers pay for production nobody really wants. A third group of losers are the third countries (as far as they are net exporters), many of them developing countries. They are facing not only lower export possibilities to the EC, but also lower revenues of their sales to world markets due to dumping by the EC. There are, however, more negative points to be mentioned.[5]

First, one result of the EC price policy is the misallocation of production factors. Agriculture and the industry producing inputs for it are using up resources that could have been better employed elsewhere. Bio-technological industries have difficulties developing, among other reasons because their input prices are too high (sugar, for instance). A considerable area of agricultural land which could have been used for other products (wood, for instance, which is in very short supply in the EC) or for nature reserves is tied up in useless production. In some countries, the high product prices are even leading to the further extension of agricultural land at the expense of woodlands.

A final point to be made refers to the growth potential of the EC economy. The large claims agriculture puts on the budget frustrate the development of programmes for the industrial and service sectors. The common agricultural policy contributes to the compartmentalisation of the EC market (indeed, the Monetary Compensatory Amounts have broken the principle of unity of the market but the programme for completing the internal market by 1992 (see Chapter 16) obliges the EC to discontinue this system).

The negative effects of the high prices on taxpayers, consumers and trade partners and of the MCA on the internal markets are all good reasons why the CAP should be reformed.

A revision of the CAP; different options

How did a policy for a major sector of the economy with considerable negative effects come to be elaborated in the first place? And how could a system so evidently incapable of correction be maintained for so long? These are points of particular interest to analyse. The answer to both questions is largely contained in the workings of the EC institutions (see Chapter 4) in general, and the specialised Council of Agricultural Ministers in particular. Special interest groups have been able (supported by their power in elections) to force decisions, and many observers are now convinced that to understand the CAP, its political rationale should be primarily considered, its economic rationale being at best of secondary importance.[6]

The gigantic production surpluses have made it clear that the policy of market control can no longer be based on guaranteed unlimited sales at fixed prices for practically all products; such guarantees are particularly out of place for products for which the EC is already or will soon be more than 100 per cent self-sufficient (Duchêne et al., 1985). Nor can the present structural policy be maintained, which tends to expand production by increasing productivity. To cope with the problem on the European level, proposals have been made based on two major ideas.

The first type of proposals are *market-oriented*, and carry on the tradition of deficiency payments. They reserve the instrument of price policy for clearing the markets, maintaining some form of market regulation to stabilise prices.[7] In that vein, schemes have been proposed by, among others: van Riemsdijk, 1972; Koester and Tangermann, 1976; Heidhues et al., 1978; Tarditi, 1984; Meester and Strijker 1985. Their evident advantage is that they would further efficient distribution of resources within Europe and between Europe and the rest of the world. Moreover, they would diminish the costs of farmer-aid schemes to both consumer and taxpayer. For some products the EC has taken the road indicated by these proposals by introducing a system of so-called 'stabilisators' (for example, for cereals, oil seeds, etc.). They imply an automatic reduction in the intervention price in case the production exceeds a certain ceiling. If this excess production continues the next year a further reduction is applied until market equilibrium is realised.

Proposals of the second type are more *interventionist*; they tend to maintain high prices while limiting production through production quotas or limited guarantees. Such schemes have now been adopted for milk and sugar (Petit *et al.*, 1987); they involve fixing maximum production levels for each country, and within each country setting a maximum authorised production level for every farmer. The advantage of quota schemes is principally to reduce budget cost. This is illustrated by Figure 11.4. At an intervention price of P_3, production will be at OF and demand at OE, the difference between the two being exported with a subsidy of $P_3 - P_1$ (intervention price minus world market price) at a cost of $IQRL$ to the budget (shaded in Figure 11.4). Introducing a quota system that limits total quantity to OW for the whole of the EC limits the budget cost to $QTIU$ (horizontally shaded in Figure 11.4). It also eases the strain on external relations because the quantity exported to world markets is reduced by WF. However, under this quota system the loss of consumer surplus remains at $ZSQK$ (the same as before in Figure 11.2b), of which QIK is deadweight loss. The deadweight loss on the producer side diminishes by about $UYRL$; as some of the most inefficient producers will continue to produce their quota while some efficient producers have to cut down, the exact amount depends on the share each group has in the quota.[8]

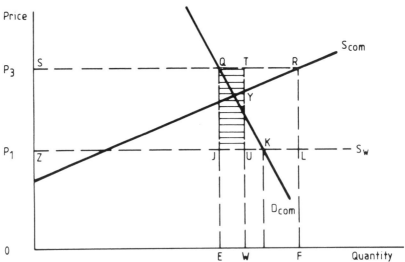

Figure 11.4 The effect of quotas

Another interventionist way to regulate quantities is to limit the use of the production factor land. One option considered is to pay the farmer for not using his land; crop-specific measures are a variation on the same theme (for example, Durand, 1980). One such measure already in operation is that the area under viniculture is not allowed to expand. Although the proposals for interventionist schemes have some appeal to those who think in political terms, most economists reject them because of their serious disadvantages (Tangermann, 1984): they tend to fossilise existing market situations, and block the entry of newcomers (such as Ireland and the United Kingdom into the dairy market). Moreover, persistent high prices tend to put industries using the products as inputs (for instance sugar in biotechnology) at a disadvantage on world markets. Finally, farms holding production authorisations may claim rents that are not economically justified.

Apart from these two major lines of attack, the EC is discussing a whole set of measures to improve the situation, including premiums for voluntary production cuts and buying up farms to take agricultural land out of production.

Measures of *structural policy* have to be revised as well, as the present policy tends to stimulate production in the long run. New measures of structural policy should aim at improving the quality of products rather than increasing productivity.

Finding *alternative products* is the aim of a last group of measures. Not an easy approach in general. One obvious solution is to increase the culture of products for which the EC is not self-sufficient, such as maize and fodder, but to that end the existing external trade relations would have to be revised. There is no such problem if marginal establishments in particular were to switch from agriculture to forestry, the Community being very short of wood and paper. Another possibility would be to put existing agricultural products to commercially sound alternative uses, for instance as input for manufacturing industries or for energy production; biomass especially comes to mind in that connection. That might be profitable notably in countries which combine a weak agricultural structure with very poor domestic energy production. However, from many studies it has become evident that for all such solutions to become operational the overall level of farm prices will have to come down substantially.

Summary and conclusions

- While in the Treaty of Rome a liberal spirit predominated in the sense that market forces were to take care of the orientation of production and the price mechanism was to play its full role, the *sector of agriculture* has been set apart and is in fact *intensely regulated.*

- Heavy pressure has been brought to bear by the farmers – the directly interested – to create mechanisms for the *transfer of money from both consumers and taxpayers* to themselves. The codification of rules in the Treaty of Rome makes it extremely difficult to realise on the political level what should be done on economic grounds.

- The *restructuring of the CAP,* started by the decision of the Council (of April 1986) to stop the raising of agricultural guarantee prices, and even to reduce some of them, together with its refusal to adopt more quota systems, has heralded a view of EC agricultural policy more in line with the rest of the Community principles.

Notes

1   For more elaborate descriptions, in English, of the CAP, readers are referred to books like Harris *et al.* (1983), Hill (1984), Pearce (1981), and Duchêne *et al.* (1985).

2   The fishery policy of the EC has some very distinctive characteristics. Interested readers are referred to CEC (1985b), Farnell and Ellis (1984), Leigh (1984), and Wise (1984).

3   In the period 1970–1980, the number of farms of between 10 and 20 ha also declined strongly in the EC9, while the number of between 20 and 50 ha remained the same and only that of establishments of more than 50 ha increased.

4   Such payments can be compared with production subsidies for industrial products, because they serve a protectionist aim: to increase home production. As farmers have taken them as income-support schemes instead of production-support schemes, the political debate is now transferred to income policies for farmers, although such schemes are practically non-existent for other socio-economic groups in Europe. For a detailed study of the effects of various schemes of income support to farmers, see OECD (1983b).

5   The other OECD countries have schemes with similar negative effects, see Winters (1987).

6   For an analysis of the political economy of the CAP: Pelkmans (1985).

7   Most of these proposals advocate the introduction of a series of new – national or European – instruments to attain other goals, such as subsidies to individual farmers threatened by too large a reduction of their income. Non–agricultural interests such as landscape preservation or maintaining the population in areas threatened by desertification are also being considered.

8   The quota system is not always easy to implement. The EC has introduced a system whereby farmers receive less than the guaranteed price for excess quantities, the difference often being claimed in the form of levies. The solution seems practical only for products with a concentrated organisation of outlets.

12 Manufacturing

Introduction

Historically, manufacturing industry grew out of craft, which in the beginning could hardly be separated from agriculture and trade. For a long time, manufacturing industry remained a relatively small sector. The great Industrial Revolution of the 18th and 19th centuries, involving thorough mechanisation and entailing scale enlargement and concentration, changed the picture drastically. In the first half of the 20th century, manufacturing industry grew into the most important sector in the economy of developed ('industrialised') countries, larger than agriculture and services.

The *definition* of industry, as given by the United Nations (UN) in the International Standard Industrial Classification, comprises all activities in factories processing raw materials into products by machines or manual power. Although formally that definition comprises craft as well, we will focus on the type of industry that uses machines. Industry is not a static concept, but subject to continuous change. The technological revolutions of the last few decades have radically changed the production apparatus as well as the tasks fulfilled within it. The large numbers of 'blue-collar' factory workers marking industry in the beginning have been replaced more and more with the grey and white collars of those concerned with management, research, control, checking, sales and organisation, working in offices, showrooms and laboratories.

Within industry, a number of *sectors of activity* are distinguished mostly by their different products and production processes. Most of them can be clearly delimited, such as foodstuffs, electronics, furniture. With some modern activities, however, the differences are steadily getting vaguer. A case in point is informatics, a sector comprising classical industrial production (like cables and side equipment for telecommunication), less classical industrial activities like the graphic arts, as well as a large number of traditional service sectors such as libraries, telecommunication, etc.

Given the importance of the industrial sector for the growth of the economy, various countries soon began to pursue a *national industrial policy*. An early example of industrial policy was Colbertism. For most countries, however, systematic intervention by governments dates from the present century. The reasons to take up an industrial policy are, in general terms: to take away negative external effects, to make markets transparent and stable, to lower thresholds and reduce the financial risks of companies. To that end, young sectors are stimulated, the conditions of mature sectors guarded, and old sectors assisted in their restructuring.

The growing importance of the industrial sector in the economy has awakened growing interest in industry *by international organisations*. After some hesitation, the United Nations founded a special organisation, UNIDO (United Nations Industrial Development Organisation), which stimulates industrial development in Third World countries by exchanging information and supporting projects. The developed – 'industrial' – countries have formalised their international industrial co-operation in the OECD. Since its foundation, this organisation has carried out comparative studies, collected statistics of various sectors, and compared national policies with respect to industry (and technology). The integration achieved in that way is limited, however.

In Europe, the *European Community* has greatly stimulated international industrial integration. One essential idea of the EC is indeed the common market for industrial products, which implies not only the free movement of goods but also a certain common market regulation and a policy with respect to the renovation of industrial structure.

Those are the points to be discussed in more detail in the next section. Afterwards, we propose first to give a concise description of general industrial development under conditions of international integration (highlighting such aspects as specialisation, concentration, and firm structure). With the help of three case studies (steel, a sector with which European industrial integration started, and two mature sectors: automobiles and white goods), we describe the dynamics of branches of industry at different stages of integration.[1] The final section will recall briefly the most important features of the analysis.

Community regime

Treaties

The Paris Treaty founding the *European Coal and Steel Community* instructs the EC to conduct both a market and a structural policy with respect to the steel sector. The Treaty has endowed the High Authority, now the European Commission, with ample powers for:

- Intervention in the market. Under certain conditions, the Commission may enact minimum prices, determine production quotas, order import restrictions, etc. (article 61, among others); in all cases a system of price transparency functions and a stringent competition policy is pursued. Competition policy covering the supervision of government subsidies is part of the system. Agreements among companies and mergers must first be submitted to the Commission for approval; they are approved only if they serve the objectives of the next point:
- Developing a sound structure. The Commission has preventive control of investments and the power to prohibit some investments. On the other hand, it may give financial support to projects improving the structure, and issue social supportive measures in the case of restructuring of firms and plants.

The Rome Treaty founding the *European Economic Community*, gives the rules for the Community policy in matters of structure and market for all other branches of manufacturing. While being explicit as to an agricultural and transport policy, the Treaty nowhere mentions an industrial policy in the sense of setting the course for and stimulating structural development. At least some of the designers of the Treaty were of the opinion that such a policy was not called for: a healthy competition would keep prices low for the consumer, assure the suppliers' efficient use of production factors, and guarantee the continuous improvement of the quality of the product. In a following section we shall see how that vision was abandoned to some degree later on.

As far as industrial policy in the sense of market regulation is concerned the Rome Treaty is clear-cut; in that area the Community has no task at all, neither with respect to prices nor with regard to quantities; in principle, market parties behave by the rules set by the national states. Only by its competition policy does the Community set the scene for the play of the actors in industry. Like the ECSC Treaty, the EEC Treaty is very explicit on that score. The competition rules in both Treaties purport to prevent companies from actions affecting trade within the Common Market and abusing dominant positions. We will go into the details of the subject in Chapter 16.

Market-control policy; prices and quantities

The *EEC Treaty* does not envisage the regulating of the market for industrial products: self-regulation through the free play of the market mechanism is the central principle. Foreign producers have in general free access to the EC market. Different import levies can be imposed for different products, however, which implies a certain element of price regulation. For certain products, quantitative restrictions can also be imposed on goods entering the Common Market from the outside.

The *ECSC Treaty*, however, permits a farther-reaching market-regulation policy for the steel sector. The Treaty of Paris introduced special rules for steel allowing certain interventions in prices and quantities (see the previous section). In the past the Commission has used its competence in that respect to conquer crises in this sector. After calling a state of 'manifest crisis', the Commission regulated directly both quantities and prices in the steel sector (by the power given it in article 58 ECSC). Quantities were controlled by introducing a system of production and supply quotas by country and by company for a large number of products. In setting the quotas, the position on the market, as well as so-called 'restructuring' aspects for efficient companies, were taken into account. Prices were directly set (by virtue of article 60 of the ECSC) through so-called 'price lists'. Not only producers but also trade are included in this system (article 95 ECSC). Close check is kept to assure that the prices declared are indeed identical to the prices actually charged.

Structural policy: motives

In due time, a mere competition policy was found insufficient to achieve certain structural changes, and a European structural policy for industry was contemplated (CEC 1970; Toulemon and Flory, 1974) and slowly realised (Franzmeyer, 1982; Hall, 1986).

What were the *reasons to proceed* after all to the designing and elaborating of a *European structural policy for industry?*[2] Five have been advanced in the past few decades with fluctuating emphasis:

- *International competitive power:* competition among the countries of the Community, often fought with such weapons as differential technical standards, government procurement, etc., has tended to weaken Europe's competitive position on world markets, especially in respect of the United States and Japan.
- *Enlarging the financial capacity:* some projects have such heavy financing requirements or carry so much risk (space travel, informatics) as to exceed the financing capacity of a single member state.
- *Enlargement of scale:* to give a European dimension to enterprise, transnational mergers of companies are furthered.[3] To that end, a 'Marriage Bureau' was founded in Brussels. The policy has not always been successful, however.
- *Restructuring of old sectors:* sectors fallen into decline through loss of sales or otherwise often cannot, or can only at very high societal cost, be restored to a healthy condition. For many of such

sectors (for instance shipbuilding, steel) the national frameworks are too limited; they need a European policy to support their adjustment.

- *Technological innovation*: when member states and companies have but limited means, the EC should step in to stimulate technology, especially for such modern sectors as computers and telecommunication.

In the first period of the EC, the emphasis was heavily on the first three arguments. During the recession of the 1970s and early 1980s, the old sectors were in the limelight. Recently the aspect of technological innovation, particularly of the modern growth sectors, has come to the fore.

Structural policy: instruments

To the Community, as to the individual member states, six *instruments* are effectively available (Rothwell and Zegveld, 1981). We shall briefly discuss how each of them can be used by the European Community.

Exchange of economic and technical information is of great value to those committed to decisions on the government or the private level, particularly in a period of fast technical progress and much uncertainty about the external environment. The Commission is active in that respect by furthering information as well as scientific and technical documentation. Accelerated technological progress and changes in the international environment have made a good insight into possible medium- and long-term developments not only more necessary, but also harder to achieve. In recent years, therefore, many more prognoses have been drawn up and pilot studies carried out than before, both in private business and on the initiative of governments or international organisations.

Financial intervention is far preferred as an instrument for governments to deal with production structures, in the form of either direct support (subsidies or favourable loans) or tax relief. The treaties of the Community leave taxes a national matter; on the other hand, they make it possible to receive two main kinds of European financial support:

- The transfer of means from the Community budget. However, for a long time budget funds reserved for structural, non-agricultural purposes used to be set aside for nuclear research. Later on, some more variety was introduced in favour of research in other areas. For some years the budget has also set aside certain funds for the financing of industrial programmes;
- The granting of loans. Although the EC's financial leeway on that score is still limited, the important thing is that the instrument

exists legally and may gain force in future. Next to the operations of the Commission, the operations of the European Investment Bank (EIB) have to be cited.

In sum, the EC's means for financial stimulation have so far been limited, and mostly served as a complement to national schemes.

Technical standards and norms count in many countries as effective protection against competition by third parties. On the other hand, such norms can stimulate endeavours towards certain social achievements, such as curbing pollution and protection of consumers or people in employment. The EC has steadily tried to harmonise such norms on the European level. However, regulation on the EC level is but rarely used as an instrument to further innovation (motorcar exhaust gas!); mostly it serves to strengthen the internal market ('1992') (Chapter 16).

Government procurement is frequently used in all countries to stimulate the development of certain production strains on the national level; especially in sectors of advanced technology, national suppliers tend to receive preferential treatment. As far as such preference implies discrimination against products from other member states, it is obviously in conflict with the Common Market. Effective use of the instrument of preferential procurement has not yet been achieved on the European level; so far, the Commission has just tried to keep the negative effects for Europe of its use on the national level within bounds. The EC policy in this respect has got a new impetus with the '1992' programme (see Chapter 16).

Trade policy, too, can be put at the service of industrial policy, but the EC has but little scope. The preamble to the EEC Treaty explicitly states the principle of 'open-door policy' towards other countries: 'Desiring to contribute ... to the progressive abolition of restrictions on international trade.' However, sectoral problems have constantly prevented full adherence to that principle. For one thing, agreements were concluded with trade partners for the voluntary export restriction of sensitive products; the multifibre agreement is a case in point. For another, in particular with respect to Japanese products some 'voluntary export restrictions' (of cars, for instance) have been agreed to. Finally, higher import tariffs are sometimes introduced for a limited time, to enable European producers to improve their competitive position by building up a home market of their own. (The last-mentioned instrument will be discussed in some more detail in Chapter 19, External Relations.)

Industrial policy tends to be organised in a cumbrous and aloof manner. Recently, the Commission is favouring more emphasis on direct consultation with industry to try and reach agreement on technical norms, future market development, and other relevant matters. The aim is to devise a policy agreeable to all those involved (including national governments and industrial associations). The new approach has proved highly effective, as could be expected from Japanese practice. The drawback is that it may be at cross purposes with the European competition policy.

Schemes to stimulate innovation

In the 1980s, the EC has progressively focused on the stimulation of modern industries. To that end, various schemes have been designed. Their common aim is to achieve real co-operation of companies, research laboratories and universities in various European countries. Consequently, European financial support is given to projects in which companies and institutions from several member states are involved. To avoid problems with European competition policy, all schemes address the so-called 'precompetitive stage' of technical development. Afterwards, each company is at liberty to exploit the common results to develop and market its own products.

Since 1986, three schemes have been in operation to stimulate the branches of activity based on the principal new technologies: informatics, telecommunication, and biotechnology. Besides, there is a scheme for rendering the results of all modern research applicable to all sectors, traditional ones included. The positive effect of the new approach induced the intensified continuation of the efforts (CEC, 1989). We must not leave unmentioned in this connection the EUREKA programme, set in motion outside the EC framework, in which 18 countries participate. This research programme covers quite a number of subjects; its objectives and means are very much like the EC programmes mentioned above. Another matter worth mentioning is that some successful co-operative associations of industries in various member states have been accomplished (with the co-ordinated support of some governments), meant to make certain products ripe for marketing. Airbus, the European consortium for civil aeroplanes, is a well-known example; Ariane, a group of companies occupying itself with space travel, is another.

Sketch of the sector

Development of branches

The manufacturing sector is of considerable importance to the economy of the EC countries, as Table 12.1 shows.

Table 12.1   Percentage share of manufacturing in total GDP and total employment, 1950–1985 (EC12)

	1950	1960	1970	1980	1985
GDP[a]	n.a.	40	36	33	32
Employment	29	32	33	28	25

[a] Inclusive of Mining, Public Utilities, Energy (approximately 3 per cent)
Sources: GDP: OECD National Account Statistics;
            Employment: 1950–1970 NEI FLEUR data base; 1970–1985 OECD
            Labour-force statistics
n.a. = not available

Although its relative importance has declined since 1970 in favour of the service sector, the manufacturing sector still accounts for one in four of all jobs in the Community, and a third of total wealth creation. For such an important sector we cannot be satisfied with only a succinct description of the totals, but have to go down to branches.

Schumpeter taught us that the life cycle of every product begins with an innovation, or rather an invention followed by an innovation.[4]

Table 12.2   Employment (million) in manufacturing by branch, (EC12) 1950–1985

Goods	1950	1960	1970	1980	1985
Food, beverages, tobacco	3.5	4.0	3.9	3.6	3.3
Textiles, clothing, footwear	8.0	7.5	6.4	4.7	3.8
Wood, furniture	2.3	2.2	2.1	2.0	1.7
Paper + printing	1.5	2.0	2.3	2.2	1.9
Chemicals + rubber	1.8	2.5	3.0	3.1	2.8
Non-metallic mineral products	1.4	1.7	1.8	1.6	1.4
Basic metals	1.6	2.1	2.1	1.8	1.3
Metal products	2.3	2.9	3.2	3.0	2.5
Non-electrical machinery	2.4	3.5	4.0	3.7	3.1
Electrical machinery	1.5	2.6	3.2	3.1	2.7
Transport equipment	3.0	4.0	4.8	4.6	3.8
Other	1.1	1.5	1.8	1.8	1.6
Total	30.4	36.5	38.6	35.2	29.9

Sources: NEI: FLEUR-data
            Eurostat: various sources
            Estimates based on national statistics.

Schumpeter saw innovation as the kingpin of the individual entrepreneur's activity: the *'Durchsetzung neuer Kombinationen!'* (realisation of new combinations). However, the individual entrepreneur is not all there is. There are indeed intervening processes, each giving rise to whole new groups of products, which frequently coincide with branches or *sectors* of industry. The economy is therefore often divided into new or growth sectors (like chemical products after the war, and informatics now), and stagnating sectors (such as furniture and lately perhaps also motorcars). The result is that the importance of sectors within total industry tends to vary considerably through time.[5]

A picture of the *long-term growth and decline of manufacturing branches* in the EC economy is given in Table 12.2 (presenting employment figures, the only indicator for which long time series could be made comparable in some detail). The metal industry (ranging from basic metals to transport equipment) is by far the largest sector. The table also indicates that employment in all sectors of manufacturing industry has declined absolutely since 1970. Much can be explained by improved productivity: in terms of production (Gross Value Added) many sectors have indeed remained stable or even grown.

In some sectors the drop in employment started early, especially in such traditional industries as textile and clothing, wood and furniture. Their share in total manufacturing employment dropped between 1950 and 1985 by almost half. By contrast, chemicals and metals were obvious growth industries in the period 1950-1980: their shares increased considerably.

Table 12.3   The ten largest manufacturing firms based in the EC (private ownership), 1972–1984, by world-wide employment

	Name	Country	1972	1984
1	Philips	Netherlands	371	344
2	Unilever	UK/NL	337	319
3	Siemens	F.R. Germany	301	319
4	Volkswagen	F.R. Germany	192	238
5	Fiat	Italy	190	231
6	British American Tobacco	United Kingdom	152	213
7	Daimler Benz	F.R. Germany	150	200
8	Peugeot/Citroen	France	n.a.	188
9	Hoechst	F.R. Germany	146	178
10	Bayer	F.R. Germany	104	175

Source: Fortune; n.a. = not available

Size of European firms

Following the development of the world's largest manufacturing firms in the past decades, one is immediately struck by the dominance of American firms. Most European firms belong to the world's sub-top (places 20 and following). Size is mostly measured by sales, but employment is another much-used indicator. Ranked by employment, the largest European firms give the following display. Table 12.3 shows that the largest firms are concentrated in very few sectors: automobiles (four), chemicals (two), electric machinery (two), and food and tobacco (two). Germany is very well represented on the list with four firms; in relative terms that is also true of The Netherlands. Most EC countries do not show up on the list at all. A final point of interest is that the ranking of the firms had hardly changed during the period of analysis.

Specialisation, economies of scale, and location

The EC was conceived as a potential for the better allocation of resources through specialisation and large-scale industrial production. Notably in manufacturing, economies of scale are very important (see, among others, Pratten, 1988), and therefore an analysis of the effects of the formation of the EC on production, direct investment and marketing is in order. To illustrate these effects, we have established Figure 12.1, that gives the differences in strategy and internal organisation of multi-product, multinational companies under different trade and direct investment regimes. A good example of a firm that has ex-

Trade regime	Location of production units for each product	Dominant part of firm
Free trade	one plant (usually home base)	production and export
Protectionism	numerous plants; one in each major national market	national companies
Integration	limited number of plants at good locations	matrix of national and product organisations
Free internal market	one optimal location	international product divisions

Figure 12.1 Production and trade patterns of multinational, multi-product companies under different trade regimes

perienced these changes in environment is Philips, and we will now briefly describe how its strategy has evolved through history (Muntendam, 1987).

As electric light became popular, Philips rapidly increased its production of light bulbs and taking advantage of *the liberalist trade environment already in the first decade of the century*, set up an international sales organisation (compare line 1 of Figure 12.1). The company moved into other products like radio sets and domestic appliances and mainly cashed in on the internalisation advantage (see Chapter 6), guaranteeing the quality of its products through horizontal and vertical integration of other production stages. As early as 1910, Philips had established sales companies in 18 European countries, and eight more in other countries of the industrialised world. Most were supplied by the plants at the home-base Eindhoven, built for low-cost, large-scale production, and some by local production plants that Philips had acquired through mergers to strengthen its market position. Under such conditions the dominant parts of the firm are the production and export department.

In the *1930s, the surge of protectionist measures* taken by European governments (see Chapter 3) compelled the company to change its strategy thoroughly. It switched to the exploitation of ownership advantage and its direct investments became of the tariff jumping type (see Chapter 6). First, assembly lines for each of the major products were set up in every individual country in whose market Philips was well established. This was soon followed by the creation of national Philips companies, which became responsible for the production and local marketing of all Philips products. Quite naturally these national companies, having to gear their production to local taste, also acquired some responsibility for product development and, needing to survive in their specific environments, also for the development of production technology. Conditions during and immediately after the war only reinforced the system of geographically decentralised combined production and selling units.

When the *formation of the EC in the 1960s* opened up the markets, Philips once more drastically revised its strategy. Now the exploitation of locational advantages became the central element. First, national companies were forced to co-ordinate their production and export policies; for this co-ordination a matrix structure of multi-product national companies and international single-product divisions was formed. Next, they were integrated in a centralised international system based on product division. Factories in different countries producing one specific product for the national market were integrated in one system, production now geared to the international market being gradually concentrated in a single plant. This reflects a direct investment behaviour of the 'optimal location type' (see Chapter 6).

The major plants which used to produce a whole array of products, now were made to specialise in only one or two products.

Recently, this European strategy of specialisation and product division has been extended all over the world for effective world-wide competition (Teulings, 1984).

Concentration

The average size of firms is generally a function of the size of the home market (Pryor, 1972). Moreover, the concentration ratios tend to be equal in markets of different sizes (Scherer, 1974). Those findings suggest that the creation of a large integrated market area like the EC will entail an increase in average firm size and a higher concentration in national and EC markets. There is evidence that this has indeed happened. An early EC study (CEC 1974) showed for the EC6 that in 1962, in 13 out of 46 sectors of activity, the four largest firms had a market share of over 50 per cent; by 1969, that number had gone up to 18 out of 46.

The European integration process has induced the creation of some very large multinational corporations, which have gradually increased their share in the EC market. One way to measure this is through the *overall top-50 ratio*. After a hesitant start (between 1960 and 1965 the ratio remained stable), the 50 largest companies increased their shares in the output of the total manufacturing sector from 15 to 30 per cent between 1965 and 1980, accounting in 1980 for about one-fifth of the sector's total employment. The next largest 50 accounted, in 1980, for another 10 per cent of jobs and 15 per cent of output (Geroski and Jacquemin, 1984). Other measures, such as the top four, eight, 30, etc. convey the same message; their share in total output increased significantly in the 1960–1976 period (Jacquemin and de Jong, 1977; Locksey and Ward, 1979).

Mergers of large firms naturally influence concentration. An analysis of the mergers among the thousand largest firms in the EC since 1976, based on the Annual Reports on Competition of the Commission (de Jong, 1987) showed that the majority of mergers are of the horizontal type. The principal motive for such mergers is 'critical mass': to increase efficiency, obtain a better competitive position, and spread R & D costs over longer series. Increased European integration did not lead to more cross-border European mergers (Lemaitre and Goybet, 1984). That is due to the differences among firms of different countries in management strategies, cultural traditions, government intervention, and legal practices. Moreover, firms tried to strengthen their position on the national market, as is illustrated by the fact that in the past period three out of every four mergers were still oriented to national markets. However, the imminent completion of the internal market has changed that: after years (1971-1983) of stability the number of mergers increased considerably and so did the share of international ones[6] (see further Chapter 16).

An interesting question is *how the large European manufacturing firms perform in comparison with their American and Japanese counterparts.* Geroski and Jacquemin (1984) report that the EC and the USA had comparable numbers of firms in *Fortune's* Top 100 (19 and 23, respectively), while Japan had only a few. That does not say much about their relative performances, however. Indeed, as the next table shows, European firms compared poorly to their competitors, their outputs by employee and their profitability ratios being much lower. The result is not due to the choice of data; indeed, Geroski and Jacquemin have shown that an analysis of figures relating to the five largest firms in each of 12 different industries, instead of the broad aggregate data of Table 12.4, gives the same results. The conclusion must be that while European firms were comparable in size to US ones and considerably larger than their Japanese sisters, European performance was much inferior to both American and Japanese achievements. This conclusion points to a significantly lower cohesion in European industrial and market structures, possibly due to cultural, legal and political differences among the member countries of the EC. This situation has convinced decision makers of the necessity of the programme to do away with a large number of such barriers to better performance (see Chapter 16).

Table 12.4 International comparison of the performances of firms by relative firm size (100 largest), 1980

	EC	USA	Japan
Output/worker (1000 Ecu)	61	75	102
Net income/sales ratio	1.4	4.8	2.7

Source: Geroski and Jacquemin (1984)

Case study 1: steel

Structure of the industry; no international integration of firms

Traditionally, technological change used to push the European steel industry towards operation on ever *larger scales*. Concentration took the form of vertical integration (coal, iron ore, iron and steel making, and metal working). At the beginning of the 1950s, the situation of the

European steel industry was marked by the existence of a large number of firms, tending to be linked (via financial groups) to other firms in the same sector, located in the same region. There was hardly any international integration. Some Belgian capital had penetrated into companies of the Lorraine district; the Dutch blast-furnace company Hoogovens controlled the German firm of Hörder, and the Luxemburg and Saar industries were to some extent controlled by French and Belgian capital. International trade in iron and steel was limited. After the creation of the ECSC in 1952, competition soon made further concentration imperative. Continued technical progress in all parts of the industry in the period 1950–1985 increased the necessity. For the years up to 1960, the exact magnitude of the development is hard to assess; the scanty information nevertheless permits the conclusion that the 1950s were marked by the disappearance of many small plants and firms. Adler (1970) shows that the process of adjusting to the new large ECSC market went hand in hand with increased intra-industry specialisation among European firms, with all countries developing certain product lines. So, the fear that one country (Germany) would use its good starting position to dominate European industry did not come true. The development after 1960 (apart from very small plants producing less than 0.5 Mt/y) is given in the next table.

Table 12.5   Estimated number of steel plants by size category (Mt/y) in the EC9

Capacity	1960	1970	1980
0.5 – 2.0	56	62	18
2.0 – 5.0	7	15	28
over 5.0	-	1	9
Total	63	78	55

Source: Boeckhout and Molle (1982); estimates based on *Iron and Steel Works of the World*. Several issues.

Ever since the war, firms have been *regrouping and merging* in a constant process of concentration; the tendency towards very few, very large-scale plants has been accentuated by the restructuring measures of the years since 1980. From the analysis of regroupings in the original EC6, at first concentration appears to have followed a regional pattern. Evidently such technical factors as economies of scale, transportation costs and labour-force adaptations induced firms to join efforts with firms close by rather than with firms in other countries. From a low spatial level (Liège, Sambre, Dortmund, for example), the concentration movement widened to operations on a larger scale. In France, the government stimulated the formation of the groups Usinor in the north and Sacilor in Lorraine; similar developments took place in the Ruhr area. Likewise, in Spain, Ensidesa regrouped firms in the Asturias, and Altos Hornos companies in the Viscaya district. Arbed integrated steel firms in the Luxemburg/Saar/Lorraine area into what became practically the only international steel company in Europe; later, Estel fused the German Hoesch group with Dutch Hoogovens.

Several factors caused the next round of concentrations to remain mostly within national borders. In Italy, the large financial holding of the State (Finnsider) assured a lively interest in the development of the national steel industry. In the United Kingdom, the nationalisation of the steel industry led to national concentration. In Belgium, France and Germany the crisis of the mid-1970s induced the governments to step in with very substantial aid, given in exchange for a certain measure of control of the developments that invariably led to concentration on the national level. The Estel group fell victim to pressure, and the German

Table 12.6 Largest European steel producing firms with a crude steel output of over 1 Mt/y and concentration ratios, 1985

Company	Country	Mt/y	% of national production
Finnsider	IT	13.5	57
British Steel	UK	13.3	83
Thyssen	FRG	11.9	29
Sacilor	FR	10.6	57
Usinor	FR	8.1	43
Hoogovens	NL	5.3	96
Ensidesa	ESP	4.5	n.a.
Klockner	FRG	4.5	11
Cockerill Sambre	B	4.5	42
Krupp	FRG	4.2	10
Hoesch	FRG	4.1	10
Arbed	LUX	3.9	100
Peine Salzgitter	FRG	3.8	9
Saarstahl	FRG	2.7	7

Source: International Iron and Steel Institute
n.a. = not available

Hoesch group was forced to participate in a 'German' regrouping.

In the EC as a whole there is not yet much concentration. The four largest companies account for about two-fifths and the eight largest for about three-fifths of total production (Oberender and Rüter, 1988). The table below gives an impression of the result of the process of growth and concentration.

Little integration of markets due to public intervention

After a period of continuous growth, in which capacity was expanded in line with demand, there was a major shock in 1974 (see Table 12.7).The total production of crude steel in what is now the EC12 dropped by 20 per cent between 1974 and 1985, and has decreased even further since. A considerable overcapacity (capacity-utilisation level: approximately 2/3) was the result, and the industry had to restructure in depth, closing down the older plants and laying off hundreds of thousands of employees. However, micro-economic as well as social factors spoke against the reduction. Given their very high fixed costs, firms were prepared for drastic price cuts to stay in the market. When that strategy threatened to make some of them go bankrupt, the government moved in with subsidies to maintain employment. In the whole of the EC, these amounted to a total of some 50 billion (10^9) Ecu for the 1980-1986 period in the whole of the EC. They have led to the*de*

Table 12.7   Some characteristic data on the Community (EC12) steel industry, 1950–1985

	1950	1960	1974	1980	1985
Capacity (effective)	n.a.	104	196	220	191
Crude-steel production (Mt/y)	49	99	168	141	135
Employment in steel industry (1000) (restricted definition)	n.a.	975	895	749	509
Net exports (third countries) (Mt/y)	6	12	21	26	21
Intra-EC trade as percentage of total trade[a]					
exports	n.a.	46	52	54	52
imports	n.a.	82	81	73	73

OECD: The Iron and Steel Industry, various years; *The Steel Market in 1981*
Eurostat: *Iron and Steel Yearbook*
[a] EC6 in 1960 and 1974; EC9 in 1980 and 1985.
n.a. = not available

facto nationalisation of large parts of the industry (over 80 per cent in the UK, France, Denmark; over 60 per cent in Italy, Belgium and Luxemburg).

Faced with this situation, the *Commission has used its powers from the ECSC treaty to restructure the industry and stabilise markets*. In the mid-1970s the EC Commission negotiated a programme of voluntary restriction of output by all producers. That was no longer sufficient when the second crisis occurred in the 1980s. Declaring a situation of manifest crisis, the Commission applied articles 58 and 61 of the ECSC treaty to introduce a system of production quotas and minimum prices.[7] The practical implication is that the European market broke down into national markets, largely fed by national production. Market integration, re-established only gradually, one product group after the other, has recently been completed. Because firms tended to remain predominantly oriented to their home (national) markets (Boeckhout and Molle, 1982), the international specialisation remained limited in the study period. The economic appraisal of the crisis management of the EC is not very positive; adaptation has taken very long and welfare costs have been very high (Oberender and Rüter, 1988).

Case study 2: cars

Firm structure; little international integration of firms

In a previous section we saw that four out the ten largest European firms were in the automotive sector. It shows how important are economies of scale in that industry. Consequently, the concentration of firms in European car manufacturing is fairly high. Between 1969 and 1986 the industry was dominated by five European 'volume' producers (Volkswagen, Peugeot, Renault, Fiat, and British Leyland), two US multinationals (Ford and GM; together taking up 76 per cent of the production in 1963 and 89 per cent in 1986), and a number of high-performance specialists (Daimler-Benz, BMW, Volvo). Concentration has not advanced much; from Table 12.8 we can calculate that the four largest producers accounted for about half of total production in 1963 and about three-fifths in 1986. The European volume producers were national champions in the sense that most of their production facilities were concentrated in one country, were controlled by capital from their home country, and very often enjoyed government support. In the 1950s and early 1960s the European volume producers concentrated on family cars with idiosyncratic national styles, which meant that they were oriented to their national markets. Since then, styles and technology have converged into one rather homogeneous product, which can be sold on national and foreign markets. More than before attention was on minimising unit cost by large production series. In the face of increased competition a tendency to concentrate along national lines prevailed (except for takeovers by US concerns), smaller firms being gradually absorbed by the larger ones. The only major attempt for an international takeover by a European firm (Citroën being acquired by Fiat) failed, and after considerable intervention of the French government, Citroën was finally integrated with Peugeot.

The following table gives an idea of the volume increase of the most important producers. The smaller producers, most of whom lost their independence in the past,[8] have been left out. The table indicates the shifts in European car making from the United Kingdom (where the industry is stagnating) to France, which recently lost ground to Ger-

Table 12.8   Production (x 1000) of the largest European car manufacturers in the EC12, (over 100 000 a year in 1986)

Country	Company	1963	1986
Germany	VW/Audi	989	1775
	GM (Opel)	360	897
	Ford	270	562
	Daimler-Benz	254	592
	BMW	44	432
France	Renault	499	1304
	Citroën/Panhard	348⎤	
	Peugeot/Talbot	237⎬	1469
	Simca[a]	251⎦	
UK	BMC-Rover	475	404
	Ford	370	346
	GM (Vauxhall)	145	162
	Rootes (Peugeot)[a]	135	58
Netherlands	Volvo	n.a.	119
Belgium	Ford	n.a.	256
Italy	Fiat (AR/Lancia)	748	1652
Spain	VW/Seat	n.a.	318
	Renault	n.a.	231
	Ford	n.a.	257
	GM	n.a.	304
	Peugeot/Citroën	n.a.	171
Total		5,125	11,309

Source: *L'Argus de l'automobile*, various years
[a] Merged first with Chrysler, later with Peugeot
n.a. = not available

many, Italy and in particular Spain, where many firms have established production facilities.

Trade structure; fair integration of markets

The *overall position vis-à-vis* the *outside world* is given in the next table, picturing how the export performance of the EC and its openness to producers from third countries have developed since 1960.

Table 12.9 Production and consumption of, and external trade in, cars in the EC 1960–1985 (millions)

	1960	1970	1978	1985[a]
Production	4.8	10.2	11.3	11.8
Imports	n.a.	0.2	0.8	1.8
Japan	(-)	(0.1)	(0.6)	(1.4)
Exports	1.1	1.8	1.8	1.2
Consumption	3.7	8.4	10.3	12.4

Source: See Tables 12.8 and 12.10
[a] Provisional,.
n.a. = not available

The European industry, while falling behind on export markets mostly in favour of the Japanese, has been able to retain much of its home market. Against all kinds of impediments the Japanese managed to capture as much as 12 per cent of the market in 1986, from a negligible beginning in the years the EC was established.

To study the *interpenetration of markets in the EC* we follow Owen (1983)[9] in using as indicator the shares the three largest producers had in total sales on their national home markets. This indicator has the advantage of also taking into account the growing openness of the EC towards third countries. Table 12.10 shows the – foreseeable – considerable and consistent decrease of the indicator between 1962 and 1986.

The European car industry presents an interesting example of the integration of markets in the EC. Initial tariffs were high (20 to 40 per cent), and international trade was hampered by the intervention of governments in car production, the absence of dealer networks, etc. Moreover, scale economies are very important in the car industry, probably even more so for parts than for final goods. So there is ample room for scale-driven exports. Indeed, large producers can use their savings on cost to penetrate foreign markets. To stop such inroads into

Table 12.10 Shares of the three largest national producers in home market sales

Country	Companies	1962	1970	1977	1986
Germany	VW, GM, Ford	78	66	62	54
France	Renault, Peugeot, Citroën	81	70	69	63
United Kingdom	BL, GM, Ford	77	76	49	43
Italy	Fiat, AR, Lancia	89	72	64	60

Source: Tatsachen und Zahlen, Automotive News, various years

their home markets, producers of other countries are forced to take up exporting as well.

The trade structure of the finished product hides, however, the enormous specialisation and hence *international trade in parts.* Dicken (1986) gives the example of the Ford Escort model, the final assembly of which takes place in the United Kingdom and Germany, but parts are provided by factories in eight EC countries, four EFTA countries, as well as the USA, Canada and Japan.

Dynamics of integration

Integration processes take a long time to take effect. As Hocking (1980) has shown, the negative relation between the size of the home market and the volume of imports in the 1960s had diminished but still persisted to some extent by the mid-1970s, some 15 years after the start of the EC.

The *pattern of integration* is heavily influenced by economies of scale. Owen (1983) shows for the period from 1955 to 1976 how the relative performance of French producers deteriorated every time their unit cost went out of line with that of their German competitors. The effect thereof in terms of change in market shares became larger the higher the penetration of the two countries in each other's markets became.

The above findings give evidence of an increasing integration of the EC car market. However, integration *is still far from perfect* for two reasons:

- Some member states maintain protectionist measures against third country producers. Italy, for one, restricts its imports of Japanese cars to 2300 a year, a quota dating from before the foundation of the EC. Furthermore, since 1977 there has been a bilateral agreement between the French and Japanese governments to restrict the Japanese share in the French market to 3 per cent. Finally, British and Japanese associations of car manufacturers have voluntarily agreed to confine the Japanese share to 10 to 11 per cent. Such Voluntary Export Restraints (CEC 1983a; OECD 1987e) have led to physical checks of all cars at some intra-EC borders.

* By their control over dealers manufacturers are able to fix different prices on different national markets, for various reasons: tax pressure leads to low net prices in Denmark; high penetration of foreign cars leads to low prices in Belgium. On the other hand, alignment to prices of the major national producer and a market protected by left-hand driving (few parallel imports) leads to high prices in the United Kingdom, producers preferring greater benefits from limited sales volumes to higher market shares at lower prices (BEUC, 1982).[9] The Commission has tried to do away with this price discrimination by favouring the possibility of parallel imports, with some success (BEUC, 1986). However, the price discrimination is also related to the tax system, companies feeling forced to reduce pre-tax prices in countries with a very heavy tax burden on cars (Murfin, 1985). This can only be solved by tax harmonisation (see Chapter 16).

To sum up: the European motor-car industry has gone through a profound restructuring process, owing to pressure from US and increasingly also Japanese firms. US firms pursued their concept of a 'global motor industry' by investing directly in Europe, while Japanese firms supplied Europe from their home factories. European producers have enjoyed substantial protection against Japanese car imports and sometimes large-scale government support for their restructuring efforts. Market integration has progressed much, but most firms remain national champions, their positions outside their home country sometimes being vulnerable.

Case-study 3: white goods

Structure of industry; European and world competitors

The white-goods industry shows in an interesting way how market integration sharpened competition, forcing European manufacturers to respond by progressive international specialisation. Following Maillet (1977), Mueller (1981), and Owen (1983), we will use the *refrigerator industry* as an illustration. The manufacture of refrigerators has greatly flourished in the last three decades: from a luxury item in the possession of only a few families, the product has become standard household equipment with a very high degree of penetration (practically 100 per cent in the higher developed West European countries).

In the late 1950s, *Italian industry*, by combining some major innovations in the production and product technology with the standardisation of the product range of refrigerators, achieved enormous economies of scale. After considerable concentration in the early 1960s, the three largest national producers (Ignis, Zanussi, and Indesit) together accounted for more than three-quarters of Italian production by the mid-1970s.

Dynamics of trade and production; full integration of markets

The cost advantage achieved by the mergers enabled the Italian producers to penetrate very quickly into the markets of the other EC countries. The next table gives an idea. By the mid-1960s the Italians had captured over two-fifths of the German and British markets and 66 per cent of the French market.

Table 12.11 Production of and trade in refrigerators, 1958–1972 (1000 units)

	Italy		Germany		UK		France	
	1958	1972	1958	1972	1958	1972	1958	1972
Production	500	5400	1550	1700	360	1110	580	500
Exports	n.a.	3900	n.a.	470	n.a.	190	n.a.	50
Imports	n.a.	30	n.a.	870	n.a.	580	8	890
from Italy	n.a.	–	n.a.	710	n.a.	n.a.	n.a.	600
Imports/ Consumption %	5	2	3	40	–	42	1	65

Source: Owen (1983), Maillet (1977), Mueller (1981), additional estimates.
n.a. = not available

Producers in the other European countries responded in three ways. Some tried to merge with others in their countries to form a company of the size required for successful competition. Others decided to give up the fridge market altogether, concentrating on other products. Others again stopped their domestic production but stayed in business by taking shares in Italian firms. The process was the same in all major European countries where companies had been shaken up by Italian competition. In the period 1965–1970, the French firms Thomson-Houston, Hotchkiss-Brandt and Claret merged to form Thomson-Brandt; firms like Frigidaire and Arthur Martin who did not join in, had to withdraw. In the same period, the German firms Bosch and Siemens merged, and so did AEG-Linde-BBC; again, several firms withdrew from the market. The United Kingdom was at the time not yet a member of the EC; in its protected market three domestic producers merged in the late 1960s to form BDA; others left the trade, so that by 1978 there were three producers left: Thorn, BDA, and Electrolux. Dutch Philips stopped its own production but took over Ignis in 1970, while AEG acquired a one-fifth stake in Zanussi in 1972. Still others continued only as commercial operators, leaving production to (Italian) large-scale producer firms.

All in all, the case of the white-goods industry shows very well how market integration permitted low-cost foreign producers to push smaller high-cost producers from their domestic markets. The additional sales thus realised enabled them to achieve further scale economies, and thus to displace (marginal) competitors.[10]

Recently, a similar development is occurring on the world level, with some very large companies (Whirlpool, Electrolux), having taken over a number of competitors, competing for world markets (Bianchi and Forlai, 1988).

Summary and conclusions

- The industry of the EC has gone through a process of *profound structural change*. New sectors of activity have developed (electronics), older ones (shipbuilding) have faded out. That has caused the creation of many new jobs and new firms on the one hand, and the loss of many jobs and firms on the other. It has also meant the relocation of activities within and outside the EC.

- The *creation of the EC has not affected all sectors* in the same way; some have responded quickly and are now characterised by firms with European dimensions and much intra-industry trade; others have been kept sheltered by various types of government intervention and are not much integrated, as witness the price differences among countries, the existence in certain sectors of national champions to which large parts of home markets are reserved, etc. This situation is likely to change now that the execution of the internal market programme (1992) is tearing down the remaining obstacles to free internal trade of goods and the free flow of production factors.

- As far as *industrial policy* is concerned, the attitude of the EC is fairly non-interventionist; market forces, regulated by competition policy, are supposed to take care of the process of change. The EC does stimulate, however, the renewal of industry by positive action in the field of innovation (R & D).

Notes

1   Another interesting case study of integration is the agricultural supply industry. See McCorrison and Sheldon (1987).
2   In legal terms, this extension of the EC competence is based on article 235 EEC, which says:

> if action by the Community should prove necessary to obtain in the course of the operation of the Common Market one of the objectives of the Community and this treaty has not provided the necessary powers, the Council shall, acting unanimously on a proposal from the Commission and after consulting the Assembly, take the appropriate measures.

3   This idea was presented first in the EC memorandum on industrial policy (CEC 1970). This document suggested facilitating the creation of large companies that could face the competition of American and Japanese firms on internal as well as external markets. The necessity of acquiring a sufficient size of operation is evidenced by the cost reduction made possible by large-scale production and marketing (Pratten, 1988); the effectiveness of liberalising trade in a common market as a tool to achieve large scale is demonstrated in Schwalbach (1988) and Helg and Ranci (1988).
4   For a number of case studies of innovative behaviour in Europe, see Sharp (1985).
5   For a general discussion of the relation between sectoral growth, life cycles and industrial policy, see de Jong (1984).
6   For an analysis of the roots of multinationalisation of European firms, see Wilkins (1986).
7   To complement these measures, the Commission also negotiated VERs with, among others, Japan and East European countries. It was in turn confronted with import restrictions on EC steel in the USA.
8   The disappearance of the independent smaller producers even in the high quality segments (SAAB, Volvo, Jaguar) is due to the ever increasing development costs which have become one of the major components of economies of scale.
9   Consult this source also for indications of the order of magnitude of the economies of scale, details of trade within the EC, and many other relevant aspects of the car and white-goods industries.
10   We shall come back to this problem in the 'internal-market' debate in Chapter 16.
11   The washing-machine industry developed very similarly to the refrigerator industry. However, because washing machines need more service after sales and because producers in other countries promptly reacted by making mergers of their own, the Italians did not manage to make as many inroads into other European markets. For a discussion of the development in later years of the white-goods industry, see Stopford and Baden-Fuller (1987).

13 Energy

Introduction

Energy is essential to economic development. Without it, most of the present production and welfare would not be possible. Energy is a collective term for many types; a common distinction is that between *primary and secondary energy*. Primary energy springs from a variety of sources. Historically, human and animal muscle power, wood, wind and water (tides and rivers) were important. In more modern times, fossil fuels have come to the fore (coal, oil, gas). Since the Second World War, nuclear energy has developed fast. Recently, other forms of energy have regained interest, in particular the so-called 'renewable resources': sun radiation, tidal energy, but also biomass, etc. Because primary energy sources are not always easy to use, they are converted into secondary ones, such as coke and gas from coal, petrol and liquified petroleum gas (LPG) from crude oil. Some of these are converted a second time for the generation of electricity in coke- or oil-fired power stations.

The external effects of the use and generation of energy are important enough to warrant *government intervention*. Besides, governments conduct an energy policy to support investors in the highly capital-intensive energy sector who, for their investment decisions, depend on a very long-term vision of societal and economic developments. An adequate government policy can relieve them of some of their uncertainties.

All West European countries pursue energy policies, but they vary widely from country to country. Two *international bodies* are trying to co-ordinate them, namely, the Organisation for Economic Co-operation and Development (OECD) in Paris, and the European Community (EC) in Brussels.

From its very creation, the *OECD* has given attention to the energy problem: indeed, energy, so vital to Europe's reconstruction, was devastatingly scarce just after the war. In the 1950s and 1960s the Organisation allowed its attention for energy to ebb; the 1973 oil crisis underlined once again that the supply of energy should be central to the economic policy of industrialised countries (Western Europe, North America, Japan, Australia, and New Zealand). A relatively advanced form of international co-operation, by OECD standards, was then initiated by the creation of the International Energy Agency. This agency was instructed to draw up an international energy programme; it tries to carry out this programme by co-ordinating rather strictly the national policies of the participating states. The OECD contents itself mostly with co-ordinating the policies of member states (OECD, various years), trying to make them match their policies voluntarily. The International Energy Agency, however, goes one better: it curtails member states' elbow-room by laying down uniform rules of behaviour which all member states are supposed to respect, their conduct being judged regularly, in meetings of government representatives, from detailed reports (for instance, OECD, 1987f). However, for energy no more than for other matters does the OECD have authority to enforce the policy agreed upon.

The *European Community*, too, has pursued an energy policy since its creation. The European Community for Coal and Steel (1952) was given wide powers to organise the European coal market. Besides, the Euratom Treaty (1958) regulated the details of the development of nuclear energy. The other energy sources come under the European Economic Community; however, the Treaty of Rome does not give any specific rules either for oil or for other energy sources; oil, gas and electricity come under the general stipulations of the Treaty, like any other product.

The *planning* of this chapter is as follows. The next section discusses in some detail the market regulation and the structural policy adopted by the EC. The third section sketches the changes which in the 1950–1985 period occurred in the consumption (total and by category) and production of energy in Europe. The fourth section treats the integration of certain submarkets in some depth; oil, coal and electricity have been chosen as examples.[1] Some conclusions will complete the chapter.

Community regime

Treaties

In 1952, when the *European Coal and Steel Community* (ECSC) was created, coal was still the most important energy source for Europe. The ECSC Treaty mentions a number of objectives (articles 2 and 3) for market regulation and a structural policy for the coal-mining sector. The High Authority's first task concerns the adequate functioning of the market; it has to 'ensure an orderly supply to the Common Market; ensure that all comparably placed consumers in the Common Market have equal access to the sources of production; ensure the establishment of the lowest prices'. In principle, the Community gives free scope to competition to govern the market process. However, in times of 'manifest crisis' or scarcity, the Community can intervene either directly in the prices (article 61), or through production quotas (article 58) and international trade (article 74); such intervention must be applied only if more indirect measures fail. The second task, to pursue a structural policy, is formulated by the Treaty as follows: 'ensure the maintenance of conditions which will encourage undertakings to expand and improve their production potential'. To attain this objective, the ECSC draws up indicative programmes, appreciates individual investment programmes, supports investments and research, and finally supports restructuring by appropriate measures (articles 46 to 56).[2]

The *European Atomic Energy Community* (EAEC) has no powers as to the regulation of the market; demand is free, and for the supply of ores, raw materials and fissionable material an EC monopoly has been given to an 'Agency' created for the purpose. The EAEC's main task is a structural–political one in which we can distinguish the following elements: to develop research (articles 4–7) – it carries on extensive research programmes in its own EC research centres, to disperse knowledge (articles 14–24), and to make investments (articles 40 and 47). Apart from supporting and co-ordinating, the EAEC can also directly participate in investments.

The treaty of the *European Economic Community* (EEC), concluded in 1958, contains no specific stipulations for the energy sector; therefore, the functioning of the (crude-)oil, (natural-)gas and electricity markets are left to supply and demand forces regulated only by the stipulations with respect to competition (articles 85 and 86). No structural measures for these sectors have been provided for at all either.

Implementation

That the situation in the energy field lacked balance was recognised quite soon after the EEC had begun to function. Since then, the Commission has submitted a series of *proposals towards a more coherent EC energy policy* along the legal principles of the three treaties. The 1962 'Memorandum on Energy Policy' was followed in 1968 by a 'First Orientation to a Common Energy Policy', which reflected the fundamental problems of the EC energy position and established the principles of EC policy, namely to ensure supply at the lowest possible price, with due regard to the specific structure of the energy sector. A common market for energy products and co-ordination of the member states' energy policy were to be the means.

The 1973 energy crisis[3] and the very divergent national responses to it (virtually disintegrating the common energy market) made the EC painfully aware of the need for further action. In a series of communications from the Commission to the Council, the former has progressively worked out the objectives and implementation of its policy. All these documents contain proposals to render consistent the objectives and measures of energy policy as pursued by national governments.

The most important objective of EC policy (CEC 1981a), is guaranteed continuous supply at fair prices. The practical purpose was to become less dependent on foreign oil, for strategic as well as economic reasons (d'Anarzit 1982). The fluctuations in the price of crude oil and the exchange rate to the dollar (see Figure 13.1) had caused huge external disturbances of the European economy in general and the energy sector in particular. Between 1973 and 1981, the oil bill of the Community had multiplied by eight (in dollars), despite a simultaneous decline of net imports by some 40 per cent. The EC tries to achieve

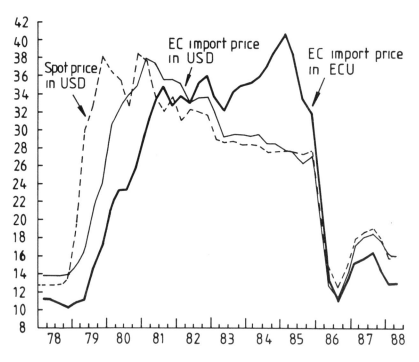

Figure 13.1 European Community import prices of energy

Source: CEC 1986f

independence by stock building, energy saving, expansion of the EC members' own production, and so-called 'fuel switching'.

The *general objectives of EC policy* as formulated recently (CEC 1988b) can be summed up in the following five concrete points:

- to diminish the ratio between the growth of energy consumption and the growth of GNP to 0.7;
- to diminish oil consumption to some 40 per cent of total primary energy consumption;
- to reduce the share of oil and stimulate the use of solid fuels and nuclear energy in electricity generation;
- to stimulate the development of permanent or renewable sources;
- to establish better and more transparent price and market conditions for the various energy sources.

The EC tries to realise these general objectives by short-term measures with a rather direct effect on the market, and longer-term measures of a more structural nature. Both types of measure aim at the co-ordination of the programmes of member states (Alting von Geusau, 1975; Lucas, 1977, 1985). To that end, the Commission organises periodical surveys of member states' energy-policy schemes (for example, CEC 1982c), thus overlapping the work of the OECD (for example, OECD 1987f).

Market control: the short term

The Commission has laid down, in regulations and directives, rules for the intervention of member states in the market. First of all, there are rules concerning *disturbances of the supply*, especially of crude oil (d'Anarzit, 1982). Member states are committed to maintain minimum stocks of oil (for at least 90 days) and in times of supply problems to introduce a rationing scheme for these stocks. To ensure that member states help one another in such circumstances, the Commission can draw on certain executive powers.

The purpose of a second group of directives is to *make the market's functioning more transparent*. The commitment of member states to inform and consult the Commission on the development of prices of oil and other energy carriers except coal (for which the ECSC Treaty already provides) comes under this heading, as does the registration of crude imports and oil-product exports. The conditions and prices of oil imports are registered as well, and the market situation is discussed regularly on the basis of the Commission's quarterly reviews. The agreement to inform the Commission of the formation and components of the price of electrical energy has the same objective; differential electricity prices can distort competition if they do not spring from evident competitive advantages of the utility companies involved. By the same agreement, data are to be collected on the importation of coal from third countries. With these data and the Euratom import data, the Commission knows exactly the position of the EC's foreign energy trade and can design its trade policy accordingly.

Structural policy: the long term

The objectives of the Common Energy Policy (CEP) cannot be realised without a rather drastic restructuring of energy production, consumption and trade. The following *measures of structural policy* are in force in the framework of the CEP:

- financing of nuclear energy (Euratom);
- measures in favour of coal-mining (ECSC) (financing and regulation);
- subsidies to research projects and demonstration programmes aiming at energy saving and alternative sources (in the last few years, some 8 per cent of public expenditure on that score was financed from EC funds);
- loans (the so-called New Community Instrument) to manufacturing industries applying new technical procedures (energy saving, rationalised production);
- information exchange with oil companies to achieve an adaptation of refining capacity to demand.

Sketch of the sector

Employment and value added

Estimating the importance of the energy sectors' constituent branches in terms of employment, we find that coal-mining, electricity generation, and oil refining each count for less than 1 per cent of total employment, which means that the entire energy sector represents perhaps 2 to 3 per cent of total employment. In terms of gross value added the percentage is certainly higher, if only because of the large contribution the sector makes to government revenue. Evidently this does not add up to a large part of total economic activity. If the EC has nevertheless decided to hammer out a common policy for energy, it is because of its strategic importance; for the same reason, we have singled the sector out for separate treatment.

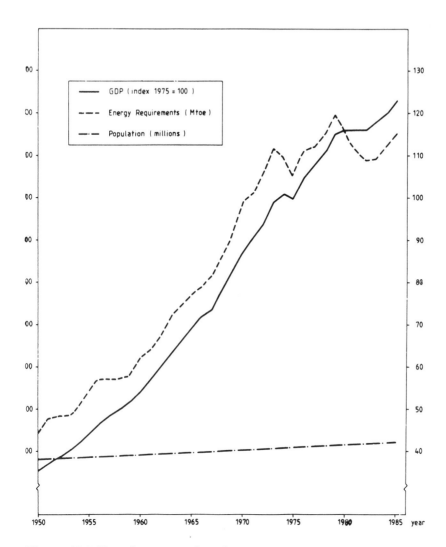

Figure 13.2 Development of total energy consumption in Western Europe, 1950–1985 (1000 Mtoe)*, and of GNP (index 1975 = 100)

* Million tons of oil equivalent

Total consumption of primary energy

In the *1950–1973 period*, which was characterised by stable economic growth, total energy consumption[4] in the European Community increased very fast (see Figure 13.2). In the 1950–1960 period, average annual growth was 3.9 per cent; in the 1960–1973 period even 5.2 per cent. The ratio between the increases of energy consumption and that of GNP (elasticity) was 0.8 in the 1950–1960 period, and somewhat higher, namely 1.1, in the 1960–1973 period.

The *1973–1982 period* started with some events which were to exert a strong effect on the entire consumption pattern. For one thing, the oil price, practically stable until then, rose almost fourfold. For another, the continuous oil supply became uncertain as some oil exporters put an embargo on oil exports to certain consumer countries. An economic recession was the result, with, in 1975, the first decline of GNP since the war. Energy consumption dropped as well: by some 7 per cent between 1973 and 1975. The high price of oil induced its substitution by other sources of energy as well as measures to diminish consumption by energy saving. As a result, energy consumption rose but slightly between 1975 and 1979. Given a growth of the EC economy by approximately 1.5 per cent in the same period, the elasticity of energy consumption in respect of GNP appears to have dropped to 0.2. In 1979 followed the second oil shock, again multiplying the oil price by nearly four. It was the main cause of a drop in energy consumption of some 10 per cent between 1979 and 1982, compared to a 1 per cent GDP increase. So, in that period, elasticity turned negative.

In recent years, *1983–1989*, with prices decreasing drastically, demand has picked up again.

Consumption by primary energy source

Consumption has developed differently for the various primary energy sources, as Table 13.1 illustrates.

Certain trends can be discerned throughout the period, with some differentiation between sub-periods. In the pre-war period almost the entire energy consumption was supplied by solid fuels, especially coal. In the second period, from 1950–1973, consumption switched fast from coal mostly to liquid fuels (crude oil), but also to (natural) gas and primary electricity, comprising hydraulic power and nuclear energy. Especially the latter is steadily progressing. The downward trend for coal and the upward trend for oil reached a turning point in 1973, when the total shares of oil and coal were 61 and 23 per cent, respectively. The year 1973 heralded a new period with the fourfold increase of the oil price, a movement that was reinforced by the 1979 events. As a result, the share of oil decreased again to 45 per cent in 1985. The increase of

Table 13.1   **Percentage shares of primary energy sources in total energy consumption in the European Community (Mtoe), 1929–1985**

Year	Coal	Oil	Gas	Electricity
1929	95	4	–	1
1937	90	8	–	2
1950	83	14	–	3
1960	63	31	2	4
1973	23	61	11	5
1979	23	52	14	11
1985	23	45	18	14

Source: OECD, *Energy Statistics, Oil Statistics*, various years, OECD, 1966, 1973

gas and primary electricity continued all through the study period; the share of solid fuels was stable from 1973 onwards. Since 1985 there has been a steep fall in oil prices due to the breakdown of the OPEC cartel, which is likely to affect the share of oil.

What are the *determinant factors behind the substitution* of one *energy source for another*? Costs, consumer convenience, and availability set the key notes; of course, the latter two can also be translated into costs.

The most important substitution has been that of oil for coal. It came not as a surprise, since their relative prices had diverged steadily from 1950 to 1973. While high labour costs of production and transportation made coal more and more expensive, the consumption prices of oil could be reduced thanks to its capital-intensive production and the economies of scale achieved in production and transportation (*Eurostat*,1974).

The steady rise of the share of gas in total consumption has been due in particular to its convenient use in many installations and to the fact that it is produced more and more in the consumption areas.

Finally, the share of primary electricity is steadily growing. The cost of electricity generated in thermal power stations, and the wish to be independent of primary-energy imports, have stimulated the development of hydro and nuclear energy. The quantities obtained in practice from other primary sources, such as wood, wind, sun, and animal force, are negligible at the moment; their limited availability and high costs and/or great inconvenience to consumers have been the main delaying factors.

Conversion of primary into secondary energy

Primary energy sources are not always convenient to users, which is why they are converted into secondary ones. *To convert energy costs energy.* On the one hand, oil refineries and coke ovens use energy to feed the production process. On the other, the return of thermal power stations is rather low: energy escapes into the cooling water and through chimneys into the air. The total 'losses' of the entire energy sector in the European Community between 1973 and 1980 amounted to about 25 per cent of the total consumption of primary energy (OECD 1987a). But why convert at all if it costs so much energy? The reason is that many processes technically require secondary energy carriers for efficient production and consumption. The primary sources differ widely in the extent to which they are converted into secondary energy. About one-half of all coal is converted, mostly in power stations, a small portion in coke factories. Brown coal is converted practically entirely into electricity. Crude oil is fully converted into oil products, of which a portion, in particular fuel oil, is processed further in electric power stations.

Apparently, then, *many primary energy sources are ultimately converted* into electricity, in spite of the heavy 'losses' incurred. The relative volumes of the various primary energy sources utilised for the generation of electricity has changed quite a bit through time, as the following table illustrates.

Table 13.2 **Percentage shares of energy sources in the consumption of power stations in the European Community (EC12) 1955–1985 (calculated on the basis of a conversion in oil equivalent)**

Source Year	Solid (coal)	Liquid (oil)	Gas	Nuclear energy	Hydro energy	Total
1955	70	3	1	–	26	100
1960	67	7	1	1	24	100
1965	62	14	2	3	20	100
1970	51	24	5	4	16	100
1975	42	25	12	7	14	100
1980	47	22	7	11	13	100
1985	41	11	6	30	12	100

Sources: 1955–1965: estimates based on OECD, *The Electricity Supply Industry in Western Europe*, various years; 1970–1985 OECD (1987g)

That the shares differ so much is due to a combination of factors such as the relative prices of primary energy sources, the technical appointment of existing power stations, and government policy (for instance stimulation of the use of coal by subsidies).

Production and importation

Along with the consumption pattern of energy in Western Europe, the pattern of production and importation, and hence the *external dependence*, have greatly changed. The first change came when coal, a predominantly domestic energy source, was replaced with an imported one, namely oil. More and more coal was imported as well, because the West European mines could not compete with foreign ones. As a result, the dependence coefficient of the EC, defined as the share of net imports in total energy consumption, rose rapidly after the war. From just 1 per cent in 1930, and 7 per cent on the eve of the Second World War, the dependence coefficient had risen to 15 per cent by 1950. From that year on it rose steadily to reach a high in 1973, when two–thirds of all energy consumed in the EC had to be imported. The oil crisis of the early 1970s opened European eyes to the risk of such a development; since then, extensive schemes have been carried out to make Europe less dependent on foreign oil, schemes to boost national production as well as reduce consumption. The effects are clearly perceptible in the figures: the dependence coefficient was down to 44 per cent in 1985 (OECD 1987g). Let us look somewhat closer at the individual energy sources.

The EC's own production of *crude oil*, practically negligible in 1950 and only 15 million tons in 1970, by 1985 had risen to 153 million tons a year. In that volume, the United Kingdom had the lion's share.[5] In fact, in 1985 the EC12 countries produced 30 per cent of their total oil consumption. By becoming increasingly self-supplying, Western Europe has diminished its total dependence on foreign oil. Moreover, it has reduced strategic risks by drawing oil from an increasing number of supplying countries. In the early 1960s, four Middle East countries, namely, Iran, Iraq, Kuwait and Saudi Arabia, still accounted for three-quarters of the oil supply to Western Europe. By 1970 their share in European imports had reduced by half, and was still dropping in the course of the 1970s because new producers, in particular in North and West Africa, but also Mexico, had joined the traditional Middle East oil suppliers to Europe (OECD, *Oil Statistics*; OECD 1973). Figure 13.3 gives an idea of the variation in the geographical pattern of European crude oil imports around 1985.

Traditionally, Northern Europe produced its own *solid fuels*. Throughout the 1950–1980 period, the largest producer countries in Western Europe were the United Kingdom and Germany, with France, Spain and Belgium following at some distance. The production in the rest of

Western Europe was negligible in comparison. In the 1950s, no more than about 5 per cent of total demand for coal needed to be imported; in the 1960s the average percentage was 10 per cent, and by 1985, when the consumption of coal had picked up again, the EC12's dependence on imports had risen to some 30 per cent.[6] Most imports came from the United States and Poland. For a long time, coal extracted in EC countries was able to hold its own against oil and imported coal with the help of supporting measures, taken mostly in the framework of the ECSC.

The development of the production of *natural gas* in the EC has been quite important as well (Lacq in the south of France, Slochteren and other places in The Netherlands, later from the North Sea (UK)). In Western Europe outside the EC, Norway is another large producer and recently, (liquified) natural gas has begun to be imported (LNG by tanker from North Africa, NG by pipe from Eastern Europe). [7]

Among the *other sources of energy*, uranium is of particular importance. Because uranium can be stocked, the fiction is often maintained that nuclear energy is a domestic source of energy; that uranium has to be imported is overlooked. For such alternative primary sources as hydro-power and wind, the EC is by definition independent of imports; given their small scale we need not give further attention to them at this place.

Consumption by category

To analyse the consumption pattern[8] we distinguish three main sectors: Industry, Transport, and Household/Commerce. The relative share of these consumer categories in total consumption were quite stable throughout the 1960–1980 period (see Table 13.3). Industry is the largest consumer category, with a share of over 40 per cent. It is followed closely by the main category of Household/Commerce, with just under 40 per cent. Transport invariably comes in third position.

Within *industry*, the more detailed basic material not presented here shows that iron and steel is the largest consumer, accounting for some 10 to 15 per cent of the total sector's 40. Coke and coal (for blast furnaces) are in the lead, but other energy sources, especially electricity, are steadily gaining in importance. A second very important sector is that of chemical products, in particular the petrochemical industry. This sector's share has risen slowly and now accounts for some 12 per cent of the EC's total final energy consumption. By far the largest consumer is the petrochemical industry, which uses mainly oil products and gases. Note that the consumption of Industry also comprises non-energetic consumption, for instance of naphtha, as a raw material of the petrochemical industry. Non-energy consumption increased quite a bit as the petrochemical industry grew in the 1960s and 1970s,

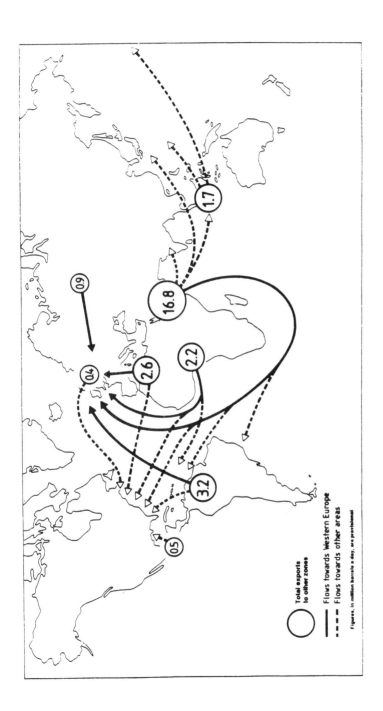

Figure 13.3. Flows of crude oil towards Western Europe (around 1985)

Table 13.3 Final domestic consumption of energy (including for non-energy purposes) in the EC12, by consumer category and secondary energy source (Mtoe), 1950–1985

Consumer category	Year	Solid	Liquid	Gas	Electricity	Total absolute	%
Industry (incl. non-energy)	1950	76	10	2	9	97	41
	1955	82	22	6	13	123	41
	1960	101	51	9	19	180	47
	1965	90	104	11	26	231	46
	1970	78	175	27	36	316	47
	1975	57	155	53	42	307	43
	1980	52	147	64	49	312	41
	1985	58	110	63	50	281	37
Household/ Commerce	1950	79	7	5	4	95	40
	1955	97	13	7	7	124	41
	1960	88	29	9	11	137	35
	1965	78	67	13	18	176	35
	1970	56	122	26	28	232	35
	1975	28	135	54	39	256	36
	1980	22	126	78	50	276	36
	1985	21	109	93	59	282	38
Transport (incl. bunkers)	1950	29	16	–	1	46	19
	1955	24	27	–	1	52	18
	1960	16	52	–	1	69	18
	1965	8	82	–	2	92	19
	1970	2	117	–	2	121	18
	1975	–	144	–	2	146	21
	1980	–	175	–	3	178	23
	1985	–	186	–	3	189	25
Total (absolute)	1950	184	33	7	14	238	100
	1955	203	62	13	21	299	100
	1960	205	132	18	31	386	100
	1965	176	253	24	46	499	100
	1970	136	414	53	66	669	100
	1975	85	434	107	83	709	100
	1980	74	448	142	102	766	100
	1985	77	405	156	112	752	100
Total (%)	1950	77	14	3	6	100	
	1955	68	21	3	8	100	
	1960	53	34	5	8	100	
	1965	35	51	5	9	100	
	1970	20	62	8	10	100	
	1975	12	61	15	12	100	
	1980	10	58	19	13	100	
	1985	10	54	21	15	100	

Sources: for 1960–1985: OECD, 1987g; for 1950–1955: estimates based on *OECD Basic Statistics of Energy*, various years

but still accounts for less than half of the sector's total demand (Molle and Wever, 1983). The industrial consumption of coal has declined fast since 1960, while that of all other energy forms has been rapidly increasing. That cannot be attributed entirely to the developments in the steel and chemical industries described above, for most sectors of other industry show the same tendency.

Within *household, commerce, etc.* household consumption ranks first, accounting for some two-thirds of the entire category's consumption in 1985. We do not know much about the structure of this main category in the years before 1975, but from fragmentary data, the household group appears always to have represented the body of the entire main category. The development of the various energy forms offers a striking picture: after a rise in the 1950s, coal was practically eliminated in the 1960s, obviously because of its inconvenience to the user. Electricity and gas, on the other hand, have grown fast, as did oil until the decline called forth by the crisis.

Within *transport*, haulage is by far the largest consumer, accounting for more than half of the category's total consumption. Moreover, its share has steadily increased through time. The demand of the haulage sector is practically entirely for oil products, which is also by far the most important source of energy compared to air and water transport. Electricity is almost completely and exclusively used for rail transport; coal has lost most of its former important position in shipping and rail transport to oil and electricity.

Case study 1: oil refining

Companies

The European oil market is dominated by a few large multinational companies, some large (state) companies operating mostly on the national markets, and a varying number of smaller companies. Molle and Wever (1983) describe these groups as follows.

- *The seven majors* (also called the 'seven sisters') (Sampson, 1977). To this group belong five American (Exxon, Texaco, Gulf Oil, Mobil Oil, and Standard Oil of California) and two European companies (Royal Dutch Shell and BP). These companies operate on a world scale and show a high degree of vertical integration. It means that they are active at all stages of the oil industry, in the exploration and exploitation of crude oil, the transport of crude and products, the refining, and finally the marketing of the finished products. They are, moreover, active in such related activities as (petro)chemicals and even in other energy sectors like nuclear energy or coal-mining. The relative position of the seven majors decreased quite a bit in the 1950–1980 period: while in 1950 they controlled 65 per cent of total European refinery capacity, in 1980 they were down to about 44 per cent. Among these majors the American company Exxon and the European companies Shell and BP are by far the greatest in terms of refinery capacity in Western Europe. In 1970, at the height of its influence, Shell possessed 23 refineries in 10 European countries; the company controlled about one-fourth of the total refinery capacity in Western Europe in the 1950s, but only 15 per cent in the 1960s and 1970s. Immediately behind comes the Exxon company, possessing 15 refineries in eight different European countries with 15 per cent of total European capacity in 1970, but by 1980 this figure had gone down to about 11 per cent. BP, the next largest, had 12 refineries in six different European countries, totalling some 10 per cent of Europe's total in 1980.

- *The State-controlled companies.* In a deliberate policy to strengthen the national position in the refinery industry with respect to the majors, a number of countries have established state-owned or state-controlled refinery companies. Most of them confine their activities (anyhow their refinery activities) within the national borders. In France there is the Total and Elf/Aquitaine[9] – two companies that together hold a very large share (between 50 and 60 per cent up to 1980) in the total French refining sector. In Italy the dominant company is the ENI, which currently possesses some 20 per cent of total refinery capacity in Italy. The Portuguese national company Petrogal even has a 100 per cent share in the refinery industry of the country. In Spain the semi-national companies are very important. Other countries also have some national or semi-national companies (Germany, Greece), but their position in the refinery sector is relatively modest.

- *Independent private oil companies.* Within this group two sub-groups can be distinguished: the Western European companies and the American companies. Within the group of Western European independents we can make a further distinction between some of the larger ones that work internationally (such as Petro/Fina), some medium-sized companies (like Gelsenberg), and a large number of smaller companies that are mostly active on a local scale only, especially in Western Germany, Italy and the United Kingdom. In the course of the post-war period many of these companies have ceased to exist, because they stopped their production or were taken over by larger companies (state, major, or chemical companies). Their market position as well as their resource base were often too weak to stand up to international competition. The refinery operations of the group of

American independents in Western Europe are limited. Conoco, Phillips, Standard Oil of Indiana, Amoco, Marathon Oil, and Occidental Oil each had in 1980 one or two refineries in Western Europe, many of these in the United Kingdom.

• *Chemical companies* with large interests in the petrochemical sector. They often depend heavily on outside supplies for their basic feedstocks, and all of them have made arrangements with one or more oil companies. Because these were not always satisfactory, some of them have integrated backwards (that is, taken an interest in refining) by participation or take-over. Examples here are the ICI's taking a 50 per cent share in the North Tees refinery of Phillips, BASF's ownership of Wintershall (with two refineries in Western Germany), and Montedison taking a share in the Brindisi and Priolo refineries in Italy.

Capacities and location pattern of refineries

The above picture of the actors involved mirrors to some extent the location pattern: the multinationals, trying to get a share in most national markets in Europe, have arranged extensions and new plants to keep the system fairly balanced and avoid large over-capacities.

Table 13.4   Number of refineries in Western Europe[10] by size class, 1950–1985

Class (Mt/y)	1950	1960	1970	1980	1985
0.1 – 1.0	61	53	37	18	10
1.1 – 5.0	11	45	64	60	50
5.1 – 10.0	–	5	19	57	41
10.1 – 15.0	–	–	6	16	12
15.1 – 20.0	–	–	1	4	3
larger than 20.1	–	–	–	4	2
Total	72	103	127	159	118
Distillation capacity	41	192	707	1000	728
Average	0.6	1.9	5.6	6.3	6.2

Source: Molle and Wever (1983), Molle (1988)

Refining is the most important activity of the European oil industry. Since the war, the total capacity of the refinery sector in Europe has increased rapidly, in line with the strongly increased demand. Part of that growth was achieved by the expansion of existing refineries, another part by the creation of new ones.

In oil refinery, as in other industries, growth was attended by a tremendous *scale enlargement*; Table 13.4 gives an impression.

The growing markets permitted a *strong orientation* of refinery activities to *national markets* and a wide spread of production in spite of the increased scale of the plants (Molle and Wever, 1983). This spread continued during the whole period 1950–1975; the orientation to national markets was consolidated by the strategy adopted by several governments to build up their own 'national' oil industries. After 1975 a slight decrease can be observed; apparently the cutbacks on capacity have not been completely in line with the decrease in demand by country.

Case study 2: electricity

Actors on the European electricity market

The European market for electric power is practically fragmented along national lines, with only little exchange among them in terms of products, and without any international integration of firms. The reason is that the manner in which electricity has to be delivered to the customers has favoured local or national monopolies, which are looked upon as a public service rather than an industrial activity. The *structure of the industry* varies widely, however. In France, Italy, Greece, Portugal and Ireland, national companies control the generation, transportation and distribution of electricity; in the United Kingdom that is true only of generation and transmission, and the other member countries show highly diversified patterns (Eurostat, several years).

Electricity companies in the EC are organised in several *international organisations*. The most important is UCPTE, which groups all but one of the continental countries of the EC, plus Austria, Switzerland and Yugoslavia. Denmark is a member of NORDEL with the other Nordic countries. UCPTE countries have an interconnected network, designed for emergencies rather than for regular trading; its capacity is calculated to cope with the need to supply electricity to a country part of whose system has broken down. UCPTE's links with NORDEL have a limited capacity; recently, a link between France and the UK was constructed.

International trade

As has been pointed out in the previous section, electricity consumption has increased very fast in the last few decades. The increase has been achieved by a considerable effort to construct generation plants and distribution lines in all countries. All the states, in their *efforts to be self-sufficient*, tend to import primary energy rather than electric power. Indeed, the figures of the next table show that only some 5 per cent of total electricity production enters into international trade. The table also shows that generation doubled in the 1970–1984 period, while exchanges increased by a factor 2.5. Exchange with third countries during this period was limited to some imports.

Table 13.5   Generation and exchanges of electricity in Western Europe[a] 1970–1984

Year	Generation (TWh)	Exchanges period	%
1970	614	1970–1974	4.9
1974	796	1974–1979	5.8
1979	952	1979–1984	6.2
1984	1223		

[a] 12 countries (members and associated members of UCPTE)
Source: Waha 1986.

International exchange of electricity is necessary to overcome several problems.

- Long-term. Power stations are, on average, large constructions which take some time to build. The generation capacity of national systems, in particular in the smaller countries, does not match demand, so that electricity has to be imported or exported. Mostly the prices agreed upon in such long-term contracts are indexed to some mix of fuel prices on international markets.
- Short-term. Thermal power plants need to be closed down at intervals for maintenance and repair; hydro power is not constantly available in the same quantities. Trading permits the utilities to economise on the total capacity needed to fulfil a certain level of demand. Prices are usually of the spot type (that is the price prevailing on the short-term market), depending on the load level, the availability of certain sources of primary energy, etc.
- Very short-term. Technical difficulties like a temporary lack of power, or peaks in demand, or technical problems of generation or transmission may occur. Such exchanges are not billed but

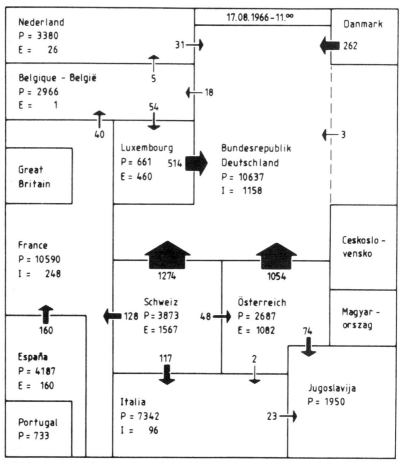

(a) Exchange of electricity (1966)

Figure 13.4 Exchange of electricity

compensated for by helping out the partner at another time; they enable utility companies to economise on stand-by capacity.

Figure 13.4 gives an impression of the European exchange pattern and its development through time. Most exchanges indicated have been made to cope with the long- and short-term problems; the very short-term difficulties having had but little effect.

The rationale for the exchange of goods and services is comparative advantage (Chapter 5), and we have indeed found clear examples of

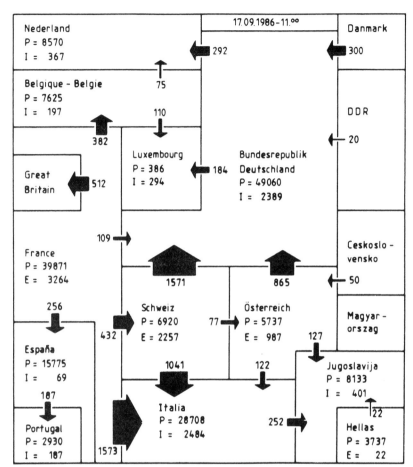

(*b*) Exchange of electricity (1986)

Figure 13.4 Exchange of electricity

this in Chapters 8 and 12. The *rationale for existing electricity trade* is to cope with an emergency need; the principle of most governments being national self-sufficiency. However, as the liberalisation of markets gets carried out as part of the completion of the internal market (Chapter 16), electricity is likely to lose that special feature, and trade will probably develop along the lines depicted for goods in previous chapters.

Prices

Market conditions being as described above, it is hardly surprising to find *important differences in price among the member countries of the EC.* Indeed, when markets are regulated to that extent, inputs (of labour, for instance) are apt to be inefficient. Moreover, there is ample scope for setting different prices for different consumer categories (joint costs; see UNIPEDE 1982 and 1985). The countries follow different strategies, based on the level of fixed costs of production and distribution and the possibilities of dividing these costs between different categories of users, taking account of market response and industrial and regional policy objectives.[11] As the differences are fairly similar for household and industrial purposes, we will confine ourselves here to the industrial sector. The differences among EC countries in the price of electricity for a typical category of industrial consumer[12] are quite substantial. In 1986, prices were much higher in Italy, Germany, The Netherlands and Ireland than in the other member states; in France and Denmark they were below average. Some relations changed considerably in the study period,[13] but France, the UK and Denmark remained consistently below, and Germany as consistently above, the European average.

No tendency to converge to a European price level can be observed. One *cause of the continuing disparity in electricity prices* is that the EC member countries use different fuel mixes to generate electricity. In France, almost three-quarters of all electricity is generated in nuclear power stations, while Denmark's power plants are almost exclusively coal-fired. The more expensive producers were those that depended on oil or gas firing. In view of the segmented markets, it is logical that the electricity prices continued to vary widely all through the period of study,[14] reflecting the industry's lack of integration. With the completion of the internal market and the likely increase in trade in electricity, it is likely that those price differences will decrease (see Chapter 16).

Summary and conclusions

- The involvement of the EC with energy is based on *three different treaties:* ECSC for coal, EAEC for nuclear energy, and the EEC for all other energy products. Gradually, a common energy policy has evolved that is largely based on the co-ordination of member-state policies.
- In the 1950s, coal was the *dominant energy source* (around which the ECSC was erected); since then, oil has taken over the lead. Electricity, generated from various primary sources, becomes ever more important.
- *Oil markets* have gone through very turbulent times, but the

market partners, in particular the multinational oil companies, seem to have responded adequately by changing exploration and exploitation methods (North Sea oil) and adapting and modernising the refining, transportation and distribution systems, taking into account the integration of the European market and the linkages with world markets.

- *Electricity*, on the contrary, is a very fragmented industry. As its importance in energy markets continues to grow, the development of a European view of production and distribution, including pricing, is becoming imperative.

Notes

1   See for a more complete description, for instance, Weyman-Jones (1986) or Jensen (1983).
2   The extended powers of the EC in the coal sector make this sector highly comparable to agriculture; here too, there is considerable intervention of public authorities both on the European and on the national level.
3   This sparked off studies like Odell and Rosing (1980), Sassin *et al.* (1983), Struls (1979), and OECD (1982d).
4   To be made comparable, the various energy sources (coal, oil, etc.) have all been converted to the energetic content of the dominant one: oil. The unit we have used is Mtoe, which stands for million tons of oil equivalent. The figures should be compared to a growth of about 1 per cent a year from 1930 to 1950.
5   In addition, some 25 million tons of oil were produced by Norway.
6   Given the very limited coal consumption in the remaining parts of Western Europe, the figure may also be considered to refer to Western Europe as a whole.
7   See for the evolution of the European gas market and its lack of competitiveness: Golombek *et al.* (1987).
8   Contrary to the OECD definition, we count bunkers to final consumption. The OECD treats this category as exports. The categories are not defined, as in Table 13.1, in terms of primary sources, but in terms of secondary sources (after conversion); 'liquid' comprises all oil products, 'solid' coal, coke and brown coal; 'gas' comprises natural gas as well as coke-oven and refinery gas, etc. and 'electricity' refers to power from nuclear as well as thermal power stations. Final domestic consumption, defined as total domestic production plus imports minus exports and minus the energy sector's own consumption.
9   Elf has a number of refineries abroad, in particular in Germany, which makes it something of a multinational.
10 OECD Western Europe without Turkey: these figures are representative also of the EC12, which accounts for some 90 per cent of the totals, and for even more in earlier years.
11 See for a detailed description of the options and choices of a major EC country: Monnier (1983).
12 See for other energy products and consumer categories, Jones and Leydon (1986).
13 The differences among agglomerations given here reflect those among countries.
14 For 1973, this applies to nine countries only, Source: CEC (1986f).

14 Services

Introduction

In recent times, the service sector has grown to predominance in the economies of the European countries. With increasing productivity and low income elasticities, the shares of the agricultural and manufacturing sectors stagnated first and dropped next, making room for the quickly expanding service sector. One reason why statistics show such a large expansion is that certain functions which had hitherto been carried out within other sectors (cleaning, auditing, etc.) were becoming independent and registered as such. This phenomenon, sometimes called 'splintering', results when technically progressive services break off from manufacturing for economies of scale or organisational advantages. When the service sector becomes dominant and many service activities concern the handling of information, the term 'post-industrial or information society' is often appropriately used.

Unlike with other sectors of activity, a *definition* of the service sector[1] is difficult to give. Services are often described as a 'rest sector' encompassing the activities not discussed in the previous chapters. Another approach focuses on the intangible nature of the output, and thus excludes, among other things, construction. Attempts have been made to overcome the problems of definition by adding such criteria as perishability and simultaneity of production and consumption,[2] but from the literature on the subject, such new criteria have all failed to make a distinction between goods and services, so that the line of severance between the two remains arbitrary. Statistical measurement is poor and hence also the possibility of quantitative analysis of the sector. Within the service sector, subsectors of activity are usually distinguished. They include such traditional ones as wholesale and retail trade, but also modern ones, like data services. A wide definition of the sector includes such government services as public administration and defence.

The service sector is subject to considerable *government regulation*, springing largely from the desire to protect consumer interests (for instance, minimum standards for the reserves of banks, or qualification standards for medical personnel). Convinced that a socially desirable organisation of quite large segments could not be left to private enterprise, governments have assumed direct responsibility, especially for services associated with the welfare state (like social security). Others (such as medical services) are a combination of public and private effort. In view of the close control that government exerts on large parts of the sector, it is hardly surprising that few countries pursue a policy for the structural development of the private segment of the service sector; indeed, that segment is mostly left to fend for itself.

The growing importance of services in the economy has not immediately brought about a greater interest of *international organisations*. For a long time, services were considered an essentially domestic sector hardly in need of international attention. Recently, however, the awareness has grown that such lack of interest has bred many protectionist measures (see also Chapter 2) impeding the internationalisation of service activities (Griffiths, 1975, among others); organisations like GATT now carry the subject on their negotiating agenda. As services are increasingly important to developing countries, UNCTAD (1983) has taken up the issue as well. The OECD has also joined in, focusing on sector-specific studies of trade impediments in services (see Chapter 2). All these organisations are trying to improve the poor data situation on international trade in services, as an essential first step towards a basis for policy making.

While the *European Community* has always looked upon services as an essential part of the integration process, it has not in practice devoted much attention to it. In the present chapter we propose to look into the service sector of the European Community in some detail.

The *pattern* of this chapter is the same as that of the previous ones. First a succinct description of the European policy environment and a general description of the service sector in Europe will be given. We will focus in this chapter on the services that can in principle be traded by private agents, thus excluding the public sector from the discussion. Transport is also left out of the present chapter; because of its special position in the European setting it will be dealt with in a separate chapter. Next we will carry out a case study of sectoral integration; the sector selected is one that has gone some way on the path of integration, namely, the insurance industry. A summary of the findings will complete the chapter.

Community regime

Treaty

The Treaty of Rome is fairly brief on services. It reflects awareness of the wide variety in products of the service branches. The general definition of services (article 60) reads: 'all these activities normally provided for remuneration in so far as they are not governed by the provisions of freedom of movement for goods, capital and persons'. They include in particular activities of an industrial or commercial nature and those of craftsmen and professions. For all these activities the treaty stipulates:

- *the freedom to provide services* (article 59a): a company of member country A can provide services in member country B without having an office there;
- *the freedom of establishment*: that is companies (or persons) wishing to set up an establishment (that is, a legal entity with, in general, premises, staff, etc.) in another member country are free to do so under the same conditions as are laid down for the nationals of the country of establishment (art. 52).

There are a few *exceptions to this general freedom*:

- activities which are connected with the exercise of official authority are excluded completely;
- medical and pharmaceutical professions; here liberalisation depends on co-ordination of the conditions for their exercise in various member states;
- transport services are governed by another title of the treaty;
- banking and insurance services: as they are closely connected with movements of capital, their liberalisation shall be effected in step with the progressive liberalisation of capital.

Contrary to the situation for goods, the Treaty is silent as to the organisation of an external policy in matters of services. Article 59 merely stipulates that the Council may extend the freedom to provide services to nationals of third countries who are *established* within the EC.

Liberalisation by the Court of Justice

In the lengthy negotiations carried on to substantiate the freedom to provide services, the equivalence of qualifications proved one difficult point, another being the way in which governments had organised certain markets (or sanctioned private groups to organise and protect them). The general result was that very little progress towards liberalisation was made up to 1970, when, in two famous cases (already cited in Chapter 9), the Court of Justice clarified the meaning of freedom of services by ruling that from January 1, 1970, anybody could claim before the national judge the direct application of article 52 EEC in matters of establishment, and of article 59 in matters of services, thus confirming that national rules discriminating by nationality are null and void. In the conflicts settled by those rulings, the country where the service was delivered had claimed the right to supervise that service or subject it to licensing, whereas the cross-border operator had maintained that compliance with the rules of his home country was sufficient. The common element in the rulings was the consideration that governments have to demonstrate clear reasons of 'public interest' before imposing requirements on a foreign trader over and above those fulfilled to receive a permit from his home authorities, or duplicating qualification checks already performed at home.

Harmonisation efforts of the Commission

The ruling of the Court has in practice liberalised almost completely all services connected with agriculture, manufacturing, craft and trade (commerce). There remained, however, quite a few problems regarding the other service branches.

- In *professional services* (rendered by lawyers and auditors, engineers, etc.), there are strong national corporations which either have themselves regulated the profession (allegedly in the interest of the consumer) or are subject to detailed government regulation concerning both the access to the profession and the type of products supplied. The instrument used to regulate access is the specification of qualification requirements (diplomas, for instance). The EC has been working on directives for the liberalisation and harmonisation of such requirements and the mutual recognition of diplomas, but progress has been extremely slow and cumbersome, and apart from a framework directive on the recognition of university degrees, little has been achieved.
- *Financial services* (banking and insurance) are regulated on a national basis to permit prudential control of the soundness of the undertakings to make sure that they will be able, for instance, to pay the client at the moment a life insurance comes to term. Finding the harmonisation of these rules extremely involved, the EC has changed its approach; now the mutual recognition of the quality of the company's control as exercised by the home country has become the leading principle (Chapter 16).
- For *other services*, harmonisation efforts have been made too; as they tend to follow the same muster as the ones just described, we will not go into them.

Market and structural policy

Apart from its efforts to liberalise intra-Community trade in services, the EC does not pursue a *market-regulation policy* for the service sector. The market for services is indeed 'organised' in much the same way as that for most manufacturing and energy activities (except steel and coal), for which EC institutions have neither responsibility, nor power to intervene in prices and quantities. Service markets come under the general rules for competition (see Chapter 16), which are considered sufficient to have European markets function properly. Many service sectors are however heavily regulated on the national level, with government influencing important aspects such as access to markets (for example, insurance, medical services), prices (insurance, etc.). The policy now pursued by the EC for these sectors in the framework of the programme for the completion of the internal market by 1992 is rather one of liberalisation and implies the tearing down of the obstacles to trade (and hence competition) that these rules imply on the EC level (see Chapter 16).

Unlike agriculture, manufacturing and energy, the sectors discussed in the previous chapters, the service sector is not subject to a *European structural policy*. There are no schemes to encourage innovation, support investments in infrastructure or production equipment, or improve human capital.

Neither was there until recently a European *external policy* to regulate service markets *vis-à-vis* third countries, in stark contrast to the very elaborate schemes operative on goods markets (Chapter 19). Recently, on the impetus of technological change (data transmission) and under pressure from third countries, questions about external trade in services have been points on the agenda of GATT for world-wide negotiations.

Sketch of the sector

Employment and value added by branch

Since the war, the service sector has rapidly advanced to the leadership in the total economy of the EC, whether measured by GDP or employment. Even by a restricted definition of the sector, excluding construction, the total sector now accounts for far more than half of total employment, as Table 14.1 shows. That spectacular growth, leading to the 'post-industrial' or 'service' economy, has been accomplished not so much in the construction or in the transport sector (the latter will be treated separately in the next chapter) as in trade, financial services and community services. The very fast growth of community services is closely related to the build-up of the welfare state and the ensuing increased involvement of the public sector in society (Saunders and Klau, 1985; Rose *et al.*, 1985).

The breakdown of these sectors into branches reveals some interesting aspects (1985 figures). The sector of commerce consists mostly of wholesale and retail trade (14 per cent), the rest being hotels and such. The financial, business-service and insurance sector is dominated by banking and insurance (3 per cent), followed by business services (3 per cent) and miscellaneous personal services (1 per cent). The large branch of community services consists of public administration (9 per cent), education (8 per cent), medical (7 per cent), and other (2 per cent).

Table 14.1 Percentage share of the service sectors in EC12 total employment

Sector	1950	1960	1970	1980	1985
5. Construction	7	8	8	8	7
6. Commerce	13	14	15	17	18
7. Transport	6	6	6	6	6
8. Finance and Business	3	4	5	6	7
9. Community and Social	9	12	18	23	26
Total services	38	44	52	60	64
Total employment (millions)	107	116	120	123	121

Sources: 1950–1970: NEI, Fleur data base
1970–1985: OECD, *Labour Force Statistics*, various years

For GDP, the branch composition of these service sectors cannot be assessed in quite the same detail, but Table 14.2 conveys largely the same configuration of services in terms of GDP as Table 14.1 does in terms of employment. Sectoral differences between the two tables may be due not only to productivity divergences but also to differences in sector delineation.

Trade in services by member country

Unlike trade in goods, trade in services constitutes a problem not only to the politician, but also to the statistician. Indeed, to measure trade in services is quite a complicated proposition. If the service is incorpor-

Table 14.2 Percentage shares of service sectors in total value added EC12, 1960-1985

Sector	1960	1970	1980	1985
5. Construction	7	8	7	6
6. Trade, Restaurants and Hotels	13	14	14	14
7. Transport	7	7	6	6
8. Finance + Community	5	6	7	8
9. Other (private)	20	24	29	30
Total	52	59	63	64

Sources: OECD, *National Account Statistics*, various years. Eurostat.

Table 14.3 Imports (M) and exports (E) of services (percentage of GDP, current prices)

Country	1960		1970		1980		1985	
	M	E	M	E	M	E	M	E
Germany	3	3	6	5	7	6	8	8
France	2	2	4	4	7	9	13	14
Italy	2	3	5	6	6	8	7	7
Belgium/Luxemburg	5	5	11	11	26	26	37	39
Netherlands	4	6	11	12	18	18	18	18
United Kingdom	5	6	7	9	10	12	19	21
Denmark	3	5	6	8	12	11	15	12
Ireland	n.a.	n.a.	6	12	7	8	23	12
Greece	n.a.	n.a.	4	5	5	10	8	8
Spain	n.a.	n.a.	3	7	4	7	5	9
Portugal	n.a.	n.a.	9	10	10	10	13	11
EC12	3	3	6	6	9	9	12	13
USA	1	1	2	2	3	5	3	4
Japan	1	1	3	2	4	3	4	3

Sources: Eurostat: *Balances of Payment*; *Global Data*. Various issues. World Bank *Atlas*, Various issues
n.a. = not available

ated in an information carrier, for instance a consultancy report, there is still some relation with goods trade, and the international transaction could in principle be recorded the moment the report passes the frontier. However, most of the time there is a question of international trade because either the consumer (a student who studies abroad) or the producer (a professor who teaches abroad) travels from one country to another. In either case the transaction is difficult to register. To overcome such difficulties, most international service transactions are registered only at the moment the payment is made (through national banks). The criterion for the international exportation of a service is then that it be paid for by a person resident or a company established in another country.

The relative importance of trade in services is given in Table 14.3. A quick look at the data in the table reveals that services are to an increasing extent traded internationally. The trend is very common

Table 14.4 Trade in services of the EC10 with third countries, 1984, thousand million Ecu

Sector	Total			With non-OECD countries		
	E	I	B	E	I	B
Transport	37.4	37.8	−0.4	13.9	15.2	−1.2
Transport insurance	1.3	1.6	−0.4	0.3	0.3	0.0
Tourism	23.4	24.1	−0.7	4.3	4.8	−0.5
Intellectual property	3.7	5.3	−1.7	0.6	0.2	0.5
Banking[a]	2.7	1.5	1.2	0.6	0.1	0.5
Insurance (other than transport)	3.4	2.7	0.7	0.4	0.3	0.1
Construction + engineering services	11.6	4.4	7.1	10.0	2.9	6.9
Film, radio, TV etc.	0.6	0.6	0.0	0.1	0.0	0.0
Other	27.9	25.0	2.7	8.6	7.2	1.5
Total	111.8	103.2	8.6	38.8	31.0	7.8
Investment Income[b]	123.6	127.0	−3.5	47.8	38.1	9.8
Labour income[b]	4.0	4.3	−0.3	1.3	1.2	0.0
Goods trade[b]	366.4	357.4	−0.9	159.1	162.7	-3.7

[a] Not including the difference between interest paid and received.
[b] For reasons of comparison with other items.
E = exports; I = imports; B = balance
Source: GATT (1987)

among all EC member countries. From the comparison of Table 14.3 with Table 8.1, which gave the same information for goods, the transactions in services appear to be relatively small (about half of those in goods). In relative terms the growth of international service transactions was quite spectacular: while goods integration (measured as a percentage of GDP) grew by somewhat more than half in the 1960–1985 period and indeed stagnated in the 1980–1985 period, service integration within the EC is now four times as high as in 1960, and the pace seems to have increased in the last few years.

Trade in services by branch and area

Table 14.4 represents the structure of the external *trade of the EC in services by sector* of activity. Transport and tourism are very important items in terms of exports as well as imports. The EC has a net surplus on its balance of trade in services, largely due to construction and other services; the latter include services related to commerce, technology, intra-firm transactions, fees, etc.

The geographical distribution shows that on average most of the external trade (about two-thirds) is with OECD countries. There are considerable differences among sectors. For most sectors, practically all trade is with OECD partners, for two (transport and other) the average situation applies, and for two others trade is practically oriented towards the non-OECD area. That situation reflects the very low degree of openness in world-wide international trade in services. In the framework of GATT, negotiations are now under way to try and dismantle such protectionism.

Europeanisation or multinationalisation of firms

The service sector is a very mixed bag, and because firms from different service branches are difficult to compare (turnover for trade, gross premium for insurance, assets for banks, etc.), rather than ranking all service firms by size, we will consider sizes and multinationalisation tendencies only by branch.

- *Construction*. There is only one very large firm (over a thousand million Ecu) in Europe, namely, the French firm Bouygues; construction is very little integrated on the European scale.
- *Commerce*. Both in wholesale and retail there are some very large firms; in terms of turnover they head the list of the largest European service firms. Most of the very large firms, like Aldi (FRG), Leclerc (France) and Marks and Spencer (UK), are still very much oriented to their national markets.
- *Banking and insurance*. For banking, integration is not very far ad-

vanced; most banks have only small international networks of branches and do limited business abroad; they are still very much oriented to national markets. Although some loose co-operative networks (consortia) exist, proper multinationalisation on the European scale is still lacking (Pecchioli, 1983; Clarotti, 1984).[3] For insurance, multinationalisation has advanced very rapidly in recent years; all the larger European companies acquired subsidiaries in most EC countries.

- *Business services* used to be organised in fairly small specialised companies. In recent years these have shown a tendency towards diversification as well as multinationalisation, much according to the pattern of manufacturing. Foremost in this group is the UK-based firm of Saatchi and Saatchi, dealers in publicity, communication, marketing and consulting, who have spread their activities in professional services world-wide.[4] Second come the large auditing firms, most of which practise, besides auditing, fiscal and management consultancy. In this branch considerable changes have taken place, due to national mergers first and world-wide mergers next. Most European companies became part of one of the American 'Big Eight'; an exception is the Dutch-centred KPMG organisation. In 1989 four of these merged again so that now only six large firms remain. The reason for that spectacular world-wide integration, which has actually bypassed European integration, is first the need for these firms to provide a world-wide service to multinational clients (there has been a clear demand pull, Leyshon *et al.*, 1987) and second to cut costs and increase market power.

- *Other services*, too, are still very much nationally oriented, partly because of the absence of economies of scale (barber shops), partly also because they are part of the (semi-)public sector (education, health, culture etc.).

Case study: insurance

Structure of the industry

The insurance business consists of two main branches, 'life' and 'non-life' (motor, fire, etc.). The latter has grown in importance in the EC in the past decades (from 56 per cent in 1960 to 61 per cent of total business in 1980). Insurance is a product for which demand is growing (income elasticity is about 1.1). The share of premiums in total GNP increased from 3 per cent in 1960 to 5 per cent in 1985. The European insurance market is still greatly segmented into national markets, and on each national market concentration tends to be fairly high. The largest firm, or group of companies, typically holds a 15 to 25 per cent share in the national market. In some countries, a large portion of the business is covered by nationalised companies (France, 37 per cent; Ireland, 50 per cent), but in most countries private firms dominate the market. In all countries, mutual-insurance companies also take a fair share of the market (CEC, 1985c).

The insurance business involves risks, and to spread these is important. Therefore, companies will try to attain a certain size. They may also try to achieve economies of scale in marketing, and use their large size as a lever in bargaining with customers and suppliers.[5] International diversification tends to spread risks even wider. To choose a reliable measure of size is difficult; we have opted for gross premium, and ranked the largest European companies accordingly in Table 14.5. The list is dominated by UK firms, followed at some distance by German and French ones.

Table 14.5 Largest European insurance companies

Rank	Company	Country	Gross premium (000 000$)	Employ- ment (000)	Assets (000 000$)
1	Commercial Union	UK	3.3	20.1	11.1
2	Prudential	UK	3.2	22.6	24.2
3	Royal Insurance Corp.	UK	3.2	8.9	6.7
4	Allianz	FRG	3.1	15.1	5.1
5	Union Assurances Paris	France	3.1	18.1	n.a.
6	Nationale Nederlanden	Netherlands	2.8	17.7	18.6
7	Willis Faber	UK	2.5	3.1	0.7
8	General Accident	UK	2.0	10.3	3.4
9	Ass. Générale France	France	2.0	15.3	5.6

Source: *Europe's Largest Companies*, London, 1985
n.a. = not available

Many insurance companies are now multi-national firms (MNF), a situation almost exclusively acquired by buying up foreign firms and transforming them into subsidiaries. A strong stimulus towards such multinationalisation has been the demand of large MNF clients of the industry for service wherever their business is located. As in the banking industry, some consortia formed as intermediate stages to the recent number of agreements of closer cooperation and take-overs.

The list of Table 14.5 is exclusive of some very large reinsurance companies, such as Münchener Re, which in 1983 handled a gross premium of 3 500 million Ecu, and is indeed the world's largest specialist reinsurance company. Nor does it include Lloyds, the British firm that occupies a very special place in insurance brokerage.

Internal market for insurance services

Within the EC countries, the insurance industry has developed on a national basis, each national submarket being protected by a whole array of measures.[6] The only exception is the UK industry, which has always been of a highly international nature. The EC has tried to bring about a European market for insurance services,[7] but has found it very difficult, given the multitude of national regulations affecting the industry. The debate about the creation of a common market for the insurance sector centres around two aspects: freedom of establishment and freedom to provide services abroad.

Freedom of establishment implies the possibility of creating a branch office in another member state; non-discrimination requires that such an office be treated on a level with national companies. Since 1973 (1978 for life insurance), EEC directives have regulated the establishment aspect, in the sense that every member state must subject all insurance business on its territory to authorisation; as a result, all companies anywhere in the EC have come under supervision. The problem is that under the old set of rules, the French authorities, applying French standards, require minimum reserves (franc-denominated and lodged in francs), which adds to the costs of the insurer. The general surveillance of the solvency margins of the whole firm is left to the home-country authorities. EC directives set minimum standards, to inspire mutual confidence in national regulations.

Freedom to provide services means that a French client can conclude an insurance contract directly with the London office of an English company. The situation is entirely different from the one prevailing for establishment. In line with the general sense of Court ruling, the Commission has proposed several schemes for liberalisation and harmonisation; however, they have all failed to get sufficient approval from the Council to reach realisation. In that situation a German broker named Steicher broke the German regulations by arranging for insurance of his German clients directly with non-German insurers. The European Court of Justice, asked to consider the case, ruled in December 1986 in favour of Steicher, considering that only for underwriting compulsory insurances – such as motor insurance – was it necessary to be established in the same country as the client, and that no such contention could be imposed on other categories, including co-insurance. The host country may insist on service authorisation, however. The implications of that case ruling are now being worked out.

On the whole, however, national regulations are well entrenched, and opposition against further harmonisation and liberalisation is quite fierce (Finsinger *et al.*, 1985). Pressure for liberalisation comes in particular from the Commission, half-heartedly supported by insurance companies. Indeed, the latter are often well settled behind protecting regulations even in foreign markets. The greatest pressure comes from UK companies who plead the liberalisation of the corporate market. We will come back to the subject in Chapter 16.

International penetration of markets in the EC

The situation described in the previous section is mirrored in the figures. Indeed, as the first column of Table 14.6 shows, the share of national markets accounted for by foreign-controlled companies is very small for all EC member states.

Table 14.6   Indicators of life-insurance market interpenetration (around 1980)

Country	Percentage of premium accounted for by foreign firms	Total number of foreign insurers from EC	Of which of UK	From third countries
Belgium/Luxemburg	12	126	39	26
Denmark	2	39	30	20
France	4	124	47	36
FRG	3	81	42	31
Greece	16[a]	64	34	15
Ireland	35	34	30	4
Italy	4	35	18	15
Netherlands	5	102	36	52
UK	11	30	n.a.	48
Spain	n.a.	21	9	12
Portugal	n.a.	25	14	1
EC12	n.a.	681	299	260

Sources: CEC (1985c); SIGMA (1985)
[a] Total industry, non-life
n.a. = not available

The above figures apply to life insurance, but were representative of the entire insurance sector in the eighties. The international relations they indicate do not seem to have increased in that period (Price Waterhouse, 1988) and possibly had even decreased somewhat in the previous decades, owing to the stricter regulating environment and new forms of protectionism, including informal barriers to entry. The small portion of the national markets of most EC countries acquired by non-nationals (column 1) were disputed by large numbers of foreign companies from other EC countries (column 2) and third countries (Switzerland, US, Japan; column 4). The lion's share of the insurance market occupied by foreign firms in all countries (column 3) was held by UK firms, some of which already get the larger portion of their premium income from foreign operations. Despite the large number of companies engaged in insurance by the end of the eighties, by far most foreign business was still done by a few very large companies with headquarters in another EC member state.

Price differences

The segmentation of markets means that the law of one price does not hold; hence large *price differences* in insurance can be expected to occur among EC member countries. That is indeed the case. To illustrate their magnitude, Figure 14.1 presents the differences for a standard life (term) insurance policy (BEUC, 1988). They show that in Portugal consumers pay nine times as much for the same product as those in the cheapest country, the UK. Similar differences in prices were found by Price Waterhouse (1988) for this and other categories of insurance (house, motor, fire and liability). Assuming that the average of the four countries with the lowest prices would be a fair indication of the average EC price after integration, they found a considerable potential for price cuts. The average cut for all fire insurance categories cited amounted to more than 50 per cent for Italy, 30 per cent for Belgium/Luxemburg and Spain, 25 per cent for France and 10 per cent for Germany.

The *causes* of the very high prices in certain countries are generally thought to be lack of competition and inefficiences due to state regulations. Full deregulation is not the answer, as the consumer needs protection against certain malpractices and in particular against the risk of the insurance company going bankrupt. BEUC has made an analysis of the situation in each country and defined the following five categories: (1) highly diversified, (2) diversified, (3) competitive, (4) cartel and (5) state-fixed tariff. The comparison of each country's scores with the prices in Figure 14.1 (see left-hand column) shows that in general high prices go indeed hand in hand with a lack of competition.

Figure 14.1 Annual premiums (best buy) of a term insurance in the EC countries (man of 30, smoker, 10 years' cover, 100 000 Ecu)

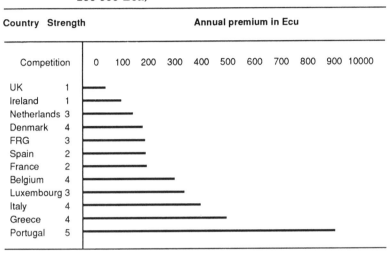

Source: BEUC: *Term Insurance in Europe*, report 51/88 Brussels

Summary and conclusions

- The EC had always considered services an essential part of the integration process, but paid little attention to it in practice. The growing importance of the sector in intra- and extra-EC trade has changed that situation, and now policies are being worked out for the liberalisation of the internal service market as well as for external trade in services.
- Many service firms have up to now been sheltered from international competition by government regulations. For that reason, little multinationalisation of firms has occurred. The sector's low degree of integration is also apparent in the fairly high differences in prices among EC countries.
- The case study of insurance, a sector in which economies of scale are important, shows that both the freedom to provide services in another country and freedom of establishment are now put into practice, leading to a growing interpenetration of markets and multinationalisation of firms.

Notes

1   There is some confusion in the literature on international trade in services whether or not to count the returns on investment and workers' remittances as such. The confusion springs from the reporting mechanism (financial flows in the balance of payments). We consider them as labour and capital transactions as dealt with in Chapters 6, 9 and 10.

2   Other criteria are often put forward, for instance output immobility, because of the important consequence of simultaneous consumption and production (Herman and van Holst, 1984).

3   There is some similarity between banking and insurance (Sametz, 1984), although the latter seems somewhat further advanced in the integration process.

4   As far as the EC is concerned, the multinationalisation of this sector may have been stimulated by the diminution of national preferences for products with certain specific characteristics and by the harmonisation of the regulatory environment for advertising (Rijkens and Miracle, 1986).

5   For an evaluation of economies of scale in the UK insurance industry, see Tapp (1986, page 56), who finds considerable economies at the lower end of the scale, a very long practically flat area in the central part, and diseconomies at the upper end.

6   A classification of protectionist measures can be made along several lines. OECD (1983a) makes a distinction between establishment and transactions on the one hand, and on the other between types of different measure (tax, solvency ratio, public sector, etc.). See also Ingo (1985).

7   For a more elaborate description of the Community's involvement, see CEC (1985c) chapter 2; for national systems of some member countries, Finsinger and Pauly (1986), and for an expert's view, van den Berghe, 1980.

15 Transport

Introduction

A great advantage of economic integration is that each member state tends to specialise in the production of those goods for which it is best equipped in terms of economic, geographical or other conditions. Specialisation within a Customs Union implies the spatial separation of supply and demand, and hence increased *international goods transport*. In the old days, goods used to be produced to meet local or national demand (see Chapter 3), and transport was limited to local or national areas. With economic integration, more goods have to pass across national frontiers. How profitable integration will be depends also on the cost of transportation. In that respect, transportation costs are not different from customs tariffs or other obstacles to the complete free trade of goods (Zippel, 1985). Logically, therefore, the transport sector should not be overlooked as integration proceeds.

The creation of the Common Market and the ensuing freedom to provide services, integration of capital markets and free movement of persons (labour), and the progress towards an Economic and Monetary Union with harmonised policies, lead to more and more contacts between workers from different member states, and hence to *increased international passenger transport*.

Because of its specific qualities and its importance to the international economy, the transport sector has drawn considerable interest from *international organisations*. Merchant shipping in particular has had the attention of such UN affiliates as ECE, UNCTAD and the International Maritime Organisation, and air transport from the International Air Transport Association. European agencies concerned with transport problems are the European Conference of Transport Ministers, the OECD Transport Committee, the European Committee for Civil Aviation and the Central Rhine Shipping Committee.

Within Europe, the *European Community* is the organisation most relevant to the transport sector from an economics point of view. European integration calls for the advanced division of tasks among member states, entailing intensified international moves of goods and passengers. Greater capacities and lower costs of transport smooth the way for progressive specialisation. Therefore, transport is a primary concern of the European Community; indeed, for full profit from the Common Market, the manifold transport regulations in the different member states need to be either abolished or harmonised.

In the period just after the Second World War there was a strong tendency to liberalise trade. Most European countries, however, did not consider the corresponding liberalisation of transport, to say nothing of positive integration, or harmonisation. Indeed, harmonisation would have been particularly difficult while most European governments continued their *intervention* in the transport sector in the form of strict regulations, which moreover differed from country to country.

In the following sections of this chapter, the transport sector in the European Community will be subjected to close analysis. The order will be the same as in the chapters on other economic sectors: first we will describe how the European markets for transport are regulated. Next some significant aspects of the sector, covering both international goods and passenger transport will be discussed. Finally, we will study in some more detail how the integration of two important submarkets – goods transport (by road, railway, inland and pipeline) and passenger transport (notably air transport) – is proceeding. A critical evaluation and some proposals for the consolidation of the common transport market will complete the chapter.

Community regime

Treaties

The few transport stipulations contained in the ECSC treaty are concerned only with preventing the distortion of fair competition by differential tariffs. The transportation of coal and steel is costly, and therefore it was of paramount importance not to have the free market (unhampered by customs tariffs) eroded by differences in transport costs. Article 70 of the Paris Treaty clearly prohibits rates or other transport conditions that are discriminating by nationality or origin/destination, but explicitly reserves transport policy to the member states. The EAEC treaty is not very important in transport matters. The EEC treaty, on the contrary, is concerned with nearly all facets of transport policy. Article 3 stipulates that the objectives of the treaty shall be pursued by a common transport policy.

A *common transport policy*, according to the Commission and many independent observers, means that (1) transport must not be an obstacle to the common market for goods and services, and (2) a common transport market has to be created. That the authors of the Treaty of

Rome set great store by transport is evident from the fact that they devoted a separate title to it (IV, articles 74–84), a privilege shared only with agriculture. Remarkably, however, the transport title applies only to the so-called inland traffic, namely 'transport by rail, road and inland waterway'. With respect to navigation and aviation, article 84 stipulates merely that 'appropriate provisions may be laid down'. While unequivocally stipulating a common transport policy (article 74), the Treaty is much less clear about the way in which it should be achieved. Let us look a bit closer at the different stipulations.

Common rules for international transport must be laid down as well as the conditions under which transport entrepreneurs are admitted to national transport in a member state in which they are not resident (article 75). This shows that the right of establishment, contrary to the right to provide services, is directly applicable to transport. Further appropriate provisions are possible. The rules and conditions referred to must be laid down in the transition period by qualified majority of votes. Unanimity is required in one case, however: the one regarding 'principles of the regulatory system for transport that would be liable to have a serious effect on the standard of living and on employment in certain areas and on the operation of transport facilities' (read: railways; see also Single European Act). On the other hand, the necessity is recognised to adjust to the economic developments resulting from the creation of the Common Market. From this article, the countries negotiating in 1957 were apparently far from being at one on the policy to be pursued; no unequivocal objectives and principles of the common policy to be drawn up can be found in the treaty. The vagueness of article 75 was made worse because some countries succeeded in having article 76 stipulate that until common rules were issued according to article 75, no member state could take measures that were more damaging to transport companies in other member states than in their own.

Market regulation concerning prices and conditions of transport is another matter dealt with by the Treaty.

- In setting prices (rates), account should be taken of the economic circumstances of carriers (art. 78) (income-policy argument, compare Agriculture);
- The general prohibition of discrimination applies also to transport (art. 79). It puts a stop to the practice of cheap tariffs for exports and high ones for imports;[1]
- Equal competition conditions (art. 80) forbids member states (unless authorised by the Commission) to impose on transport within the Community prices and conditions holding any element of support or protection of manufacturing industry or sectors.

On closer study of the Transport Title, the Treaty of Rome appears to be beset with *conflicting principles and vague stipulations.* They spring from considerable differences among member states in economic and geographical conditions and in transport–political conceptions (Erd-menger, 1981; Button 1984). Some countries (especially Germany and France) see transport as a public service or as an integral part of the social structure, affecting the distribution of population and shaping the community's social life. Others (The Netherlands and the United Kingdom) take a largely commercial view of transport; they consider that the application of market-economic principles is in the best inter-est of customers (shippers) and society.

Reaching out for a common policy

In the early days of the EC6, the Commission was striving to establish a common transport market for all inland transport modes, guided by the principles of market economics and inspired by the liberal attitude displayed in the Treaty of Rome with respect to the goods trade (*1962 Memorandum of the Commission,* and *1962 Action Programme*). A com-mon transport policy, replacing the various national policies, hope-fully would guarantee fair competition among and within branches of transport, as well as create conditions of equal competition for other sectors in the economy, such as agriculture, manufacturing industry, and commerce.

In that vein, the *Memorandum* proposed three *objectives*:

- To remove obstacles created by transport and impeding a free common market for goods and persons. The implementation of this first objective implied, among other things, the abolition of tariff discrimination for reasons of nationality.
- To integrate the transport sector on the Community level (that is, allow free movement of transport services). This implied a certain form of liberalisation. Besides, the *Memorandum* pro-posed quite detailed regulations with respect to market control, namely for tariffs, market access, etc. applicable to both national and international transport (comparable to the market regula-tions in agriculture);
- To establish a Community transport system. Obviously, that would mean adjusting the infrastructure to the demands of increased international exchange, frontier-crossing motorways, etc. Besides, the technical (axle load, carriage length, containers), fiscal (motor-vehicle tax, petrol duty), social (driving hours) and economic (professional requirements) stipulations would have to be harmonised. For many years, harmonisation was the first

concern, on the consideration that no fair competition would be possible nor liberalisation admissible without it.

In practice, these objectives and principles proved so difficult to realise that the detailed common policy advanced at a snail's pace, and the integrated market for transport services hardly if at all (see, for instance, CEC, 1973a). In the second half of the 1970s, the advance of the common transport policy was slowed down even more by the economic recession, the increased concern for the environment, the higher energy costs and the extension of the Community.

Liberalisation by the Court of Justice

Confronted with stagnation, the Commission then proposed new schemes, limiting its own involvement to laying down general principles and emphasising the harmonisation of national measures. The idea of working out a complete Community transport system, following the pattern of agriculture, was abandoned. However, the new proposals, like the earlier ones, came to nothing because of the Council's indecisiveness. In that situation, the European Parliament, always an active promotor of a European transport policy, judged that the Council of Ministers must be summoned before the Court of Justice. That this unique procedure was resorted to characterises the regrettable situation that had evolved: 25 years after the founding of the EC, and more than 15 years after the end of the transition period, there was still no EC transport policy worked out.

From the Court's verdict in the 'failure to act' case (13/83, ex-article 175 EEC) which Parliament, with the Commission's and the Dutch government's support, had instituted against the Council, we take the following significant elements:

- The Council is committed to regulate within a reasonable period the liberalisation of frontier-crossing transport within the EC (including transit);
- The Council shall also establish the conditions under which entrepreneurs from one member state are permitted to take part in transport in another member state (cabotage);
- The Council may, but is not obliged to, take complementary measures (in practice social, traffic, and other harmonisation measures).

The Court thus confirmed the application to the transport sector of the principle of freedom to provide services, but recognised also the special quality of the Treaty's stipulations with respect to transport, and finally established that freedom of transport is not enjoined in the same direct terms as free service traffic in general (Simons 1986).

The Court left the question of timing open by using the term 'within a reasonable period'. The Commission and the Council have specified the horizon, much in line with the other aspects of the internal market (Chapter 16), as the year 1992. A schedule for taking the measures required for liberalisation has been drawn up.

Market order; degree of integration by mode of transport

Up till the end of the eighties, the integration was dependent on the way in which the market was regulated, which differed widely among modes of transport.[2]

In *haulage*, national transport is reserved to national companies susceptible to national market controls. In some countries, internal long-distance carriage is subject to licensing systems. Neither cabotage nor carrying for third countries is permitted. In international transport a combined Community and bilateral system of trip authorisation with national quotas is operated. This system does not cover all goods; by 1987, a measure of liberalisation had been achieved for 35 per cent of total goods transport. The Community has regulated not only the quantities but also the prices of road transport.[3] Besides, some complementary regulations have been introduced for the harmonisation of the operating conditions for international road transport, such as: exemption from customs duties for 200 litres of fuel in the tanks of utility vehicles; social rules mainly concerned with hours of driving and resting and the use of the tachograph; conditions for admission to the profession (certificates, etc.), and a Community driving licence. That system can never respond adequately to the needs of a market. Many vehicles are forced to return empty because no return cargo may be picked up and because cabotage (carrying cargo in another member state for customers there) and transport for third countries are hardly ever permitted.[4] The number of EC authorisations is to be gradually stepped up to be large enough by 1992 for the transition to a fully free Common Market for road transport to be possible without disturbing the market.

In *rail transport*, the Community has pursued two objectives: (1) a normal price setting in commercial supply and demand situations, and (2) the abolition of subsidies. The harmonisation decision of 1965 commits member states either to reimburse the costs of charges and transport obligations foreign to the trade, or abolish the obligations. Railway companies were henceforth to be financially independent, and price formation on international segments was to be free (Council Decision 82/529, EEC).

Inland shipping was practically free when the EC was created, thanks largely to the Mannheim Convention which guarantees free traffic on the Rhine. The economic recession of 1973 inspired associations of shipowners to try and enforce, through a blockade, a rotation scheme for the proportional allocation of freight on the so-called 'north–south route'. The system already existed in France and was being introduced in Belgium and The Netherlands. The EC is opposed to such a development, which is at cross purposes with the Treaty, but so far has not taken active steps in the matter. Besides, the EC itself has laid down some rules regarding technical requirements for vessels, requirement of professional ability for captains, etc.

Maritime shipping regulation became particularly important when, with the joining of three new member states (two of them islands!) in 1972, some maritime shipping turned into intra-community transport. The Court has confirmed that sea navigation, too, comes under the general rules of the Treaty. Market control in maritime shipping mostly takes the form of so-called 'shipping-line conferences': associations of shipowners active in the same sailing area, which, in economic terms, are cartels. In the framework of UNCTAD negotiations, the EC was forced not only to accept the existence of such conferences, but also to concede a certain division of the market between developed and developing countries. Admittedly, provisos have been made to the effect that the division of cargoes will not be applied to intra-Community sea traffic and that all EC shipowners will have equal access to EC cargoes to third countries. The relevant regulations[5] have caused EC policy with respect to sea shipping to take precedence over the formulation of a common policy for other transport branches.

Finally *aviation*. The Court has confirmed that this sector, too, comes under the Treaty of Rome. Governments have a firm grip on the air-traffic market through national air companies, air-space control, landing rights, etc. Internationally, there is a veritable tangle of multilateral accords (Convention of Chicago) and bilateral agreements governing landing rights, capacity, frequency, routes, etc. In the framework of the IATA (an association of companies), tariff agreements have been concluded for passenger as well as freight services (Naveau, 1983). As a result, within the EC high prices prevail on all connections.[6] In the framework of the total programme for the completion of the internal market (Chapter 16) the Commission has submitted proposals for the further liberalisation of the air-traffic market. Progress has been made for interregional transport (Directive 83/416/EEC). The arrangement on the point of relaxation of the fifty-fifty rule by which companies share passengers on a certain route. The objective is a fully free international competition in the EC by 1992.

All those market-control schemes push up the costs for the *users* of transport services. Companies operating in protected markets are not motivated to increase their productivity, while others are not given scope to develop new initiatives. Such inefficient functioning keeps the prices of transport unduly high. If the objectives of the Treaty are to be realised after all, national government interventions must be partly harmonised and partly abolished. The experience in countries which have decided to deregulate their transport markets, is that service improves and prices drop without the market being disturbed (Auctores Varii, 1983). In Europe the navigation on the Rhine is the classical example. Economically, therefore, full liberalisation of the European transport market is the most desirable solution and one in line with the EC regime for the rest of the economic sectors.

Market control: some general aspects

Despite the specific features of transport, the general rules of the Treaty with respect to *competition conditions apply*: first and foremost, the right of free establishment; second, the general prohibition of competition-distorting state aids (articles 92–94); and third, the agreements impeding intra-community trade (article 85) or the abuse of a dominant position (86). However, special rules have been laid down for transportation by rail, road, inland shipping (Regulation 1017/68) and sea-borne shipping. Recently, the Court confirmed that the competition rules also apply to air transport.

For all transport sectors, the Community has established *systems of market observation* for easy insight into the volume, structure and development of supply and demand; the systems are helpful to market parties in reaching adequate decisions. They vary somewhat as to type of information, frequency, etc.

The co-ordination of the different modes has always been an important object of transport policy. The recovery of infrastructure costs poses moreover a difficult economic problem, for different recovery schemes can distort competition between transport modes as well as disturb international trade. Two conditions must be satisfied for the adequate recovery of costs: (1) correct computation of total costs, and (2) correct attribution to users. Levies would have to satisfy two requirements: (1) reflect marginal social costs, and (2) meet the demand of overall budget equality. The computation problem was solved in 1970, when the Council introduced a common system to establish the costs of road, railroad and waterway infrastructure. The attribution problem has not been solved yet. On the basis of the many studies made (see, among others, Allais *et al.*, 1965; Malcor, 1970; Oort, 1975), the Commission has submitted to the Council various proposals for directives; these have not yet been translated into action, however.

The outward *screening of the EC internal transport market* differs among modes. As to road transport, the bilateral deals concluded by individual member states with third countries make it practically impossible for third-country hauliers to offer their services on the EC market. The problem does not occur with rail transport, because any international transport by rail requires the co-operation of nationalised companies with monopoly power. In inland shipping, the Mannheim Act applies only to riverain states of the Rhine, which means in practice that third countries (apart from Switzerland) are banned from services on the Rhine. The regulations relevant to sea shipping have just been described. In civil aviation, national authorities have up till now regulated access to their territory for EC and third-country companies alike: a common external civil-aviation policy has not yet got off the ground.

Structural policy

EC structural policy in matters of transport has not advanced very far. The policy is concerned with both transport infrastructure (generally in the public domain) and production means (in principle in private hands, in practice also to a large extent in public hands).

The first proposals made by the Commission for intensive co-ordination of national investments in *infrastructure* were refused by the Council as an unpermissible intervention of the EC in national autonomy. The Council did reach a decision about a consultation procedure, that is to say, a far lighter form of integration. A study of the prospects for co-ordinating the investments (Gwilliam *et al.*, 1973) appeared in 1973. Present policy is directed towards improving the infrastructure from a Community point of view (CEC, 1979b). The installation of an Infrastructure Committee has improved the attuning of national projects. Since the early eighties it has become possible to give financial support to projects of which the execution is an urgent Community interest (see CEC, 1982d, 1982e). Significantly, proposals have been made to third countries (Switzerland, Austria and Yugoslavia) for the financing of infrastructure (particularly roads) in their territory as far as essential to intra-European traffic. The Commission has retraced its hesitant steps towards involvement in the financing of seaports and airports, to concentrate henceforth on what it considers the main problems of the European transport market, namely, the transportation of goods[7] by road, railroad and inland waterways. Recently, the planning of transport infrastructure regained interest through a number of large projects with evident European dimensions. The most striking is the Channel tunnel which presumably will greatly facilitate road and rail traffic from the United Kingdom to the mainland and back. Other projects are the fast trains (TGV) planned to connect towns in France with towns in neighbouring countries to the north and south. Neither the planning nor the financing of such projects are direct tasks for the Commission of the EC, however; as far as the latter aspect is concerned, the European Investment Bank will often be involved.

Policy concerned with the improvement of the *production means* varies among transport modes. In railroad transport, rolling stock is subject to many national rules, but no relevant EC measures have been taken, nor are there any EC measures to improve the production structure of road transport. To improve access to the European market, certain technical prescriptions as to axle load, brakes, permissible weight, etc., have been issued, but even on those points progress has been slow; there are still many impediments to a common structural transport policy.[8] The Commission has taken some perfunctory steps towards a structural policy for inland shipping, more specifically with respect to the demolition of obsolete ships. Its recommendations have given a European framework to the demolition schemes worked out by most member states, but European co-ordination has not always been optimum. Regarding sea and air traffic, no structure-improving programmes have been developed. So, in general there is no common policy for improving the production structure in transport at all comparable to the programmes for the agricultural and industrial sectors.

Sketch of the sector

Importance of the sector

The transport sector is of strategic importance to the EC economy, though relatively modest in terms of wealth creation and employment, accounting for a very stable 4 or 5 per cent of GDP and employment (see Table 15.1).

Table 15.1   Percentage share of transport sector[a] in total GDP and employment, EC12, 1950–1985

	1950	1960	1970	1980	1985
GDP	n.a.	7.1	6.5	6.1	6.1
Employment	5.8	5.9	6.0	6.1	6.0

n.a. = not available

[a] Including telecommunications, accounting for some 1.5 per cent of GDP and Employment

Sources: Employment:NEI FLEUR database; OECD *Labour-Force Statistics*; GDP: *National-Account Statistics*.

Table 15.2 Characteristics of the transport system (EC12), 1950–1985

	1950	1960	1970	1980	1985
Road					
Motorways (1 000 km)	2	4	13	26	30
Cars owned (x 1 000 000)	6	20	58	96	114
Cars per 1 000 population	22	72	194	300	353
Commercial vehicles (x 1 000 000)	3	5	8	10	12
Railway					
Coaches (x 1 000)	113	102	79	76	70
Goods wagons (x 100 000)	15	13	11	9	7
Track total (1 000 km)	163	148	136	129	127
Multitrack, electrified (x 1 000 km)	10	18	27	34	36
Inland waterways[a]					
Self-propelled craft (x 1 000)	n.a.	29	24	18	16
capacity (1 000 000 tonnes)	n.a.	12	11	10	10
Dumb and pushed barges (x 1 000)	n.a.	10	5	3	3
capacity (1 000 000 tonnes)	n.a.	5	4	3	4
Sea					
Total fleet (x 1 000)	n.a.	n.a.	17	18	15
Capacity (1 000 000 BRT)	n.a.	n.a.	73	121	88
Oil tankers	n.a.	n.a.	n.a.	1 657	1 200
Capacity (1 000 000 BRT)	n.a.	n.a.	n.a.	51	32
Air[b]					
Number of aircraft	367	654	628	n.a.	n.a.
Number of seats (x 1 000)	13	44	67	n.a.	n.a.
Airports with regular services	70	134	162	n.a.	n.a.
Direct links served	234	418	664	n.a.	n.a.
Average link length (km)	326	566	716	n.a.	n.a.
Average aircraft speed (km/h)	264	433	717	n.a.	n.a.
Pipe[c]					
length in service (x 1 000 km)	n.a.	6	11	17	20

Sources: UN/ECE, *Annual Bulletin of Transport Statistics for Europe*, various estimates

[a] Data indicated for 1960 apply to 1965
[b] The series for 1980/85 are not comparable
[c] Without Denmark, Ireland, FRG, Portugal
n.a. = No comparable data available.

The branches of the sector have developed differently; road transport, now accounting for almost half of employment, has taken the place that rail transport occupied in the 1950s (now some 25 per cent). The relative importance of water and air is less, but the latter is growing very fast.

Production means

The developments of production means reflect the structural changes in European transport. Table 15.2 neatly illustrates the fast rise of haulage and the decline of railroad transport. While the length of the railroad network dropped by 20 per cent and the number of wagons by 30 per cent between 1950 and 1980, the number of lorries increased fourfold in the same period. The fast growth of air traffic is also evident, as is the contraction of the European maritime fleets.

The relation between the data reveals how much the scale of transport has enlarged. The average power of pushboats and tugs for inland shipping rose from 174 kw in 1965 to 210 kw in 1980; the average capacity of aeroplanes increased from 31 seats in 1950 to 107 in 1970. Similar developments can be observed in maritime merchant shipping, rail transport, and haulage.

Government intervention

In the past, the governments' deep involvement in transport has been defended on the grounds of the special characteristics of transport in general and of certain transport modes in particular.

With respect to *transport in general* one argument is that since transportation services cannot be stocked up, capacity tends to be geared to peak demand. Because a large proportion of the costs are fixed, inelastic supply combined with a low price elasticity of demand could lead to very keen price competition. Governments will feel in duty bound to prevent such a situation (which is by no means typical of transport alone). Another argument is that transport requires expensive, long-lasting infrastructure for which the government is mostly responsible. Because the construction costs of this infrastructure and their recovery differ widely among transport modes (compare the railways with inland shipping and road traffic), measures are needed to restore a balanced competition. Finally, through the decades the objectives of transport policy have increasingly become merged with other societal objectives such as cheap transport to backward regions, for certain social groups, etc. and many sectors of transport now have so-called 'public-service obligations'.

With respect to *individual transport modes*, the traditional monopoly of the railways has led to state enterprise, to the firm hold of governments on the tariff structure, and to railroad companies' obligations to provide transport. Haulage, on the contrary, with its low entering threshold, is provided by many (small) private companies. Governments intervene mostly on social and safety considerations (driving hours, technical check-ups, etc.), or from the wish to curb the road sector's competitiveness with respect to railways. The tendency to put a check on haulage increased as (state) railways saw their market dwindle. In the past few years, concern with the environment and the wish to save energy have been new arguments to stem the growth of road traffic in favour of, among others, the railways. The sensitivity of inland shipping to cyclical fluctuations has in the past moved the government to regulate the utilisation of the collective capacity of many suppliers. Most airlines in Europe are also strictly state-controlled; aviation policy aims at protecting the national flag rather than providing optimum service. The situation varies with respect to maritime shipping: protective measures of national governments and competition control by international business companies occur side by side.

Case study 1: inland goods transport

Total volume of inland goods transport

Figure 15.1 reveals how much total transport within the EC has grown in the past 15 years. In the long term, total growth of intra-EC transport seems to follow that of GDP fairly closely (elasticity approximately 1). However, the fluctuations in the growth of *international intra-Community goods transport appears strongly correlated with industrial production.* Another observation is that transport grows faster than industrial production: its elasticity is around 1.5. Indeed, transport grew by about 3.5 per cent in the 1970–1985 period, against industrial production by an average 1.7 per cent. The impression is that before 1971, transport among the six original member states grew even faster and showed even higher elasticities. Exactly how much faster intra-Community international transport has grown (in tons) than extra-Community international transport or domestic transport, is hard to establish. From data available for some of the original six member states it can be derived, however, that

- domestic transport has indeed grown, but much slower than industrial production (elasticity approximately 0.5);
- international extra-Community transport has grown slightly less than intra-Community transport; that would confirm the data derived from international trade statistics.

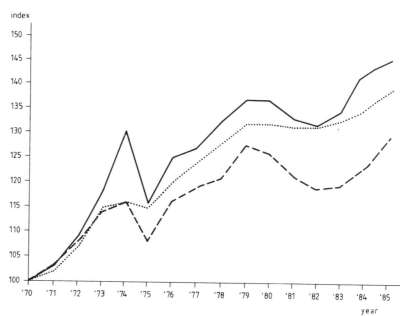

——— Intra EC transport (ton)

········ Gross National Product

— — — Industrial Production

Figure 15.1 Frontier-crossing inland goods transport among EC9 member states, on the basis of tonnage, 1970–1985

Sources: Europe Transport; Eurostat National Accounts; Statistical Bulletin EC Industrial Production.

Modal split of inland goods transport

Table 15.3 gives a survey of the changes in relative importance of the various transport modes for goods transport in Europe.

The major *shift from railroad to road haulage* is evident. Before 1957, haulage played only a modest part in goods transport among member states, amounting to less than a fifth of railroad transport (Blonk, 1968). Now, 25 years later, the roles are reversed: international haulage accounts for double the tonnage of railroad transport. Internationally (intra-EC) the tonnage carried on the road almost equals that of inland shipping. Thus, hauliers are now accounting for the greater part of transport growth among member states. Road transport has become the most important inland transport sector; in the five central member states (Germany, France, the Benelux countries), haulage contributed 86 per cent to total domestic traffic in 1985, against railroads 9 per cent and inland shipping 5 per cent (Eurostat: *Transport Statistics*). The logics of a transport policy trying to safeguard the position of the smallest mode: the railroads, by impeding the normal market development of the largest and steadily growing mode: haulage, is hard to understand (Button, 1983). Empirical studies (Voigt *et al.*,1986) suggest that all regulation with regard to prices and quantities affects modal split only marginally, and that full deregulation is the obvious policy choice.

Table 15.3 Inland goods transport in Europe EC12 by mode of transport (in percentages and in 10^9 ton/km, 1970–1985)

Mode of transport	1970	1975	1980	1984
Railroad	28	22	21	18
Road	50	57	60	65
Inland waterway	14	12	11	11
Pipeline	8	9	8	6
Total (10^9 ton/km)	750	798	965	969

Source: CEMT (1985)

Modal split of inland goods transport by product

What determines the modal split of goods transport? In the first instance, mode choice is governed by the price. However, price is not always decisive, for speed and reliability, that is to say the quality of transport, are important factors too. Their significance varies with the nature of the product to be carried. For a low-value bulk good the price comes first, while for high-value finished products speed and reliability prevail. Table 15.4 gives an impression of the relative importance of various commodity groups by mode.

Each transport mode complies in its own way with shippers' wishes. Rail and water transport are eminently suitable for the transportation of homogeneous goods, in large quantities, over long distances, especially if no connecting transport is needed. Trains and ships are the

Table 15.4 Percentage market shares of each transport mode in international goods transport among all member states of the EC10 and the remaining part of the Community by NST commodity group, 1984

NST code	Description	Road	Railroad	Inland shipping
0	Agricultural products	59	12	29
1	Other foodstuffs and fodder	66	4	30
2	Coal and coke	14	30	56
3	Oil products[a]	8	5	87
4	Ores, metal scrap	5	22	73
5	Basic metals, building materials	45	30	25
6	Crude minerals and manufactures	38	5	57
7	Fertilisers	24	20	56
8	Chemical products	68	9	23
9	Vehicles, machines, other	73	21	6

[a] Pipelines, not accounted for in this table, are also very important for this group
Source: *Europa Transport* (1984)

obvious choices for products like ores, fuel and metals; lorries cannot compete with the low costs of that type of transport. Intermediary products and finished manufactures are generally carried in smaller quantities and to more dispersed destinations. The same is increasingly true of agricultural produce and building materials. For all such cargoes, the lorry is indicated. From the table, the lorry appears to have conquered the greater part of the market for metal products, chemical products, foodstuffs and agricultural produce, and to have become important also for a series of other products. The figures in the above table refer only to 1984; consistent figures for earlier years are not available. From the limited material at hand for previous years (four central member states, total frontier-crossing transport, 1965–1981), two developments are clear, however (Eurostat *Transport Statistics*, various years):

- The growth of typical bulk goods is evidently lagging behind that of special cargo, with the obvious result that railroads and inland shipping, most suited to the transportation of bulk goods, have lost importance.
- Shifts have occurred within each commodity group. For all groups except solid fuels, natural oil and ores, the share of haulage has greatly increased, invariably at the expense of

railroads as well as inland shipping. Within the three bulk products mentioned, a shift from railroad to inland shipping has occurred.

Case study 2: passenger transport by air

Passenger transport, different modes

Passenger transport is an important economic phenomenon. In 1960, the average EC inhabitant spent 8 per cent of his total net income on mobility (purchase and use of car, moped, bicycle, etc. plus train, tram, bus and air tickets). By 1983 the percentage had risen to approximately 14 per cent. The *choice of mode* on international trips depends largely on distance. The trip purpose is also relevant (holiday, business, short stay). Passenger transport has much grown since the war, as was already apparent from the structural data of Table 15.2. The tremendous growth of passenger traffic is explained by demographic growth, increasing incomes and leisure time, and in particular by the integration of the goods and service markets of the member states. Business traffic has greatly extended as a result of increased commercial contacts. Moreover, the greater openness of the market has enhanced tourism. The explosively growing demand could be satisfied thanks to the overall adequate extension of the infrastructure (airports, motorways, etc.).

International *passenger travel* by land has grown much faster than national travel. Between 1955 and 1970, the number of international trips by car grew by a factor 8, while the number of cars rose by slightly less than a factor 3. The growth figures for bus travel are comparable. International passenger traffic by train increased in the 1960–1980 period, albeit modestly in comparison with the other traffic modes.

The growth of *air traffic* has been spectacular. In 1950 air traffic was still in its infant stage, so that very high growth rates were natural; between 1960 and 1970 the volume increased threefold. International traffic grew faster than domestic flights, which nevertheless showed a remarkable increase. Since 1970, the traffic volume has tripled again.

Air traffic; company structure

Air transport showed spectacular growth in the 1960–1985 period: the total number of passenger kilometers produced by the major European airlines increased nine times (see Table 15.5, which covers all operations, both in and outside Europe).

An analysis of the table reveals three indications of national segmentation of markets and of considerable protection.

- The low overall concentration in European air traffic. In 1985, calculated on total world operations, the C_1 index (share of largest company in total operations) = 20 per cent; C_3 (share of rank 1, 2 and 3 companies) = 50 per cent; C_6 = 77 per cent.
- The remarkable stability of the participating companies; in the 1970–1985 period the list showed neither new entrants nor departures, nor were there any mergers between companies of the list (between 1960 and 1970 only two mergers were recorded). Between 1985 and 1988 one merger was made: between British Airways and British Caledonian.
- The stability of the ranking of the major companies. Indeed, from the table it can be derived that four companies did not change places at all between 1970 and 1985, three shifted only one place and four two places in the ranking.

Table 15.5 Total passenger kilometers (1000 million) on scheduled services (international and domestic) of major European airlines, 1960–1985

Rank	Company	Country	1960	1970	1980	1985
1	British Airways	UK	5.9[a]	15.6	40.1	41.1
2	Air France	France	4.0	10.2	25.4	28.6
3	Lufthansa	FRG	1.3	8.3	21.1	24.5
4	KLM	Netherlands	2.7	5.7	14.1	18.0
5	Iberia	Spain	0.7	5.5	14.8	17.6
6	Alitalia	Italy	1.3	7.8	12.9	16.9
7	SAS	Scandinavia	2.2	5.4	11.0	12.1
8	Olympic	Greece	0.3	2.1	5.1	7.5
9	British Caledonian	UK	0.1[b]	0.6	4.0	7.1
10	Sabena	Belgium	1.3	2.4	4.9	5.7
11	UTA	France	0.8[c]	2.0	4.7	4.9
12	TAP	Portugal	0.2	2.3	3.4	4.2
13	Air Lingus	Ireland	0.4	1.8	2.0	2.5
	Total	EC	21.2	69.7	163.5	190.7
	Index		100.0	329.0	772.0	900.0

[a] BEA + BOAC
[b] BUA
[c] TAI + UAT
Source: *World Air Transport Statistics,* several years

Company response to further interpenetration of markets

The recent shifts in the EC attitude towards the (lack of) competition in air transport are bringing about great changes. The companies listed in Table 15.5 are all of the 'trunk' type, providing full scheduled service at a high price. Besides, 'charter'-type companies provide low-cost service, and 'commuter' carriers operate services between regional airports and between regional and major airports. The reactions of the three groups to further liberalisation, and the effects on the industrial landscape in passenger air transport in Europe, could be as follows (Gialloreto, 1988).

- *Trunk* carriers will have to cut costs, raise productivity and, to prevent charter companies from encroaching on their markets, match their low fares. The result may be a more differentiated service level. Of the larger trunk companies, only the better managed will keep their leading positions, while others stand to lose considerable market shares. The smaller ones, to survive in this segment of the air passenger market will have to align with, or let themselves be absorbed by, larger ones. By 1990 agreements of this type were made between BA and Caledonian (merger) BA, KLM and SABENA (financial participation) and Air France and UTA. As the European market is not the only determining factor in company strategy (competition on world routes is fierce), world-wide co-operation between carriers is likely to evolve rapidly (after the pattern of world-encompassing companies in manufacturing industry).
- *Charter* companies are likely to meet competition from trunk companies. Some of them may try to respond to this by entering into the trunk market, but as that has proved a fairly difficult strategy in countries that have already got used to liberal air transport regimes, the effect will be limited.
- *Commuter* companies will increasingly be seen by the large trunk carriers as feeder services to major routes; many independent companies that might have developed into challengers of the majors are likely to be absorbed by, or aligned with, major trunk carriers. As competition intensifies, some new entrants are likely to emerge. However, as the threshold is quite high in civil aviation, the chances of a major upheaval from that type of competition are slight.

A set of policies are necessary to make sure that such company responses to deregulation lead to more efficiency and benefits for the consumer (McGowan and Seabright, 1989).

Summary and conclusions

- The European transport market is very heavily regulated on a national basis and therefore much fragmented. There is no free access, nor are there equal competition conditions.
- A recent ruling of the Court has obliged the Council to work out a *common transport policy* along the same liberal lines that obtain for the rest of the economy under the rules of the EEC. Liberalisation is to take effect by 1992, the date set for the completion of the internal market.
- *International goods transport* by road and inland waterways has increased much faster than industrial growth, which indicates the growing integration of Europe. However, this growth has not gone hand in hand with integration of the inland transport sector; railways have stayed completely national, and in road haulage, very few multinational firms have as yet been created.
- *Passenger transport by air* has increased very rapidly in the 1960–1990 period, but the company structure has remained practically unaltered, evidencing the lack of competition and international integration. In the coming years, liberalisation and world-wide competition are likely to lead in the EC to European and world-wide mergers and linkages of European companies.

Notes

1   Such tariffs were very much in evidence in some countries. Just before the Coal and Steel Community was founded, coal produced in Germany was transported at tariffs up to a quarter below those for imported coal. An example of a low tariff for exports is that for French sodium salts, which paid up to two-fifths less for transport than salt destined for the domestic market.

2   For a complete and detailed review of the regulations in force and the various proposals for liberalisation and harmonisation, see ESS (1989).

3   Again some member states, anxious to protect their railways, have prevailed over some others which preferred to leave price formation to the market. At the moment, price formation rests on so-called 'non-obligatory reference tariffs' (price indications), but two or more member states can decide to adopt a system of so-called 'obligatory marginal tariffs' for their mutual relations (Regulations 1174/08, 2831/77 and 3568/83).

4   In the early 1980s, an estimated 40 per cent of international road haulage had no return cargo at all. Companies often tried to solve the capacity problem by taking care of their own transport, thus avoiding the capacity rules. Around 1980, more than 60 per cent of total haulage capacity in Western Germany, France and Belgium, and about 50 per cent in The Netherlands was thus organised (Source: Eurostat *Transport Statistics*, 1981). The percentages apply to total domestic and international transport; for frontier-crossing transport they are considerably lower: an average 20 to 25 per cent for the EC9 in total (*Europa Transport*). In fact, own-account transport is generally even more expensive than professional haulage, because the vehicles are less fully utilised.

5   See in that respect: Council regulations (EC) nr 4055/86, 4056/86, 4057/86 and 4058/86, *Official Journal* nr L 378, December 31, 1986, pp. 1–21.

6   For a price comparison of Europe and the US, see, among others, CEC (1979c); more recently, Gialloreto (1988) calculated that airline operating costs in Europe were 50 per cent above those in the USA.

7   The Commission gives support to infrastructure from considerations of transport policy; transport infrastructure in backward regions is supported from regional-economic considerations by the European Fund for Regional Development.

8   Nevertheless, the sector itself has made great progress on this score, as may be apparent from the next section.

PART V
CONDITIONS FOR
BALANCED GROWTH

16 Allocation, Internal Market Policies (1992)

Introduction

The main objective of the European Community is to enhance the allocational efficiency of the economies of the member states by removing barriers to the movement of goods, services and production factors. Moreover, policies have been agreed upon to make the European market, once created, function properly. In the following sections we will describe in some depth the *hard core of the European Community*, by which we understand the policies pursued to enhance the allocational efficiency of the European Common Market.

Governments may have quite different opinions about the best way to devise such policies. Some have interventionist inclinations, while others favour a *laisser-faire* approach. The *fundamental choices* the EC has made in that respect, and the major programmes drawn up to transform them into practical policy measures, will be the subjects of the first section.

Next we will go into *competition policy*, enjoined upon the EC already by the treaties of Paris and Rome to prevent private economic actors from cutting up the large market, thus cancelling the benefits of integration.

In the early 1980s it became increasingly clear that the implementation of the rules laid down in the treaties left room for many *non-tariff barriers to internal EC trade* (see Chapter 2 for a review). During the years of depression (1974–1984), member states' governments were eager to exploit the loopholes for their short-term interest. Besides, the European Community itself had created a number of such barriers by its sectoral policies. Concern about the negative effect of these barriers to European growth increased, and after several unsuccessful attempts at removing some of them individually, the Commission (CEC, 1985d) came up with a White Paper containing the bold proposal of a consistent and comprehensive attack on the barriers by *radically doing away with all controls at the internal borders of the EC by the end of 1992*.

The Commission specified a whole list of measures that have to be taken to realise that objective. They are of great importance for the completion of the European internal market and we will therefore deal with them in some detail. The White Paper groups the proposed policy measures under three headings, namely, physical, technical, and fiscal barriers, a distinction that may be convenient in a political context, but is far from convenient in economic analysis. So we prefer to discuss the various measures under the headings that we distinguished in the theoretical part of this book (Chapter 7).

Direct intervention in price and quantity and the reservation of large sections of the market for goods, services and production factors to individuals and firms of the home country are the first points to deal with.

Indirect influencing of prices through taxation, notably such indirect taxes as value-added tax and excise duties, is the subject of the following section, which will be largely in line with Chapter 3 on fiscal barriers of the White Paper. The other side of the coin of indirect influences is subsidies. As these apply to production rather than to products, they are dealt with under competition policy.

Regulating market access by defining *technical norms and standards* for the quality of products is the third major instrument by which governments have tried to protect their markets. The policy measures needed to remove such obstacles are reviewed in the next section, which runs largely parallel to the chapter on technical barriers in the White Paper.

All these barriers take a heavy toll in welfare from the Community. In a final section we will try to quantify some of the effects.

Community regime

Basic principles

European countries have very different traditions of state intervention in markets, be it control of prices and quantities, state responsibility for production and regulation of quality, or the vi·;ilance with respect to competition rules. Some countries – France for one – have a more *interventionist* tradition; others, like Germany, are more of the *liberalist* type (at least for markets of manufactured goods). However, no EC country defends a straightforward *laisser-faire* regime, nor has any country adopted a system of rigorous central planning. When the EC was created, to steer some middle course between the two extreme views was the only logical thing to expect.

The *blend of interventionist and liberalist measures in European policy making* varies for different sectors of activity, as the previous chapters have shown. Indeed, the ECSC Treaty gave the Community institutions quite some powers to intervene in coal and steel markets; the

High Authority (now Commission) can influence prices and quantities in the event of a so-called 'manifest crisis', and has the power to control investments and mergers. The EEC treaty, on the contrary, trusted mainly to market forces for the allocation function; the Commission has no powers for intervention in markets, with two noticeable exceptions: agriculture and transport. The common policy that was elaborated on the basis of the specific treaty principles for the former sector relies very heavily on both quantity and price controls. In the area of transport, many direct influences on price and quantities (quotas) persist, although the EC role is less developed on that score. Together with the coal and steel sector, that leaves three interventionist islands in the predominantly liberalist sea.

Within the general European rules set for the allocation process, national governments are free to prefer a more interventionist or a more liberal approach. Initially, EC authorities, preoccupied with such micro-economic efficiency matters as economies of scale and specialisation, did not consider diversity an obstacle to the integration of goods and production-factor markets. However, as the integration of these markets progressed, national differences in regulations were increasingly felt as an impediment to full freedom of movement, and hence to efficiency.

Persistent segmentation instead of one common market

The *unity of the market* is a basic principle of the EC, whatever the attitude chosen *vis-à-vis* a particular sector of activity. So much is clear from many articles in the Treaty, for instance the ones ordering the abolition of all customs duties and measures with equivalent effect by 1970. The obligations with respect to capital went less far, but the Treaty is again most clear on liberalising the migration of workers. In defiance of the general principles, many impediments to the free movement of goods, services, capital and labour persist, some of which imply controls at internal borders.

Indeed, *barriers persist* and the liberalisation envisaged by the Rome Treaty has not led to the complete abolition of internal borders for various reasons:

- The basic material for statistics. Although the procedure was greatly simplified by the adoption in 1988 of the so-called 'document unique' (a document containing, in code, all information on Value-Added Tax (VAT), transport, customs, etc.), it still involves a check on all intra-EC trade in goods and services, which for convenience is made at internal borders.
- The need to comply with technical standards and norms adopted by some countries for environmental reasons or to protect con-

sumers or workers. Related to it are the controls of movements of plants and animals to check whether they come up to national health standards. In the past the EC has tried to overcome such technical differences by harmonising the national regulations, that is, by making them so much alike that they do no longer present obstacles to trade. To that end, the Commission has proposed strings of draft regulations and directives. However, very few of them until recently actually reached the stage of adoption by the Council;

- Different levels of indirect taxation. Goods need to be checked to establish the amount of VAT or excise duties to be levied in the country of destination;
- EC policy measures. A case in point are the Monetary Compensatory Amounts (see Chapter 11). Sometimes, the incompleteness of EC policies does the same, an example being the national quota on third-country imports (Chapter 19);
- Public security measures, giving rise to personal checks at the internal borders (illegal immigrants, criminals, terrorists);
- Unwillingness of national politicians to give up their elbow room for electionalist policies, and of national civil servants to adopt anything else than their own set of rules.

Objective 1992

In the eighties European industry has become increasingly aware of the disadvantages of the prevailing situation. To arouse public interest, Philips' president Dekker in 1984 drew up his Plan for Europe 1990. Following his impetus, the Commission developed an ambitious project to complete the internal market by radically *abolishing all border controls on goods, services, persons and capital by 1992,* better known as the Cockfield White Paper, after the Commissioner responsible (CEC, 1985d). The paper identified all remaining barriers and presented a programme of policy measures needed to take them away. This programme has been endorsed by the Council and was made into a treaty obligation by the adoption of the Single European Act. Article 13 of this SEA (CEC, 1987a) reads:

> The Community shall adopt measures with the aim of progressively establishing the internal market over a period expiring 31 December 1992. ... The internal market shall comprise an area without internal frontiers in which the free movement of goods, persons, services and capital is entered in accordance with the provisions of this treaty.

The new approach differs from earlier attempts at coping with internal barriers by its three *distinctive characteristics*:

- *Complete comprehensiveness.* It covers all measures needed to do away with internal frontiers, irrespective of sector of activity, the field of policy, and the likely effect on individual member states or groups of society. The rationale for this approach is that the continued presence of any one reason to maintain frontier controls could be enough to keep them intact, thus jeopardising the whole idea and the advantages envisaged;
- *A clear timetable.* The target set needs to be attained by the end of 1992. This recalls the approach of the Treaty of Rome to the abolition of all tariffs and quotas on internal trade by the end of the transition period;
- *A simplified decision-making process.* The Single European Act has replaced the original Treaty requirements for decisions to be taken unanimously with a new rule that requires only a qualified majority for decisions on most measures needed to accomplish the internal market.

Competition

Basic features of the EC regime

The *rationale* for governments to pursue a competition policy is to foster the efficient allocation of production factors. As we have seen in Chapter 7, it is well established in theory. In practice, however, a set of independent national competition policies is unlikely to be sufficient for establishing a good competition regime in integration areas.[1] The need for a Common European Competition Policy has been recognised from the very creation of the European Community; both the Treaty of Paris (ECSC) and that of Rome (EEC) contain a chapter on it. In matters of competition the powers given to the Community by the ECSC reach further than those bestowed on it by the EEC Treaty. For instance, under the former, companies wanting to merge need the advance approval of the Commission, a stipulation that is unknown in the latter. The European Competition Policy is complementary to national competition policies; the former regards competition from the angle of interstate trade, the latter from whatever angle is specific to it.

The *objectives* of the European competition policy (CEC, 1985e) are threefold (and reflected in three (groups of) articles in the EEC Treaty):

- to prevent companies from re-establishing, by means of market-sharing agreements and export bans, less visible but equally effective barriers to trade to replace the customs frontiers that were abolished by the European Common Market for goods and services (article 85 EEC);

- to prevent excessive concentrations of economic power from abusing their dominant position in the market and thereby damaging the interests of consumers, competitors or subsidiaries (article 86 EEC);
- to prevent state aid from distorting competition by giving unfair advantages to certain firms and occasioning damage to firms in other member states (articles 92–94 EEC).

Three *institutions* have in the course of the years developed the fundamental competition rules laid down in the EEC Treaty: the Council by its legislation, the Commission by its administrative practice and the Court by its jurisprudence.

- The Council's role is limited to the issue of regulations and directives on the general application of the rules laid down in the Treaty.
- The Commission has been given the central role. It investigates violations of the rules on its own initiative or upon receiving complaints from member states, companies, private persons or institutions. When the Commission observes an infringement, it may order to undo it. In many cases such actions end with the company or member states voluntarily changing its conduct. In other cases, where the Commission finds a complaint well founded and the company does not change its conduct, the Commission can order changes, and member states are obliged to help the Commission enforce such ruling. All firms and public institutions are committed to allow the officials of the Commission to make any investigations it thinks necessary to gather evidence (CEC, 1985f). The Commission can impose fines, which may rise to millions of Ecu.
- The European Court deals with appeals from the allegedly infringing company. Since its creation, the Court has treated a large number of cases, and 'case law' has greatly helped to define competition law (Mathijsen, 1985) and to clear the interpretation of the three fundamental rules quoted above.

The *field of application* of EC competition rules is very wide. They apply:

- *irrespective of the company's location,* that is to say, also to companies from third countries operating in the Community;
- *whatever the legal or proprietary form,* which means that they are valid as well with respect to government companies (with the exception of public utilities); in that respect the 1980 directive is relevant, which states that the financial structure of state-owned

companies must be transparent, so that any competition-distorting effect can be identified (a rule that applies in particular to synthetic fibres, shipyards, the motor–car industry, etc.);
- *to all sectors of private economic activity,* notwithstanding the differences in market structure between them (with some complications for instance with respect to coal and steel); the exception is the public sector.

The 1992 programme foresees the integration in the competitive regime of sectors that up till now have managed to keep aloof, mostly transport and financial services.

Cartels (company agreements)

The first basic rule for competition is given by article 85.1 of the EEC treaty that bans as

> incompatible with the Common Market all agreements between undertakings, decisions by associations of undertakings and concerted practices which may affect trade between Member States and which have as their object or effect the prevention, restriction or distortion of competition within the Common Market.

The treaty says, moreover (art. 85.2), that any agreement or decision prohibited by the treaty is automatically void.
    Since 1962 (Regulation 17), *all agreements likely to come under the ban must be notified in advance in the European Commission for examination.*[2] After examining the case, the Commission can:

- give a negative clearance, which means that the Commission considers that fair competition is not threatened by the agreement;
- exempt the agreement from the overall ban because its benefits are considered more important than the possible disadvantages of limited competition. Such benefits may be the promotion of technical or economic progress and the improvement of production and distribution;
- declare the agreement illegal and order it to be terminated.

The following groups of activities are incompatible with the competition rules of article 85 (CEC, 1985e):

- Market-sharing agreements which create protected markets, dividing the Community into submarkets that coincide with single Member States;

- Price-fixing agreements of firms that control a large share of the European market (for instance, agreements to raise prices by the same amount at virtually the same time);
- Exclusive-purchase agreements involving arrangements to buy only from specified manufacturers or importers or exclusive supply agreements to sell only to certain buyers;
- Agreements on industrial and commercial property rights: the exclusive use of patents, trade marks or works of art is not necessarily exempted from competition rules;
- Exclusive or selective distribution agreements. The Commission's opposition to any form of restriction of parallel imports has been demonstrated in a number of cases. Selective distribution arrangements are sometimes permitted if they improve the quality of the service provided. But discrimination against retailers, especially for their pricing strategies, can be severely punished.

Dominant positions

The second basic competition rule is given by article 86 EEC, which reads:

> Any *abuse by one or more undertakings of a dominant position* within the Common Market or in a substantial part of it shall be prohibited as incompatible with the Common Market in so far as it may affect trade between Member States.

Forms of abuse of dominant position are unfair pricing, exclusion or limitation of supply, discrimination among trade partners, etc. This treaty provision was first applied to industrial mergers in 1971–1973; in the famous Continental Can case the Court established that a very high concentration as such can already imply abuse of dominant position. An example of the abuse of a dominant position was given by Hoffman-Laroche, who dominate the world market of vitamins in bulk (market shares of over 80 per cent). The company had passed 'fidelity' contracts with its customers which would give it a permanent position of priority or even of exclusivity as supplier to these customers. The Commission fined Hoffman-Laroche, which thereupon appealed to the European Court. However, the Court confirmed the essentials of the Commission's decision, making clear that the dominant firm may not limit a customer's supply possibilities, nor bar the entry of new suppliers which could put a downward pressure on prices.

Concentration increased in the manufacturing sector in the early period of the European integration, as could be expected. An impression of that tendency is given in the following table, which shows that the sectors in which the largest four firms (C4) control more than three-quarters (or half) of the market have increased their share in the total number of sectors in the period.

Table 16.1 Sectoral concentration[a] in the EC, 1962–1973

	1962	1969	1973
C4 larger than 75 per cent	15	17	20
C4 larger than 50 per cent	28	39	50

[a] Percentage of total number of sectors with, respectively, over 75 and over 50 per cent of C4-control
Source: de Jong (1988), based on EEC Annual Competition Reports

Since then the general tendency has stopped. Indeed, although between 1972 and 1982 some increase in concentration could be discerned for transport and electrical engineering, for most other sectors the concentration levels in the EC remained about stable. To prevent firms from acquiring dominant positions, the Commission has intensified its monitoring of *mergers*.[3] Merging activity has been fairly intense since the EC came into being, firms trying in that way to acquire quickly the size needed for the extended market. Figure 16.1 illustrates the development in numbers since the first enlargement of the EC. The perspec-

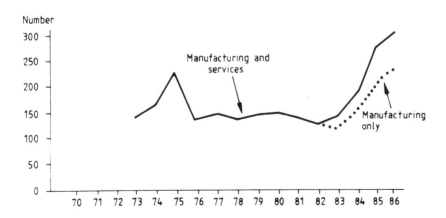

Figure 16.1 Mergers in the EC, 1973–1986
Source: de Jong (1988)

tive of the completion of the internal market has given a new impetus to merger activities, from partial data we may conclude that merging activity has again increased by some 50% between 1986 and 1989.

State aids

A third set of rules on competition is given by articles 92 to 94 EEC, which declare state aid to firms incompatible with the Common Market in so far as they distort trade among Member States or damage competing firms (CEC, 1982f). There has been a continuous debate on the subject, state aid being a major instrument for governments to intervene in the economy. Consequently, to work out articles 92–94 has mostly meant to define the *kinds of support that are permissible*. As such qualify aids that aim at:

- regional development; a maximum aid level has been established by the Commission for each problem area; the aid measures have to be public and transparent;
- environmental improvement ensuring as much as possible the principle 'the polluter pays';
- industrial restructuring; special guidelines have been established for the shipbuilding, iron and steel (the so-called 'subsidy codexes' of the ECSC), textiles and synthetic fibres. The Commission insists that such aids be exceptional, limited in duration, and geared directly to the objective of restoring long-term viability to firms or to reducing capacity in declining industries;
- research enabling companies to develop products and compete successfully on the world market;
- conservation and development of new indigenous resources of energy.

Aids are introduced to correct market failures and attain social objectives by influencing private economic decision making; they tend to multiply in times of crisis. Plans for such aids must be submitted to the EC for prior approval. The Commission forbids all forms of aid that cause too marked a distortion of competition, but in the past it has been obliged to let many trespassers go unpunished.

Direct intervention in prices and quantities

General

The European Community's underlying principle is that decisions as to production and consumption may be left to economic agents and that the public authorities do not intervene to change the price that the market establishes. However, on quite a few points neither the national governments nor the EC follow that principle, but intervene directly in prices and/or quantities on the markets of goods, services and production factors. An important instrument to control quantities is restricting the market entry for certain firms. In some cases, for instance public procurement, restrictions are such as to preclude all trade. Because national governments operate and sustain different forms of intervention, the EC market is split. Now fragmentation and the ensuing controls at the border lead to inefficiency. Hence the EC, anxious to abolish all frontier controls, wishes to do away with much of the intervention in markets on the part of national and Community authorities.

We will now briefly describe the main elements susceptible to intervention, indicating the type of measure that is wanted to remove obstacles to free movement.

Goods

In the field of *agriculture*, the CAP regulations have put some serious obstacles in the way of competition on the internal market (see Chapter 11).

- The system of Monetary Compensatory Amounts (MCAs) has effectively split the Common Market into a set of national markets, separated by a complicated system of levies and subsidies. To undo that development, automatic and complete adjustment of national prices would be required after any change of exchange rates.
- The national market regulations including price regulations (Article 4, EEC), that apply to a number of products for which the CAP has not unified the market regulations, will have to be abolished or be integrated in an EC system.
- The system of national quotas for certain products, for instance milk, will have to be adapted or abolished.

In the area of *manufacturing industry*, the principle of a Customs Union implies that a good from a third country is traded freely between member countries once it has passed the common border. Three reasons can be quoted why practice is still some way removed from this:

- The Common external trade policy (see Chapter 19) permits some countries to continue to operate quotas *vis-à-vis* certain third countries. To check whether these third countries respect their quotas, member countries often think fit to check all goods at the border. Some of these quotas are based on bilateral agreements without expiry date, concluded before the establishment of EC commercial policy and maintained since (for example the Italian quota on automobile imports from Japan). Others have been fixed on a very detailed country-to-country basis within the Multi-Fibre Agreements (MFA). The EC has to get rid of both categories by abolishing them altogether or redefining national quotas in terms of EC quotas.

- The safeguard clauses (EEC articles 108/109 and 115) permit member countries to take certain protective trade measures because of economic or balance-of-payments difficulties. Should these clauses be abolished, then alternative instruments have to be adopted to cope with economic difficulties, such as compulsory instead of voluntary mutual assistance with loans (and grants) (see Chapter 18).
- Under the rules of the ECSC (article 58), European industrial policy used national production quotas to restore equilibrium (see Chapter 12). Now that the manifest crisis in the steel industry has come to an end, these emergency measures have been withdrawn.

In the *energy* field, border controls are applied as a consequence of EC energy policy (coal quotas, among other things) because of large national differences in indirect taxation for oil products and because of safety regulations for nuclear material. However, as we have seen in Chapter 13, the greatest obstacle to free trade in energy is compartmentalisation of the EC market operated by public electric power companies. The removal of that obstacle depends on the application of the competition regime to this sector.

Services

The evidence given in Chapters 14 and 15 has made clear that there are still many obstacles to the free internal trade in services. Most of them take the form of national measures to protect consumers, or public intervention in production and trade (for reasons of economic welfare, among others).

Construction is hindered by protection through public procurement and different technical norms.

For *transport* the analysis of Chapter 15 has made plain that the free transportation of goods is not implicit in the free movement of goods (Chapter 8). Indeed, the European transport market is beset with national haulage quotas, barred access to national markets for non-national transport, quota systems for barge transport, and partitioned freight and passenger markets in the air and at sea. Liberalisation as agreed upon by the Council should put an end to all such practices, and is therefore a necessary condition for the abolition of border controls on transport. Harmonisation of technical and social rules remains necessary as well, however.[4]

For *insurance*, the case study of Chapter 14 has shown how national regulations with respect to solvency, type of products, establishment, etc., prevented the penetration of companies into foreign markets. Similar difficulties exist for the banking sector.

Production factors

With respect to *labour* (see Chapter 9), considerable difficulties have to be overcome before the internal labour market can really be completed. For employees the problem persists of mutual recognition of diplomas and of the many ways in which employers can discriminate against workers from partner countries (requiring linguistic proficiency, subtleties in the procedures, etc.). For the professions the recognition of diplomas is still a difficult matter (architects, lawyers, etc.). A lot of tedious harmonisation work has still to be done, which is likely to take more time than is available for the 1992 programme.

The European capital market has to be completely liberalised before 1992 (see Chapter 10). That means that all remaining barriers will have to be taken down. There are some complications in different fields of *capital movement*.

- Direct investment: one way of practising DI is to take over a company. Now in practice, the legal and corporate environment makes a take-over much easier in the UK than in the Federal Republic of Germany. Moreover, the taxation of companies is different in the various countries of the EC. Finally the different legal forms under which companies operate in the various countries poses problems for direct investment activity of European firms of one country in other European countries.
- Short- and long-term loans, savings: again the tax regimes that countries apply to these forms of capital movement, added to the secrecy rules of banks *vis-à-vis* the tax collector, differ among countries and can distort competition.

Public procurement

Large quantities of products in the EC are sold not to private firms and individual consumers, but to government-procurement offices. The goods range from food for school children to nuclear submarines. The total value of public procurement (both government and public enter-prise) is estimated (Atkins, 1987) at some 15 per cent of the European Gross Domestic Product. Traditionally, procurement is not decided on the basis of cost and quality alone: many other government objectives have been pursued through public contracts. Almost invariably, *con-tracts are given to national industries;* in 1985, public purchases from foreign suppliers were in the order of magnitude of only 2 per cent in the European countries (Atkins, 1987), much smaller than the import penetration of other sectors of the economy. That applies in particular to capital equipment for defence, power generation, telecommunica-tion and railways. Large parts of the 'Common Market' are thus screened off from the competitive regime installed by the EC, in spite of the general principles of free movement of goods (article 30) and services (article 59), which apply fully to public-procurement organi-sations. This has given rise to widely differing national technical standards, unexploited economies of scale in R & D and production, subsidies, and lack of competitiveness on external markets.

In the past, the EC *tried to eliminate the discrimination* practised *by government and semi-government bodies* (CEC, 1982g, 1984b). With direc-tive 77/62/EEC, in force since 1978, the EC obliges all procurement agencies of central or federal governments (and of lower government layers also) to publish in the *Official Journal* all contracts above a certain minimum amount. The directive also gives rules which the procedure must follow, criteria by which the contractor will be selected, etc. (CEC, 1982g). However, analyses carried out by the Commission (for in-stance, CEC, 1984b) have revealed that these rules are inadequately applied. Recently (1988), the Council adopted a new directive concern-ing public works costing over 5 million Ecu. They have to be made public through a new Europe-wide data-bank: Tenders Electronic Daily. The directive gives new safeguards to subscribers against dis-crimination. Directives for such large sectors as water, energy, trans-port and telecommunications are still lacking.

Indirect influence on prices, fiscal barriers

General

Fiscal barriers to internal trade are the third category which the 'White Paper' wants to see removed. These proposals are not the first to be made in the fiscal field (CEC, 1986g); on the contrary, fiscal matters have been debated from the very start of the EC. Indeed, the Treaty of the EEC already stipulated in article 99 the necessity of the harmonisation of turnover taxes, excise duties and other forms of indirect taxation to the extent that such harmonisation is necessary to ensure the establishment and the functioning of the internal market.

More specifically, articles 95–98 forbid the use of such taxes for discriminatory practices (such as high taxes on imported goods, low ones on home produced goods). From those beginnings it was clear that the fiscal policy of the EC is not an independent goal, but only serves other policy fields. Or, as the Neumark (1963) report puts it:

> It is not a problem of the structure of the tax systems, but a question of the effects and incidence of taxation operated in each country on the processes of integration and economic growth.

In practice *European tax harmonisation serves foremost to facilitate the functioning of the common market for products (goods and services) and production factors (labour and capital). In the future it may also serve the functioning of the emerging economic and monetary union* (Puchala, 1984).

The why of tax harmonisation has determined the what and how[5] of it. In Chapter 7 we have indicated how taxes affect sectors of the economy in order to identify what type of tax needs to be harmonised as integration progresses.

Indirect taxes, value added tax (VAT) and excises[6] have a direct bearing on the functioning of the internal market for goods and services. Indeed, the theoretical literature shows that different structures of indirect taxes may have quite different effects on the competitive positions of countries (Prest, 1983). It was only logical that the Treaty of the EEC, creating first a Customs Union, provided explicitly for the harmonisation of indirect taxes (article 99).

Direct taxes, such as the corporation tax and the wage tax (including social security), have an influence on capital and labour markets. Right from the start of the EEC it was recognised that unharmonised direct taxes could distort the free movement of capital and workers, thus jeopardising the effectiveness of the European Common Market. Article 220 EEC requires the member states to negotiate the abolition of all double taxation of residents and firms from other member states. However, because till recently the EC had not advanced very far towards a fully free market for capital and labour, the problems of direct taxation were considered less urgent than those of indirect taxation, and have accordingly received far less attention. Now that labour and capital mobility are becoming fully free, that consideration is no longer valid, and the positive integration of these parts of the tax systems is now due.

The EC's march along the road to an Economic and Monetary union is not yet far advanced. For its progress, national differences in the structure of taxation and social-security need to be level and reduced

(Brennham and Buchanan, 1980), but that matter has hardly begun to be studied. Recall that such tax co-ordination comes under the labels of stabilisation and redistribution rather than allocation.

Indirect taxes on goods and services: value added tax (VAT)

When the EC was created, member states were operating different systems of sales tax. The Neumark report inventoried their advantages and disadvantages. In the harmonisation process of this tax the EC has adopted the value-added principle. *A common structure of this value-added tax* has gradually been elaborated in the form of directives. The principles of, and the basis for, value-added taxation are now fairly standardised.

In 1967, the Council adopted the *destination principle* for taxation, which means that goods are taxed in the country of consumption, and that exports leave the country free of tax. As Cnossen (1987) points out, that does not mean that border controls are inevitable; indeed, the VAT adjustment can be shifted from the borders to the accounting books of taxable persons or firms. Two systems are available: the deferred-payment scheme (imports being taxable at the first inland stage), and the tax credit-clearance system (exports being taxable but a tax credit being extended to importers, payable by the exporting country). For several reasons, the latter system seems the more advantageous. It applies an accounting procedure (already operational in Benelux) coupled with the creation of a Community Clearing-House System.

With respect to the *VAT rates*, Table 16.2 indicates how widely they differ between the EC member countries. Most countries have a 'normal' or standard rate for most goods (and services) and a reduced rate for goods that are considered essentials like food, clothing or merit goods like cultural services. Some countries apply an increased rate to goods labelled as luxury goods (video recorders, for instance). The purpose of this differentiation is to achieve some redistribution. Southern member states apply luxury rates and also have more differentiation than others in the reduced and normal rates. The reason is that for redistribution purposes, southern countries rely more on VAT, northern countries more on (progressive) income tax. The EC member states have not reached agreement on the objective of complete unification of the tax rates and bases; some member states, relying very heavily on VAT for their tax revenue, fear they will not be able to raise equivalent income from other sources if they lower the VAT rates, while others on the contrary are loath to raise them (afraid of inflationary pressure). So, tax adjustment for goods crossing the borders remains necessary to prevent the distortion of intra-EC trade (Guien and Bonnet, 1987).

Table 16.2 VAT (rates and receipts) as a percentage of total GDP and total tax receipts (TAX) in member countries of the EC (around 1986)

State	Year of intro- duction	Rates (%)			Receipts (%)[a]	
		Standard (Normal)	Reduced (Essential)	Increased (Luxury)	VAT/ GDP	VAT/ TAX
Belgium	1971	19	1/6	25/33	8	17
Denmark	1967	22	–	–	10	22
Germany	1968	14	7	–	6	17
France	1968	18.6	7	33.3	9	21
Ireland	1972	25	10	–	8	21
Italy	1973	18	2/9	38	5	14
Luxemburg	1970	12	3/6	–	6	12
Netherlands	1969	20	6	–	7	15
United Kingdom	1973	15	0	–	5	14
Spain	1986	12	6	33	n.a.	n.a.
Portugal	1986	16	8	30	n.a.	n.a.
Greece	1987	18	6	36	n.a.	n.a.

Sources: Emerson *et al.* (1988), Rates: CEC, (1988c), Revenue: OECD 1987h; Rates are as of January 1987 and are tax-exclusive, that is to say, based on selling prices before tax
[a] Receipts figures 1983
n.a. = no information available

To limit the divergence, the Commission has made the following *proposals*:

- to eliminate the increased rate;
- to adopt minimum rates for the normal and reduced rates;
- to develop a common definition of the products that fall into either category (normal, reduced).

No full unification is proposed because the option chosen (national variations of rates based on the destination principle) is considered preferable in that it leaves member states free to operate their own VAT systems in line with national social and economic policy objectives, a tremendous advantage since fiscal policies are becoming increasingly important as national monetary policies are phased out with the further programme of the EMU. That individuals can freely import into high-taxation states what they have bought in low-taxation states is expected not to cause serious distortions of trade but rather to keep on the pressure to avoid any new diverging tendencies.

Indirect taxes on goods; excises

Excise taxes are far less important than value-added tax to tax revenues of member states. On the other hand, they apply to politically highly–sensitive goods, which according to many have serious negative external effects (health for alcohol and tobacco, environment for motor gasoline). Article 99 EEC stipulates that excises, like sales taxes, need to be harmonised. Harmonisation measures have focused on tobacco products, alcoholic beverages and petroleum products, which together account for almost the entire revenue. Table 16.3 pictures the differences in the most important excises in the 12 member states.

Table 16.3 Examples of excise taxes (Ecu, 1987) and importance of excise tax revenue (ETR) in total GDP (percentage, 1983), in EC member states

Member state	Cigarettes (per 100)	Beer (per litre)	Wine (per litre)	Pure alcohol (per litre)	Premium petrol (per litre)	$\frac{ETR^a}{GDP}$
Ireland	4.89	0.82	2.79	2.72	0.36	8.0
Denmark	7.75	0.56	1.57	3.50	0.47	5.7
United Kingdom	4.28	0.50	1.54	2.50	0.27	4.7
Luxemburg	0.17	0.05	0.13	0.84	0.21	4.3
Italy	0.18	0.17	0.00	0.23	0.56	3.3
Germany	2.73	0.07	0.20	1.17	0.26	2.7
Netherlands	2.00	0.20	0.33	1.23	0.34	2.6
Belgium	0.25	0.10	0.33	1.25	0.26	2.4
France	0.13	0.03	0.03	1.15	0.37	2.4
Greece	0.06	0.10	0.00	0.05	0.35	n.a.
Spain	0.07	0.03	0.00	0.30	0.25	n.a.
Portugal	0.09	0.09	0.00	0.25	0.35	n.a.
Rate proposed	1.95	0.17	0.17	1.27	0.34	3.2

Source: CEC 1988c, Emerson *et al.*, (1988)
[a] *Source*: Cnossen (1987)
n.a. = information not available

Complete unification of excise duties on the EC scale seems necessary to avoid significant distortions of EC trade under a regime of open frontiers. This means first the establishment of a European list of products subject to excise taxes; excises on all other products (for instance on soft drinks in The Netherlands) need to be abolished. Second, it means that for each product a fixed amount in Ecu needs to be set as excise. The products on the list are alcoholic beverages, tobacco and petroleum products. However, as a complete unification seems to be out of reach in the near future due to political resistance of several member countries, the Commission has put forward proposals that imply a progressive decrease of the national differences and convergence towards an EC standard by gradually imposing a minimum EC rate for each product. The harmonisation of rates presents specific problems.

With *alcoholic beverages*, member states tended to tax imported products more heavily than domestically produced ones, for instance wine versus beer in the United Kingdom, whisky versus cognac in France. The Commission in its harmonisation efforts took the view that excise taxes for different products should be based on the rationale of the excise, which is to compensate for negative health effects. Hence, the rate should be proportional to the alcohol content. The Court has in many cases ruled against discrimination, considering that all these products were in competition with one another and therefore must be taxed on an equal footing. Although the most obvious cases of discrimination have thus been removed, many specific points still remain to be harmonised.

For *tobacco* products more headway has been made with the excises (Kay and Keene, 1987): common definitions have been agreed upon and taxation systems to some extent harmonised. The relation with VAT is close: the effective tax rates (defined as the sum of excise and value-added taxes, expressed in a percentage of the tax-inclusive retail price), now lie within fairly narrow margins.

The harmonisation of *taxes on petroleum products* has proceeded very slowly. Member countries operate widely varying combinations of sales, car, road, and fuel taxes to raise money for the covering of the cost of traffic infrastructure and the removal of negative (environmental) effects. From the table, petrol excises appear to be fairly similar in the EC (between 0.23 and 0.36 Ecu, the only exceptions being Italy with 0.49 and Luxemburg with 0.20).

Direct taxes, labour

The harmonisation of wage tax (on labour income) and of the *personal income taxes*, encompassing also *independent workers*, has not raised much interest in the EC. For one thing, as we explained in Chapter 9, the free movement of labour has not created an interpenetration comparable in any way to that of the goods market, so that tax differences on that score are of minor public concern. However, for migrants and people who work away from their own country of residence, differences in taxation and different rights to social security cause a lot of private concern. As mentioned in Chapter 9, in 1971 the EC adopted regulation 1408/7, laying down in principle how discrimination and loss of social security rights are to be avoided. For income tax, things are still at the stage of study (McDaniel, 1985). Because these taxes are not levied, controlled or balanced at the internal borders, the Commission does not consider their harmonisation a necessary condition for the completion of the internal market in general and the integration of labour markets in particular, and has not been intent on it lately.

Direct taxes, capital

The European *capital market* cannot be realised without some harmonisation of tax provisions. The Segre report (CEC, 1966) pointed out that any undue direct or indirect influence of tax considerations on the choice of the country of investment should be avoided. In that respect, tax incentives, double taxation (by the countries of origin and destination) of income from investment, differential treatment of residents and non-residents and of corporate investments should be banned. The main issue in that respect is the harmonisation of *corporate taxes*. By 1967 the Commission had already proposed its 'Programme on the harmonisation of direct taxes', which envisaged a uniform corporation tax (to prevent distortions on the EC capital market). The debate on that and similar proposals has since been going on, with conspicuously little result; this is hardly surprising in view of the complexity of the systems and the fierce opposition of member states to inroads into what they consider the very core of their sovereignty. The next table shows how widely corporate taxes differ across the EC as to system, rates, dividend withholding rates, etc.

The widest cleavage is that between the systems operated; only seven members use the imputation system, which gives shareholders credits for the corporation tax to be 'imputed' to the dividends due to them. Other countries, looking upon the corporation and its shareholders as completely different entities, tax twice (classical system). Other differences are found in tax rates, tax credits and withholding rates on distributed profits. There has been some spontaneous harmonisation towards an imputation system with a broad base and low rates.

As the last two columns of Table 16.4 indicate, corporate tax does not contribute much to the revenue of EC member states. Differences may cause important losses as firms are obliged to come to grips with all the intricacies of 12 systems and important distortions as the efficiency of the investment allocation process is impeded by differences in pre-tax rates of return (Devereux and Pearson, 1989). Unfortunately, the draft directives proposed by the Commission have not yet resulted in

Table 16.4 Corporation taxes in the EC (rates as of 1985)

Country	Statutory tax rate	Tax credit as percentage of statutory	Dividend withholding rate	Revenues as *percentage GDP* 1983	1965
A Imputation system					
United Kingdom	52	39.6	0/15	4.1	2.2
Italy	40.5	34.2	0/30	3.8	1.9
Belgium	45	49.9	15	2.7	1.9
France	50	50	0/25	1.9	1.8
Germany	63.3/46.7	64.1	5/25	1.9	2.5
Ireland	50	42.9	0	1.5	2.4
Denmark	40	37.5	15	1.4	1.4
B Other systems					
Luxemburg	47.3	–	0/15	7.4	3.4
Netherlands	43	–	0/25	2.9	2.7
Spain	35	–	10/18	1.3	1.4
Greece	48.5	–	25/42	0.8	0.4
Portugal	52/40	–	10/15	n.a.	n.a.
European Community				2.6	2.1

Source: Cnossen (1987)
n.a. = not available

any harmonisation, let alone unification. Indeed, the White Paper does not contain any proposal for the harmonisation of corporate tax. The apparent lack of attention is logical, for corporate tax is not levied or controlled on the internal borders. For the same reason other elements relevant to capital markets, such as withholding taxes on dividends, have not received much attention either. The openness of the EC capital markets should be both towards other EC and world markets (Chapter 10). This implies that world-wide harmonisation is called for (Giovannini, 1989).

Access to markets, technical barriers

Origins and nature of technical barriers

Governments of member countries have always considered setting quality norms for products an important task for the protection of public health and safety as well as the environment. Historical differences have developed among countries as to essential quality requirements and the practices of testing the products' conformation to these requirements. There is a question of *technical trade barriers when differing national regulations (specifications of shape, construction or performance laid down or referred to in public law) and/or standards (codifications of shape, quality, etc. voluntarily agreed to)* prevent the free movement of goods, or when countries impose duplicative testing and certification procedures on imported goods.

Specified requirements and the ensuing technical trade barriers are often used to protect private interest groups rather than the general public. An example is the telecommunication industry, where the requirements public companies set for the equipment they purchase are such that only domestic firms are likely to comply with them.

The present situation, which compels producers to adapt their products to a number of different sets of national norms and standards, divides the market and thus costs welfare. For that reason the EC has tried several approaches to do away with the differences.

Traditional approach

To remove technical barriers to internal trade, the EC has tried two different strategies.

The first, based on *law*, is to identify technical specifications with measures of quantitative restriction. Now such restrictions are prohibited by article 30 of the EEC. In a number of famous cases, in which the objective of the regulation was clearly to protect special interest groups in one country rather than the public interest, the European Court followed that view. The trendsetter was the case of Cassis de Dijon (1979), an alcoholic product not conforming to German liquor standards in that it contained only 18 instead of the prescribed 25 per cent of alcohol. Very recent are the cases against the German 'Rheinheitsgebot', a prescription dating from the 16th century laying down that beer could only be made from certain ingredients, and against the Italian pasta regulation, prescribing the use of duram wheat, a type produced only in a small region in Southern Italy. In these cases the Court ruled that a good lawfully produced and marketed in one member country should in principle get free access to the markets of partner countries. However, this does not imply fully free movement in practice, for in the Cassis de Dijon case the Court considered that in the absence of common European rules, 'mandatory requirements' of public interest may justify national technical obstacles to free movement.

The EC's second strategy is therefore based on *harmonisation*, and envisages 'approximation of such provisions laid down by law, regulation or administrative action in member states as directly affect the functioning of the common market'. Since 1968, when the Commission proposed a general programme of harmonisation, experts of the Commission, national administrators and external institutions have exerted themselves to harmonise the technical standards for a large number of products,[7] with meagre results, however. The standards set cover only a small portion of the products for which some harmonisation is needed, small in particular for the efforts put in. The approach has indeed turned out both ineffective and inefficient. Why is the record so poor? For one thing, article 100 calls for unanimity in the Council, which proved the more difficult to obtain as the experts tended to aim for excessive uniformity and the specification of many technical details. Moreover, the procedure was frustrated by the constant stream of new national regulations and the speed of technical progress, often overtaking the work before agreement had been reached. The ministers did nothing to speed up the long and cumbersome procedure, probably because it was too technical to awaken sufficient political interest. Finally, the adoption of a directive still did not solve the problem, many member states showing themselves reluctant to take the measures necessary for implementation.

Mutual recognition and home country control

The drawbacks of the above procedures became very apparent at the moment the year 1992 was set as a target for the completion of the internal market. Indeed, in view of the poor record on harmonisation it appeared wellnigh impossible to get all the necessary work done by the end of 1992 along such traditional lines. So the EC has now adopted a new approach.

For goods, the new approach is based on mutual recognition of, and reference to, standards. Let us indicate briefly its main aspects. The directives implementing the harmonisation of legislation according to article 100 EEC do henceforth define only the essential requirements to which products must comply to circulate freely all over the Common Market. The directive refers to European standards, to be defined (by technical specifications) by the competent normalisation organisations, such as CEN, CENELEC, and CEPT. The mutual information directive (83/189 EEC) obliges member states to notify partners of, and discuss with them, any plans for new national regulations to circumvent later cumbersome procedures of harmonisation. The Single European Act solves the problems posed by the unanimity rule of article 100 EEC; for all matters concerning the internal market (except for fiscal matters) the Council now decides by qualified majority. (The voting rules of CEN/CENELEC have also been adapted in that sense.) The governments of EC member states must give free access to any product manufactured according to the European standards, and article 36 EEC (restrictions based on public interest) may no longer be invoked.

For *services the new approach is based on recognition of the quality of control in the home country.* The segmentation of service markets is due to national regulations concerning products (insurance products, among others) but also to the prudential control exerted by national authorities on all establishments located in their territory. The Commission has proposed that, in line with the 'Cassis de Dijon' judgements, financial products be accepted in all member states once they are accepted in one member state. Another proposal is to switch to a system of home country control, all member states accepting that the establishments of a multinational company are all supervised by the authorities of the member state in which the head offices are located. Of course, this presupposes a minimum standard of surveillance.

The new concept reflects a *fundamentally different view of market integration.* From a 'monolithic conception of the Community's integration process in which national legislation and powers are replaced by Community powers', the EC has turned 'to a pluralistic pragmatic and federalistic conception in which national legislation will not be replaced but framed in a way that respects minimum Community requirements' (Padoa Schioppa *et al.*, 1987).

Welfare effects

Cost of 'non-Europe'

In the early 1980s, a few attempts were made at quantifying the cost of the remaining non-tariff barriers and formalities at the internal borders of the EC and the other imperfections of the internal market (termed 'cost of non-Europe' by Albert and Ball, 1983). Hartley (1987) estimated that the large national-defence contracts reserved to firms in the home country cost 30 per cent more than would have been possible under a regime of international competition. Although defence is excluded from the rules governing the Common Market, the study gives an indication of the amounts that might be saved in other areas where governments reserve access to their markets to home firms. Owen (1983) estimated that increased competition, economies of scale, and the restucturing of firms following the opening of the European market in the 1960s had increased prosperity by between 50 and 100 per cent of the additional trade involved, or some 5 per cent of GDP.

At the end of the 1980s the European Commission, in an attempt to establish a more complete picture of the welfare gains to be obtained by the removal of the remaining obstacles, commissioned a series of detailed surveys among business firms.[8] This series deals only with the markets for goods and services, disregarding production factors. To give an idea of the *cost associated with the barriers to internal trade,* we cite the following examples:

- government procurement of telephone switching equipment in Europe. Too many suppliers made the price of a line 2.5 to 5 times higher in Europe than in the USA;
- the use of technical standards for protection purposes was illustrated before with the law prescribing the use of Italian duram wheat in pasta production. The repeal of that law could lead to a 5 per cent import penetration of the domestic Italian market, saving the Italian consumer between 20 and 60 million Ecu a year;
- different technical standards lead to double tests, which can be very costly with such complicated systems as private automatic branch exchanges used in telecommunications. Moreover, the PTT, themselves suppliers of such equipment, are nevertheless represented in some national test offices. Although the equipment cost twice as much in Germany as in France, there is practically no trade between the two countries. If only one-tenth of the German market could be captured by low-cost producers, the price there could drop by 6 per cent.

The list could be extended indefinitely, but the above examples should suffice to give an idea of the costs involved in non-tariff protection at the internal border.

Welfare effects of market integration

The Commission of the EC has made a major effort to go beyond this partial evidence of the cost of non-Europe as given in these micro studies in order to quantify the overall effects of the completion of the internal market (Emerson *et al.*, 1988). A distinction is made between three types of effects:

Border control removal will reduce the cost of administration of both importers and exporters, and the cost of delays for transporters (see Chapter 5 for theoretical underpinnings). In economic terms these costs are similar to tariffs that impede trade; their removal lowers prices for consumers of final goods and purchasers of intermediate goods, and releases resources for alternative production. Although highly visible and often cited by entrepreneurs as a major obstacle to trade, their total impact is limited and evaluated at only 0.3 per cent of GDP.

Market-entry and competition effects (discussed in theoretical terms in Chapter 5) are different for the short- and long-term. The short-term effect is that prices will drop to the level of the most efficient producer in the EC once government procurement is put on a competitive basis and the markets are no longer compartmentalised by technical regulations. The long-term effect is the further reduction of costs through increased competition, enhanced innovation and learning effects. The economic benefits associated with increased competition are considerable (Cecchini, 1988; Emerson *et al.*, 1988); they are estimated at some 4 per cent of GDP, divided about equally between short- and long-term effects.

Economies of scale (also discussed in theoretical terms in Chapter 5) are another major element. As competition leads industries to restructuring, closing down inefficient plants, investing in new plants and expanding output, production will become more efficient. In practice this effect is not always easy to dissociate from the competition effect mentioned earlier. The studies of the cost of non-Europe indicate that in certain branches of the economy there is still ample room for economies of scale, while in many others they seem to have been exploited already to the full. The estimated welfare gain on that score is some 2 per cent of total GDP.

The total welfare gains that can be reaped from the completion of the internal market of the EC may exceed the 6 per cent to which the effects, discussed before, add up, provided the right macro-economic policies are carried out. The extra benefits comprise lower unemployment figures, prices and taxes, and an increase in economic growth through the improvement of the EC's international competitive position. Although these long-term growth effects are difficult to measure, one estimate (Baldwin, 1989) suggests that they may be of the same order of magnitude as the one time effects mentioned earlier.

Summary and conclusions

- *The main rationale* for European economic integration is the enhancement of allocational efficiency; the main instrument to achieve it is the liberalisation of markets (negative integration).
- In addition to liberalisation measures, the EC needs to pursue policies of positive integration to create the conditions for the proper functioning of markets; the most important is *competition policy*.
- The European Community carries out *other policies* concerning such diverse matters as technical norms, value added tax and government procurement not because these matters need harmonisation in their own right, but because these are instrumental in achieving a better allocation of resources and hence more welfare.
- The European Community failed in the past to *complete the internal market*; a new programme is now being carried out to

succeed by 1993. It aims at the complete abolition of all controls at internal borders on goods, services, persons and capital.

* The *welfare effects* of this programme are substantial; they have been estimated at some 6 per cent of the EC's GDP. For some sectors, the effects can be achieved only by very thorough restructuring.

Notes

1. See for an introduction into the theory and a review of the competition policies practised by the EC countries (and a comparison with those of the USA and Japan), Shaw and Simpson (1987); for a good description in French, Druesne and Kremlis (1986); and for a popular introduction, CEC (1985e).
2. To limit the administrative burden, the Commission has generically exempted from notification some types of agreement considered compatible with the competition rules.
3. A good idea of such legal aspects of EC merger policy which are also interesting to economists is given by Verloop (1988); for a broader treatment, see OECD (1984b), and for the dynamics of the merger process, Mueller (1980).
4. Lorries, for instance, are held up at the internal border to check whether they meet the technical requirements specified in each country's regulations (size, tonnage per axle, etc.), whether drivers observe the limitations on work hours, and whether compensation has to be paid for the differences in excise on the diesel the tank contains. With the programme for 1992 no considerable harmonisation of the national rules applying to transport is required to dispose of border checks; the new approach of mutual recognition of standards (see the section on technical barriers) can be used to advantage for technical specifications. The social and safety checks can be made at points other than frontier crossings. Checks of the tank contents will no longer be needed after removal of the fiscal barriers (discussed in a further section).
5. For a very thorough treatment of the subject, see Cnossen (1987), from which publication large parts of this section have been borrowed.
6. Evidently, the indirect tax system has to be seen in the context of a country's overall tax system. Much information about the various national tax systems is contained in Pechman (1987); OECD (1987h) gives proposals for reform.
7. Two main approaches are followed. The first uses the specialised private European normalisation organisations of CEN and CENELEC (setting standards for products); the other is used by the EC, which by means of directives 'approximates' technical specifications.
8. The results of these detailed studies have been put together in three volumes: (1) a scientific report (Emerson *et al.*, 1988); (2) a volume containing the executive summaries of the detailed reports (CEC, 1988d), and (3) a more popular book, which became known as the Cecchini (1988) Report after the chairman of the working group.

17 Stabilisation: Macro-Economic and Monetary Policy

Introduction

The European integration process centres around the Common Market. In the previous chapters we have discussed policies intended to improve the allocation function of the Common Market, touching upon higher forms of integration only in passing. However, for balanced progress on the road from Free-Trade Area to Full Economic Union, the efforts described so far need the complement of stabilisation policies.

Stabilisation policies are pursued because adaptation to new circumstances entails cost, sometimes considerable cost (think, for instance, of the retraining of workers and the premature write-off of capital equipment). The purpose of stabilisation policies is to cushion the effects of internal and external shocks to the economy. An example is the intervention of monetary authorities in foreign-exchange markets when speculations tend to put these out of alignment with fundamental economic factors. Budgetary policies to soften the effects of the business cycle on economic activity are another example.

European countries are reputed to value stability rather highly and hence to favour such policies more than, for instance, the United States. One drawback of that preference is that if changes are mistaken as temporary rather than permanent, the unavoidable adaptation to new circumstances is retarded and will probably have to be carried through later at greater cost.

For such relatively small open economies as most EC member states are, the independent pursuit of stability is very difficult (see Chapter 7). Hence the need for a common effort in that respect. In practice this applies in particular to exchange-rate stability (monetary policy) and inflation (budget) policy, the principal objects of an Economic and Monetary Union. So, in the present chapter we will discuss stabilisation along with the EC's progress towards an Economic and Monetary Union.

First we will describe the difficult start of the EC on a narrow legal basis, the ambitious goal, the numerous difficulties encountered and the limited means to get from A to Z, as well as the deliberations held about the best road to follow.

The next section deals exclusively with monetary co-operation in Europe; it discusses the basic mechanism for creating a zone of stable exchange rates, the European Monetary System with its mechanisms for mutual support in balance-of-payment predicaments, and the European Currency Unit, increasingly used for public as well as private purposes.

Exchange-rate stability is not a goal in itself; it smooths trade in the EC, and hence contributes to the efficient use of resources. Its pursuit imposes a direct constraint on autonomous national macro-economic goals, and rules out divergent national inflation rates. Therefore, co-ordinated macro-policy in the EC must get a hold on inflation. Some major causes of inflation, and what governments can do to curb it, are the subjects of the third section.

Community regime

The beginnings: the Treaty of Rome

The foundation of the EC, the Treaty of Rome, is not very explicit on the macro-economic and monetary integration of Europe. It does not foresee a Community with a monetary identity or organisation, but stipulates only some rudimentary monetary integration, designed to facilitate the proper functioning of the Common Market for goods, services and production factors. Article 104 describes the general *objectives* of the EC in matters of economic and monetary policy as follows:

- to ensure the equilibrium of its overall balance of payments;
- to maintain confidence in its currency while taking care;
- to ensure a high level of employment;
- to ensure a stable level of prices.

To attain these objectives, three instruments were to be used:

- the co-ordination of national economic policies (art. 105) particularly cyclical policies (art. 103);
- stabilisation of rates of exchange (art. 107.1);
- initial assistance (in terms of credits) in case of balance of payments problems.

That the EC was created first and foremost as a Common Market and that monetary *policies* were only provided to safeguard its good functioning is clear from the formulation of the institutional mechanism: 'In order to promote the co-ordination of the policies of the member states in the monetary field to the full extent needed for the functioning of the common market, a Monetary Committee with advisory status is set up' (art. 105). This Monetary Committee consisted of representatives of the governments (Ministries of Finance), the National Banks, and the Commission. Its task was to review the monetary and financial situation and the payments system. The Committee was to report regularly to the Commission and the Council. More advanced ideas of a monetary union, comprising irrevocably fixed exchange rates and a common monetary (open-market) policy, had been advocated on several occasions in the 1950s, but gained too little political support to leave a mark in the Rome Treaty.

The role of the European Community in *monetary policy* is fundamentally constrained by the Treaty of Rome. While the Treaty leaves to the EC a role of some importance with respect to monetary policy, it explicitly forbids autonomous EC intervention in matters of economic policy. Article 199, for example, precludes any spending policy of the EC, stating explicitly that EC outlays and receipts must be in balance every year. Should the resources of the EC fall short of the needs, then member states have to put up the money; the EC cannot, like its member states, raise money by imposing taxes or loaning on the capital market. But even if the EC had been authorised to pursue economic policies, their effect would have been doubtful with an EC budget amounting to no more than about 1 per cent of total GDP. In fact, EC economic policy is just a matter of co-ordinating national policies.

That the Treaty was so cautious in bestowing powers of monetary and economic policy on the EC can in part be explained by the *economic conditions of the period*: the Bretton Woods system of fixed exchange rates was functioning smoothly, and the European economies were all at a stage of long-term economic growth, so that all attention was given to short- and medium-term policies.

The goal: the Economic and Monetary Union

While European integration was in progress, several proposals for the realisation of an Economic and Monetary Union were made. Experience with the co-ordination system provided for in the Treaty had shown up severe shortcomings, and further efforts were needed to cope with problems ahead. At The Hague Summit of 1969, the heads of state and government agreed in principle to the creation of an Economic and Monetary Union, and requested the Commission to work out proposals for the successive realisation of its elements (European Reserve Fund; harmonisation of economic policy).

A blueprint for such a Union was the report called *The Realisation in Stages of the Economic and Monetary Union of the Community*, submitted in 1970 by a Committee under the chairmanship of Werner. As explained in Chapter 7, such a Union implies, on the monetary side, either full and irrevocable convertibility of all currencies, coupled with a system of fixed parities (without margins) between the participating currencies, or a single EC currency. On the economic side it supposes coherence of the budgetary policies of member states, and the full mobility of production factors, in particular capital. This calls for a strong institutional structure – in practice a European Commissions' competence for macro-economic policy as well as a European system of Central Banks.

The Werner report, adopted by the Council in 1971, proposed to realise the EMU in stages, and presented an ambitious calendar, foreseeing completion in 1980. One basic weakness of the proposal was that it permitted participating countries to back out. The Werner plan soon proved an illusion. The monetary disorder of the 1970s made it very difficult to obtain adequate political support, and alternative, less ambitious proposals were made (see next section) concentrating on exchange rate stabilisation. However, the cost of the non-Europe soon became apparent on the macro-economic level as well. Albert and Ball (1983) have shown that for both small and large EC countries macro and monetary policies have lost effectiveness. Political sensitivity has made it difficult to accept the obvious conclusion of this state of affairs that only coherent co-ordinated EC policy making will permit partners to regain collectively the control that they have all lost individually.

This experience with the effects of the (lack of) macro-economic and monetary co-operation has now convinced many academic, business and political circles that further progress towards the EMU is urgently needed.

The route: controversies between 'economists and monetarists' and between 'planners' and 'free marketers'

The attainment of the very ambitious objectives of the EMU was made difficult by the deep-rooted differences in opinion among experts about the best way forward. There are two dividing lines: between economists and monetarists, and between planners and free-marketers.

The *economists* (found in particular among German and Dutch scholars) give priority to the harmonisation of economic policies, and consider results on that score an essential condition for further monetary integration. Their argument is that divergent inflation rates springing from different economic policies will sooner or later lead to exchange rate adaptations. If that option is not open any more, some countries may be forced to a very costly deflation which for internal political reasons they would rather avoid. The ensuing tensions will almost certainly break up the fragile systems agreed upon. The economists hold that the full unification of economic policies must precede full monetary integration.

The *monetarists* (chiefly found among the French, Belgians and Italians) defend the view that monetary integration (fixed exchange rates, controlled liquidity, etc.) is the best way to commit national governments to national measures of economic policy; therefore, the road to economic integration should be paved with stable exchange rates, etc. Their argument is based on the observation that governments will not start harmonising their policies unless compelled by strict monetary agreements.

The skirmishes between the two schools have been going on for quite some time now, and are likely to flare up with every step taken towards further integration. At present there seems to be a cease-fire, both parties having agreed to the compromise that the two elements need to be gradually integrated in a balanced fashion.

The second watershed was one between methods. One group of countries favoured *programming* or *planning* as the basis for government intervention with national economies, in particular with the private sector. The kind of planning they have in mind is certainly not that formerly exercised in the centrally planned economies of Eastern Europe. Indeed, many countries in Western Europe exercise some sort of indicative 'planning' in the sense that (semi) government agencies provide forecasts for key variables. France has developed an original planning system, influencing the whole economy by setting targets for several parts of the economy in co-operation with the sector (for instance, steel, banking, etc.) involved.

Other countries, not believing in such policies, just wanted to control such major economic variables as monetary mass, budget spending, etc. and let (financial) *markets* play their full part. Here, too, there seems to be a growing consensus; the belief that the economy can be finely tuned by the judicious use of an array of instruments (budgetary instruments, exchange rates, specific subsidies, etc.) has dwindled in most member countries.

The means: institutions and instruments

The institutional framework provided by the Treaty, namely an Advisory Monetary Committee, meeting monthly, soon proved inadequate.

For a smooth-functioning *macro-economic policy*, a co-ordination Committee on Short Term Economic Trends was installed in 1960, followed in 1964 by the Committee for Budget Policy and the Medium Term Economic Policy Committee; all were composed of representatives of the member states and the Commission. Later, the three Committees were merged into a new Economic Policy Committee with a view to strengthening the co-ordination between the various aspects of economic policy (including monetary matters). The work of the former three committees is now continued in three new sub-committees.

The vehicle for *monetary co-ordination* created by the Treaty, the Monetary Committee, convenes once a month. Its main tasks are to study the monetary developments in the member countries and to submit conclusions and suggestions for action to the Council and Commission. It also advises on balance-of-payment problems of member countries. Because monetary policy is executed in part independently from governments by central banks, the Monetary Committee's activity was not found sufficient, and therefore a Group of Governors of Central Banks was created in 1964. It meets regularly in Basel, the headquarters of the Bank for International Settlements, in conjunction with meetings of that Bank's Council of Governors. The European Commission is accepted only as an observer. The Group covers topics that are typically the Central Banks' responsibility, particularly with respect to credits, money and exchange markets. Its members also exchange information on the most important measures the Central Banks are taking or planning. The Group of Governors is assisted by a group of experts on monetary policy, who as a rule report to the Group twice a year. The Monetary Committee and the Group of Governors are both assisted by a Working Party on Harmonisation of Monetary Policy Instruments.

In their many meetings, the various Committees and Groups have deliberated on very important topics. All that talk has certainly produced a better understanding of one another's motives and constraints, and thus a factual co-ordination. Two basic needs have emerged from the continuous discussion on which more in subsequent sections, namely:

- the need for mechanisms to stabilise exchange rates, coupled with a closer system of monetary assistance in case of balance-of-payment problems as such first the 'snake' and next the EMS were set up;
- the need for a policy of converging inflation rates; to that end some co-ordination of budgetary policies was put into practice.

A new impetus: the Delors plan

A new plan for the realisation of the Economic and Monetary Union, focusing on stable exchange rates, has been elaborated and unanimously accepted by a Committee under the chairmanship of the president of the Commission (Delors Committee, 1989) and composed of the governors of the 12 national Central Banks and a number of independent experts. The proposal, since then accepted as guidance for further action by most of the member states, again stresses the need for a parallel development of the monetary and the economic union, and plans to realise the EMU in three stages. The proposal contains no detailed timetables for the realisation of the EMU.

At the first stage, the *present co-ordination mechanisms* are to be used as much as possible for a closer harmonisation of monetary and economic policies. That means on the monetary side:

- participation of all member states in an EMS operating with smaller margins;
- further automony of national central banks to pursue monetary policy;
- an obligation to strengthen co-operation in the Committee of Presidents of Central Banks.

On the economic side it implies the adoption of a set of objectives and actions (a system of indicators) that commit member states more strictly than at present; in particular, the budget deficits of member states will be limited for the sake of aligning their economic policies.

At the second stage, the *New EMU Treaty* (to be prepared, signed and ratified during the first stage) would come into effect. This Treaty creates a new institution, the European System of Central Banks (ESCB), replacing the present co-ordinating arrangement. This ESCB will be independent from Community and national authorities and will be responsible for monetary policy, with the present national central banks functioning as local operating units to implement ESCB policy. Economic policy co-ordination would then change from indicative to binding; member states will have to accept detailed targets as to the size of public debt, budget deficits, and the use of national instruments. This co-ordination will be accomplished by existing bodies, that is, by the co-ordination committees of the Commission. The second stage gives the opportunity to gain the practical experience needed to operate the system.

At the third stage, the decisive step towards a complete EMU is to be taken, namely, the *irrevocable fixing of exchange rates*, eventually leading to one currency.

Monetary policy: stability of exchange rates

Objectives and means

The case for international monetary co-operation rests principally on the need for *exchange-rate certainty*, a need inspired mainly by micro-economic considerations. Indeed, entrepreneurs, both investors and traders, when doing business with partner countries, incur losses from changing exchange rates (AMUE 1988). Therefore, the full benefit of specialisation, economies of scale, etc. (discussed in Chapters 5 to 10), will not be reaped until the uncertainties on that score have been taken away. Another argument is of a macro-economic nature: if governments of high inflation countries are committed to stable exchange rates, they may be able to curb the forces that tend to press inflation upwards, such as politicians (budget policy) and labour unions (wage-cost inflation).

In the past decades, the EC has worked out several systems to reduce exchange-rate uncertainty among its members. The first major attempt was the 'Snake' arrangement of April 1972. The widely varying policy responses of the European countries to the oil crisis reduced the arrangement to a small group of currencies around the German mark. The system now in force, the European Monetary System (EMS), was formally adopted by the European Council in 1978 and put into operation in 1979. Its primary aim was to create a zone of monetary stability in Europe.[1] The EMS consists essentially of four elements:

- the European Currency Unit, or Ecu;
- an exchange-rate stabilisation and intervention mechanism;
- a credit or monetary support mechanism;
- co-ordinated exchange policies towards third countries.

The following sub-sections will briefly discuss each of the first three elements, giving some attention as well to the spontaneous development of the Ecu as a private means of payment. The last point is taken up in Chapter 19.

Making a European currency: the Ecu versus national currencies

As the integration of Europe progressed, the need for a European monetary unit became pressing, since one of the member states' currencies (German mark) or a third currency (US dollar) proved hard to accept as a vehicle for financial transactions in the EC. Several forms of European units of account were developed but found inadequate for the tasks ahead, and so the Ecu, the European Currency Unit, was created.

The Ecu is often referred to as a basket-type currency, all member states putting a certain amount of their currencies in a basket to obtain one Ecu, which thus reflects the whole Community's financial identity. The 'basket' is open and ready to receive the currencies of new members as they join the EC.

How much each national currency contributes to the Ecu is given in Table 17.1, first column – 0.62 German mark, 0.09 pound Sterling etc. The size of these contributions may appear at first sight rather erratic, but in reality are dependent of a set of criteria. Each contribution or share in column 1 corresponds to a weight in column 5; the latter reflects the economic importance of the member state in question in terms of Gross Domestic Product, share in EC external trade, and quotas under the short-run monetary support system (see next section). Weights can be changed every five years; the rearrangement is such that the Ecu keeps its value on the date of change. The weights given in Table 17.1 were fixed after the adhesion of the peseta to the system; the original weights of 1974 were chosen to make the Ecu correspond to the Special Drawing Right (SDR) of the IMF (which is also a basket, but of different composition, so that the rates of Ecu and SDR have since diverged).

Table 17.1 The Ecu in relation to the component currencies (September 1989)

	1 Share	2 Exchange rate: 1$ =	3 1/2	4 Exchange rate 1 Ecu=	5 Weight
German mark	0.6242	1.9619	0.318	2.06	30.3
Pound sterling*	0.0878	0.6859	0.128	0.72	12.2
French franc	1.3320	6.5714	0.203	6.90	19.3
Italian lira	151.8000	1412.9300	0.107	1483.58	10.2
Dutch guilder	0.2198	2.2095	0.099	2.32	9.4
Bel./Lux. franc	3.4310	40.4381	0.085	42.46	8.1
Danish crone	0.1976	7.4762	0.026	7.85	2.5
Irish pound	0.0086	0.7333	0.012	0.77	1.1
Greek drachme*	1.4400	143.6095	0.010	150.79	1.0
Spanish peseta	6.8850	127.4286	0.054	133.80	5.1
Portuguese escudo*	1.3930	163.8952	0.008	172.09	0.8
Total	1 Ecu	=	1.050 $	-	100.0

* Theoretical rate
Source: CEC

The *value of the Ecu in terms of member-state currencies* is calculated daily by the Commission. To illustrate the operation, we have worked out an example in Table 17.1. First the shares (column 1) are divided by the official exchange rates of the EC currencies with respect to a reference currency, in practice the US dollar (September 1989 exchange rates in column 2). The exchange rate of the Ecu to the US dollar is obtained by adding up the resulting figures (column 3). Apparently, in 1989 the average value of 1 Ecu was 1.05 dollars. To calculate the exchange rate of each currency to the Ecu, multiply the values of column 2 by 1.05 (column 4). To permit an easier interpretation of the shares of column 1, they are usually recalculated in terms of percentages, also called the weight of each currency in the Ecu (in practice this is done by dividing the values of column 3 by 1.05, see column 5).

Exchange rate stabilisation: the short term

The main aim of the EMS is to create *short-term* exchange rate stability in Europe. In practice, this means that for all currencies reference parities (central or pivot rates) to the Ecu are defined, which also define

Table 17.2 EMS bilateral central rates and margins of fluctuation (as of September 1989)

		Amsterdam in HFL	Brussels in BFR/LFR	Frankfurt in DM	Copenhagen in DKR	Dublin in IRL	Paris in FF	Rome in LIT	Madrid in Pts
100 HFL	+2.25%		1872.15	90.770	346.240	33.887	304.440	67912.0	6125.3
	central rate	100	1830.54	88.753	338.540	33.129	297.661	63963.1	5768.8
	-2.25%		1789.85	86.780	331.020	32.394	291.040	60241.0	5433.1
100 BFR/	+2.25%	5.587		4.959	18.914	1.851	16.631	3710.2	334.62
LFR	central rate	5.463	100	4.848	18.494	1.810	16.261	3494.2	315.14
	-2.25%	5.342		4.740	18.083	1.770	15.899	3290.9	296.80
100 DM	+2.25%	115.235	2109.50		390.160	38.183	343.05	76540.0	6901.7
	central rate	112.673	2062.55	100	381.440	37.328	335.39	72069.9	6500.0
	-2.25%	110.168	2016.55		373.000	36.496	327.92	67865.0	6121.7
100 DKR	+2.25%	30.210	553.00	26.810		10.009	89.925	20062.0	1809.4
	central rate	29.539	540.72	26.216	100	9.786	87.926	18894.0	1704.1
	-2.25%	28.883	528.70	25.630		9.568	85.970	17794.0	1604.9
1 IRL	+2.25%	3.087	56.51	2.740	10.451		9.189	2050.0	184.892
	central rate	3.019	55.26	2.679	10.219	1	8.985	1930.7	174.131
	-2.25%	2.951	54.03	2.619	9.991		8.785	1818.3	163.997
100 FF	+2.25%	34.360	628.97	30.495	116.320	11.383		22817.0	2057.8
	central rate	33.595	614.98	29.816	113.732	11.130	100	21488.6	1938.1
	-2.25%	32.848	601.30	29.150	111.200	10.883		20238.0	1825.3
1000 LIT	+6%	1.660	30.387	1.474	5.620	0.550	4.941		957.6
	central rate	1.563	28.619	1.388	5.293	0.518	4.654	1000	901.9
	-6%	1.473	26.953	1.307	4.985	0.488	4.383		849.4
100 Pts	+6%	1.841	33.693	1.633	6.231	0.6097	5.479	1177.3	
	central rate	1.733	31.732	1.538	5.868	0.5743	5.160	1108.8	100
	-6%	1.632	29.885	1.449	5.526	0.5409	4.860	1044.2	
1 Ecu	central rate	2.320	42.458	2.059	7.852	0.768	6.904	1483.6	1.338

Note: The pound sterling, the drachme and the escudo do not participate in the system
Source: CEC

all bilateral exchange rates between these currencies. Together they form a grid of parities. The 1989 situation is given in Table 17.2. The market value of the currencies will change continuously as a consequence of supply-and-demand conditions. Hence differences between the real rate and the central rate will occur. Now stability is realised by the intervention of monetary authorities on the exchange markets. They have agreed to let the market rate fluctuate only within narrow margins; these margins have been fixed for all countries at 2.25 per cent above or below the central rate (in Italy and Spain, exceptionally, 6 per cent). To take an example: the central rate for the FF in Frankfurt is DM 0.298, the permitted fluctuations, accordingly, DM 0.305 and DM 0.292.

The central banks of the two member states are committed to intervene in exchange markets to contain their currencies within these margins. In practice, such intervention starts when the *divergence indicator* of the exchange rate from the central rate passes a certain threshold, which has been fixed at 75 per cent of the margin. The threshold is calculated as 0.75 x 2.25 x (100 X), X being the share of the currency in the Ecu; so, the larger the share of a national currency, the lower the divergence threshold. Warned at an early stage by the divergence indicator, the country concerned can choose its counter measures before the emergency bell tolls.

At the moment (end 1989), *not all currencies are participating* in the exchange rate mechanism (notably not the pound sterling). This causes certain complications, as a simple example may illustrate. Assume that pressure on the pound sterling, other currencies remaining stable, results in a depreciation of, say, 20 per cent. The pound-to-dollar exchange rate changes from 0.6859 to 0.8967, the corresponding value of column 3 of Table 17.1 to 0.098, and the Ecu/dollar rate to 1.02, which means a depreciation of the Ecu of 3 per cent with respect to the dollar. Although the exchange rates of the other European currencies to the dollar have not changed, the dollar exchange rates of the currencies contributing to the Ecu will drop 3 per cent. To make the Ecu value more stable and predictable, the EC tries to integrate all currencies, notably the British pound in the exchange rate mechanism of the European Monetary System.

Exchange rate stabilisation; the medium term

A structurally weak currency, that is a currency steadily valued below the 0.75 bracket of the lower margin, may call for an adjustment of the central exchange rate. Indeed EMS countries have agreed not to proceed unilaterally with respect to exchange rate changes (devaluation or revaluation), but make them subject to negotiations among all EMS partner countries and hence to their approval. The reason is that EMS members have recognised the danger of countries competing with one another by devaluation and the detrimental effect of sudden changes on the interest of partners.

An example may illustrate how such changes are realised (see Table 17.3).

Table 17.3 EMS parity changes and the Ecu

	1 Share	2 Exchange rate: 1$ =	3 1/2	4 Exchange rate 1 Ecu=	5 Weight
German mark	0.6242	1.9227	0.325	2.02	31.0
Pound sterling*	0.0878	0.6859	0.128	0.72	12.2
French franc	1.3320	6.7028	0.199	7.04	18.9
Italian lira	151.8000	1497.7100	0.101	1572.60	9.6
Dutch guilder	0.2198	2.1653	0.102	2.27	9.7
Bel/Lux franc	3.4310	40.4381	0.085	42.46	8.1
Danish crone	0.1976	7.4762	0.026	7.85	2.5
Irish pound	0.0086	0.7333	0.012	0.77	1.1
Greek drachme*	1.4400	143.6095	0.010	150.79	1.0
Spanish peseta	6.8850	127.4286	0.054	133.80	5.2
Portuguese escudo*	1.3930	163.8952	0.008	172.09	0.8
Total	1 Ecu	=	1.050 $	–	100.0

* Theoretical rate
Source: CEC

Suppose the outcome of the negotiation is a 6 per cent devaluation of the lira, a four per cent one of the French franc, and a 2 per cent revaluation of the Deutschmark and the Dutch guilder. The exchange rate of these currencies to the dollar will then change as shown in column 2 of Table 17.3. The relative importance of the changes is chosen by the Council in such a way that the value of the Ecu does not change in the operation. What has changed, however, are the Ecu weights of column 5: the DM and the guilder, before accounting for 39.7 per cent now make up 40.7 per cent, which means that these two currencies will have a greater bearing on the future development of the Ecu value than before. The preponderant position of a single currency might be objected to; therefore, every five years the shares of column 1 are brought into line with the value they should have on the basis of their GDP, trade volume, and monetary support quotas. Of course, that operation is again effected in such a way that in practice the Ecu/dollar exchange rate does not change on the day of adaptation.

Support mechanism of the EMS

Countries finding themselves unable to contain their currency within the permitted margins of fluctuation may ask for permission to use the *support mechanism* of the EMS that at present (1989) comprises three categories:

- Very short-term facilities (from one to two months) to cope with speculative capital flows; for that purpose unrestricted amounts are available on easy conditions.
- Short-term support (from three to six months), allowing Central Banks to cope with balance-of-payments difficulties. Such loans are of considerable size.
- Medium-term loans (from six months to several years), meant to ease the restructuring of the economy; their granting is no longer semi-automatic, but subject to sometimes severe restrictions and conditions for restoring the internal balance of the country in difficulty.

Out of solidarity, lending and borrowing among central banks under the mechanism described is denominated in Ecu; in that way debtor and creditor share the exchange risks. Before that arrangement was made, a country with balance-of-payments problems which had accepted a loan denominated in a strong currency, nevertheless had to devalue its own currency, used to incur an exchange loss on this loan on top of its existing financial difficulties. Now both the repayment and the interest on loans are paid in Ecu. The system adopted for fixing the rate of interest is familiar: it rests on the weighted average of the official interest rates of EMS countries, the weights being the same as used for the Ecu.

The institutional form of the EMS is weak. As is clear from the above, the EMS is not a reserve system, nor the Ecu a *reserve currency*. However, the European Council explicitly envisages such roles for the EMS and the Ecu in the future. To make a start, the central banks of the EMS countries have deposited 20 per cent of their gold and dollar reserves with the European Monetary Co-operation Fund (EMCF).

This embryo of a European monetary authority has been in existence since 1973; it handles the credit, accounting and reserve mechanisms of the EMS. In practice, the persons on its board of governors are the same as those on the Committee of Governors of Central Banks. Because the technical means required for its operations are those already employed for world-wide purposes at the Bank of International Settlements in Basel, the latter executes all practical actions for the EMCF.

Evaluation of the EMS

The EMS was created to establish a zone of stable exchange rates in Europe, with a view to enhancing the efficiency of the internal markets for goods, services and production factors, hopefully to be reflected by increased intra-union trade and capital movements (labour movement is not an objective; see Chapter 9). Let us briefly consider how far those objectives have been realised.

First, *stable exchange rates*. In the short run the system has worked satisfactorily, producing a fair balance between flexibility (daily variations of exchange rates) and stability (central rates). For the medium term the situation is more complicated. Admittedly, there have been realignments, but these have become less frequent over time (no realignments at all between 1987 and 1990). The performance of the EMS should not be measured by the ideal of fully fixed parities, however, but by the situation that would have prevailed without the EMS. This can be done by making comparisons between the period before the EMS was created and the one after, and between the performances of EMS and non-EMS currencies. Table 17.4 gives the results of both comparisons; they are very conclusive. The figures for the EMS *vis-à-vis* non EMS, and those of the control groups of the UK and the USA *vis-à-vis* both EMS and non-EMS show that the turbulence on the exchange markets after 1979 led to more variability.

Table 17.4 Index of variability of exchange rates against other currencies

		EMS		non-EMS	
		1974–78	1979–85	1974–78	1979–85
EMS	nominal	15	7	18	23
	real	16	9	20	24
UK	nominal	17	21	19	24
	real	18	24	21	28
USA	nominal	19	27	16	21
	real	20	28	18	27

Source: Ungerer *et al.*, (1986)

There is only one exception: the EMS *vis-à-vis* other EMS currencies, where variability was reduced by almost half. On the basis of an extensive statistical study Gros (1987) even concludes that the EMS has reduced intra-group exchange-rate movements to the minimum, that is to the variability of the fundamental determinants of exchange rates.

Has the exchange-rate certainty of the EMS also *contributed to intra-EC trade* ? That question is difficult to answer, as very little empirical research has been done in the field. One of the few studies is Cushman (1983), who found a negative effect of exchange-rate risk on 14 bilateral trade flows from the USA and Germany to Japan, the UK, France and Canada. This is in line with the results of inquiries among representatives of industry and commerce, which always indicate exchange-rate turbulence as a major hindrance to trade (de Lattre, 1985).[2] Let us look somewhat closer at the European evidence. European business circles are very outspoken on the negative effects of exchange-rate uncertainty on their operations (AMUE 1988). Is this also reflected in the trade pattern? The trade data given in Table 17.5 for EMS and non-EMS countries do anything but point towards a positive influence of exchange-rate stability on trade as, since 1979, intra-EMS trade has grown far slower than EMS trade with non-EMS countries. De Grauwe (1987) has pointed out that to ascribe this to the EMS would be a premature conclusion. He shows that the situation can largely be explained from other factors (for instance, slow economic growth and investment, due in turn to restrictive fiscal policies), and that trade among EMS countries would have decreased by another 1.2 per cent had the exchange rate been as variable as those of other industrialised countries. So, according to him, the EMS has created allocation benefits.[3]

Other evidence is given by Perée and Steinherr (1989) who find that exchange-rate uncertainty, defined over a medium term period does negatively effect trade flows of industrialised countries.

Table 17.5 Average percentage yearly growth rates of trade (exports + imports) in constant prices, 1973–1985, by group

	1973–78	1979–85
Intra-EMS	4.9	2.8
EMS/non-EMS	6.6	5.6
EMS/non-EMS, exclusive of USA	7.5	5.7

A partial answer to the question: has the *EMS helped to create conditions for a better functioning of capital markets?* is given by Molle and Morsink (1989) who found that for the period 1975–1983 direct investment flows between EC countries were negatively influenced by exchange rate uncertainty.

The last question is: has the EMS contributed to the *convergence of inflation rates to a low level and to convergent economic policy?* The answer seems to be positive, notwithstanding the persistent differences in inflation rates. Indeed, average inflation has decreased (see next section) and the parity changes have not fully matched the inflation differentials in EMS countries, which has gained monetary authorities in inflation-prone countries credibility for their monetary policies, intended to curb price increases (Giavazzi and Pagano, 1986).

Macro-policy: the need for convergence of inflation rates

Objectives and means

Macro-economic policy co-ordination is not a goal in itself; it is pursued to improve growth conditions for the economies of all member states, and to create the conditions for stable exchange rates, which themselves are

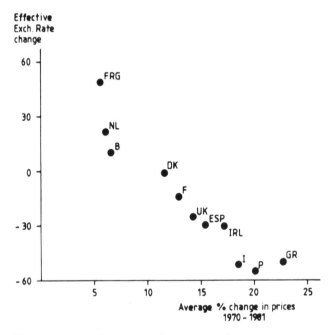

Figure 17.1 Inflation and currency depreciation or appreciation

Source: Cameron (1985)

instrumental to allocational efficiency. In that context the convergence of inflation rates is especially important. As Figure 17.1 shows, in the long run higher-than-average inflation rates of EC countries inevitably lead to a corresponding depreciation of their currencies. The opposite is also true.[4]

As discussed in Chapter 7, the mix of goals and instruments for macro-economic policies varies much among member countries; in practice the choice is between low inflation and stable exchange rates on the one side, and high nominal growth with inflation and devaluation on the other. That macro-economic co-ordination has not been very successful in the past is mostly due to the different strategies chosen by different countries.

The *actual inflation rates* prevailing in the various EC countries reflect the different policy choices (and the structural influencing factors). Table 17.6, which ranks EC countries by their performance in the 1973–1982 period, gives an idea how the inflation figures were dispersed in the 12 EC member states (as well as in the USA and Japan) in that period. The EC countries are ranked according to their performance in the 1973–1982 period.

Table 17.6 Average annual percentage inflation rate (GDP price change) by country and period

Country	1960–72	1973–82	1983–89
Germany	4.2	4.8	2.5
Netherlands	5.8	7.1	1.3
Belgium	3.9	7.2	3.9
Luxemburg	3.7	7.8	3.8
Denmark	6.3	10.1	5.5
France	4.6	10.8	5.2
United Kingdom	4.9	14.3	5.4
Ireland	6.6	14.8	6.5
Spain	6.7	16.1	8.9
Italy	4.9	17.0	8.5
Greece	3.3	17.5	16.5
Portugal	3.6	17.8	18.0
EC12	4.8	11.7	5.9
USA	3.3	7.8	3.7
Japan	5.5	7.1	1.4

Source: Eurostat, *National Accounts*, Aggregates, 1960–1985
CEC, *European Economy*, Supplements

The table clearly shows that the crisis of 1973 brought about a tremendous increase in overall EC inflation, an increase which has only recently been cut back. It also shows up three blocs of countries:

- below-average rates, inflation-shy countries, mostly in northern Europe;
- about average rates (France, Ireland);
- above average rates, 'inflation-prone' or 'inflation-permissive' countries, all lying in the Mediterranean basin.

What are the *causes of inflation and of different inflation rates among countries?* In broad terms, three different factors have been suggested in inflation theories (see Frisch, 1983, among others):

- wage push, resulting from trade-union action or tension on the labour market;
- monetary expansion, extending the quantity of money more than the total product available;
- structural inflation, dependent on the dichotomy of a sheltered and an exposed sector in the economy.

The following sections will deal separately with the three explanatory factors. No attempt has yet been made to relate the three approaches to the essential dynamics of European integration; indeed, all studies are confined to the estimation and comparison of the different models for only a limited number of (EC) countries.

Wage cost: Phillips and the institutionalists

One major cause of inflation has been the cost push resulting from changes on the labour market. Wages being a large component of most prices, wage increases beyond the rise of productivity push up the prices. The important question is, then, why should wages increase faster than productivity? Two answers suggest themselves: (1) because of the working of the Phillips curve, and (2) because of the dynamics of collective action (see Chapter 7).

According to the *Phillips curve*, wages change at a rate that is inversely related to the tension on the labour market (indicated by unemployment). This model has been estimated by several authors (Nordhaus, 1972; and Brown, 1985; Chapter 8) for the larger European countries (United Kingdom, France, the Federal Republic of Germany, Italy). They found that while for some countries the relation seemed to hold for the 1950s and 1960s, for a more recent period the curve either could not be established, or was very steep and sometimes even had the wrong sign. Nor could any evidence of a stable Phillips curve be traced for the smaller European countries (Katee, 1979; van Poeck, 1980). After severe criticism of the Phillips curve by monetarists (Friedman 1968), it was extended to include expected prices. However, including inflationary expectations in the equation gave inconclusive results: Nordhaus (1972), Katee (1979) and van Poeck (1980), Brown (1985). Consequently, most economists now believe that the Phillips curve is in the long run a vertical line and therefore hardly relevant in the European context.

In the view of *institutionalists*,[5] some countries have a higher propensity for 'wage' inflation than others because in their institutional systems pressure groups carry a lot of weight. The differences on that score among the four large EC countries have been analysed in depth by Seidel (1983) for the period from 1960 to 1975. He derived, in qualitative terms, the probable outcome of the distribution conflict, and hence the gross increase of wages, by investigating in detail the structural characteristics of the labour market. From that analysis, the decisive factors appear to be, on the one hand, organisational effectiveness (organisational structure, and the division of tasks between local and central layers) and on the other hand legal provisions (mandatory arbitration procedures, legality of lockouts, etc.).[6] Crouch (1985) carried out a similar analysis for a larger number of OECD countries, including most EC member states. He showed that countries with a strong (neo-)corporatist structure used to be less conflict-ridden than countries with an atomist or liberalist structure, where many small organisations act in an unco-ordinated way. He also showed that in both groups, the higher the percentage of unionised workers, the higher the wage claims.

Both authors agree that these factors have contributed to the low inflation figures in countries like Germany and to high inflation in the United Kingdom and Italy, France taking a middle position. However, the pursuit of a rigorous wage-increase policy by trade unions has not resulted in higher real incomes, owing to the inflationary effects of wage rises. Countermoves by employers' organisations, for instance price increases, have neutralised most of the redistributive effect that was expected from high nominal wage increases.

Will these differences among nations in institutional factors change such that the conditions for converging inflation rates in the EC can be fulfilled? Trade-union power has changed considerably in the past ten years; in all EC countries their membership did decline, which is due in part to the high growth of modern sectors with little unionisation and the phasing out of the older industries, traditionally the strongholds of the unions. With converging industrial structures, trade unions may become more alike. Government regulation has also changed considerably. In the United Kingdom, legislation has bereft trade unions of a number of action instruments. In Italy, the 'scala mobile', which automatically corrected wages for inflation, was abolished. However, to create the institutional conditions for converging inflation rates in the EC, many other measures will have to be taken, including for example, the adoption of arbitration procedures after the German model.

Budgetary deficits and money supply; the monetarist view

Important proponents of the view that inflation is a monetary phenomenon, Friedman and Friedman (1980), wrote:

> Inflation occurs when the quantity of money rises appreciably more rapidly than output, and the more rapid the rise in the quantity of money per unit of output, the greater the rate of inflation.

In that view, inflation is linked to the growth of government deficits. Let us see how far European facts support that view. A first analysis relating the development of prices to that of government deficits as a percentage of GDP for the 12 EC countries did not show any clear correlation. This may in part be due to the relation we found in the previous section between inflation levels and institutional factors. A second analysis, used the acceleration of inflation rates (difference between averages of 1973–1982 and 1960–1972) as a dependent variable, and the increase in budget deficits (as a percentage of GDP from 1965 to 1980) as an independent variable. The results are given in Figure 17.2. They show the differences between the two groups of countries distinguished in the previous section (corporatist and liberalist) and the positive influence of the deficit on inflation for both. Of course, the relation thus reproduced is only illustrative and too simple for any formal conclusions on causal relationships to be drawn.

According to monetarists, whether deficits contribute to inflation depends on their being monetised or not. To check how far that thesis holds in developed economies, Cameron (1985) related the change in consumer prices to the excess money supply and the latter to the total deficit on the government budget (for France, Italy, the UK and the FRG).

The results of his analysis of the first link in the chain seem to refute the monetarist view. For the second link in the chain the results suggest a strong relationship for all countries. Taking the two together, we find that neither deficits nor excess money can, on the whole, be blamed for inflation.

Some countries seem to escape the inflationary reaction to deficits and excess money, which means that one has to dig deeper into the causes of inflation or look for other determinant factors. One factor that is sometimes brought forward is the degree of *independence of the Central Bank*. The German and Dutch central banks are relatively

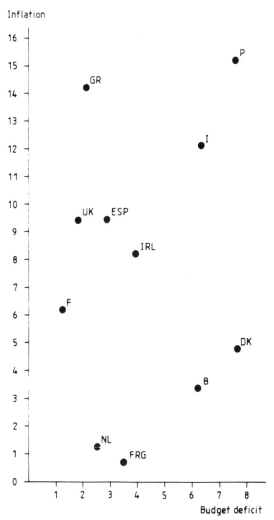

Figure 17.2 Inflation and budget deficits

Source: Deficit: OECD (1982e), *National Accounts of OECD Countries*
Inflation: Table 17.4.

independent from government, and pursue price and exchange-rate stability without needing to succumb to 'short'-term political aspects. That is all the more important as the inflexible budgetary policy in Western democracies has put relatively more weight on monetary policy (Eyzenga, 1987) to control inflation.

Structural imbalances and international transmission

While the Phillips-curve model and the monetarist theory of inflation are concerned with the problems of inflation in the narrow sense of the word (short run), the structural hypothesis attempts to explain the long-run trend in Western economies of rising price levels (Frisch, 1983). The hypothesis of structural inflation rests on the relation between the structural development of the price level and modifications in the sectoral economic structure.

The following sectoral structural factors are held jointly responsible for inflation (Maynard and van Rijckeghem, 1976; Magnifico, 1985):

- sectoral differences in the rates of increase in labour productivity. Usually productivity grows faster in the sectors producing goods than in those producing services;
- sectoral uniformity of money wage increases, generally defended on the fairness principle. The pace is set by the high-productivity (manufacturing) sectors. The service sectors follow, which owing to their low productivity change leads to a sustained cost pressure;
- price and wage rigidity (when prices and money wages are downwardly inflexible, changes in relative prices require an increase in the general price level);
- sectoral differences in price and income elasticity: services tend to have a lower price elasticity and a higher income elasticity than manufactured goods. If prices in the service sector are set by a profit-margin mark-up of rising wage costs, the relative prices of services go up;
- regional imbalances. The wage leadership of strong central areas like London or Paris pushes the wages up even if in other areas the equilibrium wage is not yet attained.

By and large, structural models are based on a two-sector division of the economy: the exposed, progressive manufacturing sector and the sheltered, conservative service sector. That structural view is developed further in the so-called 'Scandinavian model', which describes inflation as the result of *imported inflation* (working its way to consumer prices through the prices of imported goods), as well as differentials between the rates of productivity growth in the traded and non-traded goods sector. Some of these models (Dramais, 1977, among others) reveal only a slight influence of import prices on inflation, others (like Nordhaus, 1972; and Schwartz and Kooyman, 1975) find a fair influence.

Growth policy, convergence of wealth levels

Objectives and means

One of the major objectives of the Treaty of Rome is the *constant improvement of the living and working conditions of the European peoples.* Moreover, the preamble states the need to strive for a harmonious development by reducing the differences among the various regions. On the bridge between the present chapter on stabilisation policies and the next on redistribution policies, note that the national dimension of that statement is that the EC must concern itself both with the fostering of economic growth for the Community as a whole and with the convergence of wealth levels among member countries. That implies the pursuit of policies leading to higher growth rates for low-income member countries, and to lower growth rates than the EC average for the richer ones.

Table 17.7 **Average yearly growth rates of GDP (volume), and development of GDP/P (EC12 = 100), for the 12 EC member countries, 1950–1985**

Rank	Country	Growth %		Level (index)	
		1950–73	1973–85	1950	1985
1.	Denmark	3.4	1.7	153	149
2.	Germany	5.6	1.9	93	135
3.	Luxemburg	2.5	1.5	201	128
4.	France	3.6	1.6	136	122
5.	Netherlands	4.4	1.1	100	114
6.	Belgium	2.5	1.6	166	106
7.	United Kingdom	1.8	1.3	140	105
8.	Italy	4.2	1.6	71	82
9.	Ireland	2.9	2.0	81	68
10.	Spain	5.3	1.1	35	56
11.	Greece	6.7	1.5	30	43
12.	Portugal	4.3	1.3	35	28
	EC12	3.9	1.5	100	100

Source: *OECD National Account Statistics,* several years; *Eurostat Review,* several years. National figures on GDP made comparable with exchange rate figures

Let us survey briefly what the EC has achieved on that score since the war. Table 17.8 sketches for all member states of the EC, ranked by their 1985 wealth level,[7] the development of the relative levels of GDP per capita, and of real growth rates of GDP/P, through a long period.[8] The picture is very clear: immediately after the war some of the countries now making up the EC12 were very poor (Portugal, Greece and Spain, to a lesser extent Italy, and, compared to the EC9, also Germany) while others (Belgium, Denmark, the United Kingdom and France) were relatively well off.

Comparison of the growth figures of the individual countries with the EC average shows that many of the low-income countries have grown at a more than average rate whereas the growth rate of countries like the United Kingdom was below average, so that there was more equality in 1985 than in 1950.[9]

The access to the EC has had a very clear influence on the high growth figures of Spain and Portugal in recent years (larger than EC average) (CEC, 1988a).

Production factors and world markets

To find out why in different countries the output grows at different rates, economists have first of all considered the differences in the *supply of input* (following the well-known neo-classical production function). Such a model is used by Denison (1967), who further differentiates the inputs (sources of growth), distinguishing the following variables: for labour, total employment, hours worked, age and sex distribution, or education; for capital, investment in machinery, dwellings, and international assets. Productivity growth is often derived as a residual (for instance, Chenery *et al.*, 1986), in other models technical progress is traced with the help of such indicators as the progress of knowledge, or the lag in the application of the best practices (Cornwall, 1977; Cripps and Tarling, 1973). A disadvantage of the input approach (that generally explains only half the differences between countries) is that the explanatory factors are themselves in need of explanation. Indeed, to state that Germany enjoyed a very high growth rate because it increased its labour force by immigrant labour (see Chapter 9) is unsatisfactory; an explanation is also wanted why Germany could increase its output so much in the first place, to the extent that additional labour was needed.

In another view, the *growth performance is related to the terms of trade*. The hypothesis is that countries confronted with high prices on their import markets because of external shocks (oil, for instance), and with lower prices on their export markets because of fierce competition, will show lower GDP growth rates than countries in more fortunate circumstances (Bruno, 1984).

Institutionalists

Another view on the causes of differential growth comes from the institutionalist. Their principal thesis was proposed by Olson (1983). In his view, individuals and firms with similar interests tend to group together to obtain advantages for themselves at the expense of other groups of society, or of society as a whole. By their *collective action, special interest groups reduce overall efficiency and hence aggregate income.* Such distributional coalitions also reduce the rate of economic growth because they slow down a society's capacity to adopt new technology and to reallocate resources in response to changing conditions. Moreover, they raise the level and complexity of regulation and government intervention in markets, diminishing still more the capacity to adapt. The more a society accumulates special-interest groups and collusions, the lower its rate of growth.

The relevance of this theory to the EC is that it sheds some *new light on the causes of the different growth performances of the EC countries* recorded in Table 17.8. The post-war economic miracle of Germany is explained by the fact that the Nazis broke the influence of many special-interest groups, and the Allied powers did away with the influence of many others (large industrial trusts). The slow growth of the UK, on the other hand, is attributed to that country's long-term stable evolution, giving rise to a dense network of powerful special-interest groups, such as trade unions and the upper-class establishment. While the theory is very appealing, as it appears to be consistent with many situations that we are all familiar with, it is still highly deductive. Among the attempts at a rigorous test of the above theory for the EC, the one most interesting to us is that applied to the difference between two leading European member countries, namely Germany and the United Kingdom. In his study, Murrell (1983) compared different industries in the United Kingdom and the Federal Republic of Germany. His hypothesis was that special-interest groups are probably most important in old established industries and least in new industries. He found indeed that modern British industries held a better position *vis-à-vis* their FRG colleagues than the older ones.

A second point of relevance of the special-interest group theory is that it gives support to the idea of the *dynamic effects of integration,* set forth in Chapter 5. Economic integration brings in new competitors who challenge the positions created prior to the integration by special-interest groups. Collusion of firms under sanction of the government becomes more difficult, trade-union power in sheltered industries is diminished by competition from outside, etc. Hennart (1983) attributes to those factors much of the fast economic growth of France in the 1960–1973 period.

Summary and conclusions

- The EC has been slow to develop co-ordinated (let alone harmonised) stabilisation policies.
- *Stable exchange rates* are the main objective of European monetary co-operation in view of the welfare gains it provides to international traders. The structure of the European Monetary System, with its centre-piece the Ecu, has been very successful in bringing about such stability. The adaptation of exchange rates that remains necessary is of a structural nature and determined by different inflation rates.
- *Inflation* is caused by many different factors, among which stand out the behaviour of social partners, the monetary financing of budgetary deficits, and the price increases of imported goods. Differences between countries on those three scores have led to widely diverging inflation rates in the past. In recent years, the differences in causal factors have diminished and hence the inflation rates have converged.
- *Growth rates of GDP* have diverged quite a bit in the EC, but as poor countries generally grow faster, GDP levels have converged, which was one objective of the Treaty of Rome. The determinants of the differences in growth among countries are as yet insufficiently known to assess correctly the role of demand-and-supply factors and that of increased integration.

Notes

1   For a description of the genesis of the EMS, see Ludlow (1982); for the basic text: CEC (1979d), and for the workings: CEC (1986h).
2   De Lattre (1985) finds an influence of uncertainty in exchange rates on both imports (sudden increases in production cost through intermediate goods) and exports (sudden fall in a country's competitiveness when its own currency appreciates). He further distinguishes the negative influence of floating on the results of foreign investment policy, and, for MNF, the influence on the value of the balance sheet. Although financial markets have responded with different products to cover the risk of floating, it still entails cost. Moreover, for many risks coverage is difficult to obtain. So, many firms remain exposed to such a degree as to prefer exchange-rate certainty.
3   Most available evidence of the influence of short-term exchange-rate volatility on trade indicates that it is small owing to the existence of forward markets and hedging mechanisms. However, increasing doubt is cast on the negative effects of long-term misalignments; see, for instance, Crochett (1983) and Steinherr (1985).
4   The relations put forward in Figures 17.1, 17.4 and 17.5 remain the same if other OECD countries, including the larger ones, are also taken into account.
5   For the basic thoughts of this group of authors, see among others Widmaier (1974), Olson (1965), Priore (1979).
6   See for a more elaborate description of the differences in industrial relations between countries, Bamber and Lansbury (1987).

7   The figures calculated with the help of exchange rates do not take differences in purchasing power into account. If the national GDP figures are made comparable, on the European level with purchasing power parities (ppp), the differences are reduced (from 46 to 139 in 1985), but the ranking of the countries remains practically the same.

8   The period has been broken into two subperiods because of the drastic changes occurring after 1973.

9   See for further explanation of differential growth rates the country chapters in Boltho (1982).

18 Redistribution: Regional and Social Policies

Introduction

There is a general assumption, if not conviction, among economists and politicians that competitive markets (efficiency) generate considerable inequality. Government and non-market institutions are then required to reduce this inequality by redistribution, even if it means some loss of efficiency. In Okun's (1975) terminology there is a *trade-off between efficiency and equality*. These views apply also on the European level (Padoa-Schioppa, 1987).

The EC was created as a common market. The objective was to step up efficiency and stimulate economic growth by integrating the markets of goods and production factors. That the ensuing structural changes (relocation of economic activities, changing composition of sectoral activity) implied some unacceptable consequences for certain sectors of society was expected. The most vulnerable groups were concentrated, on the one hand, in particular regions or even countries (geographical dimension) and on the other in particular sectors of the labour force (social dimension). To gather the benefits of integration, the EC has taken upon itself to compensate these groups for their losses and help them adapt to the new situation.

In that spirit (see also Chapter 7), redistribution policies, in practice the *social and regional policies* of the EC, were developed. While the EC has been pledged to social policy ever since its creation, its regional policy did not really take off until after the first enlargement of the EC. Real political commitment to regional and social policy was not achieved until the 1972 Conference of the European Council. That Paris Conference called for vigorous Community action to diminish social and regional imbalances, and recognised the need to increase the finances of the Social Fund and create a Regional Fund. With the adoption of the Single European Act, the redistribution has become a treaty obligation. As a matter of fact, article 130A of this Act reads: 'In order to promote its overall harmonious development, the Community shall develop and pursue its actions leading to the strengthening of its economic and social cohesion.' With the progress of integration, the policies have changed their outlook. New elements gradually entered social policy, intended to make the EC labour market more efficient. Similarly, regional policy was expanded to cope not only with the effects of integration but also with the problems of regional disparities in Europe.

To give effect to this obligation to achieve cohesion, a new 'framework' regulation (2052/88) was adopted in 1988 that is intended to safeguard the consistent intervention by the various funds. Article 1 of this regulation indicates *five priority objectives* and the involvement of each Fund in its pursuit. These objectives are:

- to promote the development of backward regions (ERDF, ESF, EGGFA);
- to promote the restructuring of regions coping with industrial decline (ERDF, ESF);
- to fight long-term unemployment (ESF);
- to integrate young people in working life (ESF);
- to restructure rural areas (EGGFA).

Although inspired by the same philosophy, the objectives and instruments of the two policies have developed rather differently; therefore, we will deal with them in separate sections.

Regional disparities and policy

Foundations

There are *regional differences in economic development* in every country, more pronounced in some than in others. They are mostly measured by such indicators as the concentration of people and economic activities, the level of income per capita, the productivity per working person, and the availability and accessibility of environmental goods, cultural infrastructure, leisure activities, etc. On all those scores, there are also wide differences among EC countries. Consequently, welfare is unequally distributed among European regions. History (Pollard, 1981a) as well as theory (for instance Paelinck and Nijkamp, 1975) teach us that such differences are the result of a complex interplay of mutually dependent factors, which collectively determine the location of people and economic activities. Under some conditions the system tends towards less disparity, under others towards more. Because the system appears unable to achieve equilibrium, governments have stepped in.

Traditionally, *two reasons for intervention* by measures of regional policy are given.

- The efficiency argument is of a typically economic nature. In this view the concentrated regional distribution of some production factors, public goods, and economic activity, prevents an efficient allocation and hence prevents the economy from drawing full profit from the potential available. Total production would increase if the inequalities were removed.
- The equity argument is of a typical social nature. In this line of thought large groups of the population feel that inequality is socially unacceptable and morally unfair. Total welfare would increase if the inequalities were removed.

The *efficiency or economic argument* for a European regional policy was already debated at the Messina Conference, but took some time to be translated into concrete policy. Although the fathers of the EC were well aware of the regional problems (as is evident from the preamble of the Treaty of Rome, according to which the member states are 'anxious to reduce the differences existing between the various regions and the backwardness of the less favoured regions'), and in spite of repeated warnings by academics (for example, Giersch, 1949) that European integration spelled problems for certain regions, the Treaty of the European Economic Community made no provisions for a European regional policy in the proper sense. The creation of the Common Market and the development of a common foreign-trade policy deprived member states of the trade-policy instruments by which they had supported regionally concentrated industries. Exposed to foreign competition, the least efficient ones (such as the Wallonian coal mines) soon found themselves out of business. The problems were aggravated when the free movement of production factors was introduced, and capital and labour began to flow to the regions offering the best locations for investment. Furthermore, with the progress of harmonisation, especially on the industrial and social planes, national instruments lost much of their implicit power to control regional developments. The gradual realisation of an Economic and Monetary Union (EMU)[1] is curtailing even more the instruments available to national states; they are losing, for example, the authority to pursue a national exchange-rate policy (Williamson, 1976).

The effects of integration on regional equilibrium may be both positive and negative. Much depends on the initial situation, the capacity of regions to adapt, the growth effects of integration on all regions, etc. (see, among others, Williamson, 1976; Vanhove and Klaassen, 1987; Chapter 6). Measures of regional policy are necessary to compensate for the negative effects of the initial (Customs Union) and further progressive (EMU) integration. Besides, the day-to-day functioning of the European Community needs the constant accompaniment of adequate measures of regional policy. Structural changes due to economic, technological, environmental and social developments continue to occur, demanding continuous adaptation. Without measures of regional policy to compensate the afflicted regions, the very functioning of the Community may be in jeopardy. What has happened to the steel industry is illuminative. The lack of alternative activities in 'steel regions', where substantial cutbacks in employment were necessary during the latest recession, has induced certain member states to give heavy support to the established industry, to which other member states responded by threatening to close the frontiers to these products. Now that would mean a direct violation of the foundations of the Community (free market and international specialisation), jeopardising the whole European structure, on which the prosperity and welfare of Europe have largely come to depend.

The increasing attention given to the aspect of allocative efficiency through the completion of the internal market has given a new impetus to the need for an adequate regional policy. In that view, the Single European Act (article 130A) has confirmed the necessity to reduce the differences among regions to improve the economic and social cohesion of the Community.

The *equity (social) argument* for regional policy also has a European dimension, inasmuch as a regional transfer of resources would be an act of solidarity of prosperous with less prosperous regions in Europe. The recent tendency of the European Community to emphasise social and human aspects along with purely economic ones also favours efforts to improve regional equilibrium by measures of regional policy on the European level.

The question suggests itself, however, how far such arguments carry weight in the European context, where up till now neither the social dimension (see, for instance, Vandamme, 1986) nor the basis for an appeal to redistributive justice (Findlay, 1982) seem to have developed much. Traditionally, the framework for claims to solidarity has been the national state, where people feel they belong to one social system; it would be interesting to see how far the idea of the EC has come to supplement that of the nation state. Some empirical evidence on that score has come available from a survey held by the Commission (CEC, 1980). A first interesting result of that survey is that a large majority of respondents in all countries favoured social or moral arguments for measures of inter-regional transfer over efficiency arguments. The second interesting aspect is how European solidarity among regions of different countries compares with solidarity among regions of the same state. The survey shows that while four out of five respondents accept to pay a fiscal contribution for aid to regions in their own country, only one in three feels the same about aid to regions in other EC countries. That, too, is true of all the countries of the Community, with relatively slight differences among them.

Objectives

The *objectives* of European regional policy have been formulated (for example, CEC 1977) as follows:

- to diminish the problems of both the traditionally less developed regions and of regions involved in a process of industrial and agrarian restructuring;
- to prevent new regional disparities that could result from structural changes in the European and world economy.

The obvious next question is what has the EC done to attain these objectives? Little enough at first, mainly because it was poorly equipped. As a matter of fact, in 1958 nobody had a clear idea of the size and nature of regional problems at the European level. As we have seen, the Community set out without sufficient authority in regional matters from the Rome Treaty, and only got that authority by a lengthy procedure. By constant diligence the Commission has gradually acquired the necessary instruments, and the regional element has become more and more prominent among the policy areas of the EC. Now the Community regional policy is conducted in co-operation with the member states; indeed EC regional policy is not a substitute for, but a complement to, the regional policies carried out by the member states. Four main areas of EC activity in regional policy are generally distinguished (CEC, 1977); we will discuss them in succession.[2]

Assessing the regional problems[3]

The European Community is struggling with vast regional problems that vary widely and give rise to different *types of problem region*. On the one hand are the regions that so far have developed hardly any manufacturing industry and services, being still largely oriented to agriculture; especially in southern member states, agriculture is often not very productive. On the other hand are the regions which played a leading role at a certain stage of economic development, but have landed in difficulties as production conditions changed. The former type of region is generally marked by a peripheral situation and a deficient infrastructure, in particular a meagre endowment business services. The latter type is generally marked by inadequate infrastructure and serious problems in old industrial as well as residential areas. The labour-market situation also differs in the two types of region.

While agricultural regions lack skilled labour and industrial and service traditions, the trouble with the old industrial regions is that their highly specialised manpower is at odds with modern requirements.

The *disparity in income per head* is generally felt to be one of the most painful disparities among the European regions. It is indeed wide, the best favoured region in the European Community being now 10 times 'richer' than the poorest (GDP per head); the figure has increased much with the latest extension of the EC; in the EC9 it was 'only' 5 times. Extending earlier work (Molle *et al.*, 1980), Molle (1990) has analysed the development of regional disparities in income (see Table 18.1).

Table 18.1   Indices[a] of regional disparities of wealth in the EC, 1950–1985

	1950	1960	1970	1980	1985
1 disparity among regions	0.124	0.102	0.078	0.098	0.071
2 disparity among countries	0.095	0.081	0.061	0.082	0.056
3 2:1 in %	76	79	79	84	79

[a] Theil indices of Gross Regional Product by head of population
Source: Molle (1990)

As the evolution of the figures in the first row of Table 18.1 shows, the disparity between all European regions decreased considerably up to the first oil shock. The turbulent 1970s were attended by an increase in the index, largely due, however, to the increasing divergence between official exchange rates and the purchasing power of currencies. Since 1977, total disparity has again decreased.[4]

The causes of the decreasing disparity on the regional level are threefold.

- the movement of capital; in all European countries manufacturing plants have moved from central to peripheral areas (see Klaassen and Molle, 1982);
- the migration of workers; contrary to that of capital, labour movement was rather centripetal (see Chapter 9).
- the creation of the welfare state; the provision of such welfare services as schools, hospitals, transfer payments, and social security systems has strengthened the economic base of the less affluent regions (Molle, 1986).

Within that reduced spread, the ranking of European regions by their level of prosperity evidences a remarkable stability. Indeed, through the whole 1950–1985 period, the 'peripheral' regions of Mediterranean countries were always in the lowest positions, while some urban regions in northern Europe were steadily at the top. Only two significant shifts are recorded: all German regions moved strongly upward, and all regions of the United Kingdom and Belgium fell back.[5]

The disparity due to differences in GDP/P among member countries of the EC is given in the second row of Table 18.1. These international disparities are largely responsible for the interregional disparities (row 3). The underlying factors, such as resources, the level of schooling of the labour force, the access to markets, and in particular the social and economic infrastructure, are national rather than regional characteristics. Therefore, to consider merely regional factors, as would be proper for regions within one single country, is not sufficient to cope with the regional problems within the EC; the so-called 'national factors' should be given at least as much attention. Indeed, only by national factors can we explain why Mediterranean countries are so much inferior to northern Europe in income by head, and why the relative positions of the United Kingdom and Germany have changed (see Chapter 17).

Co-ordination of EC policies with a regional impact

Specific policy measures have different effects on regions. That holds also for the EC. If, for instance, the tariff on textiles is reduced as a measure of common trade policy, textile activities that happen to be concentrated in a few regions may bear the brunt. That policies may have an adverse effect on regional equilibrium was made eminently clear by Henry (1981), who showed that the measures of agricultural policy, which consume three-quarters of the EC budget, mainly benefit the rich regions. Woken up, the EC now tries to assess the probable regional impact of its other policies before implementing them.

Molle and Cappellin (1988) have tried to *establish the regional impact of the most important EC policies*. Given the complexities of the detailed studies on which they based their research (for instance trade, macroeconomics, industry), only approximation proved possible. They have made a geographical division between north (N) and south (S) (based on the general welfare differences in Europe), and distinguished the usual four types of region: metropolitan, intermediate, agricultural/peripheral, and old industrialised. The scores of Table 18.2 indicate the effects found in the detailed studies.[6]

Two major *conclusions* are warranted: (1) that Community policies tend to have contradictory effects, and (2) that the combined scores tend to accumulate more positive points to some regions (intermediate north) and negative points to others (in particular the problem regions of long standing in southern Europe). Thus, the urgency attached by the EC to the analysis of policy impacts seems justified.

The response of European regional policy to the problems indicated has been inspired by the idea of compensation. That is hardly surprising, as in a sense the entire EC regional policy owes its existence to the UK claim to be compensated for losses due to integration. More specifically, European regional programmes like VALOREN (for energy), try to compensate the regions in the very sector which has caused the regional problem in the first place. For instance, if European energy policy has aggravated a region's problem, a programme is drawn up to improve its energy situation. Molle and Cappellin (1988) favour an approach without that pronounced link, an approach by which regions are helped by all practical means to overcome their problems, whatever the cause. In such an 'endogenous' approach, the potential sources of conflict between Community, national and regional objectives and instruments seem to be far less virulent than in the compensation approach.

Table 18.2   Schematic view of impacts by policy area and type of region[a,b]

Policy area	Metro-politan		Inter-mediate		Agri/periph.		Old indus-trial	
	N	S	N	S	N	S	N	S
Agriculture	0	0	+	0	0	-	0	0
Industry	-	0	+	+	0	0	-	-
Energy	0	-	0	-	-	-	0	0
Transport/Telecommunications	+	0	+	-	0	-	0	0
Trade (external)	0	0	0	0	0	0	0	0
Macro and Monetary	+	0	+	0	0	-	0	0

[a] + = beneficial; 0 = neutral; - = negative
[b] N = north; S = South
Source: Molle and Cappellin (1988)

Co-ordination of member states' regional policies

All countries in Western Europe have taken up regional policy in the course of the past decades. According to the gravity of their regional problems and the socio-economic views held, they started sooner or later, and more or less intensively, as is apparent both from the number of instruments used and from the vigour with which they were applied. Gradually, however, the multiple ideas on tools of regional policy developed in the member states of the European Community are settling in a kind of pattern, and some consensus is gradually crystallising out, so that now a few general characteristics can be given of eligible regions and instruments.

In all member states, *the instruments of regional policy* can be divided into (1) instruments addressed to people, and (2) instruments addressed to industries. The former category, which is practically abandoned everywhere, concerned mainly financial support to persons willing to move house. To the important group of instruments applied to economic activities belong, first, financial benefits (loans, grants, etc.) meant to encourage investments in certain regions, and second, the large category of instruments encouraging location in certain regions. The latter instruments refer traditionally to infrastructure (roads, ports, industrial sites, training of workers, public utilities, etc.) (Yuill and Allen, 1985); recently, aspects of research and innovation have come to the fore.

If all governments are broadly agreed on the causes and remedies of regional problems, that does not mean they also take a European view. Actually, the national views tend to be distorted. What from a national point of view may seem a grave problem justifying a substantial money outlay, may seem trifling from the EC point of view. So, the first task of the EC was to define the *priority regions on the EC level*, that is, the regions that are eligible for aid from the European Regional Fund. Figure 18.1 gives those so qualified in 1987.

The second task was to prevent governments from outbidding one another with subsidies, which would mean in practice that the richer member states would be able to match any package allowed to the poorer ones. The EC has put a *ceiling on aid levels* in each type of problem region, that is high in a very poor region and low in relatively prosperous areas.

Because the regional policy of the EC is complementary to that of the member states, national measures need to be co-ordinated. Once that need had been recognised, *the regional programme* was introduced as a policy instrument.[7] Its purpose is to integrate the measures taken by competent organisations in the regions with respect to infrastructure, schooling, housing, etc. so that the EC can co-ordinate them, identify any gaps, and design schemes to fill these up.

For the smooth co-ordination of more general issues between the EC and the member states, and as a platform for regular discussions on priorities, programmes, and other matters, a *Committee for Regional Policy* has been installed, consisting of officials of the Commission and the national governments of the member states.

The European Regional Development Fund

For effective help to regions in distress, the EC must have financial means. After years of negotiation,[8] the EC finally obtained the necessary funds with the creation, in 1975, of the European Regional Development Fund.[9] The *tasks of the ERDF* are to grant subsidies to stimulate investment in economic activities and develop the infrastructure in

Figure 18.1 Areas eligible for ERDF assistance at the beginning of
1987

specific regions designated as EC problem areas (see Figure 18.1). These areas are selected for their below-average wealth levels and above-average unemployment levels. Eligible for investment support in these regions are those activities which are already receiving aid from the member state in question or one of its agencies; the EC intervention is indeed meant to complement such aid. Apart from works directly related to manufacturing (industrial sites and such), more general infrastructure works, for instance the construction of roads and canals, also qualify for support. Member states are invited to submit projects, which are then compared with the 'regional programme' to evaluate their contribution to the solution of the region's problems. The Fund (approximately 12 000 millionEcu for the 1975–1984 period) is fed by the EC budget, the Community's own financial means.

The *financial means of the Regional Fund are attributed in such a way as to strongly favour low-income countries.* Table 18.3 compares ERDF aid per capita to GDP per capita (in index figures). (When interpreting the figure for Greece, keep in mind that Greece only started to benefit from the ERDF after 1981.)

Table 18.3 **Concentration of ERDF aid (EC10), 1975-1984 (Indexes; EC = 100; aid per head and GDP per head) and shares of EC countries in ERDF (as of 1986)**

Country	Concentration		Shares		
	ERDF/P	GDP/P	Min	Max	Pivot
Greece	261	40	8.4	10.6	9.2
Ireland	477	51	3.8	4.6	4.1
Italy	181	67	21.6	28.8	24.5
United Kingdom	116	90	14.5	18.3	16.4
France	74	117	7.5	10.0	8.5
Belgium	58	125	0.6	0.8	0.7
Denmark	28	115	0.3	0.5	0.4
Netherlands	25	116	0.7	0.9	0.8
Luxemburg	*	121	0.0	0.1	0.1
Germany	21	128	2.6	3.4	2.9
Spain	*	*	18.0	23.9	20.3
Portugal	*	*	10.6	14.2	12.1
EC10	100	100	88.6	117.1	100.0

Source: Concentration calculated from data in CEC (1985g); Shares Regulation EEC 3641.85
* not yet members

The enlargement of the EC with two low-income countries, the need to step up the efficiency of regional policy, and the introduction of other EC policies with regional effects (internal market and EMU) have forced the EC to make a number of changes.

The *size of the ERDF* was increased, in 1987, to 3 000 million Ecu a year to cope with the increased range of regional problems. For a prompter response to new exigencies, the distribution of the funds among countries has been made more flexible, with shares varying between a maximum and a minimum (as shown in the right-hand part of Table 18.3). The present distribution is stronger than the former oriented to low-income countries. Indeed, some 66 per cent of the Fund is reserved to the four Mediterranean countries Greece, Italy, Spain and Portugal, which accommodate 36 per cent of total population, but contribute only 22 per cent of GDP to the EC12. The size of the ERDF is to increase considerably in the early 1990s in order to cope with the possible negative effects of the completion of the internal market.

The ERDF responded to *the need for regional innovation*. Indeed, regions have to be innovative, using their own indigenous potentials, as standard solutions from outside are not always forthcoming. A new regulation of the Fund (EC 1787/84) introduced three new types of measures:

- aid to companies in management and organisation questions, and allowances for the development of new products;
- stimulation of the creation of agencies that compile and distribute information on product and process innovation;
- support to companies by evaluating the technical feasibility and marketing prospects of new products and production processes.

The main concern of the three types of measure is to assist small and medium-sized companies, which otherwise would have no access to such essential information.

Evaluation

Many authors have already posed the question *how effectively regional policy helps to realise certain objectives*. Several types of studies have been carried out to find the answer. The simplest approach is to measure the effect of regional policy as the sum of all employment in activities that have been supported. But the question is how much of that employment would have been created anyhow, without support. To measure that, models have been developed to isolate the effects of regional policy from 'normal' development. From such studies, the importance of regional policy seems to be limited. Another approach has been to interview the firms concerned, asking them how far their choice of location had been influenced by measures of regional aid. Again, the general conclusion is that current regional-policy measures cannot hope to affect the spatial distribution of economic activities in a big way (Folmer, 1980; Uhrig, 1983).

Clearly, the EC regional policy is carried out in the form of programme aid. There are no block grants allotted to countries (Chapter 7), which indicates that redistribution is not the only effect envisaged; on the contrary, all measures need to help improve allocational efficiency. Whether the policy measures are effective on that score is doubtful (ECA, 1988).

Social policy

Foundations, objectives and means

European social policy is a complement to national social policies developed to attend to such social problems as unemployment, poverty, illness, etc. Social policy is closely associated with, and may even encompass, labour-market policy.

The *rationale for a European social policy* is based on efficiency and equity arguments already put forward in the section on regional policy:

- The efficiency argument is that measures of social policy help towards the efficient allocation of resources. An example is a programme for the retraining of workers for taking up jobs in a new industry after having been made redundant in an old industry. Such social policy measures are the oil in the economic machinery.
- The equity argument is that wide differences in welfare are morally unacceptable and that, therefore, redistribution should take place by transfer payments from the most to the least affluent. In all countries, this argument has led to detailed schemes of social security: old-age pensions, unemployment benefits, insurance against illness, etc. – schemes generally associated with the welfare state. Moreover, the equity argument has led to the definition of basic social rights of workers, including minimum standards for the quality of occupations (such as safety, health, hours of work, length of paid holidays, etc.) and industrial relations (such as collective bargaining, strikes and employee co-management) (Kolvenbach and Hanau, 1988).

Most international efforts with respect to social policy are made in the framework of the *International Labour Organisation*. Convention no. 102 of the organisation (adopted as early as 1952) commits ratifying states to certain minimum standards for social-security systems. For Europe, these standards were raised somewhat in 1964 when the Council of Europe adopted the European Code of Social Security (IEE, 1978).

European social policy can be traced back to the *European Coal and Steel Community*. Its activities in the field were inspired mainly by the efficiency argument; the objective was to make the labour force more easily adjustable to the exigencies of the Common Market. Indeed, article 56 of the Treaty of Paris permits the ECSC to provide non-repayable aid towards:

- the payment of tide-over allowances to workers;
- the payment of resettlement allowances to workers;
- the financing of vocational training to workers having to change their employment; in 1960 complemented with;
- the payment of allowances to undertakings to enable them to continue paying such of their workers as may have to be temporarily laid off as a result of the undertakings' change of activity.

The equity aspect was given scant attention; article 46 only authorised the High Authority to obtain the information required to assess the prospects for improving the working conditions and living standards of workers in the industries within its province, and the threats to them.

The experience of the ECSC proved profitable when the social policy of the *European Economic Community* was devised. While the countries of Europe were still discussing the need for economic integration, the need for a complementary social policy had already been recognised (ILO, 1956). However, the preparatory discussions for the Treaty of Rome did not produce a clear-cut view on such a policy, so that the relevant Treaty's articles form rather a mixed bag. Social policy deals with two different subjects:

- Co-ordination of social-security systems (article 15) to secure freedom of movement for workers. Workers who migrate from one national system of social security to another need protection to safeguard their rights, but that does not necessarily mean that the systems themselves need to be changed. Also important are articles 117 and 118 on the harmonisation of social-security systems that reach far beyond article 51 in that they envisage the adoption of certain common principles and set certain common standards.
- The Social Fund, which has the task of 'rendering the employment of workers easier and of increasing their geographical and occupational mobility' (article 123).

The Treaty of the EEC seems in two minds as to the *aims and means* of social policy, especially with respect to the harmonisation of the social-security systems of member states. The first paragraph of article 117 sets broad and ambitious aims as it states:

> the member states agree upon the need to promote improved working conditions and an improved standard of living for workers, so as to make possible their harmonisation, while the improvement is being maintained.

However, the second paragraph of the same article merely goes on to say that

> the member states believe that this is largely to be achieved through the beneficial effects of the Common Market

which puts paid to the hopes of a full-dress European Social Policy. The same dichotomy of aims and means is found in article 118. The first part of this article states that the Commission's tasks are to promote close co-operation in the social field, particularly in employment, labour law and working conditions, basic and advanced vocational training, social security, prevention of occupational accidents and diseases, occupational hygiene, and the right of association and collective bargaining between employers and workers. The second part of the same article allows very limited means to realise these tasks: the Commission is asked to undertake studies, arrange consultations, etc. The Commission has indeed done so, but up till the end of the 1980s with little practical result.

Recently, the work on the *European Social Charter* that lays down a number of fundamental rights for workers in the European Community has given a new impetus to the elaboration of a European Social Policy that goes beyond merely coping with the social effects of the economic policies of the EC. (We will come back to this point in Chapter 20.)

All social issues do not have the same importance in economic terms. For that reason we will not discuss all matters further but limit ourselves to social security, the Social Fund and workers' participation; the last is an issue which has attracted much interest from the European business community.

Social security

In the debate provoked by the provisions of the Treaty in matters of social security, broadly two views can be distinguished (Holloway 1981), the 'economic' and the 'social-progress' view.

In the *economic view*, the provisions of the Treaty (articles 117 and 118) demand only that the social-security systems be harmonised as far as necessary for the proper functioning of the Common Market. Some understood this to mean that the charge to employers should be to some extent equalised across Europe to prevent distorted competition. Others believed that the differences would be compensated for by the exchange rate, their only concern being of a macro-economic nature: since a high proportion of total state expenditure is taken up by social security benefits, the equilibrium among states could be upset if the amounts involved in social security rose too fast. In general, economists have tended to warn the EC from any major action. The only exception, explicitly foreseen by the Treaty, concerns the protection of migrants against the loss of social-security rights. We have seen in Chapter 9 that the Common Market, while not meant to set large flows of migrants in motion, nevertheless has led to several millions of migrant workers. The geographical reallocation of the labour force in Europe would have been an empty word without measures to protect migrant workers against the risk of losing social-security rights. So, the Treaty of Rome commits the EC to co-ordinate the relevant systems of the member states[10] by:

- removing nationality and residence restrictions;
- deciding that the law of the place of work is applicable;
- organising mechanisms of co-operation among the agencies administering the various schemes in the member states;
- regulating the aggregation and proration of insurance periods in different member countries.

The *social-progress view* takes for granted that the EC is more than a Common Market, and has the clear task of enhancing welfare. This view has led to claims from trade unions demanding harmonisation in the form of upward alignment to the highest level in any member state of the EC, or at least elimination of the gravest shortcomings of the systems in certain member states. First, the Commission should carry out cross-fertilising studies, and next, draw up proposals for European regulations setting minimum levels. Proposals for a redistribution from the rich to poor member countries by means of a European Social Security Fund have been put forward, but due to the obvious lack of political support they have not been realised. However, such transfers would be perfectly in line with the increasing solidarity among member states of the European Community.

The *outcome of the debate between economists and social-progressists* was clear-cut; the economists won. The Commission, which had associated itself initially with the social-progress approach, was forced, in 1966, to adopt the economic line advocated by all member states. Consequently, little progress has been made since, despite the declaration of the Paris summit of 1972 that the EC should take on a more human face and that social goals might therefore be important. Only two recommendations on minor points have been issued. Some consider that this does not do justice to the real situation (Holloway, 1981) because by the mere study and exchange of information that has been going on since the creation of the common market, some quite natural harmonisation has been achieved.

Employee participation

The Commission's main activity with respect to workers' participation has been to propose to the Council, in 1980, a directive on *procedures for informing and consulting the employees in multinational firms*. It is generally called the Vredeling directive, after the commissioner then responsible for social affairs. The reason for the proposal was that a parent multinational company had closed down a subsidiary without warning, let alone consulting, the employees. In many EC countries, trade unions had concluded agreements with employers' associations on the participation of employees in important decisions, such as mergers, major investments or disinvestments, etc. To give substance to these agreements, governments had laid down legal obligations for managements to inform and consult their employees. Many subsidiaries of multinationals tried to get around these obligations by disclosing only partial and incomplete information to trade unions, preventing the latter from forming for themselves a good idea of what was going on on the European level. The Vredeling directive aimed to put an end to such practices by obliging the management to explain to the employees of the subsidiary companies the grounds for and the *legal, economic and social consequences of the following decisions:*

- the closure or transfer of an establishment or major parts thereof;
- restrictions or substantial modifications in the activities of the enterprise;
- major modifications with regard to organisation, working practices, or production methods, including modifications resulting from the introduction of new technologies;
- the introduction of long-term co-operation with other enterprises or the cessation of such co-operation;
- measures relating to workers' health and to industrial safety.

The Vredeling proposal has met with very fierce *opposition from the associations of employers,* who argued that the directive completely failed to understand the responsibility of company directors. Opposition was particularly heavy against the so-called 'bypass' clause (article 6, paragraph 5), which authorised the employees' representatives to open consultations with the management of the parent company if the management of the subsidiary failed to produce the relevant information. This was said to misinterpret the role of the managers of subsidiaries of multinational firms, who for most of their actions are in practice completely independent. Empirical research, however, has produced only partial support for that view (van den Bulcke, 1984). American multinational companies in particular, not used to such social commitments, exercised much pressure to kill the proposals. The discussions in the Economic and Social Committee and the European Parliament have not contributed much to a consensus; on the contrary, they have only shown up the profound differences in opinion among the members of both assemblies. Within the Council, opinions differed so much that, in spite of some adaptations by the Commission, the proposal has so far failed to get sufficient support.

European Social Fund

The *original objective* of the European Social Fund (ESF) as stated in article 123 EEC is to increase the occupational and geographical mobility of workers in the Community, thus serving both an allocational purpose (to increase the efficiency of the European labour market) and a redistribution purpose. By article 125 EEC this was to be achieved mainly through vocational retraining and resettlement allowances, but aid could also be granted for the benefit of workers whose employment was reduced or temporarily suspended as a result of conversion. The Fund was to be administered by the Commission, assisted by a committee of representatives of governments, trade unions and employers, an arrangement that is still valid. The Treaty allows the Fund to be used for new tasks after the transitional period (article 126 EEC), which indicates considerable foresight of the authors: the tasks of the Fund have indeed been continuously changed under the influence of new political demands and new economic and social circumstances (see Collins, 1983). Three periods can be distinguished.

1.   The *'first'* Fund covers the period of the EC6, from 1958 to 1972. While the treaty mentioned three purposes, in practice the Fund became almost entirely devoted to enhancing the allocational efficiency of the labour market, in other words, occupational mobility. In the period considered, 97 per cent of the Fund's resources went into the financing of vocational training or retraining schemes. Only a minor portion (10 million Ecu) of the total amount of 320 million Ecu of grants paid in this period were channelled into schemes for resettlement, for the purpose of stimulating geographical mobility. The reasons are not hard to find: indeed, the shortages on the labour market were already calling forth large migration flows which needed no incentives. Nothing was done to encourage reconversion, mostly because member states

could not agree on the type of project that would be eligible for aid.

2.   The *'second' Fund* came into operation after the reforms of 1971, and lasted, with major adaptations, until 1983. In that period, its financial scope was gradually increased from some 250 million Ecu in 1972 to 1500 million Ecu in 1982. The Fund was able to contribute up to 50 per cent to the training and related costs of specific groups in society. To show up the priorities, Table 18.4 quantifies the distribution of the available funds among countries and target groups.

Table 18.4   Social Fund Aid, in percentages, by category and member state, 1976–1980

	Agriculture	Textiles	Migrants	Women (1978/80)	Young	Handi-capped	Regions	Tech-nical progress
Percentage of total EC=100	3	3	4	1	29	8	50	2
Germany	16	20	28	55	7	24	6	-
France	49	10	23	23	22	12	14	-
UK	4	28	9	3	33	21	27	17
Italy	23	26	34	14	26	19	39	41
Netherlands	1	10	4	2	1	4	2	-
Belgium	1	5	2	1	2	4	1	3
Denmark	-	-	1	1	2	4	2	39
Ireland	6	1	-	1	7	12	9	-
Luxemburg	-	-	-	-	-	-	-	-
EC9	100	100	100	100	100	100	100	100

Source: Collins (1983) various tables

From the table, redistribution apparently has overtaken allocation. Indeed half the Fund's money went to the less developed regions. In that realm, the European Social Fund works alongside the ERDF, the latter helping to create job opportunities, the ESF assisting the labour force to acquire the skills needed for the new jobs. Almost 30 per cent of the grants paid by the ESF were used to improve employment prospects for young people, because much of the burden of rising unemployment appeared to be shouldered by the young.

The *'third' Fund* came into operation after a major revision in 1983. Its volume was increased to 2500 million Ecu in 1986 (EC12). The priorities set tend to continue and accentuate the aspect of redistribution practised by the previous Fund. First priority are young people: on their education, training and initial hiring, 75 per cent of the Fund must be spent. Next come the distressed regions in Europe; 45 per cent of total ESF aid accrues to the following: all regions of the three poorest countries of the EC (Greece, Portugal, Ireland), the Italian Mezzogiorno, and large parts of Spain. As an example we give the division of the Fund for 1986.

Evaluation

From the preceding sections, European social policy consisted up to the end of the 1980s mainly of: (1), a set of rules defining the rights of migrant workers to social-security benefits; (2) a loose co-operation in the form of exchange of information on social policy, including social-security systems; and finally, (3) a means of redistributing European funds among member countries for the retraining of workers.

The various elements of European social policy have drawn mostly unfavourable critiques. Laffan (1983) and Steinle (1988) are among those who argue that at best, the ESF serves the redistribution of European money, but fails to attain any specific Community objectives in matters of training (allocation function).

Those who set very high objectives[11] for a European social policy (to remedy the employment situation, remove disparities in welfare among social groups,[12] all-Europe collective bargaining and agreements,[13] full democratisation of the economy, not to speak of more immaterial aims) look upon the progress as very limited, and hardly worth attention. On the other hand, those who set their objectives otherwise, and many would say more realistically, will join the conclusion of Vandamme (1985) 'that it was quite evident from the outset that all social improvements that were not the outcome of the spontaneous evolution of economic realities, would be both very difficult to achieve and inevitably limited'.

However, as the internal market develops (Chapter 16) and the work on higher objectives of integration, such as the Economic and Monetary Union (Chapter 17) advances, gradually the conditions for a more developed European social policy are likely to establish themselves. The codification of a set of basic social rights for workers in the European Social Charter may lay the foundations for this (Chapter 20).

Summary and conclusions

- The most important policies carried out by the EC to improve the redistribution of wealth are regional and social policies. The instruments used for both reflect the wish of the EC to make these policies instrumental to more allocational efficiency as well.

- *Regional disparity* in the EC12 has gradually decreased in the past decades, but considerable differences in wealth remain. The effect of the Regional Fund on that development is uncertain. The effect of European integration in general is not solidly documented either, but the impression (see Chapter 17) is that the EC has helped to diminish the disparity in national wealth, and that is a major determinant of disparity in regional wealth.
- *Social policy* in the EC has limited objectives and consists mostly of a redistribution of resources through the European Social Fund for the retraining of workers of depressed regions.
- Evaluations of the *effectiveness* of both policies are fairly critical; although the redistribution effect in budgetary terms is certain, the contribution to growth and efficiency appears to be limited.

Notes

1 Giersch (1949) has already argued that the creation of a Monetary Union would transform balance-of-payment problems into regional problems.
2 The basic texts of the Regional Policy are collected in CEC (1985h). For a more extended treatment including theoretical bases and empirical results of EC regional policy, the reader is best referred to the *locus classicus* in the field, Vanhove and Klaassen (1987). For a shorter treatment, for example, Pinder (1983).
3 From the beginning, the Commission has been active in assessing the regional situation and regional developments in the Community by carrying out or commissioning several studies (CEC, 1961, 1964, 1971, 1973b). The main purpose of the reports is to keep knowledge of the old problems up-to-date and to recognise new problems as soon as they present themselves. They also serve as a foundation for discussions with member states about priorities in regional policy and the changes to be carried through in it. Recently it was agreed that the Commission would periodically write reports on the regional situation in the Community (CEC 1981b/1984c/1987). See also Clout (1986).
4 When the GDP/P figures are calculated with purchasing-power parities instead of exchange rates, they are reduced by about half; however, a situation in which the richest region is five times wealthier than the poorest is to most observers still unacceptable. Another indicator of regional disparity is *unemployment*. As it appears to be highly concentrated in the same regions that also show a low GDP/P level we will not pay attention to it.
5 For the causes of the slow growth of the UK, see among others Kaldor (1966) and Hudson and Williams (1986); for the causes of the level of growth rates of other countries, Boltho (1982).
6 For many of the detailed studies, quantitative results either were not available or their underlying concepts could not be made comparable. That is why we have to be content with these fairly crude indicators.
7 CEC (1979e) reviews the older programmes, CEC (1984d) the more recent ones.
8 Discussed at the Messina Conference back in 1956, proposed by the Commission in 1969.
9 See for a description of the creation of the Fund, Talbot (1977), for the restructuring CEC (1981c), and for a review of its performance in the first 10 years the EC brochure CEC (1985g). Recently, the Single European Act (article 130) has reinforced the position of the ERDF in the EC institutional framework.

10   An extensive and detailed system of regulation has been developed by the EC, corroborated by countless decisions of the European Court of Justice. As the details are more interesting to lawyers than to economists, we will not go into them here.
11   See part two of Holloway (1981) for some details.
12   For a discussion of the perception of poverty by different social groups in European countries, see Hagenaars (1986).
13   Often claimed by the trade unions. See for a discussion of their action, Barnovin (1986).

19 External Relations

Introduction

In this chapter we will look into the external relations of the EC, starting from the assumption that the scope of foreign policy differs with the stage of economic integration. That assumption rests on the principle that a matter which has been regulated by the Community cannot be treated internationally without the participation and consent of the EC. Or, as Wellenstein (1979) put it: 'All fields in which the Community fixes its own rules are potential fields of external activities or foreign policy.'

As the EC is first and foremost a customs union, trade policy will receive the most attention. Three sections will be devoted to aspects of the common external trade policy: the general principles, the instruments, and the specific relations with different (groups of) trading partners.

However, the EC is developing from a customs union into a full economic and monetary union and possibly a political union, which means that matters other than trade are the object of gradual integration and are thus becoming the concern of common external policy. The final section of this chapter therefore briefly reviews labour and capital movements, and international economic and monetary co-ordination. There we will also enter the field of development aid as well as that of external policies less associated with economic issues, such as foreign and defence policy. Some general conclusions will complete the chapter.

External policy: general issues

Major categories

The importance of the categories of an economic community's external relations can be derived from its balance of payments, which is the financial record of its transactions with the rest of the world. These transactions include current ones concerning merchandise, services, etc. as well as long- and short-term capital transactions. We have rearranged the headings in the statistics of the current account of the European Communities to fit the general organisation chosen earlier in this work; the results are given in Table 19.1.

A few brief comments on the results are in order. The first is that the structure of the external transactions has been stable through time. The prominence of merchandise exports is striking; they account for about two-thirds of total current transactions. That justifies the considerable attention we will devote to EC trade relations in the next sections. Services, while increasing in importance, still come second but occupy a modest place in comparison. Among the payments associated with production factors, the returns on capital invested abroad are growing in importance; the payments made by, and to, the EC for labour (earnings from work and remittances by emigrant workers, etc.) are very small in comparison. Official transactions, finally, cover on the one hand payments for embassies and international organisations, and on the other the financial aid given to developing countries. Next to these current-account transactions there are those of the capital account, whose total volume, as a matter of fact, is by far the greater. Although this would in principle justify a considerable involvement of the EC in world policies on capital transactions, the reality is different,

Table 19.1   Transactions of the EC with third countries by
category; average assets and liabilities[a] 1976–1984

	1976[b]	1984[c]
Merchandise	66	62
Services (commercial)	18	21
Labour (inc.)	2	2
Capital (inc.)	8	12
Official	6	3
Current account (CA)	100	100
CA:GDP x 100	17	21

[a]   Figures of assets being very much like the liability figures for all headings, we have preferred this presentation to the more common one of net figures (assets minus liabilities)
[b]   EUR9 with third countries
[c]   EUR10 with third countries
Source: Eurostat (1977) , *Balance of Payments; Geographical Breakdown, 1972–1976* and Eurostat (1987) *Balance of Payments G.B. 1981–1985*

as will emerge from our brief description in the last section of this chapter, which also deals with policies in matters of development aid.

International setting: the rules of GATT

All member countries of the EC are contracting parties to the GATT, the General Agreement on Tariffs and Trade. GATT came into being after the Second World War as a second best option, the International Trade Organisation having failed. At the moment almost a hundred countries have signed the agreement. GATT has two main objectives: (1) to lay down a set of rules of conduct for international trade, and (2) to provide a framework for international negotiations on the reduction of tariffs and other impediments to trade.[1]

Central to GATT is the so-called *'most-favoured-nation clause'*, which obliges all contracting parties to adopt a policy of non-discrimination. In the terminology of GATT, it means that

> any advantage, favour, privilege or immunity affecting tariffs or other trade regulation instruments which is granted to one of the GATT members, must immediately be granted to all other members as well.

Another important GATT rule is that *changes in trade policy*, such as the imposition or raising of tariffs, the setting of quotas, etc. cannot be decided unilaterally by one national government, but *must be subjected to international negotiation*. That rules out unilateral increases in protection which might lead to retaliation and tariff wars, and at the same time provides countries prepared to make concessions in the direction of free trade with a lever to obtain similar concessions from other nations (reciprocity). The GATT has engaged the contracting parties in some major rounds of international negotiation, in the course of which the protecting tariff walls have been substantially taken down. GATT has also set rules for other instruments of international trade, prohibiting import quotas (art. 11) and limiting export subsidies (art. 16), but the negotiation rounds on those scores have not been so successful. In the late 1970s and early 1980s , there has been an upsurge of protectionism, mostly in the form of non-tariff measures (Greenaway, 1983).

At the moment, negotiations are under way to find out how far agriculture and services can be put under the GATT umbrella. For agricultural products, many developed countries including the EC refuse to expose their agriculture to international competition. With respect to services, on the contrary, some developed countries (the United States, Japan, the United Kingdom) are urging liberalisation according to GATT rules, but on that score developing countries are afraid to lose growth possibilities.

Community regime

The preamble of the Treaty of Rome already states the desire to 'contribute by means of a *common commercial policy* to the progressive abolition of restrictions on international trade'. One major instrument for such a policy is the Common External Tariff (CET), for which article 29 gives the following motives:

- the need to promote trade among Member States and third countries;
- the possible improvement of the competitive capacity of undertakings;
- the avoidance of competitive distortions in finished-goods markets, related to supplies of raw materials and semi-finished goods;
- the avoidance of serious disturbances in the member states' economies, while ensuring the growth of production and consumption within the Community.

That Common Commercial Policy (CCP) is indeed a concern of the EC follows from article 113, which states: 'The common commercial policy shall be based on uniform principles'. The often-posed question whether the CCP covers only tariffs or other trade instruments as well, was clearly decided when the Court of Justice ruled in 1975 that it covers all trade instruments. That decision implies that all powers regarding changes in tariff rates, conclusion of trade agreements, export policy, the achievement of uniform liberalisation, and anti-dumping or counter-vailing duties should be transferred to the institutions of the EC. Nevertheless, the mixed nature of their economies causes member states to use independently all sorts of instruments on the borderline of trade policy, a development that gives rise to lengthy competence battles between the Commission of the EC and member-state governments.[2]

The extension of EC external relations to *other policy areas* follows also from article 113 EEC, which in section 9 deals with the conclusion of international agreements in the setting of a common commercial policy. The scope of this article has been a source of multiple conflicts between the Council and the Commission, many of which have been submitted to the Court. Schwarze (1987) summarises the consequences of the case law of the European Court as follows:

> The implied powers (of the EC) to conclude treaties with third countries does exist when: a) the Community holds the respective internal power and b) the treaty is necessary for the attainment of any objective recognised by Community law. This concept has become known as the principle of

parallel powers whereby the Community's treaty making powers are congruent with its internal competences in any given field.

In practical terms this means that the European external policy will be extended with new subjects as integration progresses through the stages we distinguished in the second chapter (see also Ward, 1986; Molle and van Mourik, 1987).

Trade policy: a fan of instruments

Common External Tariff

The Common External Tariff (CET) of the EC was established for each category as the arithmetic average of the tariffs applied by the member states (art. 19.1 EEC). Thus, the first CET reflected the whole history of the trade relations of all member countries. Since then, there have been some major changes, mostly due to GATT negotiations. The so-called Dillon Round of 1960–62 and the subsequent Kennedy Round of the mid l960s cut the tariffs by about half. A further tariff cut of some 30 per cent of the 1978 level was agreed upon during the so-called Tokyo Round of the mid-1970s. The general level of tariff protection of the EC is now very low, about 3.5 per cent. For many imported products coming under the preferential agreements to be reviewed in the next section, the EC tariff is even nil or negligible. Moreover, the dispersion has become very narrow; only for very few products does the EC import tariff exceed 20 per cent.

The conclusion may be that as far as tariffs are concerned, the EC has effectively worked towards free trade, as the Treaty of Rome had enjoined upon it. However, the *scope of the reductions is severely restricted*. For one thing, the GATT-Round reductions applied to industrial products only. The agricultural sector remains the most protected sector in the Community: substantial tariff and non-tariff barriers (NTBs) exist for most agricultural products (see Chapter 11). For another, several industrial products were excluded from liberalisation. No significant tariff reductions could be agreed upon for textiles and wearing apparel, steel, footwear, ships. For many products of these so-called 'sensitive' sectors import barriers prevail, mostly in the form of quotas and voluntary export restraints. 'Sensitive' sectors are composed of low-technology manufacturers, using relatively standardised, labour-intensive production technologies, the very sectors for which LDCs are gaining an increasing comparative advantage. Finally, the tariff reductions are not applied across-the-board. Indeed, the tendency has been for greater reductions of duties on primary commodities and raw materials than of duties on finished goods.

Non-tariff barriers

Less visible than tariffs but no less effective as instruments of trade policy are the so-called 'non-tariff barriers' (NTBs). In line with its Treaty obligations, the EC tries to *free international trade* not only from tariffs but also from NTBs such as border formalities, import quotas, administrative and technical regulations, tax laws, aid programmes, and discriminate government procurement. Many NTBs applied to non-EC members date from pre-EC times, when quotas in particular were popular among the present EC member states. Although the Treaty of Rome allows member states to retain such pre-EC quotas on imports from non-member countries, the Commission has been pushing to dispose of them. Its efforts towards liberalisation have not been very successful – as a matter of fact, a recent inventory of the Commission shows some 500 national quotas still remaining. The number varies considerably among members. A special case is Italy, which imposes import controls on a large number of Japanese goods.

Despite the EC's principles, the use of NTBs by the EC and its member states has increased in recent years, which means that the EC is taking an active part in the 'new protectionism'(Greenaway, 1983). It is practised in the form of so-called *'voluntary' export restraints* (VERs) (by one exporting country) and *orderly marketing arrangements* (OMAs) (multilateral voluntary restraint agreements). VERs and OMAs exist outside the GATT framework, and are therefore, from a political point of view, more expedient than quotas. Tariff quotas, applied under the GSP (Generalised System of Preferences; see next section), constitute another well-known form of NTB protection. The GSP treatment allows a limited volume of duty-free exports, the excess being subject to customs duties. Many such controls come under the *Multi-Fibre Arrangement* (MFA), negotiated between the EC and the principal textile-exporting developing countries. The latter have agreed to a voluntary restriction of their textile exports to the EC. In practice, the MFA has deteriorated into a scheme by which the individual EC member countries have fixed how many textile products they will import from each separate exporting country.

Not only the EC but also the other major trading countries of the world have increased NTB protection. As we have indicated in Chapter 5, these NTBs can be expressed in a tariff equivalent. Several studies have empirically measured tariff equivalents; the results are summarised in the following table.

The upper part of the table shows that results of different studies vary quite a bit not only as to the level of protection for each block, but even as to their relative positions. From the bottom part, NTBs appear to be highest in agriculture, food and raw materials.

Table 19.2 New Tariff Barrier equivalents (in percentages) for
various countries and products

	EC	US	Japan
All products (weighted)			
Balassa and Balassa (1984)	15	13	7
Deardorff and Stern (1981)	n.a	22	57
By *product group* (Whalley, 1985)			
Food, beverages	33	44	72
Raw materials	49	0	46
Mineral fuels	28	6	38
Chemicals + other manufactured goods	8	8	8
Machines + transport equipment	2	0	2

n.a. = not available

Protection against unfair trade practices

In their attempts to conquer a new export market, firms sometimes adopt the strategy of first selling at a loss in foreign markets to force local producers out of business, and afterwards raising their prices to very profitable levels. The practice is known as *dumping*. GATT rules allow the importing country to take protective measures against such practices, in particular to impose anti-dumping duties which level off the difference between the selling prices the dumping firm charges in its home and export markets. Much in the same way, the importing country may put on a countervailing duty to the amount of the subsidy on products subsidised by the exporting country. GATT rules require that such measures be taken only if it can be shown that:

- imports have increased substantially;
- there is a substantial price difference;
- the imports cause material injury to the home producers.

These general rules have inspired the EC anti-dumping regulation (Regulation 3017/79).
The *procedure* is as follows (Gijlstra, 1983):

- A complaint is lodged by (groups of) firms directly concerned. The regulation indicates in detail what information the Commission requires to judge whether the complaint is justified.
- Investigation by the Commission; the Commission verifies the

information given by the complaining party (analysis of their accounts), and, if the exporting country is agreeable, sends an investigation team to that country.

- If a dumping margin is found to exist and if damage has been done, the Commission may either accept the exporters' offer to adjust prices and/or subsidies, or, if the adjustment is insufficient, impose an anti-dumping or countervailing duty.
- Should the duties have to extend to a longer period than 6 months, the Council must make them permanent.

The anti-dumping rules have been increasingly applied in the last few years. A detailed analysis of their country and sector incidence is given in Tharakan (1988), a very critical evaluation in Messerlin (1988). Cases of anti-dumping and countervailing duties represent less than 1 per cent of total EC imports, but the percentage is rising. Only for five countries have such measures affected more than 1 per cent of their exports to the EC. In the entire period 1968–1978, only five procedures were settled every year; the number gradually increased to 43 in 1983. So far, most procedures have been concluded by a *'solution à l'amiable'*, that is, by the acceptance of a price undertaking by the producer under pressure from the Commission.

When the EC or a member country is faced with a sudden increase in imports, they may take *safeguard measures*. The procedure is much the same as for anti-dumping measures. Safeguard measures are mostly of the surveillance type, which means that importers must apply for licences. The statistics thus obtained allow the EC to follow closely how the imported quantities develop. Licensed imports can still flow into the EC free of quotas or extra duties. More severe safeguard measures are of the quota type. However, GATT rules preclude discriminating quotas, which means that they cannot be made country-specific. For that reason, the EC has often preferred negotiating VERs to having recourse to safeguard quotas.

The above procedures may not be sufficient to make a trading partner change its behaviour. However, if presumed unfair trading practices of third-country exporters threaten to disrupt the EC market, quick EC action may be vital to European firms. To be able to respond instantly, the EC has adopted the so-called *'New Community Trade Instrument'*, intended as an immediate answer to unfair trading practices. While GATT procedures tend to take much time, during which considerable and sometimes irreparable damage can be done, the EC can now retaliate faster: the Commission initiates actions upon which the Council has to agree within 30 days.

Export promotion and controls

Export promotion is often achieved through export credits (soft loans), implying a government subsidy. Other forms of direct export subsidy are also used, as well as indirect ones (subsidies to production, permitting producers to work at lower cost and thus obtain a better export position). The EC has used the instrument very overtly in the case of agriculture (direct subsidy). It has given production subsidies to steel, and accepted or regulated national large-scale subsidies for ships, aeroplanes, arms and other products. Like the OECD (Ray, 1986), the EC has tried to check the efforts of member countries to outbid one another on export markets with finance subsidies. Some alignment has been accomplished, but there remain widely different, detailed national arrangements. National subsidies are given to shipbuilding and steelmaking and some other sectors. By its industrial and competition policy, the EC tries to reduce such practices. As export promotion is generally considered to fall outside the realm of EC Common Commercial Policy, the Commission has little power to harmonise, let alone unify, this aspect.

Export *controls* take the form of export quotas or even embargoes. Outside the arms sector, very few national export quotas survive, and there exists only one EC export restriction (on copper scrap) outside the agricultural domain.

Effects of less protectionism

There are sound economic arguments for the abolition of all protective measures. Theoretical analyses (for instance, Greenaway, 1983) have shown that trading partners can obtain a net welfare gain from getting rid of protective measures (see Chapter 8 for the effects of trade liberalisation in the framework of the EC). To find out whether such effects indeed occur in practice, we will give the results of two studies (Deardorff and Stern, 1981; Whalley, 1985) that have analysed with general equilibrium models the effects of the Tokyo Round (see Table 19.3).

The results concur as to the slightness of the effects on the welfare levels of the individual partners and the world as a whole, but diverge as to the effects on the EC and the developing countries: the first study concludes to positive effects for the EC and negative ones for LDCs, the second to the opposite. From a further analysis of Whalley's results, the revocation of the NTBs in particular appears to be responsible for the adverse effects on the EC and the positive ones on LDCs.

One of the principal impediments to trade (other than agriculture) of the EC is the *Multi-Fibre Arrangement* (MFA). Koekkoek and Mennes (1988) have estimated the effects of the liberalisation of the MFA for the

EC as well as the LDCs. Dependent on the assumptions made, the EC's annual welfare gain for textiles and clothing together is estimated at 1 000 – 3 000 million Ecu. The larger part of this amount comes from the transfer of rents earned by foreign producers under the present MFA. Exports from LDCs to the EC could increase by 2 000 – 6 000 million Ecu, and LDC employment in the sector by between 20 and 45 per cent.

Table 19.3   Yearly welfare effects of the Tokyo Round by country, in percentage of GNP

Category	Authors	EC	USA	Japan	LDC	World NIC
Tariffs	Deardorff + Stern[a]	0.1	0.05	0.03	-0.01	0.1
	Whalley[b]	0.2	0.0	0.2	-0.2	0.0
Tariffs + NTB	Whalley	-0.2	0.2	0.2	0.2	0.1

[a]   Refers to 1976
[b]   Refers to 1973

There are a few estimates of the *cost to the EC of non-tariff protection* for specific industries. Kalantzopoulos (1986) calculated that VERs concluded by the EC for video-cassette recorders cost consumers about 500 million dollars; the same amount has to be added for the more general welfare cost of protecting the EC market for this product. For clothing, his estimate of the welfare cost of EC protection was as high as 1400 million dollars.

Causes of persistent protection

Now, if economic considerations plead so convincingly against the use of protective instruments, then why are they so widely used, even by the EC? The reason is that negative effects of protection on welfare in terms of jobs lost are plain to see and directly attributable to trade, while the positive effects are more general and diffuse and hence less visible. That makes it relatively easy to convince policy-makers of the need for protection. To analyse the mechanism, we must turn to political rather than economic science. The theoretical basis for such analysis is given in Caves's (1975) model of interest groups, worked out later by several other authors (Frey and Schneider, 1984; Baldwin, 1984). In their models, the level of protection is determined in a political market. Protection is demanded by pro-tariff interest groups, which from empirical evidence consist mainly of declining industries, using low-technology production techniques, that is, large pools of low-skilled, low-wage labour, and losing out to international competitors. Claims for protection were found to be higher as: 1) industry is more concentrated corporately or regionally, 2) the historical levels of protection are higher, 3) the industry is better organised, and 4) the macro-economic performance (including the balance of payments) weaker. Export industries and consumers have no interest in protection. However, in contrast to the sectors demanding protection, they tend to be poorly organised and have little influence. Politicians anxious to be re-elected, whatever their ideology, tend to listen more to the slogans of well-organised pro-protection pressure groups than to the pleas of anti-protectionists. There is now some historical evidence (Borchardt, 1984) that the state will only override the pro-protection interest groups if considerations of international relations carry enough weight.

Empirical work along those lines has confirmed the validity of the arguments. Weiss (1987), among others, has tried to test the hypothesis for the EC (actually the FRG) that the change in effective protection by sector of activity (account taken of tariffs, subsidies, etc.) between 1972 and 1982 depended on a number of sectoral characteristics. In line with the hypothesis, there is a negative relation for the human capital intensity and a positive one for the size of the labour force and for the concentration both on the firm and the regional level.

Trade policy: differentiation by area

A hierarchy of trade relations

All EC member countries are also contracting parties to GATT. Therefore, EC trade relations are governed by GATT rules. The trade relations of EC member states, apart from those with other members coming under the EC customs union, are essentially governed either by the most-favoured nation agreement for GATT partners, or by the rules applying to non-GATT partners. However, there have been factors at work to make the practice far more involved, very specific rules being worked out for specific groups of countries, some that are not always compatible with GATT rules. Table 19.4, adapted from Hine (1985)[3], gives a summary idea of the highly complicated system.

How trade with these country groups has developed has been shown in Table 8.4. Rather than repeating what has been said in Chapter 8, we will evoke the historical backgrounds and describe how the EC relates to each layer of trade advantages[4] in the next sections.

Table 19.4 The hierarchy of EC trade relations

Countries concerned	Form of trade relationship	Trade and aid[a] conditions	Share[b] in EC external trade (%)	Population 1985 (millions)
EFTA	Free trade area	M R	21	40
Mediterranean	Mixed[c]	a A M r	12	250
ACP[d]	One-way preferences[e] special	a A M	6	360
Other Third World	generalised preference	mg[f]	18	2900
USA, Japan, etc.	MFN[g]	q[h]	34	400
East European	Other	Q	9	390

[a] A: covers agricultural trade; M: covers trade in manufacturers; R: reciprocal (that it, partner must offer concessions on EC members' exports);
  EC provides financial aid; Q: EC imports are controlled by quotas or voluntary export restraints (VERs). Upper-case letters signify full, lower case partial, application of the measure
[b] See Table 8.4; 1985 imports and exports divided by two
[c] Customs unions, free trade areas, reciprocal and non-reciprocal (one-way) tariff preferences
[d] African, Caribbean and Pacific countries
[e] One-way (non-reciprocal) preferences: the EEC reduces/eliminates its tariffs on imports from the partner country but obtains no reciprocal (reverse) concessions on its exports; generalised preferences apply to all developing countries, special preferences to a selected group
[f] VERs on NICs' exports, quotas on textiles, tariff quotas/ceilings on other goods
[g] Most-favoured-nation (MFN) treatment: trade; subject to the (non-discriminatory) tariffs negotiated and bound in GATT
[h] National quotas on some imports from Japan; some products subject to VERs

EFTA (Other Western Europe)

EFTA countries have paralleled the members of the EC in the liberalisation of their internal trade in manufacturing goods. In 1966, some years ahead of schedule, their *free-trade area* was successfully established. That quick success was helped by the generally good economic environment as well as by the limitation to manufactured goods only; indeed, the agricultural sector was left out entirely.The EFTA share in EC exports and imports increased greatly in the period 1958–1972, and has been stable since. As a free-trade area, EFTA did not establish a common external tariff. The problem of trade deflection, imports tending to pass through the country with the lowest tariff, was solved by a system of rules of origin. Goods produced in the area (containing, in value terms, less than 50 per cent of non-area components) are allowed to move freely among all member countries.

When at the end of the 1960s the United Kingdom and three other EFTA member countries applied for EC membership, a major problem arose: trade among former free-trade partners risked being greatly disturbed by the trade barriers still remaining between the EC and EFTA. Evidently, relations among the West European countries of the two groups had to be reformulated. Several factors have influenced the outcome. The first was the general conviction that the introduction of new trade barriers would be harmful to all concerned, but particularly to the remaining EFTA members, which would be greatly dependent on the enlarged EC. Harm could be circumvented only by installing some form of free-trade area among all concerned. Because the remaining EFTA countries were unable to join the EC for reasons of foreign policy (neutrality, lack of democracy), a customs union was out of the question. For that matter, the EC clearly stated that it was not prepared to share its responsibility for trade matters in the framework of the CCP with countries that were not full members. The formula eventually chosen was that of a large European free-trade area, of which the EC is the core. The EC has negotiated *free-trade areas on a bilateral basis with the individual EFTA countries* (of which remain, after the latest enlargement, Iceland, Norway, Sweden, Finland, Switzerland, and Austria), with largely similar provisions. The remaining EFTA countries have maintained free trade among themselves on the multilateral basis of the EFTA. In that way, full free trade in manufactured goods in Western Europe took effect in 1977; as in EFTA, agricultural goods were excluded from the arrangements. A few additional rules were laid down concerning the incompatibility of state aids and restrictive business practices, to safeguard the proper functioning of the agreements.

Recently the completion of the internal EC market has encouraged EFTA-EC relations to become even closer. Most EFTA countries tend to follow the EC regulations and directives, although they have no formal influence on their elaboration. The EC may however consult these countries in the framework of an ill-defined concept (without legal status) the so-called *'European Economic Space'*. This encompasses all EC and EFTA countries that have the same regime for many parts of the economy. EFTA countries seem to be able to reap considerable benefits from such types of relations (Norman, 1989).

Relations with Mediterranean countries (mixed)

For several reasons, EC trade relations with Mediterranean countries are of a *special nature* (Shlaim and Yannopoulos, 1976; Pomfret, 1986).

The first is that some North African countries used to have colonial ties with one of the EC member countries, and wanted to maintain the special trade relations that had been established. Some European countries had applied for EC membership, and agreements were concluded with them in the mean time. Yet others wanted to obtain advantages on the EC market similar to those their neighbours had obtained. The EC gave way to the strong political pressures for preferential treatment, the *form* chosen depending on political aspirations on the one hand and GATT limitations on the other. As the GATT rules allowed such preferential treatment only as the precursor of a genuine free-trade area or customs union, many trade agreements between the EC and the Mediterranean countries were made to fit that framework. When after a while that method proved difficult to continue, the EC made efforts to put the agreements on a more uniform basis.[5] That, together with the second enlargement of the EC with Greece, Spain and Portugal, has simplified the picture enough for the following classification to be possible:

- *Co-operation agreements* have been concluded with the Maghreb (Morocco, Algeria and Tunisia) and Mashreq (Egypt, Lebanon, Jordan and Syria) countries and Yugoslavia. The parts concerned with trade are in the form of a one-way preference scheme, which means that these countries have tariff-free access to the EC market for industrialised goods. The EC has settled for an MFN treatment of EC goods on the home markets of these countries. For some sensitive goods, the imports into the EC are limited by quotas or import ceilings. The advantages of the trade agreement with the EC should not be overestimated: for limited quantities these countries already had tariff-free access by their generalised-system-of-preference (GSP) status.
- *Association agreements*, possibly leading to full EC membership, have been concluded with Turkey, Cyprus and Malta. Under these agreements, these countries have obtained tariff-free access to the EC for manufactured goods. As these agreements aspire to a full-fledged customs union, the EC requires in principle full reciprocity. That proved too hard a condition for Cyprus and Malta, so that the next stage of the association has been postponed for them. The same applies to Turkey, for which country progress was moreover blocked by political problems.
- *A free-trade agreement*, on the principle of full reciprocity, has been concluded with Israel.

Examining the total picture, we observe that fully reciprocal trade relations exist only between the EC and Israel, and partial reciprocity applies to Turkey, Malta and Cyprus; with North Africa there is no reciprocity. Thus, the relations with Mediterranean countries are hybrid forms of EFTA and ACP models; indeed many Mediterranean countries, like the ACP, receive aid in various forms from the EC.

From Table 8.4, the Mediterranean countries appear to have been able, in the last 25 years, to increase their share in EC imports considerably, while their share in EC exports has stagnated, which is an indication of their improved position *vis-à-vis* the EC and other countries exporting to the EC.

The Lomé Convention (Africa, Caribbean, Pacific)

Under the *colonial regimes*, the colonies had protected access to the markets of the mother country. Especially under French pressure, the EC has taken over the responsibility for easy access of producers of the former French colonies in black Africa to the EC market. After the UK had joined the EC, the schemes were extended to the former British colonies, whose economic structure resembles that of the associated states. The present scheme was concluded in Lomé between the EC and 64 countries, and covers the so-called ACP (African, Caribbean and Pacific) area, including practically all countries in sub-Saharan Africa and some few, very small countries scattered across the Caribbean and Pacific areas.

The *main provisions* of the present scheme are: tariff preferences, special treatment for products coming under the CAP (Common Agricultural Policy) and development aid (to be dealt with in the last section of this chapter).

Tariff preferences are fairly generous for ACP countries; indeed almost their entire exports have access to the EC market free of any tariff or quota. In that sense the ACP countries have a better deal than the other developing countries (GSP, see next section), which are sometimes subject to formal and informal quantitative restrictions (tariff preference quotas). However, access is granted only for goods which can be shown to originate for more than 50 per cent of the value added in the country itself, in other ACP countries, or in an EC country. The tariff preferences are non-reciprocal; the agreement stipulates only that the ACP countries grant imports from the EC the same favourable treatment that is allowed to the most favoured developed country.

The *special treatment of products coming under the CAP* involves a reduction of the levies which the EC puts on many agricultural imports. Although imports are not unrestricted, the quotas are applied in a 'relatively liberal' way.[6] The most important product involved is sugar. The EC has agreed to buy specified quotas of cane sugar from each country at a price approximating the one paid to EC farmers. The advantage of the arrangement is largely offset, however, by the 'dumping' of EC sugar on world markets, which negatively affects the price of ACP exports to other than EC countries.

The Lomé agreement has been somewhat disappointing to ACP countries, not least because it has failed to prevent their share in total EC imports falling from 10 to 7 per cent, and in EC imports from non-oil-exporting developing countries from 27 to 20 per cent in the past 25 year period.

Generalised System of Preferences (GSP) (Latin America and Asia)

The wish to do something about the problems of developing countries in general has been a fourth motive for differentiated trade relations with groups of countries. The UNCTAD adage 'trade instead of aid' has been important in that context. Indeed, developing countries participating in world trade face several problems.

- In the developed countries, demand for agricultural products grows but slowly because of the low income elasticity for food, while the share of indigenous production is increasing owing to support schemes and increased productivity; world markets are distorted by dumping and export subsidies to agricultural production in the developed world. Prices tend to fluctuate very heavily.
- On non-agricultural commodity markets, a similar situation prevails: economic growth is now accumulating to the less material and energy-intensive activities. These markets, too, are highly unstable: prices, and hence export earnings, tend to fluctuate very much.
- On markets for manufactured products, developing countries face heavy protective tendencies on the part of developed countries, because the very competitiveness of their new industries threatens the viability of the older sectors in developed countries.

In successive UNCTAD negotiations, the developing countries of South America and Asia have tried to obtain better prospects of penetrating the markets of developed countries. The EC market was more open than those of the USA and Japan, as the following table shows.

The European system of preference (GSP) has some distinctive features (Hine, 1985, Langhammer and Sapir, 1987), which we will briefly analyse.

- *Status.* The GSP is not a uniform world system, applied in the same way by all developed countries; on the contrary, the EC, the

Table 19.5 **Market penetration by imports from LDC into the EC, USA and Japan,1973 and 1983 (in percentage of apparent domestic production)**

ISIC code	EC		USA		Japan	
	1973	1983	1973	1983	1973	1983
Textiles	5.5	13.0	3.7	10.9	5.8	5.0
Clothing	8.6	21.2	5.9	17.2	8.0	9.0
Iron and Steel	0.7	0.8	0.7	2.7	0.3	2.2
Non-ferrous metals	13.3	9.9	2.9	4.8	7.5	10.2
Shipbuilding	2.4	7.3	0.6	4.1	0.4	1.1
Motor vehicles	0.2	0.8	0.0	0.5	0.0	0.0
Other	5.7	17.5	4.9	11.1	4.9	4.6
All manufactures	2.7	3.5	1.6	3.1	1.5	1.4

Source: Kol (1987)

USA and others have created their own systems, albeit broadly on the same principles. The EC version of GSP is autonomously granted to a number of beneficiary countries. As it is not an agreement concluded between two or more parties after negotiations, the EC can unilaterally decide to change it or even withdraw it completely.

- *Instrument*. The scheme offers a tariff preference: in general, goods coming under the GSP are imported into the EC tariff free, whereas non-GSP countries face the full Common External Tariff. Access is mostly limited to certain quantities, beyond which the full CET is applied. There is no reciprocity, EC exports to GSP countries receiving MFN treatment.
- *Product coverage*. The GSP is confined to semi-manufactured and manufactured goods. For sensitive goods,[7] it is limited to sometimes fairly restricted quotas. Moreover, some products are completely excluded from the application of the GSP, such as textiles, which are ruled by the Multi-Fibre Arrangement(MFA).[8] On the other hand, some agricultural products are included. A critical look at the product structure reveals that the products that are of most interest to GSP countries receive the least benefits; they tend to be the products from sectors for which the pressure to protect European production is heaviest.
- *Countries selected*. The GSP is in principle available to all developing countries, but the EC has specified those to which it agrees to give GSP status. In practice, some countries coming under the GSP, such as ACP and Mediterranean countries, prefer other

more advantageous schemes; that leaves Latin American and Asian countries as the most important beneficiaries.
* *Discrimination.* Although the GSP was initially a non-discriminatory scheme, in practice it has developed into a highly complicated and selective arrangement. Indeed, the trade advantages are differentiated according to the level of development of the country involved.

The EC attitude towards developing countries must be judged, not by the GSP alone, but by *the evaluation of its total trade record.* What EC policy has meant for GSP countries in terms of trade in industrial goods has been indicated in Table 19.5, which shows that on average the penetration of LDCs into the EC market has improved. In agriculture, the CAP has pushed external suppliers from the EC market, it has also thrown its huge agricultural surpluses on the world market. Unlimited subsidies to exports have driven developing countries out of their traditional markets, and caused a steep drop in world-market prices, and hence in the export earnings of developing countries (see, for instance, Matthews, 1985; and IBRD, 1985).

Most favoured nation (MFN) (USA, Japan, etc.)

There is a group of countries with which the EC has established trade relations on the basis of the most-favoured-nation treatment. To this group belong all non-European industrialised countries. Among these, the USA and Japan take pride of place, while others, like Australia, are less important to the EC. We have already indicated that trade among GATT partners has been considerably liberalised in successive rounds of tariff reductions.

The trade relations with the *USA* have for a long time been strained over the CAP, the Americans arguing that Europe prevents their exploiting its advantages to the full, the EC complaining that the USA subsidise their farmers with amounts at least equivalent to the protection given to the EC farmer. In the latest round of discussions on trade, the USA was again pushing for the liberalisation of agriculture. It has also brought much pressure to bear on the liberalisation of trade in services, to which the EC's reaction has been only lukewarm, owing to the different positions of its member states.

The trade relations of the EC with *Japan* are strained for one major reason, namely, the growing deficit on the commercial balance between the two. While in 1970 the trade balance was still practically in equilibrium, now EC exports to Japan cover only 30 per cent of its imports from that country. According to some observers, Japanese exporters owe their success to protection. They claim that the Japanese practice is to target certain industries (such as computer printers) for which they protect their own market, quickly achieving profitability and economies of scale there, and then invading other markets, including the EC market, with low-cost products. Without better access to the Japanese market, many EC countries are not prepared to give up their protectionist measures against the flood of Japanese goods (notably cars), measures that sometimes date from pre-EC times, and sometimes like the VER have been introduced since. That attitude has prevented an EC-wide approach; naturally, divergent national approaches do not make for the best possible bargaining position.

Eastern Europe, centrally planned countries

The trade relations of the EC with centrally planned countries are of a special nature. Up till the end of the 1980s most of these countries were not contracting parties to the GATT (Lopandic, 1986). Trade among CMEA (Comecon) member countries was conducted in the form of barter, and that is the form which has become dominant in East–West trade as well. The EC applied the MFN treatment (tariffs) to imports from Comecon countries, paying special attention to customs value. As trade was a matter of the state in CMEA countries, much East–West trade was based on bilateral co-operation agreements between individual EC and Comecon member countries. As consultation with the EC has been difficult till recently, the EC has found itself compelled to set the conditions for imports from Comecon countries unilaterally, in the form of import quotas, which are revised every year, again unilaterally.

The situation has improved since 1988 when the EC and Comecon concluded an agreement in which they recognise each other's specific authority in trade matters. Since the political changes that have occurred since 1989 in the CMEA countries, the EC has taken up a new responsibility for Eastern European countries that are in the process of developing both market-oriented economies and representative democracies. Trade relations on a completely new footing are now being elaborated that witness the commitment of the EC to let these countries participate in the European economic integration process.

Economic analysis of differentiation

The previous sections have shown that the EC has developed a complicated system of trade relations with (groups of) trading partners, mainly on the assumption of the *discriminatory benefits of differentiated tariffs (and quotas)*. Many would argue that such discrimination can hardly be effective what with the low level of tariffs on the one hand, and the uncertain prices and exchange rates involved in international trade on the other. From the vehemence of the political debate on changing the clauses of discriminatory arrangements, however, the advantages accruing to their beneficiaries do seem to be well worth-while. Let us dig somewhat deeper into the question by analysing the results of some empirical studies.

EFTA has benefited from free trade with the EC; the effect of free–trade areas among highly developed countries has been analysed in some depth in Chapter 8 (on the effects of integration).

Mediterranean countries' preferential access to the EC market has stimulated their exports, with substantial gains for these countries; to that conclusion has come Pomfret (1986) on the basis of various sets of studies (including agricultural and industrially-sensitive products). The EC itself appears to pursue mainly political objectives; the economic effect of its Mediterranean policy seems to be small. However, the GSP countries have suffered from the policy's trade-diversion effects.

Yaoundé/Lomé: Young (1972) found that the main effect of the early association agreement has been to produce windfall gains (due to higher export prices) to exporters in ACP countries. He estimated the advantage at around 2.5 per cent of the 1969 export value. He did not find, however, any diversion of EC imports to associated countries. Similar small trade effects were also found more recently by Moss (1982), who studied the performance of the new countries joining the first Lomé convention. The countries involved registered small trade-creation effects, and even smaller trade-diversion effects (from Latin American countries to ACP). On the other hand, the former Yaoundé countries have not benefited from the extension of the EC; their losses on EC6 markets were hardly offset by their gains on the UK market.

GSP: Baldwin and Murray (1977) calculated that the EC's GSP had led to a trade expansion of some 15 per cent of all eligible exports; trade diversion was slight (about 2 per cent). That positive effect on GSP exports is confirmed by the recent work of Davenport (1986), who, using the trade-creation/trade-diversion concepts calculated welfare gains due to the GSP of some 2 per cent for the beneficiary countries and a loss of about 0.5 per cent for the EC; third countries had lost no welfare as far as the manufacturing sectors were concerned, but about 1 per cent in agriculture. Langhammer and Sapir (1987) also found that the trade effects of the European GSP scheme were inconclusive,[9] and that the aid equivalent of the tariff preferences was almost negligible as a consequence of the multitude of controls for sensitive products.

Developing countries: these countries have concluded an 'unholy alliance' with the EC according to Wolf (1988) by creating a system of preferential liberalisation and discriminatory protection, which tends to weaken the world's liberal trade system. Both the EC and the developing countries start from the belief that this is beneficial to them. Yet there is evidence (van Wijnbergen, 1985) that trade intervention not only shifts the terms of trade of LDCs adversely, but also leads to higher interest rates. Indeed, the protection of the EC *vis-à-vis* LDC countries has considerable negative effects on GDP in both developed and developing countries.

CMEA (Comecon): Yannopoulos (1985) remarked that

> the proliferation of EC preferential trade agreements with various groups of countries place CMEA exporters at increasingly disadvantageous market access conditions. However, this does not seem to have exerted a restrictive influence on EEC–CMEA trade. CMEA exporters appear to have managed to overcome the damaging effects of the commercial policies of the EEC by linking issues, bargaining for loopholes and mobilising transnational and transgovernmental allies. One instance of linking issues is the growth of industrial co-operation agreements.

From trade to foreign policy

Production factors and economic policies

The EC has been given distinct powers in external trade matters (negotiations with the Commission, treaty with the Council), and the previous sections have given an idea of the complex system that has evolved. There is no such thing for the external relations engendered by the Common Market and the Economic and Monetary Union. Let us briefly review the situation with respect to the most important elements.

With respect to *production factors* (*Common Market*) we have already noted in Chapters 9 and 10 that the internal situation of the EC is a complicated one, leading to equally complicated external situations.

- For labour the EC resembles a free-trade area, internal freedom of movement and external relations being governed by the law of individual member countries. That implies that there is no free movement within the EC of nationals of third countries working in a member country. Evidently, this is a problem if the controls of the inner frontiers are abolished, and the EC will have to work out a common policy towards immigration (permanent stay) and a common visa policy (temporary stay). There is no institution on the world level that is empowered to deal with such matters, so the EC is likely to proceed by unilateral rules or bilateral agreements with the most concerned third countries.
- For capital, the situation is largely the same, albeit that internal and external free movement of capital still awaits full realisation. As we have seen in Chapter 10, much of the integration in capital markets was not achieved by EC countries among themselves, but by individual EC countries with the off-shore capital market

for bonds and deposits and with the USA for stock markets. The efficiency of these markets requires that the full liberalisation of the capital market be *erga omnes*, that is, towards partner and third countries alike. Indeed, the capital-diversion effects of any EC-wide control would be too costly to be acceptable for countries that are now open to the rest of the world.

Given the variety of national standpoints it is hardly surprising that, contrary to the situation in goods trade, the EC lacks external identity with respect to labour and capital. The lack of financial identity is evident from the fact that the EC cannot participate in the IMF or the Bank of International Settlements.

Little progress has been made with the external relations of an *Economic and Monetary Union*:

- Allocation policies are hardly co-ordinated with third countries. The noteworthy exception is the co-ordination between the EC and the EFTA in the framework of the 'European Economic Space' on matters regarding the completion of the internal market (1992).
- Redistribution policies are not subjects of external co-ordination either; apparently the political basis for solidarity has not developed even among very close trade partners, apart from development aid, the subject of the next section.
- For stabilisation however, international co-ordination is starting, albeit slowly. The EC involvement in the work of the groups charged with co-ordinating the macro and monetary policies (the Group of Five or Seven Largest Developed Countries) is increasing. Although the preliminary consultation of all EC partners before Economic Summits has not always been realised in the past (Merlini, 1984) in recent years the involvement of the president of the Commission in many of these meetings has strengthened the role of the EC as a whole. In Chapter 7 we discussed the need for stabilisation policies, and in Chapter 17 we focused on the economic cost of exchange-rate changes. On the world scale, the same need for co-ordination obtains with the objective to stabilise the key currency, that is, the US dollar. The variations (see Figure 19.1) of the $/Ecu exchange rate have indeed been particularly wide in the past ten years, leading to conflicts between the USA and the EC. Stabilisation of this parity by co-ordinated action, the EC operating as one block, would certainly be beneficial to European trade and industry.[10] The group of the seven largest industrial countries has defined so-called 'target zones' for the exchange rates of the principal currencies (Frenkel and Goldstein 1986). However, there is con-

siderable disagreement about the policies that should be pursued to maintain them. The systematic use of indicators of international policy targets (such as internal demand, interest rates, etc.) and rules for policy response to certain situations, would greatly enhance the effectiveness of the policies of individual countries (Williamson and Miller, 1987). Co-ordination of exchange-rate policies is practically limited to the countries of the OECD area and virtually non-existent with other areas.

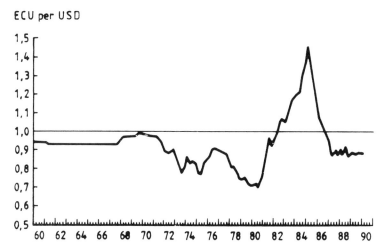

Figure 19.1 Ecu/$ exchange rate through time

Clearly, the further development of the EC identity will have to lead to a definition of a common EC policy *vis-à-vis* third countries on all matters that follow from the internal development of the Common Market and the Economic and Monetary Union. It will also logically lead to the increased participation of the Commission in the relevant 'negotiations' on behalf of the member states. Given the diversity of third countries it may be necessary to *differentiate the EC regime vis-à-vis* the outside world in a similar way by groups as has been done for goods trade. If such structural discrimination is inevitable for lack of world standards, incidental short-term changes in the regime for specific countries for policy considerations should at any rate be avoided (Molle and van Mourik, 1987).

Development-aid policy

The EC member states have the moral obligation to co-operate in the redistribution of wealth on the world level. However, to support the development of Third World countries could not be solely a matter of national states; as a matter of fact, the EEC treaty (articles 3.k and 227) imposed the same obligation on the Community as a whole. Some theoretical reasons[11] are that the EC is the organisation responsible for commerce; that the gains from international trade may be unevenly distributed among partners, and moreover that the protectionism which the EC maintains on some scores for reasons of internal redistribution may have a negative effect on world equilibrium. The EC ought to compensate for all this by a development-aid policy.

The EC's policy of aid to developing countries is complementary to that of the member countries, but it is limited to the associated ACP countries. The EC policy in matters of international co-operation with these countries dates back to the creation of the EC. Abstracting from trade, which was dealt with earlier, and from balance-of-payment aid, which the EC does not give, we may say that initially the aid primarily envisaged was that for investment (Faber, 1982). Afterwards new aspects were added, namely, the stabilisation of export earnings and food aid. These elements are paid for by the *European Development Fund* (EDF), which was created by a special agreement annexed to the Treaty of Rome. It is administered separately from the EC budget, and fed through a specific arrangement among member countries.

The main objective of association is the contribution to *investments* that are needed for the gradual development of the associated countries (art. 132, Rome Treaty). The European Development Fund provides loans and grants to facilitate investment in economic (roads, ports, water) and social (hospitals, schools, information and trade-promotion institutions) infrastructure. The scope of the EDF was extended by the first Lomé agreement to productive investments in agriculture, mining, industry and energy (Stevens, 1981). Investment is also promoted by loans from the EIB and by the Centre for Industrial Development.[12]

The development aid of the EC to associated countries comprises also the *stabilisation of export earnings*. The STABEX mechanism for agriculture and the SYSMIN system for mineral products are simple. If the value of an ACP country's exports to the EC drops by more than a certain minimum percentage, the EC compensates for the loss with a transfer of money. The schemes apply only to products contributing substantially to the country's total export earnings. Although the schemes represent an improvement on the situation with regard to non-associated countries, their impact has been reduced by worldwide inflation, which has concealed the price drops in real terms that have occurred for some commodities. Moreover, the schemes give only temporary support, cushioning the first shock rather than compensating losses in the long run. STABEX and SYSMIN transfers represent a special budget line of the EDF.

The third element, *EC food aid*, concerns among other things the provision of food to people in areas struck by acute famine, from the EC stocks (or surpluses from the farm policy – see Chapter 11). Besides its evident humanitarian effects it has also the side effect of disrupting the indigenous system of production and commerce, and undoing the efforts of agro-industrial development aid (Eussner, 1986).

In view of the limited value of the trade arrangements for development purposes, the aid programme is looked upon as the centre-piece of the Lomé arrangements. While the aid component of Lome is often cited as an example of good policy, it is also the object of much criticism. One criticism concerns the effectiveness of aid. In general, EC aid does not seem less effective than other aid schemes (Hewitt, 1984), although rigorous assessments are not available. However, as EC grants to development projects are often softer than those of other sponsors, their effectiveness depends critically on the policy environment of the receiving country. In that light, the EC logically tries to influence this policy environment by a so-called 'dialogue on policies'. There are no systematic evaluation studies of the contribution EC aid has made to economic growth in ACP countries and thus to narrowing the wealth gap between them and the EC.

Foreign policy

The European Community has become increasingly aware of two facts:

- third countries tend to look upon the Community as one political entity, also in non-economic matters, and expect a common stand of the member states on a wide variety of diplomatic issues (such as apartheid in South Africa);
- co-ordinated foreign policies tend to increase the effectiveness of individual member states (for instance in the fight against terrorism; for a theoretical treatment of the advantages of co-operation versus single action, see Chapter 7).

These led in the 1960s to regular meetings of the Ministers of Foreign Affairs of EC countries regarding questions external to the EC. Next, in 1970, the *European Political Co-operation* (EPC) was created as an inter-governmental 'institution', not linked to the EC framework, and working essentially through information and consultation. The centre-piece of the EPC is the commitment to consult partners before adopting final positions or launching national initiatives on all important questions of foreign policy common to EC member countries, and to the joint implementation of actions. This specifically includes the preparation of international conferences. In the course of the years the co-operation has steadily intensified and its scope continually broadened. The work of the Conference of Ministers is complemented by meetings of the Political Committee (high-rank civil servants) and expert groups. Presidency and secretariat alternate with the presidency of the Council of the EC. The dissociation of the normal EC institutions was increasingly felt as a problem. This led, first, to the regular participation of the President of the Commission and the Commissioner for External Relations in the EPC conferences. Recently, however, the EPC was formally brought within the EC institutional framework by Title III of the Single European Act. This has been accomplished without changing many of its objectives or its intergovernmental features. Indeed, the EPC has no institution of its own apart from a small secretariat in Brussels; the work is done by national civil servants. It means that the Commission (although 'fully associated' in the work) and Parliament ('closely associated' through regular information by the Presidency) play a very limited part.

How important is this EPC in *economic terms*? Two sides of the problem can be distinguished in that respect:

- The use of economic instruments by third countries to pursue non-economic foreign-policy objectives may directly affect the European internal market or endanger the security of supplies to the EC. An example was the selective oil embargo of Arab states against some EC countries in the 1970s. Sometimes the EC uses sanctions (for instance, against South Africa), or imposes export restrictions on strategically important goods.[13]
- Progress towards further integration by completing the internal EC market implies common foreign-policy measures. A case in point is the common visa policy for foreign visitors, which becomes necessary as soon as the controls of persons at internal borders are abolished.

External economic and diplomatic issues are closely intertwined. Therefore, the Single European Act (article 30.5) enjoins upon the Presidency and the Commission to ensure the consistency of the two policies.

Security policy

A particularly important matter in the context of EC external policy is *defence*. Now although a major objective envisaged with the creation of the EC was to contribute to durable peace, its pursuit was to be made by economic means.

We may bring to mind that after the failure of the European Defence Community in the 1950s, European defence matters have been treated in international bodies such as the NATO (North Atlantic Treaty

Organisation) and the *WEU (Western European Union)*. All EC12 member states except neutral Ireland are members of NATO, in which moreover two other West European countries are grouped, namely, Norway and Turkey. The WEU was created by the Treaty of Brussels in 1954 to strengthen peace and security. Its members are the original six EC members plus the United Kingdom, Spain and Portugal. Attempts to extend WEU membership to all new EC members and merge its institutional structure with that of the EC have been opposed from two sides. Some of the present members fear that the centrifugal forces resulting from such extension might jeopardise co-operation, difficult enough among the nine present members. On the other hand, in a country like Ireland there is doubt whether its constitution permits WEU membership. Superseded by NATO, the WEU had long been a rather dormant institution. In 1984 its members decided to reactivate it to get more say in such questions as arms control and disarmament.

The *defence issue is closely related to economic policy*, and two articles in the EEC treaty deal with such matters (see also Steenbergen, 1987).

- *Arms industry* (article 223 EEC). Member states are allowed to take the measures concerning the production of, and trade in, arms they consider necessary for the protection of their essential interests. It follows that the EC as such has no powers in either industrial or trade policy with respect to arms. Moreover, the EC rules of competition, state aids, etc. have proved difficult to apply to the category in hand. With a view to the completion of the internal market, however, the situation becomes more and more difficult; hence the need for a better co-ordination of production of, and trade in, arms within the EC. Such a common strategy can ensue only from a common defence strategy.
- *Disturbances* (article 224). If the functioning of the Common Market is affected by a (threat of) war, or by internal disturbances, member states have to consult one another on the way the effect can be minimised. This may imply consultations about the way to take away the cause of such events (defence policy).

It also seems logical for the EC to be increasingly involved in the political aspect of defence. As a matter of fact, the single European Act opens the possibility of discussing defence issues in the framework of the EPC.

Summary and conclusions

- The EC is still mainly a customs union, which means that its external relations are mostly *trade relations*. However, its progress towards an economic and monetary union has drawn other areas, such as immigration, international capital and monetary matters, into the domain of EC external policy. Moreover, defence and other elements are increasingly integrated in a full-dress EC foreign policy.

- A complicated system of trade advantages, differentiated according to specific groups of countries, has been drawn up. Although the system has some economic effect and has been established for political reasons, it would seem advisable to simplify it considerably.
- The common commercial policy uses a fan of instruments to regulate trade and protect EC industry. However, the EC has consistently moved towards greater liberalisation of world trade, and, apart from agricultural matters, is fairly open to third country suppliers. The trade policy has become more streamlined as the Commission gradually acquired the status and the instruments for the implementation of the necessary measures.
- The external relations implied in the establishment of the Common Market (labour capital) and the Economic and Monetary Union (currency policy) are still dealt with by the member states. The growing identity of the EC in these matters calls for an elaboration of common policies in the near future.
- Foreign and security policies are the object of intergovernmental co-operation, largely outside the EC institutional framework.

Notes

1   For a good introduction into the principles of GATT, see Kock (1969), Dam (1970), and McGovern (1982).
2   For a description of the legal basis, easily accessible to economists, see Völker (1983).
3   The book by Hine (1985) is to be recommended to those who desire more detailed information about the subject matter of this section. See also Stevens (1981) and Long (1980).
4   The idea of hierarchy, layer, etc. is also found back in the pyramid concept proposed by Mishalani *et al.*, (1981).
5   For a more elaborate discussion, see Pomfret (1986).
6   Concessions the EC made in the past towards ACP countries for agricultural trade are well accounted for in Ritson (1978) and Hoffmeyer (1982).
7   There is a list of so-called 'sensitive products', defined as goods whose increased imports would cause serious damage to certain European producers. That means in practice that for these goods the quotas are set on a national basis, both at the EC (importer) side and on that of the exporters. Davenport (1986) reports that the EC GSP involves some 40 000 different EC-wide and bilateral quotas and ceilings.
8   Although MFA protection was tightened a great deal (quotas specified for individual exporting countries and EC importing countries in the 1970s), no great change of trade flows has resulted from it (Kol, 1987). There was a swift growth of imports from LDCs into the EC, but also of EC exports to the former.

9   The outcome is not surprising, as the structure of exports is very dissimilar for developing (GSP) and industrialised (non-GSP) countries (Yannopoulos, 1986).
10 See for an introduction to this problem, Artis and Ostry (1986) and for a description of the political aspects of 'Summitry': Merlini (1984).
11 See for a more elaborate discussion, among others, Faber (1982).
12 The principal task of this organisation is to help small and medium-sized firms to establish joint ventures in ACP countries; the EIB can only help to finance profitable projects.
13 See for the limited effectiveness of economic sanctions, Hufbauer and Scott (1985) and van Bergeijk (1987).

PART VI
CONCLUSIONS

20 Evaluation and Outlook

Introduction

The objective of this book was to present an economic analysis of the process of European integration. To that end we described first the conceptual basis, historical roots and institutional framework of integration, continuing on with the theoretical foundations at its different stages. The freedom of movement of goods, services, labour and capital, and the organisation of economic activity in the various sectors of the economy are the pivots of economic integration, and therefore rightly occupy the central place in this book. But freedoms cannot flourish nor economic sectors be organised to advantage unless government has created the proper conditions. So, a discussion of the policies pursued with that goal in mind completes the book.

At the end of this detailed analysis, a more general view of the whole process and a broad evaluation of the progress of integration in the past period seem in order. The progress of integration can be measured by several indicators. We will make a distinction between indicators of a more economic nature, such as the share of trade in total GDP, and the more policy-oriented indicators such as the limitation of power of national states in different segments of economic policy. Economic integration is not an objective in its own right, but instrumental to the growth of welfare. In that spirit, Waelbroeck (1976) considered trade and factor movements 'irrelevant variables in the study of integration' and proposed to concentrate on the creation and distribution of welfare. We will devote a separate section to each of these aspects.

The economic integration of Europe is a process of long duration that is far from completed. In the *future*, integration will enter new fields and become more intensive in the fields already covered. In the last section of this chapter we will look ahead along the roads laid out in the previous chapters, basing our outlook on published plans and ideas. Unlike the rigorous presentation of the theoretical and empirical results of all previous parts of the book, a more projective and speculative approach characterises this outlook. We shall be intrigued to find out in a few years time how far the speculations presented here have come true. In new editions of this book such changes will be included

471

as new developments in the various chapters, leaving room for speculations on new horizons.

Progress of integration : economic indicators

Quantities

One way to measure the progress of integration is by quantities traded or exchanged. For goods and services this is done in practice by measuring the extent to which the production of one country is consumed in another. In much the same way, the advance of integration on

Table 20.1   Growth of integration in the EC (goods, services, labour and capital), 1960–1985 (percentages)

			1960	1970	1980	1985
Customs Unions						
1 Goods[a]		Intra	6	8	13	14
		Extra	9	10	11	12
2 Services[a]		Intra	n.a.	4	7	9
		Extra	n.a.	1	2	3
Common Market						
1 Labour[b]		Intra	2	2	2	2
		Extra	1	3	3	2
2 Capital						
	DI[c]	Intra	n.a.	1	1	1
		Extra	n.a.	1	2	2
	Investment Income[d]	Intra	n.a.	-	1	2
		Extra	n.a.	1	2	3

[a] average of imports and exports as a percentage share of GDP
[b] Non-nationals as a percentage of total labour force
[c] Direct investment; three-year averages (1970 = average of 1969–1970–1971); Average of imports and exports as a percentage share of gross fixed capital formation
[d] Income from investments abroad as a percentage of GDP
Sources: Goods: Chapter 8
            Services: Chapter 14 plus some estimates based on balance-of-payments data for 1970 and 1980.
            Labour: Chapter 9
            Capital: Chapter 10, Matisse (1988), plus some estimates based on balance-of-payments data.
n.a. = not available

the markets for production factors can be assessed by measuring the extent to which the labour and capital of one country are put to work in another. Both indicators have been employed in the detailed analysis of the preceding chapters.[1] Table 20.1 combines the dispersed results.

For *goods and services* the figures leave little room for doubt: by 1985, EC countries had become far more integrated with their EC partners than in 1960 (6 versus 14 per cent), and the same can be said of the integration of the EC countries in the world economy (9 versus 12 per cent). Apart from its relative size, the orientation of trade is an important indicator of integration. Recall in that respect the finding of Chapter 8, confirmed by Table 20.1, that in 1960 trade in goods was more oriented to third countries than to (potential) partner countries. Under the influence of the integration process the situation changed: countries were orienting themselves more to partners, with the result that by 1980 intra-EC relations outweighed the extra-EC ones.

For *labour* the situation is different. The figures indicate that only a small percentage of labour in EC countries is of foreign origin, and that this percentage has been very stable through the last 25 years. The percentage share of labour from other countries in the total labour force of the EC oscillated within a narrow band of around 2 per cent between 1960 and 1985. For workers from outside the EC, the level is rather low too; the figures show a steep increase in the 1960s, followed by a decrease in recent years. Before yielding to the temptation to interpret this as an indication of limited integration, we should remember that massive migration flows were never an objective of the EC; on the contrary, the movement of capital to, and the differential growth of, the economies of poor member countries were intended to keep intra-EC migration in check (see Chapter 9), while national admittance laws regulated integration with third countries.

For *capital*, the only way to analyse movements effectively is to break them down by type. The most important category for our purpose is direct investment (DI). Within the EC, foreign direct investment has been fully liberalised since the 1970s. Although its volume increased considerably between 1961 and 1978 (Pelkmans, 1983), its relative share is still modest. The stock of DI in total GDP amounted to some 6 per cent in 1975 and some 8 per cent in 1983. DI stock data being very hard to obtain, we cannot extend that series of observations. However, flow data are available for the 1970–1985 period. We have compared these to data on Gross Fixed Capital Formation (GFCF) in preference to GDP, because the latter gave very low percentages, and the relation of DI to total investment is more relevant anyway. The bottom part of Table 20.1 shows, first, that in terms of DI, EC countries are less oriented to their partners than to third countries; that is due as much to heavy EC investment activity abroad as to foreign (third-country) investment in EC countries. Moreover, the interrelations with third countries are developing much faster than those among EC countries: the latter stagnated in the 1970–1985 period, while the former doubled in that span of time. Figures of the quantities exchanged are available for DI but not for other forms of capital movement (Euromarkets).

Another indicator of the integration of capital markets (not used in Chapter 10) is the income received from investments abroad (both DI and Portfolio). The balance-of-payments figures available show a very fast increase for both external and internal EC relations. In line with the DI levels found, the relations of the EC with third countries appear to be far more important than the relations among EC countries themselves.

Prices

The progress of integration can be measured not only by the growth of the quantities exchanged among partner countries, but also by the convergence of prices for the same goods and services and production factors in the various countries of the EC.

The comparison of prices for *goods* is beset with difficulties. However, we do have some figures for a short period; they are given in Table 20.2 opposite. They indicate very clearly the convergence of prices for consumer and producer goods in that period. Whether this convergence is entirely attributable to economic integration is not certain. Indeed, the integration effect is difficult to isolate from the effects of the many other factors that influence the structure of prices.

For *services* we have only very little data to compare the prices through time. What we do have do not suggest any convergence, which is in keeping with the still rudimentary integration of this sector evidenced in Chapter 14.

The price of labour, *the wage rate*, although difficult to measure appears to have shown a gradual convergence, but whether that is indeed an integration effect remains highly uncertain at this stage. To establish the possible convergence of *capital* prices, several indicators suggest themselves. We have opted here for the indexes of parallelism of prices on stock markets and on the markets for long- and short-term loans. Although these data, too, are beset with uncertainties, the results of their analysis seems to permit a straightforward interpretation: the prices of stocks and short-term credits have converged. For long-term credit the situation is more involved; here the turbulence of the first oil shock brought a clear divergence; after 1979, however, the prices converged as well. Although the figures suggest that the EC has to some extent liberalised capital markets, no studies are known to have established rigorously how much increase in DI or other capital flows is due to integration. The same holds for the price convergence on capital markets. Nevertheless, the fact that the figures clearly began to

Table 20.2 Price convergence for goods, services and production factors, 1965–1985

Indicator			Year	
Customs Unions[a]		1965	1975	1985
Consumer goods	(tax-inclusive)	n.a.	20.5	19.4
	(tax-exclusive)	n.a.	16.5	15.2
Equipment goods	(tax-inclusive)	n.a.	13.7	12.4
	(tax-exclusive	n.a.	13.7	12.4
Services	(tax-inclusive)	n.a.	27.3	27.2
	(tax-exclusive)	n.a.	n.a.	n.a.
Common Market		1963/74	1973/79	1980/86
Wages[b]		n.a.	n.a.	n.a.
Capital[c]				
Stock values		n.a.	0.63	0.89
Long-term real interest rate		0.94	0.81	0.92
Short-term interest rate		0.42	0.61	0.71

[a] Index of dispersion (see Chapters 8 and 14); lower indices show higher integration
[b] See Chapter 9
[c] Different indicators (see Tables 10.5 and 10.7); the closer they come to 100 the higher the integration
Sources: Emerson *et al.*, (1988)
n.a. = not available

change soon after major measures of liberalisation had been taken suggests that the recent convergence is probably due to integration.

Progress of integration: policy indicators

Institutions: growth of operations

Looking at the European Community as an organisation, we can measure the progress of integration in several ways, of which we have picked out three.

The most obvious indicator is the increase in the *number of members*. Membership has increased almost at regular 14-year intervals and by the same number (three). The Benelux, a precursor of the EEC, was created by three countries in 1944; the EEC was created by the original six members in 1958; its first extension came in 1973 when the three northern countries joined, and the second extension with the three Mediterranean countries was a fact in 1986.

An indicator of integration that visualises growth even to the casual observer, is the *number of people* involved in the EC policy-making machinery (input). The civil servants employed by the Commission and other EC institutions have rapidly increased in number: with the Commission, from 1000 to 15 000 between 1960 and 1988. (In the same period the total number of civil servants in the countries of the EC12 rose from 4 to 8 million persons.) The meetings of the Council of Ministers, its working parties, and experts of the Commission also have become more and more frequent. New lobbyist groups were regularly established, and older ones have increased their efforts to influence European policy and decision making by extending their membership and consolidating their presence in the centre of EC decision making. Evidently, the growth and exact number of lobbies is not known,[2] but from an EC publication (CEC 1986i) we are able to gather how some of the more important ones have developed. Almost half the groups with industrial, commercial, and professional spheres of interest whose establishment can be dated, were set up between 1955 and 1965, the period of creation of the EEC. From 1965 to 1985, the rate of increase was much lower (see Table 20.3). Recently a new upsurge in the growth of lobby groups has occurred.

Table 20.3 Growth of European administrative and related organisations 1960–1988

Indicator	1960	1970	1980	1988
Permanent civil servants (x 1000) of Commission	1	5	11	15
Official Journal (pages x 1000)	2	12	26	32
Number of lobby organisations (producers and professional)[a]	167	309	410	435[b]

[a] *Sources*: CEC (1986i), CEC *General Reports*, *Official Journal* (several years)
[b] 1985

A third indicator is the yearly *production of directives and regulations* (output). Its increase is also difficult to measure, but as details are not necessary to our purpose, a cursory analysis of the number of pages of the EC's *Official Journal* between 1960 and 1988 will do (see line 2 of Table 20.3). The advance of integration is also manifest from the volume of preparatory work that precedes the actual publication: the continuous growth of the total output of expert studies, committee reports, white papers, communications, etc. in the past 30 years has indeed been impressive. Quantification, if feasible, would probably reveal a growth pattern very similar to that of the number of pages of the *Official Journal*.

Subject matters: the movement to higher stages

There are sound economic as well as political reasons to start economic integration with goods markets (Customs Union, CU), continue with production factors (Common Market, CM), and conclude with intensified policy integration (Economic and Monetary Union, EMU). In that view, the progress of economic integration in Europe can be measured by the stage it has reached at different moments in time. Remember, however, that the stages are not strictly successive in the sense that the lower ones have to be fully realised before the higher ones can be tried for. Rather, as remarked before, progress in the later stages is a condition for the full realisation of the earlier ones.

The *Customs Union* was to be realised before the end of the 1960s (art. 3a.b EEC). The evidence from internal and external trade in goods (Chapters 8, 14 and 19) shows that for large parts of the economy (manufactured goods) that objective has indeed been realised, but for various reasons services and some other sectors remained protected. For these sectors the CU is now being implemented in the framework of the 1992 programme (see Chapter 16). Once this programme is completed, the CU will also be fully realised.

The *Common Market*, implying the abolition of most obstacles to the free movement of capital and workers (article 3c EEC), is an old target. Progress on it has been fairly quick for large parts of both the labour and capital markets (see Chapters 9 and 10). However, large sections remained excluded. For production factors, too, the 1992 Programme sets the objective of complete abolition of barriers, the attainment of which implies the completion of the Common Market.

The *Economic and Monetary Union* became an objective of the EC in the 1970s. Before that time, a number of common policies (foreseen by the EEC Treaty, for instance 3d to 3g) had been adopted and monetary policy co-ordinated in preparation. Notably, the creation and successful operation of the EMS has paved the way for further integration.

Recently, some concrete proposals for the creation of the EMU were once more put forward.

Full Economic Union: work has already started on an even closer integration than the CM and the EMU, the EC penetrating now into environment, culture, education, and other fields.

Instruments; the shift of competence from national to Community institutions

All progress of integration tends to curb the freedom of action of the member states' policy-makers. The higher the instrument's rank in the hierarchy from consultation to unification (Chapter 2), the more its use will limit the autonomy of the member states, and the further integration has apparently progressed. To illustrate the progress made since the EC came into existence, we have indicated in Table 20.4 how the use of three types of instruments – C, Consultation; H, Harmonisation; and U, Unification – has developed in the policy fields identified earlier in this book (namely, allocation, stabilisation, redistribution and external, to which we have added a group 'other' described in the first section of each chapter). The first column presents the situation at the moment of birth of the EC; the last column describes the present situation; the middle benchmark year describes the situation just before the first extension. Evidently, each situation is liable to be characterised differently by different observers; we think, however, that the table gives a fair overall picture. Let us briefly comment on each policy field.

For the *four freedoms* – of goods, services, labour, and capital – the situation is clear: from the outset the EEC treaty provided for full uniformity of their regimes; in principle the member states have ceded all relevant authority to the Community (although many rudiments of their power remain so that the freedoms are far from perfect; Chapter 16). An exception was made for capital, of which the movements were liberalised only as far as necessary for the functioning of the Common Market. That restriction was recently lifted, which means that the whole block now comes under uniform rules.

Under the heading of *allocation* we have classed the policies that aim at the proper functioning of the common (internal) market, including those that try to improve the structure of productive activity. The Treaty of Rome (articles 3f, 85–90) partly unified competition policy in the EC; the situation has remained virtually unchanged since. For fiscal, technical and related internal-market policies, a timid start with consultation (based on EEC 3c, d and h) was soon followed by intensive harmonisation efforts, and although the outlook was recently changed ('new approach'), the instrument stayed the same. The EC accepted very early responsibility for a limited part of structural policy (agriculture, and coal and steel), but for most sectors, integrating efforts of

Table 20.4 Synoptic view of the development through time (1958–1988) of the degree of policy integration by activity area*

Field of action	1958	1973	1988
Four freedoms			
goods	U	U	U
services	U	U	U
labour	U	U	U
capital	U*	U*	U
Allocation			
competition	U*	U*	U*
fiscal	C	H	H
technical	C	H	H
structural	C	C	H
Stabilisation			
monetary	C	C	H*
macro + budgetary	C	C	C
growth policy	C	C	C
Redistribution			
regional	O	C	H
social	H*	H*	H*
External			
trade ⎱ goods	U	U	U
⎰ services	O	C	H
production factors ⎱ labour	O*	C	H
⎰ capital	O*	C	U*
development aid	U*	U*	U*
foreign (EPC)	O	O	C
defence	O	O	C
Other			
environment, etc.	O	C	H
culture	O	O	C

* The asterisk indicates that only part of the policy field is affected by the indicator given
O: means that there was no EC involvement; C: Consultation; H: Harmonisation;
U: Unification

industrial policy have not passed beyond the stage of consultation. However, as recently some large-scale European supply-side programmes have been implemented (Esprit, Monitor, etc.), 'harmonisation' aptly describes the present situation.

For *stabilisation* policies – mostly monetary and macro-economic – consultation was foreseen right from the start (article 3g of the EEC Treaty refers to co-ordination). In the past 30 years, consultation has intensified but the pattern has remained largely the same as in 1958. The only exception is the EMS, created to stabilise exchange rates.

In *redistribution*, we have distinguished regional and social policies. The EC started in 1958 without a clear idea about regional policies.[3] By 1973 a consultation procedure (study etc.) had been put into practice. With the creation of the European Regional Development Fund, ERDF, national regional policies were subjected to European harmonisation. The situation is different for social policies; the European Social Fund, ESF, was created right at the start of the EEC, and there has been little development since. Some important fields of redistribution (social security) remain largely unaffected.

Among *external policies* we have grouped a whole array of policies from trade to defence. The common trade policy (implying uniformity) is a treaty obligation (articles 29–113). It has been realised for goods trade, but as far as services are concerned, there are quite a few uncertainties, which make 'harmonisation' a more appropriate term. In the 1960s, there were no external policies for production factors. Some co-ordination began in the 1970s. Recently, a common policy for capital was decided on (full external freedom). Part of development aid has been uniform right from the beginning, but the better part of it remained in national (unco-ordinated) hands. Recently some consultation on diplomatic and defence matters has been practised (EPC).

Other policies that were non-existent in 1958 have become the object of EC harmonisation efforts, cases in point being environment and education.

Summarising the information contained in Table 20.4, we find that the use of higher instruments clearly increased through time (the number of H scores rising from 1 to 9), while the number of unco-ordinated areas diminished (0 scores going down from 8 to 0), a development that reflects the progress of policy integration in the EC. Actually, the speed increased, seven scores moving up in the 1958-1973 period against 10 in the 1973–1988 period.

Welfare effects

Total growth

The calculation of the income effects of integrated *product markets* has been confined mostly to the markets of manufactured goods, leaving agriculture, energy and services largely out of account. All relevant studies have come to the conclusion that the static income effects of the free movement of goods are rather small, somewhere in the order of 1 per cent. However, those studies have disregarded the effects of economies of scale, efficiency, and learning by doing. In another analytical set-up, that of a macro model, Marques-Mendes (1986a, 1986b) shows that about half the growth of the EC6 countries up to the crisis of the 1970s had been due to the effects of the EC; how much the EC has since contributed to keeping growth slow is highly uncertain.

In a recent attempt to complete the picture of the effects of further integration (removal of persistent barriers to internal trade), the European Commission (Emerson *et al.*,1988) estimated that the combined effects of better market entry and increased competition, more innovation, learning and economies of scale amounted to some 6 per cent of GDP.

The welfare effects of the integration of *labour markets* spring in particular from the immigration of people, many of them coming from third countries. Migration among EC countries has on the whole been on a low level. The employment of immigrant workers has had a positive effect on total production and GDP (the expansion of production about equals that of the labour force). The average contribution of migration to the economic growth of EC countries (Askari, 1974) has been rather small, approximately 1 per cent. The dynamic effects of labour immigration are not known very well (Böhning and Maillat, 1974), but some believe that immigration, by removing certain bottlenecks from the economy, has led to a permanently higher growth of GNP (UN/ECE, 1977). Negative aspects have also been pointed out but rarely quantified. The most important point is that immigration has prevented the economies of the EC from adjusting structurally to the new world conditions in comparative advantages.

The empirical evidence on the welfare effects of the integration of European *capital markets* is very thin, and differs from one submarket to another. For direct-investment flows the attention has been limited to employment effects: these seem invariably positive for the host country, but for the home countries vary from negative (when exports from the home bases are replaced) to positive (when the DI facilitates penetration into a foreign market, thus enhancing activity at home as well; Buckley and Artisien, 1987). For short- and long-term capital markets, the welfare effects resulting from the completion of the internal market were found to be very positive (Price Waterhouse, 1988). For the integration of stock markets, we can only quote an early study (Levy and Sarnet, 1970), estimating the increase in return that would ensue from passing from a national to a world market; we do not know of any more recent studies of the subject.

For *common policies* the situation is very unclear. Although some headway has been made with the study of their efficiency, the growth and welfare effects have received very little attention so far.

Welfare effects: redistribution

A major objective of the EC is to achieve the harmonious development of the European economy by reducing the differences in wealth among the various countries and regions. It implies the pursuit of policies leading to higher-than-average growth rates for low-income countries and regions. Let us see what the EC has achieved on that score.

Immediately after the war, some of the countries now making up the EC12 were very poor (Portugal, Greece, Spain, and to a lesser extent Italy, and also, compared to the EC9, Germany), while others (Belgium, Denmark, the UK and France) were relatively well off.

Comparison of the growth figures of the individual countries with the EC average shows that many of the low-income countries have grown at a more than average rate, while others, the United Kingdom for one, remained below the average, so that in 1985 there was more equality than in 1950.

Access to the EC is believed to have had a marked influence on the high growth figures of Italy in the 1960s and Spain and Portugal in more recent years (higher than the EC average; CEC, 1988a). However, no formal proof of any equalising effect of EC integration has as yet been given.

Towards new objectives

Allocation: the 1992 programme

The advance of the EC towards new goals of integration has been made possible by the progress achieved in its *hard core*, which is the internal market for goods, services, labour and capital. In the future as in the past, the essential policy objective of the EC is to create optimum conditions for the internal market to fulfil its resource-allocating function. In that respect the programme for the completion of the internal market (adopted formally by the European Council and inserted in the Single Act) is particularly important. In Chapter 16 we already discussed its essential characteristics. The following important points will call for closer future attention:

- *Direct intervention in markets* (prices and quantities). The analyses given in Chapters 11 to 15 have made clear that the EC leaves most of resource allocation to the market. Only in three noticeable areas do public authorities intervene in prices and quantities, namely, agriculture, coal and steel, and transport. The justification for those exceptions seems to have been gradually eroded by social and technical change. Agriculture is more and more mechanised and increasingly resembles the manufacturing sector. The importance of coal and steel as strategic products has dwindled. Transport is increasingly regarded as a normal service activity. For all these reasons, we expect public intervention in these markets to diminish, and the market regimes of these sectors to adopt a uniform pattern: that of the manufacturing sector.
- *Competition policy.* The role of the EC as the guardian of the fair play of market forces will gain in importance. Indeed, wherever governments lose the possibility of direct intervention, they will be inclined to employ such indirect means as subsidies to firms threatened by international competition. Firms, on their part, may collude to try and restrict competition, jeopardising the beneficial effects of integration.
- *Taxation (indirect intervention in prices).* This was discussed in Chapter 16, where the suggestion was made that the different national regimes of indirect taxation (value added and excises) may distort Europe-wide allocation. Although different rates and structures can co-exist in practice (see USA) and will probably have to for some time to come (given the difficulty of arriving at unanimity in the Council and the sensitivity of the issue), we nevertheless think that economic factors (efficiency) will force the EC to move gradually towards uniform rates and structures of VAT, excises and corporate taxation alike.
- *Market access.* Mutual recognition and home-country control are now the fundamental rule. The critique is often heard that such an approach, while benefiting the countries with deficient quality standards and prudential requirements, spells harm to European consumers. On the other hand, consumers are likely to be increasingly well informed about products, and by their preferences may steer the process towards efficiency. Moreover, as Giersch (1987) argued, the system will engender a competition of rules. Products made under efficient government rules will be preferred to those manufactured under excessive regulatory systems that cause high costs to the producer and the taxpayer,

and hamper instant adaptation to new circumstances. Such excessive rules will lead to pressure from inside to adjust the national regulation. Thus the dynamics of international systems leads quite automatically towards efficiency. The previous harmonisation efforts required considerable and constant bureaucratic and political negotiations on the European level, and the compromises thus reached seldom proved efficient.

Stabilisation; the objective of the Economic and Monetary Union

The EC set out with a very limited objective in terms of stabilisation policies. As a matter of fact, only some loose co-ordination of budget, cyclical and monetary policies was envisaged. However, the growing interdependence of the goods, service and factor markets led to a considerable increase in international commercial and financial transactions; European companies especially became aware of the costliness of such transactions due to the uncertain exchange rates. So to increase allocational efficiency on these markets, a mechanism for exchange-rate stabilisation was created, which presupposed a minimum degree of co-ordination in economic policy.

This mechanism, the *EMS*, has been very successful. It has created a zone of stable exchange rates in Europe and obliged member states to approximate their economic policies. However, the stability is still far from perfect, and European enterprise, aware that in a completed internal market the number of international transactions will increase even more (capital transactions will be completely free by 1990), is lobbying for the irrevocable fixing of exchange rates or the creation of one currency, efficiency being one argument used. Support of the general public for that idea is growing too. Some early plans for the gradual realisation of the Economic and Monetary Union had not gained sufficient support.

The new *Delors plan* for an *EMU*, published in 1989, has given a new impetus to the idea of a monetary union. Notwithstanding the progress made with the first stage, there are still many question marks for the later stages. These are related to issues like the political sensitivity of the subject, the external influences, the redistribution effects and the complexity of the mechanism. However, as many economic forces are pushing towards the EMU its realisation may, in our view occur quite soon, this century yet.

Redistribution and the 'social dimension'

The EC has been some time getting really involved in redistribution policies. However, with the Single European Act the *economic and social cohesion* of the EC has become a Treaty obligation. The programme for the internal market as well as the document on the Economic and Monetary Union stress the need to strengthen the role of redistribution, lest the internal market and the EMU aggravate the present imbalance. The instruments qualified to add a 'social dimension' to both projects would be the present (probably extended) Regional and Social Funds.

There are many advocates of another social dimension (for example, CEC 1988c), which has less to do with the redistribution aspects and more with *social policy in the broad sense*. The ideas and plans put forward in that respect concern a so-called 'European Social Charter' laying down minimum rules for such diverse matters as workers' participation (the Vredeling directive), the safety and health conditions at work (important progress being made already by the EC as a complement to the 1992 Programme), the mutual recognition of diplomas (slow progress), and finally the position of women and migrants. As these plans are in line with a basic structural feature of most Western European societies, we think that they will gain increasing support. However, as the issues involved are not the mainstream of economic redistribution we will not go further into them.

Social security, on the contrary, is truly an issue as it is the centre-piece of redistribution policies on the national level. There are fierce discussions about the role of social security on the European level, but no clear plans. Articles 100, 118 and 121 EEC permit the harmonisation of the national systems of European social security to go far beyond the mere solution of the 'problems' due to migrant labour. Although the European Council has decided that the systems of social security need no further harmonisation, many people think that a certain harmonisation is needed to set so-called 'minimum standards'.[4] They argue that in future more and more Europeans in different countries will cultivate the feeling that they belong to one union, and want to give substance to European solidarity by contributing to more equal claims to social security through intra-European transfer payments. Member states that cannot afford to improve their systems enough to meet such minimum standards should receive aid from other countries.[5] A European system for help to individuals would become superfluous as transfers via the European budget (an adapted ESF, for instance) to the national executive agencies become possible. As far as opposition to this proposal is ideological, it falls outside the scope of this book. However, there is also a financial aspect: some people consider the extra outlay of money for this project unacceptable. The fact should be borne in mind, however, that a substantial transfer of money by way of a social-security programme could be effected without extra cost to the EC budget if resources were no longer wasted on agriculture, with its perverse redistribution effects.

External relations: fortress or crossroads?

The European Community was created with two objectives in mind: to establish the conditions for durable peace and to enhance the economic development of Europe. Right from the start the EC has been aware that promoting integration with non-member countries would serve the same objectives on the world level.

The external *trade* relations of the EC have been dominated in the past by its participation in the GATT rounds to combat protectionism on the world scale. The EC has committed itself to continue the policy of openness towards third countries. The first implication is that the EC co-operates in the GATT round towards a more liberal trade in the products of agriculture and the service sector, two sectors that so far have been screened from international competition, the former by the CAP, which will have to be restructured, and the latter by very opaque protection systems. The second is that the EC must continue its efforts to do away with the remaining protection for manufacturing goods (so-called 'sensitive products'). The political changes that have occurred in Eastern Europe call for a drastic revision of the trade relations of the EC with these countries. That may involve quite important changes in the patterns of specialisation, not only between the EC and this group of countries, but also between the EC and its other trade partners.

With respect to *production factors*, the EC is not likely to change its policy a great deal. Capital movements will shortly be completely free and require no major further steps. For labour movements, the present situation of nationally regulated access is likely to continue in the near future. In some time the logic of the completed internal market will, however, push towards the unification of the external dimension of the labour market, that means European immigration laws. It is unlikely that the European Community will open up for large-scale external migration, it will rather count on trade and development assistance as instruments to alleviate the employment and wage situation in third countries.

For *common economic policies* however, substantial changes are on the cards for the near future. As the range of matters treated within the EC expands, so does the need to discuss them externally. Likely fields of greater EC activity are:

- *international allocation*: co-ordination of technical norms and standards, negotiations on landing rights in civil aviation, tele-communications, etc.;
- *stabilisation*: monetary co-ordination, some form of EMS for the major world currencies, or – less drastic – target zones;

- *redistribution*: EC involvement in development aid is likely to expand.

Common non-economic policies are likely to expand greatly in the future (see next section), and so will their external scope, as the EC involves itself in an increasing number of matters.

From the previous sections, international co-operation in quite a few matters is likely to intensify in the future. The question then arises whether the present institutions are still adequate or need reinforcement to handle these new tasks. So far, few proposals have been submitted to set up entirely new organisations, but proposals to adapt existing structures (IBRD, IMF, etc.) abound .[6]

Beyond economics; towards a people's Europe

The final stage of integration is the Full (Political) Union. As the present book is concerned with economics, we might stop at this point. However, as the Treaty of Rome places the economic integration of the EC in the perspective of such a political Union ('determined to lay the foundations for an ever closer union among the peoples of Europe') we will briefly indicate what actions are already being undertaken towards such a Union. These actions have been proposed by the special committee appointed by the European Council in 1984 to suggest ways and means to strengthen the EC's identity in the eyes of the ordinary individual citizen. The recommendations of this committee, which have been endorsed by the European Institutions (European Council, Parliament, and Commission, etc.), concern:

- *Living and travelling.* The freedom to move from one EC country to another is as yet limited to workers. The right to move and stay for long periods in another member state should be extended to all people with sufficient means not to burden the social security of the host country. To facilitate immigration checks for temporary and extended stays in another EC country, the EC passport has been adopted for easy establishment of the bearer's EC identity. To facilitate formalities for car travellers, the same has been done with the drivers' licence.
- *Democratic rights.* EC citizens living in another EC member state than their own should have the right to participate in elections for the EP and to vote and stand in local elections in their country of stay.
- *Care of the environment.* The emission of polluting matter in one member country often results in emission in another; in other words, the negative external effects are exported. To combat pollution and avoid distortion of the environmental costs and

benefits of production, the EC has launched several programmes, and plans to extend its action in the field;

- *Protection of the consumer*. Several directives specify the essential health and safety conditions for products. Other elements of EC action are: to safeguard after-sales services in the country of residence irrespective of the place where the product was bought, to outlaw improper clauses in standard contracts, etc. Some progress has been made on those scores, but the EC has made little headway in protecting the economic interest of consumers (see agriculture, external trade etc.);
- *Educational exchange*. To improve understanding among cultures, EC schemes to support the exchange of university students (ERASMUS) and other young people (YES) have been drawn up;
- *The European identity*. This is strengthened by the use of signs and symbols helping people to express themselves. In that philosophy, the Community has adopted its own flag (blue with twelve golden stars) and its own official anthem (Schiller and Beethoven's *Ode to Joy*), and proclaimed its own public holiday (9th May).

Summary and conclusions

Integration has made *considerable progress* in Europe in the last 30 years. That is evidenced by many indicators:

- economic ones, such as the interpenetration of markets and the convergence of prices;
- policy ones, such as the fields covered, and the strength of instruments used by Community Institutions.

New objectives have been set for future economic integration. After the completion of the internal market, the most important goal will be the gradual build-up of the Economic and Monetary Union. The emergence of a Community in which increased solidarity leads to more international redistribution seems to be somewhat farther down the road.

Notes

1   We used that method for instance for goods in Chapter 3 (Table 3.3) and Chapter 8 (Tables 8.1 and 8.2).
2   The growth of European lobby groups by category and their relative strength *vis-à-vis* national lobby groups is clearly an under–researched area that would deserve close attention from political economists and political scientists alike.

3   Although the EEC (Treaty, article 3c) set regional equilibrium as a common objective to cope with the negative side effects of EC allocation policies.

4   This would extend the work of the Council of Europe (European Charter of Social Security) and of the International Labour Organisation (Treaty, w102).

5   This idea was already put forward in the McDougall report of 1977.

6   Tinbergen and Fischer (1987) recently drew up a plan to reform UN agencies, equipping them to cope with the increasing demand for world-wide co-ordination. See in this respect also Vosgerau (1989).

ANNEXES

List of Abbreviations

ACP	African, Caribbean and Pacific Countries
BEUC	Bureau Européen des Unions de Consommateurs
BIS	Bank of International Settlements
CAP	Common Agricultural Policy
CCP	Common Commercial Policy
CEC	Commission of the European Communities
CEN	Comité Européen de Normalisation
CENELEC	Comité Européen de Normalisation Electronique
CEP	Common Energy Policy
CEPT	Conference Européenne des Postes et Télécommunication
CET	Common External Tariff
CM	Common Market
CMEA	Council of Mutual Economic Assistance (Comecon)
CMU	Capital Market Union
CPE	Centrally Planned Economies
CU	Customs Union
COREPER	Committee of Permanent Representatives
DI	Direct Investment
EAEC	European Atomic Energy Community (Euratom)
EAGGF	European Agricultural Guidance and Guarantee Fund
EC	European Community
ECA	European Court of Auditors
ECE	Economic Commission for Europe
ECJ	European Court of Justice
ECSC	European Coal and Steel Community
ECU	European Currency Unit
EDC	European Defence Community
EDF	European Development Fund
EDIE	European Direct Investment in Europe
EDIUS	European Direct Investment in the US
EEC	European Economic Community
EFTA	European Free Trade Association
EIB	European Investment Bank
EMCF	European Monetary Co-operation Fund

EMS	European Monetary System
EMU	Economic and Monetary Union
EP	European Parliament
EPC	European Political Community/Co-operation
ERDF	European Regional Development Fund
ESC	Economic and Social Committee
ESF	European Social Fund
EU	Economic Union
FCMA	Free Capital Movement Area
FEU	Full Economic Union
FLMZ	Free Labour Movement Zone
FPCE	Foreign-Profit Creation Effect
FPDE	Foreign-Profit Diversion Effect
FRG	Federal Republic of Germany
FTA	Free Trade Area
GATT	General Agreement of Tariffs and Trade
GDP	Gross Domestic Product
GI	Gigajoule
GNP	Gross National Product
GSP	Generalised System of Preference
HFL	Dutch Florin
IATA	International Air Transport Association
IBRD	International Bank for Reconstruction and Development (World Bank)
IIT	Intra-Industry Trade
ILO	International Labour Organisation
IMF	International Monetary Fund
LDC	Less Developed Country
LEC	Labour-Exporting Country
LIC	Labour Importing Country
LMU	Labour Market Union
MCA	Monetary Compensatory Amounts
MFA	Multi-Fibre Arrangement
MFN	Most-Favoured-Nation
MNF	Multi National Firm
MU	Monetary Union
Mt/y	Millon (1 000 000) tons per year
Mtoe	Million (1 000 000) tons of oil equivalent
NATO	North Atlantic Treaty Organisation
NIC	Newly Industrialising Countries
NORDEL	Nordic Electricity
NTB	Non-Tariff Barriers
OCA	Optimum Currency Area
OECD	Organisation for Economic Co-operation and Development

OEEC	Organisation for European Economic Co-operation
OMA	Orderly Marketing Arrangements
OPEC	Organisation of Petroleum Exporting Countries
PTT	Post Telegraph Telephone
QR	Quantitative Restrictions
R & D	Research and Development
RCA	Revealed Comparative Advantage
RIR	Real Interest Rates
SDR	Special Drawing Right
SEA	Single European Act
SITC	Standard International Trade Classification
SSR	Self Sufficiency Ratio
TWh	Tetra Watt hour
UCPTE	Union for the Coordination of the Production and Transmission of Electric Power
UK	United Kingdom
UNCTAD	United Nations Conference on Trade and Development
UNIDO	United Nations Industrial Development Organisation
UNO	United Nations Organisation
USA	United States of America
USDIE	United States Direct Investment in Europe
VAT	Value-Added Tax
VER	Voluntary Export Restraint
WEU	Western European Union

Bibliography

Adler, M. (1970), Specialisation in the European Coal and Steel Community, *Journal of Common Market Studies*, vol. 8, pp. 175–91.

Adler, M. and Dumas, B. (1983), International Portfolio Choice and Corporation Finance, *Journal of Finance*, vol. 38.3, pp. 925–84.

Aitken, N.D. (1973), The Effect on the EEC and EFTA on European Trade; a Temporal Cross-Section Analysis, *American Economic Review*, vol. 63, pp. 881–91.

Akhtar, A.M. (1986), Recent Changes in the Financial Systems; a Perspective on Benefits versus Costs, in D.E. Fair (ed.), *Shifting Frontiers in Financial Markets*, Nijhoff, Dordrecht, pp. 31–41.

Albert, M. and Ball, R. (1983), *Towards European Economic Recovery in the 1980's*, European Parliament Working documents 1983/84, Luxemburg.

Allais, M., Duquesne de la Vinelle, L.,Oort, C.J., Seidenfus, H.S. and del Viscoro, M. (1965), Options in Transport Policy, *The EEC Studies*, Transport Series no. 4, Brussels.

Allen, P.R. (1983), Policies to Correct Cyclical Imbalance within a Monetary Union, *Journal of Common Market Studies*, vol. 21.3, pp. 313–27.

Alting von Geusau, F.A.M. (ed.) (1975), *Energy in the European Communities*, Sijthof, Leiden.

AMUE (1988) (Association for the Monetary Union of Europe): *European Business and the ECU*; Results of a survey carried out by FAITS and OPINIONS among 1036 business leaders in the European Community with the help of the Ecu Banking Association and the European Commission, Paris.

Anarzit, P. d' (1982), *Essai d'une politique petrolière européenne*, Editions Techniques et Economiques, Paris.

Arge, R.d' (1969), Note on Customs Union and Direct Foreign Investment, *Economic Journal*, vol. 79, pp. 324–33.

Artis, M. and Ostry, S. (1986), *International Economic Policy Co-ordination*, RIIA/RKP, London.

Askari, H. (1974), The Contribution of Migration to Economic Growth in the EEC, *Economica Internazionale*, vol. 27.2, pp. 341–5.

Atkins (1987) The cost of non-Europe in public sector procurement, *Research on the cost of non-Europe*, vol. 5 part A, CEC, Brussels.

Atkinson, P., and Chouraqui, J. (1985), Real interest rates and the prospects for durable growth, *OECD Working Paper* no. 21, Paris.

Auberger, B. (1980), Quelle politique agricole commune pour demain? *Revue du Marché Commun*, vol. 23.241, pp. 519–26.

Aubrey, B. (1984), 100,000 travailleurs frontaliers, *Economie et Statistique* no. 170, pp. 13–23.

Auctores, Varii (1983), Issues and Experience of Transport Regulation Reform, *International Journal of Transport Economics*, vol. 10.1–2.

Ayling, D.E. (1986), *The Internationalisation of Stock Markets; the Trend towards Greater Foreign Borrowing and Lending*, Gower, Aldershot.

Bairoch, P. (1976), *Commerce extérieur et développement économique de l'Europe au XIXᵉ siècle*, Mouton, Paris.

Balassa, B. (1961), *The Theory of Economic Integration*, Irwin, Homewood, Illinois.

Balassa, B. (1966), Tariff Reductions and Trade in Manufactures among Industrial Countries, *American Economic Review*, vol. 56, pp. 466–73.

Balassa, B. (ed.) (1975), *European Economic Integration*, North-Holland/American Elsevier, Amsterdam.

Balassa, B. (1976), Types of Economic Integration, in Machlup, F. (ed.), *Economic Integration, Worldwide, Regional, Sectoral*, Macmillan, London, pp. 17–31.

Balassa, B. (1977), Revealed Comparative Advantage Revisited: an Analysis of Relative Export Shares of the Industrial Countries 1953–1971, *The Manchester School*, pp. 327–44.

Balassa, B. (1986), Intra-Industry Trade among Exporters of Manufactured Goods, in Greenaway, D. and Tharakan, P.K.M. (eds), *Imperfect Competition and International Trade*, Wheatsheaf, Sussex, pp. 108–128

Balassa, B., and Balassa, C. (1984), Industrial Protection in the Developed Countries, *The World Economy*, pp. 179–96.

Balassa, B. and Bauwens, L. (1988), The Determinants of Intra European Trade in Manufactured Goods, *European Economic Review*, vol. 32.7, pp. 1421–1439.

Baldwin, R. and Murray, T. (1977), MFN Tariff Reductions and Developing Country Trade Benefits under GSP, *Economic Journal*, vol. 87, pp. 30–46

Baldwin, R.E. (1984), Trade Policies in Developed Countries, in Jones, R.W. and Kenen, P.B. (eds), *Handbook of International Economics*, vol. I, North Holland, Amsterdam, pp. 571–621.

Baldwin, R. (1989), The growth affects of 1992, *Economic Policy*, vol. 2, pp. 247–81.

Bamber, G.J. and Lansbury, R. (1987), *International and Comparative Industrial Relations*, Allen and Unwin, London.

Barnovin, B. (1986), *The European Labour Movement and European Inte-*

gration, Graduate Institute of International Studies, Pinter, Geneva-London.

Bartel, R. (1974), International Monetary Unions, the 19th Century Experience, *Journal of European Economic History*, vol. 3.3, pp. 689–723.

Batchelor, R. (1982), Expectations, Output and Inflation: the European Experience, *European Economic Review*, vol. 17.1, pp. 1–25.

Baumol, W.J., Panzar, J.C. and Willig, R.D. (1982), *Contestable Markets and the Theory of Industry Structure*, Harcourt, Brace Jovanovitch, San Diego.

Bergeijk, P.A.G., van (1987), *The determinants of success and failure of economic sanctions, some empirical results*, Development and Security, Groningen.

Bergh, P., van den *et al.*, (1987), Deregulering van de internationale financiele stromen en valutastelsel, in Auctores Varii, *Sociaal-economische deregulering*, 130e Vlaams Economisch Congres, pp. 843–78.

Berghe, L., van den (1980), *The European Insurance Market; some considerations*, Reports and Studies of the International Insurance Seminars, IIS Inc., Paris, pp. 143–56.

Bergstrand, J.H. (1983), Measurement and Determinants on Intra Industry International Trade, in P.K.M. Tharakan, *Intra-industry Trade: Empirical and Methodological Aspects*, North Holland, Amsterdam, pp. 201–55

Bernard, P.J. (ed.) (1978), *Les travailleurs étrangers en Europe*, Mouton, The Hague.

BEUC (1982), *Report on Car Prices and private Imports of Cars in the EC Countries*, BEUC 105892, Brussels.

BEUC (1986), *Car Price Differences in the EEC*, Brussels.

BEUC (1988), *Term Insurance in Europe*, (Report nr. 51/88), Brussels.

Beuter, R. and Pelkmans, J. (1986) (eds), *Cementing the Internal Market*, EIPA, Maastricht.

Bhagwati, J. (1982), Shifting Comparative Advantage, Protectionist Demands, and Policy Response, in Bhagwati, J. (ed.), *Import Competition and Response*, University of Chicago Press, pp. 153–95.

Bhagwati, J.N. (1987a), Trade in Services and the Multilateral Trade Negotiations, *The World Bank Economics Review*, vol. 1.4, pp. 549–69.

Bhagwati, J. (1987b), International Factor Mobility, in (ed.) Feenstra, R.C., *Essays in International Economic Theory*, vol. 2, MIT Press, Cambridge Massachusetts.

Bhagwati, J., Schatz, K.W. and Wong, K. (1984), The West German Gastarbeiter System of Immigration, *European Economic Review*, vol. 26, pp. 227–94.

Bianchi, P. and Forlai, L. (1988), The European Domestic Appliances Industry 1945-1987, in de Jong, H.W. (ed.), *The Structure of European Industry*, 2nd edn., Kluwer, Dordrecht, pp. 269–96.

Black, J. and Dunning, J.H. (eds) (1982), *International Capital Movements*, Macmillan, London.

Blaise, J., Fouchard, P. and Kahn, P. (1981), *Les Eurocrédits; un instrument du système bancaire pour le financement international*, Librairies Techniques, Paris.

Blitz, R.C. (1977), A Benefit-Cost Analysis of Foreign Workers in West Germany 1957–1973, *Kyklos*, vol. 30, pp. 479–502.

Blonk, W.A.G. (1968), *Enige aspecten en problemen van het goederenvervoer tussen de lidstaten van de Europese Economische Gemeenschap, met name ten aanzien van de kwantitatieve beperkingen en kwalitatieve belemmeringen*, Born, Assen.

Boeckhout, I.J. and Molle, W.T.M. (1982), Technological Change, Location Patterns and Regional Development, *FAST Occasional Papers* no. 16, EEC, DG XII, Brussels.

Böhning, W.R. (1972), *The Migration of Workers in the U.K. and the EC*, Oxford University Press, London.

Böhning, W.R. (1979), International Migration in Western Europe, Reflections on the Last Five Years, *International Labour Review*, vol. 118.4, pp. 401–15.

Böhning, W.R. and Maillat, D. (1974), *The Effects of the Employment of Foreign Workers*, OECD, Paris.

Boltho, A. (ed.) (1982), *The European Economy; Growth and Crisis*, Oxford University Press, Oxford.

Borchardt, K. (1984), Protektionismus im historischen Rückblick, in A. Gutowski (ed.), *Der neue Protektionismus*, Weltarchiv, Hamburg, pp. 17–47.

Bordo, M. and Schwartz, A. (1984), *A Retrospective on the Classical Gold Standard*, NBER, New York.

Bourguignon, F., Gallast-Hamond, G. and Fernet, B. (1977), *Choix économiques liés aux migrations internationales de main d'oeuvre; le cas européen*, OECD, Paris.

Bourrinet, J. (1981), L'explication économique de la genèse des Communautés Européennes, in Lasok, D. and Soldatos, P. (eds), *Les Communautés Européennes en fonctionnement*, Bruylant, Bruxelles, pp. 65–84.

Bouteiller, J. (1971), Comparaison de structure inter-industrielles de salaires dans les pays du marché commun, *Annales de l'INSEE*, no. 8, pp. 3–24.

Brennan, G. and Buchanan, J.M. (1980), *The Power to Tax, Analytical Foundations of a Fiscal Constitution*, Cambridge University Press, Cambridge.

Breyer, S. (1984), Analysing Regulatory Failure; Mismatches, Less Restrictive Alternatives, and Reform, in Ogus, A.I. and Veljanovski, C.G. (eds), *Readings in the Economics of Law and Regulation*, Oxford, pp. 234–239.

Bröcker, J. (1984), *Interregionaler Handel und ökonomische Integration*, Florentz, München.

Brown, A.J. (1985), *World Inflation Since 1950, An International Comparative Study*, Cambridge University Press, Cambridge.

Browne, F.X. (1984), The International Transmission of Inflation to a Small Open Economy under Fixed Exchange Rates and Highly Interest Sensitive Capital Flows, *European Economic Review*, vol. 25, pp. 187–212.

Brugmans, H. (1970), *L'idée Européenne 1920–1970*, De Tempel, Brugge.

Bruno, M., (1984), Stagflation in the EC Countries, 1973–1981: a cross-sectional view, in Emerson, M. (ed.), *Europe's Stagflation*, Clarendon Press, Oxford, pp. 33–58.

Buchanan, J.M. (1968), *The Demand and Supply of Public Goods*, Rand MacNally, Chicago.

Buckley, P.J. and Artisien, P. (1987), Policy issues of intra-EC direct investment; British, French and German multinationals in Greece, Portugal and Spain with special reference to employment effects, *Journal of Common Market Studies*, vol. 26.2, pp. 207–30.

Buckwell, A.E., Harvey, D.R., Thomson, K.T. and Parton, K.A. (1982), *The Cost of the Common Agricultural Policy*, Croom Helm, London.

Buiter, W.H. and Marston, R. (eds) (1985), *International Economic Policy Coordination*, Cambridge University Press, Cambridge.

Bulcke, D. van den (1983), Multinationale ondernemingen en Europese Gemeenschap; impact en respons, *Maandschrift Economie*, vol. 47, pp. 304–26.

Bulcke, D. van den (1984), Decision Making in Multinational Enterprises and the Consultation of Employees; the Proposed Vredeling Directive of the EC Commission, *International Studies of Management and Organisation*, vol. 14.1, pp. 36–61.

Bulmer, S. and Wessels, W. (1986), *The European Council Decision Making in European Politics*, Macmillan, Basingstoke.

Butler, A.D. (1967), Labour Cost in the Common Market, *Industrial Economics*, vol. 6.2, pp. 166–183.

Button, K.J. (1983), Regulation and Coordination of International Road Goods Movements within the European Common Market; an Assessment, *Transportation Journal*, vol. 22.4, pp. 4–16.

Button, K.J. (1984), *Road Haulage Licensing and EC Transport Policy*, Gower Press, Aldershot.

Cairncross, A. (1973), *Control of Long-Term International Capital Movements*, Brookings Institution, Washington.

Cameron, D.R. (1985), Does Government Cause Inflation? Taxes, Spending and Deficits, in Lindberg, L. and Maier, C.S. (eds), *The Politics of Inflation and Economic Stagnation*, Brookings Institution, Washington, pp. 224–79.

Caramazza, F. (1987), International Real Interest Rate Linkages in the 1970s and 1980s, in Tremblay, R. (ed.), *Issues in North American Trade and Finance*, North American Economic and Finance Association, vol. 4.1, pp. 123–50.

Carson, M. (1982), The Theory of Foreign Direct Investment, in Black, J. and Dunning, J.H. (eds), *International Capital Movements*, Macmillan, London, pp. 22–58.

Castles, S, and Kosack, G. (1985), *Immigrant Workers and Class Structure in Western Europe*, Oxford University Press, London.

Caves, R.E. (1975), Economic Models of Political Choice: Canada's Tariff Structure, *Canadian Journal of Economics*, vol. 9, pp. 278–300.

Caves, R. (1982), Multinational Enterprise and Economic Analysis, Cambridge University Press, Cambridge.

Caves, R. and Jones, R. (1984), *World Trade and Payments*, Little, Brown, Boston (3rd edn).

CEC (1961), *Document de la Conference sur les économies regionales*, vol. II, Brussels.

CEC (1964), *Reports by Groups of Experts on Regional Policy in the European Economic Community*, Brussels.

CEC (1966), *The Development of a European Capital Market*, Segré Report, Brussels.

CEC (1967), *Critère à la base de la fixation des salaires et problèmes qui y sont liés pour une politique des salaires et des revenus*, Brussels.

CEC (1968), *Memorandum sur la reforme de l'agriculture dans la Communauté Economique Européenne, Agriculture 1980*, COM 68/100e, Luxemburg.

CEC (1969), *A Regional Policy for the Community*, Brussels

CEC (1970), *De industriepolitiek van de Gemeenschap*, memorandum van de Commissie aan de Raad, Brussels.

CEC (1971), *Regional Development in the Community: Analytical Survey*, Brussels.

CEC (1972), *La libre circulation de la main-d'oeuvre et les marchés du travail dans la CEE*, (DG V), Brussels.

CEC (1973a), Communication from the Commission to the Council on the Development of the Common Transport Policy, *COM* (73), Brussels.

CEC (1973b), *Report on the Regional Problems in the Enlarged Community; (Thomson Report)*, Com.73/550, Brussel.

CEC (1974), *Third Report on Competition Policy*, Brussels.

CEC (1977), The Regional Policy of the Community, New Guidelines, *Supplement 2/77 to the Bulletin of the EC*.

CEC, (1979a), *Etude comparative des conditions et procedures d'introduction et d'accès à l'emploi des travailleurs de pays tiers dans les états membres de la Communauté*, Brussels.

CEC (1979b), A Transport Network for Europe, Outline of a Policy, Supplement 8/79 to *Bulletin of the European Communities*.

CEC (1979c), Air Transport, A Community Approach, Supplement 5/79 to the *Bulletin of the European Communities*.

CEC (1979d), *The European Monetary System: Commentary Document*, European Economy no. 3.

CEC (1979e), The Regional Development Programmes, *Regional Policy Series*, no. 17, Brussels.

CEC (1980), *The Europeans and their Regions*, internal EC document DG XXVI nr 9.

CEC (1981a), *Energy Strategy to be Adopted by the Community*, Brussels.

CEC (1981b), *The Regions of Europe: First Periodic Report*, Brussels.

CEC (1981c), *Proposal for a Council Regulation Amending the Regulation (EEC), no. 724/75, establishing a European Regional Development Fund*, Brussels.

CEC (1982a), *The Competitiveness of the Community Industry*, Brussels.

CEC (1982b), The Agricultural Policy of the European Community, *European Documentation*, no. 6.

CEC (1982c), *Review of Member States' Energy Policy Programmes and Progress towards 1990 Objectives*, Brussels.

CEC (1982d), Experimenteel programma betreffende de vervoersinfrastructuur, COM 82/828 def., Brussels.

CEC (1982e), European Transport, Crucial Problems and Research Needs, a Long Term Analysis, *Series FAST* no. 3, Brussels.

CEC (1982f), The Community and State Aids to Industry, *European File*, no. 9, Brussels.

CEC (1982g), Public Supply Contracts in the European Community, *European Documentation*, Luxemburg/Brussels.

CEC (1983a), *Commission activities and EC-rules for the Automobile Industry 1981–1983*, Com 83/633 final, Brussels.

CEC (1983b), Wine in the European Community, *European Documentation* 2/3.

CEC (1983c), The Customs Union, *European Documentation* 6/1983, Luxemburg.

CEC (1984a), The European Community's Legal System, *European Documentation* 1984/5, Luxemburg.

CEC (1984b), *Public Supply Contracts, Conclusions and Perspectives*, COM 84/717, Brussels.

CEC (1984c), *The Regions of Europe; Second Periodic Report on the Situation and Socio-economic Evolution of the Regions of the Community*, Brussels.

CEC (1984d), *Les programmes de développement regional de la deuxième génération pour la période 1981–1985*, Collection Documents, Bruxelles.

CEC (1985a), Migrants in the European Community, European File 13.85, Brussels.

CEC (1985b), The European Community Fisheries Policy, Luxemburg.

CEC (1985c), *The Insurance Industry in the Countries of the EEC, Structure, Conduct and Performance,* (by Aaronovitch, S. and Samson, P.) Documents, Brussels.

CEC (1985d), *Completing the Internal Market,* White Paper, Brussels/ Luxemburg.

CEC (1985e), European Competition Policy, *European File no. 6,* Brussels.

CEC (1985f), The European Commission's Powers of Investigation in the Enforcement of Competition Law, *European Documentation,* Luxemburg.

CEC (1985g), *The European Community and its Regions; 10 Years of Community Regional Policy and the ERDF,* Luxemburg.

CEC (1985h), *Main Texts Governing the Regional Policy of the EC, Collection Documents,* Brussels.

CEC (1986a), European Act, *Bulletin of the European Communities,* Supplement 2/86.

CEC (1986b), The ABC of Community Law, *European Documentation* 1986/2, Luxemburg.

CEC (1986c), The Court of Justice of the European Community, *European Documentation* 1986/5, Luxemburg.

CEC (1986d), The European Communities' Budget, *European Documentation* 1986/1, Luxemburg.

CEC (1986e), *Programme for the Liberalisation of Capital Movements in the Community,* Brussels.

CEC (1986f), *Bulletin of Energy Prices,* Luxemburg.

CEC (1986g), The Approximation of European Tax Systems, *European File no. 9,* Brussels.

CEC (1986h), The European Monetary System, *European File 15,* Brussels.

CEC (1986i), *Directory of European Community Trade and Professional Associations* (3rd edn), Brussels.

CEC (1987a), *Treaties Establishing the European Communities,* (abridged edn), Luxemburg.

CEC (1987b), *Regional Disparities and the Tasks of Regional Policy in the Enlarged Community (Third Periodic Report),* Brussels.

CEC (1988a), The Catching-up Process in Spain and Portugal, *European Economy Supplement* A, no. 10.

CEC (1988b), *Major Results of the Survey of Member States' Energy Policies,* COM 88/174 fin.

CEC (1988c), *La dimension sociale du Marché Intérieur,* Rapport d'Etappe du groupe interservices présidé par M.J. Degimbe, Brussels, 1988.

CEC (1988d), Research on the 'Cost of Non Europe' – Basic Findings Vol. 1; *Basic Studies; Executive Summaries,* Brussels.

CEC (1988e), Europe without frontiers; completing the internal market, *European Documentation* 3/88, Brussels.

CEC (1989), *European Community Research Programmes; France, work programme* 1978–1981, Status 1989, DG XII, Brussels.

Cecchini, P., *et al.* (1988) *The European Challenge 1992*, Gower, Aldershot.

CEMT (1985), *Trends in the Transport Sector*, 1970–1984, Paris.

Centi, J.P. (1984), *Integration européenne et concurrence des monnaies*, Economica, Paris.

CEPS (1986), *The Future of Community Finance*, Centre for European Policy Studies, Brussels.

Chabod, F. (1961), *Storia dell'idea d'Europa*, Laterza, Bari.

Chenery, H. (1960), Patterns of Industrial Growth, *American Economic Review*, vol. 50, pp. 624–54.

Chenery, H., Robinson, S. and Syrquin, M. (1986), *Industrialisation and Growth; a Comparative Study*, Oxford University Press, Oxford/New York.

Cheng, L. (1983), International Trade and Technology: A Brief Survey of the Recent Literature, *Weltwirtschaftliches Archiv*, vol. 120, pp. 444–69.

Cherif, M. and Ginsburgh, V. (1976), Economic Interdependence Among the EEC Countries, *European Economic Review*, vol. 8, pp. 71–86.

Chipman, J.S. (1965/66), A Survey of the Theory of International Trade, *Econometrica*, part I, vol. 33.3, pp. 477–519; part II, vol. 33.4, pp. 685–761; part III, vol. 34.1, pp. 18–76.

Cho, D.G., Enu, C.S. and Senbet, L.W. (1986), International Arbitrage Pricing Theory: an Empirical Investigation, *Journal of Finance* vol. 41.2, pp. 313–29.

Claassen, E-M., and Wyplosz, C. (1982) Capital controls; some principles and the French experience, *Annales de l' Insee*, no. 47/48, pp 237–77.

Clark, C. (1957), *Conditions of Economic Progress*, Macmillan, London.

Clarke, W.M. and Pulay, G. (1978), *The World's Money; How it Works*, Allen & Unwin, London.

Clarotti, P. (1984), Progress and Future Development of Establishment and Services in the EC in Relation to Banking, *Journal of Common Market Studies*, vol. 22.3, pp. 199–226.

Clout, H. (1986), *Regional Development in Western Europe*, J. Wiley Chichester.

Cnossen, S. (ed.) (1987), *Tax Coordination in the European Community*, Kluwer, Deventer.

Collins, D. (1983), *The Operations of the European Social Fund*, Croom Helm, London.

Cooke, T.E. (1988), *International Mergers and Acquisitions*, Basil Blackwell, Oxford.

Cooper, R.N. (1983), Economic Interdependence and the Coordination of Economic Policies, in Jones, R. and Kenen, P.B. (eds), *Handbook of International Economics*, North-Holland, New York.

Corden, W.M. (1971), *Theory of Protection*, Clarendon, Oxford.

Corden, W.M. (1972a), Economies of Scale and Customs Union Theory, *Journal of Political Economy*, vol. 80.1, pp. 465–75.

Corden, W.M. (1972b), Monetary Integration, *Essays in International Finance* no. 93, Princeton University, Princeton, N.J.

Corden, W.M. (1974), *Trade Policy and Economic Welfare*, Clarendon, Oxford.

Corner, D.C. and Tonks, I. (1987), The Impact of the Internationalisation of World Stock Markets on the Integration of EC Securities Markets, in Macmillan, M., Mayer, D.G. and van Veen, P. (eds), *European Integration and Industry*, Tilburg University Press, Tilburg, pp. 229–46.

Cornwall, J. (1977), *Modern Capitalism*, Robertson, London.

Council of Europe (1980), *European Migration in the 1980s, Trends and Policies*, Strasbourg.

Council of Europe (1983), *The Situation of Migrant Workers and their Families; Achievements, Problems and Possible Solutions*, Strasbourg.

Cripps, F. and Tarling, R. (1973), *Growth in Advanced Capitalist Economies 1950–1970*, Cambridge University Press, Cambridge.

Crochett, A. (1985), Exchange Rates and Trade; is there a Problem for Policy?, in Peeters, T., Praet, P. and Reding, P. (eds), *International Trade and Exchange Rates in the Late Eighties*, North Holland, Amsterdam, pp. 267–99.

Crouch, C. (1985), Conditions for Trade Union Wage Restraint, in L. Lindberg and Ch.S. Maier (eds), *The Politics of Inflation and Economic Stagnation*, Brookings Inst., Washington, pp. 105–39.

Cushman, D.O. (1983) The Effects of Real-Exchange-Rate Risk on International Trade, *Journal of International Economics*, vol. 15, pp. 45–63.

Dam, K.W. (1970), The GATT: *Law and International Economic Organisation*, UCP, London.

Davenport, M. (1986), *Trade Policy, Protectionism and the Third World*, Croom Helm, Beckenham.

Deardorff, A. and Stern, R. (1981) A disaggregated model of world production and trade; an estimate of the impact of the Tokyo Round, *Journal of Policy Modelling*.

Delors Committee (1989), *Report on Economic and Monetary Union in the European Community*, CEC, Brussels.

Demsetz, H. (1982), *Economic, Legal and Political Dimensions of Competition*, North Holland, Amsterdam.

Denison, E.F. (1967), *Why Growth Rates Differ*, Brookings, Washington.

Denton, G. (1984), Restructuring the EC Budget, *Journal of Common Market Studies*, vol. 24.2, pp. 117–40.

Devereux, M. and Pearson, M. (1989), Corporate Tax Harmonisation and Economic Efficiency, *Report Series* no. 35, Institute of Fiscal Studies, London.

Dicken, P. (1986), *Global Shift, Industrial Change in a Turbulent World*, Harper and Row, London.

Dornbusch, R. (1976), Expectations and Exchange-Rate Dynamics, *Journal of Political Economy*, vol. 84, pp. 1161–1176.

Dornbusch, R. (1980), *Open Economy Macro-Economics*, Basic Books, New York.

Dosi, G. and Soete, L. (1988), Technical Change and International Trade, in Dosi, G. *et al.*, (eds), *Technical Change and Economic Theory*, Pinter, London, pp. 401–31.

Dosser, D. (1966), Economic Analysis of Fiscal Harmonisation, in Shoup, C.S. (ed.), *Fiscal Harmonisation in Common Markets*, Columbia University Press, New York.

Drabeck, Z. and Greenaway, D. (1984), Economic Integration and Inter-Industry Trade, the CMEA and EEC compared, *Kyklos* vol. 37, pp. 444–69.

Dramais, A. (1977), Transmission of Inflationary Pressures between the E.E.C. Members, *European Economic Review*, vol. 9, pp. 21–42 .

Druesne, G., and Kremlis, G. (1986), *La politique de concurrence de la CEE*, ed. Paris.

Duchêne, F., Szczepaniak, E. and Legg, W. (1985), *New Limits on European Agriculture; Politics and the Common Agricultural Policy*, Croom Helm, London.

Duchêne, F. and Shepherd, G. (eds) (1987), *Managing Industrial Change in Western Europe*, Pinter, London.

Dufey, G. and Giddy, I.H. (1981), *The Evolution of Instruments and Techniques in International Financial Markets*, SUERF, Tilburg.

Duncan, M.G. and Hall, M. (1983) *Proposals for a European Equity Market through Linkage of the Community Stock Exchanges*, CEC, Brussels.

Dunning, J.H. (1979), Explaining Changing Patterns of International Production; in Defence of an Eclectic Theory, *Oxford Bulletin of Economics and Statistics*, vol. 41, pp. 269–95.

Dunning, J.H. (1980), A note on Intra-Industry Foreign Direct Investment, *Banca Nazionale del Lavoro Quarterly Review*, vol. 34, December.

Dunning, J. and Cantwell, J. (1987), *IRM Directory of Statistics of International Investment and Production*, Macmillan, London.

Durand, A. (1980), The Quantum, in Smith, L. (ed.), *Alternative Proposals for the Common Agricultural Policy*, Dublin.

Duroselle, J.B. (1965), L'idea d'Europa nella Storia, *Collana Europa* Una, Edizione Milano Nuova, Milano.

Duroselle, J.B. (1987), L'Europe dans l'historiographie 1815–1914, in Rijksbaron, A. *et al.*, *Europe from a Cultural Perspective*, Nijgh en Van Ditmar, The Hague, pp. 31–32.

ECA (1988), *European Fund for Regional Development*, (*Official Journal* 12-12-1988).

Edye, D. (1987), *Immigrant Labour and Government Policy*, Gower, Aldershot.

El-Agraa, A.M. and Jones, A.J. (1981), *Theory of Customs Unions*, Philip Allan, Oxford.

El-Agraa, A.M. (1985), International Economic Integration, in Greenaway, D. (ed.), *Current Issues in International Trade, Theory and Policy*, Macmillan, London, pp. 183–207.

Eliasson, G. (1984), The Micro Foundations of Industrial Policy, in Jacquemin, A. (ed.), *European Industry, Public Policy and Corporate Strategy*, CEPS, Clarendon, Oxford, pp. 295–326.

Emerson, M. with Aujean, M., Catinat, M., Goybet, P., and Jacquemin, A. (1988), The Economics of 1992; an assessment of the potential economic effects of completing the internal market of the European Community, *European Economy*, no. 35/3 pp. 5–222.

Erdmenger, J. (1981), *The European Community Transport Policy*, Gower, Aldershot.

ESS (1989), *EEC Transport Policy within the Context of the Single Market*, European Study Services, Rixensart.

Eurostat (1974), *Statistics of Energy*, Special nr 4, Luxemburg.

Eurostat (1983), *Monthly Bulletin of Foreign Trade*, Special issue 1958-1982, Luxemburg.

Eurostat (1985), *Foreign Population and Foreign Employees in the Community*, Luxemburg.

Eurostat (1987), *Employment and Unemployment*, Theme 3, Series C, Luxemburg.

Eurostat (several years), *Electricity Prices*, Luxemburg.

Eussner, A. (1986), Agro-industrial Cooperation between the EC and ACP countries, *Journal of Common Market Studies*, vol. 25.1, pp. 51–73.

Eyzenga, W. (1987), The Dependence of the Deutsche Bundesbank and De Nederlandsche Bank with regard to Monetary Policy; a comparative analysis, Series: *SUERF Papers on Monetary Policy and Financial Systems*, No. 2, Tilburg.

Faber, G. (1982), *The European Community and Development Cooperation*, Van Gorcum, Assen.

Faber, M. and Breyer, F. (1980), Eine ökonomische Analyse konstitutioneller Aspekte der europaischen Integration, *Jahrbuch fur Sozialwissenschaft*, vol. 31, pp. 213–27.

Farnell, J. and Ellis, J. (1984), *In Search of a Common Fisheries Policy*, Gower, Aldershot.

Findlay, R. (1982), International Distributive Justice, a Trade Theoretic Approach, *Journal of International Economics*, vol. 13, pp. 1–14.

Finsinger, J., Hammond, E. and Tapp , J., (1985), *Insurance: Competition on Regulation, a Comparative Study*, The Institute for Fiscal Studies, London.

Finsinger, J. and Pauly, M.V. (eds.) (1986), *The Economics of Insurance Regulation*, Macmillan, Houndsmill.

Fisher, M.R. (1966), *Wage Determination in an Integrating Europe*, Sijthoff, Leyden.

Fisher, S. (1987), International Macro-Economic Policy Coordination, *NBER Working Paper* no. 2244, Cambridge, Massachusetts.

Fishwick (1982), *Multinational Companies and Economic Concentration in Europe*, Gower, London.

Fleming, M. (1971), On exchange rate unification, *Economic Journal*, vol. 81, pp. 467–88.

Folmer, H. (1980), *Regional Economic Policy; Measurement of its Effects*, Kluwer, Deventer.

Forte, F. (1977), Principles for the Assignment of Public Economic Functions in a Setting of Multi-Layer Government, EC, *Report of the (McDougall) Study Group on the role of Public Finance in European Integration*, vol. II, Collection of Studies of Economics and Finances, Series no. B 13, Brussels.

Francko, L.G. (1976), *The European Multinationals; a renewed challenge to American and British business*, Harper and Row, London.

Franzmeyer, F. (1982), *Approaches to Industrial Policy within the EC and its Impact on European Integration*, Gower, Aldershot.

Frenkel, J.A. and Goldstein, M. (1986), *A Guide to Target Zones*, IMF Staff Papers, vol. 33.4.

Frey, B. (1984), *International Political Economics*, Basil Blackwell, Oxford.

Frey, B. (1985), The Political Economy of Protection, in Greenaway, D. (ed.), *Current Issues in International Trade*, Macmillan, London, pp. 139–57.

Frey, B. and Schneider, F. (1984), International Political Economy, a Rising Field, *Economia Internazionale*, vol. 37.3–4, pp. 308–47.

Friedman, M. (1968), The Role of Monetary Policy, *American Economic Review*, vol. 58.1, pp. 1–17.

Friedman, M. and Friedman, R. (1980), *Free to Choose, a Personal Statement*, Harcourt-Brace Jovanovich, p. 154.

Frisch, H. (1983), Theories of Inflation, Cambridge Surveys of Economic Literature, Cambridge.

Fukao, M. and Hanazaki, M. (1987), Internationalisation of Financial Markets and the Allocation of Capital, *OECD Economic Studies*, no. 8, pp. 35–92.

Gaab, W., Granziol, M.J. and Horner, M. (1986), On Some International Parity Conditions: an Empirical Investigation, *European Economic Review*, vol. 30.3, pp. 683–713.

GATT (1987), *The European Community's External Trade in Services*, Geneva.

Geist, Ch.R.(1979), *Raising International Capital, International Bond Markets and the European Institutions*, Saxon House, Farnborough.

Gerbet, P. (1983), *La construction de l'Europe*, Imprimerie Nationale, Paris.

Gerloff, W. (1920), *Die deutsche Zoll- und Handelspolitik von der Gründung des Zollvereins bis zum Frieden von Versailles*, Glöckner, Leipzig.

Geroski, P. and Jacquemin, A. (1984), Large Firms in the European Corporate Economy and Industrial Policy in the 1980s, in Jacquemin, A. (ed.), *European Industry: Public Policy and Corporate Strategy*, CEPS; Clarendon, Oxford, pp. 343–67.

Geroski, P. and Jacquemin, A. (1985), Industrial Change, Barriers to Mobility and European Industrial Policy, *Economic Policy*, vol. 1.1 pp. 170–218.

Gialloreto, L. (1988), *Strategic Airline Management*, Pitman, London.

Giavazzi, F. and Pagano, M. (1986), *The Advantages of Tying one's Hands; EMS Discipline and Central Bank Credibility*, Centre for Economic Policy Research, London.

Giersch, H. (1949), Economic Union between Nations and the Location of Industries, *Review of Economic Studies*, vol. 17, pp. 87–97.

Giersch, H. (1987), *Internal and External Liberalisation for Faster Growth: Economic Papers*, Commission of EC, Brussels.

Gijlstra, D.J. (1983), Dumping Policy of the EC in Practice, in Bourgeois, J.H. *et al.*, *Protectionism and the European Community*, Kluwer, Antwerp, pp. 147–79.

Giovannini, A. (1989), National Tax Systems versus the European Capital market, *Economic Policy* pp. 346–86.

Glejser, H. (1972), Empirical Evidence on Comparative Cost Theory from the European Common Market Experience, *European Economic Review* vol. 163, pp. 247–59.

Golombek, R., Hoel, M. and Vislie, J. (eds) (1987), *Natural Gas Markets and Contracts*, North Holland, Amsterdam.

Gomes, L. (1987), *Foreign Trade and the National Economy; Mercantilist and Classical Perspectives*, Macmillan, London.

Grauwe, P. de (1975), Conditions for Monetary Integration, a Geometric Interpretation, *Weltwirtschaftliches Archiv*, vol. 3, pp. 634–44.

Grauwe, P. de (1987), International Trade and Economic Growth in the European Monetary System, *European Economic Review*, vol. 31, pp. 389–98.

Greenaway, D. (1983), *International Trade Policy, from Tariffs to the New Protectionism*, Macmillan, London.

Greenaway, D. and Milner, C. (1986), *The Economics of Intra Industry Trade*, Basil Blackwell, Oxford.

Greenaway, D. (1987), Intra-industry Trade, intra-firm Trade and European Integration; evidence, gains and policy aspects, *Journal of Common Market Studies*, vol. 26.2, pp. 153–72.

Gremmen, H. (1985), Testing Factor Price Equalisation in the EC: An Alternative Approach, *Journal of Common Market Studies*, vol. 23, pp. 277–86.

Griffiths, B. (1975), *Invisible Barriers to Invisible Trade*, Macmillan, London.

Grinols, E.J. (1984), A Thorn in the Lion's Paw; Has Britain Paid too much for Common Market Membership?, *Journal of International Economics*, vol. 16, pp. 271–93.

Groeben, H. von der (1982), *Aufbaujahre der Europäischen Gemeinschaften*, Nomos, Baden-Baden.

Gros, D. (1987), On the Volatility of Exchange Rates: a test of monetary and portfolio balance models of exchange rate determination, *Economic Working Document*, vol. 32, CEPS, Brussels.

Gros, D. (1989), Paradigms for the Monetary Union of Europe, *Journal of Common Market Studies*, vol. 27.3, pp. 219–30.

Grubel, H.G. (1974), Taxation and the Rates of Return from some US Assets Holdings Abroad, *Journal of Political Economy*, vol. 82, pp. 469–87.

Grubel, H.G. and Lloyd, P. (1975), *Intra-Industry Trade: the Theory and Measurement of International Trade in Differentiated Products*, Macmillan, London.

Grubel, H.G. (1981), *International Economics*, Irwin, Homewood, Illinois.

Guieu, P. and Bonnet, C. (1987), Completion of the Internal Market and Indirect Taxation, *Journal of Common Market Studies*, vol. 25, pp. 209–23.

Gwilliam, K.M., Petriccione, S., Voigt, F. and Zighera, J.A. (1973), Criteria for the Coordination of Investments in Transport Infrastructure, *The EEC Studies, Transport Series Nr 3*, Brussels.

Haack, W.G.C.M. (1983), The Selectivity of Economic Integration Theories; a Comparison of Some Traditional and Marxist Approaches, *Journal of Common Market Studies*, vol. 21.4, pp. 365–86.

Hagenaars, A.J.M. (1986), *The Perception of Poverty*, North-Holland, Amsterdam.

Hall, G. (ed.) (1986), *European Industrial Policy*, Croom Helm, London.

Hamada, K. (1985), *The Political Economy of International Monetary Interdependence*, Cambridge University Press, Cambridge.

Hammar, T. (1985), *European Immigration Policy*, Cambridge University Press, Cambridge.

Harding, S., Philips, D. and Fogarty, M. (1986), *Contrasting Values in Western Europe, Unity, Diversity and Change*, Macmillan, London.

Harris, S., Swimbank, A. and Wilkinson, G. (1983), *The Food and Farm Policies of the European Community*, J. Wiley, Chichester.

Hartley, K. (1987), Public Procurement and Competitiveness: a Community Market for Military Hardware and Technology?, *Journal of Common Market Studies*, vol. 25, pp. 237–47.

Hartog, F. (1979), *Hoofdlijnen van de prijstheorie* (Main Lines of Price Theory), Stenfert Kroese, Leiden.

Hawtrey, R. (1947), *The Gold Standard in Theory and Practice*, Longmans, London.

Heidhues, T., Josling, T., Ritsen, C., *et al.* (1978), Common Prices and Europe's Farm Policy, *Thames Essays* no. 13, Trade Policy Research Centre, London.

Heijke, J.A.M. and Klaassen, L.H. (1979), Human Reactions to Spatial Diversity, Mobility in Regional Labour Markets, in Folmer, H. and Oosterhaven, J. (eds), *Spatial Inequalities and Regional Development*, Nijhoff, The Hague, pp. 117–30.

Helg, R. and Ranci, P. (1988), Economies of Scale and the Integration of the EC, the Case of Italy, in *Research into the Cost of Non-Europe, Basic Findings*, vol. 2, pp. 205–85.

Helpman, E. and Krugman, P.R. (1985), *Market structure and foreign trade; increasing returns, imperfect competition and the international economy*, Wheatsheaf, Brighton.

Hennart, J.F. (1983), The Political Economy of Comparative Growth Rates; the Case of France, in Mueller, D. (ed.), *The Political Economy of Growth*, Yale University Press, New Haven, pp. 176–203.

Henry, P. (1981), *Study of the Regional Impact of the Common Agricultural Policy*, Luxemburg.

Herbst, L. (1986), Die zeitgenössische Integrationstheorie und die Anfänge der europäischen Einigung 1947–1950, *Vierteljahreshefte für Zeitgeschichte II*, vol. 34, pp. 161–204.

Herman, B. and van Holst, B. (1984), International Trade in Services; some theoretical and practical problems, *Series Occasional Papers and Reprints*, NEI, Rotterdam.

Herman, V. and van Schendelen, M.P.C.M. (eds) (1974), *The European Parliament and the National Parliaments*, Saxon House, Farnborough.

Hewitt, A. (1984), The Lomé Conventions: Entering a Second Decade, *Journal of Common Market Studies*, vol. 23.2, pp. 95–115.

Hill, B.E. (1984), *The Common Agricultural Policy; Past, Present and Future*, Methuen, London.

Hill, B.E. and Ingersent, K.A. (1982), *The Economic Analysis of Agriculture* (2nd edn), Heinemann, London.

Hine, R.C. (1985), *The Political Economy of European Trade*, Wheatsheaf, Brighton.

Hirsch, S. (1974), Hypothesis Regarding Trade Between Developing and Industrial Countries, in Giersch, H.(ed.), *The International Division of Labour*, Mohr, Tuebingen, pp. 65–82.

Hirsch, S. (1981), Peace Making and Economic Interdependence, *The World Economy*, vol. 4, pp. 407–17.

Hocking, R. (1980), Trade in Motorcars between the Major European Producers, *Economic Journal*, vol. 90, pp. 504–19.

Hodges, M. and Wallace, W. (eds.) (1981), *Economic Divergence in the EC*, Allen & Unwin, London.

Hodget, G. (1972), *A Social and Economic History of Medieval Europe*, Methuen & Co., London.

Hoffmann, S. (1982), Reflections on the Nation State in Western Europe Today, *Journal of Common Market Studies*, vol. 21.1, pp. 21–39.

Hoffmeyer, B. (1982), The EEC's Common Agricultural Policy and the ACP States, *Research Report no. 2*, Centre for Development Studies, Copenhagen.

Holland, S. (1980), *Uncommon Market, Capital Class and Power in the European Community*, Macmillan, London.

Holloway, J. (1981), *Social Policy Harmonisation in the European Community*, Gower, Aldershot.

Holtfrerich, C-L. (1989), The monetary unification process in nineteenth century Germany, in de Cecco, M. and Giovannini, A. (eds), *A European Central Bank?*, Cambridge University Press, Cambridge, pp. 244–74.

Hudson, R. and Williams, A. (1986), *The United Kingdom*, Harper and Row, London.

Hufbauer, G.C. (1968), The Commodity Composition of Trade in Manufactured Goods, *Conference on Technology and Competition in International Trade*, NBER, New York.

Hufbauer, G.C. and Scott, J.J. (1985), *Economic Sanctions Reconsidered; history and current policy*, Institute for International Economics, Washington

Hughes Hallett, A.J. (1985), Autonomy and the Choice of Policy in Asymmetrically Dependent Economies, *Oxford Economic Papers* no. 38, pp. 516–45.

IBRD (1985), *World Development Report*, Oxford University Press, New York.

IEE (1978), *La charte sociale européenne: dix années d'application*, Editions de l'Université, Bruxelles.

ILO (1956), *Social Aspects of European Economic Cooperation*, Report by a group of experts, Geneva.

Ingo, W. (1985), Barriers to Trade in Banking and Financial Services, *Thames Essay*, no. 41, Trade Policy Research Centre, London.

Ingram, J.C. (1973), The Case for European Monetary Integration,

Essays in International Finance no. 98, Princeton University, Princeton N.J.

Isaacs, G. (1986), *Les ressources financières de la Communauté Européenne*, Economica, Paris.

Ishijama, Y. (1975), The Theory of Optimum Currency Areas, a Survey, *IMF Staff Papers*, vol. 22, pp. 344–83.

Jacquemin, A.P. and de Jong, H.W. (1977), *European Industrial Organisation*, Macmillan, London.

Jacquemin, A. (1979), *Economie industrielle européenne; structures de marché et stratégies d'entreprises* (2nd edn), Dunod, Paris.

Jacquemin, A. (1982), Imperfect Market Structure and International Trade, Some Recent Research, *Kyklos* vol. 35, pp. 73–93.

Jacquemin, A. and Sapir, A. (1988), European Integration or World Integration? *Weltwirtschaftliches Archiv*, vol. 124, pp. 127–39.

Jansen, E. and De Vree, J.K. (1985), *The Ordeal of Unity, the Politics of European Integration 1945–1985*, Prime Press, Bilthoven.

Jensen, W.G. (1983), *Energy in Europe 1945-1980*, Fouls, London.

Johnson, H.G. (1958), The Gains from Freer Trade in Europe, an Estimate, *Manchester School*, vol. 26.3, pp. 247–55.

Johnston, R.B. (1983), *The Economics of the Euromarket, History, Theory and Policy*, Macmillan, London.

Jones, A.J. and El Agraa, A.M. (1981), *The Theory of Customs Union*, Philip Allen, Oxford.

Jones, C.L. and Leydon, K. (1986), Developments in Gas and Electricity Prices in the EEC, in Odell, P. and Daneels, J. (eds), *Gas and Electricity Markets in Europe: Prospects and Policies*, BAEE, Brussels, pp. 8–122.

Jones, K. (1984), The Political Economy of Voluntary Export Restraint Agreements, *Kyklos*, vol. 37, pp. 82–101.

Jong, H.W. de (1981), *Dynamische Markttheorie*, Stenfert Kroese, Leiden.

Jong, H.W. de (1984), Sectoral Development and Sectoral Policies in the EC, in Jacquemin, A. (ed.), *European Industry; Public Policy and Corporate Strategy*, CEPS, Clarendon, Oxford, pp. 147–71.

Jong, H.W. de (1987), Market Structures in the European Economic Community, in: Macmillan, M., Mayes, D.G. and van Veen, P. (eds), *European Integration and Industry*, Tilburg University Press, Tilburg, pp. 40–89

Jong, H.W. de (ed.) (1988), *The Structure of European Industry* (2nd edn), Kluwer, Dordrecht.

Jong, H.W. de (1989), *De overname markt; protectie of vrij handel?* ESB, pp. 939.

Kaelble, H. (1986), *Sozialgeschichte der europaischen Integration, 1880–1980*, Freie Universitat, Berlin.

Kalantzopoulos, O. (1986), The Cost of Voluntary Export Restraints for Selected Countries, cited in the World Bank's *World Development Report*, 1987, Oxford University Press, New York, p. 150.

Kaldor, N. (1966), *The Causes of the Slow Growth of the United Kingdom*, Cambridge University Press, Cambridge.

Kane, D.R. (1982), *The Euro-Dollar Market and the Years of Crisis,* Croom Helm, London.

Kapteyn, P.J.G. and Verloren van Themaat, P. (1980), *Inleiding tot het recht van de Europese Gemeenschappen*, Kluwer, Deventer.

Katee, S. (1979), De Phillips-curve in Nederland, 1959–1979, *Maandschrift Economie*, vol. 43, pp. 484–99.

Kaufman, P.J. (1987), The Community Trademark, its Role in Making the Internal Market Effective, *Journal of Common Market Studies*, vol. 25.13, pp. 223–35.

Kay, J. and Keene, M. (1987), Alcohol and Tobacco Taxes, Criteria for Harmonisation, in Cnossen, S. (ed.) *Tax Coordination in the European Community*, Kluwer, Deventer, pp. 85–112.

Kayser, B. (1972), *Cyclically Determined Homeward Flows of Migrant Workers*, OECD, Paris.

Kennedy Brenner, C. (1979), *Foreign Workers and Immigration Policy*, OECD/DC, Paris.

Kenwood, A.G. and Longheed, A.L. (1983), *The Growth of the International Economy 1820–1980, an introductory text*, Allen and Unwin, London.

Keynes, J.M. (1936), *The General Theory of Employment, Interest and Money*, Harcourt, Brace & Co., New York.

Kindleberger, C. P. *et al.* (1979), *Migration, Growth and Development*, OECD, Paris.

Kindleberger, C.P. (1984), *A Financial History of Western Europe*, Allen & Unwin, London.

Kindleberger, C.P. (1987), *International Capital Movements*, Cambridge University Press, Cambridge.

Klaassen, L.H., and Drewe, P. (1973), *Migration Policy in Europe,* Saxon House, Farnborough.

Klaassen, L. H. and Molle, W.T.M. (eds.) (1982), *Industrial Migration and Mobility in the European Community*, Gower Press, Aldershot.

Klein, L. (1985), Trade and Sectoral Adjustment Policy Problems, in Peeters, T., Praet, P. and Reding, P. (eds), *International Trade and Exchange Rates in the Late 1980s*, North Holland, Amsterdam, pp. 111–30.

Kock, K. (1969), *International Trade Policy and the GATT, 1947–1967*, Almquist and Wicksell, Stockholm.

Koekkoek, K.A. and Mennes, L.B.M. (1988), Some Potential Effects of Liberalising the Multi-Fibre Arrangement, in Mennes, L.B.M. and Kol, J. (eds), *European Trade Policies and the Developing World*, Croom Helm, Beckenham, pp. 187–213.

Koester, U. (1977), The Redistributional Effects of the Common Agricultural Financial System, *European Review of Agricultural Economics*, vol. 4.4, pp. 321–45.

Koester, U. and Tangermann, S. (1976), *Alternative der Agrarpolitik*, Hiltrup, Münster.

Kol, J. (1987), Exports from Developing Countries; Some Facts and Scope, *European Economic Review*, vol. 31, pp. 466–74.

Kol, J. (1988), *The Measurement of Intra-Industry Trade*, Erasmus University Press, Rotterdam.

Kolvenbach, W. and Hanau, P. (1988), *Handbook on European Employee Co-Management*, Kluwer, Deventer.

Kottis, A. (1985), Female/Male Earnings Differentials in the Founder Countries of the EEC; an Econometric Investigation, *De Economist*, vol. 132.2, pp. 204–23.

Kozma, F. (1982), *Economic Integration and Economic Strategy*, Nijhoff, The Hague.

Kragenau, H. (1987), *Internationale Direktinvestitionen*, IFW, Weltarchiv, Hamburg.

Krauss, H.B. (1979), *The New Protectionism, the Welfare State and International Trade*, Basil Blackwell, Oxford.

Krauss, L.B. (1968), *European Integration and the US*, Brookings, Washington.

Kreinin, M.E. (1973), The Static Effects of EEC Enlargement on Trade Flows, *Southern Economic Journal*, vol. 39, pp. 559–68.

Krugman, P. (1979), A Model of Innovation, Technology Transfer, and the World Distribution of Income, *Journal of Political Economy*, vol. 87, pp. 253–67.

Krugman, P. and Obstfeld, M. (1988), *International Economics*, Scott, Foreman and Co., Glenview.

Kuznets, S. (1966), *Modern Economic Growth; Rates, Structure and Spread*, Yale University Press, New Haven.

Laffan, B. (1983), Policy Implementation in the European Community: The European Social Fund as a Case Study, *Journal of Common Market Studies*, vol. 21.4, pp. 389–408.

Lamfalussy, A. (1981), Changing Attitudes towards Capital Movements, in Cairncross, F. (ed.), *Changing Perceptions of Economic Policy*, Methuen, London, pp. 194–217.

Lane, J.E., and Ersson, S.O. (1987), *Politics and Society in Western Europe*, Sage, London.

Langhammer, K.J. and Sapir, A. (1987), *Economic Impact of Generalised Tariff Preferences*, TPRC, Gower, Aldershot.

Lannes, X. (1956), International Mobility of Manpower in Western Europe (I + II), *International Labour Review*, vol. 73, pp. 1–24 and 135–51.

Lattre, A. de (1985), Floating, Uncertainty and the Real Sector, in

Tsoukalis, L. (ed.), *The Political Economy of International Money: In Search of a New Order*, Sage, London, pp. 71–103.

Lebergott, S. (1947), Wage Structures, *Review of Economics and Statistics*, vol. 29, pp. 247–85.

Lebon, A. and Falchi, G. (1980), New Developments in Intra-European Migration Since 1974, *International Migration Review*, vol. 14.4, pp. 539–73.

L.E.I. (1987), *Landbouw-economisch bericht*, The Hague.

Leigh, M. (1984), *European Integration and the Common Fisheries Policy*, Croom-Helm, Beckenham.

Lemaitre, P. and Goybet, C. (1984), *Multinational Companies in the EEC* (IRM Multinational Report no. 1), John Wiley, Chichester.

Levi, M. and Sarnet, F. (1970), International Diversification of Investment Portfolios, *American Economic Review*, vol. 60, pp. 668–75

Levi, M. (1981), *International Finance; financial management and the international economy*, McGraw-Hill, New York.

Leyshon, A., Daniels, P.W. and Thrift, N.J. (1987), *Internationalisation of Professional Producer Services; the case of large accountancy firms.* Working Papers on Producer Services, Universities of Bristol and Liverpool.

Lindbeck, A. (1981), Industrial Policy as an Issue of the Economic Environment, *The World Economy*, vol. 4.4.

Lindberg, L.N. and Scheingold, S.A. (1970), *Europe's Would-Be Polity*, Englewood Cliffs, N. J.

Linder, S.B. (1961), *An Essay on Trade and Transformation*, Almquist and Wicksells, Uppsala.

Lindert, P. (1986), *International Economics*, (8th edn), Irwin, Homewood, Illinois.

Linnemann, H. (1966), *An Econometric Study of International Trade Flows*, North-Holland, Amsterdam.

Lipgens, W. (with contributions from Loth, W. and Milward, A.) (1982), *A History of European Integration, vol. 1, 1945–1947, The Formation of the European Unity Movement*, Clarendon and Oxford University Press, London and New York.

Lipsey, R.G. (1960), The Theory of Customs Unions: a General Survey, *Economic Journal*, vol. 70, pp. 496–513.

Lloyd, P.J. (1982), 3 x 3 Theory of Customs Unions, *Journal of International Economics*, vol. 12, pp. 41–63.

Locksey, G. and Ward, T. (1979), Concentration in Manufacturing in the EC, *Cambridge Journal of Economics*, vol. 3.1, pp. 91–7.

Long, F. (1980), *The Political Economy of EEC Relations*, Oxford.

Lopandic, D. (1986), The European Community and Comecon, *Review of International Affairs*, nr. 876, 3, pp. 12–14.

Lucas, N. (1977), *Energy and the European Communities*, Europa Publications, London.

Lucas, N. (1985), *Western European Energy Policies, a Comparative Study,* Oxford University Press, Oxford.

Ludlow, P. (1982), *The Making of the European Monetary System,* Butterworth, London.

Lunn, J. (1980), Determinants of US Investment in the EEC; Further Evidence, *European Economic Review,* vol. 24, pp. 93–101.

MacBean, A.I., and Snowden, P.N. (1981), *International Institutions in Trade and Finance,* George Allen and Unwin, London.

MacDougall, G.D.A. *et al.* (1977), *Report of the Study Group on the Role of Public Finance in European Integration,* CEC, Economy and Finance Series vol. 1, General Report, Brussels.

Machlup, F. (1977), *A History of Thought on Economic Integration,* Macmillan, London.

Macmillan, M.J. (1982), The Economic Effects of International Migration; a Survey, *Journal of Common Market Studies,* vol. 20.3, pp. 245–67.

Magnifico, G. (1985), *Regional Imbalances and National Economic Performance,* Office of Official Publications of the EC, Luxemburg, pp. 85–95.

Maillet, P. (1977), *The Construction of a European Community,* Praeger, New York.

Maillet, P. (1983), *L'Europe à la recherche de son avenir industriel,* Dunod, Paris.

Maillet, P. and Rollet, Ph. (1986), L'insertion de l'Europe dans la division internationale du travail; appréciations et suggestions, *Revue du Marché Commun,* no. 299, pp. 371–86.

Malcor, R. (1970), Problèmes posés par l'application pratique d'une tarification pour l'usage des infrastructures routières, *The EEC Studies,* Transport Series no. 2, Brussels.

Mark, N.C. (1985a), Some Evidence on the International Inequality of Real Interest Rates, *Journal of International Money and Finance,* vol. 4.2, pp. 189–208.

Mark, N.C. (1985b), A Note on International Real Interest Differentials, *Review of Economics and Statistics,* vol. 67.4, pp. 681–84.

Marques-Mendes, A.J. (1986a), The Contribution of the European Community to Economic Growth, *Journal of Common Market Studies,* vol. 24.4, pp. 261–77.

Marques-Mendes, A.J. (1986b), *Economic Integration and Growth in Europe,* Croom Helm, London.

Mathijsen, P.S.R.F. (1985), *A Guide to European Community Law* (4th edn.), Sweet & Maxwell, London.

Matisse, T. (1988), *The European Community's External Trade in Services,* Eurostat, Luxemburg.

Matthews, A. (1985), *The Common Agricultural Policy and the Less Developed Countries,* Gill and Macmillan, Dublin.

Mayes, D. (1978), The Effects of Economic Integration on Trade, *Journal of Common Market Studies,* vol. 17.1, pp. 1–25.

Maynard, G. and Ryckeghem, W. (1976), Why inflation rates differ, a critical examination of the structural hypothesis, in Frisch, H. (ed.) *Inflation in small countries*, Springer, Berlin. pp. 47–72.

McCorrison, S. and Sheldon, I.M. (1987), EC Integration and the Agricultural Supply Industries, in Macmillan, M., Mayes, D.G. and van Veen, P. (eds), *European Integration and Industry*, Tilburg University Press, Tilburg, pp. 119–52.

McDaniel, P.R. (1985), Personal Income Taxes; the treatment of tax expenditures, in Cnossen, S. (ed.), *Tax Coordination in the European Community*, Kluwer, Deventer, pp. 319–33.

McGovern, D. (1982), *International Trade Regulation, GATT, the United States and the European Community*, Exeter.

McGowan, F. and Trengrove, C. (1986), *European Aviation; a Common Market?* Institute of Fiscal Studies, Report Series no. 23, London.

McGowan, F. and Seabright, P. (1989), Deregulating European Airlines, *Economic Policy* vol. 2, pp. 284–344.

Meade, J.E. (1955), *The Theory of Customs Unions*, North Holland, Amsterdam.

Meerhaeghe, M.A.G. van (1980), *A Handbook of International Economic Institutions* (3rd edn.), Martinus Nijhoff, The Hague.

Meerssele, P. van de (1971), *De Europese Integratie 1945–1970*, Standaard, Antwerp.

Meester, G. and Strijker, D. (1985), *Het Europees landbouwbeleid voorbij de scheidslijn van zelfvoorziening* (WRR, V46), State Publishing Office, The Hague.

Merlini, C. (ed.) (1984), *Economic Summits and Western Decision Making*, Croom Helm, London.

Messerlin, P.A. and Becuwe, S. (1986), Intra Industry Trade in the Long Term; the French Case 1850–1913, in Greenaway, D. and Tharakan, P.K.M. (eds), *Imperfect Competition and International Trade*, Wheatsheaf, Brighton, pp. 191–216.

Messerlin, P.A. (1988), *The EC anti-dumping regulations; a first economic appraisal 1980–1985*, paper presented to the first International Seminar on International Economics, Oxford, August, 1988.

Meyer, F.W. and Willgerodt, H. (1956), Der wirtschaftspolitische Aussagewert internationaler Lohnvergleiche, in *Internationale Lohngefaelle, wirtschaftspolitische Folgerungen, und statistische Problematik*, Bundesministerium fur wirtschaftspolitische Zusammenarbeit, Deutscher Bundesverlag, Bonn.

Meyer, G. (1973), *Problems of Trade Policy*, Oxford University Press, London.

Meyer, P.A. (1967), Price Discrimination, Regional Loan Rates and the Structure of the Banking Industry, *Journal of Finance*, vol. 22.1, pp. 37–49.

Mihailovic, K. (1976), Migration and the Integration of Labour Markets, in Machlup, F. (ed.), *Economic Integration, Worldwide, Regional, Sectoral*, Macmillan, London, pp. 163–86.

Miller, M.H. and Spencer, J.E. (1977), The Static Economic Effects of the UK joining the EEC, a General Equilibrium Approach, *Review of Economic Studies*, vol. 44, pp. 71–93.

Mishalani, P. *et al.* (1981), The Pyramid of Privilege, in Stevens, C. (ed.), *The EEC and the Third World, a Survey I,* Hodder and Stoughton and ODI/IDS, London, pp. 60–82.

Mishan, E.J. (1982), *Introduction to Political Economy*, Hutchinson, London.

Mishkin, F.S. (1984a), The Real Interest Rate; a Multicountry Empirical Study, *Canadian Journal of Economics*, vol. 17.2, pp. 283–311.

Mishkin, F.S. (1984b), Are Real Interest Rates Equal Across Countries, an Empirical Investigation of International Parity Conditions?, *Journal of Finance*, vol. 39.5, pp. 1345–1357.

Mitchell, B. (1981), *European Historical Statistics 1750–1975*, (2nd edn), Sythoff/Noordhoff, Alphen a/d Rijn.

Molle, W. (1980), with the assistance of van Holst, B. and Smit, H., *Regional Disparity and Economic Development in the European Community*, Saxon House, Farnborough.

Molle, W.T.M. and Wever, E. (1983), *Oil Refineries and Petrochemical Industries in Western Europe*, Gower Press, Aldershot.

Molle, W.T.M. (1983), Technological Change and Regional Development in Europe (Theory, Empirics, Policy), *Papers and Proceedings of the Regional Science Association, European Congress*, pp. 23–38.

Molle, W.T.M. (1986), Regional Impact of Welfare State Policies in the European Community, in Paelinck, J.H.P. (ed.), *Human Behaviour in Geographical Space*, Gower Press, Aldershot, pp. 77–90.

Molle, W.T.M. and van Mourik, A. (1987), Economic Means of a Common European Foreign Policy, in de Vree, J.K. *et al.* (eds), *Towards a European Foreign Policy*, Nijhoff, Dordrecht, pp. 165–92.

Molle, W.T.M. (1988), Oil Refining and Petrochemical Industry, in de Jong, H.W. (ed.), *The Structure of European Industry*, 2nd edn. Kluwer, Dordrecht, pp. 41–60.

Molle, W.T.M., and Cappellin, R. (eds) (1988), *Regional Impact of Community Policies in Europe*; Avebury/Gower, Aldershot.

Molle, W.T.M. and van Mourik, A. (1988a), International Movements of Labour under Conditions of Economic Integration; the Case of Western Europe, *Journal of Common Market Studies*, vol. 26.3, pp. 317–42.

Molle, W.T.M. and van Mourik, A. (eds) (1989a), *Wage Structures in the European Community, Convergence or Divergence?* Gower, Aldershot.

Molle, W.T.M., and van Mourik, A. (1989b), A Static Explanatory Model of International Labour Migration to and in Western Europe, in Gordon, I. and Thirlwall, A. (eds), *European Factor Mobility, Trends and Consequences*, Macmillan pp. 30–52.

Molle, W.T.M. and Morsink, R. (1990), European Direct Investment in Europe: an Explanatory Model of Intra-EC Flows, in Bürgermeier, B. and Mucchielli, J.M. (eds), *Multinationals and Europe 1992*, Routledge, London.

Molle, W.T.M. (1990), Will the completion of the internal market lead to regional divergence?, in Siebert, H. (ed.), *The completion of the internal market*, Institut für Weltwirtschaft, Kiel.

Monnet, J. (1976), *Mémoires*, Fayard, Paris.

Monnier, C. (1983), *La tarification de l'électricité en France*, Economica, Paris.

Moss, J. (1982), *The Lomé Conventions and their Implications for the US*, Westview Press, Boulder, Colorado.

Moulaert, F. and Derykere, Ph. (1982), The Employment of Migrant Workers in West Germany and Belgium, *International Migration Quarterly*, vol. 2, pp. 178–197.

Mourik, A. van (1987), Testing Factor Price Equalisation in the EC: An Alternative Approach: A Comment, *Journal of Common Market Studies*, vol. 26.1, pp. 79–86.

Mourik, A. van (1989), Countries, a neo-classical model of international wage differentials, in Molle, W. and van Mourik, A. (eds), *Wage Differentials in the European Community, Convergence or Divergence?* Gower Press, Aldershot, pp. 83–103.

Mueller, C. (1980), *The Economics of Labour Migration, a Behavioral Analysis*, Academic Press, New York.

Mueller, D. (1981), Competitive Performance and Trade within the EEC, Generalisations from several case studies with specific reference to the West German economy, *Zeitschrift für die gesamte Staatswissenschaften*, vol. 137.3, pp. 638–63.

Mueller, D. (ed.) (1983), *The Political Economy of Growth*, Yale University Press, New Haven.

Mueller, D.C. (ed.) (1980), *The Determinants and Effects of Mergers; an International Comparison*, Oelgeschlager, Cambridge, Massachusetts.

Mundell, R.A. (1957), International Trade and Factor Mobility, *American Economic Review*, vol. 47.3, pp. 321–35.

Mundell, R.A. (1961), A Theory of Optimum Currency Areas, *American Economic Review*, vol. 53, pp. 657–64.

Muntendam, J. (1987), Philips in the World, a View of a Multinational on Resource Allocation, in B. van der Knaap and E. Wever (eds), *New Technology and Regional Development*, Croom Helm, London, pp. 136–44.

Murfin, A. (1985), Price Discrimination and Tax Differences in the European Motor Industry, in Cnossen, S. (ed.), *Tax Coordination in the European Community*, Kluwer, Deventer, pp. 171–95.

Murrell, P. (1983), The Comparative Structure of Growth in West Germany and British Manufacturing Industries, in Mueller, D. (ed.), *The Political Economy of Growth*, Yale University Press, New Haven, pp. 109–32.

Musgrave, R.A. and Musgrave, P. (1985), *Public Finance in Theory and Practice*, McGraw-Hill, Auckland.

Myrdal, G. (1956), *An International Economy, Problems and Prospects*, Harper and Bros, New York.

Myrdal, G. (1957), *Economic Theory and Underdeveloped Regions*, Duckworth and Co., London.

Naveau, J. (1983), *L'Europe et le transport aerien*, Bruylant, Brussels.

Neary, P. (1987), *Tariffs, Quotas and VER With and Without Internationally Mobile Capital*, Paper to the European Economic Association Conference, Copenhagen.

Neary, P. and Ruane, F.P. (1984), International Capital Mobility, Shadow Prices and the Cost of Protection. *Working Paper 32, Center of Economic Research*, University College Publication, Dublin.

Neumark (1963), Report of the Fiscal and Financial Committee, *The EEC Reports on Tax Harmonisation*, International Bureau of Fiscal Documentation, Amsterdam.

Noel, E. (1988), Working Together; the Institutions of the European Community, *European Documentation*, Luxemburg.

Nordhaus, W.D. (1972), The Worldwide Wage Explosion, *Brookings Papers on Economic Activity*, 2, pp. 431–65.

Norman, V. (1989), EFTA and the Internal European Market, *Economic Policy*, vol. 2, pp. 424–65.

Oates, W. (1972), *Fiscal Federalism*, Harcourt, New York.

Oberender, P. and Ruter, G. (1988), The Steel Industry, a Crisis of Adaptation, in de Jong, H.W. (ed.), *The Structure of European Industry* (2nd edn), Kluwer, Dordrecht, pp. 81–105.

Odagiri, H. (1986), Industrial Policy in Theory and Reality, in de Jong, H.W. and Shepherd, W.G. (eds), *Mainstreams in Industrial Organisation*, Book II, pp. 387–412.

Odell, P., and Rosing, K. (1980), *The Future of Oil, a Simulation Study of the Interrelationship of Resources, Reserves and Use, 1980–2080*, Kogan Page, London.

OECD (1964), *Industrial Statistics 1900–1962*, Paris.

OECD (1965), *Wages and Labour Mobility*, Paris.

OECD (1966), *Energy Policy*, Paris.

OECD (1968), *Capital Market Study*, (five volumes), Paris.

OECD (1973), *Oil, the Present Situation and Future Prospects*, Paris.

OECD (1978), *The Migratory Chain*, Paris.

OECD (1979), *International Direct Investment; Policies, Procedures and Practices*, Paris.

OECD (1980), *Controls on International Capital Movements; the Experience with Controls on International Portfolio Operations in Shares and Bonds,* Paris.

OECD (1981), *International Investment and Multinational Enterprises, Recent International Direct Investment Trends,* Paris.

OECD (1981), *Regulations affecting International Banking Operations,* (2 volumes), Paris.

OECD (1982a), *Controls on International Capital Movements, the Experience with Controls on International Financial Credits, Loans and Deposits,* Paris.

OECD (1982b), *Code of Liberalisation of Capital Movements,* Paris.

OECD (1982c), *Controls and Impediments Affecting Inward Direct Investment in OECD Member Countries,* Paris.

OECD (1982d), *World Energy Outlook,* Paris.

OECD (1983a), *International Trade in Services; Insurance: Identification and Analysis of Obstacles,* Paris.

OECD (1983b), *The Implications of Different Means of Agricultural Income Support,* Paris.

OECD (1984a), *International Trade in Services; Banking: Identification and Analysis of Obstacles,* Paris.

OECD (1984b), *Merger Policies and Recent Trends in Mergers,* Paris.

OECD (1985a), Relative Wages, Industrial Structure and Employment Performance, *Employment Outlook,* pp. 83–99.

OECD (1985b), *Tourism Policy and International Tourism,* Paris.

OECD (1985c), *Cost and Benefits of Protection,* Paris.

OECD (1986a), *International Trade in Services; Audiovisual Works,* Paris.

OECD (1986b), *SOPEMI; Continuous Reporting System on Migration,* Paris, (also 1973–1986).

OECD (1987a), Science and Technology, *Newsletter* no.10, Paris.

OECD (1987b), *International Trade in Services; Securities,* Paris.

OECD, (1987c), *Recent Trends in International Direct Investment,* Paris.

OECD (1987d), *National Policies and Agricultural Trade,* Paris.

OECD (1987e), *The Cost of Restricting Imports; the Automobile Industry,* Paris.

OECD (1987f), *Energy Policies and Programmes of IEA Countries,* 1986 Review, Paris.

OECD (1987g), *Energy Balances of OECD Countries 1970–1985,* Paris.

OECD (1987h), *Taxation in developed countries,* Paris.

Okun, A. (1975), *Equality and Efficiency; the Big Trade Off,* Brookings, Washington.

Olson, M. (1965), *The Logic of Collective Action, Public Goods and the Theory of Groups,* Harvard University Press, Cambridge, Massachusetts.

Olson, M. (1983), *The Rise and Decline of Nations (Economic Growth, Stagflation and Social Rigidities),* Yale University Press, New Haven.

Oort, C.J. (1975), *Study of the Possible Solutions for Allocating the Deficit which may occur in a System of Charging for the Use of Infrastructures Aiming at Budgetary Equilibrium*, CEC, Brussels.

Owen, N. (1983), *Economies of Scale, Competitiveness and Trade Patterns within the European Community*, Clarendon, Oxford.

Padoa-Schioppa, T.,*et al.* (1987), *Europe in the 1990's Efficiency, Stability and Equity, a Strategy for the Evolution of the Economic System of the European Community*, Oxford University Press, Oxford.

Paelinck, J.H.P. and Nijkamp, P. (1975), *Operational Theory and Method in Regional Economics*, Saxon House, Farnborough.

Page, S. (1981), The Revival of Protectionism and its Consequences for Europe, *Journal of Common Market Studies*, vol. 20, pp. 17–40.

Palmer, M., Lambert, J., *et al.* (1968), *European Unity; a Survey of the European Organisations*, P.E.P., Unwin University Books, London.

Papadimetriou, D.G. (1978), European Labour Migration (Consequences for the Countries of Workers' Origin), *International Studies Quarterly*, vol. 22.3, pp. 377–408.

Pearce, J. (1981), *The Common Agricultural Policy*, Chatham House, London.

Pecchioli, R.M. (1983), *The Internationalisation of Banking, the Policy Issues*, OECD, Paris.

Pechman, J.A. (ed.) (1987), Comparative Tax Systems; Europe, Canada and Japan, *Tax Analyst*, Arlington, Virginia.

Peeters, T., Praet, P. and Reding, P. (eds.) (1985), *International Trade and Exchange Rates in the Late Eighties*, North Holland, Amsterdam.

Pelkmans, J. (1980), Economic Theories of Integration Revisited, *Journal of Common Market Studies*, vol. 18.4, pp. 333–54.

Pelkmans, J. (1982), The Assignment of Public Functions in Economic Integration, *Journal of Common Market Studies*, vol. 21.1, pp. 97–121.

Pelkmans, J. (1983), European Direct Investments in the European Community, *Journal of European Integration*, vol. 7.1, pp. 41–70.

Pelkmans, J. (1984), *Market Integration in the European Community*, Nijhoff, The Hague.

Pelkmans, J. (ed.) (1985), *Can the CAP be Reformed?* EIPA, Maastricht.

Pelkmans, J. (1986), Completing the Internal Market for Industrial Products, CEC, Brussels.

Pelkmans, J. and Vollebergh, A. (1986), The Traditional Approach to Technical Harmonisation: Accomplishments and Deficiencies, in Pelkmans, J. and Van Heukelen, M. (eds) (1986), *Coming to Grips with the Internal Market*, EIPA Maastricht, pp. 9–30.

Pereé, E. and Steinherr, A. (1989), Exchange Rate Uncertainty and Foreign Trade, *European Economic Review*, vol. 33, pp. 1241–64.

Peschel, K. (1985), Spatial Structures in International Trade; an Analysis of Long-Term Developments, *Papers of the Regional Science Association*, vol. 58, pp. 97–111.

Petit, M., *et al.* (1987), *The Agricultural Policy Formation in the European Community; The Birth of Milk Quotas and the CAP Reform*, Elsevier, Amsterdam.

Petith, H.C. (1977), European Integration and the Terms of Trade, *Economic Journal*, vol. 87, pp. 262–72.

Phelps-Brown, H. (1977), *The Inequality of Pay*, Oxford University Press, Oxford.

Philip, A.B. (1978), The Integration of Financial Markets in Western Europe, *Journal of Common Market Studies*, vol. 16, pp. 302–22.

Phylaktis, K. and Wood, G.E. (1984), An Analytical and Taxonomic Framework for the Study of Exchange Controls, in Black, J. and Dorrance, G. S. (eds), *Problems of International Finance*, St. Martins Press, New York, pp. 149–66.

Pinder, D. (1983), *Regional Economic Development and Policy; Theory and Practice in the EC*, G. Allen & Unwin, London.

Pinder, J. (1986), The Political Economy of Integration in Europe, Policies and Institutions in East and West, *Journal of Common Market Studies*, vol. 24.1, September, pp. 1–14.

Pirenne, H. (1927), *Les villes du Moyen-age*, Lamertin, Brussels.

Poeck, A. van (1980), De Belgische inflatie (1960–1977): Een interpretatie aan de hand van de moderne Phillips-curve, *Maandschrift Economie*, vol. 44.3, pp. 122–40.

Polachek, S.W. (1980), Conflict and Trade, *Journal of Conflict Resolution*, vol. 24, pp. 55–78.

Pollard, S. (1974), *European Economic Integration*, Thames & Hudson, London.

Pollard, S. (1981a), *Peaceful Conquest, the Industrialisation of Europe 1960–1970*, Oxford University Press, Oxford.

Pollard, S. (1981b), *The Integration of the European Economy since 1815*, George Allen & Unwin, London.

Pomfret, R. (1986), *Mediterranean Policy of the European Community; a Study of Discrimination in Trade*, Macmillan, London.

Pratten, C. (1988), A Survey of the Economies of Scale, in *Research into the Cost of Non-Europe, Basic Findings*, vol. 2, Luxemburg, pp. 11–165.

Prest, A.R. (1983), Fiscal Policy, in Coffey, P. (ed.), *Main Economic Policy Areas of the EEC* (2nd edn.), Nijhoff, M., The Hague, pp. 59–90.

Price Waterhouse (1988), The Cost of Non-Europe in Financial Services, *Research into the Cost of Non-Europe; Basic Findings*, vol. 9, Document CEC, Brussels.

Priore, H.J. (ed.) (1979), *Unemployment and Inflation; Institutionalists' and Structuralists' Views*, Sharpe, White Plains, New York.

Pryce, R. (1973), *The Politics of the European Community*, Butterworth, London.

Pryor, F. (1972), An International Comparison of Concentration Ratios, *Review of Economics and Statistics*, vol. 54.2, pp. 130–40.

Puchala, D.J. (1984), *Fiscal Harmonisation in the European Communities, National Policies and International Cooperation*, Pinter, London.

Raux, J. (ed.) (1984), *Politique Agricole Commune et Construction Européenne*, Economica, Paris.

Ray, J.E. (1986), The OECD 'Consensus' on Export Credits, *The World Economy*, vol. 9.3, pp. 1–14.

Reder, M.W. (1962), *Wage Differentials, Theory and Measurement*, Princeton, N.J.

Resnick, S. and Trumann, E. (1975), An Empirical Examination of Bilateral Trade in Europe, in Balassa, B. (ed.), *European Economic Integration*, North-Holland, Amsterdam, pp. 41–78.

Richardson, J. (1987), *A Subsectoral Approach to Services Trade Theory*, SWF Pergamon.

Ricq, C. (1983), Frontier Workers in Europe, in Anderson, M. (ed.), *Frontier Regions in Europe*, Frank Cass, London, pp. 98–108.

Riemsdijk, J.F. van (1972), A System of Direct Compensation Payments to Farmers as a Means of Reconciling Short Run to Long Run Interests, *European Review of Agricultural Economics*, vol. 1.2, pp. 161–189.

Rijke, R. (1987), *Competition among International Airlines*, Gower, Aldershot.

Rijkens, R. and Miracle, G.E. (1986), *Supernational Regulation of Advertising in the EEC*, North-Holland, Amsterdam–New York.

Rijksbaron, A., Roobol, W.H. and Weisglas, M. (eds) (1987), *Europe from a Cultural Perspective Historiography and Perceptions*, Nijgh and Van Ditmar, The Hague.

Ritson, C. (ed.) (1978), The Lomé Convention and the CAP, *Commonwealth Economic Papers* no. 12, Commonwealth Secretariat, London.

Robson, P. (1988), *The Economics of International Integration* (3rd edn.), Allen & Unwin, London.

Rollet, P. (1984), *Spécialisation internationale et intégration économique et monétaire dans les pays CEE*, CREI, Lille.

Rollo, J.M.C. and Warwick, K.S. (1979), The CAP and Resource Flows among EEC Member States, *Working Paper* no. 27, Government Economic Service, London.

Rose, R. (1985), *Public Employment in Western Nations*, Cambridge University Press, Cambridge.

Rothwell, R. and Zegveld, W. (1981), *Industrial Innovation and Public Policy; Preparing for the 1980s and 1990s*, Pinter, London.

Rugman, A.M. (ed.) (1982), *New Theories of the Multinational Enterprise*, Croom Helm, London.

Sachs, J. (1980), Wages, Flexible Exchange Rates and Macro-Economic Policy, *Quarterly Journal of Economics*, vol. 94, pp. 731–47.

Salt, J. (1976), International Labour Migration, the Geographical Pattern of Demand, in Salt, J. and Clout, H. (eds), *Migration in Post-War*

Europe, Geographical Essays, Oxford University Press, Oxford, pp. 126–67.

Sametz, A.W. (ed.) (1984), *The Emerging Financial Industry*, Lex Books, De Heath and Cy, Lexington, Massachusetts.

Sampson, A. (1977), *The Seven Sisters*, Corgi, London.

Samuelson, P.A. (1948), International Trade and the Equalisation of Factor Prices, *Economic Journal*, vol. 58, pp. 163–84.

Samuelson, P.A. (1949), International Factor Price Equalisation Once Again, *Economic Journal*, vol. 59, pp. 181–97.

Sannucci, V. (1989), The Establishment of a Central Bank; Italy in the Nineteenth Century, in: de Cecco, M. and Giovannini, A. (eds), *A European Central Bank?*, Cambridge University Press, Cambridge, pp. 244–74.

Sassin, W., Hölzl, A., Hogner, H.H. and Schrattenholzer, L. (1983), *Fuelling Europe in the Future; the Long Term Energy Problem in the EC Countries, Alternative R & D Strategies*, IIASA, Luxemburg.

Saunders, C. and Marsden, D. (1981), *Pay Inequalities in the European Communities*, Butterworth, London.

Saunders, P. and Klau, F. (1985), The Role of the Public Sector, Causes and Consequences of the Growth of Government: *OECD Economic Studies*, no. 4, pp. 1–239.

Scaperlanda, A.E. (1967), The EEC and US Foreign Investment; Some Empirical Evidence, *Economic Journal*, vol. 77, pp. 22–6.

Scaperlanda, A.E. and Mauer, L.J. (1969), The Determinants of US Direct Investment in the EEC, *American Economic Review*, vol. 59 pp. 558–68.

Schäfers, A. (1987), The Luxemburg Patent Convention, the Best Option for the Internal Market, *Journal of Common Market Studies*, vol. 25.3, pp. 193–207.

Schendelen, M.P.C.M. van (1984), The European Parliament; Political Influence is more than Legal Powers, *Journal of European Integration*, vol. 8, pp. 59–76.

Scherer, F. (1974), The Determinants of Multi-Plants Operations in Six Nations and Twelve Industries, *Kyklos*, vol. 27.1, pp. 124–39.

Schippers, J.J. and Siegers, J.J. (1986), Women's Relative Wage Rate in the Netherlands, 1950–1983; a Test of Alternative Discrimination Theories, *De Economist*, vol. 134.2, pp. 165–80.

Schmitz, A. (1970), The Impact of Trade Blocks on Foreign Direct Investments, *Economic Journal*, vol. 80, pp. 724–31.

Schmitz, A. and Bieri, J. (1972), EEC-Tariff and US Direct Investment, *European Economic Review*, vol. 3, pp. 259–70.

Schwalbach, J. (1988), Economies of Scale and Intra-Community Trade, in *Research into the Cost of Non-Europe, Basic Findings*, vol. 2, pp. 167–204.

Schwartz, A. and Kooyman, J. (1975), Competition and the International Transmission of Inflation, *De Economist*, vol. 123.4, pp. 723–48.

Schwarze, J. (1987), Towards a European Foreign Policy; Legal Aspects, in de Vree, J.K., *et al.* (eds), *Towards a European Foreign Policy*, Nijhoff, Dordrecht, pp. 69–97.

Scitovsky, T. (1958), *Economic Theory and Western European Integration*, Allen & Unwin, London.

Scott, N. (1967), *Towards a framework for analysing the cost and benefits of labour migration*, Institute for International Labour Studies, Bull., February.

Seers, D., Schaffer, B. and Kiljunen, M.L. (1979), *Underdeveloped Europe: Studies in Core-Periphery Relations*, Harvester Press, Hassocks.

Seers, D., Vaitsos, C. and Kiljunen, M.L. (1980), *Integration and Unequal Development, The Experience of the EC*, St. Martin's Press, New York.

Segré, C., *et al.* (1966), *The Development of a European Capital Market*, Commission of European Economic Community, Brussels.

Seidel, B. (1983), *Wage Policy and European Integration*, Gower, Aldershot.

Sellekaerts, W. (1973), How meaningful are empirical studies on trade creation and trade diversion: *Weltwirtschaftliches Archiv*, Vol. 109.4 pp. 519–51.

Sharp, M. (ed.) (1985), *Europe and the New Technologies, Six Case Studies in Innovation and Adjustment*, Pinter, London.

Shaw, R.W. and Simpson, P. (1987), *Competition Policy; Theory and Practice in Western Economies*, Wheatsheaf, Brighton.

Shelp, R.K. (1981), *Beyond Industrialisation; Ascendency of the Global Service Economy*, Praeger, New York.

Shepherd, G., Duchêne, Fr. and Saunders, Ch. (1983), *Europe's Industries, Public and Private Policies for Change*, Cornell, New York.

Shepherd, W.G. (1985), *Public Policies Towards Business* (7th edn), Irwin, Homewood, Illinois.

Shlaim, A. and Yannopoulos, G.N. (1976), *The EC and the Mediterranean Countries*, Cambridge University Press, Cambridge.

SIGMA, (1985), *Wirtschaftsstudien der Schweizerischen Rückversicherungsgesellschaft*, Zürich.

Simons, J. (1986), *Recht en onrecht in het Europese vervoerbeleid*, Tjeenk Willink, Zwolle.

Sleuwaegen, L. (1987), Multinationals, the European Community and Belgium; Recent Developments, *Journal of Common Market Studies*, vol. 26.2, pp. 255–72.

Sleuwaegen, L. and Yamawaki, H. (1988), European Common Market: Structure and Performance, *European Economic Review*, vol. 32, pp. 1451–75.

Smith, A. and Venables, A.J. (1988), Completing the Internal Market in the EC, Some Industry Simulations, *European Economic Review*, vol. 32, pp. 1501–25.

Södersten, B. (1980), *International Economics* (2nd edn.), Macmillan London.

Soete, L. (1987), The Impact of Technological Innovation on International Trade Patterns: the Evidence Reconsidered, *Research Policy*, pp. 101–130.

Steenbergen, J. (1987), Legal Instruments and External Policies of the EC, in de Vree, J.K. *et al.* (eds), *Towards a European Foreign Policy*, Nijhoff, Dordrecht, pp. 109–43.

Steinherr, A. (1984), Convergence and Coordination of Macro-Economic Policies: Some Basic Issues, *European Economy*, no. 20, pp. 71–110.

Steinherr, A. (1985), Competitiveness and Exchange Rates; some Policy Issues for Europe?, in Peeters, T., Praet P. and Reding P. (eds.), *International Trade and Exchange Rates in the late Eighties*, North Holland, Amsterdam, pp. 163–190.

Steinle, W. (1988), Social Policy, in Molle, W. and Cappellin R. (eds), *Regional Impact of European Community Policies*, Gower, Aldershot, pp. 108–123.

Stevens, C. (ed.) (1981), *EEC and the Third World; a Survey*, Hodder and Stoughton, London.

Stonham, P. (1982), *Major Stock Markets of Europe*, Gower, Aldershot .

Stonham, P. (1987), *Global Stock Market Reforms*, Gower, Aldershot.

Stopford, J.M. and Baden–Fuller, Ch. (1987), Regional Level Competition in a Mature Industry; the Case of European Domestic Appliances, *Journal of Common Market Studies*, vol. 26.2, pp. 173–192.

Strasser, D. (1982), The Finances of Europe, *European Perspectives*, Brussels/Luxemburg.

Strauss, R. (1983), Economic Effects of Monetary Compensatory Amounts, *Journal of Common Market Studies*, vol. 21, pp. 261–281.

Strijker, D. and de Veer, J. (1988), Agriculture in Molle, W. and Cappellin, R. (eds.), *Regional Impact of Community Policies in Europe*, Gower, Aldershot, pp. 23–44.

Struls, A. (1979) (ed.), *Energy Models in the European Community*, IPC Science and Technology Press, Guildford.

Swoboda, A. (ed.) (1976), Capital Movements and their Control, in *IUHEI, CEI*, no. 3, Sijthoff, Leiden.

Talbot, R.B. (1977), The European Community's Regional Fund, *Progress in Planning*, vol. 8.3, pp. 183–281.

Tangermann, S. (1984), Guarantee Thresholds, a Device for Solving the CAP Surplus Problem? *European Review of Agricultural Economics*, vol. 11.2, pp. 159–168.

Tapp, J. (1986), Regulation of the UK insurance industry, in Finsinger,

J. and Pauly, J. (eds), *The Economics of Insurance Regulation*, Macmillan, Houndsmill, pp. 27–64.

Tarditi, S. (1984), La crise de la PAC: un point de vue italien, *Economie Rurale*, vol. 163, pp. 28–33.

Teulings, A.W.M. (1984), The Internationalisation Squeeze: Double Capital Movement and Job Transfer within Philips World Wide, *Environment and Planning*, A, vol. 16, pp. 597–614.

Tharakan, P.K.M. (ed.) (1983), *Intra-Industry Trade; Empirical and Methodological Aspects*, North Holland, Amsterdam.

Tharakan, P.K.M. (1988), The Sector/Country Incidence of Anti–Dumping and Countervailing Duty Cases in the EC, in Mennes, L.B.M. and Kol, J. (eds), *European Trade Policies and the Developing World*, Croom Helm, Beckenham, pp. 94–135.

Thugesen, N. (1990), The Benefits and Costs of Currency Unification in Siebert, H. (ed.) *The Completion of the Internal Market*, IWW/Mohr, Tübingen, pp. 347–75.

Tims, W. (1987), EC Agricultural Policies and the Developing Countries, in Kol, J. and Mennes, L. (eds), *European Trade Policies and the Developing World*, Croom Helm, Beckenham, pp. 135–187.

Tinbergen, J. (1954), *International Economic Integration*, Elsevier, Amsterdam.

Tinbergen, J. (1959), Customs Unions, Influence of their Size on their Effect, *Selected Papers*, North Holland, Amsterdam, pp. 152–164.

Tinbergen, J. (1962), *Shaping the World Economy; Suggestions for an International Economic Policy*, The 20th Century Fund, New York.

Tinbergen, J. and Fischer, D. (1987), *Warfare and Welfare, Integrating Security Policy into Socio-Economic Policy*, Wheatsheaf, Brighton.

Tironi, E. (1982), Customs Union Theory in the Presence of Foreign Firms, Oxford, *Economic Papers*, vol. 34, pp. 150–171.

Toulemon, R. and Flory, J. (1974), *Une politique industrielle pour l'Europe*, PUF, Paris.

Tovias, A. (1982), Testing Factor Price Equalisation in the EEC, *Journal of Common Market Studies*, vol. 20, pp. 165–181.

Tsoukalis, L. (1977), *The Politics and Economics of European Monetary Integration*, Allen & Unwin, London.

Tucker, K. and Sundberg, M., (1988), *International Trade in Services*, London.

Tuma, E.H. (1971), *European Economic History, 10th Century to Present*, Harper & Row, New York.

Twitchett, K.J. (ed.) (1976), *Europe and the World, the External Relations of the Common Market*, Europe Publisher, London.

Uhrig, R. (1983), *Pour une nouvelle politique de développement régional en Europe*, Economica, Paris.

UN (1979), *Labour Supply and Migration in Europe; Demographic Dimensions 1950–1975 and Prospects*, UN/ECE, Geneva.

UN (1980), *Tendencies and Characteristics of International Migration since 1950*, Geneva.

UNCTAD (1983), *Protectionism and Structural Adjustment; production and trade in services, policies and their underlying factors bearing upon international service transactions*, Geneva.

UN/ECE (1967), *Incomes in Postwar Europe: Economic Survey of Europe in 1965*, part 2, Geneva.

UN/ECE (1977), *Intra-European Temporary Migration of Labour; its Consequences for Trade, Investment and Industrial Co-operation, TRADE R 341*, Geneva.

UN/ECE (1980), *Economic Role of Women in the ECE Region* (Chapter 4), Geneva.

UN/ECE (several years) *Annual Bulletin of Electric Energy Statistics for Europe*, Geneva

Ungerer, H., *et al.* (1986), The European Monetary System, Recent Developments, *Occasional Paper* no. 48, IMF, Washington.

UNIPEDE (1982), Influence des prix sur la consommation d'électricité, *Rapport du groupe 60.02*, Brussels.

UNIPEDE (1985), *Compte rendu d'activités du groupe d'experts pour l'étude de l'influence entre prix et consommation de l'électricité*, Athènes.

Urban, G. (1983), Theoretical Justification for Industrial Policy, in Adams, F.G. and Klein, C.R. (eds), *Industrial Policies for Growth and Competitiveness: an Economic Perspective*, pp. 21–40.

Vandamme, J. (ed.) (1985), *New Dimensions in European Social Policy*, TEPSA, Croom Helm, London.

Vandamme, J. (1986), *Employee Consultation and Information in Multinational Corporations*, Croom Helm, London.

Vanhove, N. and Klaassen, L.H. (1987), *Regional Policy, a European Approach* (2nd edn), Gower, Aldershot.

Vassille, L. (1989), Similarity among Countries; an International Comparison Based on Data from the 1978/79 Survey; and Industries; the Role of Productivity, Skill and Other Factors, in Molle, W. and van Mourik, A. (eds), *Wage Differentials in the European Community, Convergence or Divergence?*, Gower Press, Aldershot, pp. 65–83 and 139–63.

Verdoorn, P.J. (1952), Welke zijn de achtergronden en vooruitzichten van de economische integratie in Europa en welke gevolgen zou deze integratie hebben, met name voor de welvaart in Nederland? *Overdruk no. 22*, Centraal Planbureau, The Hague.

Verdoorn, P.J., and Schwartz, A.N.R. (1972), Two Alternative Estimates of the Effects of EEC and EFTA on the Pattern of Trade, *European Economic Review*, vol. 3.3, pp. 291–335.

Verloop, P.J.P. (ed.) (1988), *Merger Control in the EEC*, Kluwer, Deventer.

Vernon, R. (1966) International Investment and International Trade in the Product Cycle, *Quarterly Journal of Economics*, vol. 80, pp. 190–207.

Verrijn Stuart, G.M. *et al.* (1965), Europees kapitaalverkeer en Europese kapitaalmarkt, *European Monographs*, no. 5, Kluwer, Deventer.

Viaene, J.M. (1982), A Customs Union between Spain and the EEC, *European Economic Review*, vol. 18, pp. 345–68.

Viner, J. (1950), *The Customs Union Issue*, Stevens and Sons, London.

Voigt, F., Zachcial, M. and Rath, A. (1986), *Regulation and Modal Split in the International Freight Transport of the EC*, mimeo University Bonn, CEC, Brussels.

Völker, E. (1983), The Major Instruments of the CCP, in Bourgeois, J.H. *et al.* (eds), *Protectionism and the European Community*, Kluwer, Antwerp, pp. 17–49.

Vosgerau H.J. (1989), *New Institutional Arrangements for the World Economy*, Springer, Berlin.

Waelbroeck, J. (1976), Measuring the Degree of Progress of Economic Integration, in Machlup, F. (ed.), *Economic Integration, Worldwide, Regional, Sectoral*, Macmillan, London, pp. 89–99.

Waha, J.P. (1986), Intra-European Trade in Electricity, in Odell, P. and Daneels, J. (eds), *Gas and Electricity Markets in Europe: Prospects and Policies*, BAEE, Brussels, pp. 330–44.

Wallace, H. *et al.* (eds) (1983), *Policy making in the European Community* (2nd edn), J. Wiley, Chichester.

Wallace, W. (1982), Europe as a Confederation: the Community and the Nation State, *Journal of Common Market Studies*, vol. 21.1, pp. 57–69.

Ward, E. (1986), A European Foreign Policy, *International Affairs*, no. 4, pp. 573–82.

Warneke, S.J. and Suleiman, E.N. (eds) (1975), *Industrial Policies in Western Europe*, Praeger, New York.

Warner, H. (1984), EC Social Policy in Practice; Community Action on Behalf of Women and its Impact in the Member States, *Journal of Common Market Studies*, vol. 23.2, pp. 141–67.

Weiss, F.D. (1987), A Political Economy of European Community Trade Policy against the LDCs, *European Economic Review*, vol. 31, pp. 457–65.

Wellenstein, E. (1979), 25 Years of European Community External Relations, CEC, *European Documentation* 4/79, Brussels.

Weyers, G.J. (1982), *Industriepolitiek*, Stenfert Kroese, Leiden/Antwerpen.

Weyman-Jones, T.G. (1986), *Energy in Europe; Issues and Policies*, Methuen, London.

Whalley, J. (1979), Uniform Domestic Tax Rates, Trade Distortions and Economic Integration, *Journal of Public Economics*, vol. 11, pp. 213–21 (see also the further debate in *J.P.E.*, December 1981, pp. 379–90).

Whalley, J. (1985), *Trade Liberalisation among Major World Trading Areas*, MIT Press, Cambridge, Massachusetts.

Whichart, O.G. (1981), Trends in the US Direct Investment Position Abroad, 1950–1979, US Department of Commerce, *Survey of Current Business*, vol. 61.2, pp. 39–56.

Widmaier, H.P. (ed.) (1974), *Politische Oekonomie des Wohlfahrtstaates, eine Kritische Darstellung der neuen politischen Oekonomie*, Frankfurt.

Wijnbergen, S. (1985), Interdependence Revisited; a Developing Countries' Perspective on Macro-Economic Management and Trade Policy in the Industrial World, *Economic Policy, a European Forum*, vol. 1.1, pp. 81–137.

Wilkins, M. (1986), The History of European Multinationals, a New Look, *The Journal of European Economic History*, vol. 15.3, pp. 483–510.

Williamson, J. (1976), The Implication of European Monetary Integration for the Peripheral Areas, in Vaizey, J. (ed.), *Economic Sovereignty and Regional Policy*, Gill and Macmillan, Dublin, pp. 105–21.

Williamson, J. and Bottrill, A. (1971), The Impact of Customs Unions on Trade in Manufactures, *Oxford Economic Paper*, vol. 23, pp. 323–51, reprinted in Kraus, M. (ed.) (1973), *The Economics of Integration*, Allen & Unwin, London, pp. 118–51.

Williamson, J. and Miller, M.H. (1987), *Targets and indicators; a blueprint for the international coordination of economic policy*, Institute for International Economics, Washington DC.

Winsemius, A. (1939), *Economische aspecten der internationale migratie*, Bohn, Haarlem.

Winters, L.A. (1985), Separability and the Modelling of International Economic Integration, *European Economic Review*, vol. 27, pp. 335–53.

Winters, L.A. (1987), The Economic Consequences of Agricultural Support; a Survey, *OECD Economic Studies*, pp. 7–54.

Wise, M. (1984), *The Common Fisheries Policy of the European Community*, Methuen, London.

Wittelloostuyn, A. van, and Maks, J.A.H. (1988), Workable Competition and the Common Market, *European Journal of Political Economy*, vol. 16, pp. 1–19.

Wolf, Ch. (1987), Market and Non Market Failures; Comparison and Assessment, *Journal of Public Policy*, vol. 7.1, pp. 43–70.

Wolf, M. (1988), An Unholy Alliance: the European Community and Developing Countries in the International Trading System, in Kol, J. and Mennes, L.B.M. (eds)., *European Trade Policies and the Developing World*, Croom Helm, Beckenham, pp. 31–57.

Wonnacott, P. and Wonnacott, R. (1981), Is Unilateral Tariff Reduction Preferable to a Customs Union? The Curious Case of the Missing Foreign Tariffs, *American Economic Review*, vol. 71, pp. 704–14.

Woolly, P. (1974), Integration of Capital Markets, in Denton, G. (ed.),

Economic and Monetary Union in Europe, Croom Helm, London, pp. 23–55.

WRR (1986), *The Unfinished European Integration,* Netherlands Scientific Council for Government Policy, The Hague.

Yannopoulos, G.N. (1985), The Impact of the European Economic Community on East–West Trade in Europe, *University of Reading Discussion Papers in Economics,* Series A, no. 165.

Yannopoulos, G.N. (1986), Patterns of Response to EC Tariff Preferences; an Empirical Investigation of Selected non ACP Associates, *Journal of Common Market Studies,* vol. 25.1, pp. 14–30.

Young, C. (1972), Association with the EEC; Economic Aspects of the Trade Relationship, *Journal of Common Market Studies,* vol. 1,1, pp. 120–35.

Ypersele, J. van and Koene, J.C. (1985), The European Monetary System; Origins, Operation and Outlook, *CEC Series European Perspectives,* Luxemburg.

Yuill, D. and Allen, K. (eds) (1985), *European Regional Incentives,* CSPP, Glasgow.

Zippel, W. (1985), Die Bedeutung einer Harmonisierung der einzelstaatlichen Verkehrspolitiken im Hinblick auf den Integrationsprozess, in Voigt, F. and Witte, H. (eds), *Integrationswirkungen von Verkehrssystemen und ihre Bedeutung für die EG,* Duncker und Humblot, Berlin, pp. 21–35.

Index